THE HUNS, ROME
AND THE BIRTH OF EUROPE

The Huns have often been treated as primitive barbarians with no advanced political organization. Their place of origin was the so-called 'backward steppe'. It has been argued that whatever political organization they achieved they owed to the 'civilizing influence' of the Germanic peoples they encountered as they moved west. This book argues that the steppes of Inner Asia were far from 'backward' and that the image of the primitive Huns is vastly misleading. They already possessed a highly sophisticated political culture while still in Inner Asia and, far from being passive recipients of advanced culture from the West, they passed on important elements of Central Eurasian culture to early medieval Europe, which they helped create. Their expansion also marked the beginning of a millennium of virtual monopoly of world power by empires originating in the steppes of Inner Asia. The rise of the Hunnic Empire was truly a geopolitical revolution.

HYUN JIN KIM is the Australian Research Council DECRA Fellow at the University of Sydney. His first book, published in 2009, was a comparative analysis of Greece and China: *Ethnicity and Foreigners in Ancient Greece and China*. He has taught Greek history and Greek literature at Sydney University, and has also given numerous invited talks and special seminars in the US, UK, Australia, New Zealand, Greece and Kazakhstan on topics related to Comparative Literature, Greece and the Near East, and the importance of wider Eurasia to the study of Greco-Roman civilization. He is currently undertaking a new research project funded by the Australian government titled 'Transfer of Hegemony: Geopolitical Revolutions in World History'.

THE HUNS, ROME AND THE BIRTH OF EUROPE

HYUN JIN KIM

CAMBRIDGE
UNIVERSITY PRESS

CAMBRIDGE
UNIVERSITY PRESS

University Printing House, Cambridge CB2 8BS, United Kingdom

Cambridge University Press is part of the University of Cambridge.

It furthers the University's mission by disseminating knowledge in the pursuit of education, learning and research at the highest international levels of excellence.

www.cambridge.org
Information on this title: www.cambridge.org/9781107009066

© Hyun Jin Kim 2013

This publication is in copyright. Subject to statutory exception and to the provisions of relevant collective licensing agreements, no reproduction of any part may take place without the written permission of Cambridge University Press.

First published 2013
3rd printing 2014

A catalogue record for this publication is available from the British Library

Library of Congress Cataloguing in Publication data
Kim, Hyun Jin, 1982–
The Huns, Rome and the birth of Europe / Hyun Jin Kim.
pages   cm
ISBN 978-1-107-00906-6 (hardback)
1. Huns – Asia, Central – History.   2. Huns – Europe – History.   3. Asia, Central – Civilization.   4. Rome – Civilization – Asian influences.   5. Europe – Civilization – Asian influences.   I. Title.
D141.K59   2013
936′.03–dc23
2012040702

ISBN 978-1-107-00906-6 Hardback

Cambridge University Press has no responsibility for the persistence or accuracy of URLs for external or third-party internet websites referred to in this publication, and does not guarantee that any content on such websites is, or will remain, accurate or appropriate.

Contents

List of maps	*page* vi
Acknowledgements	vii

1	Introduction	1
	Steppe empires and their significance in the history of wider Eurasia and Late Imperial Rome	1
	The Huns, a new world order and the birth of 'Europe'	5
2	Rome's Inner Asian enemies before the Huns	9
	The Parthian Empire	9
	The Partho-Sassanian confederacy	14
3	The Huns in Central Asia	17
	Inner Asian empires before the fourth century AD	17
	Contemporary Inner Asian empires (fourth, fifth and sixth centuries AD)	35
4	The Huns in Europe	43
	The Hunnic Empire, the Germanic tribes and Rome	43
	The impact of the Hunnic Empire and Roman military collapse	69
5	The end of the Hunnic Empire in the west	89
	Civil war and the rise of Ardaric	89
	Odoacer the king of the Torcilingians, Rogians, Scirians and the Heruls	96
	Valamer the king of the Huns and founding king of the Ostrogoths	105
	Orestes the royal secretary	127
	New invasions from the east	131
6	The later Huns and the birth of Europe	137
	The later Hunnic Empire of the Bulgars, Oghurs and Avars	137
	The birth of a new Europe	143
	Conclusion	156

Notes	159
Bibliography	276
Index	333

Maps

1 Eurasia in the late fourth century AD *page* 18
2 The Hunnic Empire in Europe at its maximum extent under Attila 44
3 The breakup of the Hunnic Empire in Europe 90

Acknowledgements

I would like to thank first of all my old friend and DPhil thesis supervisor Doctor Timothy Rood at Oxford whose assistance and advice have been instrumental in my finishing two books over the past five years. Due to a clumsy error in editing, I was not able to thank him sufficiently when I published my first book. I would therefore like to take this occasion to express my deep gratitude.

Special thanks also to Professor Peter Golden, the greatest scholar I know of Inner Asian history. I would like to thank him profusely for his patience and sound advice concerning various etymologies and questions relating to Inner Asia. I am heavily indebted to him in many ways, not least in my understanding of Steppe history in general. All possible errors and assertions made in this book are however naturally my own.

I would like to thank Professor La Vaissière for his insights on the Hephtalites and other aspects of Central Asian history.

I would also like to thank Professor Sam Lieu for his advice regarding etymologies and Professor Dan Potts for introducing me to critical literature that greatly facilitated my understanding of Iranian history. I would like to thank Professor Alison Betts for providing me with insights into Central Asian archaeology, Professor David Christian for comments on my final chapter, and also my friend Doctor Selim Adali for his helpful insights into Turkish etymologies.

I would also like to acknowledge the assistance provided by people I met during field research in Kazakhstan, in particular my translator Galiya Biltayeva and the academic staff at Ablaikhan University, Almaty.

Thanks also to all my friends and colleagues in the Sydney University Classics and Ancient History Department, in particular Dr. Julia Kindt, Professor Peter Wilson, Professor Margaret Miller, Dr. Peter Brennan and Professor Eric Csapo.

I am grateful to the University and also to the Centre for Classical and Near Eastern Studies of Australia for providing the funding and facilities that made this project possible.

I owe a debt of gratitude also to my mentor Professor Vivienne Gray. Thanks also to Dr. Angus Bowie, Doctor Stephanie West, Professor G. E. R. Lloyd, Dr. Rosalind Thomas and Dr. Robert Chard at Oxford University.

I would like to acknowledge the insights provided by Professor Nicola Di Cosmo in our email correspondence several years ago.

Last but not least I thank my parents who have encouraged me to persevere and complete this book.

CHAPTER 1

Introduction

STEPPE EMPIRES AND THEIR SIGNIFICANCE IN THE
HISTORY OF WIDER EURASIA AND LATE IMPERIAL ROME

In the heyday of the Mongol Empire in the late thirteenth century AD, the Grand Vizier of the Ilkhan Ghazan (the Mongol King of Persia), the famous Rashid al-Din, set about writing a history of the known world – the whole world, not just of Islam or Europe, as many previous histories claiming to be world histories had been, and even today often are. Rashid, a Jewish physician turned Muslim and later Prime Minister of a Mongol Khanate, working in union with scholars and administrators from every corner of Eurasia subdued by the Mongols, set about his task declaring:

Today, thanks be to God and in consequence of him, the extremities of the inhabited earth are under the dominion of the house of Chinggis Qan and philosophers, astronomers, scholars and historians from North and South China, India, Kashmir, Tibet, (the lands) of the Uighurs, other Turkic tribes, the Arabs and Franks, (all) belonging to (different) religions and sects, are united in large numbers in the service of majestic heaven – This book –, in its totality, will be unprecedented- an assemblage of all the branches of history. (Rashid al-Din/ Alizade, vol. 1, pt. 1, pp. 16–17)[1]

It was indeed an unprecedented undertaking[2] and no similar work was to emerge until the twentieth century. A history which covered the whole of Eurasia from the realm of the Franks, i.e. western Europe, through Muslim lands into India and past the Nomadic world of the steppe to the plains of China and beyond. Even places as far as Java, Korea and Japan are included in this grand survey. This was a historical undertaking made possible by the dominance of the Mongols, the greatest of the steppe empires, over the whole of Eurasia. The world had indeed become one under the Mongols, not just in terms of political unification of most of the known world under the dynasty of Chinggis Khan (better known as Genghis Khan), but intellectually and economically.[3]

1

Strangely enough this intellectual unity in our age of globalization and fervent cultural exchange is sadly lacking in the discipline of history. The branches of history that Rashid referred to are today in discordant disunion in a way that would have appalled our thirteenth-century predecessors. World history of the type Rashid engaged in, in our age of departmentalization and compartmentalization, has without doubt lost something of its former allure. The monumental works of intellectual giants such as Max Weber and Arnold Toynbee, never mind distant luminaries of the past, the likes of Rashid, Ibn Khaldun, Sima Qian and Herodotus, are well and truly relics of the past. Those who dare to engage in work that is broad-ranging enough to be categorized, perhaps, as world history, do so with fear that their work may be castigated for lacking specialist knowledge or be lampooned as a random collection of trivial generalizations.[4] However, fortunately (or alas!) for those historians who engage in the history of the fourth and fifth centuries AD (i.e. Late Antiquity), the centuries characterized by the rise of steppe empires and the collapse of the western half of the Roman Empire, departmentalization and selective specialization are wishful thinking and in fact wholly inappropriate.

Many in fact have tried to engage in such limited research and have arguably produced erroneous conclusions as a consequence. Dependence on nothing but Greco-Roman sources has produced valuable insights to be sure, but has fallen short of providing satisfactory answers to one of the key issues raised in this book: why indeed did the imperial structure of Rome, which had held firm for so many centuries previously, fail miserably in the last century of its existence? To unravel this 'mystery' a much broader interdisciplinary and comparative analysis, the type that calls to mind some of the ambitious eclecticism of Rashid al-Din's enterprise, is needed. In short 'a Eurasian perspective' must again be adopted.

Such an analysis would prove the main argument of this book – that the most important historical development of Late Antiquity, which was of critical importance to the later history of the world, was not the fall of the Western half of the Roman Empire, which was one of its consequences, but the world-changing dynamics or convulsions, a veritable revolution in the strategic and political balance of the global power structure,[5] which originated in a region that Central Asian specialists identify as Inner Asia,[6] the steppe region that has historically linked the main civilizations of Eurasia: China, the Greco-Roman world, Iran and India. Indeed the fifth century AD, which saw the collapse of Western Rome, saw these cultural zones linked together by and under the domination of four well-organized and long-lived empires: the Hunnic Empire in Europe; the White Huns (Hephtalites) in Central Asia,

Northwestern India and Eastern Iran; the Rouran Khaganate in Turkestan and Mongolia; and finally the Xianbei Toba Empire in Northern China.[7] Of these, the first three had a core Hunnic/Xiongnu element and the fourth (Xianbei) had likewise originated from the Xiongnu/Hunnic political entity.

We will return to these empires shortly, but first a brief and by no means comprehensive overview of the background to these world-changing developments is needed. Scholars have already discussed at some length what the remarkable polymath Hodgson[8] and after him Chase-Dunn and Hall identify as the Afro-Eurasian interactive system.[9] Between the fifth century BC (perhaps even earlier) and the fifteenth century AD, before the discovery of the New World, this interactive system, in essence a network of trade routes (the most famous being the Silk Road)[10] across the Eurasian continent and sea lanes which linked China and India to the Middle East and East Africa via which to the Mediterranean, constituted the most vital avenue of cultural exchange and economic prosperity in the world. This system expanded and contracted over nearly two millennia and arguably reached its climactic apogee with the establishment of the pan-Eurasian Empire of the Mongols under Chinggis Khan.[11] The Mongols, as Rashid al-Din so accurately demonstrates, dominated virtually all the traditional continental trade routes and created an unprecedented mechanism for cultural exchange across the known world.[12] Their contribution (in fact that of all the steppe polities that had preceded it) to the birth of what is now called the Modern world is somewhat underrated[13] and a vast amount of historical data and information concerning this remarkable Eurasian Empire still remains under-researched.[14]

Tempting as it is to discuss this matter further, the Mongol Empire is only of peripheral concern to the main subject of this book and hence it is hoped that more scholarship will in the future further highlight the importance of this critical phase in world history.[15] However, it must be noted in passing that the Mongol Empire was the culmination of nearly a millennium of domination of much of Eurasia by Turkic or Mongolic empires (with a greatly heterogeneous population base[16]) of the Eurasian steppe. Between AD 311, arguably the beginning of the great Inner Asian incursions into China,[17] and AD 1405, which marked the death of perhaps the most brutal of the numerous inner Asian conquerors of the known world Timur or Tamerlane,[18] every corner of Eurasia from Gaul (France) to the Pacific, from the deep frozen recesses of Siberia to the fertile plains of the Ganges in India, had at one stage or another been ruled by a Turkic (heavily mixed with Iranian[19]) or Mongolic ruling elite.[20] This is surely remarkable and there is simply no parallel in world history to this persistent and millennium-long dominance by a single cultural group originating from basically the same region, the eastern steppes (from the Altai to eastern Mongolia). Arguably, not even the Romans or the Chinese at their height under the Tang Dynasty (seventh to ninth centuries AD) came close to exerting such a far-reaching and long-lasting influence geographically or in temporal terms.

With the exception of the significant, but in fact comparatively brief, interlude of Arab Muslim and Tang Chinese dominance between the seventh and ninth centuries AD (roughly 200 years),[21] the millennium that we identify as the Dark Ages-cum-Middle Ages was without a doubt the era of Turco-Mongol supremacy. In this world order Inner Asia formed the core and Europe, China and the Middle East merely the periphery.[22] Such a reality was difficult to accept for most historians in both the West and also the East. No Sinocentric or Eurocentric writer could ever admit that their world was of secondary importance in the grand scheme of things and that the 'nomadic', steppe barbarians, whom they despised, were at one stage even in the distant past their superiors and overlords.

The solution had been to basically ignore this period of history altogether (as the relative dearth of scholarly interest in the so-called Middle Ages in comparison to the previous 'Classical Period' of Greco-Roman pre-eminence and the later Pre-Modern European era shows) or relegate the Turks and the Mongols to oblivion by attributing to them unbelievably primitive and bestial levels of cultural development and a comprehensive lack of any redeeming civilized features.[23] To be sure, the Huns and the Mongols were extremely cruel in their conquests and caused substantial destruction,[24] but can we argue that the Romans or even the Macedonians destroyed any less? The Persians at Persepolis, the Greeks of Thebes, the Phoenicians of Tyre, the Sogdians of Cyropolis and the countless thousands of innocent victims in India and Central Asia who were massacred by Alexander's conquering army[25] could hardly appreciate the argument that 'Greek'[26] Macedonian conquest brought them the benefits of a superior civilization.[27] The brutal efficiency of Roman conquest doesn't even need a survey. The ruins and mass slaughter of Carthage, Etruria, Gaul and Jerusalem would be sufficient evidence of that.

However, any student of Classical civilization would certainly reply that the Romans and the Macedonians, after the initial brutality of conquest, left behind them shining monuments of cultural brilliance that are the heritage of the Western world. That is certainly true too. But by the same logic the Seljuks, the Timurids, the Moghuls, the Mongol Yuan Empire and the Ottomans, after the initial terror, all bequeathed to posterity architectural and artistic wonders and a fabulously rich cultural legacy,

The Huns, a new world order, the birth of 'Europe'   5

no less significant than the Romans'.[28] They were a brutally efficient and capable group of conquerors and rulers, in every way the equals of the Roman Caesars or the Macedonian kings.

Yet in the plethora of rhetoric concerning racial/ethnic superiority, democracy, western orientalism, Chinese nationalism etc., the group that was the real instigator of momentous changes in the millennium before European dominance has been largely forgotten. The public in both the West and the East are vaguely aware of them, if at all, as simple savages who killed, looted and plundered their ancestors. It is perhaps time to give the steppe empires their due and acknowledge the fact that their world constituted another, important civilization,[29] which made a significant contribution to our 'modern' civilization by first bringing together the disparate cultural centres of Eurasia out of their comparative isolation into a Eurasian whole and then contributing to the moulding of a new global culture. Central Asians, though they certainly weren't peace-loving sages, were also certainly not the paradigm of unrestrained barbarism.[30] In this book I seek to introduce the reader to the people who began the legend of the 'rapacious' and fearsome nomad in the West, the Huns who brought down the Roman and Chinese Empires and ushered in the era of Turco-Mongol pre-eminence.

THE HUNS, A NEW WORLD ORDER AND THE BIRTH OF 'EUROPE'

Between the year AD 311, when Luoyang the capital of the Jin Dynasty of China was sacked by the eastern Huns (Southern Xiongnu),[31] and the 450s AD when the last vestiges of Western Roman military supremacy over Europe vanished as a consequence of losses inflicted on the Empire by the European Huns, in the space of little over a century the steppe powers, mostly referred to as Huns ('hiungnu', Hunas, Chionites, etc.) in our various sources, caused the total or partial collapse of four sedentary empires: Rome, Jin (China), Sassanian Persia (which lost its eastern territories to the Hephtalite and Kidarite Huns) and the Guptas (India). The Huns, who brought about these cataclysmic changes and threatened the borders of all the major powers of the ancient world simultaneously across the whole length of the immense boundaries of Inner Asia, were, as mentioned earlier, the forerunners of a whole millennium of military and political dominance emanating from the steppe in world affairs. Han China and Rome, the superpowers of the ancient world, were eclipsed by the third power group, the Huns and other steppe peoples.

This revolutionary shift in the balance of power from the sedentary world to the steppe or rather from the Eurasian periphery to its centre, turned what had once been the poorest and most desolate region of world civilization into the very core of the Eurasian interactive system. Through the 'nomads', much maligned and underrated, the Eurasian world became further integrated.[32] The concept of east and west was rendered irrelevant and peripheral. Steppe empires ruled both East and West and under the Mongols a truly universal empire was brought into existence. In effect both East and West became merely the wings of the central Inner Asian core.

This dominance of Inner Asia was only broken gradually between the fifteenth and seventeenth centuries by a combination of factors, one of which was European maritime activity from the fifteenth century onwards.[33] Until in some cases the twentieth century the residual states of this old order, e.g. the Manchu Qing Empire, the Ottoman Turkish Sultanate[34] and the Uzbek Khanates of Bukhara and Khiva, survived. The green 'oceans' of the steppes and the steppe horse, the old vehicle of rapid movement, were gradually replaced by blue oceans and mechanized ships. East and West Eurasia, in large part due to the unity brought about by Central Eurasians (steppe peoples), which alerted them to the existence of each other and the great benefits (i.e. trade and exchange) that could be gained through greater interaction, chose to meet directly and no longer via Central Asian intermediaries. The world became closer than ever before. In a way the histories of both Greco-Rome and China became the history of the whole world, not just their parochial locality. Steppe history, however, made this later development possible.[35] A fourteenth-century sinicized immigrant in Jiangxi, southeastern China, from the west called or rather renamed Wang Li (1314–89), aptly sums up the impact of the steppe empires in the following way:

The land within the Four Seas had become the territory of one family, civilization had spread everywhere, and no more barriers existed. For people in search of fame and wealth in north and south, a journey of a thousand li was like a trip next door, while a journey of ten thousand li constituted just a neighbourly jaunt. Hence, among people of the Western Regions who served at the court, or who studied in our south-land, many forgot the region of their birth, and took delight in living among our rivers and lakes. As they settled down in China for a long time, some became advanced in years, their families grew, and being far from home, they had no desire to be buried in their fatherland. Brotherhood among peoples certainly reached a new plane.[36]

Yet while the impact of later steppe empires is finally getting some belated recognition at least among interested academics, the significant historical, cultural and political contributions made by earlier steppe empires, especially the Hunnic Empire, to world history and civilization, are still almost entirely neglected by both many academics and the general public. It is the argument of this book that the political and cultural landscape of early medieval Europe was shaped by the fusion of Roman and Inner Asian (Hunnic and Alanic) cultural and political practices. Most importantly, this book will trace the origins of certain elements of early medieval 'feudalism' in Inner Asia.[37] It will demonstrate that the Hunnic Empire played a decisive role in the unravelling of Roman hegemony over areas that would later become Western Europe and actively facilitated the political formation of the so-called 'Germanic' successor kingdoms. It proposes that early medieval Europe was as much Inner Asian as Roman and that this has significant ramifications for how we should view and categorize 'Europe' and our 'modern' civilization. The book will address these critical issues specifically and is not intended to be a full history of the Huns or the later Roman Empire, though substantial information about the history of Late Antiquity and the early Middle Ages will be provided as part of the effort to elucidate the main arguments of the book.

For the sake of clarity it is also necessary to explain here in the introduction the relevance of the concept of 'ethnicity' to the subject matter of this book. I have already used terms such as 'Germanic', 'Iranian', 'Turkic' and 'Turco-Mongol'. All these terms are broad linguistic terms referring to speakers of groups of languages (belonging to language families[38]) and not specific ethnic appellations. In contrast terms such as Goth, Hun, Alan, Parthian, Scythian, Frank, etc., which will regularly appear, refer to primarily political and ethnic categories. I need not remind the reader that the term ethnicity is a neologism coined in the middle of the twentieth century. Yet in scholarship the ideas and concepts embraced by this neologism have often been used to define and categorize historical ethnic entities and political groupings.[39] An extended discussion of ethnicity is out of place here and I must refer the reader to my earlier publication[40] on the subject, but a brief overview will be provided to clarify just what is meant when terms such as Hun and Goth are used in this book.

Scholarship on ethnicity is divided among those who follow the model of the Norwegian ethnologist F. Barth, the so-called Modernists (or instrumental approach), who argue that an ethnic group is in reality purely a self-created, artificial entity formed to protect specific political and economic interests[41], and the primordialists (sometimes also called the perennialists) who tend to argue that ethnic groups are the product of specific cultural and historical realities such as blood ties ('race'), language, common territory, common religion and common historical memory that function as 'primordial' ties.[42] A synthesis of aspects of both positions is now generally accepted as best reflecting the reality of ethnicity and ethnic consciousness in history.[43]

As will be shown in due course, groups such as the Huns, the Goths and the Franks were neither entirely concrete ethnic entities in the sense advocated by the primordialists, nor simply artificial political-economic constructs as proposed by the modernists. They were a complex agglomeration of peoples who were united for a number of different reasons: political, economic, military, putative blood links, at times by common language(s) and historical memory. Multilingualism was very often a feature of a number of these groups, especially those originating from Inner Asia, and heterogeneity both in terms of language and 'genetic' makeup, especially of the elite, was common. Therefore, when reference is made to the Huns or Goths, one should not consider automatically a racial category or a clear-cut ethnic identity. The reality was much more complex, fluid and ever-changing. Identity (both ethnic and political) was inherently unstable. A Hun could transform himself into the leader of the Goths or Franks whom he dominated, as we shall see, and become a Frankish or a Gothic leader. A Goth could also become a Hunnic noble. Such complexities should therefore be recognized when reference is made to 'ethnic' names such as the Huns and the Goths.

CHAPTER 2

Rome's Inner Asian enemies before the Huns

THE PARTHIAN EMPIRE

Before we begin our inquiry on the Huns, however, it is necessary to examine briefly the steppe peoples who came into contact with the Romans before the Huns. Firstly in order to determine how the strategic situation in Western Eurasia was altered by the rise of the Hunnic Empire and secondly to determine what influence, if any, Inner Asian peoples had on the political organization of Rome's most formidable sedentary enemy, Persia.[1] This section is not intended to be a full-length or in-depth history of the Parthians and the Sassanians, but will focus specifically on the steppe characteristics of the Parthian and to a lesser extent Sassanian political systems. It will also attempt to show how these traces of Inner Asian practices in the Persian (i.e. Parthian and Sassanian) political landscape bear witness to the political complexity of Inner Asian society from which the Huns later emerged. It is often taken for granted that the Parthian Empire was a state-level entity that possessed a complex political organization. Yet the Huns, who like the Parthians originated from Inner Asia, are often viewed as politically primitive by modern ancient historians. In this chapter and the following chapter the myth of a politically primitive and backward Inner Asia will be refuted.

Among the handful of steppe peoples in whom the Romans had any interest, without a doubt the Parthians were the most famous or most dreaded. The military power and organization of the early Parthian state, before its precipitous decline in the second century AD, was formidable and stable enough to sustain this steppe-derived political entity for half a millennium, all the while gaining the respect of its rival, the Roman Empire.[2] Yet the steppe origins of the Parthians have not received the attention that they deserve and are not widely regarded as an essential element of the imperial structure that the Parthians created,[3] despite the attestations of our ancient sources regarding the persistence of steppe customs and institutions among the Parthians (Strabo (11.9.2; 16.1.16, 743 C) and Trogus/Justin (41.2–4)).

One could of course argue that the Achaemenids, who preceded the Parthians before the Macedonian/Seleucid interlude and without a doubt provided a model for imperial rule on which both the Seleucids and later the Parthians built, being Indo-Iranians, also had an Inner Asian origin.[4] The critical impact of Inner Asian Saka (Scythian) nomads[5] on the culture and administrative practices of the Median and later Achaemenid Empires has indeed been vigorously argued for by Vogelsang.[6] It has been proposed that the highly militarized population of Eastern Iran, who are likely to have included a significant Saka/Scythian element and were governed in ways very reminiscent of practices found in later steppe political entities and tribal confederacies, may in fact have provided the framework within which the Persian kings built their administration and empire.[7]

The political system of this Persian Achaemenid empire has been called 'feudal' or quasi-feudal[8] because it was a system in which the king ruled through local intermediaries (in the eastern half of the empire possibly military lords of Scythian/Saka origin) who provided levies for the king's army[9] and were tied to the central government by an intricate web of land grants in return for providing military resources (as in later Medieval Europe), tribute payments and gift exchanges[10] (a system which, as we shall see later, strikingly resembles the Xiongnu imperial structure in Central Asia and the Hunnic imperial system in Europe). Now of course the use of the term 'feudal' with its Marxist and 'ahistorical' connotations is highly problematic and it is very questionable whether the term is applicable to pre-modern societies outside Western Europe without serious qualifications. However, as outlined in the introduction, part of the aim of this book is to trace the origins of elements of early Medieval 'feudalism' in Inner Asia. Therefore, before we progress any further, I will take this opportunity to briefly clarify what is meant by early medieval 'feudalism' and whether modified variations of that term can legitimately be used to describe similar political systems and practices in Ancient Inner Asia and Inner Asian dominated Ancient Iran.

The 'feudalism' that I am referring to is 'feudalism' in the political sense of a formal division of state power between the king and his subordinate great vassals (sub-kings and great nobles) within the upper aristocratic elite, so centralized 'feudalism', and not the fragmented political-economic system which we identify with later medieval Europe, the *seigneurie* or manorialism.[11] Manorialism is a system in which there is a near complete breakdown of central government authority, where small local fief holders

The Parthian Empire

exercise virtual de facto independent power. Some call the earlier centralized form of 'feudalism', 'proto-feudalism' to distinguish it from the manorial feudalism of the late Middle Ages, but this early 'feudalism' or proto-feudalism of the early Middle Ages was instrumental in bringing about the formulation of late medieval, feudal society and its political and economic culture. Often the difference between early and later versions of feudalism[12] is understood as that between what has been called early Frankish 'incipient feudalism', a centralized feudalism which allowed the king to increase his power by distributing land to his followers, thereby gaining their loyalty, but nonetheless bestowing on the ruler the absolute right to take the lands back,[13] and the 'seigneurial-type' power structures in the tenth century, in which there was virtually no central control over the fiefs distributed to vassals.[14]

As we shall see throughout the rest of this book and as Cribb points out, a system very similar to this early medieval centralized feudalism or proto-feudalism definitely existed also in ancient Inner Asia, where a small powerful elite owned vast numbers of animals that they farmed out to 'tenant' households. Political power and large grants of land and peoples were likewise concentrated in the hands of a very select group of royalty and associated aristocratic families. Cribb uses the term 'pastoral feudalism' to describe this Inner Asian political model.[15] The appropriateness of using the term 'feudal' here is debatable, but the similarities are so strong that a case can be made for using modified terms such as 'quasi-feudal' or 'proto-feudal' to describe this Inner Asian political system. The same could also be said about Iranian Parthian and Sassanian political models, which we will discuss below. Therefore, from this point onwards I will use the term 'proto-feudalism' to refer to the earlier centralized version of feudalism that existed in the early Middle Ages in Europe, and use the term 'quasi-feudal' and the associated term 'fiefs'[16] to describe similar political practices found in Inner Asia and Iran.

As in Inner Asian states which we shall examine in detail in later chapters, the Achaemenid Persians distributed major 'fiefs'/satrapies to members of the royal clan and usually other important, minor 'fiefs' to Persian nobles who had intimate connections with the ruling dynasty, while allowing a limited number of local, native rulers to rule under Persian supervision in more remote regions difficult to control (e.g. Inaros and Amyrtaios in Egypt, Geshem of Kedar in Arabia, and local chiefs in Ionia, Macedonia and the Central Asian Saka territories on the fringes of the empire).[17] The Persian military would also possess six pre-eminent commanders/marshals,[18] a decimal system of organization (under chiliarchs,[19] Old Persian *hazarapatish* (commander of a thousand)),[20] and under Cyrus the Great it may have been divided into three parts.[21] These structures or structures closely resembling them, as we shall see repeatedly henceforth, typify Inner Asian military states from the Scythians and Xiongnu to the later Huns.

Even more noteworthy for our purposes is the fact that Central Asia as early as the middle of the first millennium BC already possessed organized political structures in regions conquered and later loosely controlled by the Achaemenids: Sogdia, Parthia, Bactria and Chorasmia.[22] The Parthians therefore did not originate from a political backwater. Advanced political structures and institutions already existed in Central Asia at the time of the Parthian invasion of formerly Seleucid lands.[23] As we shall see in the next chapter, the superbly organized steppe empire of the Xiongnu and the kingdom of the Yuezhi (later the Kushans) were already fully established at the time of Parthia's founding under Arsaces.[24] To what extent then was the political structure of the Parthian state Inner Asian?

The Parthian state was formed after the conquest of the satrapy of Parthia by an Inner Asian people of Iranian extraction called the Parni,[25] which was itself a member of the three-tribe confederation of the Dahae.[26] The kingdom of the Royal Scythians immortalized by Herodotus two centuries earlier interestingly enough also possessed three tribes, which, as will be shown in the next chapter, was probably a reflection of the tripartite division of political power among the dominant tribes that characterized Inner Asian political entities like the Xiongnu. Were the Parthians while they were still in Central Asia similarly organized? This is as yet difficult to ascertain. However, what is clear is that the Parthian state became a full-fledged imperial entity under Mithradates I (171–138 BC) in the mid second century BC.[27]

The new masters of Iran and Mesopotamia soon came under intense pressure from new arrivals from Inner Asia, the formidable Saka tribes and the Tochari.[28] The Yuezhi who had pushed these peoples into Parthia would eventually triumph in Central Asia under Kushan leadership, becoming the immediate Eastern neighbours of the Parthians.[29] Under pressure from steppe enemies, the Parthians were forced to adapt their political and military structures to cope with the threat.[30] Significant numbers of Saka and other Inner Asians also entered the Parthian state and became part of its political and military establishment.[31]

It was with this steppe type army which included large Saka contingents that the great Surena destroyed the numerically superior Roman army under Crassus at Carrhae. In this battle Surena employed the tactics that one would see again and again in steppe warfare: a constant rain of arrows from a distance by mounted archers to wear down the opposing force, feigned retreats to entice an infantry formation to break ranks, and then the devastating charge of the cataphract, heavy cavalry, to deliver the coup de grâce.[32] Surena was a member of the Suren noble house that was one of the six elite families of the Parthian Empire.[33] The six chiefs of these noble households (curiously resembling the six marshals of the Achaemenid military) supported the original Arsaces in founding the Parthian state and it was the chief of the house of Suren who placed the royal tiara on the head of Arsaces, a function that became hereditary in this family.[34]

The Suren lords were largely responsible for checking the Saka invasions to the East and they became the hereditary lords of Drangiana (Sistan).[35] According to Plutarch (*Crassus* 21.6), Surena commanded a personal armed retinue of 1,000 heavily armed cataphract cavalry[36] and 10,000 other horsemen (his vassals and slaves,[37] mainly mounted archers). This system of quasi-feudal appanages and distribution of military commands among elite aristocratic families is also a feature we will discover among other steppe peoples. The Saka ruler Azes I in AD 57 would decorate his coins with the images of cataphract horsemen[38] who played such a notable role in the defeat of Roman armies further to the west. Bivar is probably correct in identifying the heavy horsemen in Surena's cavalry with troops levied among the Saka in Margiana and Sistan (the Surens were marcher lords in charge of the East and hence lived among the Saka).[39]

The Inner Asian nature of the Parthian state becomes even clearer when we examine the ways in which the empire was governed. First of all, as among other steppe peoples, we find among the Parthians the notion of the divine charisma of the ruling dynasty, which endows it with the unique right to allocate power to subordinate rulers. The Arsacid 'Great King' is represented in Parthian iconography as the mediator between the gods and his vassal kings.[40] The authority of the Great King was thus seen as paramount, but also at the same time conditioned by the very Inner Asian practice of power distribution among members of the ruling family and nobility.

Instead of the large satrapies of the Achaemenid Empire (twenty in all) we see in the Parthian state an increasing number of smaller satrapies (seventy-two according to Appian by the first century AD) and the new feature of semi-autonomous, but vassal kingdoms (eighteen in the days of Pliny).[41] This was without a doubt the result of allocating 'fiefs' to members of the royal family and other noble clans,[42] a characteristic feature of steppe empires. Feuding over 'fief' (territories or peoples) allocations was an endemic feature of steppe political life and the Parthians were no exception, as can be seen from constant struggles between brothers and cousins over the succession to the throne and appointments of royal kinsmen as sub-kings. As in many other steppe polities there was no strict primogeniture. Any male of Arsacid lineage was acceptable as monarch and this reflects the steppe political notion of regarding the state as the property not of the individual monarch, but of the royal clan.[43] This in turn led to the creation of a state structure that closely resembled later medieval feudal realms[44] in Europe and this would ultimately contribute to the empire's demise,[45] since it encouraged centrifugal tendencies and decentralization in the last two centuries of the Parthian state.[46] The eighteen kingdoms mentioned by Pliny were organized into two groups, the upper (eleven kingdoms) and the lower (seven kingdoms), possibly reflecting the two wings of the traditional Inner Asian political organization[47] which is also found among the contemporary Xiongnu in the east.[48]

Moses of Chorene[49] gives us a good example of how the Parthians organized their kingdom and in his descriptions we find the typical Inner Asian state apparatus. In Armenia when it was taken over by the Arsacids, the Parthian ruler Tiridates reorganized his new realm on the Parthian model. We find: the common Inner Asian institution of royal bodyguards (comitatus); high positions that relate to the aristocratic, military interests of the Parthian, steppe elite – e.g. master of the royal hunts (an important feature of steppe life and also military training)[50] and the falconer (another hobby common among Inner Asian elites); and other positions such as the chamberlain, head of sacrifices, guardian of summer residences (indicative of the semi-nomadic lifestyle of the steppe ruler), etc. These important posts were distributed among members of the great families in ways, as we shall see in the next chapter, remarkably similar to the contemporaneous Xiongnu. This distribution of high offices among nobles, which in effect gave them an important stake in the preservation of the central government, prevented the quasi-feudal nature of the state from degenerating into anarchy. 'Fiefs' were granted to vassals and to the four territorial Wardens of the Marches.[51] The army thus consisted of the standing army of the king and quasi-feudal levies.[52]

THE PARTHO-SASSANIAN CONFEDERACY

The Sassanians who replaced the Parthians preserved most of the political institutions of their Parthian predecessors.[53] In fact the great Parthian noble families continued to rule under a different dynasty,[54] that of the Sassanians which simply filled the void left by the declining Arsacids. The powerful Parthian families: Karen, Suren, Mihran, Ispahbudhan, Kanarangiyan were in effect co-partners in imperial rule with the reigning Sassanians.[55] Thus the so-called Persian Empire of the Sassanids was in fact a Sassanian–Parthian confederacy,[56] a quasi-feudal empire,[57] which closely resembled the Inner Asian state polity of the Parthian Arsacids that had preceded it.[58] The Parthian nobility, which provided the Sassanids with their heavy cavalry, formed the backbone of the Persian military establishment.[59] They were so powerful that towards the end of the Sassanian Period the Mihranid Bahram-i Chubin (AD 590–1) dethroned Khusrow II Parviz and briefly ascended the throne. Another Parthian noble, Vistahm of the Ipahbudhan family, would again threaten Khusrow II with a huge revolt that spread from Khurasan to Azerbaijan (595–600).[60]

Like the Arsacids the Sassanians would maintain a comitatus, a royal bodyguard, and would frequently employ mercenary troops from the steppe to augment their cavalry force.[61] Their empire, like the Arsacid state before it, had its vassal kings (*sahrdaran*),[62] princes of the royal blood (*waspuhragan*), grandees (*wuzurgan*) and minor nobles/knights (*azadan*), who made up the elite mounted warriors of the Sassanid armies.[63] The grandees, as during the Arsacid era, were loaded with various honours and high positions at court to tie them to the central government. They were the viceroys, chiliarchs and chiefs of cavalry, and together with the princes of the blood (who were the sub-kings),[64] these select few families monopolized high appointments at court. The great clans would often display their clan emblems or coats of arms on their caps, approximating the practices we find later in medieval Europe.[65] Scribes (*dibiran*) also performed important roles in the Sassanian system and often functioned as the bureaucratic apparatus of government.[66] Again we will see echoes of this in the later Hunnic Empire.

The courtly life of the Sassanian nobility brings us even closer to the medieval, feudal world. Various instruments including flutes, harp, cither and drums were used to liven up the feasts of the king and his nobles with the mandatory accompaniment of dancing and bard recitations.[67] Juggling and various other performances that one would expect to find in a medieval European court were all to be found in the court of the Sassanians. These 'medieval' courtly ceremonials were also practised in the court of Attila on the Danube.[68] The aristocracy, the grandees and the knights of Sassanian Iran, as during the Parthian period, engaged in riding (*aswarih*), archery (*kamanwarih*), polo, jousting with spears (*nezagwarih*) and more importantly royal hunts that imitated military manoeuvres.[69] The same kind of customs of course also characterized the nobility of Medieval Europe.

Did these Achaemenid-Parthian-Sassanian quasi-feudal practices influence the Hunnic Empire in any way? Probably not directly, but certainly via other Central Asian Iranian[70] states (in what is now Kazakhstan and ancient Sogdia and Chorasmia), who were first neighbours of both the Sassanians and the Huns and then later subjects of the growing Hunnic Empire in Central Asia, and perhaps also via the Yuezhi Kushans[71] (who possessed a remarkably similar political structure to the Huns and Xiongnu, as we shall see in the subsequent chapter) and Kangju, the Iranian culture (political and material) of the Persians–Parthians and Sassanians seems to have had an impact on the Hunno-Alanic culture[72] that spread into Europe and thereby heralded the dawning of the Middle Ages.[73] It is certainly no accident that in the grave of the seventh-century Bulgar Hunnic Khan Kubrat, discovered in Pereshchepyne, Sassanian silverware was discovered alongside weapons and exquisite dress accessories.[74] The empire of the Parthians and to a certain extent that of the Sassanians are also good examples of the adaptation and imposition of steppe political structures and practices on a conquered, sedentary population and provide us with an interesting precedent for examining Hunnic practices in Europe.

On the strategic level the armies of the Inner Asian Parthians and the Sassanians, although they undoubtedly did pose a serious challenge to Rome, did not constitute a mortal danger to the Roman Empire between the first century BC and the sixth century AD. The Sassanians, it is true, inflicted one embarrassing defeat after another on the Romans in the third century AD (most famous of all being the capture of emperor Valerian in AD 260) and were without a doubt Rome's most formidable opponent until the arrival of the Huns. As we shall see in Chapter 4 the Sassanians (together with the military pressure from the Sarmatian and Germanic[75] barbarians on the Danube) were largely responsible for the excessive concentration of Roman military resources in the east, which placed imperial defences in the west at a comparative disadvantage.[76] When Rome's enemies in the west were disorganized Germanic tribes this was a manageable situation for the Roman Empire, but when an Inner Asian Empire organized similarly to the Parthian Empire emerged in Europe, Rome could not hold its frontiers or avoid military collapse. The establishment and impact of this Inner Asian Empire, the Hunnic Empire, will be the topic of discussion of the rest of the book. However, before embarking on the examination of the Hunnic Empire it is necessary to locate its origins in Central Asia, in the original political milieu that gave rise to the empire's imperial organization.

CHAPTER 3

The Huns in Central Asia

INNER ASIAN EMPIRES BEFORE THE FOURTH CENTURY AD

Introduction

The altering of the strategic balance across Rome's European borders in the fourth century AD, which should rightfully be examined in the broader Eurasian context of Hunnic expansion across the entire landmass of Eurasia, has until now been analysed with an excessive focus on the Germanic migrations or Roman internal collapse. The Huns, more barbarous and primitively organized than the Germanic tribes, so we are told, have at best been allotted a peripheral role in what was arguably the single most important event in the formation of Western Europe.[1] They are never considered as the prime agents of the cataclysmic changes that they brought about.

It is the argument of this and subsequent chapters that the events of the fourth and fifth centuries AD in Western Eurasia, from Central Asia to the Atlantic, can only be accurately understood if we place the Huns at the centre of the debate and analyse historical developments from a Central Eurasian perspective. The diminution or neglect of the Hunnic Empire in modern historiography largely stems from the myths concerning their society and culture spread through the absurdly literal reading (now often rejected, it is true, but nonetheless so internalized in our understanding of the Huns that it prevents a more objective assessment of Hunnic political organization) of the mythological account on the Huns written by Ammianus Marcellinus. Famously in Ammianus, our principal source (sadly) for the early history of the Huns in Europe, the Huns are mythologized to the extent that they become practically unidentifiable in the real world. They are the most primitive savages conceivable who instead of resorting to 'normal' food for their sustenance eat roots of wild plants and

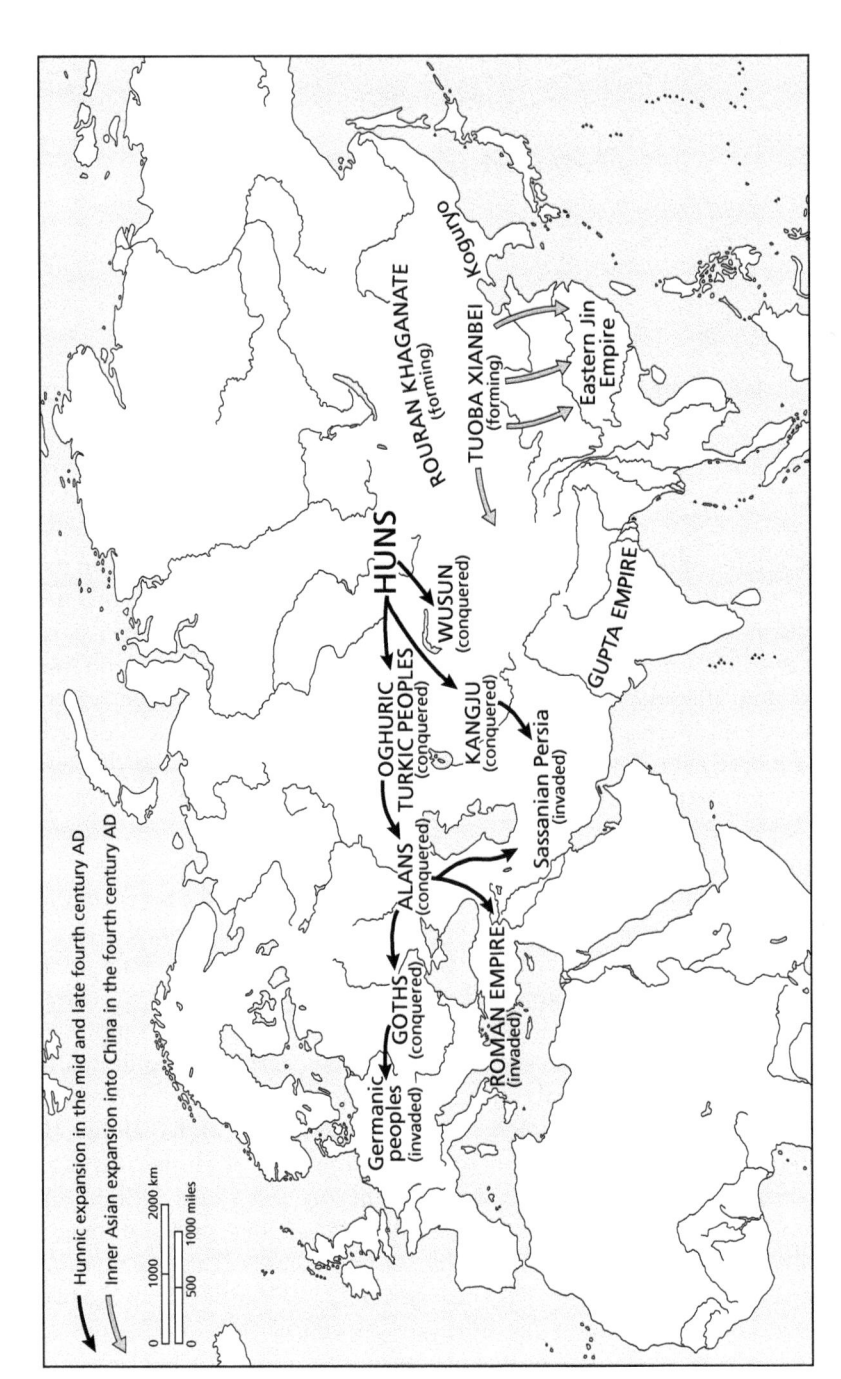

1 Eurasia in the late fourth century AD

half-raw meat of any kind of animal, use bone tips instead of iron for their arrowheads,[2] and most importantly lack any rudimentary form of kingship. According to Ammianus they improvise policy on the spot as a common body under the disorderly leadership of their important men and are therefore at the lowest possible level of social evolution:

Et deliberatione super rebus proposita seriis, hoc habitu omnes in commune consultant. Aguntur autem nulla severitate regali, sed tumultuario primatum ductu contenti, perrumpunt quicquid inciderit.

And when deliberation is called for about weighty matters, they all consult as a common body in that fashion. They are subject to no royal restraint, but they are content with the disorderly government of their important men, and led by them they force their way through every obstacle.[3]

The obvious inadequacy of this distorted representation, that was taken rather literally many years earlier by Thompson, who envisaged the absurdity of the Huns conquering the Goths and Alans without sufficient iron weaponry,[4] has often been pointed out. Maenchen-Helfen has already identified clearly anachronistic and outright mythical elements in Ammianus' account.[5] It is surely amazing that his analysis, though always acknowledged in passing, is not taken up as seriously as it should be in the latest works that discuss the Huns. On another level the lack of enthusiasm among many historians of late Roman history for comparative research and for Central Asian historical data already available (concerning what is arguably the single most important shift in strategic balance across the Eurasian continent, which heralded the millennium of dominance of steppe empires), has caused immense difficulties in accurately assessing the real impact of the Huns. A more in-depth comparative analysis that critically examines both late Roman history and Central Asian history can shed new light on the much distorted and misunderstood nature of Hun society and its political and social organization. It will be argued henceforth that the Huns, contrary to Ammianus' mythical account, possessed a highly sophisticated state or 'early state' structure originating from state or 'early state' models already available in the steppe region since the time of imperial entities such as the Royal Scythians and more importantly the great, universal steppe empire of the Xiongnu.

Before we progress any further, however, it is necessary to address the argument that early steppe empires such as the Xiongnu, which, it will be argued, provided the political models on which the Huns later built their empire, were super-complex chiefdoms or tribal confederacies with imperial dimensions rather than supra-tribal state entities.[6] No historian with specialist knowledge of steppe empires, to my knowledge, now contests the reality of the existence of political complexity within steppe empires. However, the need to accurately define what exactly constitutes a 'state' has created a slight divergence in opinions as to how exactly steppe polities before and after the Huns should be defined. Kradin has applied the most rigorous criteria in his definition of what exactly a state should be and claims a state should have the following characteristics: (1) access to managerial positions by a form of merit-based, extra-clan and non-kin-based selection; (2) regular taxation to pay wages to officials; (3) a special judicial power separate from political power; (4) a 'class' of state functionaries engaged in running a state machinery consisting of services for the administration of the whole political community. Kradin argues that the earliest steppe empire of the Xiongnu only fulfilled these requirements at best at an embryonic level and therefore cannot be defined as a state.[7]

This view is, however, quite erroneous and as Di Cosmo points out the Xiongnu Empire even by Kradin's definition was much closer to a state than to a chiefdom. As we shall see shortly the Xiongnu state administration possessed distinct military and civilian apparatuses separate from kin-based hierarchies (1). Top commanders and functionaries received their wages (in various forms) from a political centre headed by the Xiongnu emperor (Shanyu/Chanyu) (2), who was also in charge of ceremonies and rituals that were meant to include the entire political community. The incredibly complex organization of Xiongnu armies, its imperial rituals, government structure and politically centralized functions of trade and diplomacy all bear witness to a political machinery and supratribal, imperial ideology.[8] Kradin himself acknowledges that special judicial manpower (i.e. judges) was also available in the Xiongnu Empire (3) and that there were special state functionaries (Gu-du marquises) who assisted the emperor in the overall administration of the empire (4).[9] In short, even on the basis of the scant information we do have on Xiongnu political organization, it is possible to argue that the Xiongnu Empire in all likelihood met the definition for a state or an 'early state'.[10]

Also, there is absolutely no doubt at all that the Xiongnu constituted an empire, 'a political formation that extended far beyond its original territorial or ethnic confines and embraced, by direct conquest or by the imposition of its political authority, a variety of peoples and lands that may have had different types of relations with the imperial centre, constituted by an imperial clan and by its charismatic leader'.[11] It is difficult to see how without even a rudimentary state structure and state institutions of some sort the Xiongnu could have accumulated the political ability and military power to create a vast empire and maintain it for centuries. The same principle applies also to the later Huns,[12] who, as I will demonstrate, possessed very similar organization to the Xiongnu which they in all probability inherited directly from the Xiongnu. It is logical to assume, therefore, that the Xiongnu Empire was a state or an 'early state'. The comparative analysis which follows will offer an explanation as to why the Huns alone of all the 'barbarians' north of the Danube managed to provide a political system that integrated all the peoples in barbaricum and to pose a persistent political as well as a military threat to the Roman Empire.[13]

The question is, how can one even contemplate governing an empire that stretches from Gaul to the Volga without sophisticated political structures even for a single generation (i.e. Attila's reign, the length of time many scholars erroneously grant for the life-span of the Hunnic Empire)? This is obviously impossible. Has any state even tried to govern nearly half of Europe for nearly eighty years without any advanced apparatus of government? This is, however, the picture that is created, if we accept what many historians up until now have been suggesting. Yet the Huns held their empire together for a substantial length of time in non-Roman Europe, where, especially in Germania, there was simply no precedent for imperial, political unity. We will elaborate on the organization of the Hunnic Empire later, but what is clear is that former models proposed for the nature of the Hunnic Empire are vastly misleading and wrong.

The Xiongnu, the Scythians and the Sarmatians

The mistaken assumptions regarding the organization of steppe societies have led to the persistence of these many myths concerning the Huns and their empire. When we observe, however, the level of administrative sophistication achieved among the Xiongnu and the Scythians[14] long before the appearance of the Huns in Europe, such myths can be swiftly dispatched. Many historians and literary critics, who simply ignore Central Asian history in their analysis of Classical texts which discuss steppe nomads, typically assume that 'a nomad power is something inconceivable: if it is a power, it cannot be nomad'.[15] Such an assumption derives from the mistaken presupposition that nomadism is an insurmountable obstacle to sophisticated social organization and centralization of authority.

Yet many Classical authors, even as early as the historian Herodotus, had no such presuppositions. Herodotus in his discourse on the Scythians mentions the existence of a *nomarch* in each province of the Scythian kingdom (4.66). In Book 4.62.1 he also mentions the *nomes*. This is all the more important in that the same word is used to denote administrative units of Egypt and Persia.[16] To many critics, who refuse to believe that the Scythians could have developed such a level of organization, this is simply an example of Herodotus observing the principle of symmetry between Egypt and Scythia and explaining Scythian practices in Egyptian terms. However, the level of administrative sophistication achieved by the Eastern Xiongnu,[17] (Early Middle Chinese (EMC), pronounced Hun-nu[18]) in Mongolia and Turkestan, whose empire co-existed with that of the Scythians, should radically alter our interpretation of Herodotus' early account of Scythian administrative organization.[19]

The Xiongnu (匈奴, as a united imperial entity third century BC – 48 AD[20]), despite their 'nomadism', managed to achieve an astonishing degree of centralization and pioneered the classic model of imperial rule for later steppe empires to imitate.[21] Their society was essentially quasi-feudal,[22] characterized by a complex hierarchy which is outlined in detail by the first-century BC Han Chinese historian Sima Qian:

Under the *Shan-yü*[23] are the Wise Kings of the Left and Right, the left and right Lu-li kings, left and right generals, left and right commandants, left and right household administrators, and left and right Ku-tu marquises. The Hsiung-nu word for 'wise' is 't'u-ch'i', so that the heir of the *Shan-yü* is customarily called the 'T'u-ch'i King of the Left'. Among the other leaders, from the wise kings on down to the household administrators, the more important ones command ten thousand horsemen and the lesser ones several thousand, numbering twenty-four leaders in all, though all are known by the title 'Ten Thousand Horsemen'. The high ministerial offices are hereditary, being filled from generation to generation by the members of the Hu-yen and Lan families, and in more recent times by the Hsü-pu family. These three families constitute the aristocracy of the nation. The kings and other leaders of the left live in the eastern sector, the region from Shang-ku east to the land of the Hui-mo and the Ch'ao-hsien peoples. The kings and leaders of the right live in the west, the area from Shang province west to the territories of the Yüeh-chi and Ch'iang tribes. The *Shan-yü* has his court in the region of Tai and Yün-chung. Each group has its own area, within which it moves about from place to place looking for water and pasture. The Left and Right Wise Kings and the Lu-li kings are the most powerful, while the Ku-tu marquises assist the *Shan-yü* in the administration of the nation. Each of the twenty-four leaders in turn appoint his own 'chiefs of a thousand', 'chiefs of a hundred', and 'chiefs of ten', as well as his subordinate kings, prime ministers, chief commandants, household administrators, *chü-ch'ü* officials and so forth. (*Shiji* 110: 9b–10b)[24]

From what is known about the Xiongnu we can deduce the following about their administrative system. The supreme power rested in the hands of the Shanyu/Chanyu (單于, meaning 'emperor', likely to have been pronounced dàn-wà, representing darγwa in EMC[25]) who was assisted in his duties by the

Gu-du (Ku-tu in the Wade–Giles transliteration above) marquises who ran the central imperial government and co-ordinated the affairs of the empire. As in the contemporary Parthian–Sassanian system to the west mentioned in the previous chapter, in the Xiongnu Empire in the east, flanking the central government there seem to have been four principal, regional governorships in the East and West (later called in the *Hou Hanshu*, 'the four horns' or 'angles'[26]): the Worthy King of the Left and the Luli King of the Left in the East and the Worthy King of the Right and the Luli King of the Right in the West. Each of these four governorships had its own government bureaucracy[27] and the kings (sons or brothers of the reigning Shanyu) constituted the highest ranking aristocrats in the empire.[28] The Xiongnu also possessed (or perhaps gradually added after 97 BC to the system described in the *Shiji* above) six more eminent aristocratic titles (the six horns or angles,[29] perhaps by coincidence (?) slightly reminiscent (though with obvious differences) of the system of six great aristocratic families in the Parthian Empire), consisting of the Rizhu kings of the Left and Right (titles reserved also for the sons and younger brothers of the Shanyu),[30] Wenyuti kings of the Left and Right, and the Zhanjiang Kings of the Left and Right.[31]

Below these top-ranking nobles or including them there were the so-called twenty-four imperial leaders/ministers[32] (each titled Ten Thousand Horsemen), who acted as imperial governors for the major provinces of the empire and were (and this will also have important ramifications for the Hunnic political system later on) usually close relatives of the Shanyu or members of the Xiongnu aristocracy (probably related to the royal house).[33] These princes and senior nobles were divided into Eastern and Western groups (dualism)[34] and the successor to the throne was usually appointed the Wise King of the Left, i.e the ruler of the Eastern half of the empire (again we will see echoes of this in the Hun system later on). All the appointments were made by the Xiongnu central government under the direction of the Shanyu.

At the bottom of the administrative hierarchy was a large class of subordinate or vassal tribal leaders (sub-kings, prime ministers, chief commandants, household administrators, *chü-ch'ü* officals etc.) who were under the command of the twenty-four imperial governors, but enjoyed a level of local autonomy.[35] A non-decimal system of ranks was used for the political administration of tribes and territory within the empire which included groups of many different sizes.[36] However, a more rigid system of decimal ranks (thousands, hundreds, tens) was used in times of war when large armies were formed from troops drawn from different parts of the steppe under a single command structure.[37] A census was also taken to determine the empire's reserves of manpower and livestock.[38]

It is highly probable that Herodotus was in fact referring to a similar organization among the Scythians.[39] The nomarchs are likely to have been division commanders of the kind found among the Xiongnu. The Scythian legend of their origin which divides their nation into three parts (Hdt. 4.7) may also reflect a similar tripartite division of power among the leading tribes/clans which characterized the Xiongnu form of government.[40] Ivantchik notes that the element *-xais* with which all three names of the brothers in the Scythian foundation legend end (Lipoxais, Arpoxais and Colaxais), is etymologically connected to the Iranian word *xsaya* (king).[41] He also suggests quite plausible etymologies which would connect the names Cola, Arpo and Lipo with the Iranian words for sun, water, and mountain.[42] The names are probably indicative of the division of the world into three levels, which is one of the principal ideas of Indo-Iranian cosmology found in various Vedic and Zoroastrian texts and traditions.[43] The three levels may correspond to the three castes mentioned in various Indian and Iranian texts (priest, farmer and warrior).[44] The Scythians of Herodotus, therefore, probably possessed a highly stratified, politically organized state[45] and as Bichler puts it 'sehr festen herrschaftlichen Institutionen'.[46]

At the pinnacle of the Scythian political structure was the king whose power, contrary to what critics like Hartog believe, was in all probability very real and certainly not a mere product of the narrative constraint which imposes the need to assign a king to every non-Greek power.[47] Among the Xiongnu, to use once again the same analogy, the political power wielded by the Shanyu was truly formidable. Chinese sources report that Modun, the Shanyu, could boast of having subjugated twenty-six states and reduced them to obedience as a part of the Xiongnu nation.[48] In war the Shanyu could reputedly mobilize an army of 140,000 men from among his subjects.[49] Herodotus portrays the Scythian king in a similar way. As the head of the so-called Royal Scythians[50] who held supremacy over all other groups of Scythians the king, like the Shanyu, was the military leader in times of war, as is demonstrated by Idanthyrsus' direction of the war against the Persians. In times of peace the king was also apparently the distributor of justice and presided over duels between relatives (4.65.2). Furthermore, the taking of the census by King Ariantes (4.81) and the punishment he used to enforce his decree (4.81.5) reveal the substantive nature of royal power which turned Scythia into a real state with the necessary means to impose order and control.[51] In fact archaeological excavations from Arzhan in Tuva, northwest of Mongolia, from the Scythian period (eighth century BC), have revealed the existence of highly organized steppe polities in Central

Asia that corroborate Herodotus' observations. A huge Scythian or rather Saka type tomb that included 70 chambers and 160 saddle horses buried with the king, who obviously ruled a large and powerful steppe confederacy, was brought to light. That he ruled over a more or less typical steppe hierarchical state/quasi-state entity is confirmed by the fact that subordinate princes or nobles were buried to the north, south and west of the king and his wife.[52]

One startling difference between the Xiongnu and the Scythians, though, was the degree to which they absorbed the political institutions of their sedentary neighbours. The Scythians do not seem to have adopted any institutional features from either the Greeks (highly disorganized in any case) or even the Persians (that is unless their organization mentioned above in some way can be seen as an imitation of Achaemenid administrative ideas).[53] The Xiongnu in contrast seem to have absorbed some of the sophistication of their Chinese neighbours when it came to state organization and administration.[54] The essentially 'feudal' character of their empire with its hierarchy of kings and marquises, the highest ranks of which were reserved exclusively for members of the royal clan and the lesser ranks for leaders of other leading clans that intermarried with the royal clan (of immense significance for our later examination of the Hunnic Empire and its successor kingdoms in Europe),[55] has obvious analogies with the kingdoms and marquisates of the Han Empire, but with clear differences in functions. The Xiongnu territorial divisions which favoured the left, i.e. the east (when viewed with orientation towards the south in the Chinese manner or right when viewed with orientation towards the north in the steppe manner[56]), over the west may also reflect the influence of Chinese ideas of rulership which identified the left (east) with the *yang* (as in *yinyang*) forces of generation and growth. The use of colours as symbolism for territory, blue for east, white for west, black for north and red for south, correspond to the symbolism of Chinese cosmology (Wuxing, five elements theory).[57]

In the west the Scythian political tradition was to some extent continued by the Sarmatians and Alans (considered a branch of the Sarmatians,[58] who seem to have been somewhat more fragmented in comparison to other steppe nomadic peoples further to the east[59]), later conquered by the Huns upon their entry into Europe.[60] According to Strabo,[61] the Sarmatians at one stage in their history (possibly from the late second century BC to *c*. 60 BC), before they fragmented, possessed tighter organization and a ruling royal tribe who were situated in the centre of the Sarmatian tribal confederacy/empire and surrounded by a protective ring of vassal tribes (Iazyges to the south, Urgi to the north and the Roxolani to the east).[62] The Alans further to the east, like the Scythians and western Sarmatians in the second century BC, also possessed a royal clan[63] and regiments of professional warriors in the Scythian manner (presumably in the usual decimal system).[64] The kings, like the Scythian Ariantes of old, carried out a general census of male warriors (*Martyrdom of Sukuasyants*[65]) and even built royal palaces[66] and city fortifications. An inscription at Olbia also bears witness to their observance of the steppe custom of collective or joint rule among brothers who are referred to as the 'greatest kings of Aorsia'.[67] Furthermore, the Alans apparently possessed a ranking system, in much the same way as the Scythians and the Xiongnu. The kings used a royal title similar to the Scythian *ksais*, local princes or chiefs were titled *ardar* (literally 'holding in a hand', perhaps related to sceptre holders mentioned in Tacitus *Annals* 6.33) and were distinguished from the class of slaves called *čagar*.[68] We also learn that the Alans used colour to designate segments of their tribal confederation in the same way as the Xiongnu. Thus we find Ptolemy making reference to white (hapax) Alans.[69]

Even if we were to discount the Alans, who may well have possessed similar though obviously more haphazard political and social institutions in comparison to the Xiongnu, it is nonetheless clear that in the territory from which the Huns derived there were already historical precedents for highly sophisticated organization, both social and military, that facilitated the emergence time and again in the steppe region of formidable empires. Han Chinese administrative and political practices, more complex than even the Roman model,[70] also seem to have had a profound effect on the early Huns/Xiongnu. If so, then what is the evidence for the possibility of this organization being transmitted to the Huns in the fourth century AD?

The Hun–Xiongnu connection

To fully understand the nature of our European Huns, it is necessary first of all to re-examine their possible links to the above-mentioned Xiongnu. The now almost legendary work of Deguignes, *Histoire générale des Huns, des Turcs, des Mogols et des autres Tartares occidentaux* (1756–1824), sparked a debate that has raged for centuries. Were the European Huns the political and physical descendants of the imperial Xiongnu? Deguignes with remarkable intuition asserted that they were, but later scholarship tended to voice scepticism concerning this link between Huns and Xiongnu. Renowned and distinguished historians of the Huns and Central Asia openly rejected any links other than possible cultural affinities between the Huns and the

Xiongnu.[71] For our purposes cultural links, and in particular the preservation of political institutions, are obviously of greater importance and sufficient for the argument that the Huns were politically organized. However, it is possible to strengthen this cultural link with actual physical, 'genetic' links between the later Huns and the earlier Xiongnu.

In 1948 Henning published a remarkable text from the year AD 313, a letter sent by a Sogdian merchant by the name of Nanaivandak from Gansu in China concerning the fall of the Chinese capital of Luoyang to the Southern Xiongnu in AD 311. In the letter, without a shadow of a doubt, the Xiongnu are called Huns.[72] The response to this amazing discovery has been equally amazing. Sinor suggests that this only proves that the name Hun was a general term used by Sogdians for all nomads.[73] Bailey for his part, believing the Xiongnu to be Iranians, not Turkic like the western Huns presumably were,[74] argues that the name Hun derives from the term *Hyaona*, a designation used in the *Avesta* to denote a hostile people. This he assumes was used by the Sogdian merchant to refer to the Xiongnu, as a generic term for nomads.[75]

However, as La Vaissière points out, both Sinor and Bailey are wrong to attribute the use of the name Hun as a general designation for all nomads before the time of the great Hunnic invasions.[76] It was only after the fourth- and fifth-century exploits of the Huns, which made their name famous, that historians in the West would start to use their name in a generic sense to designate nomads. There is no evidence whatsoever that their name was used as a generic term for nomads before the sixth century AD. It is also highly problematic to treat the name Hun as a fourth-century pan-Iranian term for steppe nomads. For starters the 'h' in the Avestic initial 'hy-' (as in *Hyaona*) disappears in Sogdian and words that derive from Avestic with the 'hy-' initial prefix never commence with 'X' in Sogdian, with which the name Hun begins in the letter of Nanaivandak.[77] In other words there are formidable linguistic problems with associating the term *Hyaona* with the Huns.

Another problem with the Iranian theory is that the term Hun was without a doubt the self-designation adopted by the Huns themselves. *Hyaona* may possibly be a Zoroastrian term applied to hostile enemies, but it by no means designated exclusively nomads, who were more often referred to as the *Tuirya*.[78] If so, why on earth would the Huns adopt this name as their own ethnonym and why would non-Zoroastrian Sarmatians and Goths refer to the Huns in this manner? And we must also take note of the fact that there were plenty of other nomadic tribes in eastern Turkestan at the time when Nanaivandak travelled through it, who were not called

Huns, but referred to themselves as the Dingling, Var, Xianbei etc. Are we to assume that Nanaivandak, who was an eye-witness to the events of AD 313, was ignorant of the proper name of the invading horde? This surely can't be right and it is totally unacceptable to dismiss primary evidence like this in a cavalier manner.

In fact recently further evidence has come to light, this time from India and Tibet, which in my view renders the identification of the name Hun with Xiongnu highly probable, if not certain. Two texts, the *Tathagataguhya-sutra* and *Lalitavistara*, translated into Chinese by Zhu Fahu, a monk from Dunhuang, by origin of Bactrian descent (translations AD 280 and AD 308 respectively, i.e. roughly contemporaneous with Nanaivandak's letter), identify the *Huna* (Huns), then a distant people to the Indians, with the Xiongnu, as a specific political entity adjacent to China.[79] There is no indication at all that the use of the term Xiongnu for *Huna* here is generic in any sense. Given this contemporary evidence, it seems quite natural to agree with La Vaissière and Pulleyblank that the imperial Xiongnu and the European Huns had the same name.[80]

Having the same name is a start, but this certainly does not prove that the Huns and the Xiongnu were culturally linked. Archaeological evidence, however, in this case supports the link and leaves no doubt as to the cultural connections between the European Huns and the old territory ruled by the Xiongnu. Most serious scholars of the Huns and Xiongnu are in agreement that Hunnic cauldrons, an archaeological marker of Hunnic presence, derive from Xiongnu cauldrons in the Ordos region in Inner Mongolia.[81] Remarkably, the placement of the Xiongnu and Hunnic cauldrons are virtually the same, on the bank of rivers, a fact which proves that the continuity between the old Xiongnu and the European Huns is not only artistic or technological, but also cultural.[82] Furthermore, both the Huns and the Xiongnu practised a very similar sword cult (in Xiongnu the cult of the *kenglu*).[83] In other words, even if one were to reject an ethnic/genetic link between Huns and Xiongnu,[84] it is impossible to deny a cultural continuity or affinity between the Xiongnu and the Huns. Of course it might be possible that the Huns residing in Kazakhstan (from where they would in the fourth century AD move into Europe)[85] had no blood links with the Xiongnu of Mongolia, though how this could be given the history of prolonged Xiongnu presence, migration to and rule of the very regions occupied by the Huns, is problematic to say the least.[86]

It must, however, be recognized that the Hunnic confederation that entered Europe, despite having the same name as the Xiongnu and also very likely a similar mix of ethnic groups (at least initially) and cultural traditions to those which characterized the latter, was not the exact replica of the old Xiongnu Empire. During their migration west the Xiongnu (Huns) seem to have undergone a transformation. Whereas the original Xiongnu in Mongolia, according to Pulleyblank and Vovin, may have had a Yeniseian core tribal elite[87] which ruled over various Iranian and Altaic (Turco-Mongol) groups,[88] if the names of Hunnic tribes and rulers are a rough guide to ethnicity[89] (poor indicators at best in the steppe region), the Huns seem to have had a core Turkic element, ruling over initially a large Turco-Iranian population (in the east) and then after their conquests in Europe a largely Germanic population in the western half of their empire.

The heavier concentration of Turkic peoples[90] in the western half of the old Xiongnu Empire is likely to have contributed to this shift from a Yeniseian core language group to a Turkic one.[91] A very similar transformation can be noted in the later history of the steppe in the Golden Horde and the Chagatai Khanate where the Mongol ruling elite from the east rapidly adopted the Turkic language which was the dominant spoken language of the tribes that made up the bulk of their armies in the West.[92] The Xiongnu who migrated west are likely to have done the same.

Yet the fact that the Huns chose to hold on to the name of the imperial Xiongnu as their own ethnonym or state name, even after the probable Turkification of the elite, is a clear indication that they regarded this link with the old steppe tradition of imperial grandeur as valuable and significant, a sign of their original identity and future ambitions no doubt. The preservation of Xiongnu cultural identity (as the preservation of Xiongnu-type cauldrons all the way from the eastern steppe to the Danube shows) among the western Huns suggests also that a culturally dominant inner core of Xiongnu/Huns remained intact through their long migration from Inner Asia to Europe.[93] The old Xiongnu confederation was in any case highly heterogeneous,[94] a polyglot empire containing Yeniseian, Turkic, Mongolic, Tungusic, Iranian and even Chinese elements. The name Xiongnu/Hun could also refer to either a specific ethnic entity or more frequently to all dwelling within the political entity established under the name Hun.[95] The later descendant of this imperial confederacy, the Hun Empire would, following the old traditions of the Xiongnu, be equally heterogeneous, containing mainly Turkic, Iranian and Germanic elements, but also Slavic, Baltic, Finno-Ugric and even Greco-Roman minorities.[96]

This heterogeneity of the Hunnic state in Europe has led numerous scholars (most recently Heather) to make the unverifiable assertion that the official language of the Hunnic Empire was Gothic due to the rather disputable assumption that the names of three Attila era kings – Ruga (or

Roga/Rua/Rugila), Bleda and Attila – are Gothic.[97] Naturally we also have more probable Turkic etymologies for these names, especially for those of Attila and Bleda.[98] However, even if they were Germanic or Germanicized Turkic names,[99] this does not allow us to make any hasty assumptions about the official language of the empire, if it ever existed. What Heather ignores is the fact that we have convincing or highly probable Turkic etymologies for the names of many of the other Hunnic kings and nobles before and after Attila, e.g. Mundzuk[100] (Attila's father, from Turkic *Munčuq* = 'pearl/jewel'), Oktar/Uptar (Attila's uncle, *Öktär* = 'brave/powerful'), Oebarsius (another of Attila's paternal uncles, *Aïbârs* = 'leopard of the moon'), Karaton (Hunnic supreme king before Ruga, *Qarâton* = 'blackcloak'), Basik (Hunnic noble of royal blood, early fifth century, *Bârsiğ* = 'governor'), Kursik (Hunnic noble of royal blood, from either *Kürsiğ*, meaning 'brave or noble', or *Quršiq* meaning 'belt-bearer').[101] All three of Attila's known sons have probable Turkic names: Ellac, Dengizich, Hernak, and Attila's principal wife, the mother of the first son Ellac, has the Turkic name Herekan, as does another wife named Eskam (*Ešqam* = 'companion of the Shaman').[102]

It seems highly likely then from the names that we do know, most of which seem to be Turkic, that the Hunnic elite was predominantly Turkic-speaking.[103] However, in the western half of the empire, where most of their subjects spoke Germanic languages, the Huns may have used both Hunnic (Oghuric Turkic[104]) and Gothic. Thus fief holders and royal family members in the west who ruled Germanic tribes often bore Germanic or Germanicized titles (of great significance, as we will discover later on in the book), e.g. Laudaricus and Ardaric.[105] Priscus, who is our only reliable source, being an actual eye-witness, tells us that at the Hunnic court Hunnic, Gothic and Latin were spoken, but with Hunnic always mentioned before Gothic. All three languages were apparently understood by the elite to some degree,[106] so much so that Zercon the Moor could provoke laughter by jumbling all three together at a Hunnic banquet in the presence of Attila.[107] There is, however, no indication anywhere that any of these three languages was the lingua franca.

It is highly probable that like the later Ottoman Turkish Empire, in which Persian was used for administration, Arabic for religion and Turkic for the army, and as in the contemporary Hunnic Kidarite Empire in Central Asia which used Sogdian, Bactrian, Middle Persian and Brahmi on different occasions for administrative purposes,[108] the Hunnic Empire used three (possibly four: Hunnic, Gothic, Latin, Sarmatian (i.e. Alanic)) languages at various levels in order to govern its vastly polyglot army and population.[109] All levels of Hunnic society are also likely to have been heavily mixed through inter-marriage. Some of that mixing would have taken place as far back as old Xiongnu times.[110] Thus to refer to Hun–Xiongnu links in terms of old racial theories or even ethnic affiliations simply makes a mockery of the actual historical reality of these extensive, multiethnic, polyglot steppe empires.[111] It is nonetheless clear that the ancestors, if they need to be mentioned at all, of the Hunnic core tribes (mostly Turkic and Iranian) were part of the Xiongnu Empire and possessed a strong Xiongnu element, and that the ruling elite of the Huns, as their very name indicates, claimed to belong to the political tradition of this imperial entity.

However, as many historians have pointed out there is a historical gap of about two centuries between the final defeat of the Northern Xiongnu confederation at the hands of the Xianbei[112] and the Hunnic invasions of the mid fourth century AD.[113] The *Hou Han-shu* (89.2953–4) records that the last known Shanyu (emperor) of the Northern Xiongnu in AD 91 either disappeared in the west or moved to the territory of the Wusun in modern day eastern Kazakhstan.[114] The *Wei Shu* (102.2268) indicates that he moved further west to Kangju (Tashkent region) and that the Yueban (悅般, Weak Huns, east of the Kangju) who dominated the old territory of the Wusun in the fifth century AD were Xiongnu/Hun remnants.[115] The Xianbei under their leader Tian Shi-huai,[116] however, defeated the remaining Xiongnu feudatories in the Tarim basin *c.* AD 153.[117] After this, due to the decline of Chinese interest in the West, nothing more is heard of the western Huns until the fourth century. Some might question whether the western Huns, despite their pretensions to Xiongnu heritage, could still have had the capacity after this lull to create an imperial structure with the sophisticated social and military organization that was the distinguishing feature of the early Xiongnu polity.

The Yuezhi (Kushans), Kangju and the Wusun

In order to address this issue it is first necessary to observe the political situation in Inner Asia before and at the time of the Hunnic onslaught on the Alans and Goths. During the so-called two-hundred-year gap in our records we find in close proximity to the Xiongnu residing in the Altai (from where the European Huns would start their long trek west), not immediately adjacent, but to their southwest from the Tarim basin[118] to Northern India, the formidable empire of the Kushans founded by the five Da Yuezhi (大月支) tribes.[119] The Yuezhi[120] were steppe nomads driven out of Chinese Turkestan by the Xiongnu *c.* 162 BC.[121] Their migration west,[122] according to the *Han Shu*, caused a chain reaction which drove the Sai (Saka[123])[124] into the Greco-Bactrian kingdom[125] and then even further west into Parthia.[126] In the end the Yuezhi migration resulted in the permanent conquest of Bactria by the Yuezhi[127] (Tochari[128] led by the Asiani/Asi[129]) and the establishment of Scythian/Saka states all over Afghanistan and northwestern India. The Parthian kings Phraates II (Justin 42.1.5) and Artabanus II (Justin 42.2.2, combating the Tochari) were killed by the invading 'Scythians'[130] and only in the reign of Mithradates II (beginning *c.* 124 BC, Justin 42.2.4–5) could the Parthians contain the Saka in Sistan.[131]

The Yuezhi would later in the first and second centuries AD struggle with other Tocharians, 'Scythians' and even the Han Empire in Central Asia. The Chinese interestingly refer to the five *xihou* or Lords of the Yuezhi who rule the five tribes of their imperial confederation.[132] According to Pulleyblank, this *xihou* corresponds in the EMC pronunciation to what would later become the Turkic title *yabgu*[133] and this originally Yuezhi royal title appears on the coins of the Yuezhi rulers, Kujula Kadphises, as 'IAPGU/yavuga'.[134] Of the five Yabgus,[135] the Lord of the Guishuang/Kushan tribe[136] would become the ruling power under the above mentioned Kujula.[137]

These rulers of steppe origin, who on their coins proudly depicted themselves wearing the typical Central Asian/Scythian peaked headdress and long boots,[138] fascinatingly possessed political institutions that closely resemble the Xiongnu and later Hunnic models. Like the Xiongnu the Yuezhi had a political and ceremonial centre even when they were ruled by the five Yabgus.[139] In AD 90 we learn that a *fu-wang* (sub-king) called Xie was sent out by the Kushan king to attack the Han Chinese military commander in the Tarim basin, Ban Chao.[140] Another Kushan ruler Vima Kadphises, the father of the famous Kanishka,[141] would appoint a general to supervise the administration of the Upper Indus Valley,[142] which is probably a demonstration of the overlapping of military and civilian administration so typical of the Xiongnu system of government. Kushan inscriptions also show that officials with titles such as *dandanayaka* and *mahadandanayaka* performed both civil and military functions throughout India.[143]

Even more revealingly we learn that among the Kushans collateral succession to the throne and some form of joint rulership and association of sub-kings in the imperial administration were persistently practised right up to the end of the empire in the third century AD.[144] By way of example, Kaniska I was succeeded by Huviska, but Vasiska and Kaniska II appear to have been associated with them respectively as joint rulers and used the same imperial titles.[145] Thus, as among the Xiongnu and later steppe empires, the Yuezhi/Kushans may have practised dualism and collective rule and possessed an elaborate hierarchy of sub-kings and officials. The Kushans even practised the custom of artificial cranial deformation which would later be introduced into Europe by the Huns and Alans and was also practised by the Hephtalite Huns.[146]

Kushan power in Central Asia (Transoxiana and the Tarim Basin[147]) southwest of the Northern Xiongnu/Huns in the Altai would fade under Sassanian pressure in the mid third century AD (Shapur I, r. AD 240–70, would dissolve the Kushan Empire), but their remnants would continue to rule in various capacities as Kushanshahs[148] under Sassanian overlordship until the Hunnic conquest in the fourth century.[149] The Yuezhi Kushans, however, were by no means the only Inner Asian steppe people (possibly of Tocharian origin[150]) to possess an elaborate political structure during the second and third centuries AD. We also know that the Dayuan (大宛, perhaps pronounced in EMC as *Taxwār*[151]), who were situated in Ferghana,[152] and the Kangju (康居, in modern Uzbekistan around Tashkent, south of the Dingling (as mentioned earlier, probably Oghuric Turks in Kazakhstan who were gradually absorbed by the Huns some time during the so-called two-hundred-year gap[153])), who may have been ruled by an elite called the Asi[154], also possessed state level organization.

The Dayuan would submit to the Han Empire and then later to the Kushans,[155] but the Kangju would become a power to be reckoned with in the first century AD[156] and would also subjugate the Yancai (later the Alans[157]) further west and keep them in that state until at least the second century AD and possibly even the third century AD.[158] The Kangju were also ruled by a *Yabgu* like the Kushans with whom they were dynastically related by marriage[159] and at least during the Early Han Period they possessed a system of five 'lesser kings',[160] indicating that they too had very similar political institutions to their southern neighbours.[161] In ways reminiscent of the Xiongnu/Huns, the Kangju would impose their ruling elite upon the conquered Alans. Thus we find among the western and Caucasian Alans the ruling clan/tribe of the Dukhs-As (Asi).[162] These Kangju were in direct contact with the Xiongnu (Huns) who had moved west and in the first century BC we hear of the migration of a Xiongnu Chanyu called Zhizhi who went west with his people to the Kangju and borrowed troops from them with which he attacked the Wusun.[163] Zhizhi would be killed by the Han Chinese in 36 BC, but the Xiongnu of the Altai (the later Huns of Central Asia and Europe) in the second–fourth centuries AD, as they gradually absorbed the Dingling

(Oghuric Turks) in northern and central Kazakhstan, came to share a common boundary with the Kangju and continuously interacted with them.[164]

The Wusun (direct neighbours of the Huns to the southwest in the Ili basin),[165] who had earlier in the second century BC expelled the Yuezhi/Kushans from the Ili basin[166] and whose territory the Xiognu/Huns would later absorb in their expansion west and south in the fourth century AD, also possessed a highly developed political structure. Their political structure was apparently modelled after that of the Xiongnu.[167] There was a hereditary king who was assisted by a council of elders, which could also act as a restraint on the powers of the sovereign. There was likewise a fairly developed administrative apparatus consisting of sixteen graded officials, who were recruited from the ruling nobility. Social stratification and the concentration of wealth in the hands of a small elite class, some of whom possessed as many as 4,000–5,000 horses in a pastoral economy, evidently caused social tensions among the Wusun,[168] noted by Chinese visitors. The officials and nobles of the realm maintained themselves by taxes/tribute collected from subordinate tribes, war booty and profits from trading activities (much the same as the Hunnic elite, as we shall see later). The Kunmo or the Great king[169] and his two sons, the rulers of the left and right domains (again in exactly the same way as the Xiongnu), each commanded a personal force of 10,000 horsemen.[170] The remnants of the Wusun seem to have survived until AD 436 (that is, unless this is an anachronistic reference to the Yueban (Weak Huns), who occupied their former lands[171]). Most of the Wusun, however, seem to have been either absorbed or assimilated by the Xiongnu/Huns.

It is unclear as to exactly when the Kangju disintegrated,[172] but they too like the remnants of the Kushans and the Wusun were caught up in the Hunnic expansion west and south. Until then the Kangju for several centuries ruled over a large political entity stretching from the steppes of western Kazakhstan to the borders of the Huns and Wusun in eastern Kazakhstan with its core situated around Tashkent in modern Uzbekistan. The sophisticated inhabitants of this empire, many of whom were actually urban dwellers or only semi-nomadic[173] like the later Yueban (Weak Huns to the east, who were surprisingly enough deemed to be the most civilized people among the barbarians by the Chinese in the fifth century AD), were under heavy Xiongnu/Hun influence.[174] Is it possible then to defend the illogical idea of a primitive Hun society with no political organization whatsoever, when in fact the peoples and states conquered or vassalized by the Huns while they were still in Central Asia possessed high levels of civilization and sophisticated political structures?

In the first and second centuries AD the Xiongnu/Huns were indeed at the nadir of their political and military fortunes. They were practically under siege in the Altai region. To the west and south the Dingling, Kangju and Wusun exerted pressure. To the east the powerful Xianbei and the Han Empire had expelled them from their eastern domains. However, remarkably after the third century AD these menaces disappeared one after the other. To the east the Han Empire descended into civil war following the Yellow Turban revolt. The Xianbei who had earlier exerted such pressure on the Huns during the second century AD were divided into feuding tribes and their confederacy would completely disintegrate by AD 350.[175] To the west and southwest the Kangju state was slowly disintegrating.[176] Is it then an accident that we find the Huns up in arms and expanding west and south in the fourth century? In fact archaeological evidence from the Ural region seems to point to the expansion of the Huns into that area by the early fourth century AD,[177] suggesting that the nations between the Altai and the Urals had succumbed to Hunnic conquest by the early fourth century. This was then followed by Hunnic thrusts in two directions, one into Kangju and Wusun territories to the south and the other into Alan territory to the west. What is clear from all this is that during the so-called gap between references to the Huns in our sources (of c. 200 years) the Xiongnu/Huns were in constant contact with imperial and state-level (or early-state-level) entities (in particular the Kangju and the Wusun), all of whom possessed elaborate political structures.

CONTEMPORARY INNER ASIAN EMPIRES (FOURTH, FIFTH AND SIXTH CENTURIES AD)

The White Huns (Chionites, Kidarites and Hephtalites)

The eventful fourth century AD, as already pointed out towards the beginning of this book, opened with the Southern Xiongnu/Hun sack of the capital of the Chinese Jin Empire in AD 311. The Southern Xiongnu power in China (Earlier/Later Zhao Empire[178]) quickly collapsed as other ethnic groups (The Murong Xianbei, Chiang etc.) and Chinese resistance drove them from their domains.[179] In the meantime in the steppe further north and northwest new nomadic confederations called the Rouran (situated later firmly in Mongolia, possibly the Avars[180]) and Hua (EMC either Var or Ghor[181]), originally vassals of the Rouran,[182] were gradually taking shape. The *Liangshu* (54.812) provides evidence that would link the latter confederation (Hua) to the Hephtalites[183] of the fifth century AD who ruled the

White Hun Empire. If the name Hua was transliterated as *Var* and not *Ghor* in EMC, the Hua may also be considered as the forerunners of the later Eurasian Avars.[184]

Czeglédy, regarding the Hua to be Vars (Avars), argued that a migration wave of Vars/Avars may have reached western Turkestan in the middle of the fourth century AD and this may have had some kind of an impact on the Hun migration west.[185] More recently it has been proposed that the Huns started moving west out of the Altai in the fourth century AD, not because of renewed military pressure from the east, but because of radical climate deterioration in the Altai region in that century.[186] Neither explanation is satisfactory since the Hunnic expansion west may have commenced well before the fourth century. Érdy, on the basis of archaeological evidence provided by Hunnic cauldrons, has argued for a Hunnic presence in the Tobol, Irtish, Middle Ob region already in the third century AD.[187] However, the drastic change in climate in the fourth century may have had something to do with the sudden thrust of the Huns remaining in the Altai region in an opposite direction into Central Asia. As La Vaissière shows in his excellent analysis of the Chinese sources on the early migration of the Hephtalites, the Huns from the Altai suddenly moved south in the 350s AD.[188] The invasion of these Huns would have dire consequences for the Kangju (based in Tashkent and Sogdia), the Sassanians and Kushan remnants in Central Asia.

The Kidarite[189] Huns[190] appear on the scene sometime in the middle of the fourth century and are in firm possession of Bactria by AD 360.[191] According to an embassy from Sogdia that visited the Toba Wei court in AD 457, the Huns (called Xiongnu in the *Wei Shu*, proving without a shadow of a doubt that the White Huns (Central Asian Huns) at least were Xiongnu and that the people whom our sources call Huns and Hunas in Central Asia and India are Xiongnu in origin[192]) conquered Transoxiana in the mid fourth century AD (three generations before the embassy).[193] These Huns, whom the Persians would call collectively Chionites,[194] at a later stage in the fifth century AD,[195] under the name White Huns (or Western Huns), were all ruled by a new royal clan named the Yeda/Yanda (嚈噠)[196] or Hephtalites[197] (sometimes also identified with the Eurasian Avars[198]).

There is general consensus among historians that the Chionites and the Huns were one and the same.[199] In AD 350 the Sassanian King Shapur II had to call off the siege of Nisibis to deal with a grim threat developing to the east. In fact this was an eight-year-long conflict (AD 350–8) that brought the Persian Empire to the brink of destruction.[200] After somehow managing to forge an uneasy alliance with them, Shapur used Hunnic allies to augment his army in the siege of Amida in AD 360. There Grumbates, the king (probably a sub-king) of the Chionites (his name being possibly Kurumpat: Turkish, 'ruling prince'),[201] lost his son.[202] The subsequent reign of Bahram IV saw the Sassanids losing almost all of their east Iranian lands taken earlier from the Kushans[203] to the western Huns. Later incursions, especially those during the reigns of Bahram V (421–38), Yazdegard (438–57) and Peroz (457–84)[204], in other words at exactly the same time when the European Huns were menacing the Romans under Rua, Bleda and Attila, reduced the mighty Persians to tributary status to the Huns.[205]

In AD 454, a year after the death of the European Hunnic King, the Hephtalites (by now having more or less displaced the previous reigning dynasty, the Kidarites,[206] except in Gandhara and India[207]) won a decisive victory over the Sassanians. The next Sassanian King to reign, Peroz, was placed on the Persian throne by a Hephtalite army.[208] Later Peroz bravely tried to free himself of Hephtalite dominance and tried his luck against them. He was defeated by a Hephtalite king called Akhshunwar by Tabari and Khushnavaz by Firdausi.[209] He escaped death on that occasion (AD 469), but according to Procopius he was afterwards slain with most of his army in another encounter with the Huns (AD 484),[210] who placed his only surviving son Kubad on the throne as a vassal king.[211] In AD 487 Kubad was temporarily dethroned and again with Hephtalite support he was able to regain his kingship.[212] However, the price was high and in order to pay the required annual tribute to the Huns he asked the Romans, with whom Persia had good relations for about half a century (largely due to Hunnic pressure which prevented the Persians from upsetting the Romans and vice versa the Romans the Persians due to the European Hunnic threat), for loans. The Roman refusal would later in AD 502 lead to renewal of ancient hostilities between the two empires.[213]

The Chinese historical records mention the vast extent of the Hephtalite Hunnic Empire. The *Liangshu* 54 lists among their domains Persia, Kashmir, Karashahr, Kucha, Kashgar and Khotan, and the *Bei Shi* 97: Kangju (Sogdia), Khotan, Kashgar and Persia.[214] More than thirty lands of the west are seen as being subject to the White Huns in our sources.[215] The Hephtalites by the year AD 500 would also deal the death blow to the Indian Gupta Empire.[216]

In India the terrified Indians identified two branches of the Hunnic nation: the Sveta Huna (White Huns, i.e the Hephtalite Huns) and the Hara Huna (possibly Black Huns), the word *Hara*, according to some scholars, being a corruption of the Turkic word *Kara* (black).[217] Although it is far from certain, it has been speculated that the Hara Huna is a reference to Attila's Huns in Europe.[218] All sorts of bizarre ideas have been put forward by historians from Procopius onwards about this identification: white and black. Procopius notes that the Hephtalites were ruled by a king and were guided by a lawful constitution,[219] i.e. that they had a sophisticated state structure comparable to those of the Sassanians whom they had vassalized. But he then misinterprets the appellation 'white' to mean that the Hephtalites were white and not swarthy like the European Huns supposedly were.[220] As Pulleyblank[221] points out white was symbolic of west among the steppe nomads. Black signified north and red the south, hence the existence also of Red Huns (Kermichiones).[222]

As Pritsak points out, in steppe societies the colour black signifying north and the colour blue signifying east, both of which carried connotations of greatness and supremacy,[223] always had precedence over white (west) and red (south). Thus whoever the Hara Huna were, they are likely to have had precedence over their formidable cousins the White Huns, at least initially. The fact that the term *kara* suggested elevated status among the European Huns too, as it did among other Inner Asian Turkic peoples, seems to be confirmed by the report in Olympiodorus that the supreme king of the Huns was called Karaton.[224]

The examination of the Chionite and later Hephtalite conquests also shows clearly that these White Hunnic conquerors (claiming Hunnic heritage like Attila's Hun), who according to the *Wei Shu*[225] (103. 2290; 102.2278–9[226]) originated from exactly the same area as the European Huns (from the Altai region[227]) in the same time period *c*. AD 360,[228] possessed a military and social structure that matched those of the Xiongnu in the past. Without them it is impossible to explain how they managed to defeat formidable opponents such as the Sassanians and the Guptas. The *Wei Shu* as mentioned above even specifically states that the fifth-century rulers of Sogdia,[229] i.e. the White Huns, are Xiongnu in origin (102.2270), thereby confirming the link between Central Asian Huns and the Xiongnu of old, and calls the country *wen-na-sha*, pronounced 'Huna sha' in EMC, i.e. King of the Huns.[230]

A fifth-century Chinese geographical work called the *Shi-san zhou ji* by a certain Gan Yin preserved in *Sung Shu* 98, furthermore insists, on the basis of information derived probably from Sogdian merchants,[231] that the Alans of Europe and the Sogdians (whom the Chinese had just learned had been conquered by the Huns three generations earlier) were under different rulers. As Pulleyblank notes, the need to clarify this implies the misapprehension that both peoples were ruled by the same ruler. In fact this is only natural given the fact that both had been conquered within the space of some ten years by the same people called Huns.[232] Also in ways remarkably similar to the European Huns, the succession to the Hephtalite throne could pass from uncle to nephew[233] and artificial cranial deformation was practised among their elite, as among the European Huns and Alans.[234] They also practised the Xiongnu system of appointing vassal kings, e.g. the king of Zabulistan who held an autonomous fief within the empire and was instrumental in spearheading the Hephtalite thrust into India,[235] and collective governance of the empire was practised by several high-ranking *yabgus* and *tegins*.[236] In India the Kidarites and then the Hephtalite Huns also introduced the rule of multiple rajas and rajputs who held territories in 'fief' to their overlord the Hunnic supreme king. Thus a form of quasi-feudalism was introduced to India and a transformation in the administration of revenues took place.[237] In subsequent chapters we will see very similar transformations occurring in Europe after the Hunnic arrival.

The Rouran Khaganate

However, this is not yet the whole story. Some forty years before Attila ascended the throne of the Huns in Europe, in the East in Mongolia and Turkestan another mightier and even more formidable empire was being created by a Chinggis Khan-like figure, Shelun Khagan of the Rouran.[238] The Rouran like the Hephtalites and the European Huns contained a strong element of Huns (Xiongnu remnants[239]) who collaborated with certain Xianbei tribes to form the Khaganate under Shelun.[240] In AD 394 Shelun broke free from vassalage under the Toba Xianbei Empire (also steppe nomads) whose centre of power had begun to shift south away from Mongolia after the Toba conquest of Northern China.[241] In just six to eight years Shelun subdued almost twelve powerful, nomadic tribal confederacies or states in the vast region stretching from the borders of Koguryo (Korea) in the east to Dzungaria in the west (the original homeland of the White Huns and the European Huns). Even the great Hephtalites were for a while vassals of the Rouran Empire.[242]

As Kradin points out, the Rouran Empire was very much a typical steppe empire. Its organization and hierarchical structure was almost a complete replica of former Xiongnu practices. The empire, like that of the Xiongnu, was divided into two wings in a dual system with the ruler of the east holding greater prestige and overall authority,[243] though later the western ruler seems to have reversed the equation, thus mirroring a similar process among the Huns under Attila, who overthrew his Eastern overlord Bleda.[244] The empire had a core Rouran tribe leading ethnically related tribes as vassals and holding in servitude conquered tribes like the Uighurs under

Zhi-paye-zhi.[245] Shelun enforced in the Xiongnu manner a compulsory registration of all warriors, who were instructed to follow strict rules of conduct in battle. Disobedience was punished with severe penalties which mirror the policies of the Great Xiongnu Shanyu Modun.[246]

The entire nation was organized in a decimal system, again exactly like the Xiongnu. The 1,000 formed the detachment (*run*/military head) and 100 the banner (*Zhuang* commanded by the *Shawu*/leader or commander). In all in times of full mobilization between 100,000 and 300,000 horsemen could be raised for military service (again approximating the size of earlier Xiongnu armies).[247] Political power was concentrated in the hands of a charismatic, ruling clan. The ruler, Khagan, was chosen usually from among the direct male heirs of the previous ruler or from a collateral line within the royal family. The closest relatives of the Khagan were given fiefs, usually in the form of large military units with the title of *Xielifa*.[248] Under them were the leader of the 1,000 and 100, usually tribal chiefs and clan elders of different levels. Among them were chosen the *dachen*, the grandees of the empire, classed as high and low ranking with titles distributed at the will of the Khagan. 'It was a complex hierarchical multi-level system.'[249]

The succession to the Rouran throne also shows the features that we discover in Hunnic contexts. The ruling Khagan would always try to pass on his throne to his sons. However, if a close relative had greater prestige, this could lead to a succession struggle, which in most cases ended without bloodshed,[250] though there were notable exceptions. Thus out of sixteen Khagans, eight were collateral members of the royal family, nephews who, like Attila and Bleda, inherited the throne from an uncle. Under the rule of Doulun Khagan, however, the system could not prevent bloodshed. The Uighurs under a Rouran ruler Abuzhiluo (we see here the typical steppe practice, also found among the Xiongnu and later the Huns and Gokturks as well, of appointing a member of the royal clan or a close subordinate from the ruling tribe, Rouran, Hun or Turk, as the ruler of a vassal horde[251]), 100,000 tents in all, revolted and had to be suppressed (the constant Hun demands to the Romans for the return of fugitives comes to mind and also the destruction of the horde of fugitive Goths under Radagaisus by Uldin in AD 406).[252] In the process two armies were raised to suppress the rebellion. One was led by the Khagan, the other by his uncle Nagai. The Khagan suffered defeat, but Nagai had success. This was interpreted by Rouran troops to be a sign that heaven's favour had left the Khagan and passed to Nagai. Nagai murdered the Khagan and ascended the throne in a coup,[253] demonstrating the extraordinary importance attached to military success in steppe politics, which as we shall see later explains a lot of the behaviour of Hunnic kings in Europe.[254]

We also hear that a Rouran Khagan Anagui[255] later built a capital city, Mumocheng encircled with two walls (*Liangshu* 54), and hired Chinese defectors as clerks to maintain written records (*Song Shu* 95). We are no doubt reminded of Attila's Roman secretaries Orestes (the father of the last Roman emperor Romulus Augustulus) and possibly also Onegesius.[256] The Khagan was also guarded by a staff of bodyguards (which mirror the institution of intimates (*epitēdeioi*) among the Huns of which the Hun king of the Sciri, Edeco, was a member) who watched over the person of the ruler in shifts.[257] This Rouran institution would be inherited by the Turks who overthrew them in the sixth century. Curiously these guards would be referred to as the *böri* (wolves), the wolf being the traditional sacred totemic symbol of the Turco-Mongol peoples.[258] The Ashina ruler of the Gokturks and the later Mongols all held the wolf in reverence.[259] What is intriguing is that the son of Attila's bodyguard, Edeco, was called Hunoulphus ('the Hun wolf'). It is to be wondered whether this name is suggestive of his father's association with the imperial bodyguard.[260]

Sedentarism among steppe peoples

Another important aspect of steppe empires contemporaneous with and prior to the Huns is the presence of a sedentary, agrarian element in their polities.[261] The early Iranian-speaking 'nomads' collectively named the Scythians/Saka in our sources were often by no means pure nomads.[262] In the fifth century BC Herodotus claimed that certain Scythians had become settled farmers (4.17–18) and this observation has been proved correct by archaeology.[263] Herodotus relates that the Budinians, who are part Greek and part Scythian, had established a town called Gelonus (4.108.1) which was later burned down by Darius (4.123.1). According to Rolle, archaeologists have discovered 'more than a hundred – fortified settlements – in the forest steppe region'[264] which closely resemble the wooden town described by Herodotus.[265] Some scholars even believe that they have found in the large ancient settlement of Bel'sk the town of Gelonus.[266] There is evidence of craft industry, agriculture and even horticultural activity in this town.[267] The Xiongnu, who are often viewed as quintessential nomads,[268] also possessed a strong sedentary element. Modern archaeology has shown that, like the Scythians, part of the Xiongnu had become settled or was from the very beginning sedentary and engaged in agriculture and craft production.[269]

The steppe confederations and empires originating from Central Asia were particularly hybrid in the sense that their economy had always been sustained from very early on by a combination of pastoralism and irrigated agriculture,[270] which was introduced into southern Central Asia as early as the middle of the first millennium BC. The combination of nomadic conquerors and agriculturalists triggered the rise of the first political federations or empires in Central Asia around the seventh century BC.[271] Following in their footsteps the steppe empires of the Yuezhi (Kushans) and the Kangju (overlord of the Alans) in fact presided over the highest level of development in Central Asian irrigation systems.[272] The Kangju (which intermittently controlled Sogdia) and also the neighbouring state of Khwarezm,[273] were hybrid polities that contained both pastoral elements and long-established communities (some dating back to the fifth century BC) with irrigation systems, agriculture, mining and manufacturing centers.[274]

Although their military power was dependent upon the nomadic population in the steppe, the elite of the Kangju spent their winters in a capital city and their culture shows a considerable level of sophistication.[275] The neighbouring Wusun, whose territory would be seized by the Xiongnu/Huns, also possessed a walled capital city, which functioned as the political and administrative centre of their state. They also practised agriculture to supplement their semi-nomadic pastoral economy.[276] This symbiosis of pastoralism[277] and sedentary agriculture would continue to be a regular feature of steppe polities in the Middle Ages.[278] The European Avars, who displaced the Hunnic Empire in the sixth century in the western steppe, were noted by the Romans for their grain-producing capacity which distinguished them from Germanic federates of earlier centuries. The Avars on several occasions supplied defeated Roman armies and populace with food and deported Roman civilians (270,000 (!) in c. 619 alone, so we are told[279]) to areas north of the Danube in order to augment their agricultural base.[280] Mahmud al-Kashgari, a member of the Karakhanid Turkish dynasty that ruled Transoxiana (centred around modern Uzbekistan) in the eleventh century,[281] who wrote the famous *Diwan Lugat at-Turk* (written c. AD 1075), in his overview of medieval Turkish tribes, also alerts us to the fact that of the twenty Turkic tribes, ten were sedentary.[282] Thus the domination of a core of steppe pastoralists was by no means a hindrance to co-existence/symbiosis with a subject sedentary population and the steppe political system was structurally not incompatible with stable tributary administration. The longevity and essential stability of steppe-based empires like the Xiongnu and steppe-derived entities such as the Parthian Empire are a telling reminder that the myth of political anarchy and rampant disorder that dominates our perception of Central Asian steppe societies requires a radical re-evaluation.

CHAPTER 4

The Huns in Europe

THE HUNNIC EMPIRE, THE GERMANIC
TRIBES AND ROME

We have observed that two extraordinarily complex and well-organized steppe empires, both of which contained a strong Hunnic element, co-existed with the European Huns and were their eastern neighbours.[1] If we also count the Xianbei (the ancient nemesis of the Huns) state of Northern Wei[2] that originated in Mongolia and ruled Northern China between AD 386 and 535, we have a situation where steppe powers rule virtually all of Eurasia in the fifth century, either directly or indirectly (over tributary vassals), from Gaul in the west to Manchuria in the east and Siberia in the north to India in the south.[3] Is it a coincidence that simultaneously with the Hunnic ascendancy in the west we have steppe imperial rule across the whole of Eurasia?

We have also noted that all these steppe empires, like those that preceded them, always possessed a strong sedentary element as well as the core nomadic/pastoral population, the backbone of their military power. The sedentary base no doubt contributed to the development of more stable political, social and economic institutions within these steppe empires and allowed them to become largely self-sufficient both in food production and weapons manufacturing. The symbiosis of pastoral and agricultural elements also facilitated the development of the apparatus of state administration and regular collection of revenue for the imperial governments. Are we to assume then that the Huns of Europe, who created a vast empire that was only rivalled in size by that of the Rouran and was more extensive than the other two empires, alone of those who had originated from the territory of the former Xiongnu Empire, at the very time when these other states were expanding, had no organization comparable to that of virtually all nomadic confederacies in Central Asia and the eastern steppe before, contemporaneous and after?[4] Surely this is

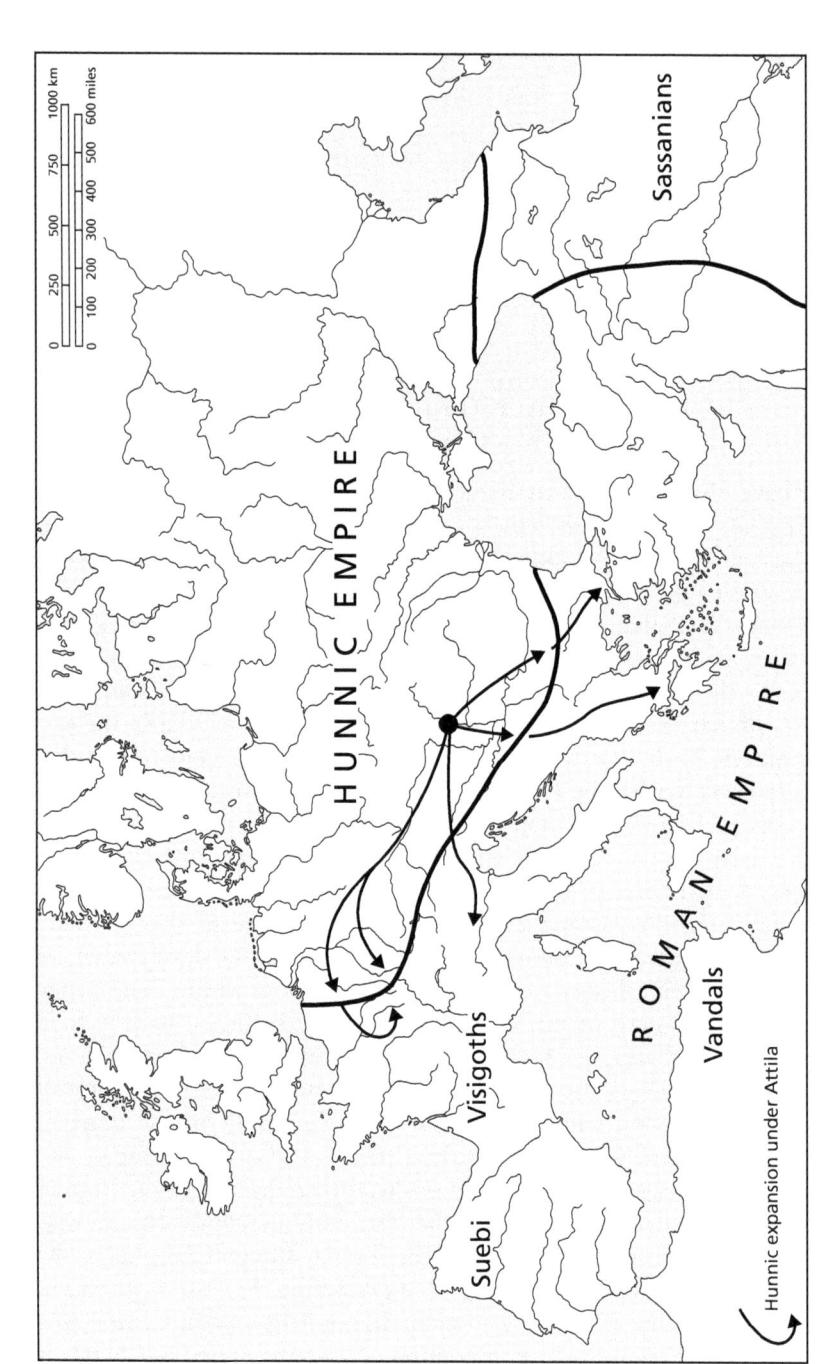

2 The Hunnic Empire in Europe at its maximum extent under Attila

an absurdity that defies belief. The unsustainable consensus, based on internalized readings of Ammianus (whose description of the Huns should rightly, as Bona notes, be relegated to the realm of fairy tales[5]) that attribute primitive levels of cultural and political development to the Huns, has been sustained in scholarship for so long that even among those who fully recognize the danger of taking Ammianus literally, no viable alternative has been postulated.

For instance, Heather, whose great scholarship makes a large contribution to our understanding of Late Antiquity and rightly re-emphasizes the role of the Huns in the demise of the Western Empire, unfortunately in my opinion does not go far enough in his conclusions. To Heather, who in general accepts, though with an admirable degree of caution,[6] the story of the primitive Huns, the Huns are a primitively organized group of independent war-bands when they enter Europe, whose political structure is as haphazard as, and very likely more rudimentary than, those of the Goths and the Alans whom they defeat in their migration west.[7] This analysis of Hunnic political organization is, I would argue, quite unacceptable. If this was the case, we have no way of explaining how the Huns managed to both conquer the Goths and the Alans and maintain their imperial structure in Europe.

Is there then evidence that the Hunnic Empire existed as a political unit before Attila's famous or infamous rule in the mid fifth century in our sources? The sources that we do have are often confused, but by comparing what they tell us with what we have discussed thus far regarding other contemporary steppe empires, we can actually see glimpses of Hunnic organization and political structure. If the following analysis shows that the Huns did indeed possess a political, social and military structure of the level of sophistication we have seen among the Rouran and also the Hephtalites, White Huns, this has immense implications for our interpretation of their role in the political and military convulsion that engulfed the whole of Europe in Late Antiquity and the early Middle Ages, and calls into question the validity of many assumptions and theories regarding historical developments of the period.

Recent scholarship on the Late Roman Empire has rightly emphasized the relative strength of the Roman state and its armies in comparison to those of their Germanic neighbours, who were highly disorganized and had nowhere near the capacity of, say, the Great Sassanian Empire, the archenemy of Rome since the third century AD, to pose a significant, mortal threat to the empire.[8] In Heather's analysis, the Huns were the main catalyst for bringing about the fall of the Western Roman Empire in the sense that they kept occupied the Roman armies that would otherwise have been deployed in destroying the barbarians who had entered its territory, thereby allowing the Germans to become more entrenched and rob the empire of its vital tax revenues, especially those of Africa.[9] This he argues was the cause of the fall.

Because to Heather and to virtually all other non-Hungarian scholars[10] the Huns were never a unified[11] and well-organized political entity, the level of threat they posed to the Empire and the severity of the damage they inflicted on imperial power, which is so obviously stated in our sources, are minimized. Thus Heather argues that Attila was not a mortal threat to the Eastern Empire and could never have conquered it.[12] He argues that Attila did not even come close to conquering the Western Empire.[13] Thus at best to Heather the Huns are the 'nursemaid' of the 'Germanic Revolution' that supposedly brought down the West.

Halsall, who is actually far more dismissive of the Huns than Heather, however, sees inadequacies in Heather's reasoning. He removes the Huns from the equation and without them it becomes obvious that the Germanic tribes could not possibly have brought down the Roman edifice. Thus Halsall attributes the events of the fifth century mainly to internal Roman political problems (for instance incompetent emperors and the misuse or lack of imperial patronage in the western provinces) combined with economic fragmentation that created a rift between local elites and Rome in the Western Empire[14] and allowed an 'inventive experiment' of settling Germanic troops ('barbarian protectors' says Goffart[15]) in Roman territory[16] to get way out of hand.[17] Thus he envisages the scenario of Roman internal collapse triggering barbarian migrations into the Roman Empire.

Both theories are in my opinion inadequate, though it must still be acknowledged that they have no doubt contributed greatly to our overall understanding of the Late Roman world. To explain away the Hunnic success against his formidable Germans, without attributing sophisticated organization to the Huns, Heather finds himself in a dilemma. He explains the fact that the Huns so obviously did manage to conquer the Germanic tribes and the Alans and keep them in a state of subjection for extended periods of time by pointing to the 'wonder weapon' of the steppe, the Hunnic composite, reflex bow.[18] This supposedly gave them a tactical advantage over the Germans.[19] Maybe it did, but how then did they also manage to overwhelm other steppe nomads such as the Alans and more importantly the various Turkic tribes that also formed a part of their confederacy who are likely to have possessed similar weapons?[20] Heather wrongly takes the example of the somewhat exceptionally disorganized

Sarmatians (in steppe terms that is) as an example for the Hunnic polity.[21] But these Sarmatians when they first appeared on the scene had no knock-on effect, as it were, that triggered the Germanic tribes to migrate en masse into the Roman Empire. Heather thus attributes this exceptional turn of events as an indication that the Germanic tribes had simply developed better organization and social stratification that allowed them to overwhelm previously solid Roman defences.

However, this assessment conflicts with Heather's own analysis on the state of the Roman Empire in the fourth century. Although it might be a slight exaggeration, the fourth century in terms of administrative organization, advanced bureaucracy and buildup of military manpower[22] may have marked the high point of Roman imperial rule.[23] Certainly, as Matthews suggests, the imperial government of the mid fourth century AD was unmatched in Greco-Roman history 'in its scale and complexity of organisation'.[24]

Kelly adds that there was a slow, but significant transition from 'soft' to 'hard' government which brought about an unparalleled centralization of the imperial government that was both more effective and intrusive.[25]

This centralization of imperial authority also brought about the revival of Roman military strength after the near collapse of imperial rule in the third century, which saw Germanic, Sarmatian and Persian incursions into virtually all of the empire's frontier provinces in Europe and Asia in addition to chronic and almost fatal military usurpations within the empire.[26] Under Diocletian and his colleagues in the early fourth century AD the number of legions in the Roman army compared to the third-century armies under the Severan emperors increased dramatically from 33 to over 67.[27] In the Eastern provinces alone there were 28 legions, 70 cavalry units, 54 auxiliary *alae* and 54 cohorts.[28]

Of course, this does not necessarily mean that the legions of the fourth century were exactly the same size as the legions of old. They were in fact doubtlessly smaller in size. However, the reduction in the overall number of infantry in the legions was more than compensated for by the buildup of the cavalry wing of the imperial army. The cavalry, which became the core of the newly established mobile field armies that were led by experienced, professional soldiers,[29] was essential for combating more mobile barbarian invaders of the fourth century.[30] As Lactantius comments, the size of the army had indeed been greatly increased, if not by as dramatic proportions as the number of legions may suggest.[31] By the end of the fourth century the Roman army, at least on paper, numbered anywhere between 400,000 and 600,000 men. In other words, Rome was an even more formidable opponent for the Germanic tribes in the fourth century than it had been in the third.[32]

True, a significant portion of these Roman troops may in reality have been ineffective[33] and a not negligible portion of the empire's best troops were progressively Germanic or Alan in origin.[34] However, nothing in the history of the fourth century AD suggests that Germanic or Alanic troops in the regular Roman army were any less loyal or dependable than 'native' Roman troops.[35] If anything they were often the most effective and devoted of the imperial troops, that is until the latter half of the fifth century when the Western Roman Empire had almost entirely lost its political authority. The barbarian federates and mercenaries, who in the mid fifth century were not at all integrated into the Roman military in any meaningful sense, were largely autonomous under their own rulers[36] and later delivered the *coup de grâce* on the Western Roman state, should not be taken as the standard for measuring the nature and effectiveness of the barbarian troops in the Roman army in earlier times.[37]

Economically also, at least in the Eastern Empire, the fourth and fifth centuries AD were a time of prosperity, economic recovery and even population increase.[38] Thus in a situation in which the Romans had actually managed to increase their economic and military strength, the Germanic tribes, though perhaps more sophisticated than they were in earlier centuries, were, contrary to what Heather suggests, far from constituting a mortal threat to the Empire in terms of military potential and political unity.[39] The tough challenge posed to Rome by a newly resurgent Persian Empire under the Sassanians in the third century had also been successfully dealt with by the fourth.[40] There is absolutely no evidence that either the Goths or the Sassanians were any more formidable in the fourth than they were in the previous third century AD. So what went wrong for the Romans?

Can internal factors such as the alienation of the Roman provincial elite from the central government or the incompetence of leadership at the top in the fifth century alone explain the sudden failure of the Roman state? There were arguably plenty of comparable dissensions, incompetence, local separatism and economic disasters in the Roman Empire of the preceding third century. The empire in such dire straits with huge internal revolts in the provinces (Gallic Empire and Palmyra), socio-economic crises and one military coup after another (more chaotic than the usurpations of the fourth or fifth centuries AD) still managed to recover and contain the barbarians.[41] If external powers simply did not intrude to exploit the 'pre-existing faultlines' within the Roman imperial system, all evidence that we have from the fourth century, both historical and archaeological, would point to a lasting continuation of Roman imperial rule without radical disturbances.[42]

The Hunnic Empire, the Germanic tribes and Rome

The slow, ongoing process of settling troops of Germanic origin, who had been granted land in return for military service, in Roman territory, which began well before Adrianople,[43] was also not necessarily detrimental to Roman interests.[44] Even mass immigration or rather invasion, like that of the Visigoths and Vandals, as the Roman handling of invasions of the Alamanni and Goths in the third century show, was manageable for the Roman state in the fourth and fifth centuries. As we shall see shortly, it was the Hunnic interventions in Roman internal affairs, for which the Romans were totally unprepared and which could hardly have been predicted, that time and again prevented the empire from effectively resolving the barbarian problem within the empire and decisively eroded the military capacity of the Roman state to reverse the barbarian tide as it had done in the third century.

Naturally in any disaster that involves a collapse of such magnitude as the fall of the Western Empire, a multiplicity of causes is likely to have contributed to the final outcome.[45] The most significant internal cause, among the many that are suggested and which seems somewhat reasonable compared to the rest, may perhaps have been the growth in power of the provincial landowning elite, who by the constraints they could have imposed on the availability of manpower and taxable land (especially in the Western Empire, argues Jones[46]) might have in some way hindered the empire's efforts to militarily and economically manage the barbarian problem in the fifth century.[47] However, even if this was the case, it is doubtful whether such internal deficiencies were powerful enough to radically alter the political map of the Roman world.

These were problems accentuated by external pressures and which exacerbated the difficulties facing the empire. If there were no Hunnic pressure in the east, the Visigoths, Vandals, Alans and Suebi would never have entered the empire in the first place and even if they somehow had, it is inconceivable that the empire could not have managed to eventually destroy the Visigoths and the Vandals. Even as late as the sixth century AD Justinian, with only half of the empire intact (the Western Empire having disappeared completely), could still destroy long-established barbarian states such as the Vandal kingdom in North Africa and the Ostrogoths in Italy. He even recovered parts of Spain from the Visigoths.[48]

With the Western Empire still intact the job would have been infinitely easier to accomplish and although the two halves of the empire were more or less separate states in reality by the fifth century AD, the notion/ideal of a single Roman Empire lingered and precipitated periodic Eastern support and substantial military aid to the West to punish barbarian incursions and seizures of Roman territory.[49] Without further Hunnic interventions in

Roman affairs, the barbarians in the West would have been either exterminated or pacified by superior Roman economic and military resources and these incursions would have been remembered in the same manner as those of the earlier third century, a devastating barbarian disturbance extinguished with some difficulty and great loss of life by imperial troops, and nothing more.

As will be shown henceforth, unless we place this imperial disaster in its proper context, that is a Eurasian one, the essential components and the very nature of the post-Roman world in the West become unintelligible. If the 'barbarians' are the context of imperial collapse, then we are left with the same question that had baffled the earliest critics of the history of Roman collapse. How could primitive, badly organized barbarians effectively combat and bring down the imperial edifice? Heather emphasizes the political progress made by the Germanic tribes and argues that they had developed a more cohesive socio-political structure through what he calls the economic revolution of the third and fourth centuries AD[50] among them. Certainly there were over-kings and other loose forms of hegemony among the Tervingi Goths and the Alamanni. However, it is also notable that essentially the same type of loose tribal organization with unstable kingship as in the first and second centuries AD[51] still prevailed among the Germanic tribes in most of Germania in the third and fourth centuries AD.[52]

There is no evidence that the Tervingi Gothic, Frankish[53] and Alamannic confederations[54] of the fourth century differed in any significant way in their organization and political structure from the same confederations in the previous third century. Nor can it be convincingly argued that the greater interaction with the Romans in the space of less than a hundred years made the Germanic recipients of Roman civilization more dangerous to Rome. If that were the case, then how can we explain the fact that the Tervingi Goths and the Vandals, who were all eastern tribes, i.e. furthest away from Roman influence and with the shortest time of exposure to Roman civilization among the Germanic tribes, were the most menacing and persistent opponents to the Romans among the Germanic tribes in the fourth and fifth centuries AD and furthermore were also probably the best organized?[55] Even they in the late fourth century AD could not be said to be much better organized and further along the road to statehood than the elaborately organized Royal Scythians almost seven centuries earlier or even the more recent Dacian kingdom destroyed by Trajan in AD 106.[56] True, Germanic warbands do seem to sustain their unity longer in the fourth century than in the second or even perhaps the third, and this may, as Heather argues, suggest the growing power of a strong aristocratic element among the Germanic tribes in the fourth century whose influence brought about greater cohesiveness in the once chaotically organized warbands.[57] But whether this level of cohesiveness and perhaps better socio-economic conditions rendered the Germanic tribes formidable enough to overwhelm the Romans is highly questionable. Other than the Goths who, as we shall see shortly, were strengthened by steppe elements and also the Vandals (likewise led by the steppe Alans) none of the Germanic tribal confederacies in the fourth century made any noticeable impression on Roman defences in the fourth century and this is surely significant.

The Marcomanni and other Danubian peoples together with some of the Sarmatians in the second century (the Marcomannic and German wars of AD 166–8, 169–74, 177–80) could contain for a while the might of the Roman Empire at its height and force Marcus Aurelius to spend most of his reign along the empire's borders.[58] In the third-century military crisis, when Roman generals marched with ever-increasing frequency to Rome to claim the imperial title at the head of frontier armies[59] and thereby left the borders undefended to Germanic incursions, the Alamanni and the Goths pulled off feats of daring intrusion that matched and in some cases surpassed the exploits of their later descendants: e.g. the invasion of the Alamanni and the Franks in the year 269–70 when the barbarians almost reached Rome and the extraordinary maritime ventures of the Goths.[60] The defeat and death of Valens at Adrianople, over-dramatized and over-emphasized due to Ammianus, already had a precedent in Decius' defeat and death at the hands of the Goths in AD 251.[61] The occasional military successes of the Tervingi Goths in the late fourth century AD, then, can hardly be used as evidence for better organization than in the third century.[62]

Centralization of the kind needed for an advanced state structure does not seem to have existed above the Danube and east of the Rhine before the arrival of the Huns. Only in times of war do the Germanic confederations of the fourth century show organization that approaches the type of control found among steppe empires. However, even then what we find is not a cohesive military force with a clear command structure, but rather a loose conglomeration of numerous *reguli* (petty kings[63]) or war chiefs. Thus when Chonodomarius, the strongest of the Alamannic chiefs, gathers an army of Alamanni to fight the Romans at the battle of Argentoratum in AD 357, he is given neither magisterial nor official power over the army.[64] He is simply the strongest among numerous independent chiefs who are categorized by Ammianus as great or small on the basis of their martial ability and the size of their retinue. Thus Chonodomarius is accompanied by his nephew who is equal to him in power, five other kings who approach his power and ten more petty kings (*regales*) who are weaker. There are also a host of 'nobles' (*optimatum*) and troops who are fighting not because of state or royal authority that compels them to give military service, but partly for pay (*mercede*) and partly because of an agreement (*pacto*) to fight for the kings.[65]

In fact the power of Alamannic 'kings' over their people is so weak that before the battle the 'royals' are shouted down by the visibly offended rank and file for being presumptuous enough, i.e. considering themselves to be superior to the rest, to remain mounted on their horses, instead of fighting on foot with the people.[66] Followers also bully the kings to act in accordance with their wishes as in the case of Vadomarius, who is forced to join Chonodomarius by his people, while Gundomadus is actually killed for disagreeing with the majority view.[67] This is not the picture of an organized state entity. As in earlier centuries, these so-called kings of the fourth century were the representatives of their respective kin-based clans. Thus kings are called *cynings* in the West, i.e. 'the man who represents the cyn (kin)'.[68] In fact it is only after the Alamanni went through a period of Hunnic domination that in the latter half of the fifth century we find evidence for a stable kingship among them, possibly due to the influence of the Danubian Suebi (heavily accustomed to the lifestyle and political order of steppe societies) under their prince Hunimund.[69]

The early Franks were as decentralized as the Alamanni, being composed of multiple independent groups such as the Chamavi, Chattuarii, Bructeri and Amsivari. In the late fourth century the Franks were ruled by a host of petty kings (*reguli*) and *duces*[70] in dispute with one another. Thus Arbogast the Frankish war leader would feud with the *reguli* Marcomer and Sumno.[71]

The Germanic tribes to the east (Tervingi Goths, Vandals and Longobards, often referred to as Scythians and Getae, not Germans) were probably better organized than the Alamanni and the Franks due to influences from the steppe region,[72] but even among the Tervingi Goths central authority was highly limited. Athanaric the judge (*iudex*) of the Tervingi had only superficial control over the various tribes supposedly under his authority and could not prevent lesser leaders from acting independently or even making their own agreements without his authorization.[73] The Goths, like other Germanic tribes to the west, were ruled by numerous tribal chiefs (*reguli*) who only occasionally, depending on military circumstances, obeyed the *iudex*. We learn from the church historian Socrates that there were frequent internal disputes and civil war among the Tervingi tribes between those led by Athanaric and those following Fritigern.[74] It was only after the Tervingi encountered the Huns and adopted the mounted warfare and other military–political practices of the steppe region (from the Huns, Alans and possibly also the Greuthungs) that they become the well-organized Visigoths of the fifth century AD.[75]

It is, however, very likely that the Greuthung Goths who inhabited the Pontic steppe possessed superior organization vis-à-vis their western cousins, with an increasing trend towards associating kingship with a specific dynasty.[76] This was primarily due to their early contact with the advanced Scythian–Sarmatian, political culture of the steppe region[77] and their virtual symbiosis with the Sarmatians.[78] The Goths and other east Germanic tribes such as the Vandals and Gepids were so thoroughly Sarmatianized that Procopius would later argue that they were in fact separate from the Germanic peoples and were originally Sarmatians and Getae[79] like the Iranian Alans.[80]

Many east Gothic noble clans were also in all probability of Alan or Sarmatian mixed origin. For instance, the famous clan name Amal (the ruling clan of the east Goths after the breakup of the Hunnic Empire and maybe also before the Hunnic invasion) could be of Iranian origin from the Avestic *ama* 'powerful, strong', which is also the name of a Mithra-deity.[81] Of course this fits in nicely with the information given by Jordanes that the mythical ancestors of the Amal dynasty, of which Amal the eponymous ancestor stands out, were demi-gods.[82] Even if this etymology is rejected, further indications of an Alanic/Sarmatian element in the Amal clan can be found in Jordanes who tells us that Andag, an Amal of the mid fifth century AD, was married to the sister of Candac, the Alan king.[83] What is interesting is that even the name Andac, a scion of the Amali, itself is almost certainly a Sarmatian name as the appearance of the Sarmatian name Andaakos in a third-century Tanais inscription shows.[84]

The later Ostrogoths, who doubtlessly included the Greutungs, certainly show all the features of a typical steppe people: mounted warfare, hunting, falconry, shamanism and the wearing of Iranian–Central Asian royal vestments by the powerful royal dynasty of the Amals.[85] This is of course the picture of the Greutungs after nearly a century of Hunnic rule. Whether Ermanaric's Greutungs were similar to the better-organized, later Ostrogoths is still debatable.[86]

The weakness of central authority and loose political integration limited the military effectiveness of the Germanic tribes (even the Goths) who in most cases also lacked the proper siege engines to successfully besiege Roman fortified towns.[87] They thus posed only a marginal threat to the maintenance of Roman political authority. The Hunnic ability to besiege towns in protracted siege warfare would radically alter this situation.[88] The Germanic cavalry, of particular importance to Gothic (Theodoric's army consisted primarily of horsemen) and Vandal armies of the late fourth and fifth centuries, would also develop into a competent fighting force only after the Germanic contacts with and imitation of the tactics of Central Asian invaders, the Huns and Alans.[89] It was of course this steppe-style cavalry (Alan and Greuthung) that brought the Goths their great victory over the Romans at Adrianople.[90]

Thus, although it is necessary not to underestimate the political progress made by the Germanic tribes, it is also important to realize that they were still politically fragmented and far from constituting a mortal threat to the Roman Empire. So if the Germanic tribes did not pose a mortal threat to Rome, then what about the Huns? Let us now observe the actual Roman assessment of Hunnic power. Ammianus, as mentioned earlier, knew virtually nothing about the Huns and it is clear that he had never seen a Hun in his life. However, in the fifth century we find in Priscus an excellent eyewitness to the Hunnic polity. In the account of his participation in the East Roman embassy to the Hunnic court, he gives us a contemporary Roman, not modern, assessment of Hunnic power. He states, 'he (Attila) has a military force which no nation can withstand'.[91] Contrary to the somewhat mistaken assessment of many modern critics who would limit Attila's realm to basically Hungary and no further east or west, an underestimation that results from their refusal to countenance Hunnic capacity for state organization,[92] Priscus clearly points out that Hunnic territory in the east stretched to an area very close to that of the Medes (i.e. the Persians in Iran).[93] He records an invasion, probably in the 420s[94] into Media (Iran), launched under the command of Basich and Kursich, members of the 'royal family' (τῶν βασιλείων Σκυθῶν) and 'commanders of a large force' (πολλοῦ πλήθους ἄρχοντας). Attila according to Priscus' source, a man from the Western Empire called Constantiolus whom Priscus met during the embassy (another eyewitness source, not hearsay), ruled over the whole of Scythia and even the islands of the ocean (presumably Scandinavia).[95]

Attila was apparently toying with the idea of conquering Persia, treated as a real possibility by Priscus.[96] The Sassanians were at this time under severe pressure from the Hephtalite Huns (the eastern cousins of the European Huns) and were reduced to vassal status to the Hephtalites shortly after the death of Attila. A combined invasion from the east and west, therefore, could indeed have destroyed Persia. Priscus' premonitions were not an exaggeration at all. With enough co-ordination this was a militarily feasible operation. When the Romans with Priscus pray that God will induce Attila to attack the Persians and not the Romans, Constantiolus warns them that if the Huns conquer Persia, Attila will no longer tolerate Roman independence (!) and

The Hunnic Empire, the Germanic tribes and Rome 55

'holding them to be obviously his servants' he will force the Romans to call him an emperor.[97] So contemptuous was he of Roman power that Attila regarded his generals as equals to the emperors of the Romans.[98]

The account left by Priscus tells us several critical things about the Hunnic state. First we see two members of the royal family holding important commands over large military forces in the same way as we have observed among the contemporary Rouran in the east. Earlier in the account Priscus mentions that Edeco was one of the intimates (*epitēdeioi*)[99] of Attila, who guarded the person of the king on a rotational basis. Again we see a mirror image of the Rouran practice of royal bodyguards.[100] We also hear of Attila's *logades* (picked men) who feature again and again in our sources on the Huns.[101] The frequent, sumptuous ceremonial banquets of Attila's court also remind us of the steppe custom that requires all rulers to have an open table for their subjects as a sign of their generosity.[102] A sign of bureaucratic organization is available from the important role given to Onegesius[103] (who was held in such high regard as to sit on the right of the Hunnic king in banquets, in the position of honour, and enjoyed considerable power,[104] as shown by the courteous treatment of his wife by Attila and the possession of the second biggest palace in the capital, which all point to his influence at court and also the power of the state bureaucracy[105]) and possible ex-Roman defectors such as Rusticius, Constantius and Orestes, the father of the future Roman emperor Romulus Augustulus. The absorption of the Romanized population of conquered Pannonia and other Danubian provinces would have strengthened the bureaucratic base of the Huns[106] and Altheim suggests that the Huns, contrary to what we would expect, may even have possessed their own written script that was adapted from Ancient Sogdian,[107] which doubtlessly would have facilitated a much more efficient administration of their empire.

Did the Huns have the hierarchical, stratified structure of government along tribal lines which we have seen among the earlier Xiongnu and the contemporary Rouran? Eunapius records vaguely that there were certain Hunnic units in Thrace in the reign of Theodosius the Great, who took part in the emperor's campaign against the usurper Eugenius. They are said to have served in units under their tribal chieftains.[108] Olympiodorus,[109] a more reliable eyewitness, who also travelled on an embassy to the Huns before the time of the rule of Rua (Attila's uncle), in order to negotiate with the Hunnic sub-king Donatus,[110] is clearer. He records that Donatus who was in unknown circumstances murdered, presumably by Roman agents, was a vassal of the 'ὁ τῶν ῥηγῶν πρῶτος' (the first of the kings) Charaton,[111] who being enraged at the treachery had to be appeased with fantastic gifts.

Here we have definitive proof that the Huns practised the hierarchical division of power among the supreme ruler (Khagan or Shanyu, as among the Rouran and the earlier Xiongnu) and lesser vassal kings. The same type of organization is found again among the Hunnic vassal horde in the East along the shores of the Black sea, the Akatziri Huns. Obviously disaffected by the coup of Attila, who murdered the supreme ruler Bleda, the king of the eastern half of the Huns,[112] the Akatziri plotted a revolt with Roman support. However, the Roman ambassadors made an error while distributing gifts from the emperor. Kouridachus,[113] who was senior in office (πρεσβύτερον ὄντα τῇ ἀρχῇ), was given his gifts second, which was interpreted as denying him proper honours due to his rank (οὐ κατὰ τάξιν).[114] This slight led him to inform Attila about the planned rebellion and the Hunnic king quickly quelled the revolt after which he set up his own son Ellac as overlord of this eastern 'fief'.[115] The references to ranks, office and precedence clearly suggest that the system of rule that existed among the Huns was of a different nature from the relatively speaking more haphazard organization found among the Germanic tribes, where there is no clear division or gradation of rank between various kings or rather chiefs that make up the tribal confederation.[116]

Ellac's appointment to rulership over the Akatziri also shows the steppe practice, noted also among the Rouran and the earlier Xiongnu, of giving key fiefs to members of the royal family.[117] Indeed Attila's empire later fell precisely because of bitter disputes regarding the distribution of fiefs among his sons.[118] We also have the case of Laudaricus (Germanic: Laudareiks)[119] who according to the *Gallic Chronicle* of 511 was a blood relative of Attila (*cognatus Attilae*).[120] He was killed in battle at Mons Mauriacus. Bona points out that he was in all likelihood a vassal king of an affiliated Germanic tribe in the same way that Ellac was ruler over the eastern Akatziri and Edeco over the Sciri.[121]

Dualism, representing the two wings (Left and right or East and West) of the steppe imperial system,[122] which we have already noted as a feature of Xiongnu and Rouran kingship, was also very much a feature of the Hunnic Empire. Right from the very beginning of Hunnic history, dualism was a key feature. Firstly we encounter Donatus, who may have been a western representative of his eastern overlord Charaton.[123] Again and again in Hunnic history we find two rulers. Rua rules in the company of Oktar, his brother, who is active in the west in Gaul as the ally of Aetius,[124] suggesting that he was the ruler of the western realm, whereas Rua, who was quite clearly the more prominent king, in the traditional manner ruled the east. They were followed in the Hunnic kingship by their nephews Bleda, who ruled the east, and

Attila, who succeeded to Oktar's realm.[125] That Attila ruled the western half seems confirmed by the note in Priscus that Attila was of the Gepid Huns (i.e. his personal fief was the Gepids situated in modern Hungary, the core of the western half of the Hunnic Empire).[126]

Attila's unusual dictatorship after the murder of his overlord Bleda, though we do find him apportioning the East to his son Ellac in the familiar dual system during his lifetime, meant that the traditional balance of power had been upset and as we shall see later this had tremendous repercussions for the stability of the empire after his death.[127] Attila is of course referred to by Priscus as the *praecipuus Hunnorum rex*,[128] the chief/high king of the Huns,[129] which again shows us that there were other Hunnic kings who ruled under him, Ellac as his eastern co-ruler (dualism) and sub-kings ruling over lesser sub-divisions of the empire.[130] After a period of chaos following Attila's death, dualism again reasserted itself in the succession of Dengitzik and Ernak (west and east respectively). The successors to the Hunnic Empire in the east, or rather probably the continuation, also featured two wings, the Kutrigurs (west) and the Utigurs (east), ruled presumably by Ernak's descendants.[131]

The *logades* (picked men), commanding military units (presumably organized along tribal lines) in the Hunnic Empire, mentioned earlier, deserve further attention. These *logades* of the Hunnic king, which include eminent men such as Edeco the ruler of the Sciri, Berik 'the ruler of many villages in Scythia' due to his noble birth,[132] and even men with possibly Roman origins like Orestes, the father of the last Western Roman Emperor, were, as Thompson rightly notes, primarily responsible for the government of the empire.[133] The *logades* were clearly directly responsible to the central government of the two supreme kings of the two main wings of the empire (Attila and Ellac, the crown prince) and were in all likelihood the equivalent of the twenty-four governors of the Left and Right which we have seen among the Xiongnu, who administered the main provinces (in the steppe often groups of tribes situated in a fixed region, rather than a strictly defined territorial block) and regulated the relations between the centre and the peripheral vassal sub-kingdoms. This seems to be confirmed by the fact that Edeco and others like him often functioned as ambassadors and communiqués[134] to vassal tribes (Onegesius for instance is sent to the Akatziri to supervise the instalment of Ellac, the Hunnic crown prince, as direct overlord of the tribe[135]) and also by the fact that they were *logades*, picked men from among other eminent nobles of the Hunnic realm, who like the governors of the Xiongnu Empire (called 'ten thousand horsemen') commanded a considerable portion of horsemen allocated to them specifically to govern.[136]

What is revealing is the fact that these *logades* did not suddenly turn up under Attila. Thompson suggests probably correctly that the *oikeioi* (retainers) and *lochagoi* (captains) of Uldin, the western Hunnic king of the early fifth century, who betrayed him during his campaign against the Romans were the same as the *logades* under Attila. These captains/governors during military campaigns not only commanded specific squadrons of Huns assigned to each of them, but also contingents from subject peoples provided by the districts/provinces that they governed.[137]

There was also a distinct and regulated hierarchy among the *logades* themselves. This is shown by the distinctly Inner Asian seating arrangements during the feasts organized by Attila for the Roman ambassadors. Onegesius and Berik, both *logades*, were seated to the right and left of the Hunnic king, but Onegesius outranking Berik sat to the right of the king which was considered more honourable. This is highly significant since in the old Xiongnu Empire and also all other steppe societies the right (signifying the east, with orientation towards the north) had precedence over the left (west).[138] Members of the royal family who ranked even higher than the *logades* such as Oebarsius, the paternal uncle of the king, and the king's eldest son were seated in conspicuous positions of honour as befits their rank right next to the king on the same couch.[139] Taxes and tribute were also collected from subject peoples either by the *logades*[140] or more probably lower-ranking officials under their administration, usually it seems in kind (agricultural produce of various kinds) and often, as in the Roman Empire, in ruthless fashion.[141] As in the case of the Xiongnu Empire the Huns, despite their reputation for being 'nomads', also had an agricultural base to exploit composed mainly of the conquered populations in the Ukraine (like the Goths and others) who had practised agriculture from the time of the ancient Scythians and also a not inconsiderable number of agricultural workers imported into the empire from Roman territory (usually captives).[142]

Even more striking is the possible inheritance from the Xiongnu among the Huns of the aristocratic institution of the six horns,[143] a group consisting of six top-ranking nobles, the membership of which was exclusively limited to members of the royal family (Xulianti) and the highest-ranking noble families, the Huyan, Lan, Xubu and later also the Qiulin that intermarried with the imperial clan.[144] When rendered in Turkic this institution would have been called *Alti*[145] (six) *cur* (nobles). In the Greek transliteration this was rendered *Oultizouroi*.[146] The College of six *boliades* (boyars/nobles) would also become the distinguishing feature of the Danubian Bulgarian Empire formed by Hunnic descendants[147] and in Volga Bulgaria founded by a branch of the Proto-Bulgars, as in the old Xiongnu Empire, there would be four pre-eminent sub-kings (the equivalent of the old Xiongnu four horns kings, representing the four main divisions of the Empire), who sat to the right of the supreme ruler.[148]

The ruling family of Old Bulgaria in their prince list would name Ernak, Attila's son, as one of their earliest ancestors and call their clan Dulo. This name Dulo is accepted by most experts as being the same as the name Tu-lu, which was later in the sixth to seventh centuries AD the designation of one of the two major subdivisions of the Western Turkish Khaganate.[149] Pritsak goes one step further and argues for a connection between the name Dulo and the name of the old Xiongnu ruling house, T'u-ko (in EMC *d'uo'klo*).[150] If correct, this could validate the as yet hypothetical, dynastic links between the old Xiongnu and the European Hun-Bulgars,[151] in addition to the clear parallels in political organization that we have seen thus far. Pritsak also suggests that the Vichtun mentioned in the Prince list is none other than the famous Xiongnu emperor and founder of Hunnic greatness Modun (EMC *bəktun/biktun*).[152] Furthermore, we find among the Ostrogoths, who derive from the Hunnic Empire and may well have had a Hunnic royal house,[153] the decimal system of military and social organization which, as Wolfram accurately points out, derives from the steppe, i.e the Huns and Alans.[154]

It is then clear that the Huns had pretty much the same organization as their forebears the Xiongnu and also their eastern, contemporary neighbours, the Rouran (the overlord of virtually the whole of Inner Asia) and the Hephtalite White Hun Empires, all of whom had a Hunnic (Xiongnu) element within their polity.[155] It was this complex, quasi-feudal[156] social system and superb organizational ability which enabled the Huns to bind innumerable subject peoples, Germanic, Iranian, Slav, Finno-Ugric, Turkic etc., to their vast empire and allowed them to wage continuous, successful wars of conquest in Europe. It is absolutely no accident that the Huns created the first unified empire in European barbaricum beyond the Roman border and presented a real, viable alternative to Roman hegemony for the peoples of Europe.

The lack of knowledge of steppe institutions has led many scholars to misinterpret the information given by our sources. They envisage a primitive collection of tribes at the beginning with no political unity or centralized kingship, a chaotic agglomeration of chiefs later developing into a system of fewer kings by the time of Rua and then absolute kingship under Attila.[157] However, as we have shown thus far, Attila's sole rule was actually an aberration from the traditional steppe system of dual kingship presiding over fiefs ruled by sub-kings. If the Huns were primitive savages without organization, then how do we explain the fact that in less than half a century from the 370s onwards, with supposedly rudimentary institutions, if any, they develop into a massive empire that stretches from Gaul to Persia? In terms of sheer landmass it was an empire rivalling the size of the Roman Empire. Is it really possible to govern this huge territory with no advanced organization and institutions whatsoever? Surely this is an absurdity.

Maenchen-Helfen is right to point out that the Huns were already highly organized when they entered Europe,[158] but he and many others have not fully grasped the imperial dimension of the Hunnic state. The very name Hun implies the tradition of empire. It is not an ethnic appellation as such, but rather like the name Rome or Roman, an indicator of steppe imperial ideology.[159] This understanding is important when we assess the early history of the Huns, especially since many have been misled by reports in our sources of Hunnic auxiliaries operating within Roman territory, seemingly independent of the main Hunnic polity, and considered this as a sign of political fragmentation among the early Huns.

Ammianus, who is usually confused when it comes to the Huns, provides us with the first such instance of independent action by 'some Huns'. He tells us that other Huns (*hunis aliis*) were hired by the Gothic King Vithimiris to fight the Alans invading his lands.[160] Does this imply that the Huns were so disorganized that some of them even offered their services to the Goths whom they had just defeated? Maenchen-Helfen notes correctly that these 'other Huns' of Ammianus were not the Huns who had defeated the Goths but the Chunni (mentioned by Ptolemy in the second century AD) who may have included some Turkic tribes such as the Alpidzuri, Alcidzuri, etc., who were already living west of the Volga at the time of the Hunnic invasion and joined the Goths in resisting the new invaders.[161] The 'Huns' who may have formed a part of the three-tribe confederation of Alatheus and Saphrax,[162] probably also belong to this category of 'Huns', as do the Thracian Huns (possibly the same as those with Alatheus and Saphrax) who serve Theodosius under their own chiefs. There were also runaway slaves and deserters from the Roman army who called themselves Huns to exploit the terror inspired by that name. This group of vagabonds ravaged Thrace in AD 401 until they were wiped out by the regular Roman army under Fravitta.[163]

However, whether these so-called Huns were independent tribes of Turkic speakers who were resisting imperial Hunnic invasion or whether they were part of the Hunnic wave who seceded from the main body hardly makes a difference in our assessment of the nature of the early Hunnic state. When the Hephtalite White Huns invade Persia, there are affiliated, related or rival groups who often act independently of the main imperial horde (e.g. the Kidarites Huns in Gandhara and the Tchols), either as advance guards in reconnoitring new territories or in rebellion/resistance.[164] In many cases these tribes are formally conquered subjects or defeated enemies of the empire who are fleeing the domination of the main horde, e.g. the Kidarites who flee into northwestern India to avoid Hephtalite domination, the 100,000 Uighurs who try to flee west to escape Rouran rule, and later the Naimans and other Mongol tribes that try to form links with the Kara–Khitan Empire and the Khwarezm-Shah to resist the onslaught of the imperial Mongols under Chinggis Khan.[165] In other words the existence of wayward subject tribes or fleeing enemies of the same ethnic provenance, by no means indicates that the imperial Huns lacked overall leadership or were primitively organized.[166] If so, are Roman rebels and renegades who flee into non-Roman territory an indication of Roman impotence and lack of organization?

Further analogies from steppe history can again help us to better understand the phenomenon of seemingly wayward tribes acting independently of the main steppe power and determine whether or not this is indicative of political fragmentation. The best case study for this phenomenon is the Inner Asian state of the Khitans who originated in Inner Mongolia and gradually came to dominate Manchuria and parts of northern China. Their expansion and behaviour vis-à-vis the Chinese dynasties of the Central Plains (Zhong Yuan) can shed light on Hunnic activities and behaviour once they entered the orbit of the Roman Empire.

The Khitans were the remnants of the once mighty Xianbei (the nemesis of the Huns) possibly mixed with some Xiongnu (Huns) who joined them during the Han Period.[167] After the fourth century AD all vestiges of Xianbei power in Mongolia completely vanished as the major Xianbei clans created empires in China and departed for good leaving the steppe in the hands of the Rouran. The Khitans, although descended from the Xianbei and presumably inheriting their martial and political traditions, were for a long time a weak people who were subjected successively to the Rouran, Koguryo,[168] Sui-Tang China[169] and then most importantly the Gokturk[170] and Uyghur Turkish Khaganates[171] that ruled most of the eastern steppe from the sixth to the ninth centuries AD. Thus as in the Hun–Xiongnu case there is an even bigger hiatus between the rise of the ex-Xianbei Khitans in the ninth century AD and the demise of Xianbei power in Mongolia in the fourth century AD.

Yet, in contrast to the divergence in opinion about Hun–Xiongnu connections, interestingly enough most scholars now accept the Khitan links to the Xianbei[172] and few have ever contested the complexity of their political organization (both before and during the reign of Abaoji,[173] the founder of Khitan power), which all agree originated from the Inner Asian world that they came from. Despite a 500-year hiatus that separates the Khitans from their Xianbei forebears their society and polity are deemed complex because all agree (as I would argue was also true in the case of the Huns) that there were plenty of prior and contemporary state models in the steppe that the Khitans could draw from, even without necessarily harking back to the memory of the old Xianbei. Like the Huns of Europe who mainly consisted of the western fringe populations of the Xiongnu Empire (Turkic and Iranian-speaking tribes) the Khitan state was a confederation of tribes made up of mainly the eastern fringe elements of the Uyghur Khaganate.[174]

What is striking about the rise of the Khitans is that like the Hunnic rise in Central Asia it occurs in the context of a power vacuum. In the same way that in the third and fourth century AD the Huns saw their traditional Inner Asian and sedentary rivals disappear one after the other, the Khitans in the ninth century witnessed the dissolution of the domineering Uyghur Khaganate at the hands of the Kyrgyz and the collapse also of the Tang Empire to the south.[175] This also coincided with the decline of the main power to the east of the Khitans, the largely sedentary Manchurian–Korean kingdom of Balhae, which the Khitans eventually destroyed (we are reminded of course of the Hun conquest of the semi-sedentary Kangju). Lesser nomadic tribes such as the Xi (recall the Alans) were also quickly absorbed into the growing Khitan Empire, whose military success was only realized through the centralization of authority and political reorganization achieved by Yelu Abaoji and the dynasty he founded,[176] yet another indication that comparable Hun successes earlier in history could not have occurred without organized leadership and a corresponding political structure. Tellingly, the pre-dynastic Khitans were weak and unable to expand precisely because they possessed inferior and fragmented sociopolitical organization in comparison to their better organized neighbours.[177] In other words, the Huns could hardly have conquered the Alans and the Goths without superior political organization and centralization of authority.

The conquests of Yelu Abaoji made the Khitans the undisputed military power north of China, which amazingly enough was at this time also in a fragmented state (recall the East–West division of the Roman Empire when

The Hunnic Empire, the Germanic tribes and Rome 63

the Huns arrived), with the south rendering only nominal allegiance to the Five Dynasties that ruled one after the other in rapid succession in the north (Wudai Shiguo Period AD 907–60). Like the Roman military of the fourth and fifth centuries who recruited heavily among barbarians, the main strength of the armies of the northern Chinese dynasties (Later Tang, Later Jin and Later Han) lay in their naturalized Shatuo Turks who provided the empire with both its emperors and military elite.[178] Like Stilicho and later Aetius to Attila's Huns, some of these military strongmen (most notably Shi Jingtang, the founder of the Later Jin Dynasty) in China would appeal for military aid to the Khitans in order to resolve internal power struggles.[179] The Khitans for their part, like the Huns, were primarily Inner Asian pastoralists, but they like the Huns already had ample exposure to sedentary societies before their arrival in China (via their own rather flourishing agricultural base[180] and the conquest of Balhae). Thus in the Khitans we have a state entity that closely resembles the Hunnic Empire of the west and also a correspondingly similar sedentary rival.

What is notable is the fact that the Khitans, even when they possessed military superiority over the Chinese, did not make the absorption of Chinese territory their primary goal. As Standen correctly points out, the Khitan rulers behaved in China like the steppe potentates that they were and focused their efforts on forcing the Chinese to recognize their suzerainty and overlordship.[181] The Chinese emperor was treated like a vassal steppe chieftain who owed 'feudal' homage to the Khagan.[182] Even after capturing the Later Jin capital in AD 947, Deguang, the Khitan ruler, after looting the treasury and deporting prisoners and captives to the north, withdrew when the campaigning season drew to a close, leaving the Chinese to retrieve what they could of their battered empire.[183]

This closely resembles the Hunnic incursions under Attila into the Roman Empire. We see the Huns dutifully returning to their base in Hungary when the campaigning season draws to a close. Of course, in both cases the sedentary power left behind with the ashes of ruined cities and decimated armies claimed 'victory' due to this customary withdrawal, but the nomads were ready to return the following year to finish the job. Luckily for the Romans and the Chinese both Attila and Deguang died before they could return at the peak of their military success, leaving their descendants busy with internal conflicts and quite unable to resume military campaigns against their sedentary neighbours. It would take nearly half a century before the Khitans would resume their invasions of China. The Bulgar and Kutrigur descendants of the Huns would likewise return after a similarly long interlude.[184]

What is even more interesting is that prior to the great inroads by the main Khitan army, although it is clear that all nomads north of China were at this stage under Khitan control, there are still small groups of nomads that make incursions into China and enter into dealings with the Chinese authorities without being directed to do so by the Khitan central government. This does not imply that these groups did not owe allegiance to the Khitans, but merely that tribes or rather frontier guards on the fringes of the empire were often given a greater degree of autonomy in carrying out military action to test the strength of potential, new targets of fresh conquest without bringing direct danger to the Khitan core.[185] This type of reconnaissance or periodic nomadizing on the borders to test targets of raids or invasions is a routine feature of nomadic conquests and is seen also in the context of Mongol expansion west in the thirteenth century.[186]

Another intriguing analogy, this time in the west, can also be helpful to our understanding of the Hunnic situation. If we compare their conquest and expansion to that of the Oghuz Seljuk Turks and the Karakhanids[187] from Kazakhstan (the same region from which the Huns originated) in the eleventh century AD, we immediately discover astonishing similarities and possible explanations to Hunnic behaviour in the early years of their drive west as they moved out of Central Asia. The Oghuz confederation from which the Seljuk dynasty originated was formally part of the Great Gokturk Khaganate, the successor state of the Rouran Khaganate which had co-existed with the Hunnic Empire in the west. After the collapse of this imperial entity in AD 741 (we are reminded of course of the collapse of the Xiongnu Empire in the case of the Huns), the Oghuz migrated further west and their leader assumed the military office of Yabghu of the 'right wing of the horde',[188] a position that is subservient to that of Khagan which the Oghuz lords, being non-Ashina (i.e. non-royal) in origin, could not acquire. The Khaganate was claimed by their eastern neighbours, the more powerful Qarluks who in the eleventh century conquered Transoxiana and became known as the Karakhanids.[189]

The Karakhanids were never strong enough to apply any real control on the more westerly Oghuz (just as the Huns remaining in Central Asia seem to have had no effective influence on the activities of the European Huns), but they did preserve the old Turkish double system of Great Khan and Co-Khan (dualism), a double khanate supported by the familiar six supreme nobles,[190] in which subordinate kings from the ruling family held fiefs in various regions (again a mirror image of the Xiongnu model).[191] The Oghuz also possessed the same political model and once their conquests in the west had elevated their status significantly among the Turkish peoples, the Seljuk dynasty of the Oghuz in a manner reminiscent of the Karakhanids[192] divided their new conquests in Persia into two zones, the west under the control of Toghril Beg (younger brother) with Chagri Beg (elder brother) ruling the east.[193] The conquests were deemed to be the inheritance of the royal clan, not the exclusive property of the supreme ruler, Toghril.[194] Thus, as observed among the Xiongnu, Rouran and the Huns, 'fiefs' were distributed to various princes of the blood. Musa Yabghu was invested with control of Sistan.[195] To Qavurt, the elder son of Chagri Beg, fell Kirman[196] and Alp Arslan (the younger son of Chagri Beg and the chosen successor of Toghril Beg) inherited the sultanate. Once established in power Alp Arslan distributed more 'fiefs' in strategically vital regions such as Khwarezm, Khurasan and the upper Oxus lands to his sons and relatives.[197]

So far what we see here is a typical Inner Asian quasi-feudal empire reminiscent of the Xiongnu, but the Seljuk state had several critical weaknesses that would ultimately bring about its early demise and render it more unstable than the Karakhanids to the east. The Karakhanids were in the eyes of all Turks a legitimate royal dynasty that had a long pedigree stretching back to the days of the Great Gokturk Empire.[198] The Seljuks in contrast were not the legitimate ruling clan of the Oghuz, but merely the Sü-Bashï, a high-ranking military vassal under the rule of the Yabghu (vassal king) of the Oghuz (whose capital was at Yengi-Kent in the Syr Darya delta region).[199] With approximately 7,000–10,000 Oghuz under their control the Seljuk lords who had been expelled for rebellion usurped the title Yabghu.[200] Thus the Seljuks were originally a group of fugitive renegades, who after many years of bitter conflict overthrew the previous ruling family of the Oghuz (AD 1042 in Khwarezm).[201] In other words, they lacked prestige and more importantly legitimacy in the eyes of their steppe neighbours.

The Oghuz left in the steppe were crushed by the combined pressure from the Seljuks from the south and the Kipchaqs invading from the north and east.[202] The surviving Oghuz tribes either fled west into the Pontic steppe or joined the Seljuks who now claimed to be the overlords of all the Oghuz.[203] The Seljuk claim to supremacy, however, was not universally accepted, though certainly not because they lacked political organization. Many Oghuz clans were resentful of the success and monopoly on power of these upstarts whom many viewed as their equals, not superiors.[204] Turbulence and rebellion among the 'Turkmen' was a chronic feature of the Seljuk Empire.[205] In the periphery of the Seljuk state, especially in regions like Anatolia in the extreme west, the various Oghuz bands acted independently of the Seljuks and even served as auxiliaries (*foederati*) of the Byzantines in opposition to the Seljuks.[206] Some of them would set up famous dynasties of their own in Anatolia such as the Danishmenids and Mangüjekids.[207] The last effective Seljuk ruler in Iran, Sultan Sanjar, would fall precisely due to such Turkmen intransigence. He was arrested by rebellious Turkmen and his empire did not survive his captivity.[208]

The rebellious nature of the Oghuz was, however, not the only problem faced by the Seljuk state. Potentially more dangerous were the ambitions of royal princes, who being unsatisfied with their own fiefs contested power with the reigning sultan and his heirs. This was a chronic menace to stability and central authority. For instance Alp Arslan's accession to the throne was contested by his relatives Yabghu b. Mikail and Qutlumush.[209] Qutlumush was defeated and executed, but his sons survived and would later set up an independent Seljuk sultanate in newly conquered lands in Anatolia which remained hostile to the Great Seljuks in Iran and Iraq.[210] We are of course reminded of the fact that the Huns themselves fell victim to such internecine struggles after the death of Attila.

Were the European Huns more like the Karakhanids who had directly inherited the imperial traditions of the Gokturks[211] or were they like the Seljuks, upstarts who were nonetheless familiar with steppe imperial practices and who modelled their new conquest state on the institutions of the old Gokturk and Iranian empires of their region? Either could be possible, since we have no way of knowing why the European Huns separated from the Central Asian Huns and marched west. However, when we consider the fact that their expansion west happened almost simultaneously with the Hunnic expansion south into Persia, it does seem likely that their departure was not due to political divisions as in the case of the Oghuz mentioned above. The Oghuz were under pressure from the Kipchaqs and rocked by internal civil war between the Yabghu and the Seljuks. This precipitated the migration of the Seljuks and other Oghuz clans into Persia. However, the Huns in contrast, as shown earlier, were probably under no such external pressure in the mid fourth century AD. The Xianbei, Kangju and the Wusun, the traditional neighbours and rivals of the Huns in Inner Asia, were all either destroyed or dispersed at this stage and the empire of the Rouran was yet to take shape. In fact the Huns were supreme in their local region. Their expansion therefore in my opinion resembled more closely the purposeful campaigns of the Khitans, Mongols and Gokturks than the desperate push south by the Seljuks.

The arguments for a loosely organized Hunnic horde in its early years in Europe are contradicted by three developments. Firstly, there is the rapid stabilization of western conquests. Although Heather is correct in noting that the main body of the Hunnic nation lay further east until the opening years of the fifth century,[212] as Maenchen-Helfen argues, at least an advance guard of the Huns were already active on the Danube in the 370s.[213] According to Zosimus, in the year AD 381/2 the Sciri and Carpodacians under the probable direction of the Huns attacked Roman territories across the Danube.[214] In 384, according to Ambrose, the Huns with some Alans, at the request of the Romans, attacked the Suebic Juthungi in Raetia and then rode on in the direction of Gaul, where they were induced by Valentinian to turn back and fall upon Alemannia.[215] After the breakout of Odotheus' Greuthungi in AD 386, there are no serious tribal movements on the Danube which indicates that the Huns were by AD 387 at the latest the masters of the Hungarian Plains.[216] In other words it took the Huns just over ten years to conquer the immense region stretching from Hungary to the Volga and also to largely secure this turbulent region. Such rapid conquest and also stabilization, though imperfect, is surely impossible without an organized system of rule.

There would indeed be rebellions against Hunnic rule in the early fifth century when the Alans led a secessionist group of Vandals and Suebi on a track towards Gaul (AD 405/6)[217] and Radagaisus led his Goths into Italy.[218] The imposition of Hunnic princes and nobles as rulers replacing native ones is likely to have led to this emigration.[219] The Huns could not stop the Alans from leaving, which shows that their power did not reach as far west as Germany at this stage, but in collusion with the Roman general Stilicho, Uldin the king of the Huns in the west[220] annihilated the rebel tribes under Radagaisus,[221] thereby demonstrating the basic stability of Hunnic control in the Danubian region and its ability to punish in detail secessionist tendencies among newly conquered subjects. Uldin would shortly afterwards (AD 408) engage in an ill-fated adventure into Roman territory with unreliable Germanic and Alanic levies,[222] but this doesn't alter the picture of Hun rule stabilizing in this western extremity of their empire by the early 400s.

The second development is related to the first. As imperial rule stabilizes in the west we see shortly thereafter in the reigns of Rua and Attila (and there is little doubt that this was also happening to a limited degree even earlier under Uldin, as demonstrated by the mass conscription of conquered non-Hunnic tribal groups like the Alans and Sciri in Hunnic armies on the Danube) the forced relocation of whole tribal communities away from their original habitat to the Danubian region. Thus the Ostrogoths for instance are moved en masse by the Huns, by presumably either Rua or his nephews Bleda and Attila, from the Ukraine to Pannonia after the conquest of that area to form what Heather calls part of a protective ring around the central Hunnic core lands on the middle Theiss.[223] What is important about this development is that such controlled mass movements of populations can only be undertaken by a well-organized state with a functioning apparatus of government.[224]

We see a very similar policy of mass deportations of tribal groups being enacted by Shah Abbas, the Safavid ruler of Iran in the early seventeenth century. The Safavid state, despite its Iranian pretensions, was in fact a state founded by Turkic tribes, the so-called Kizilbash. Once the state was founded, however, the Turkoman and other nomadic tribes in western Iran increasingly became a menace to the authority of the Safavid dynasty. Shah Abbas came up with a brilliant solution to this dilemma and that was to move tribal groups, both Turkish and Kurdish, from Azerbaijan (the original heartland of the dynasty) to the eastern border region of Khurasan. The unruly tribes thus displaced in many cases lost their original cohesion in an alien environment, becoming less of a threat and more dependent on the government, and at the same time acted as excellent buffers against Uzbek and Turkmen raids from the North and East.[225]

Later Nadir Shah, an Afshar Turk, who took control of Iran following the collapse of the Safavid state, enacted the same policy by moving rebellious, recently conquered Sunni tribal groups such as the Afghans and Turkmens, as well as Shia Azeri Afshars and the Bakhtiyari from Luristan to his power base in Gurgan and Khurasan.[226] The Hunnic relocations of the Goths, Sciri and Gepids appear to have served the same purpose. However, such controlled deportations in the Iranian case were only possible because of internal stability and the administrative capacity of the Safavid state. To expect any less control and significantly inferior administrative capacity among the Huns who carried out a similar relocation program some 1,200 years earlier would be nonsense.

Lastly, years before the Hunnic deportations of conquered tribes to the Danubian region in AD 395 the main eastern wing of the Huns launched a major offensive through the Caucasus against both the Sassanian Empire and the Roman Empire.[227] The assault on the Roman Empire in particular even included a simultaneous incursion into the Balkans in the west, proof of the extraordinary Hunnic capacity for military planning and organization on a gigantic scale and over immense distances.[228] The sheer scale of this invasion, which terrified Saint Jerome and Ephraim the Syrian,[229] is surely an unmistakable indication of Hunnic unity and military cohesion. The Huns in just a few decades had conquered much of eastern and central Europe. They were invading Persia and the Roman Empire at will, possibly in collusion with

The Hunnic Empire and Roman military collapse 69

their eastern cousins the White Huns. Only the blind could regard as primitive this formidable military machine; and to maintain such a war machine, social and political organization is an imperative in any age.

Even if the Hunnic state approximated the Seljuk and Oghuz state model, described above, more closely than the better organized steppe empires such as the Xiongnu and Rouran, one cannot define their early polity as primitive or poorly equipped to govern an empire. The army that the Seljuks led obviously had the capacity to turn itself into a state entity as soon as they entered Iran. With astonishing rapidity they structured their new political entity into an Inner Asian and Iranian quasi-'feudal', bureaucratic state. This organizational structure was imperfect and unstable, but despite serious internal problems, the Seljuk state persisted for over a century and only fell due to a new migration from the east, that of the Kara-Khitans. The quasi-feudalism of the Seljuks and their practice of handing out important 'fiefs' to family members often created struggles over inheritance and this profoundly weakened the Seljuks, but even so the Seljuk state remained a formidable military machine capable of administering and controlling a far-flung empire. Similarly the Hunnic political structure, like that of many other steppe empires, had its flaws and the ruling clan was often fractious and this sometimes led to civil war.[230] However, once united in purpose, usually after some bloodletting over the succession, the military and political organization that formed the backbone of all steppe confederacies and empires would be reactivated with devastating effect.

THE IMPACT OF THE HUNNIC EMPIRE AND ROMAN MILITARY COLLAPSE

If then it is accepted that the Hunnic Empire was an immensely powerful, well-organized, military machine, as our sources and historical, comparative analysis show, what was its impact on the Roman Empire? As mentioned earlier misconceptions regarding the nature of the Hunnic Empire have led many to minimize the role of the Huns and attribute their role to others, i.e. the Germanic tribes and even incompetent Roman emperors. Most recently Goldsworthy has claimed that Rome never met a serious challenger to its superpower status.[231] It is, however, not to be doubted that in the Hunnic Empire Rome did indeed face a serious challenge, which in the end brought down the Roman imperial edifice in the West and through political, as well as cultural transformations, heralded the dawning of a new age that historians in the West call quite erroneously the Dark Ages or, slightly more invitingly, the Middle Ages.[232]

As noted earlier in the chapter, if the Romans had been able to concentrate their forces effectively against the barbarians who had infiltrated into the empire, the Visigoths and the Vandals, there is no doubt that they would have succeeded in wiping out or absorbing these minor troublemakers in much the same way that the empire had dealt with earlier third-century invaders. Even as late as the sixth century AD, when the West had long since fallen, Justinian the emperor of the East could still marshal enough resources to re-conquer much of the old Western Empire. However, as was also the case in the fifth century AD, the Eastern Empire by itself could not hold together these disparate territories. Even though the Eastern Empire by the fifth century was vastly wealthier and in military terms the superior to the Western half, by itself it could not revive the entirety of the Roman state. The Western Empire and its military establishment were still needed.

By AD 440 the Romans with some solid assistance from allies, none other than the Huns,[233] were in the process of achieving what was expected, the destruction or pacification of the barbarian intruders, albeit with occasional mishaps such as the embarrassing defeat in Spain against the Suebi. Gaul was largely back in Roman hands after the chaos of the early fifth century. The Visigoths, Alans, Burgundians and Franks as well as the troublesome Bacaudae[234] in Northern Gaul had largely been brought to heel within the Roman system.[235] Much of Spain was also recovered and then lost again through a military disaster precipitated by Visigothic treason against the empire. The Vandals in Africa though were the most serious problem and were depriving the Western Empire of much-needed tax revenues and grain supplies. To remedy this situation both halves of the empire were in the process of assembling troops in Sicily to finish off the Vandals in Carthage. If this operation had succeeded the full recovery of the Western Empire would have been in sight.

But then in 441 disaster struck. The Persians, the ever-present foe of the Eastern Empire, waged war. By itself this was manageable. However, when the Huns sensing imperial weakness in the Balkans joined the war against the Romans, it was a catastrophe.[236] The army under Areobindus sent to attack Geiseric and his Vandals was called back to defend Constantinople.[237] By the end of AD 442 the war drew to a close and Rome agreed to pay tribute to the Huns.[238] The Persians had earlier withdrawn from the war. In fact after this war they would not engage the Romans again in open warfare for the remainder of the century.[239] The

The Hunnic Empire and Roman military collapse 71

Sassanians were in a life or death struggle with the White Huns, who would soon reduce them to vassalage. In such a crisis the Persians were no longer in any position to threaten Rome.

Some historians have remarkably downplayed the Hunnic successes in the 440s by attributing their success to the Persian concerns of Constantinople. If so, then how are we to explain the Roman disasters of the greater war of AD 447[240] and the destruction in that year of all Roman forces in the Balkans?[241] There were no Persian armies this time[242] or any other significant military menace. The East Roman field army in full force fought against the Huns and was systematically wiped out. The Huns after having destroyed the Roman army under Arnegisclus near the river Utus and sacked their base of operation, Marcianople, then trapped and destroyed the last field army immediately available to the Eastern Empire (presumably under the command of Aspar and Areobindus, Arnegisclus having died in battle at Utus) at Chersonesus (Gallipoli).[243] Theophanes reports that all three generals were badly defeated and Attila advanced to both seas, the Black Sea and the Hellespont, forcing the Eastern emperor Theodosius to sue for terms.[244]

The *Gallic Chronicle* of 452 records that the Huns captured some seventy cities in the Balkans.[245] Every city in Thrace was sacked except Adrianople and Heracleia[246] and Constantinople was threatened. This was then followed by Hunnic raids deep into Greece which reached Thermopylae.[247] The events were so shocking that even Western Romans took notice and the *Gallic Chronicle* would castigate Western generals for not coming to the aid of the East.[248] The losses sustained by the Empire were so serious that the Balkans would be virtually defenceless to roaming bands of barbarians right up to the end of the fifth century.[249] Marcellinus Comes, one of our sources, summed it up as follows: *Ingens bellum et priore maius per Attilam regem nostris inflictum paene totam Europam excisis invasisque civitatibus atque castellis conrasit* ('A mighty war, greater than the previous one, was brought upon us by king Attila. It devastated almost the whole of Europe and cities and forts were invaded and pillaged.')[250]

Priscus as usual is our best source and provides a summary of the outcome. 'The Romans pretended that they had made the agreements [i.e. to increase payments of tribute] voluntarily, but because of the overwhelming fear which gripped their commanders they were compelled to accept gladly every injunction, however harsh, in their eagerness for peace.'[251] Thompson downplays the severity of the burden imposed on the empire by the tribute payments, but a closer reading of Priscus' text yields a different conclusion. Thompson argues that the annual revenue of the Eastern Empire was 270,000 pounds of gold, of which 45,000 was spent on the army.[252] The money that the Romans agreed to pay Attila, 2,100 pounds of gold per year and 6,000 pounds of gold in arrears (2.2% of the imperial budget), was thus, he argues, insignificant.[253]

However, as Wickham points out, more like half of the entire imperial budget usually went to feeding and paying the army.[254] The impressive figures for tax revenue collected in the Eastern Empire are also at times unreliable, suggesting that they were often optimistic estimates of the ideal figures rather than accurate sums.[255] Expenditure would have been much greater than usual in AD 447 and the years following due to the need to re-equip and virtually re-build the entire army that had been wiped out in the war. The permanent need to feed the imperial capital, which was the second largest expenditure, would then have consumed most of the remaining reserves. Add to this the cost of restorations of fortifications and other defensive structures that were immediately required to prevent future Hunnic incursions and the enormous loss in revenue from the devastated Balkan provinces, then the tribute starts to look ominous.

To make matters worse the 8,100 pounds of gold mentioned above was, it seems, not the only payments due to the Huns. Ransom would have had to be paid for the immense number of prisoners of war taken by the Huns (the peace treaty even provided for the payment of ransoms for Roman prisoners who had fled Hunnic territory and were no longer under Hunnic jurisdiction[256]) and visiting Hunnic dignitaries like Edeco had to be paid off and lavishly entertained.[257] In addition Priscus specifically mentions that tribute was paid not just to the Scythians (i.e. Huns), but also the other barbarian neighbours of the Romans, further draining imperial resources.[258]

It is in this context that Priscus' account of senators selling their wives' jewellery, rich men their furniture and some even committing suicide because they could not meet the required contributions demanded of them by the emperor for the payment of tribute to the Huns, becomes intelligible. True 8,100 pounds of gold was not enough to suddenly empty the treasuries of the empire as Priscus records. It was its combination with other expenditures that were brought on by the defeat in the Hunnic war that made the Romans cringe.

Later in AD 545 the hard-pressed Eastern Empire under Justinian, with its armies still relatively intact, would buy peace for five years with the Persian Sassanian Empire by offering a payment of 2,000 pounds of gold. In AD 551 a further five-year treaty was signed at the price of 2,600 pounds of gold, which was considered by the Persians, the most formidable power of the age, as a substantial sum,[259] enough to refrain from war for five years. If that is the case then a lump sum of 8,100 pounds plus unspecified other expenditures and the cost of rebuilding the entire army is no small figure. The losses suffered in the Great Hunnic War were enough to cripple the empire militarily for a decade.

The Battle of Chalons, the salvation of Western Civilization?

Four years later the Huns invaded Gaul. The battle of Chalons of AD 451 has often been called one of the most decisive battles in history.[260] It was probably nothing of the sort.[261] However, virtually all writers even now are in agreement that the battle was a great defeat for the Huns and in popular literature the battle is to some extent still portrayed as a defining moment that saved Western Christendom/civilization from an alien culture. The depiction of the battle in this manner commenced in the nineteenth century when historians like Thierry argued that through the victory of the Visigoths and Aetius, civilization in the West was saved from total destruction.[262] His line of thought, which was somewhat typical, that saw in the Huns only wanton savagery and destruction, was perpetuated in the twentieth century. In his *Fifteen Decisive Battles of the World*, Sir E. S. Creasy would define what was saved by the 'victory' of the Goths (surprisingly the Romans under Aetius are passed over in this analysis[263]). He states that the Germans differ from the 'Sarmatics' (Iranians) as well as the 'Slavs' (!) because of their 'personal freedom and regard for the rights of men'.[264] They are distinguished over other races because of their respect for the female sex and the 'chastity for which the latter were celebrated'. These things, i.e. Germanic respect for personal freedom and the chastity of their women, are in his words 'the foundations of probity of character, self-respect and purity of manners' among the Germans. Even while they were pagan, this chivalry and nobility of the Germanic stock was self-evident and it was this Germanic element of Western civilization that was supposedly threatened by Asiatic invaders at Chalons.[265] General Fuller in his *Decisive Battles of the Western World* would repeat the same message: Attila was nothing but a plunderer.[266] Chalons was a victory of the Romans and the Teutonic peoples, who being Europeans, as in the case of the European Greeks at Salamis, had set aside their private quarrels in order to face the common foe of the West, the 'Asiatics'.[267] This was, he argues, one of the most decisive moments in Western history.[268]

More recent and definitely more serious analyses of the battle have avoided these grotesque racial and ethnic clichés. Instead they categorize the battle as a Hunnic defeat that broke the myth of Hunnic invincibility[269] or as *The Cambridge Illustrated History of Warfare*, with the subtitle *The Triumph of the West*, puts it, a decisive triumph of Roman defensive strategy.[270] The rationale behind this excessive importance attributed to 'victory' over the Huns, is amply summed up by Thompson, who argues that the Huns 'were mere plunderers and marauders' from the east who being savages made no direct contribution to the progress of Europe and 'offered nothing'.[271] In other words, a Hunnic victory and conquest of Europe would have doomed Europe to a savage, barbarous future.

We will discuss in greater detail what exactly these 'plunderers and marauders' had to offer and more importantly the political and cultural impact the Huns and the Alans (Asiatics as it were) had on European medieval culture in Chapter 6, but turning first to the issue of race that troubled our nineteenth- and early twentieth-century historians, it need not be pointed out that the Asian Huns themselves actually constituted a tiny fraction of the population of the Hunnic Empire. Even among upper class Huns 'Caucasoid' elements made up the bulk of the presumably 'Mongoloid' in origin ruling elite that had mixed heavily with the 'Europoid' Iranians and Germans. In other words by the time the Huns reached Gaul, their army and their officer core, with the possible exception of the Hunnic king (who according to Jordanes may have had a Mongoloid appearance of sorts[272]) and his immediate family, had an overwhelmingly European, whatever that implies, Caucasoid visage and appearance.[273] The battle of Chalons was certainly no race war.

It wasn't a religious one either.[274] The Hunnic state, like all steppe empires, was pluralistic and conciliatory towards all forms of religious expression. There were plenty of Arians and Catholic Christians within the Hunnic state and the strange idea that Huns were a threat to the Christian religion of the Romans and the Goths is absurd when we consider the fact that all physical descendants of the Huns in later centuries, perhaps with the exception of some of the Volga Bulgars, converted to Christianity.[275] The Huns who entered the West were an extreme minority and just as the Mongols rapidly became Muslim or Buddhist monarchs in their new territories and quickly took on the trappings of sedentary rulers, the Huns would doubtlessly have undergone the same process after their conquest of the Romans. In fact this is exactly what happened to the Hunno-Germanic princes Theodoric and Odoacer in Italy.[276]

If the battle of Chalons had no racial, religious or even cultural significance, then what is its significance, if any? The most visible consequence of the battle was the virtual annihilation of what was left of the Western Roman military establishment.[277] The issue of who exactly was the victor in this battle has been a highly contentious one for centuries. Jordanes, who has heavily embellished and altered the original account of the battle in Priscus,[278] of course attributes victory to the Goths and only the Goths as usual.[279] The Western Romans under Aetius, who were the main opponents of the Huns, and the Alans who actually fought the Hunnic contingent (i.e. the strongest) within Attila's army in the centre, receive scarcely any attention at all in the battle narrative. The account is on the whole hopelessly confused, but what we can notice from this distorted tale told by Jordanes is that Theodorid the king of the Visigoths is slain at the beginning of the battle.[280] After some forced rhetoric concerning Visigothic military prowess[281] after this calamity, we see subsequently the Visigoths withdrawing from the battlefield and returning to Toulouse, leaving the battlefield in the possession of the Huns.

Most historians, taking Jordanes for his word, have attributed this to Thorismud's anxiety over his inheritance in Toulouse or the machinations of Aetius who persuaded him to let the Huns go because he was now afraid of the power of the Visigoths and needed the Huns as a counterweight.[282] It is hard to believe that this kind of nonsense (presumably Visigothic retelling of their contribution to the battle long after the event when they had become masters of most of southern Gaul and Spain,[283] or even literary embellishment added either by Cassiodorus or Jordanes himself to make Aetius the new Themistocles[284]) has persuaded so many scholars until now.[285] Such an unrealistic series of decisions and persuasions can hardly have been possible. The numbers engaged in the battle were massive for the standards of the day and the heterogeneous nature of both armies would have made it impossible for commanders, especially on the Roman side (where a unified command structure had in haste only recently been improvised), to accurately grasp the actual situation on all flanks. Victory or defeat was always uncertain.[286] In such mayhem and confusion with desperately poor communication between troops, would political manipulation have been possible when an enemy of the magnitude of the Huns still remained on the battlefield? This is surely pushing at the limits of plausibility.

In fact we find in Jordanes' own account the curious situation of both Thorismud (Gothic commander after the death of Theodorid, his father) and Aetius losing track of their troops during the battle. Both of them, according to Jordanes, after the supposed rout of the Huns during the day, which forced Attila to withdraw into his camp, became separated from their respective commands. Thorismud somewhat inexplicably ends up in the Hunnic camp during the night after the battle, is almost killed and is dragged from his horse by the Huns before being rescued by his followers.[287] Aetius also finds himself separated from his men in the confusion of night and wanders about in the midst of the enemy (i.e. Huns, *noctis confusione divisus cum inter hostes medius vagaretur*), until he finds refuge in the Visigothic camp. He feared, according to Jordanes, that a disaster had happened.[288]

Now if the day had been a Roman–Visigoth triumph, as Jordanes insists, how could both commanders of the allies have simultaneous lost track of their armies? Aetius, the commander in chief, became lost because of the dark and as a consequence found himself among the Huns? Weren't the Huns supposed to have retreated into their camp? How on earth could Aetius have gone all the way down to the Hunnic camp bypassing without recognizing all his troops from the very rear of the army where he would have held his command? Or was it, as we are naturally led to suspect, the other way around? It is clear that these details more properly describe not a situation in which the Goths and the Romans are chasing the Huns downhill into their camp, but the Huns chasing the fugitive allies who had been defeated into the Roman camp. It was presumably during this rout that both Aetius and Thorismud became separated from their rapidly disintegrating armies.[289] This is confirmed by the rather curious piece of information in Jordanes that the Huns, after their supposed defeat, were unable to approach the Roman camp because of the hail of arrows from the Romans.[290] Weren't the Huns supposed to be trapped inside their ring of wagons, all desperate and fearing annihilation by this stage? What on earth are they doing lurking around the Roman camp?

In fact the day after the battle Jordanes tells us that the Romans, seeing the battlefield piled high with corpses, thought the victory was theirs, but knew Attila would not flee from the battle unless overwhelmed by a great disaster.[291] Didn't Jordanes just before say that the Romans and the Goths had carried the day? So why does Attila the following day need to be overwhelmed by another disaster? Even more perplexingly Jordanes says that Attila at this juncture did nothing cowardly, like one that had been defeated, but with clash of arms sounded the trumpets and threatened an attack. 'This warlike king at bay terrified his conquerors'.[292] The Romans and the Goths decide what to do next and that decision is to retreat!

So what really happened here? The death or disappearance of the commanding general in antiquity usually meant certain defeat and despite Jordanes' inordinate fixation with Gothic victories the death of their king in all likelihood meant the end of the battle for the Visigoths. Not only Theodorid, but also Thorismud, his son, goes missing and finds himself among the Huns. Keeping his throne would have been the least of Thorismud's worries at this point. His very survival was at stake! Even more interestingly Aetius the overall commander, supposedly in order to keep the booty for himself, sends away his Frankish allies[293] and at some point loses track of his own army and ends up spending the night at the Gothic camp. After some discussion both the Romans and the Goths leave the battlefield to the Huns and depart. So who then was the victor? Quite obviously the Huns who had possession of the battlefield after the battle.[294] Indeed the only relic of the battle found at Chalons is a Hunnic cauldron, used probably for the burial of Attila's relative Laudaricus after the battle.[295]

We can now attempt to reconstruct what actually happened in the battle. The Goths did not win the day as Jordanes says, but they actually seem to have abandoned the battlefield after Theodorid was killed. Note that after the death of the king Jordanes tells us that they separated from the Alans who held the centre.[296] In other words, they broke formation and left a glaring gap for the Huns to exploit. Far from deciding the battle in favour of the Romans, the Visigoths were primarily responsible for a military disaster by withdrawing from the battle. Jordanes tries to place the onus of the Hunnic breakthrough on the Alans and argues that the Alans were placed in the centre because they were unreliable, but as Bachrach notes, this is simply false. If anything the Alans bore the brunt of the battle (directly against the Hunnic contingent) precisely because they were the most reliable group among the allied forces.[297] It was the Alans not the Visigoths in Toulouse who were under direct attack from the Huns, since it was their territory in the Orléanais (given to king Goar and then to his successor Sangiban by Aetius for the Alan assistance in subduing Armorican rebels[298]) that was being invaded. The spirited resistance of Orléans before the battle[299] was also due to Alan intransigence in the face of Attila's threats.

The inglorious performance of the Goths at Chalons is the real reason why their exploits are so inflated and magnified by Jordanes.[300] The downgrading of the Alans is also due to the fact that it was the Alans who were the backbone of Roman defences in Aquitaine and hence the greatest hindrance to Visigothic hegemony in the region.[301] He over-emphasizes the deaths suffered by the Goths (especially that of their king) and even brings in the Huns as witnesses to the glorious nature of the Gothic war effort.[302] Many sceptics obviously needed some persuading.

In fact the whole battle narrative is clearly modelled on the narrative of the Battle of Marathon in keeping with the classicizing bent of Cassiodorus–Jordanes. The Huns, like the Persians of Herodotus, are situated in the middle, the weak Athenian centre (read unreliable Alans) gives way, allowing the wings to sandwich the Huns/Persians in the centre and save the day. No particular credit is given to the left wing (Plataeans/Romans) and all glory is bestowed on the heroic right wing (Goths under Theodorid and the main Athenian army under the war archon Callimachus). Both Theodorid and Callimachus, as if by coincidence, get killed during the battle, leaving the hero Miltiades/Thorismud to secure victory. Then after the victory the Athenians/Goths rapidly return to their home city Athens/Toulouse to secure it from the Persian navy which is aided by Athenian traitors who send a signal by raising a shield/sedition at home threatening Thorismud.[303] The sequence of events, troop deployments, and deeds attributed to participants in Jordanes' narrative exactly matches that of the Marathon narrative. This cannot be a coincidence.

The purpose of the Hunnic campaign west too has been long misinterpreted and this has also affected the assessment of the outcome of the battle. Jordanes as usual inflates to an unrealistic degree the contemporary power of the Goths and attributes the entire campaign to the machinations of Geiseric the Vandal, who fearing the revenge of Theodorid, the Visigothic king, for the barbarities committed on Theodorid's daughter by him and his son Huneric, had supposedly bribed Attila to attack Toulouse.[304] As if the Huns would launch an entire expedition west just to please Geiseric.[305] A fragment of Priscus, the authenticity of which is somewhat doubtful,[306] also asserts that Attila decided to attack the Western Empire to gain Honoria and her wealth and to attack the Goths to do a favour (why is not stated) to Geiseric.

However, the real purpose of the campaign into Gaul becomes more obvious in another more genuine fragment of Priscus, which tells us that the initial clashes occurred around the issue of the Frankish succession. Aetius and Attila, both looking to control the Franks, had supported different candidates and this sparked a conflict between them. However, Priscus tells us this was only an excuse for the main invasion which aimed at nothing less than rule over half of the Western Roman Empire.[307] Although this was feasible for the Hunnic ruler, a careful examination of Hunnic policy towards Rome shows a distinct unwillingness to permanently occupy Roman territory. For instance Attila abandoned most of his Balkan conquests after his victory over the Eastern Empire in AD 447 and satisfied himself with setting up a defensive ring around his core territory by creating a series of Hunnic fiefs south of the Danube, which he then officially claimed as Hunnic territory. Even this narrow strip of Roman territory that he had annexed he quickly showed a willingness to give back. The main objective all throughout seems to have been to prevent his own barbarian subjects from defecting to

The Hunnic Empire and Roman military collapse

the Romans, to create a defensive ring of barbarian vassals around his core territories and to subject the empire to vassalage and the payment of tribute (somewhat reminiscent of the policy adopted by his Xiongnu ancestors towards the sedentary empire of the Han Chinese much earlier in the East, which we have discussed above). Therefore, it is highly unlikely that Attila wanted to annex large chunks of Western Roman territory. Rather the objective seems to have been to consolidate Hunnic control over all barbarians within what he regarded as the Hunnic sphere of influence, that is the tribes of the Rhine region (mainly the Franks), and to subject the Western Empire to tribute. That the first of the main objectives was the Franks is confirmed by the route taken by the Huns in their invasion of Gaul. Tournai, Cologne and Trier, all areas with heavy concentration of Franks, are attacked first and occupied, the cities sacked.[308]

To fulfill these objectives Attila needed to accomplish two things. First, as in the case of the war with the Eastern Empire, a clear military victory over the main army of the Western Empire (in this case the army of Aetius in Gaul, hence the prior invasion of Gaul over the more tempting target of Italy where the Western Roman government was situated) to force other barbarians leaning towards the Romans into obedience and to stop the Romans from accepting defectors and fugitives from the Hunnic Empire. This would then be followed by an invasion of Italy itself to force the Western emperor into vassalage and the payment of tribute. Thus the target was not the Visigoths of Toulouse, which Jordanes' inflation of the importance of his Goths has long made historians suspect,[309] but the far more potent and dangerous Western Roman army under Aetius.[310] The destruction of this army was achieved at Chalons and the effectiveness of this expedition is brought to light by Aetius' total inability to offer any resistance to the Huns when they invade Italy the following year.

The sudden withdrawal of the Mongols from Central Europe, due most probably to a succession crisis back home in Mongolia, caused the Poles and the Hungarians to celebrate their military disasters in the 1240s as pyrrhic victories over the Mongols, simply because the Mongols returned home after winning the battle.[311] I would suggest that the same phenomenon had occurred in the case of Chalons. The main body of the Huns, as was their standard practice, returned to their home base in Hungary after the conclusion of the campaigning season (we see this also in Attila's campaign against the Eastern Romans in 447 and again in the Italian campaign of 452, when he withdrew from Italy without taking either Ravenna or Rome which lay defenceless before his army). Then because of the succession crisis following Attila's death in AD 453, the Huns ultimately failed to exploit any of the advantages gained from their earlier victories. This probably allowed the Romans and the Visigoths to represent their defeat as a costly victory.

Many have erroneously taken the withdrawal from Gaul to Hungary of the main body of the Hunnic army after the battle to be a clear indication that Attila was defeated. Hydatius, Sidonius Apollinaris[312] and other sources would claim a Roman victory for this reason and also the situation discussed above. Prosper of Aquitaine, a contemporary, in fact provides us with the clearest insight into how the Romans assessed the outcome of the battle. He says the slaughter was incalculable – for neither side gave way – and '*it appears that the Huns were defeated* in this battle because those among them that survived lost their taste for fighting and *turned back home*'.[313] In other words the Romans claimed victory, not because the outcome necessarily favoured them, but because the main Hunnic army returned home.

We must first note the fact that the Huns did not commence their march homeward because of the battle of Chalons. After a long drawn-out siege at Orléans that failed due to the tenacity of Alan resistance, and otherwise having largely fulfilled his objective (conquest of the Franks, though the reluctance of Aetius to engage him in battle until that point (due to Roman military weakness vis-à-vis the Huns as Sidonius observed[314]) had robbed him of the decisive battle he had wanted), Attila had apparently already decided to withdraw. This is confirmed by the location of the battle of Chalons which is to the east of Orléans and en route to the territory of the Huns. The battle was therefore either the result of a feigned retreat (typical steppe strategy) by the Huns in order to draw the evasive Romans into a decisive battle, or a pursuit by the allied army under Aetius of the Hunnic army already returning to winter bases in Hungary. Thus the return of the main Hunnic army to Hungary was by no means the result of a military defeat. Also what many have not noticed is that the Huns did not in fact completely withdraw from Gaul after Chalons.

In the story of Odoacer's extraordinary life, we have a curious episode in Gaul, most probably concerning him or implausibly another man bearing the same name, a certain Adovacrius/Odovacrius.[315] Between the battle of Chalons and the Visigothic success in the Loire region under Euric in the 460s, Gaul was fought over by the Franks under Childeric (the father of the famous Clovis), the Visigoths, a Roman general called Paul (succeeding Aegidius, the father of Syagrius[316]) and the above-mentioned Adovacrius/Odovacrius. Sometime after the battle of Chalons at Angers,[317] deep in western Gaul, a massively confused encounter takes place. Paul fights off the Visigoths in the area with Frankish aid,[318] but is then killed by Adovacrius and the Franks. The Franks and the 'Saxons' under Odovacrius then fight it out among themselves and in the end the Franks emerge victorious. Then, in a considerable leap of time and space, the account of Gregory of Tours, our source, moves on to an agreement between Childeric and Odovacrius to attack the Alamanni who were threatening Italy.[319] Gregory obviously regards Odoacer in Italy to be the same man as the Odovacrius in Gaul.[320]

What exactly is happening here? And to add to the puzzle we encounter the amazing story in Jordanes about the Visigoths beating off a second Hunnic invasion, after Chalons and the Hunnic invasion of Italy. Historians have pointed out that this is from a military point of view highly implausible and they are indeed correct. Two invasions from Hungary in the same year are hardly likely or even feasible. However, if this event is not made up, then where did these Huns come from and why is Odoacer, the Hunnic general (whose father Edeco and brother Hunulphus with their Sciri would later be found in modern day Romania and Bulgaria in the Balkans, then in Hungary, clearly the location closer to their original 'fief'), roaming about in western Gaul after the battle of Chalons? And furthermore, who exactly was Childeric the Frank and who was he fighting for at the time of the Battle of Chalons?

The Hungarian scholar Bona has argued that Childeric was a former vassal of Attila.[321] The founder of the Merovingian dynasty is identified by Bona with the elder of the two claimants to the Frankish throne mentioned in Priscus[322] who became king of the Franks thanks to the support of Attila and his Huns.[323] Interestingly Childeric, according to the somewhat garbled story of his life preserved in the Chronicle of Fredegar, at some point early in his career is said to have been taken into 'captivity' along with his mother by the Huns. He was 'freed' from 'captivity' by a faithful retainer named Wiomad, who would feature prominently in his rise to power.[324] According to both Fredegar and Gregory of Tours, Childeric was also expelled by the Franks, allegedly for his licentious behaviour, and had to live in exile in Thuringia for eight years[325] (if we accept Bona's chronology, then at the time under Hunnic rule). If Bona's theory is correct then Childeric presumably fought for Attila at Chalons, as a commander in Attila's army.[326] This seems to be confirmed by the fact that the mysterious Wiomad, who was powerful enough to be recognized as a sub-king of the Franks,[327] who supposedly rescued Childeric from captivity among the Huns and then later was instrumental in the establishment of the Merovingian dynasty, was himself a Hun and represented a Hunnic element in the Frankish army.[328]

In fact Fredegar tells us that it was the cunning Wiomad who stirred up the Franks against Aegidius (supposedly then ruling the Salian Franks during Childeric's exile[329]), engineered Childeric's return from exile and persuaded the emperor Maurice (probably a garbled reference to Attila) to give Childeric a vast treasure with which to defeat Aegidius and kill many Romans.[330] Furthermore, we find in Fredegar a curious origin myth for the Franks that attributes a common ancestry to the Franks and the Turks, by which term Fredegar was obviously referring to the Huns. The original united group had allegedly separated into two at the Danube, one migrating further west to become the Franks and the other remaining in the Danubian region to become the Turks.[331] As Hummer points out, the claim to kinship with the Turks (Huns) in the origin-myth reflects the real, historical absorption of oriental, steppe elements in the fifth century.[332] All of this and the strong Hunnic Danubian influence on grave goods found in Childeric's tomb suggest that Childeric was strongly associated with the Huns in some way and his rise to power was not unrelated to the Hunnic invasion of Gaul.

What is intriguing is the fact that those who benefit most from the war of AD 451 are the Franks and Burgundians, who until then had been marginal in comparison to the Visigoths and the Alans in Western affairs,[333] but now emerge in the form of Gundobad (nephew of the kingmaker Ricimer)[334] and Childeric as major powers due to their participation on the winning side of the war, i.e. the Hunnic.[335] Thus Childeric's activity in Gaul with Odoacer was the later side-effect of the Hunnic invasion of the region. Here we have another reasonable indication that Attila had not been defeated. Far from it, he had actually left troops behind to rule the newly conquered territory (or form a buffer between Roman territory further to the west and the main Hunnic realm[336]) and they were Odoacer's troops and possibly those of Childeric. The second Hunnic army that Thorismud supposedly defeated in AD 452 is also likely to have been part of this force left behind by Attila to govern Gaul.[337] The Visigoths, or rather the Alans with limited Visigothic support,[338] probably won a skirmish against them and then the Visigoths conflated this small victory into a myth that they had beaten Attila himself at Chalons and once again in the following year.[339] In reality Attila himself after his victory over Aetius returned to Hungary to pursue the main invasion (that of Italy) and left his lieutenants in Gaul to mop up the situation.

However, while the Huns in Gaul were dealing with pockets of Roman, Alan and Visigothic resistance in what was left of Roman Gaul, the Hunnic civil war broke out in AD 453–4 and this isolated Odoacer's army in Gaul, as

The Hunnic Empire and Roman military collapse 83

Hunnic control over the Rhine region vanished. Thus Visigoths, Alans, Roman remnants and Franks managed to oust the outnumbered Huns from Gaul during the Hunnic civil war, now that the Huns under Odoacer, or rather the mainly Germanic troops under Odoacer's Hunnic command, could no longer be reinforced from Hungary. Odoacer despite being cut off seems to have held his own for a long time until his defeat *c*. AD 469 at Angers, which probably induced him to return to his father's kingdom (that of the Sciri) in Pannonia[340] after striking a deal with Childeric in Gaul. It is then no accident that Childeric and Clovis became the rulers of Gaul[341] after the Hunnic invasion. Childeric was one of the governors left behind by Attila.[342]

Roman military impotence post AD 451

Returning to Attila, the year after Chalons in AD 452, after his supposed defeat in AD 451, the King of the Huns invaded Italy in full force. The *Gallic Chronicle* of 452 records that resistance collapsed completely and Aetius forever lost his *auctoritas*.[343] He had no troops to speak of to defend Italy, let alone Gaul, which as mentioned above was awash with Hunnic troops left behind by Attila following his victory at Chalons. Though the Hydatius Chronicle records that Marcian sent auxiliaries to assist Aetius and says the Huns were slaughtered by plague and the army of Marcian, this brave action from the East seems to have had little effect.[344] There are no records of any victories won by the Romans in open battle with the Huns. Marcian probably just claimed victory because the Huns at the end of their campaigning season, as was their standard practice, withdrew back to winter quarters in Hungary, laden with plunder and tribute from Pope Leo.[345] Since subjecting the Romans to tribute and vassalage was the main aim of the expedition, it can be said that the campaign was largely successful for Attila.

There is no doubt that the invasion of Italy had been a fiasco for Aetius. He even seems to have suggested that the emperor should abandon Italy altogether.[346] He never recovered from the twin blows of Chalons and Italy and neither did the Western Roman army.[347] As mentioned earlier, the East could not by itself win back the entirety of the empire. The vital Western contribution that was needed for this effort was forever lost through defeats sustained at the hands of the Huns. Never again would a Western Roman army fight effectively against a barbarian army. In fact from this point on it was almost entirely made up of unreliable barbarians, ironically mostly of elements drawn from former subjects of the Huns who had drifted away from Hunnic overlordship after Attila's death, e.g. the Heruls, Sciri, Rugi etc.[348]

Despite the bravado of Hydatius, according to Priscus, Marcian, who was in any case the handpicked puppet of the Alan general Aspar,[349] feared the coming encounter with the Huns who would no doubt retaliate for the Eastern involvement in the futile defence of Italy.[350] This is far from the triumphal emperor that one would expect if Hydatius' account of victory was true.[351] Marcian had the incredible good luck of Attila dying in AD 453 right before his intended attack on Constantinople. The civil war which followed nullified for a while the threat from the Hunnic quarter. An indication of East Roman military impotence at this stage is given by the fact that Roman reoccupation of territory seized by the Huns south of the Danube only began c. AD 458, nearly four years after the commencement of the Hunnic civil war.[352] Even as late as the mid 460s, more than ten years after the commencement of the Hunnic civil war, the Romans were still having difficulty containing even minor Hunnic bands like that of Hormidac who operated well south of the Danube and sacked Sardica.[353] Marcian's supposedly victorious campaign against Attila then was not even a real threat at all to the Hunnic king. The Romans didn't even get past the Huns south of the Danube.[354] The disastrous effect that the Hunnic invasions had on both halves of the empire is clearly shown by what happened next. In AD 454 Geiseric invaded Italy and sacked Rome with a thoroughness that would later make the name Vandal notorious. Neither of the emperors could do anything and it was not until AD 467 that the Eastern Empire could again assemble its forces for, as it turned out, a disastrous punitive expedition against the Vandals.

The Roman emperors to be sure tried their best to deal with an impossible situation, but the tide had turned irreversibly on the fortunes of the Roman superpower. Losses suffered in the Hunnic war were for Rome decisive. The Western field army was virtually destroyed in AD 451–2. At least three Eastern field armies between AD 441 and 447 had been wiped out. In other words a minimum of four consecutive defeats like Adrianople in roughly ten years and at least a hundred cities destroyed in the Balkans, Gaul and Italy! Not even the East could take such losses and recuperate quickly, let alone the West.[355] During the time of Roman impotence in the West, the Western barbarians, the Vandals in particular, began to consolidate their position and become entrenched in their territories.[356] The Western Empire was now reduced to a mere 'fief' of the Eastern empire. The East itself had been so weakened (though in its case temporarily) that it was forced to pay roughly the same tribute paid to Attila personally (not counting all other payments due to the Hunnic Empire) to a nonentity like Theodoric Strabo, a Gothic soldier of fortune in Roman service. This is not, as many would have it,[357] an indication of Hunnic insignificance, but East Roman panic and weakness under Zeno during the Isaurian coup. The mighty Eastern Roman army was in such dire straits and critically short of manpower that they couldn't even handle Gothic armies of probably fewer than 10,000 men operating in the Balkans,[358] a far cry from the immense numbers fielded by the Hunnic king earlier in the 440s.

A closer examination of the period allows us to examine the extent to which Eastern Roman military strength had been weakened due to the Huns. The overblown importance attached to the African expedition of AD 468 and the highly suspicious rounded figures of the number of troops involved, has allowed many to simply bypass the Huns and treat the Vandal takeover of Africa as the decisive cause of the collapse of the West and the impotence of East Roman armies in the last quarter of the fifth century.[359] The rounded number for the troops under Basiliscus,[360] 100,000, is, however, clearly nonsense.[361] Belisarius and Narses campaigning in the West during the period of Eastern resurgence in the sixth century could barely manage 20,000 troops.[362] Even an army commanded by an emperor in person in the late fourth and fifth centuries AD, like the one at Adrianople under Valens, rarely numbered over 30,000.

This number is therefore clearly another exaggeration of titanic proportions. If the imperial army had been that large, there is no way the Vandals could possibly have survived the offensive, even with the spate of good fortune at sea that is attributed to them by our sources. A force of around 10,000 or 20,000 sounds more like the real figure[363] and even this was an impressive number for an empire sorely depleted of manpower and resources following the Hunnic wars.[364] The abject failure of the expedition suggests clearly that the lower figure is correct. The 600 ships supposedly lost echo the number of ships that Datis and Artaphrenes used to invade Attica in the Marathon campaign in Herodotus[365] and the 1,113 ships echo the number of Persian ships supposedly at Salamis![366] These are without a doubt fictitious, classicizing numbers and hardly tell us anything about the real state of affairs in the Empire.[367]

In the same year as this fiasco we see the western wing of the Huns invading the empire under Dengizich.[368] Dengizich's enterprise fails and his severed head is brought back to Constantinople in AD 469, quite fittingly by the Romano-Gothic general Anagast, the son of Arnegisclus who died at the hands of Attila, Dengizich's father. This event is treated by many historians as proof that at this stage the empire had the overwhelming military strength to effortlessly defeat the remnants of the Huns, but the reality was in fact very different. First of all Dengizich's forces were seriously depleted due to the opposition of his brother Ernak, his overlord, who rejected the war against the Romans because he was at the time preoccupied with other wars in his own territory.[369] Thus during the invasion of AD 467–8 Dengizich was forced to depend inordinately on recently reconquered Ostrogoths[370] and equally unreliable Bittugurs.

Their unreliability and the lack of support from Ernak would prove decisive. The Romans, according to Priscus, somehow managed to corner the Goths in a 'hollow place' and then foster rebellion among them by sending a Hunnic officer called Chelchal in Roman service to incite them.[371] The revolt of the Goths instigated by this subterfuge apparently forced Dengizich to withdraw. Shortly after this he is killed in mysterious circumstances, probably murdered, and this is how Anagastes grabbed hold of the greatest trophy of his lifetime, the head of the son of Attila.

What happens next fully demonstrates the sorry state of the Eastern Roman army. The old strong man of the East Aspar the Alan, who had made and broken several emperors already, was finally assassinated in AD 471 and with him fell out of imperial favour a certain Theodoric Strabo,[372] the leader of a band of Goths who had sought service under the Romans. Heather argues that some of his troops were Goths settled in the Balkans earlier than the 'demise' of the Huns in the West in AD 454.[373] With his ragtag force Theodoric holds the empire to ransom for over ten years until his death in AD 481, not from Roman vengeance, but a nasty fall from his horse while pillaging Rome's Balkan territories.[374] He had the good luck to be sure of having another band of Goths under Thiudimer, Theodoric Amal's father and brother of Valamer, enter the scene after AD 471[375] and cause trouble in Macedonia. But even when we combine their two armies we have barely 20,000 Goths and allies. Thiudimer, as we shall see later, was not leading a band of conquering Goths as Jordanes' distorted account would have us believe, but actually a group of defeated warriors who had been expelled from the Danubian region by the Suebi, Rugi, Sciri, Heruli and Gepids.[376] Compared to the mighty hosts of the Attilid Huns and the Persians, this was a paltry force that Rome in its better days before the Hunnic invasions could easily have annihilated. Not so, however, in the 470s.

Thiudimer penetrates the Balkans right up to the gates of Thessalonica on the coast of the Aegean without meeting any effective Roman resistance. The Romans were simply too busy dealing with Theodoric Strabo's Thracian Goths (barely 10,000 strong). Only at Thessalonica is Thiudimer stopped, but not beaten.[377] The other Goths under Strabo attack Adrianople and

The Hunnic Empire and Roman military collapse 87

Philippopolis, again without meeting an imperial army. In AD 473 the empire, supposedly mighty, pays off both bands with bribes. Theodoric Strabo, who is closer to the capital and thus a greater threat, is given a bribe of 2,000 pounds of gold per annum, almost the amount given to Attila the Hun personally (Malchus fr. 2, p. 408.22 ff.), and Thiudimer is given lands in Macedonia.[378] What has happened to the Eastern Roman army? Where is it?

The answer is that it hardly exists as a viable fighting force in the Balkans.[379] The only 'Eastern Roman' army around Constantinople is actually Theodoric Strabo's Goths in revolt (!) and a force of probably comparable numbers under the Isaurian general Illus who sets up Zeno, a fellow Isaurian,[380] on the throne (after initially having favoured the coup d'état of Basiliscus (AD 474–6)[381]) and then plays the role of Aspar (the former kingmaker). In AD 478 Zeno tries to put together an army to tackle Strabo, 50,000 on paper, but including *c.* 10,000 or fewer Goths under Theodoric the Amal. It turns out that no army can in reality be put together. Troops simply don't turn up or desert en masse (Malchus fr. 18.2, p. 426. 1–2) and the Amals find themselves alone against the Thracian Goths under Strabo.[382] Heather argues that Zeno was trying to play a double game and to set off one band of Goths against the other.[383] Indeed maybe he was, but the very fact that he needed to resort to such underhand tactics tells us something about the state of the Roman army in the Balkans.

Theodoric Amal feeling betrayed marches on Constantinople[384] and then despite Heather's unrealistic emphasis on the fallback plan of Zeno, supposedly to trap the Goths as they retreated, the tiny army of Theodoric after making a brief demonstration before the imperial capital marches off virtually unscathed across the length of the entire Balkans to the Adriatic Sea where he seizes the port city of Dyrrhachium in AD 479.[385] The Romans need to resort to Hunoulphus (the son of the Hunnic noble Edeco and brother of Odoacer) and the troops he led into Illyricum to inflict a minor loss on a column of Goths led by Theodoric's brother Theodimundus at Candavia.[386] To deal with the other Goths under Strabo/Triarius, Zeno turns to the Huns now called Bulgars.[387] They attack Strabo in 480, but for some mysterious reason make little impression on the Goths. Strabo probably bribed them off with more money than the Romans had offered them. Strabo then, still unscathed, like his namesake Theodoric the Amal, marches on Constantinople, threatens the imperial city, and like the previous horde marches away virtually uncontested to the western Balkans. In the space of three years two small Gothic armies roamed the entire breadth and length of the Balkans and twice threatened Constantinople without meeting a significant Roman force other than those situated before the capital itself. It is clear that even these troops at the capital were nowhere near numerous enough to even actively pursue the Goths once they withdrew.

In AD 483/4 Theodoric Amal, taking advantage of the accidental death of his rival Strabo in 481[388] and having assassinated Strabo's successor Recitach,[389] unites the Goths into a single army of some 20,000 warriors.[390] The empire is powerless before this relatively small army. Zeno grants the Amal Goths land in Dacia Ripensis and Lower Moesia and appoints Theodoric MVM Praesentalis and consul for 484 (Marcellinus Comes s.a. 483 (CM ii.92)). Four years later in AD 487 Theodoric again attacks Constantinople, this time setting up his camp at Rhegium and harrying the city's suburbs. The Goths even cut a major aqueduct.[391] Again the imperial army in any substantial numbers is nowhere to be seen other than within Constantinople. Zeno has to make a pact with Theodoric and induce him to leave the Balkans, probably devastated by decades of warfare and pillaging and therefore no longer a desirable place to the Goths, for the acquisition of the realm of another Hunno-Germanic potentate, Odoacer of Italy.[392]

These events in no way bear witness to the mighty Eastern Roman state that historians have been claiming to have been in existence in the late fifth century AD. East Rome could not even manage small Gothic armies in the Balkans. If the Persians had anywhere near their former military strength in the late fifth century, East Rome might even conceivably have been finished long before 1453. In the end the eastern Hephtalite Huns, who were rightly so praised by Procopius (who had recognized their strategic value to the Romans), gave the Eastern Empire a gift through which it managed to recover from the war waged by the Huns in Europe. The Hephtalites neutralized the Persian threat, the only real danger to the Eastern Empire once the Huns had temporarily disappeared from the picture. Because of this and the accident of geography[393] that happened to separate, by a stretch of water and the almost impregnable defences of Constantinople, the Asian provinces from the barbarian armies ravaging the Balkans, the bulk of the Eastern Empire was given the time to recuperate. The West, now totally exposed and virtually defenceless, was nowhere near as fortunate. Thus in every sense the Huns destroyed the Roman Empire in the West and as we shall see shortly, they also probably delivered the *coup de grâce*. As John Malalas and the Paschal Chronicle tell us, Attila's claim to be the lord and master of the Roman emperors was not entirely empty rhetoric.[394]

CHAPTER 5

The end of the Hunnic Empire in the west

CIVIL WAR AND THE RISE OF ARDARIC

The breakup of the Hunnic Empire in the west after Attila's death has in many cases provided fodder for those who argue for a flimsy and badly organized Hunnic Empire. Heather has argued that the Hunnic Empire was inherently unstable and easily collapsed because it lacked the bureaucracy to control its subjects and was dependent on the flow of Roman gold, which, he argues, was essential to lubricating the whole 'creaky structure.'[1] Thus the Hunnic Empire, it is argued, was not a real state at all, but rather, as Kelly argues, a vast, primitive protection racket[2] that endured for a time because of its success in blackmailing the Romans and paying off restless subjects with gold taken from them. Heather states categorically that the Hunnic Empire 'was dependent on broad flows of Roman wealth in the form of plunder and tribute, and collapsed when these were cut off. Non-Roman levels of economic development by themselves were insufficient to sustain political structures of the scale necessary for carving out a successor state on Roman soil.'[3] If one were to see the Hunnic Empire in exclusively Roman terms, this is a plausible explanation. However, what are we then to make of the existence, with minimum influx of Roman gold, of the Hunnic *imperium* in the western steppe for half a century before the beginning of regular tribute payments from Rome under Rua and then Attila?

The structural weaknesses of the Hunnic Empire should not be exaggerated. The Hunnic state in Europe from its foundation as an imperial entity in the 370s persisted in continuous expansion until the 450s. In other words it kept itself together as a single political unit for around eighty years. After this prolonged period of unity its western half fragmented and seceded from central control, while the east hung on in various forms for another century before being absorbed into the Avar Khaganate. The Avar Empire was essentially a revival of the old Hunnic Empire. The Avars in fact spoke essentially the same language as the

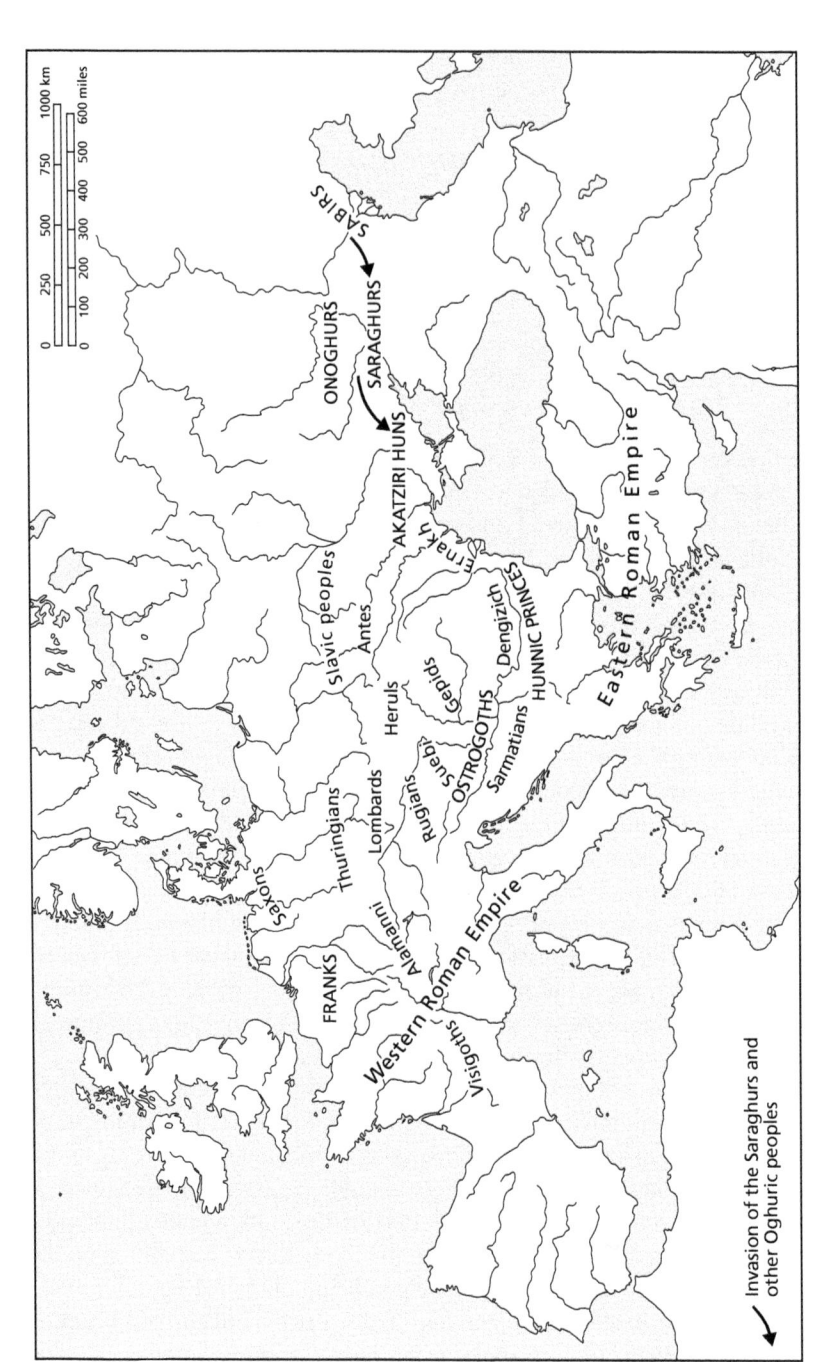

3 The breakup of the Hunnic Empire in Europe

Huns[4] and what had transpired was not the end of the Hunnic state, but a new royal clan superimposing itself over the old royal house of Attila which now became vassal rulers of the subordinate Bulgars.[5]

The Hunnic polity in various forms thus remained alive for nearly two hundred years and would revive itself as Great Bulgaria and the Avar Khaganate after its demise. It did not suddenly disappear as many historians have erroneously claimed. Kradin notes that most steppe empires last 100–150 years.[6] However, quite a few of them lasted even longer. The Xiongnu state would last for four centuries, the Golden Horde in Russia for nearly 300 years and the empire of the Ottomans (of Inner Asian steppe origin) would transform itself and enjoy a remarkable longevity of some 600 years! The Moghul Empire, founded with an army drawn largely from Moghulistan (in the steppe) would rule in India for well over 300 years. Compared to them the Hunnic Empire was relatively short-lived, but compared to other steppe empires its life-span was pretty normal and in fact quite so in comparison to so-called sedentary empires. Does one need to be reminded that the British Empire, as a fully-fledged imperial entity with the vast advantage of 'modern apparatus' of government and organization, barely lasted longer? Napoleon's ephemeral French Empire lasted a mere two decades. The fall of the Huns then cannot be used as an indicator of the weakness/flimsiness of Hunnic military or political organization. It is simply an endemic feature of all empires. They eventually fall apart.

So why then did the Hun Empire fall and what was the nature of its so-called collapse? According to Jordanes' rather distorted account (in favour of his Goths, naturally), we see a revolt of Germanic subjects who overthrow the 'tyranny' of the Huns and regain their freedom after defeating Ellac, the Hunnic crown prince in battle at Nedao in AD 454. Is this really what happened? To get some clarity on what happened we must first determine the main actors in this drama that unfolded north of the Danube. It will be argued henceforth that the majority of the great political figures that emerged in the Germanic world during and after the breakup of the Hunnic Empire were either Hunnic nobles in origin or at the very least closely related to the Huns. Because of the dearth of information about this period, etymologies and onomastic evidence in addition to information provided by historical sources will be utilized extensively to determine as far as possible the likely ethnic origin of these post-Hunnic political figures. Some may ask, what does it matter if these men were Germanic or Hunnic in origin? It does matter greatly, because the question of ethnic origin alters our entire perception and appreciation of the nature of the post-Hunnic world. What occurred in AD 454 was not a 'national uprising' among the

Goths and other Germanic tribes against the Huns. It was certainly not a rejection of the Hunnic political system either. Indeed many Goths were still under the rule of the eastern Huns as late as Dengizich's invasion of the Eastern Roman Empire in the late 460s.[7]

Ardaric and the Gepids

The only personality that figures prominently at Nedao other than Ellac is Ardaric, the ruler of the Gepids,[8] who in alliance with possibly some of the Suebi, Rugii and Sarmatians[9] kills Ellac, the eldest son of Attila. He gathers around him a coalition of Attila's subjects against another coalition put together by Ellac. Virtually all the tribes in the west seem to have sided with Ardaric against those of the east.[10] Thus it was a war between the two principal wings of the Hunnic Empire. How on earth did so many tribes side with Ardaric against Ellac in what was, according to Jordanes, a crisis precipitated by quarrels among Attila's heirs over fief distributions?[11]

It is first necessary to identify who exactly Ardaric was. We have already noted earlier that Attila was probably the Hunnic quasi-feudal king of the Gepids[12] before he became the Great King of the Hunnic Empire after overthrowing his brother Bleda. The Gepids who were under Attila's direct rule would have contributed significantly to this revolution and this explains their importance in Attila's army in the west and the prominence of their ruler Ardaric (appointed by Attila) in the post-Attila struggle over Hunnic 'fiefs'. We have also already encountered a blood relative of Attila called Laudaricus.[13] His name is the entirely Germanic *Laudareiks* (*Lauda* king)[14] and this alerts us to the pitfalls of identifying as Germanic every notable figure at Attila's court with a Gothic-sounding name or vice versa.[15] Given the Hunnic (Inner Asian) practice of distributing 'fiefs' to members of the royal family and also the importance of the Gepids to Attila himself personally, it is more than likely that the Hun king would have bestowed this important appanage on a close relative or noble he could trust. Was Ardaric like Laudareiks a Hunnic prince with a Gothic or rather a Germanicized name?

It is noteworthy that in the west of the Hunnic Empire where the population was overwhelmingly Germanic, Hunnic princes almost uniformly have Germanic-sounding names. As Maenchen-Helfen points out, these are in all likelihood not their real names, but rather, as the title *reik* (king) in their names suggests and the addition of the Gothic suffix -*ila* in the name of the Hunnic king Ruga/Roas (Roila/Rugila[16]) points out, Germanicized or Germanic versions of their originally Turkic names.[17] The Turkic names of virtually all the princes who rule Hunnic fiefs in the

Civil war and the rise of Ardaric 93

east – such as Attila's sons Ellac, Ernak/Irnik and Dengizich; Attila's kinsmen who reside in the Danubian region after Attila: Emnetzur and Ultzindur (who hold Oescus, Utum and Almus on the right bank of the Danube);[18] also of Attila's uncle and father Octar and Mundzuk, and Hunnic royal family members Kursich and Basich – are proof that the names of the Hunnic princes were originally Turkic, right up to the time of Attila's death, not Germanic. The Germanicization of Hunnic (Oghuric Turkic) names may have been a conscious policy among the Hunnic elite in the west in order to ease the transition to their rule of formerly independent German tribal unions. The same process is observable in the later Mongol Empire where the Mongol Khans, especially those in Russia where the Mongols were an extreme minority, gradually adopt the language and names of their Turkic subjects who make up the bulk of their army in the west.[19] The Khazars, who replaced the Avars and Bulgar-Huns in the Pontic steppe, would likewise adopt the Bulgar-Hunnic language of the majority of their subjects after conquest.[20] The Huns when they first entered Kazakhstan in the second century AD also had probably done the same when they adopted Oghuric Turkic instead of their native Yeniseian/Xiongnu language upon becoming rulers of northern Central Asia, mainly populated by Turkic speakers.

The suffix *-ik/ich* with which many of the Turkic names of Hunnic princes end is also very interesting. The name of Ellac, Attila's eldest son, is a corruption of the Turkic *älik* (*ilik*) meaning 'ruler, king'.[21] Ernak/Irnik the youngest son also has the variation of the same suffix in his name. His name is probably Turkic *är-näk*, meaning 'great hero', with the suffix here functioning as an augmentation of the Turkic *är-än* (hero).[22] Thus the suffix *-ik/ich* was used in Hunnic to imply greatness (i.e. ruler or kingship). These names were, it seems, formal court titles rather than personal names. The name Ellac meant 'king' and Ernak has the same meaning as the Inner Asian title Bagatur (hero/knight).

More relevant for our purposes is the rendition of the name of the third of Attila's sons, Dengizich (meaning 'lake,'[23] with the implied meaning of 'broad, great', possibly etymologically connected with the title Genghis (oceanic) as in Genghis Khan, again with the same suffix *-ik*). This name was pronounced by his Germanic contemporaries as Dintzic[24]/Denitsik, reflecting the frequent practice of dropping the 'g' in Germanic transliterations of Hunnic names, and was then rendered Dintzirichus (i.e. Dintzik the *reik*/king).[25] What this shows is that the Turkic suffix *-ik* was replaced by the Germanic suffix *-reik* to Germanicize a Hunnic name. This is by no means an isolated instance of this practice. Jordanes tells us clearly that the

Goths took over many of their names from the Huns[26] and we will later see a surprising example of this in the name of one of the mythical founding kings of the Goths, Berig, who supposedly led the prehistoric Goths out of Scandinavia.[27] His name is almost identical with the name of the Hunnic noble Berik (meaning 'strong' in Turkish),[28] the Lord of many villages (a Hunnic fief holder), mentioned by Priscus, and is likely to be a borrowing of a Hunnic name by the Goths.[29]

I would argue that there is also a case for regarding the name Ardaric as a Germanicized version of a former Hunnic name (Iranian in origin[30]). There are numerous Sarmatian names that are attested which closely resemble that of Ardaric, e.g. Ardagdakos, Ardarakos, Ardariskos, Ardaros, etc. Vernadsky argues that the first element of the name Ardaric *ard* is linked to the Ossetian (the only surviving language that derives from ancient Alan and possibly Sarmatian[31]) *ard*, meaning 'oath'. To this was added the Germanic suffix *-reik*, through the usual practice of Germanicizing Hunnic/Alanic names.[32] His name would thus mean a king bound by an oath (oath king), which instantly reminds us of Jordanes' repeated assertion that Ardaric shared in Attila's plans and was famous (i.e. notable) due to his great loyalty.[33] What could be a greater assurance of loyalty than an oath of loyalty? This explanation for the meaning of Ardaric's name is infinitely more plausible than the Germanic 'king of ploughman' that has been suggested thus far.[34] It also suggests that the name Ardaric is not a personal name, but a court title (meaning loyal king, bound by an oath of loyalty to Attila).

Let us now then try to answer why Ardaric raised a coalition against Ellac. The Icelandic *Hervararsaga*, which many historians agree preserves some faint historical memory of fifth-century events, provides us with a curious piece of information. It says that Heithrek king of the Goths had two sons, Angantyr (whose mother is not mentioned) and Hloth from his marriage to a Hunnic princess, the daughter of Humli king of the Huns. Heithrek has been identified by some historians with none other than Ardaric the Gepid king,[35] but from what happens next it would seem that actually his son Angantyr is the more likely candidate.

Interestingly enough one of Ardaric's grandsons Mundo, the nephew of the Gepid king Trapstila (or Thraustila), was called both a Gepid and a Hun and was in fact a descendant of both Attila and Ardaric.[36] Pohl points out that Mundo was the son of Giesmos, a son of Attila who married a daughter of Ardaric.[37] This implies of course that the historical Ardaric as well as the part mythical Ardaric in the saga had royal Hunnic connections either by marriage or by birth. The saga goes on to tell us that Hloth, the son of the

Civil war and the rise of Ardaric

Hunnic wife, who had grown up at the court of his Hunnic maternal grandfather demanded an equal share of the Goths after the death of Heithrek, his father. When Angantyr refused to comply the Huns attacked to enforce the rights of Hloth by force, but were defeated. Both Hloth and Humli, the Hun king, were killed in the engagement with the Goths.[38]

The Hunnic civil war was precipitated by disputes over inheritance of 'fiefs' among Attila's heirs and the information in this saga seems to capture the gist of what actually happened. Ellac (presumably Humli of the saga), the new king of the Huns, is certain when he ascended the throne to have tried to impose his authority over his father's entire domain. Ardaric, like Angantyr in the saga, either stood to lose from the new settlement imposed by Ellac (i.e. ceding part of his people and territory to Hloth) and consequently revolted or possibly even supported another claimant to the Hunnic throne (perhaps Giesmos, his son-in-law,[39] which could provide an explanation for the dual kingship found among the later Gepids). There were also plenty of Hunnic princes who had a grudge against Attila (e.g. those who favoured Bleda, the actual legitimate Lord of the Huns) and plenty of collateral princes who hungered for their own estates. Ardaric was thus not necessarily a rebel against Hunnic rule, but, as a member of the Hunnic royal family, a key player in the succession struggle. The fact that his state after its victory over Ellac became Gepid, not Hun, is hardly surprising as the western half of the Hun Empire was almost entirely Germanic.

However, it is clear that Ardaric continued to use the trappings of Hunnic imperial rule to solidify his rule in the Carpathian basin. Interestingly enough the Gepid system of rule in the Carpathian basin was almost identical to the political structure found among the Huns, whereby there is a supreme king in the eastern core territory in the Tisza region, who is supported in his duties by a subordinate western king in Sirmium (dualism[40]). In AD 504 Thrasaric, the son and successor of the western Gepid king Trafstila of Sirmium (who held the city in fief from the end of the 480s, presumably occupied some time after the flight of the Ostrogoths c. AD 470), after being defeated by the Ostrogoths, fled back to his suzerain.[41] When the city was recovered some forty years later Turisind, the then Gepid king, appointed his son, the heir apparent, as the Duke of Sirmium. Under the two Gepid kings there were the Dukes (i.e. sub-kings, later there would be three dukes who each had their own military retinue) such as Omharus of Transylvannia, who were often powerful enough to threaten the throne. There was also a council of nobles, again in the same manner as among the Huns, which limited the power of the king.[42]

96   *The end of the Hunnic Empire in the west*

Furthermore, the identity of the three other prominent non-Attilid figures to emerge out of the struggle for Attila's patrimony, whose careers we will examine in detail in the remainder of this chapter, will make it even clearer that what occurred after Attila's death was a civil war over the succession and 'fief' distribution among Hunnic princes and not a rebellion of Hunnic subjects against the Huns. The first prominent figure, Edeco, king of the Sciri, was obviously, as Priscus tells us, a Hun.[43] He seems to have sided with Ellac after Attila's death and later became the enemy of Valamer (founder of the Ostrogothic Amal dynasty). After Edeco established a short-lived Scirian state the tribes he governed would later be responsible for the death of Valamer[44] and the foundation of the first barbarian kingdom in Italy. His famous son Odoacer would deliver the coup-de-grâce on the moribund Western Empire.

ODOACER THE KING OF THE TORCILINGIANS, ROGIANS, SCIRIANS AND THE HERULS

In 1946 Reynolds and Lopez published a ground-breaking article which identified Edeco, the lieutenant of Attila, as the Hunnic father of the first 'Germanic' king of Italy, Odoacer,[45] and his brother Hunoulphus (Hun wolf). This became, due to the plethora of evidence that supports their analysis, quite rightly, general consensus among scholars. That is until 1983 when McBain tried to argue that Edica, the father of Odoacer, was not the same person as Edeco the Hun. He argued that the various references to Edeco in our sources could actually refer to three distinct contemporary personages: (1) the Hunnic ambassador Edeco, (2) the Scirian chieftain Edica, and (3) Edico/Aedico[46] or Idikon,[47] the father of Odoacer. McBain thinks that (2) and (3) are identical, but not (1), the Hunnic Edeco.

The crux of his argument lies in the fact that none of the contemporary sources identifies Odoacer as a Hun, but instead they link him to the Sciri,[48] Torcilingi, Rugii/Rogii,[49] Heruls[50] and even Goths.[51] He feels that it is inconceivable that had anyone among his contemporaries known that Odoacer was the son of a famous Hun, they would have omitted reference to this fact. Orestes, who had been Attila's secretary, is after all recognized as having been such by the Anonymus Valesianus.[52] He also argues that the anti-Odoacer ecclesiastical rhetorician Ennodius who served Theodoric the Great in Italy does not use the Hunnic origin of Odoacer to denounce him in his *Panegyric to Theodoric*.

Another piece of evidence he brings forward is the reference in the *Suda* (a late Byzantine source) to Hunoulphus being a Thuringian on his father's side and a Scirian on his mother's side.[53] The identification of Hunoulphus' father Aedico as a Thuringian in the *Suda* is rejected as a scribal error for Torcilingi by the *PLRE* II (p. 806), but McBain takes this to be correct by assuming that the record derives from Malchus, a contemporary historian.[54] He also thinks that the absence of references to Edica as being Hunnic in Priscus, in the record of the war between the Goths and the Sciri north of the Danube after Nedao, is proof that the Edica commanding the Sciri and other barbarians is not the same person as Edeco the Hun, whom Priscus had met during his embassy to Attila.[55] He even proposes the idea that since in the account of the meeting between Odoacer and Saint Severinus in Noricum in the *Life of Saint Severinus* Odoacer is represented as a tall man,[56] he couldn't have been a Hun because there are no tall Huns! Finally the fact that Odoacer was an Arian Christian is held as evidence that he was not a Hun.

The idea that Christianity and Huns somehow don't go together is a bizarre one and, as seen before in the context of the battle of Chalons, the notion forms a part of the racial ideology of the West and supposedly Western values which were protected by the 'defeat' of the Huns. What are we then to make of Gordas or Grod, the Christian convert king of the Huns in AD 528[57] and also the masses of north Caucasian Huns who converted in AD 535 or 537 when an Armenian missionary team headed by bishop Kardost baptized them en masse?[58] The Huns had been in touch with Arian Christians through the Goths and other Germans for nearly a century before Odoacer's takeover of Italy. Are we to assume that there were no Hunnic converts? As mentioned earlier there were definitely Hunnic converts to Christianity before the fifth century and these later successes in conversions and indeed Odoacer's exceptional preoccupation with the West, as borne out by his sojourn in Gaul and his Scirian mother, who could conceivably have been an Arian Christian, make it likely that he of all Huns had sufficient exposure to Christianity.

The argument that Odoacer may have been tall and therefore could not have been a Hun (by which McBain is thinking Mongoloid East Asian) is also obviously absurd and it need not be pointed out to the reader that there are plenty of East Asians who are in fact taller than the average European. Has anyone seen Yao Ming? The Huns like all other peoples in Europe had mixed to a considerable degree, in their case with their conquered Germanic, Iranian and Slavic subjects. The Hunnic graves in Europe have revealed that only 30 per cent or less of the upper class Huns had some Mongoloid features.[59] Thus physically the majority of the Huns were not easy to distinguish from the rest of their European subjects. We certainly hear of Attila marrying a Germanic woman called Ildico; and Edeco, assuming that he is the same as the Scirian Edica, married a Scirian woman, hence their sons Odoacer and Hunoulphus were at least half Germanic, Iranian, Balt or Finnish,[60] that is if Edeco himself did not already have some Germano-Alanic blood already through marriages in earlier generations, which is also quite likely. Then of course there is the marriage of the Hunnic king Balamber with a Gothic princess Vadamerca. More on Balamber and his Gothic marriage later, but let us for the moment return to Edeco.

The entry in the *Suda* that calls Edeco a Thuringian is almost certainly a scribal error as previous scholars have pointed out. By the late tenth century when the *Suda* was compiled the Torcilingi no longer existed, but the Thuringians certainly still did. A scribe may have noted the similarity between the two names and simply equated the two.[61] The confusion is in fact highly likely given the renewal of Byzantine concerns with events in Germany during this period, due to the imperial pretensions of the Ottonians. Theophano, possibly the niece of the Byzantine emperor John II Tzimisces, married Otto II shortly before the *Suda* was compiled.[62] She brought with her to Germany a retinue of Byzantine courtiers who had ready access to information about contemporary Germany. They would no doubt have encountered Thuringians and a scribe referring to events that happened somewhere north of the Danube may easily have been confused. Furthermore, it is difficult to believe that Jordanes, in origin a Germanic barbarian from the region beyond the Danube, of all people could have made an error about the tribal affiliation of Odoacer, not once, but three times, and confused Thuringians with Torcilingi. He of all people is likely to have known pretty well, even if all other Romans didn't, who the Germanic Thuringians were! He in fact mentions the Thuringians (Thuringos/ Thoringos) in his *Getica* (55.280), surely an indication that he had no reason to confuse them with the Torcilingi. Furthermore, the Lombard historian Paul the Deacon (eighth century AD) also calls the tribe affiliated with Odoacer Turcilingi.[63] The Lombards and the Thuringians were direct neighbours before the Lombard migration into Italy in the mid sixth century AD. Is he also in error?

Thus three of the arguments raised by McBain can be dismissed as excessively forced. The other emphasis on the lack of contemporary reference to Odaocer's Hunnic origin can also be explained quite quickly. First it is clear that poking fun at the Hunnic origin of Odoacer would not necessarily have pleased the patron of contemporary sources like Cassiodorus and Ennodius, the great Theodoric, who was himself descended from a Hunnic prince Valamer/Balamber, as Odoacer was from the Hun Edeco.[64] Regarding Edeco, as Thompson points out and McBain himself acknowledges, Priscus meant exactly what he wrote when he called Edeco a Hun, since he uses the word Hun very judiciously and identifies Edeco's Hunnic origin specifically in order to explain the different treatment he had received from his non-Hunnic entourage.[65]

To argue that Priscus, as he is preserved in Jordanes, does not spell it out that Edeco in the context of the Sciri-Gothic conflict is a Hun and therefore this latter Edica is not the Hunnic Edeco, is also far-fetched. We only have very sparse fragments of Priscus for this part of his histories and most of that via Jordanes. We simply have no idea whether he had other things to say about Edeco or not. Jordanes certainly mentions someone with the same name as the leader of the Sciri and the fact that he isn't explicitly mentioned as 'he who went on the embassy' is only natural. Why bother? He was already well known enough to be identified as 'that famous figure'. This is confirmed by the fact that both the Anonymus Valesianus and John of Antioch cited above refer to Odoacer as the son of Edeco, clearly expecting the name to ring a bell for their readers. If Edica of the Sciri is not the same person as Edeco the Hun, then is it conceivable that another important figure with the same name existed in the same Hunnic court and chose to follow the sons of Attila even after the Hunnic defeat at Nedao in AD 454 (*Getica* 50.265)[66] in the same area as the above-mentioned Hun? Possible perhaps, but highly unlikely to say the least, especially given the nature of the conflict that followed Attila's death, which was essentially a civil war among Hunnic princes, not an uprising of Hunnic subjects.

The very name Edeco/Edico[67] or Edica in fact has no Germanic etymology and it is clearly a non-Germanic name. It does, however, have excellent Turco-Mongol etymologies. For instance, the name is probably linked to the old Turkish name *ädgü*[68] and the Mongolic *Edgü*.[69] In Turkish this name means 'good'. Unless the name has been borrowed by a non-Hunnic chieftain (an unlikely scenario in this case as we will see shortly), even if the two are not identical, we still have either someone close to the Huns or a Hun with a clearly Turkic, i.e. Hunnic, name, ruling the Sciri.[70] In fact all major critics who have discussed the issue are in agreement that the two Edecos are one and the same.[71] There is no reason to disagree with a perfectly logical identification.

The absence of contemporary identification of Odoacer as a Hun also need not trouble us. The army that Odoacer commanded was almost entirely non-Hun, perhaps with the exception of the Torcilingi.[72] He himself was probably more Scirian and many other things in terms of blood lineage, especially on his mother's side, than a Hun which was part of his paternal legacy. He was without a doubt of a very mixed ethnic background, but Odoacer's main power base when he was in Italy was clearly the Sciri,[73] his mother's people, something which would probably have strengthened his inclination to stress on occasions his maternal ancestry over his paternal one. After the Scirian entry into Italy, to ensure the prolonged loyalty of his troops to himself, Odoacer would have emphasized, as Theodoric would do later among the Goths, his status as a king of the Sciri and various other tribes that made up his army; hence the confusion about his ethnic affiliation.[74]

His father's Hunnic ethnicity and his standing in Attila's court would have guaranteed his family a prominent place in the post-Attila civil war and redistribution of fiefs and peoples among Hunnic princes. Edeco's marriage to a Scirian noblewoman would only have strengthened his claims to the Sciri. However, by the time his son Odoacer took over the helm of the Scirian ship, the Huns (as an ethnic group) were no longer the main power in the region. It was time to stress the other side of the family lineage and this is probably what Odoacer did, though not always. His contemporaries, whose writings are sparse and fragmentary, may have commented on the issue of his descent from the Huns, but this does not survive down to us. Even if they did not, it is perhaps only to be expected given the confusing ethnic identity of Odoacer himself and of his army.

His identification in Jordanes as the 'king of the Torcilingi'[75] and 'by race the Rugii or rather Rogii',[76] is also interesting. The Torcilingi, who as argued above were definitely not Thuringians, may have been a Turkic tribe that was linked to the Huns.[77] Jordanes mentions the Torcilingi three times in relation to Odoacer's conquest of Italy.[78] Reynolds and Lopez suggest (though their etymologies for this ethnonym and other names associated with Odoacer have been contested[79]) that Torcilingi is very likely connected with the Turkic *Türk-lük* (Turkdum) or possibly the widespread Turkic name Toghrul/Toghril (the name of the eleventh-century Seljuk Turkish Sultan of Persia) with the Germanic suffix *-ling* added to it[80] as part of the regular practice of Germanicizing Hunnic names. The idea is compelling, though the etymologies seem unlikely.

Closer to Europe we find names that are etymologically much closer to the name Torcilingi such as *Turcae* (first-century AD tribe in the Azov region)[81] and *Tyrcae* (a people in the same area).[82] Then there is of course the name *Torci* (also *Turqui*) given by Fredegar in the middle of the seventh century AD to refer to a people in the Danubian region whom we have discussed in the previous chapter.[83] Fredegar also mentions a king by the name of *Torcoth* (*Torquotus*) in the same passage. Wagner argues that these *Torci* in Fredegar are a reference to the Hunnic Bulgars in the Danubian region and that *Torcoth* and *Torquotus* are approximations of the name Turxanthos, a contemporary western Turkic ruler.[84] Ewig suggests that knowledge of the western Turks in Central Asia was conveyed via Byzantium to the Frankish court and that Fredegar used this information to describe the Turkic-speaking Hunnic Bulgars.[85] Meserve for her part rejects the possibility that the *Torci* are the Hunnic Bulgars, since the Bulgars never called themselves Turks or were known to others as Turks.[86]

Now Meserve has a point, but she fails to realize that a significant portion of the Hunnic Bulgars was absorbed by the western Turks (later the Khazars) both before and after the reign of Kubrat (mid seventh century AD) who established the short-lived Great Bulgaria in the Ukraine.[87] Many of the Bulgars were, during the late sixth and early seventh century AD, at times included under the blanket term Turks by virtue of being subjects of the western Turkic Khagan. Some may have conceivably even been called Turks, though this can't be proven. So the etymological links between *Torcoth* and Turxanthos and between *Torci* and the name Turk suggested by Wagner certainly cannot be dismissed easily. However, the geographical distance between the Franks and the eastern Bulgars under the rule of the western Turks makes the identification of Fredegar's sixth- and seventh-century *Torci* with the western Turks or Bulgars in the Ukraine unlikely. Rather, as Cahen rightly points out, the *Torci* are most likely none other than the Torcilingi[88] (probably remnants of the tribe in the Danubian region, then under Avar rule).

The etymological links between the name *Torci* and Torcilingi (Torc + connecting vowel *i* + Germanic suffix *-ling*) are clearly undeniable, so too the links between *Torci* and the name Turk. The name Turk was frequently rendered Torc or Tork, as in Tork[89] (designating a western Oghuz Turkic tribe that fought for the Kievan Rus as part of the Chernii Kloboutsi confederation[90]), as late as the twelfth century AD.[91] Thus it is highly likely that the Torcilingi were indeed a Turkic-speaking tribe under Hunnic rule. The Germanicization of its name suggests that the Torcilingi were probably of mixed origin, like the man who ruled them, with possibly a Germanic and Turkic (Hunnic) mixture of some sort.[92]

The Rugii, called Rogii in relation to Odoacer, in Italy offer another tantalizing possibility. They are usually identified with the Germanic Rugians who were located in the Pomeranian region along the Baltic Sea coast in the first century AD by Tacitus.[93] It is assumed that their descendants came to occupy Noricum in the fifth century and that it was these people who had an ongoing feud with Odoacer.[94] The Rogians who serve Odoacer in Italy against the Rugians in Noricum are usually taken to be a splinter group from the main Rugians further north. However, Reynolds and Lopez have made the interesting suggestion that the Rogians under Odoacer should be sharply differentiated from the Rugians in Noricum. They consider the Rugii in Noricum to be a Germanic tribe, while the Rogii mentioned in Jordanes in relation to Odoacer to be a tribe or a clan named after the Hunnic king Roga/Ruga/Rua, understanding the discrepancy in spelling between 'u' and 'o' to signify different entities.[95] Is there any validity to this interpretation?

In one of the two references to Odoacer's association with the Rogii, Jordanes calls him Odoacer, *genere Rogus*.[96] He then on another occasion refers to the tyranny of the king (i.e. Odoacer) of the Torcilingi and Rogii, *sub Regis Torcilingorum Rogorumque tyrannide*.[97] In the first instance one could interpret *genere Rogus* as meaning a descendant of Rogus (a person), whom Reynolds and Lopez wish to identify with Ruga/Rua/Roga, the Hunnic king. However, the other passage seems to refer to a Rogian tribe, *Rogorumque*. Is this a reference to a ruling clan that named itself after Rua/Roga as Reynolds and Lopez argue or is it an identification of an old Germanic tribe called Rugii mentioned by Tacitus in the first century AD?[98] To confuse matters we also have references to a powerful tribe (Celtic in origin) called the Lugii, with a name similar enough to invite confusion with the Rugii, in the vicinity of Noricum, who once held the Gutones (Goths) under subjection when the Goths and the above-mentioned Rugians were inhabiting the Baltic region before the presumed Gothic migration to the Ukraine.[99] The Lugians are often identified with the later Vandals[100] and the Rugians of Noricum are sometimes associated with the later famous Longobards, their vassals.[101]

So who are these Rogians with Odoacer? The Lugians can probably be ruled out as a possibility given the mass migration of the Vandals to the west from this region in AD 405 to avoid Hunnic domination. This leaves us with the Rugii from the Baltic region deemed to be identical with those later in Noricum and the alternative theory of a Hunnic royal clan named after Ruga. The belief that the Germanic Rugii of the first century AD are the ancestors of all the peoples called Rugii or Rogii in the fifth century AD has been so pervasive that virtually all serious commentators have taken it for granted that the names Rogii and Rugii in Jordanes are referring to the same Germanic tribe.[102]

It is necessary at this point to consider what we actually know about the Baltic Rugians before the fifth century. Other than Tacitus' brief reference to them in the *Germania*, there is a reference to a town called Rougion somewhere in the Baltic region in Ptolemy.[103] After this in the fourth century according to the Verona List the Rugians were still somewhere in the Baltic region.[104] Then in the fifth century a group with a similar name reappears in the context of the breakup of the Hunnic Empire in the west. However, there are some problems with identifying these Rugians of Noricum with those mentioned by Tacitus, Ptolemy and the Verona List.

First of all Jordanes in *Getica* 4.26 makes no connection whatsoever between the Rugians of Noricum, whom he knew well enough, and the coast-dwelling tribe called the Ulmerugi (Island Rugii),[105] whom he identifies in the context of a war fought against them by the Goths while living in the Baltic region and who are without a doubt the Baltic Rugians mentioned in Tacitus.[106] In fact Jordanes actually mentions a people called Rugii, geographically distinct from the Rugians of Noricum, still in the Baltic region in the late fifth or early sixth century AD under the rule of a certain Rudolph, who later sought refuge in Italy with Theodoric the Great.[107] With the Rugii (close to Scandza, i.e. the Baltic region[108]) there are also the Grannii, Augandzi, Eunixi, Taetel, Arochi and Ranii in the same area, all supposedly ruled by Rudolph who it is said despised his kingship among them and left for Italy (in other words, he was thrown out). The Rugii are only mentioned fourth on this list, which implies that they were by no means formidable.

The fact that the Rugians in Noricum first emerge within the Hunnic Empire is also highly problematic. Even if we were to accept the possibility that some of the Baltic Rugians may have formed a part of this group, the political entity of the fifth century in Noricum was obviously a different one from the old Baltic Rugian tribe given the certainty of Hunnic political interference.[109] That the Rogians or Rogus are so intimately linked to Odoacer's personal ancestry is also an important issue. Odoacer is called a king of the Torcilingi, Rogii, Sciri and Heruls in our sources. We know that Odoacer was Scirian on his mother's side and that he was Torcilingian on his father's side (i.e. Turkic/Hunnic). How can he then be by race Rogus?

There is also one more important fact which we must consider. In the steppe there were a plethora of tribes throughout history who named themselves after a famous figure, e.g. the Nogais after Nogai, the Uzbeks after Uzbek Khan and the Seljuks and Ottomans after Seljuk and Osman, the tribal founders. Closer to our period we know that Ultzinzures, a group that lived along the Danube around AD 454, were named after Ultzindur the relative of Attila.[110] Were the Rogii in Italy and also the Rugii in Noricum named after a famous historical figure like the Ultzinzures? Thus to summarize we have three possibilities concerning the Rogii in Italy: (1) they were members of a Germanic tribal confederation formed from a core of the Rugii from the Baltic region unconnected with the Hunnic king Ruga/Roga; (2) they were a largely Germanic tribal group with the name of the Hunnic king Ruga/Roga/Rua as its new self-designation to mean the men of Ruga, residing in both Noricum and in Italy; (3) they comprised just the family of the Hunnic King Ruga and their followers in Italy.

The first option is, as explained up until now, though favoured by most scholarship, unlikely. Reynolds and Lopez obviously accept the third option, but not the second or the first. The fact that Odoacer is a Rogus by race suggests the strong possibility that there was actually a family of Rogus (i.e. a specific individual, as Reynolds and Lopez argue), but the *Rogorumque* in the other reference to the Rogii in Jordanes implies the existence of a people called Rogii. I would argue that both existed and that the tribe was the creation of a clan descending from king Roga. The eventual victors who grabbed control of the core western territories of the Hunnic Empire, Noricum and Pannonia, after driving out the powerful Ostrogoths and the Sciri, were the Rugii and the Gepids. The Rugii took Noricum and the Gepids most of Pannonia. In other words they were among the most prominent groups to emerge in the Hunnic civil war in the west.[111] We have already observed the reasons behind Ardaric the Gepid's prominence, his blood ties with Attila, his prominence at the Hunnic court and the strong Gepid participation in Attila's usurpation of the Hunnic throne.

Odoacer and his brother Hunoulphus later in their struggle against the Rugii would kill the Rugian king Feva and chase away his son Fredericus, who found refuge with Theodoric's Ostrogoths in Novae (Moesia).[112] What exactly was the origin of this dynasty of Rugii presumably founded by Flaccitheus after Nedao, and why is it so powerful after the breakup of the Hunnic Empire? The only possible answer to this is that like the Gepids (led by the Hunnic or partially Hunnic noble Ardaric) and the Sciri (led by the Hun Edeco), the Rugii too in accordance with the Hunnic practice of distributing important tribes to royal family members were led by a Hunnic prince or a ruler closely associated with the Huns. The fact that the Rugii also seem to have possessed a very similar political organization to the Huns and had a system of apportioning 'fiefs' to royal family members like the Huns, supports this line of reasoning.[113]

The name Ruga was certainly prestigious enough in the West, given the fame of that particular Hunnic king, who was essentially the first ruler to rule over all of Barbaricum from the Rhine to the Pontic steppe and more importantly was the king under whom the Huns conquered territories west of Hungary, i.e. the lands where we find our Rugii and Rogii, so there is a strong possibility that his name was adopted by a collection of tribes under the rule of a prince claiming descent from Ruga. The fact that there is strong centralized authority among the Rugii (in contrast to the disorganized tribalism that characterized the northern Germans including the Germanic Rugii mentioned by Tacitus before the Hunnic invasion) directly after the fall of the Huns is indicative of the likelihood of this hypothesis.[114] Thus what we have might be a Germanic kingdom with a Hunnic prince who named his people after a prominent dynastic member to whom he traced his descent: Ruga. It might well be that Odoacer and Edeco were also descendants of Ruga or related to him in some way and contested the control of the tribes allocated to Ruga's descendants in the distribution of fiefs after Attila's death. This would partially explain the later deadly feud between the Rugians of Noricum and the Rogians under Odoacer.[115]

Other interesting hypotheses have been suggested by Reynolds and Lopez concerning Odoacer's name which they link to the name of the Hunnic prince Octar, the brother of Ruga and Mundzuk, and the Turkic name *Ot-toghar*.[116] This is clearly a possibility, but not certain. Other interesting etymologies are Oghlan (Turkic 'youth') for Oklan, the son of Odoacer.[117] Although further research is needed on this topic, we should not be surprised if the etymologies turn out to be correct. Names are certainly not always an indicator of ethnicity and many Germans did take up Hunnic names and probably some Huns Germanic or Iranian names. However, the heavy concentration of possible Turkic/Hunnic names in virtually every group or individual closely associated with Odoacer tells us that his identity was indeed much more deeply immersed in the former Hunnic Empire than many thought possible.[118]

VALAMER THE KING OF THE HUNS AND FOUNDING KING OF THE OSTROGOTHS

The third and perhaps the most interesting figure to emerge from the Hunnic civil war is Valamer, the king of the Ostrogoths. Who exactly was this person? The Amal dynasty that Valamer founded or took over was in all probability not connected with the old ruling house of the east Goths, the house of Ermanaric.[119] The name of Ermanaric was later inserted into Amal genealogy, presumably, it has been suggested, either to legitimize the succession of Theodoric's son-in-law, who may have claimed descent from him, to the Ostrogothic throne or one could argue due to the archaizing tendency of Roman historians like Cassiodorus or even the Goth Jordanes[120] who wanted to make the dynasty look as ancient as possible, found that Ermanaric was the oldest east Gothic king they could find in Greco-Roman sources (Ammianus), and connected the Amals to him without a further thought. Indeed a majestic seventeen-generation genealogy was created for the Ostrogothic kings of Italy by Cassiodorus (*Variae* 9.25.4–5),[121] obviously in imitation of the seventeen generations of kings that separate Romulus from Aeneas in Roman mythography.

As Merrills notes, genealogies of the type we find in the *Getica* (often based on ever-changing oral traditions or the writer's own imagination) were susceptible to dramatic changes and realignments 'in order to justify the redefinition of the status quo'. In other words, the distant past was often reconfigured with fictitious familial links that were designed to bind contemporary rulers to the shared heroic myths or perceptions about the past of the people.[122] Also political and physical upheavals, in the case of the Goths the eighty years of Hunnic domination, without a doubt had a significant impact on the formulation of the Amal genealogical tradition.[123]

When we examine the Amal genealogy in the *Getica* with these observations in mind, several things become immediately obvious. Firstly, the earliest so-called Amal kings listed in the genealogy (*Getica* 14.17) are clearly fictitious additions drawn from Gothic popular mythology. Gapt, the first on this list, is a semi-divine hero, not a historical figure.[124] The second king Hulmul is another hero common to Germanic folklore,[125] while the fourth king Amal and the sixth Ostrogotha are obviously eponymous figures invented as the ancestors of the Amals and Goths respectively. Hisarnis (the iron one),[126] the fifth king, again is a non-historical mythical hero.[127] More on this later, but what is clear is that the later 'Amals' were not an ancient Gothic dynasty, but rather newcomers who became rulers of the Goths most likely during Hunnic domination or after the Hunnic civil war in the 450s.[128] As Heather rightly points out, the Hunnic conquest had profound implications for the former political order of the Goths before conquest.[129]

If this was the case, how then should we interpret the information in Jordanes that Valamer along with Ardaric were the most honoured members of Attila's court?[130] Is this Jordanes simply glorifying the Amal ruler before he actually became prominent, i.e. after Attila's death? Exaggeration is probable, but as we shall see, there are some good reasons for believing

Valamer the king of the Huns and Ostrogoths

that at least this comment in Jordanes has some claims to validity. We have already noted that Ardaric was related by blood or marriage to the Hunnic royal family. If Valamer was prominent, given the nature of the Hunnic state which, as in the Rouran Khaganate and the earlier Xiongnu Empire mentioned earlier, allocated major conquered peoples as 'fiefs' to members of the royal family (e.g. the Akatziri to Ellac) and the long period during which the Goths (like the Sciri who lived under the rule of a Hunnic prince at least as early as AD 381 when they campaigned under Hunnic direction in the Balkans) in particular had been under Hun domination, it is highly likely that Valamer like Ardaric was in some way related to the Hunnic royal house. Was Valamer a Hunnic prince?

To find out the exact origins of Valamer we must examine in some detail the information provided by Jordanes.[131] In his record of the history of the Ostrogoths before the reign of Attila Jordanes states:

48.246 – Quos constat morte Hermanarici regis sui, decessione a Vesegothis divisos, Hunnorum subditos dicioni, in eadem patria remorasse, Vinithario tamen Amalo principatus sui insignia retinente. 247 Qui avi Vultulfi virtute imitatus, quamvis Hermanarici felicitate inferior, tamen aegre ferens Hunnorum imperio subiacere, paululum se subtrahens ab illis suaque dum nititur ostendere virtute, in Antorum fines movit procinctum, eosque dum adgreditur prima congressione superatus, deinde fortiter egit regemque eorum Boz nomine cum filiis suis et lxx primatibus in exemplum terroris adfixit, ut dediticiis metum cadavera pendentium geminarent. 248 Sed dum tali libertate vix anni spatio imperasset, non est passus **Balamber, rex Hunnorum**, sed ascito ad se Gesimundo, Hunnimundi magni filio, qui iuramenti sui et fidei memor cum ampla parte Gothorum Hunnorum imperio subiacebat, renovatoque cum eo foedere super Vinitharium duxit exercitum; diuque certati primo et secundo certamine Vinitharius vincit. Nec valet aliquis commemorare, quanta strage de Hunnorum Venetharius fecit exercitu. 249 Tertio vero proelio subreptionis auxilio ad fluvium nomine Erac, dum utrique ad se venissent, Balamber sagitta missa caput Venetharii saucians interemit neptemque eius Vadamercam sibi in coniugio copulans iam omnem in pace Gothorum populum subactum possedit, ita tamen, ut genti Gothorum semperum proprius regulus, quamvis Hunnorum consilio, imperaret.[132]

It appears that at the death of their king, Hermanaric, they were made a separate people by the departure of the Visigoths, and remained in their country subject to the sway of the Huns; yet Vinitharius of the Amali retained the insignia of his rule. (247) He rivalled the valor of his grandfather Vultuulf, although he had not the good fortune of Hermanaric. But disliking to remain under the rule of the Huns, he withdrew a little from them and strove to show his courage by moving his forces against the country of the Antes. When he attacked them, he was beaten in the first encounter. Thereafter he did valiantly and, as a terrible example,

108   *The end of the Hunnic Empire in the west*

crucified their king, named Boz, together with his sons and seventy nobles, and left their bodies hanging there to double the fear of those who had surrendered. (248) When he had ruled with such license for barely a year, *Balamber, king of the Huns*, would no longer endure it, but sent for Gesimund, son of Hunimund the Great. Now Gesimund, together with a great part of the Goths, remained under the rule of the Huns, being mindful of his oath of fidelity. Balamber renewed his alliance with him and led his army up against Vinitharius. After a long contest, Vinitharius prevailed in the first and in the second conflict, nor can any say how great a slaughter he made of the army of the Huns. (249) But in the third battle, when they met each other unexpectedly at the river named Erac, Balamber shot an arrow and wounded Vinitharius in the head, so that he died. Then Balamber took to himself in marriage Vadamerca, the grand-daughter of Vinitharius, and finally ruled all the people of the Goths as his peaceful subjects, but in such a way that one ruler of their own number always held the power over the Gothic race, though subject to the Huns.[133]

It would perhaps surprise the reader, but historians have with good reason suspected that Balamber, who is called in this passage 'King of the Huns' of the late fourth century AD, is the same person as the Ostrogoth Valamer in the mid fifth century AD, whose name in Greek was written βαλαμηρ.[134] This then would yield the natural conclusion that Valamer was a Hun, though amazingly none have even raised the obvious idea. Peter Heather sees the events surrounding Balamber as strictly an internecine Gothic affair.[135] Let us look further. The passage records also that Vinitharius, an Amal Goth, campaigned against the Antes (Slavs, possibly under Sarmatian domination) independently of the Huns in the late 370s, but was, as a consequence of his impertinence, after barely a year attacked by his overlord Balamber who allied himself with another Gothic princeling Gesimund, son of Hunimund. Vinitharius is killed by Balamber himself who then takes as his wife Vadamerca, the dead man's grand-daughter.

If Vinitharius existed and was indeed an Amal, as Jordanes tells us, then Theodoric the Great who is the nephew of Valamer/Balamber is only an Amal via his uncle's marriage, a dubious connection at best. The conquest of the Antes is also probably not an Ostrogothic achievement in the fourth century, since the Antes (Slavs or slavicized Sarmatians[136]) only start to move into the southern Ukraine and Moldavia from somewhere in the north well after the Hunnic conquest in the 370s AD and are first attested in the area in the late fifth century (presumably they moved into the region vacated by various Germanic tribes fleeing the Huns some time in the fifth century).[137] If Vinitharius (as his name implies the Wend-fighter, i.e. Slav fighter) did fight the Antes, then he is likely to be a fifth-century figure, not a fourth-century one.¹³⁸ It therefore soon becomes apparent that the events relating to Gesimund, Balamber and Vinitharius could not have taken place in the fourth century. Jordanes goes on to comment:

250 Et mox defuncto Venethario rexit eos Hunimundus, filius quondam regis potentissimi Hermanarici, acer in bello totoque corpore pulchritudine pollens, qui post haec contra Suavorum gente feliciter dimicavit. Eoque defuncto successit Thorismud filius eius flore iuventutis ornatus, qui secundo principatus sui anno contra Gepidas movit exercitum magnaque de illis potitus victoria casu equi dicitur interemptus. **251** Quo defuncto sic eum luxerunt Ostrogothae, ut quadraginta per annos in eius locum rex alius non succederet, quatenus et illius memoriae semperum haberent in ore et tempus accederet, quo Valamer habitum repararet virilem, qui erat ex consubrino eius genitus Vandalario; quia filius eius, ut superius diximus, Beremud iam contempta Ostrogotharum gente propter Hunnorum dominio ad partes Hesperias Vesegotharum fuisset gente secutus, de quo et ortus est Vetericus. Veterici quoque filius natus est Eutharicus, qui iunctus Amalasuenthae filiae Theodorici, item Amalorum stirpe iam divisa coniunxit et genuit Athalaricum et Mathesuentam. Sed quia Athalaricus in annis puerilibus defunctus est, Mathesuenta Constantinopolim allata de secundo uiro, id est Germano fratruele Iustiniani imperatoris, genuit postumum filium, quem nominavit Germanum.¹³⁹

(250) And later, after the death of Vinitharius, Hunimund ruled them, the son of Hermanaric, a mighty king of yore; a man fierce in war and of famous personal beauty, who afterwards fought successfully against the race of the Suavi. And when he died, his son Thorismud succeeded him, in the very bloom of youth. In the second year of his rule he moved an army against the Gepidae and won a great victory over them, but is said to have been killed by falling from his horse. (251) When he was dead, the Ostrogoths mourned for him so deeply that for forty years no other king succeeded in his place, and during all this time they had ever on their lips the tale of his memory. Now as time went on, Valamir grew to man's estate. He was the son of Thorismud's cousin Vandalarius. For his son Beremud, as we have said before, at last grew to despise the race of the Ostrogoths because of the overlordship of the Huns, and so had followed the tribe of the Visigoths to the western country, and it was from him Veteric was descended. Veteric also had a son Eutharic, who married Amalasuentha, the daughter of Theodoric, thus uniting again the stock of the Amali which had divided long ago. Eutharic begat Athalaric and Mathesuentha. But since Athalaric died in the years of his boyhood, Mathesuentha was taken to Constantinople by her second husband, namely Germanus, a cousin of the Emperor Justinian, and bore a posthumous son, whom she named Germanus.

Now according to this tangled chronology both Hunimund (who definitely cannot be the son of Hermanaric as Jordanes asserts¹⁴⁰ and who has two grown sons Gesimund, who allies himself with Balamber, and Thorismud his successor) and Vinitharius (who already has a grand-daughter), are men well advanced in their years by the 370s or 380s, if we were to grant a few years of inactivity before Vinitharius' supposed campaign against the Antes that triggered the Hunnic reaction under Balamber. Thorismud and Gesimund, sons of Hunimund, already commanding armies, are thus at least in their twenties in the 370s or 380s, if Jordanes' dates are to be believed, and this must also mean that Vandalarius, their cousin and supposedly the father of our Valamer, is of a similar age in the 370s/80s. According to Jordanes, Thorismud is succeeded by Valamer after an improbable forty-year (!) interregnum.

Interestingly enough Vinitharius who is killed by Balamber (Valamer) is entered into the Amal genealogy as the father of Vandalarius (*Getica* 14.79). This is completely implausible. The fact that Balamber/Valamer married Vinitharius' grand-daughter after defeating him must have contributed to the oddity of Vinitharius being designated as the grandfather of his adversary. Valamer was thus not Vinitharius' grandson, but grandson-in-law and due to this relationship Vinitharius was later inserted into the royal genealogy for, presumably, some political expediency once Valamer/Balamber and his descendants became kings of the Goths.[141]

Heather makes the very perceptive observation that Jordanes must have wrongly identified Vithimeris, the short-lived successor of Ermanaric in Ammianus, (a fourth-century historical figure) with Vinitharius (a fifth-century opponent and grandfather-in-law of Valamer),[142] hence the confusion in the chronology and the separation of our historical Valamer into two separate individuals, Gothic Valamer and an earlier Hunnic Balamber. This separation into two individuals was also presumably the result of his dual identity, as both a Hun royal and a Gothic king. Jordanes, when he later read his sources or heard the accounts of Goths about Valamer, due to either confusion or deliberate attempt to obscure the Hunnic origin of the Amal dynasty, made a single king appear as two individuals.

Though Eckhardt, in a desperate attempt to skirt over the chronological inconsistencies of Jordanes and defend his authority as a historian, actually sees Vithimeris as Vinitharius, and Vithericus (Vithimeris' underage son) as Vandalarius (supposedly son of Vinitharius and father of Valamer),[143] as Christensen rightly points out, the *Getica* does not identify Vandalarius as a king, which is inconceivable if Jordanes or Cassiodorus, who knew their Ammianus, had thought the king Vithericus mentioned by Ammianus was the same person as Vandalarius.[144] This also means that the ancestry given in Jordanes (*Getica* 14.79) which links Vinitharius to an earlier prince called

Valamer the king of the Huns and Ostrogoths

Vultuulf, supposedly the brother of Ermanaric and great-great-grandfather of Valamer, and thus to the old Gothic royal house, is a highly distorted one.

In fact in a later passage (*Getica* 48.252) Jordanes actually leaves out both Vinitharius and his father Valaravrans from the 'Amal' ancestry and calls Vandalarius the son of a brother of Ermanaric, i.e. Vultuulf. In other words, Vinitharius and his father have been inserted into the Amal genealogy to make the 'Amals', Amals (i.e. Gothic kings). Now who then are Vultuulf and Vandalarius, the grandfather and father of our Valamer? We have already noted the Germanic practice of Germanizing or Gothifying Hunnic royal names by adding Germanic suffixes. Thus the Germanic suffix *-ila* is added to names like Att-ila[145] and Ruga, which becomes Rug-ila, and Dengizich becomes Dintzirich by adding the suffix *-reik* (king). In addition, as Schramm points out even the names themselves were often substituted by similar sounding Gothic names. For instance the name of Attila's father Mundzuk[146]/Munčuq = 'pearl/jewel' (Turkic) was turned into Mundiuks[147] with the *dz* sound altered to make the name sound more Gothic, like the *mund* element in Gothic names such as Munderich. A similar process can also be suspected for the name of Attila from Turkic *As-til-a* (great river/sea[148]) to Gothic *atta-ila* (little father).

It is to be wondered whether the same has happened in the case of the name Vultuulf. The name Vultuulf is clearly a combination of two elements *Vult* and the suffix *-ulf*, as in Hun-oulphus (*-ulf*, the Germanic word for 'wolf'). Now the *Vult* component appears in names such as Sigis-vultus (Ostrogothic, fifth century[149]) with the *vultus* (Gothic *wulþus*) meaning 'grandeur/fame'.[150] So Vultuulf would be *wulþ(u)-wulfs* (famous/glorious wolf). However, we also learn that the *Vu-* in *Vult* was often rendered *Uld* as in Gib-uldus and Uldida.[151] Now there is a plethora of Hunnic names with the element *Uld/Ult* in our sources for the fifth and sixth centuries: Uld-in, Ult-zin-cur (Ernak's cousin), Ult-zia-giri (Hunnic tribal name),[152] Ould-ak (Hunnic general in the East Roman army in AD 550)[153] etc. The name Vultuulf therefore, despite its Gothic appearance could well be a Hunnic name that has been gothified (Hunnic name *Uld/t* + Germanic suffix *-ulf*, then assimilated into the more familiar Gothic word *wulþus* to form Vultuulf). What is interesting is that in the early fifth century when Vultuulf must have been active we find the figure Uld-in (the *in* being a Greek suffix added to his name), the king of the western Huns in Hungary who died *c.* AD 410. Equally interesting is the fact that all Germanic names with the element *wulþus* as prefix appear after the career of Uldin, just as those containing the element *iok* (probably deriving from the *juk* or *dzuk* element in Hunnic names such as Mundzuk[154]) as suffix in Germanic names such as Gundiok appear after the career of the Hunnic king/prince Mundzuk, the father of Attila. Could Valamer then be a descendant of the western Hunnic king/prince Uldin?

This becomes even more likely when we consider the name of his supposed son Vandalarius (meaning 'he who conquered the Vandals'). The Vandals of course deserted their central European abode with the Alans and the Suebi in AD 405 to avoid Hunnic domination. There is no Ostrogoth who could have fought the Vandals after the Hunnic conquest of 376, except possibly Odotheus (killed AD 386) and Radagaisus (killed AD 405/6 by Uldin and his Romano-Alan allies). However, these two chieftains were fighting the Romans and the Huns in Italy and the Danubian provinces, not the Vandals, and they are certainly not the ancestors of the Amals. There is simply no other record anywhere of any conflict between the Ostrogoths and the Vandals around the time that Vandalarius would have been active (early fifth century AD), that is before the Vandal flight to Gaul in AD 405. Who could possibly have conquered or beaten the Vandals at this stage? Obviously Uldin, who chased them away. Uldin is thus likely to be Vultuulf and Vandalarius is presumably his son who participated in the conquest of the Vandals before AD 405. Valamer, who is active in the mid fifth century, is either a descendant or the son of Vandalarius. His direct forebear Vandalarius was clearly not a king, since kingship fell to the related house of Hunimund. Into this original geneaology was later inserted the Amal Vinitharius.

Therefore, Jordanes' genealogy, if accepted at face value without identifying these insertions and confusions over names, creates innumerable chronological inconsistencies.[155] Jordanes himself was obviously aware of this problem and he thus adds in a forty-year interregnum among the Goths after Thorismud's death, no doubt to make up for some of the awkward chronological inconsistencies resulting from the transferring of fifth-century events into the fourth century.[156] These so-called 'Gothic' kings who controlled the Goths after Ermanaric – Vinitharius, Hunimund and Thorismud – are thus all historical figures who were active in the fifth century, not the fourth. This indicates another crucial fact, that the Goths were under the direct rule of the Huns during this time and not 'always ruled by kings of their own stock' in direct succession from Ermanaric, as Jordanes asserts.

In fact it is clear that the Goths were always ruled directly by the Huns from the time of the Hunnic conquest in the 370s.[157] This will become apparent when we later discuss the identity of Thorismud's father, Hunimund, the king of the Goths, who Jordanes records became famous for his victory over the Suebi. However, for now let us return to Valamer. Jordanes next tells us that Valamer and his brothers Thiudimer and

Vidimer, ruled their portions of the Goths under Hunnic overlordship.[158] They were, in other words, Hunnic quasi-feudal lords.[159]

After the breakup of the Hunnic Empire the Goths of Valamer, again according to Jordanes, fought against the Huns at Nedao in AD 454 and then came into conflict with Attila's sons sometime after AD 455.[160] Valamer and his entourage are said to have engaged the sons of Attila (who regarded him and his Goths as deserters) in battle alone without the assistance of Valamer's brothers, but still managed to emerge victorious. Jordanes claims that Valamer was able to inform his brother Thiudimer about the great news shortly thereafter and that this happened to coincide with the birth of Theodoric the Great, Thiudimer's son and Valamer's nephew.[161]

Is this what really happened? First of all, we should note that the date of Theodoric's birth, if we take this version of events to be accurate, must be c. AD 456[162] at the earliest, but this would throw into disarray all records of Theodoric's age and subsequent activities in the early 470s, by making him lead armies at fifteen years of age![163] Theodoric was almost eight years old when he was sent to Constantinople as a hostage in AD 459.[164] This means that he must have been born c. AD 451/2. This is when the Goths were still ruled by Attila. So what are we to make of the story in Jordanes of Thiudimer rejoicing at the news of his brother's victory over the sons of Attila and also the birth of his newborn son Theodoric?[165]

The answer is obvious. The story is clearly a forged one that deliberately falsifies what really happened during and after the Hunnic civil war. Valamer certainly did not throw off the Hunnic 'yoke' (he was a Hun after all[166]) directly after the death of Attila, as Jordanes tells us. In the epic poem *Lied von Frau Helchens Söhne* we see the Ostrogoths marching under the banners of the Huns at Nedao, not the so-called anti-Hunnic coalition of Ardaric. Pohl and Wolfram are both of the opinion that the Valamer Goths only parted ways with the sons of Attila after the battle of Nedao.[167] In fact I would argue that the definitive break between Valamer and the sons of Attila only came after either AD 459 (when Theodoric was sent to Constantinople as a hostage) or AD 461 when Valamer concluded a *foedus* with the Romans.[168]

Jordanes, in his eagerness to create the impression that Valamer and his brothers immediately broke free from the control of Attila's sons right after the death of Attila in AD 453,[169] seems to have invented a phantom encounter between the Huns and the Goths in the mid 450s. He would obviously have liked to attribute the victory at Nedao over Ellac's Huns to Valamer and the Ostrogoths. However, the tradition that attributed that victory to Ardaric and the Gepids was too well known for even Jordanes to distort the facts. The only real clash between the Huns under Attila's sons and Valamer's Goths was the war that took place in the mid 460s, which we will discuss shortly. Jordanes needed a battle earlier in the 450s to extricate his Goths from Hunnic rule immediately after Nedao, so just as he has created two Valamers (one Hunnic, one Gothic) out of the same person he has created two wars out of a single conflict which occurred in the 460s.

This is confirmed by information that Jordanes himself provides. He tells us that after Nedao in AD 454 the Huns swarming about everywhere betook themselves into Romania, i.e. Rome's Balkan territories south of the Danube that they seized without Roman authorization.[170] In other words, the Huns expelled from Hungary by the Gepids started a conflict with the Romans. Jordanes says that the Ostrogoths, like the Gepids who had formed an alliance with the Romans against the Huns *c.* AD 454, in vivid contrast to the Huns who simply seized Roman territory after AD 454, asked for land from the Romans and peacefully received Pannonia from the emperor Marcian.[171] Valamer did indeed conclude some kind of a peace treaty with the Eastern Romans (that is before the more definite *foedus* involving a payment of 300 pounds of gold per year from the Romans to the Goths agreed to in AD 461) during the reign of Marcian, but this had nothing to do with authorization to settle in Roman territory, rather it was an agreement not to invade Roman territory in return for a small monetary compensation![172] When he was not paid his due 'tribute' Valamer did not hesitate to attack the Romans. In AD 459 he devastated Illyricum and raided as far south as Epirus.[173] It was only after this clash when he agreed to send his nephew Theodoric to Constantinople as a hostage that his stance towards the Romans started to change for the better, culminating in the *foedus* of AD 461. Thus it was only in the brief period after AD 459 and before the mid 460s when Valamer was killed by the Sciri that there was a momentary separation of Valamer's Goths from the Attilids. Partial reassertion of East Roman authority in areas south of the Danube in the late 450s, e.g. the absorption of the Hunno-Gothic fief formally controlled by Tuldila by the Romans around AD 458[174] (fear of which may well have been part of the reason behind Valamer's initially belligerent stance against the Romans in the following year), may explain Valamer's decision to make peace with the Romans and desert the sons of Attila.

However, the sons of Attila and the Huns with them, who were far from finished, did not quietly tolerate this situation. We read the following in Jordanes:

LIII. 272 Postquam ergo firma pax Gothorum cum Romanis effecta est, videntes Gothi non sibi sufficere ea quae ab imperatore acciperent simulque solitam cupientes ostentare virtutem, coeperunt vicinas gentes circumcirca praedari, primum contra Sadagis, qui interiorem Pannoniam possidebant, arma moventes. Quod ubi rex Hunnorum Dintzic filius Attilae cognovisset, collectis secum qui adhuc videbantur quamvis pauci eius tamen sub imperio remansisse Vltzinzures, Angisciros, Bittugures, Bardores, venientesque ad Basianam Pannoniae civitatem eamque circumvallans fines eius coepit praedare. 273 Quod conperto Gothi ibi, ubi erant, expeditionemque solventes, quam contra Sadagis collegerant, in Hunnos convertunt et sic eos suis a finibus inglorios pepulerunt, ut iam ex illo tempore qui remanserunt Hunni et usque actenus Gothorum arma formident. Quiescente vero tandem Hunnorum gente a Gothis Hunumundus Suavorum dux dum ad depraedandas Dalmatias transit, armenta Gothorum in campis errantia depraedavit, quia Dalmatia Suaviae vicina erat nec a Pannonios fines multum distabat, praesertim ubi tunc Gothi residebant. 274 Quid plurimum? Hunimundus cum Suavis vastatis Dalmatiis ad sua revertens, Thiudimer germanus Valameris regis Gothorum non tantum iacturam armentorum dolens quantum metuens, ne Suavi, si inpune hoc lucrarentur, ad maiorem licentiam prosilirent, sic vigilavit in eorum transitu, ut intempesta nocte dormientes invaderet ad lacum Pelsodis consertoque inopinato proelio ita eos oppressit, ut etiam ipsum regem Hunimundum captum omnem exercitum eius, qui gladio evadissent, Gothorum subderet servituti. Et dum multum esset amator misericordiae, facta ultione veniam condonavit reconciliatusque cum Suavis eundem, quem ceperat, adoptans sibi filium, remisit cum suis in Suavia. 275 Sed ille inmemor paternae gratiae post aliquod tempus conceptum dolum parturiens Scirorumque gente incitans, qui tunc super Danubium consedebant et cum Gothis pacifice morabantur, quatenus scissi ab eorum foedere secumque iuncti in arma prosilerent gentemque Gothorum invaderent. Tunc Gothis nihil mali sperantibus, praesertim de utrisque amicis vicinis confisi, bellum exurgit ex inproviso coactique necessitate ad arma confugiunt solitoque certamine arrepto se suaque iniuria ulciscuntur. 276 In eo si quidem proelio rex eorum Valamir dum equo insidens ad cohortandos suos ante aciem curreret, proturbatus equus corruit sessoremque suum deiecit, qui mox inimicorum lanceis confossus interemptus est. Gothi vero tam regis sui mortem quam suam iniuriam a rebellionibus exigentes ita sunt proeliati, ut pene de gente Scirorum nisi qui nomen ipsud ferrent, et hi cum dedecore, non remansissent: sic omnes extincti sunt.

LIV. 277 Quorum exitio Suavorum reges Hunimundus et Halaricus vereti, in Gothos arma moverunt freti auxilio Sarmatarum, qui cum Beuca et Babai regibus suis auxiliarii ei advenissent, ipsasque Scirorum reliquias quasi ad ultionem suam acrius pugnaturos accersientes cum Edica et Hunuulfo eorum primatibus habuerunt simul secum tam Gepidas quam ex gente Rugorum non parva solacia, ceterisque hinc inde collectis ingentem multitudinem adgregantes ad amnem Bolia in Pannoniis castra metati sunt. 278 Gothi tunc Valamero defuncto ad fratrem eius Thiudimer confugerunt. Qui quamvis dudum cum fratribus regnans, tamen auctioris potestatis insignia sumens, Vidimer fratre iuniore accito et cum ipso curas belli partitus, coactus ad arma prosilivit; consertoque proelio superior pars

116   *The end of the Hunnic Empire in the west*

invenitur Gothorum, adeo ut campus inimicorum corruentium cruore madefactus ut rubrum pelagus appareret armaque et cadavera in modum collium tumulata campum plus per decem milibus oppleverunt. **279** Quod Gothi cernentes, ineffabili exultatione laetantur, eo quod et regis sui Valameris sanguinem et suam iniuriam cum maxima inimicorum strage ulciscerentur. De vero innumeranda variaque multitudine hostium qui valuit evadere, perquaquam effugati vix ad sua inglorii pervenerunt.[175]

(53.272) Now after firm peace was established between Goths and Romans, the Goths found that the possessions they had received from the Emperor were not sufficient for them. Furthermore, they were eager to display their wonted valor, and so began to plunder the neighboring races round about them, first attacking the Sadagis who held the interior of Pannonia. When Dintzic, king of the Huns, a son of Attila, learned this, he gathered to him the few who still seemed to have remained under his sway, namely, the Ultzinzures, and Angisciri, the Bittugures and the Bardores. Coming to Bassiana, a city of Pannonia, he beleaguered it and began to plunder its territory. (273) Then the Goths at once abandoned the expedition they had planned against the Sadagis, turned upon the Huns and drove them so ingloriously from their own land that those who remained have been in dread of the arms of the Goths from that time down to the present day. When the tribe of the Huns was at last subdued by the Goths, Hunimund, chief of the Suavi, who was crossing over to plunder Dalmatia, carried off some cattle of the Goths which were straying over the plains; for Dalmatia was near Suavia and not far distant from the territory of Pannonia, especially that part where the Goths were then staying. (274) So then, as Hunimund was returning with the Suavi to his own country, after he had devastated Dalmatia, Thiudimer the brother of Valamir, king of the Goths, kept watch on their line of march. Not that he grieved so much over the loss of his cattle, but he feared that if the Suavi obtained this plunder with impunity, they would proceed to greater license. So in the dead of night, while they were asleep, he made an unexpected attack upon them, near Lake Pelso. Here he so completely crushed them that he took captive and sent into slavery under the Goths even Hunimund, their king, and all of his army who had escaped the sword. Yet as he was a great lover of mercy, he granted pardon after taking vengeance and became reconciled to the Suavi. He adopted as his son the same man whom he had taken captive, and sent him back with his followers into Suavia. (275) But Hunimund was unmindful of his adopted father's kindness. After some time he brought forth a plot he had contrived and aroused the tribe of the Sciri, who then dwelt above the Danube and abode peaceably with the Goths. So the Sciri broke off their alliance with them, took up arms, joined themselves to Hunimund and went out to attack the race of the Goths. Thus war came upon the Goths who were expecting no evil, because they relied upon both of their neighbors as friends. Constrained by necessity they took up arms and avenged themselves and their injuries by recourse to battle. (276) In this battle, as King Valamir rode on his horse before the line to encourage his men, the horse was wounded and fell, overthrowing its rider. Valamir was quickly pierced by his enemies' spears and slain. Thereupon the Goths proceeded to exact vengeance for the death of their king, as well as for the injury done them by the rebels. They fought in such wise that there remained of all the race of the Sciri only a few who bore the name, and they with disgrace. Thus were all destroyed.

(54.277) The kings [of the Suavi], Hunimund and Alaric, fearing the destruction that had come upon the Sciri, next made war upon the Goths, relying upon the aid of the Sarmatians, who had come to them as auxiliaries with their kings Beuca and Babai. They summoned the last remnants of the Sciri, with Edica and Hunuulf, their chieftains, thinking they would fight the more desperately to avenge themselves. They had on their side the Gepidae also, as well as no small reinforcements from the race of the Rugii and from others gathered here and there. Thus they brought together a great host at the river Bolia in Pannonia and encamped there. (278) Now when Valamir was dead, the Goths fled to Thiudimer, his brother. Although he had long ruled along with his brothers, yet he took the insignia of his increased authority and summoned his younger brother Vidimer and shared with him the cares of war, resorting to arms under compulsion. A battle was fought and the party of the Goths was found to be so much the stronger that the plain was drenched in the blood of their fallen foes and looked like a crimson sea. Weapons and corpses, piled up like hills, covered the plain for more than ten miles. (279) When the Goths saw this, they rejoiced with joy unspeakable, because by this great slaughter of their foes they had avenged the blood of Valamir their king and the injury done themselves. But those of the innumerable and motley throng of the foe who were able to escape, though they got away, nevertheless came to their own land with difficulty and without glory.

Valamer, having gained Roman support in AD 461, then sometime in the mid 460s attacked the Sadages (one of the subject groups still under Attilid control).[176] This, however, provoked a counter-attack from Dengizich, the western ruler of the reduced Hunnic Empire. In this war in the middle of the 460s, Dengizich, with the Ultzinzures, Angisciri, the Bittugures and the Bardores, penetrates far into Gothic Pannonia and we see the Goths also becoming entangled at this time with a figure named Hunimund, king of the Suebi/Suavi and the Sciri under Edica.[177] What exactly is happening here, and what is the relation between this Hunimund and Hunimund the Great (who was successful in war over the Suebi, presumably around the time of their conquest by the Huns c. AD 405) mentioned earlier, the ruler of the greater portion of the Goths before the reign of Balamber (Valamer)?

In the above passages we learn that either Hunimund the Great himself (highly unlikely)[178] or more likely, as I will show henceforth, his descendant with the same name, is ruling the Suebi in Pannonia (who were previously under the rule of Hunimund the Great). This younger Hunimund is said to have disturbed the original peace between Edica (the Hunnic prince Edeco) of the Sciri and the Goths of Valamer after a quarrel with Valamer's brother

Thiudimer. The Scirians, it must again be noted, had sided with Ellac and Ernak in the civil war in opposition to Ardaric and his Gepids.[179] The Angi-Sciri are indeed listed in the names of tribes accompanying Dengizich in his campaign against the Ostrogoths.[180] The Suebi and Goths ruled by the house of Hunimund the Great were definitely allies of the Sciri before the above-mentioned feud between the younger Hunimund and Thiudimer (*Getica* 53.275), since Jordanes records that they (Sciri) were until then at peace with the Goths. As allies of the Sciri (who closely followed the fortunes of Attila's sons), it is certain that the Goths of Thorismud (according to Jordanes, predecessor of Valamer as king of the Goths[181]), son of Hunimund the Great, were anti-Gepidae (i.e. Hunnic vassals who had fought under Ellac at Nedao in AD 454). This is the real reason why Hunimund the Great's son and successor Thorismud is killed while fighting the Gepids,[182] an event which supposedly heralded the beginning of the forty-year interregnum among the Goths in the early years of the fifth century, but which definitely happened after AD 453, presumably at the Battle of Nedao.

Despite Jordanes' massive distortion of history, his attribution of unending victories to the Ostrogoths over everybody else north of the Danube[183] and the unrealistic sudden collapse of the Huns, which has misled many historians, closer scrutiny of Jordanes' own text leaves us with no doubt that the Ostrogoths were clearly only one among many players in this drama unfolding in the Danubian region. From our reconstruction of events it seems likely that the 'Amal' Goths (i.e. Valamer's Goths) initially played a secondary role to the Goths under Hunimund the Great (who also ruled the Suebi) and their allies the Sciri who fought the powerful Gepids of Ardaric in support of their common overlord Ellac, Attila's heir.

After the death of Thorismud in battle in AD 454 Valamer took over his cousin's Goths as well as those under Vinitharius, mentioned earlier, and then in AD 461 renounced the suzerainty of Attila's sons after concluding an alliance with the Romans. He is then attacked by both the Huns under Dengizich and the Sciri under Edica/Edeco. Jordanes again boasts of a Gothic victory, but again as in the cases of Thorismud against the Gepids and Theodorid at Chalons, the king of the Goths, Valamer, is killed (i.e. he was defeated). Now Dengizich's invasion of Eastern Roman territories in the Balkans took place c. AD 467–8, after his fight with Valamer and I would argue after the Scirian killing of Valamer. Given the pro-Attilid bent of the Sciri explained above, it is highly likely that the Sciri were acting in tandem with Dengizich's Huns when they killed Valamer c. AD 465/6.[184]

According to Priscus, the Roman emperor Leo had sided with the Sciri in this war, though Aspar, the wiser man, had advised him to remain neutral. Priscus also tells us that both the Goths and the Sciri after an indecisive first encounter appealed to many, including the Romans, for aid. Despite Leo's orders to assist the Sciri, little seems to have been done by the Roman military to inconvenience the Goths.[185] As usual Jordanes has muddled the whole chain of events to create a string of victories for his Goths, but what this fragment of Priscus suggests is the strong likelihood that the Hunnic clash with the Goths did not happen before the Goths fought with the Sciri, but after the indecisive encounter between the Goths and Sciri mentioned in Priscus which induced both the Sciri and Goths to appeal for aid from their neighbours. In other words, the Goths in an attempt to expand east clashed with the Suebi, Sciri and the Sadagis *c.* AD 465, and this caused the Sciri and also the Sadagis to invite the Huns to intervene. This then led to a surprise attack on Valamer by the combined army of Huns and Sciri which resulted in defeat and death for the Gothic king.

After Valamer's death, though Jordanes speaks of Valamer's triumph over Dengizich (and also over the Sciri of course), which made the ferocious Huns supposedly dread the name of the even more valiant Goths, a significant portion of Valamer's Goths seem to have submitted to Dengizich's Huns. This is why we find the Ostrogoths with the Huns in AD 467 (they were not included by Jordanes in the previous list of tribes under Dengizich's rule when he fought Valamer, so this is clearly an indication of the surrender of substantial numbers of Goths to the Huns after the conflict[186]) and why Beremud (grandfather of Eutharic), the cousin of Valamer and son of the previous king Thorismud, leaves the Ostrogoths for Gaul, because, as Jordanes says, he disliked the rule of the Huns and was ashamed of Gothic subservience to them.[187] Wolfram trying to make sense of Jordanes' chronological inconsistencies identifies a certain Vetericus in Gaul in AD 439 who quarrels with Theodorid, the then Visigothic ruler, with Videric or Veteric, the son of Beremud and the father of Eutharic (son-in-law of Theodoric the Great and father of Athalaric king of the Ostrogoths in the sixth century).[188] This is, however, surely implausible. If this were the case, then Videric must have been at least seventy or eighty years old when Eutharic was born in AD 480! The Videric who is the father of Eutharic is a different individual from Vetericus.

Dengizich, his power now augmented, sent an embassy to Constantinople in AD 466[189] demanding some of the rights that his father had enjoyed in his heyday, indicating thereby that the Huns had secured the Danube region well enough to finally recommence offensive operations against the Romans.[190]

Dengizich's defeat by the Romans in AD 467–8 and his sudden death in AD 469,[191] however, allowed the Amals to break away once and for all from the Attilid Huns. In fact the Amal Goths probably facilitated Dengizich's defeat and death by leading the Gothic revolt against him during the campaigns against the Romans.[192] This explains why Theodoric, Thiudimer's son (or perhaps Valamer's son), was released and sent back to his father shortly after this event by Constantinople *c.* AD 469.[193] The alignment of the Bittugurs (one of Dengizich's subject tribes) with the Amal Goths after Dengizich's fall also cannot be a coincidence.[194] The Bittugurs, whose name suggests that they were part of the Oghurs who had recently been fighting the Huns in the east, but presumably defeated and forced to serve the Hunnic king Dengizich in the west, must have colluded with the Ostrogoths in bringing about the demise of Dengizich.

Now finally rid of their overlords, the Ostrogoths, according to Jordanes, just before Theodoric's return *c.* AD 469, in late AD 468 undertook a campaign against the Suebi and their federates the Alamanni, presumably somewhere in Noricum.[195] The Goths were, however, soon forced to abandon their home base in Pannonia altogether presumably due to pressure from an alliance of Sciri, Rugii, Suebi and the Gepids.[196] Jordanes places this grand alliance and the great battle against it at the river Bolia right after the death of Valamer in *c.* AD 465. However, the fact that Vidimer, whose only real exploit is leading a group of Goths to Italy after AD 470, plays a role in this battle, suggests that it happened *c.* AD 470, as does the fact that the Sarmatians under Babai also feature prominently in the battle (Theodoric of course is said to have attacked them *c.* AD 470 after returning from Constantinople).[197] The battle it seems did not go completely the way of the Goths. Jordanes as usual says that the Ostrogoths under Thiudimer won all their battles and then decided to take on a bigger challenge, the Roman Empire.

However, this is again, like most of the things Jordanes has to say about battles involving the Goths, nonsense. If it was the Ostrogoths who won, then why do Vidimer and Thiudimer become separated after their 'victory'? Vidimer moving into western Noricum[198] and then on to Italy and Thiudimer to Macedonia? And why do we find the former lands of the Ostrogoths in the hands of their supposedly defeated enemies (eastern Noricum under the Rugii, Pannonia under the Gepids, Sciri and Suebi)?[199] Thiudimer led not a victorious army that had triumphed over all the tribes north of the Danube, but the bloodied remnants of his battered tribal confederacy into Roman territory shortly after AD 471. His former lands in Pannonia and eastern Noricum had been carved up by his enemies, the Gepids, Sciri, Suebi and the Rugii.

Valamer the king of the Huns and Ostrogoths 121

Going back to Valamer, further attention must be given to the fact that he is the son of a cousin of Thorismud, the Gothic king and son of Hunimund the Great. He was in other words the relative of the earlier kings of the Goths and the Suebi. We have already seen that Valamer is likely to be a descendant of Uldin the Hunnic king. If he is also the relative of Hunimund the Great and his sons Thorismud and Gesimund, this means that these 'Gothic' princes are not, as Jordanes would have it, descended from Ermanaric the Goth at all, nor can Uldin/Vultuulf (the Hunnic king) be the brother of Ermanaric. Indeed revealingly in a document dated to early AD 533 Cassiodorus, who presumably provided Jordanes with some of the genealogy of the Amals, does not include either Ermanaric or the Scandinavian demi-gods of Jordanes in his Amal genealogy.[200] They are without a doubt later additions and this means that Hunimund and his sons are like Vultuulf/Uldin Hunnic princes, not Goths.

Therefore, it seems plausible to argue that Valamer and his brothers were in fact originally affiliated with the Suebi–Goths who were ruled by a related dynasty, that of Hunimund the Great, who presumably became the ruler of the main patrimony of Uldin (Goths) when Uldin died *c.* AD 410. The kingship therefore bypassed Valamer's direct ancestor Vandalarius (the Vandal-conqueror), a common feature of Hunnic and Central Asian steppe laws of succession. It is in this context we should also consider the record in Cassiodorus (*Variae* 8.9.8, addressed to a certain Tuluin) about the hero Gensemund, who is loyal to the Amals, but whom some of the Goths wanted to crown king in his own right. He is subsequently adopted as a son-at-arms (i.e. vassal) by the Amals. This Gensemund is none other than Gesimund, the son of Hunimund, the ally of Balamber mentioned earlier, who was faithful to his oath of loyalty to the Huns, according to Jordanes.[201] Gensemund/Gesimund is considered worthy of kingship precisely because he represents the senior line of the Hunnic dynasty to which both he and Valamer belonged.[202]

It is no accident then that Hunimund the elder is called 'the Great' by Jordanes, the father of the ally (Gesimund) of the Hunnic king Balamber (Valamer) who helps Balamber to crush a separate Gothic tribe under Vinitharius. The confusing saga of the time before and after the Hunnic civil war has been projected backwards into the 370s and it disguises the fact that Valamer was very likely a highly aristocratic (enough to see him honoured as part of Attila's inner circle), junior partner or a member of the cadet branch of the Hunnic royal dynasty that ruled the Suebi and the Goths. He was clearly initially indebted to his cousin Gesimund in his conquest and rule (by virtue of his marriage to the grand-daughter of

Vinitharius after the conquest) of the Amali tribe of the Ostrogoths. In his conflict with Vinitharius, Valamer received crucial assistance from his cousin Gesimund, who would remain loyal to his leadership.

We can now provide an answer as to why Valamer is so closely associated with the Huns in Jordanes. In an earlier passage in Jordanes on the ethnogenesis of the Huns we encounter the story of Gothic witches copulating with evil spirits and giving birth to the Huns.[203] This implies that the Goths regarded the Huns and themselves (or their royal family at least, which as this story indicates had or claimed a sacred or 'devilish' origin in ways reminiscent of the concept of sacred kingship among steppe royal clans) to be blood related.[204] This should also remind us of Balamber/Valamer the Hun's marriage to a Gothic princess. Note that Hunimund the Great, the king before Balamber (Valamer), is likewise closely associated with the Huns. His very name contains the element 'Hun' and means literally 'under the suzerainty of the Hun'.[205] This of course, however, does not necessarily tell us anything about his ethnic provenance.[206] However, when we take into consideration the steppe tradition of fief distribution among members of the Hunnic royal family and his blood ties to the Hun Valamer, it is more than likely that, like Edeco among the Sciri and Ellac among the Akatziri, Hunimund was also a Hunnic prince or noble who had been allocated his fief among the Goths and who later added the Suebi to his list of subjects, hence the title King of the Suebi borne by his descendant Hunimund the younger.

Later in the Mongol Empire the Mongol rulers of Persia would call themselves Ilkhans (subordinate Khans) to indicate their vassalage and loyalty to the Great Khanate in Mongolia. Jordanes tells us that Hunimund was at peace with the Huns and that his son Gesimund was loyal to the Huns. Like the meaning of his name, Hunimund was indeed subservient to the main Huns and in fact it is highly probable that his name is not a personal name, but a title, like the title Ilkhan, meaning vassal king. The Hunnic origin of this dynasty is made even more likely by the name of the first non-divine ancestor of the Amals in their genealogy,[207] Hunuil. Hunuil may be a Turkic term combining the imperial name *Hun* with *il*, meaning 'people' or 'state' in Turkish.[208] In the Amal genealogy we find eponymous names that indicate the ruling dynasty's affiliation with the political entity/people of the Ostrogoths (Ostrogotha) and the clan or sub-tribe of the Amals (Amal). If the dynasty was indeed originally Hunnic we can expect this fact also to be reflected by a name such as Hunuil (meaning 'Hunnic people/empire/state').[209]

Just as remarkable is the fact that Berig/k (Turkic 'strong'), the name of one of Attila's Hunnic magnates in Priscus, which we have noted earlier, somewhat surprisingly appears as the name of the original Gothic king who supposedly led the Goths out of Scandinavia, Berig.[210] Maenchen-Helfen, while noting the astonishing similarity between the two names, rejects the identification from the reasoning that although the Goths did take over many Hunnic names, they could not have renamed one of their half-mythical kings with a Hunnic name. This is insufficient reasoning obviously for rejecting the identification. Christensen, on the other hand, concludes that the myth of Berig, if it is a Gothic myth at all, does not belong to any authentic Gothic tradition.[211] Certainly the Visigoth Isidore of Seville, who wrote the *History of the Goths*, and was born shortly after Jordanes wrote the *Getica*, shows no knowledge of any such legend linking the Goths with either Berig or Scandza, but identifies Scythia and the Getae in Scythia as the origins of the Goths, which is remarkable given the fact that the Visigoths and the Ostrogoths lived under the rule of the same Theodoric the Great in the early sixth century.[212]

Christensen reasonably identifies the name Berig as either a borrowing from Hunnic or perhaps Celtic. There was apparently a Celtic name, Bericos, which is used by Cassius Dio to refer to a Briton in the early first century AD, who participated in the conquest of the island by Claudius.[213] The location of Scandza as the place of Gothic origin is also clearly a guess on the part of Cassiodorus, who had knowledge of the region via his reading of Ptolemy and his involvement in the handling of the Hesti embassy from the region.[214] The legend is unlikely to be Celtic, given the vast time gap between Dio and Jordanes, but Priscus was a source that Jordanes directly used. What if this ancestor is not a Goth at all, but the leader who led the Huns in their migration west? What if the dynastic tradition of the Hunnic royal family has been superimposed on the vague memory of the Goths migrating from somewhere in the north? There are plenty of instances of such phenomena throughout history.[215] This would explain why this supposedly Gothic myth is unknown to the Visigoths. It is purely an Ostrogothic or rather Amal/Hunnic tradition of origin.[216]

Returning once more to Valamer, it seems that Valamer had greater ambition than his cousin Hunimund and claimed the greater title of King of the Huns, not just Hunimund 'vassal king', hence the reference to him in Jordanes as Balamber, King of the Huns. After he rebelled against the sons of Attila Valamer seems to have toyed with the idea of becoming heir to Attila's empire. After AD 461 we see the Amal Goths campaigning against the Suebi to the north (*Getica* 53.273–4) and the Sadagis (interior of Pannonia) to the east.[217] However, his ambition and expansionism provoked punitive measures from Attila's son Dengizich. He also found himself fighting not just the Huns, but also the Sciri (under Edica and

Hunoulphus), Suebi (under the younger Hunimund) and perhaps also the Gepids (either reconciled to Dengizich and Ernak or more likely forced at the time once more to recognize Dengizich and Ernak as heirs to Attila's former domains[218]). Valamer's death seems to have forced his brother Thiudimer to briefly submit to Dengizich,[219] as mentioned earlier.

After Dengizich's demise yet another defeat at the hands of the coalition of their enemies forced the Goths to flee into Roman territory.[220] The disaster of AD 470, when the Goths were faced with a combined army of Rugians,[221] Scirians, Sarmatians and Gepids, was serious and this prompted Vidimer and Thiudimer to part ways. After abandoning their ancestral domains in Pannonia, Vidimer seems to have first headed to western Noricum where we hear of his Pannonian Goths besieging and then failing to take the city of Tiburnia (Teurnia) in AD 472[222] and then into Italy in AD 473, while Thiudimer headed to the south into Macedonia. Vidimer died upon entering Italy, probably due to a military defeat, though Jordanes naturally skirts over the issue.[223] His son with the same name moved into Gaul and took refuge with the Visigoths thereby joining another cousin Beremud, the son of Thorismud (son of Hunimund the Great), already in Gaul, whose descendant Veteric was the father of Eutharic, the son-in-law of Theodoric the Great.[224]

Sidonius Apollinaris, a contemporary of Vidimer and Thiudimer and writing around AD 476, provides us with a clue as to why exactly Vidimer and his east Goths fled to Gaul from Pannonia. In a poem that is designed to flatter the Visigothic king Euric, Sidonius writes that the Ostrogoths had been in conflict with the Huns.[225] Sidonius talks about a victory of the Ostrogoths, who with the support of Euric (reigned from AD 466 onwards) triumphed over the 'neighbouring (*vicinosque*)' Huns. Now the Ostrogoths who received help from Euric against the Huns cannot have been in Pannonia since there the Visigoths of Euric would simply be too far away to offer any help to the Ostrogoths.[226] They must have been somewhere close to Gaul and the only Ostrogoths close enough to have appealed to the Visigoths for aid during the reign of Euric were those under Vidimer who entered Italy *c.* AD 473 and then moved on to Gaul. However, which Hunnic group could possibly have attacked the Goths this far west? It is surely no accident that in the path of Vidimer we find the figure of Odoacer and his Torcilingi Huns accompanied by the Sciri, Rugii and Heruls (Sidonius calls them the hordes of Scythia[227]), who had entered Italy just before the Ostrogoths in *c.* AD 472 when Odoacer became the leader of the *foederati*.[228] Glycerius, the emperor of the West, managed to throw out Vidimer from Italy into Gaul, but with what army?

We later learn that the so-called Western Roman army at the time was actually largely made up of Odoacer's troops: the Torcilingi, Sciri, Heruls and some Rugii. We of course know from Jordanes that the Rugii had joined the anti-Ostrogothic alliance together with the Sciri *c.* AD 469/70.[229] Odoacer, who seems to have been operating in Gaul until this time,[230] then returned to Pannonia to link up with the Sciri and the Rugii around AD 470/1, presumably after hearing news of the death of his father which suddenly left him with part of the Sciri as his inheritance. It was this army that Odoacer led into Italy and which later was used to destroy Vidimer's invasion force at the request of Glycerius. After ridding himself of Vidimer, these 'Scythians' of Odoacer (very likely the Huns mentioned by Sidonius), took over Italy. His brother Hunoulphus would likewise fight against the Amals in the Balkans under the auspices of the Eastern Roman government in AD 479. The feud between the Hunno-Gothic Amals and Hunno-Scirian house of Edeco ran deep.

The sudden volte-face of the Sciri from imperial enemies to imperial generals and federates was due obviously to the death of Dengizich, their former overlord. With Dengizich's death in AD 469, Hunnic unity in the west definitely ended. Noricum and Italy fell to the Hunnic princes of the house of Ruga, Odoacer and Feletheus, and the Gepids under the Hunnic noble Aradaric, if he was still alive, continued to control the Hungarian plains and took over former Ostrogthic possessions in Pannonia, parts of which were given to the Heruls and the Suebi. The Ostrogoths under another king of Hunnic origin, Theodoric the Great, would, however, have their revenge. In AD 487 the feud between former allies Odoacer and Feletheus reached a bitter conclusion. Odoacer destroyed the Rugian kingdom of Noricum[231] and expelled the son of Feletheus, who had shortly before murdered his uncle.[232] In addition he brought the Gothic princess Giso (probably a relative of the Amal kings), Feletheus' wife and very likely the instigator of the feud between the Rugii, to Italy and cruelly executed her.[233] This was *casus belli* for the Ostrogoths and Theodoric would avenge the king of the Rugians and his two uncles Valamer and Vidimer by defeating and then murdering Odoacer and Hunoulphus.[234]

Returning for the last time to Valamer, his eminence in Attila's court and his activities and associations after Attila's death tell us that he was among the intimates of Attila, i.e. at the least a Hunnic nobleman or more likely a collateral member of Hunimund's branch of the Hunnic royal family descended from Uldin. The title King of the Huns given to Balamber[235] (Valamer) in Jordanes' account is therefore an accurate ethnic appellation.[236] The Goths were certainly not ruled by members of their own ethnic stock under the Huns. Who ruled them during the so-called interregnum? Obviously the Huns exerted direct rule. Did these Hunnic rulers just disappear? Surely not. Gesimund the ally of Valamer and son of Hunimund the Great is said to have been faithful to his oath of loyalty to the Huns. This can only mean that he was either loyal to the house of Attila or more likely to Valamer himself, who claimed Attila's mantle as the King of the Huns, unlike other members of Hunimund's family, who used the title of sub-king (Hunimund). Valamer was thus a Hunnic prince and not originally a Goth.

As noted before, the story of the founding king has been projected backwards into the distant past to explain what Heather claims was the union between the so-called house of Ermanaric[237] and the Amals under Theodoric the Great's successor in Italy. Or was it in fact the union of two related Hunnic royal houses? It appears that the line of Hunimund, the original, senior branch of the Hunnic royal family of the Ostrogoths, was either ousted by the line of Valamer or forced to migrate west after Valamer's defeat at the hands of Dengizich and other Danubian tribes. Thorismud's son, prince Beremud, fled to Gaul and was later joined there by Vidimer, the nephew of Valamer (*Getica* 56. 283–4).[238] This explains why Theodoric later chose Beremud's descendant as the husband of his daughter and his eventual successor. They were blood relatives of the same royal family, but that of the Huns, not the legendary Ermanaric.

One may then ask, is this genealogy that links the Amals to Ermanaric in the *Getica* the product of the conscious work of the Amals themselves or is it the work of Cassiodorus or Jordanes, who created it simply to make the dynasty look more Gothic and ancient? The Hunnic ancestry of the ruling prince would certainly have been an asset during the Hunnic civil war when no one knew how things would eventually turn out and Hunnic prestige was still at its height. The Hunnic Empire could conceivably have been restored in the west, as we learn from the activities of Dengizich, even after the death of Ellac at Nedao. Under such circumstances being associated with a Hunnic royal was valuable to any budding political entity eager to carve out a realm from the former empire of the Huns. However, after the Ostrogothic ethnic identity had somewhat solidified, the association of the ruling family with the Huns could have become problematic. The more Turkic Huns of the east under Dengizich and Ernak were dangerous enemies of the nascent Ostrogoths, and in the same way that even in modern times the British Windsors during the First World War would suppress their German origins and even change their name to appease their subjects then fighting Germany, the Amals may well have appealed to their maternal 'Gothic' ancestry which they then linked artificially to the old Gothic King Ermanaric.[239]

The fact that Valamer, the founding king, was a Hun was evidently well known, as the records of the activities of Balamber (Valamer) king of the Huns show. However, by the time Jordanes came to write his history of the Goths, this was no longer acceptable, at least not to someone like Jordanes who regarded the former Gothic subjection to the Huns as a mark of shame. The Hunnic half of the founding king Balamber was thus repositioned in the distant past in the fourth century and artificially separated from Valamer, his Gothic half. Of the four post-Attila potentates of the west, all originating from the Hunnic Empire, three – Ardaric, Edeco and Valamer – were Hunnic nobles or princes and the fourth Orestes was Attila's secretary. It was these men and the troops that they governed that ended the Western Roman Empire and heralded in the 'Middle Ages'.

ORESTES THE ROYAL SECRETARY

The last noteworthy figure to emerge from the Hunnic civil wars is Orestes, Attila's secretary.[240] His Greek name has made most scholars simply assume that he was Roman in origin, but the name of his father given by Priscus, Tatoulos, is in all likelihood not Roman (Greek or Latin) in origin and Altheim suggests that he was only Greek on his mother's side.[241] In other words he is likely to have been at least in part barbarian. Orestes would, with the support of barbarian troops then making up most of the so-called 'Roman' army in Italy, gain the Western imperial throne for his son Romulus Augustulus, the last Western Roman emperor to rule in Italy. The elevation of Orestes to the post of *magister militum* to replace Gundobad[242] who had departed (or fled) for his father's kingdom in Gaul in 473, which in turn allowed Orestes to make his son the emperor in AD 475, was due largely to the support he received from the now familiar Odoacer, the Hunnic prince, who ruled the Torcilingi, Rogii, Sciri and the Heruls. What was called the Western Roman army after AD 473[243] was actually the tribal confederacy ruled by Odoacer which consisted of the above-mentioned tribes, all of which derived from the Hunnic Empire. Orestes' previous career as the imperial Hunnic secretary under Attila probably made him an ideal candidate for these former Hunnic troops and their leader Odoacer to use as a figurehead.[244]

The nature of this arrangement between Orestes and Odoacer's ex-Hunnic army has long been rendered obscure due to what appears at first glance to be two contradictory accounts in our sources about how

Odoacer came to Italy: one as a conquering king of barbarians, the other as a barbarian officer in the imperial bodyguard of Anthemius.[245] Jordanes describes Odoacer as the king of the Torcilingi, by race a Rogian, who invaded Italy as leader of the Sciri, the Heruli and allies of various races, and overthrew Orestes.[246] John of Antioch (fr. 209.1), a seventh-century chronicler, tells us that Odoacer the son of Edeco was with Ricimer when the latter overthrew Anthemius in AD 472. Procopius, however, describes Odoacer as being one of the emperor's bodyguards.[247] This has led Goffart to argue that when Jordanes talks about Odoacer invading Italy (*Italiam invasit*) he used the verb *invadere* in the sense of seizing Italy from within, by coup d'état.[248] This is, however, a forced translation and is not corroborated by the context.

König, who also believes that the account of Odoacer invading Italy with a barbarian army is incorrect, notes that in the *Vita S. Severini* 7, Odoacer is presented in shabby clothes. From this he speculates that Odoacer at that stage before he entered Italy did not have a great retinue which he could lead into Italy.[249] However, the rhetorical purpose of the passage also needs to be considered before we reach such a hasty conclusion. The account is not concerned with giving an accurate assessment of Odoacer's power or his retinue, which it does not even mention, but with highlighting the holiness and miraculous powers of the saint who can predict Odoacer's future greatness in Italy. All the more dramatic then it would be to suggest that Odoacer was no more than a powerless pauper before he received the words of wisdom of the saint which led him become a king, i.e. a rags to riches tale that does not reflect the true nature of the meeting. A similar presentation is given of the meeting between the king of the Rugii and the saint. Flaccitheus the Rugian king is likewise presented as being powerless, in tears in fact, and only saved from the hostility of the Goths through the foresight and the warnings given by the saint (*Vita S. Severini* 5). Quite obviously this is again rhetorical and not true.

The probable answer to the dilemma is that both accounts about Odoacer's arrival in Italy are correct to an extent, but they view Odoacer from different perspectives, Jordanes from the perspective of the 'barbarians' and John and Procopius from that of the 'Romans'. That Odoacer was not a mere officer in the Roman army is made clear by the ethnic composition of the so-called Roman army that overthrows Orestes: Torcilingi, Rugii/Rogii, Sciri and Heruli. All these tribes, as noted above, originate in the east from the former territory of the Huns and all of them are in one way or another linked to Odoacer. He was personally king of the Torcilingi, the Sciri are his mother's people and the subjects of his father Edeco; the Rogii, as explained earlier, were allied to the Sciri in their conflict with the Goths in

Pannonia and Noricum; and the Heruli were also in all probability part of this alliance, since they receive a portion of Pannonia after the expulsion of the Goths. This explains the prominence of Odoacer already in AD 472 in the overthrow of Anthemius. A significant portion of the 'Roman' army of Italy was controlled by him, giving him the power to intervene in Roman internal politics.

Thus it is likely that Odoacer first entered Italy during the reign of Anthemius with an army that he had gathered in Pannonia and Noricum (he had presumably returned to the east from Gaul after learning of his father's death *c.* AD 469, hence the account in Jordanes of him invading Italy with an army of Sciri etc. and the story of him meeting Saint Severinus before his departure to Italy), consisting of the Sciri in Pannonia and other tribes formerly allied to his father Edeco that had not joined his brothers Hunoulphus and Armatus in entering Eastern Roman service in the early 470s. He probably entered Italy at the invitation of Anthemius (*c.* AD 472) who may have wished to check the power of Ricimer's 'Roman' army within Italy by introducing a new barbarian army. This entry of Odoacer's forces into Italy to 'protect' the emperor was then possibly misrepresented in Procopius, which makes Odoacer the emperor's 'bodyguard'. However, once he arrived Odoacer colluded with Ricimer in overthrowing the emperor (John of Antioch's account) and then Odoacer's 'Huns' seem to have played a key role in defeating the invading army of Vidimer's Goths during the later reign of Glycerius (AD 473–4). Odoacer then probably fell out with both Gundobad, Ricimer's nephew and successor, whom he likely expelled (AD 473), and subsequently Glycerius whom he replaced with Nepos in AD 474 at the instigation of Orestes,[250] his long-time acquaintance at the court of Attila.

If we therefore accept the assumption, made also in the previous section about Valamer and the Ostrogoths, that the Huns that drove out Vidimer, the brother of Thiudimer, from Italy during the reign of Glycerius were indeed Odoacer's troops, then the circumstances behind the sudden departure of Gundobad, the deposition of Gundobad's puppet Glycerius, and the subsequent enthronement of Nepos, then Romulus, all become intelligible. Gundobad was a member of the Gibichung royal house of the Burgundians and he inherited his power in Italy from the barbarian general-kingmaker Ricimer who had ties with the Gibichungs.[251] However, once Ricimer and Vidimer (who invaded Italy in AD 473) had both died (late 472 and 473 respectively) the presence of a more powerful 'barbarian' army under Odoacer might well have precipitated Gundobad's departure from Italy. After all, why would Gundobad have given up his lucrative and more appealing position of kingmaker of Roman Italy (de facto ruler) for an uncertain future as one of the many contestants for the throne in the tiny principality ruled by his father (died in AD 473),[252] which he could have left to his brothers? The almost immediate deposition of Gundobad's puppet Glycerius after his departure supports this line of reasoning.[253]

Once he had thrown out first Vidimer and then Gundobad from Italy, Odoacer in order to consolidate and legitimize his position in Italy appears to have accepted the Eastern candidate for emperor of the West, Nepos, who may in fact have had in his entourage our Orestes.[254] It is likely that Orestes persuaded Odoacer to drop his support for Glycerius and back Nepos. Soon afterwards Orestes seems to have become a figurehead for Odoacer's army, now refashioned as the 'Roman' army of Italy. Orestes then, after promising to cede land to Odoacer and his men, used their military strength to dethrone Nepos who had reigned for just a year. Orestes' unwillingness to share Italian land[255] or more probably his power with Odoacer and his followers then precipitated Orestes' quick demise and the end of Western Roman rule in Italy.[256] Thus as can be clearly seen from this final episode of Western Roman history, the Roman Empire in the West was definitively ended as a political entity by former Hunnic troops governed by a prince of Hunnic origin.[257] The final ruler of the moribund Western Empire was the son of the secretary of Attila the Hun, and the eventual rulers of Italy the Ostrogoths and the Lombards were also political units formed out of the former Hunnic Empire. There can be no doubt then that the end of the Western Roman Empire was caused by the Huns.[258]

The notion that Odoacer and Theodoric ruled Italy as nominal viceroys of the Eastern emperor and therefore there is no significance in the deposition of Romulus Augustulus or that the new Italy was politically still Roman[259] is surely a slight exaggeration. The two kings were in reality for all intents and purposes independent monarchs of a new political entity.[260] The Eastern empire under Zeno might have claimed that it commissioned Theodoric to overthrow Odoacer[261] and therefore Theodoric ruled as the emperor's viceroy in the West,[262] but this was quite clearly empty rhetoric. Zeno in the 480s, as we have seen in the previous chapter, was in no way capable of forcing or even influencing (other than through bribery) the behaviour and decision-making of the two kings.[263] He was in no position to send an army to Italy that would make the slightest impression on either Odoacer's armies or later those of Theodoric. On the other hand Theodoric used this 'commission' from Zeno to subjugate and render docile the Roman population of Italy who considered the authority of the emperor of the East to be legitimate and still entertained the illusion that nothing had really changed in Italy, a misconception that Theodoric and before him Odoacer had for their own convenience no doubt actively encouraged.[264] In the same way Odoacer before Theodoric's arrival even minted coins in the name of Nepos (nominal Western Emperor exiled from Italy) whom he had helped overthrow and later those of Zeno, the Eastern emperor, for the same purpose.[265]

To be sure the two Hunno-Germanic kings retained much of the paraphernalia and the trappings of Roman imperial rule like the consulship, flattered the senatorial elite of Italy by offering them jobs,[266] retained much of the former Roman administrative structure[267] and paid lip service to 'respecting' the Roman political tradition and the emperor of the East,[268] thereby creating a deliberate ambiguity that served their purpose well.[269] But did not Alexander when he conquered the Persian Empire do exactly the same thing? He retained old Persian administrative practices and ceremonials, employed Iranians as satraps, wore Persian royal garb and pretended that he was the legitimate heir to the Achaemenid kings by marrying the daughters of previous Persian kings.[270] He did this to minimize resistance from the conquered population and because the Macedonians had no first-hand experience of administering a large empire. Thus for most people then living within the Persian Empire, the shift away from the Persian Empire to a Macedonian one was not keenly felt, at least initially. However, no one could argue that Alexander's conquest of Persia and the deposition of the last Achaemenid king, despite important institutional and administrative continuities between the former Achaemenid and later Macedonian/Seleucid Empires, were not significant for the future of the Near East.[271] In the same way the Hunno-Germanic kings of Italy softened the impact of their conquest by conciliating old Roman elites and playing along to the tune of old Roman customs and practices as long as this helped strengthen their control over the new Italy which they gradually brought about. In this sense their conquest was every bit as subtle and significant as the Macedonian takeover of Persia.[272]

NEW INVASIONS FROM THE EAST

One other factor that needs to be taken into account in the assessment of events that took place after the death of Attila is the invasion of the western steppe by new arrivals from the east around the time of the civil wars. In the year AD 434 the Rouran, the greatest imperial power in the east, together with the Hephtalites invaded Bactria and crushed the Kidarite Huns who were pushed into India.[273] Not just the Kidarites, but also elements of the Tiele Turkic federation, the Oghurs in Kazakhstan (i.e. the immediate neighbours of the Huns in the mid fifth century AD) came under intense pressure.[274] The Sabirs[275] had likewise been defeated by the Rouran (probably the Avars) and they forced the various Oghurs (tribes) to fight their way into the western steppe controlled by the Huns.[276] Priscus informs us that in AD 463 the Saragurs (an Oghur tribe)[277] had overwhelmed the Akatziri, the tribe formerly ruled by Ellac, the eldest son of Attila.[278] The defeat of the Akatziri was likely to have been a drawn out process like the defeat of the Alans earlier in the saga of Hun migration into Europe. It is likely to have occurred over a long period of time before the culmination of events in AD 463.[279] Thus just after the battle of Nedao, the main tribe of the eastern faction in the Hunnic civil war was preoccupied with fighting a greater menace than the western Germanic tribes under Ardaric. The inability of the Huns in the steppe region to effectively prevent the secession of militarily inferior western tribes in the decades following Nedao becomes intelligible when we consider these pressing concerns on their eastern flank.

Dengizich, the ruler of the western wing of the Huns in the mid 460s, returns to the offensive in the west, vanquishing the Ostrogoths of Valamer in the process. Later he wages war against the East Romans.[280] However, his activities in the west met with the opposition of Ernak/Hernak, his brother and ruler of the eastern half of the Hun realm (i.e. his superior), who wished to concentrate on his eastern enemies.[281] Priscus' record of Ernak's preferential treatment by Attila, due supposedly to a prophecy that he would restore the fortunes of the Huns,[282] may actually have been coloured by hindsight, an indication of his success in the decades following Nedao and Dengizich's failed expedition against Rome. He apparently became the ruler of the Bulgars according to the Bulgar Prince list,[283] the progenitor of a dynasty that presided over a newly formed confederation of Huns and incoming Oghurs.[284]

As Golden points out, the names of the two greatest powers in the western steppe to emerge out of the confusion of the civil wars, the Kutrigur (nine Oghurs) Huns and the Utigur Huns (thirty Oghurs),[285] both contain the element Oghur in their ethnonym.[286] They were also according to Procopius and Menander of the same origin, that is Hunnic (no doubt with a heavy Oghur admixture).[287] In ways reminiscent of old Hunnic and Xiongnu practices these two formed the western (Kutrigur) and eastern (Utigur) wings of the revived Hunnic state.[288] The Khazars who would eventually become rulers of the region much later in the seventh century AD would still speak the Hunno-Bulgaric language[289] of the Oghur tribes that were ruled by Ernak and his descendants, indicating the lasting impact their immigration had on the eastern territories of the Hunnic state.

The dissolution of the Hunnic state: an analysis

We have noted thus far that the Hunnic state in the west dissolved in the context not of a national uprising of Germanic tribes against the Huns, but rather a dispute over the imperial succession and distribution of 'fiefs' among Hunnic princes, a civil war among Hunnic lords. Civil war arising from succession disputes was an endemic feature of Turco-Mongol steppe polities and the Hunnic Empire was no exception. However, this instability cannot be viewed as proof of the flimsiness of Hunnic state institutions or lack thereof. By the same logic we could argue that the Roman Empire, perennially plagued by civil war over the throne, an empire of coup-d'état, had no stable state institutions, which would be nonsense. The intriguing question is, why indeed did the Hunnic Empire at that particular juncture in history fail to resolve its succession dispute and recover its former position of strength?

The invasion of the Oghurs from the east has already been cited as a major reason behind the inability of the Huns to react effectively against the Germanic tribes or rather fiefs seceding in the west. Another important factor in the failure of Hunnic restoration in the west attempted by Dengizich is geography and the location of human resources. The Hunnic Empire was the product of the political culture and resources of the Eurasian steppe. Its heartland, therefore, was the Pontic steppe, from the inhabitants of which it derived its military power. If the Huns had limited their conquests to eastern Europe and had governed the periphery, i.e. the Balkans and Hungary, from afar, there is no reason to doubt that their empire would have enjoyed the longevity that characterized the later empire of the Khazars who did exactly this.[290]

However, under Attila the Hunnic centre of power shifted permanently to the west to Hungary. The connection between the Hunnic state and its original power base, the steppe, was thus weakened, giving rise to secessionist tendencies among the eastern tribes like the Akatziri and the various Oghurs. We see the same phenomenon in the Avar Khaganate that succeeded the Hunnic Empire in Hungary. Once the Khagans moved their political centre to the Carpathian basin their control over the Ukrainian steppe slowly slipped away, leading to the formation of an independent Bulgar state. The Avars, however, were able to maintain stability by concentrating their resources in a relatively compact area around Hungary and thus preserve their state for another two centuries after the Bulgar secession. The Huns in the west in contrast indulged in over-expansion towards the west into Germany and Gaul.

The result was the decline in the Hunnic ability to access the military resources of the steppe and the unenviable task of having to govern new warlike subjects in the west with an ever-decreasing number of effective Hunnic troops, spread thin over a vast area.[291] This would then lead to over-dependence on unreliable Germanic troops in the far west, who had only recently been conquered, and that translated into military weakness and political instability in the western half of the Hunnic realm. The rapidity of the conquests under Rua and Attila in the west also meant less time to consolidate newly added provinces. What was needed at this juncture was a prolonged period of political stability, which would allow for the Hunnic state to deal with some of these pressing issues. However, the violent usurpation by Attila of the Hunnic throne, after assassinating his elder brother and overlord Bleda, seems to have alienated the traditional Hunnic peoples of the east, the most reliable upholders of the imperial order, and augmented the importance of the western tribes who had provided him with assistance in his coup d'état.

The elevation of non-Huns such as Orestes and possibly also Onegesius to the status of *logades* was also perhaps part of the conscious policy adopted by Attila to weaken the traditional Hunnic aristocracy by building a power base of men who were dependent upon him alone personally for their political status and fortunes. The frequent execution of Hunnic royals under Attila's rule bears witness to the possibility of this scenario. However, when Attila disappeared from the scene old grievances among disaffected Hunnic princes and the troops they governed shattered the political unity of the state, and the western feudatories, already empowered during Attila's reign to dangerous levels, easily broke away under rebellious Hunnic princes and allied potentates.

Almost a mirror image of this Hunnic collapse can also be found in the later history of the steppe. The Chaghatai Khanate of Central Asia underwent a similar breakdown of central authority in the 1330s after over a century of relative stability. The eastern half of the empire, Moghulistan (largely steppe territory inhabited by Mongols), remained intact under legitimate Chaghatai Khans and would endure for another 300 years. However, the more sedentary areas in the west, Transoxiana, descended into chaos.[292] By the year AD 1346 the Chagatai Khans of the west lost all real political power and were replaced by the Qaraunas (Turkified Mongols) emirs, the most famous of whom was the notorious Tamerlane.²⁹³ This situation bears a striking resemblance to the Hunnic survival in the eastern steppe after Attila and the dissolution of the empire's western half under Hunno-Germanic princes.

Another useful analogy is the dissolution also in the 1330s AD of another Mongol empire, that of the Ilkhans in Persia. Other than the Mongol Yuan dynasty in China, the Persian Khanate was the best governed, most sedentary and most sophisticated of the Mongol states in terms of bureaucracy and administration.²⁹⁴ Mongol control, however, was the strongest in three areas, Khurasan, Azerbaijan and Iraq, where the bulk of the invading Mongol armies had been settled. The peripheral areas such as Herat (western Afghanistan, under the Kartids), and Anatolia (under the Seljuks of Rum who ruled with the aid of a Mongol military governor) were governed through local rulers or long-term governors. This again resembles the Hunnic situation under Attila, when the core region of Hungary and tribes in surrounding areas were ruled directly by the Huns and Hunnic princes (e.g. Ellac over the Akatziri in the Ukraine, Ardaric over the Gepids in the Carpathian basin, Hunimund and Valamer over the Ostrogoths and Suebi in Pannonia, Edeco over the Sciri in Romania, and possibly also the Rogii over Germanic tribes in Lower Austria), while the more distant territories of the empire were ruled via vassal rulers of native origin such as Childeric the Frank under the supervision of the Hunnic general Wiomad.

When a succession crisis tore apart the Ilkhanate after the death of Abu Said, the core regions fell to Mongol lords and princes who either claimed the throne for themselves – like Arpa Ke'un (Azerbaijan), Musa (Iraq) and Togha Temur (Khurasan), Chingizids and therefore eligible for the throne – or raised their own Chingizid puppets for the succession, e.g. the Chobanids in Anatolia and later Azerbaijan (Mongol nobility related to the Chingizids by marriage) and the Jalayirids in Iraq.²⁹⁵ The peripheries of the empire on the other hand gradually asserted their independence when it became clear that none of the contestants for the throne could overpower other claimants. Thus the Muzaffarids and Injuids (former Mongol governors) became rulers of Yazd, Fars and Isfahan,²⁹⁶ the Kartids of Herat and the various Turkmen dynasties of Anatolia broke free and set up their own beyliks. After five decades of conflict, the successors to the Ilkhans were then swept away by the conquests of the eastern Turco-Mongols under Timur.²⁹⁷

The same sequence of events can be seen in the Hunnic civil war and aftermath. The core regions are fought over by Hunnic princes. Ellac, Dengizich and Valamer, Hunnic royals, claim the throne for themselves like Arpa Ke'un, Musa and Togha Timur, the Chingizid royals. Ardaric, related by marriage to the Attilids (like the Chupanids), possibly raised his own puppet claimant to the throne. The peripheral regions break away when it becomes clear that no one power would prevail. Thus the Franks, Alamanni, Burgundians and Thuringians break free and become independent under presumably native princes (like the Injuids of Fars, and the Kartids of Herat). The eastern core meanwhile is reunited by Ernak, just as the core areas of Azerbaijan and Iraq were reunited in the end under Jalayirid (Mongol) rule following the end of the Ilkhanate. After nearly nine decades of division, the former territories of the Hunnic Empire are then swallowed up by an invasion from the east led by the Avars (read Timur's invasion from Central Asia that virtually finished off the Jalayirid Mongol dynasty).

Both the Chaghatai Khanate and Ilkhanate were sophisticated state entities that collapsed due to political instability caused by civil war. Their collapse was a long drawn out process and was neither inevitable nor irreversible. No one in their right state of mind would claim that these states fell due to the lack of political institutions and the apparatus of government. Their dissolution shows a remarkable degree of similarity to the saga of Hunnic demise and this surely cannot be an accident. When the civil war came the Hunnic state, as explained earlier, was ill-prepared to manage its western territories. The steppe-based eastern realm was able to recuperate, but for the more alien lands of central Europe, where Hunnic institutions had much less time to take root, the wounds inflicted by a full-blown conflict were harder to heal. However, the civil war by no means ended the Hunnic Empire, and the Huns certainly did not just disappear as a people.[298]

CHAPTER 6

The later Huns and the birth of Europe

THE LATER HUNNIC EMPIRE OF THE BULGARS, OGHURS AND AVARS

The various Oghurs (Utigurs and Kutrigurs) and the Bulgars, who are mentioned in our sources after the so-called 'total disappearance' of the Huns, as noted earlier, are likely to have been either the same people or at least members of the same, related political entity.[1] The name Bulgar, which in Turkic means 'stir, confuse or mix',[2] probably referred to the process of tribal union of the Oghurs and the Huns under the Attilids.[3] The name Bulgar first appears when the emperor Zeno appeals to them for aid against the Ostrogoths in AD 480, indicating that by this stage some ten years after Dengizich's death Ernak had successfully moulded the various Oghur tribes and Huns into Bulgars.[4] Their raids become more frequent thereafter (AD 491, 493, 499, 502).[5]

In AD 514 the usurper Vitalian, called a Scythian (presumably either a Hun or Alan),[6] appeals to them for aid against the Emperor Anastasius.[7] Further raids would follow and Justinian in AD 531 had to specifically appoint a household confidant, a certain Chilbudius, as general of Thrace to guard the river Danube against repeated incursion by the Huns, who along with their Antes and Sclaveni subjects or allies had 'done irreparable harm to the Romans'.[8] In the 530s, however, the Romans would see the Kutrigur Huns in Moesia and Illyricum (AD 538/9) and by AD 540 near Constantinople and Thessaly. Procopius tells us that the Huns had invaded the Empire frequently before this, but never had the calamity for the Romans been so great.[9]

In AD 539 they capture a total of thirty-two fortresses in Illyricum alone, taking 120,000 captives.[10] Zabergan, the king of the Kutrigur Bulgar Huns,[11] in AD 558 would launch a devastating raid into the Balkans, all the way to the long Walls of Constantinople.[12] Justinian would just barely fight off this invasion due to the ingenuity of Belisarius.[13] These last two campaigns are of a magnitude to warrant comparison with the invasions of the earlier Huns[14] and again such offensives and the taking of immense numbers of captives into Hunnic territory could never have been undertaken by primitive hordes without political organization. Malalas indeed informs us that when the Gepid-Hun Mundo inflicted a rare defeat on the Bulgars in AD 530 he captured one of their kings, suggesting the possibility that the Bulgars like the Huns maintained a system of graded kings.[15] The Huns probably did possess a state in the sixth century AD.

At any rate in the seventh century the Bulgar prince Kubrat,[16] who revived the Bulgarian state after its temporary demise at the hands of the Avars and the Turks in the latter half of the sixth century, is referred to in Theophanes as the king of the Ounnogoundour Huns[17] (probably the Onogur (ten Ogurs))-Bulgars[18] and Kotragoi.[19] Historians who believed that the Huns had simply vanished after the defeat at Nedao have often ignored these references in our sources to the Huns as anachronisms. True Agathias, one of our sixth-century sources, suggests that certain steppe tribes such as the Oultizouroi and the Bourougoundoi who had existed during the time of Emperor Leo (AD 457–74) in the fifth century had vanished by his time.[20] However, for starters the Oultizouroi are, as mentioned earlier, actually not a specific tribe, but most probably the Hunnic (Oghuric Turkic) aristocratic council of six nobles and presumably also the tribes they govern. They did not disappear but actually reappear later in Danubian Bulgaria set up by Asparukh, the son of the above-mentioned Kubrat, as an aristocratic institution.[21] The Bourougoundoi or Ourougoundoi[22] are not mentioned afterwards which implies that they were absorbed by the Kutrigurs and Utigurs (i.e. Bulgars)[23] under Ernak and later Attilids.

It is also true that Byzantine writers in later centuries would at times use the name Hun as they had previously used Scythian to designate steppe nomads. However, it is hard to agree that Procopius, Jordanes, Menander, Agathias and Pseudo-Zacharias Rhetor, all living in the sixth century, who were familiar with tribal designations of the northern steppe, always use the name Hun as a generic term for nomads.[24] This is highly implausible given the existence of actual Hunnic tribes, in all likelihood independent of the Attilids (Utigurs and Kutrigur Bulgars) in the northern Caucasus in the sixth century AD.[25]

Separated from the main Hunnic realm by the powerful Sabirs[26] to the north, we see their activity in the Caucasus in association with the ongoing East Roman–Sassanian conflict. In AD 503 the invasion of Huns into northern Persia, i.e. the Caucasus region, forces Kabad, the Persian king,

The later Hunnic Empire

to prematurely break off his until then successful campaign against the Romans.[27] Kabad is preoccupied with matters in this region for decades and the East Romans were only too glad to incite the various Caucasian kingdoms (Iberia and Lazica) and especially the Huns to cause trouble for the Persians.[28] In AD 522 Boareks, the widow of king Balach, called a Hun by Malalas,[29] but most likely a Sabir,[30] on behalf of the Byzantines attacked two Hunnic leaders in succession, King Styrax in AD 528 and then later Glones,[31] who were then allies of the Sassanians and anti-Byzantine. A Caucasian Hunnic king (or rather a sub-king) by the name of Askoum entered imperial service in AD 530 and was appointed *magister militum per Illyricum*. He was assigned the task of repelling the invasion of his cousins the Hunnic Bulgars in the Balkans. He failed, was captured and had to be ransomed by Justinian for an enormous sum of gold.[32] A Hunnic mini-state in the area north of Derbent in modern-day Dagestan is quite frequently mentioned in the sixth century.[33]

Real Huns then did indeed survive into the sixth century,[34] even if we were to treat the Utigur, Kutrigur and Onogur Huns[35] (in all probability ruled by the Attilids) as mainly Bulgars or Turkic Oghurs,[36] and they would continue to loom large in the political and military horizons of the Byzantines and the Sassanians. At the great battle of Daras, Belisarius defeats the Persian host mainly through the battle prowess of his 600 Massagetic (i.e. Hunnic) horsemen under Sunicas and Aigan[37] and a further 600 horsemen under the Hunnic commanders Simmas and Ascan.[38] Even in situations where the name Hun is clearly used in a generic sense to mean steppe horsemen from the Pontic region, Procopius and others usually take care to specify who they are. Thus, in response to the Roman use of Hunnic cavalry the Persians later retaliate by sending an army including 3,000 'Huns' into Armenia. Here the name Hun is generic, but Procopius quickly explains that they are Huns called Sabirs, thereby demonstrating his knowledge of specific tribal affiliations of these northern steppe peoples.[39]

When sixth-century authors really wished to be anachronistic they would use the term Scythian[40] or Massagetae, not Huns. This is demonstrated again by the following episode. In AD 531 Justinian manages to get hold of intelligence through a spy who had defected from the Persians that the Massagetae had decided to ally with the Persians against the Romans and were marching into Roman territory to join up with the invading Persian army. He, however, cleverly uses this against the Persians and deceives the Persian army besieging Martyropolis into believing that these Massagetae have been won over with money by the Roman emperor. Massagetae here are clearly anachronistic references to the Huns and we learn shortly afterwards that the Persians are terrified by the advance of these hostile 'Huns' and withdraw.[41] Later in Book 3 of his histories Procopius calls Aigan, the officer in command of Belisarius' cavalry, a Massagetan by birth, 'whom they now call Huns' (11.9). All these references and the fact that Procopius accurately records the sixth-century self-designation of the Hephtalites, 'White Huns', as we have seen in an earlier chapter, clearly show that the name Hun was not yet anachronistic in the sixth century AD or purely generic.

It must also be noted again that the name Hun was, like the name Rome or Roman,[42] the appellation of imperial status among steppe nomads. Thus even the original Hunnic state cannot strictly be identified as an ethnic state of the 'Huns' because a Hun was a member of the Hunnic Empire whose status was recognized by the ruling imperial clan, not necessarily a member of a fixed tribe. The core Turkic tribes of the Hunnic Empire from very early on all possessed different names: Akatziri, Alpidzuri, etc. in addition to their Hunnic identity. Thus although the later Huns bear different tribal names like the Utigurs or Kutrigurs, this does not mean that they had disappeared as a political entity.[43] It simply means that the constituent members of their imperial confederacy had been augmented and altered by the infusion of new elements from the East.[44] They were as before led by the Attilid charismatic clan and the attribution of the name Hun to these peoples in the sixth century at least is likely to have been the result of their own self-designation of their polity, not always anachronistic attestations by Byzantine scribes.

We have already observed the fact that the original Huns of the fourth century had adopted the name Hun (Xiongnu) to signify their imperial status in memory of the old empire of the Xiongnu.[45] The same is likely to have been the case among the Utigurs and Kutrigurs who under Attilid rule had even more justification for claiming the imperial mantle of the Huns of Europe.[46] Some may, however, argue that the 'large' number of tribal names mentioned by sixth-century writers in the steppe region, especially west of the Volga and east of the Danube, is indicative of anarchy, not the continuation of the Hunnic political legacy. However, this is not an accurate assessment of the situation.

First of all, we should consider the size of the region that is under discussion. Less than half a dozen peoples (excluding the Slavs who generally lack political cohesion, situated in modern Romania and the northwestern Ukraine), according to Jordanes (*Getica* 5.36–7), inhabit the huge area between Romania and the Volga: the Akatziri[47] (old subjects of the Huns situated somewhere north of the Bulgars), the Bulgars (i.e. the Attilid-

The later Hunnic Empire 141

ruled Kutrigur and Utigur Huns between the Dnieper and the Volga[48]), the Hunni (i.e. tribes with rightly or wrongly Hunnic origins) who are divided into Altziagiri[49] near Cherson in the Crimea[50] and the Sabirs[51] (in the Volga region and independent of the Attilids), and finally the Hunuguri (the Onogurs[52] living to the northwest of the Sabirs in the middle Volga region, who control the trade in marten skins with the Ural region[53]). Utigurs, Kutrigurs and Onogurs were in all likelihood identical with the Bulgars.[54]

Pseudo-Zacharias Rhetor gives us another list of thirteen nomadic tribes north of the Caucasus around AD 555:[55] Onoghurs, Ogurs, Sabirs, Bulgars, Kutrigurs, Avars, Acatziri, Itimari, Saragurs, Barselts, Choliatae, Abdelae (Hephtalites) and Hephtalites.[56] The Hephtalites, whose name is duplicated in this list as both Abdelae ('bdl') and Hephtalites ('ptlyt'),[57] obviously due to some kind of confusion, can safely be removed from our consideration of tribes west of the Volga since they are situated in Central Asia. The Avars and the Choliatae[58] were newcomers in the 550s. This leaves us with nine instead of the five or six tribes given by Jordanes.

However, it quickly becomes apparent that pseudo-Zacharias, in the same way that Jordanes frequently indulges in anachronisms, is simply naming all the tribes that were historically known to the East Romans up to that point rather than illuminating contemporary political reality in the steppe.[59] It is doubtful whether the Itimari and Saragurs still existed in AD 555.[60] Their absence in Jordanes' list, despite Jordanes' love for naming anachronistic tribes, is telling. The Ogurs (Turkic 'tribe, arrow') designate simply Turkish-speaking tribes in the region, rather than a distinct political group (or maybe they refer to the Utigurs, since the name is listed beside that of the Onogurs who were in close proximity to the Utigurs). The Bulgars and Kutrigurs also likely refer to the same horde or reflect subdivisions of the same confederacy (the western half of the confederation (possibly including the Akatziri, Hunnic subjects), which to the east also may have contained two divisions: Utigurs in the Kuban and the Onogurs to their north, thus forming the traditional four divisions of an Inner Asian confederacy which we have already noted among the earlier Xiongnu and the later Göktürks).[61] The Barselts[62] were a group that was situated in the Volga region. The Sabirs and the Onogurs[63] were to the east and northeast of the Utigurs. The Akatziri were probably situated to the northwest of the Bulgar Huns. Thus we have roughly the same number of tribes again: five or six between Romania and the Volga, with the Altziagiri in the Crimea excluded from Zacharias' list.

We can note from these lists that all of these peoples, except the powerful Sabirs and perhaps the Barselts, are in all likelihood ruled by the Attilids, as their names and history suggests. The Akatziri and the Hunuguri/Onogurs were probably vassal hordes, distributed as fiefs to collateral members of the royal family, as is customary among steppe nomads. Thus we can count just four groups, all ruled by the Attilids or at least associated with the original Huns in the region stretching from Romania to the eastern end of the Kuban steppe, a huge area for anyone who can read a map! Is this chaos? The only thing that makes us feel that there is no order in this region is general unfamiliarity with names which baffle us, not actual realities. In a region as large as Germany and Italy put together, there existed a Hunnic confederation under Attila's heirs.[64]

They were, it must be acknowledged, a rather fractious bunch. Internal squabbles are an endemic feature of steppe polities (as they are for sedentary societies as well I might add) in which rivalries within the royal clan often led to civil war. Such divisions were exploited by the Byzantines in the mid sixth century AD. Justinian, hard-pressed by the Kutrigurs, induced their cousins the Utigurs under their king Sandilch to attack the Kutrigurs in the rear.[65] The resulting fratricidal war between them left them vulnerable to Avar[66] conquest shortly afterwards.[67]

The Avars[68] in effect, as mentioned earlier, recreated the old Hunnic Empire in its entirety.[69] Within ten years of taking over the Hunnic confederacy in the east in AD 557 and receiving the submission of the Sabirs, Onogurs and Barsils[70] (the inhabitants of the Volga region), they would conquer all of central Europe. In AD 565/6 they defeated and captured the Frankish king Sigibert.[71] In AD 567 they would destroy the Gepids and in AD 568 occupy Austria from the departing Lombards.[72] In the same year 10,000 Kutrigur Bulgar Huns under the command of the Avar Khagan Bayan sacked the cities of Dalmatia. By the end of the century they had also conquered much of the Balkans[73] and all the Slavs up to the Baltic Sea.[74]

As the superpower ruling most of Central and Eastern Europe[75] they would lay siege to Constantinople in AD 626[76] in union with the Sassanians and almost succeeded in bringing down the Roman Empire once and for all. After the aborted siege, however, their empire would split into two halves,[77] the Avar Khaganate in Hungary and Great Bulgaria under the leadership of the Onogurs ruled by Kubrat[78] (from the Dulo clan[79] which claimed Attilid descent from Ernak) in the Ukraine.[80] In the 790s AD the Avar state would fall victim to the combined invasions of the Bulgars and the Franks[81] and remnants of their once mighty empire would join the Hungarians when they arrived in Hungary under the Arpads in AD 896.[82] Curiously the Hungarians whose name possibly derives from the Onogurs[83] who were linked to the Bulgars, i.e. the Attilids, claimed Attilid descent for their royal family the Arpads.[84] Attila's legacy and the fame of the Huns would live on in Hungary until modernity. The Bulgars, the other ethnicity claiming ties to the Huns, would dominate much of the Balkans until their dissolution at the hands of their old enemies the East Romans in the early eleventh century under Basil II, the Bulgar-Slayer.[85]

THE BIRTH OF A NEW EUROPE

The early Middle Ages, often erroneously characterized as the 'Dark Ages', were a time of immense change for Western Europe. Europe of the early Middle Ages witnessed the end of the long domination by Mediterranean-based powers of the geographical region that came to be known as Western Europe.[86] This precipitated fundamental changes in the political and cultural fabric of the region. That this new 'Europe' was heavily influenced by the cultural and political legacy left by the Romans is obvious and nobody could possibly dispute this fact. However, another fundamental influence that helped shape Western Europe of the early Middle Ages has thus far received scant attention. In this last section it will be argued that the political and cultural traditions of Inner Asia brought to Europe by Central Asian immigrants, the Huns and the Alans, were just as fundamental to the formation of Western Europe as the rich legacy left behind by the Roman Empire. The political and cultural landscape of early medieval Europe was shaped by the fusion of Roman and Inner Asian influences.

What follows is mainly an analysis of the impact of Inner Asian political practices on state formation in early medieval Europe. Most importantly it will trace the origins of early medieval 'feudalism' in Inner Asia.[87] The influence of Inner Asian material culture and artistic traditions on Europe as a whole was arguably equally profound. However, not being an art historian by training I leave closer scrutiny of that topic to future art historians and archaeologists. Only a brief summary of the significant impact of Inner Asian material culture and art on Europe will be provided in this book. The polemical rhetoric and faulty methodology employed by Strzygowski did immense damage to the study of artistic links between Europe and Central Asia by tainting the discipline with absurd racial theories.[88] However, the general observation that art styles and material culture of Central Asian and Iranian provenance had a profound influence on Germanic Europe, for reasons that will be specified shortly, cannot be rejected. It is necessary also to counter the chauvinism we find in some circles which privileges Mediterranean, Greco-Roman art over other art originating further to the east, calling the latter 'barbaric', primitive etc. Now that we have finally (or hopefully) cast aside all these unnecessary preconceptions based on regional and racial prejudices, it is hoped that in the future archaeologists and art historians of both the Mediterranean world and Inner Asia will collaborate to further illuminate the dynamic cultural interactions between the two worlds that gave birth to early medieval Europe.

While the Bulgars were struggling with the East Romans for supremacy in eastern Europe, in western Europe the rise of the Franks definitively brought to an end the long political domination by Mediterranean powers of areas that now constitute Western Europe. The rise of the Franks also brought into being a new imperial entity. Heather regards this dramatic development as the direct consequence of significant social, economic and political transformations that took place within the Germanic world on the periphery of the Mediterranean basin in the fourth and fifth centuries AD.[89] The strategic realignment of the Western Eurasian world is thus viewed as the result essentially of an increased, internal Germanic capacity for state formation. The Huns in Heather's estimation merely sped up the inevitable rise of Germanic Europe which would, even without the Huns, have gradually displaced the Roman superpower in western and northern Europe.[90]

However, a more in-depth analysis of historical and political developments of the fourth and fifth centuries AD yields a slightly different conclusion. Indeed the 'Germanic' world in these two centuries developed the capacity for forming states that were well organized enough to challenge the old dominance of the Mediterranean region. Yet this capacity for organization and the political culture of the early Middle Ages came not from the Germanic world itself, but from Inner Asia via the Huns. In the same way that the Avar invasion from Central Asia marked a watershed in the political history of the Slavic peoples in the sixth century AD[91] (and also later Khazar and Bulgar incursions in subsequent centuries on the political organization of the eastern Slavs[92]), the Hunnic conquest was a catalyst for momentous, revolutionary changes in the political structure of the Germanic tribes. The transfer of political institutions and cultural capital from the Eurasian Huns to the Germanic tribes may appear somewhat unbelievable to many, but when we consider the fact that what we now identify as central and even western Europe had constantly been on the receiving end of cultural influences from the eastern steppe for almost nine centuries before the arrival of the Huns, this new interpretation of the post-Hunnic European political world will become much more compelling.

Much of southeastern Europe from Hungary to the Ukraine was originally inhabited by peoples who probably spoke languages related to Thracian.[93] This largely settled agricultural population was at some point in the mid first millennium BC conquered by the Iranian-speaking Scythians from what is now western Kazakhstan, i.e. exactly the place from which the Huns would later make their move against the Alans and Goths in the same region.[94] These Central Asian Scythians, who possessed an elaborate culture that was heavily influenced by west Asian (Assyrian, Caucasian, Medo-Persian)[95] culture (a result of centuries of contact and invasions of western Asia by the Scythians) – we are no doubt reminded of the Huns' long interaction with the Iranian world (west Asian) before their own entry into Europe – were, as mentioned at the beginning of this book, politically complex, well organized and ruled like so many other steppe polities after them by a charismatic royal clan that claimed absolute, sacred authority derived from the gods.[96]

Incredibly in ways that mimic the situation before the arrival of the Huns, as there were Turkish-speaking tribes already in Europe before the main Hunnic invasions, so too was the Pontic steppe in the pre-Scythian era home to non-Scythian Iranian tribes that co-existed with the original inhabitants.[97] After progressively overwhelming both the Iranian and Thracian elements in eastern Europe, the Scythians like the Huns after them set about imposing an Iranian (presumably Scythian) ruling elite on the conquered peoples. Thus among the Agathyrsi who were subject to the Royal Scythians,[98] a king with a clearly Iranian name, Spargapeithes, ruled as a vassal king. Archaeological evidence also points to the dissemination of Scythian culture and possibly political domination not just in the Ukraine and Romania, but also in Hungary and Slovakia in Central Europe by the late sixth century BC.[99] However, again like the Huns, the Scythians did not halt there but expanded further west. Destroyed earthworks and Scythian arrowheads from around 500 BC, found sticking out of outer defensive walls, were excavated in Germany in the area labelled by archaeologists as the Lusatian culture. Scythian arrowheads and armaments from the same period are even found as far west as France. This Scythian intrusion into central Europe was in effect a forerunner of the later invasions of the Huns, Avars and Mongols from Central Asia, and like all their successors the Scythians left a tangible cultural impact in Europe which manifests itself in the influence of Scythian art (including elements borrowed from west Asia) on Celtic art.[100]

Thus there were elements of Central Asian culture already deeply ingrained in the artistic traditions of central and even western Europe before the arrival of the Huns. As we shall see shortly this influence from the steppe on Europe would continue via the Sarmatians[101] who succeeded the Scythians and ultimately in dramatic fashion culminate, via the Huns, in the creation of a steppe-derived political and cultural *koine* in early 'medieval' Europe. So what then is the evidence for this *koine* brought to Europe by the Huns?

In 2001 Golden made the very astute observation that what seem like typical steppe political customs are detectable in various European polities that emerge after the fall of the Huns. The notion of the collective sovereignty of the royal clan,[102] a concept intimately associated with the sacred power accorded to kings, that we find in most steppe empires before and after the Huns,[103] is also found among the Franks, Danes,[104] and the various Slav peoples. Thus amongst the Polabian Slavs,[105] in Greater Moravia,[106] Poland,[107] and maybe also in Bohemia,[108] a system of fraternal rule and succession developed which gave each of the king's sons his own appanage,[109] but which maintained the outward political and territorial integrity of the state.[110] This is exactly the type of system we have already seen among the Huns and other steppe peoples. Can this be a coincidence?

The Hunnic Bulgars would also make a great contribution to Slavic political organization in Russia and the Balkans. The title and institution of Zhupan used in medieval Croatia and Serbia derive from the Hunnic Bulgars or the Avars who became the overlords of the Hunnic Bulgars,[111] as does without a doubt the aristocratic class system of boyars.[112] Furthermore, the Croats and Serbs would use colour designation for their political divisions in exactly the same way as the Central Asian Huns and Alans, hence we discover through the testimony of Constantine Porphyrogenitus the existence of 'White' Croats and 'White' Serbs next to Frankia.[113] We cannot due to confines of space discuss in greater detail the impact of Hunno-Bulgar-Avar political tradition and practices on early central and eastern European political entities. However, less well known and perhaps entirely unexpected is the impact of Hunnic political organization on the Frankish Merovingian kingdoms.

The sacred, hereditary charisma of the ruling clan which we have already noted among the various Turco-Iranian steppe polities[114] is especially pronounced in the dynastic tradition of the Merovingian Franks.[115] We find among them the notion of the sacred charisma of the long-haired kings.[116] As Ganshof points out, in vivid contrast to the limited power of the old Germanic *reguli*, whose authority was largely confined to leadership in war time, the Merovingian Frankish kings in a way reminiscent of the old Inner Asian steppe rulers exercised (at least in theory) absolute power within the territories they governed.[117] Gone was the vague Germanic practice of selecting separate leaders/kings for the sacred assembly of the people, the so-called *thing* kingship or *thiudans*, and for war (*reiks/duces*),[118] which usually meant the agglomeration of

The birth of a new Europe 147

quasi-equal and almost completely autonomous petty kings/chiefs. Instead we have kingship and hierarchy of the steppe, Inner Asian sort with a supreme monarch (ruling in conjunction with his brothers (fraternal, collective rule)) and a clearly stratified ranking system for sub-kings and dukes.[119] The steppe custom of regarding the state as the property of the ruling family led to a system of rule in which partition of territory is an endemic feature, where any male member of the ruling dynasty can claim kingship and territory. This is also exactly what is found among the Franks.[120] Thus after Clovis' death in AD 511 the kingdom is divided among his four sons.[121] Another partition occurs at the death of Clovis' last surviving son Chlotar I in AD 561[122] (when the kingdom was again divided into four parts[123]) and again at the death of Dagobert I in AD 639.[124]

However, curiously among the Franks, as among steppe peoples, despite the numerous succession disputes and partitions, the notion of an undivided dynastic state endures intact[125] and leads to periodic reunifications under a single strong ruler, e.g. Chlotar II in AD 613.[126] Thus what we have is in essence centralized 'feudalism'[127] of the Hunnic sort in sharp contrast to virtual local independence and paralysis of central government found in later medieval Europe.[128] Revealingly enough the Franks also followed the Hunnic practice of appointing sub-kings and distributing appanages/fiefs[129] among members of the royal family. The above-mentioned Dagobert was appointed sub-king in Austrasia in 623–9, before his father's death and later Dagobert in AD 629 appointed his half-brother Charibert II (629–32) king of part of Aquitaine.[130] This practice was continued by the succeeding Carolingians and Charlemagne in AD 781 would appoint his two younger sons Louis and Pepin sub-kings of Aquitaine and Italy.[131] More distant fiefs and buffer zones between the Franks and other powers such as the Avars in Hungary – Bavaria, Thuringia, Rhaetia, Provence, Alemannia and sometimes also Aquitaine – were distributed to Frankish dukes many of whom developed or already had local connections.[132] This clearly resembles what we have seen in steppe and Iranian empires, where more important fiefs close to the central core of the empire are given to royal family members and more distant fiefs given to trusted vassals selected from the nobility or local dynasts who have submitted.[133] The oath of loyalty of the vassal/subject to his lord that typifies the Merovingian political order and later feudal Europe also already had precedents in the Hunnic Empire where sub-kings and vassals had to swear loyalty to the supreme Hunnic King.[134]

The annual Frankish assemblies, where the Franks determined whether or not to wage war and also resolved legal disputes before the king and the nobles of the realm accompanied by their armed retinue,[135] also resembles closely steppe Turco-Mongol assemblies like the Kuriltai where the imperial succession, key military decisions and legal issues were discussed.[136] The practice of levying tribute on conquered or vassalized peoples (like the Lombards who paid the Frankish kings an annual tribute of 12,000 gold *solidi* until 617–18, and the Saxons who were required to pay an annual tribute of 300 cattle) and even on native inhabitants of Gaul itself,[137] rather than just taxing them in the Roman way, is also reminiscent of the practice found in Inner Asian and Iranian tributary empires examined at the beginning of the book.[138]

The dissolution of the Frankish Kingdom[139] also followed closely the precedents set by the Hunnic Empire. Over-expansion into Italy, Hungary and Spain following the usurpation of the Frankish throne by the Carolingians from the legitimate Merovingians (a more radical political upheaval than the usurpation of Attila) stretched the resources of the state beyond manageable limits and regionalization again began to raise its head.[140] This fragile situation was then made progressively worse by civil wars among Charlemagne's descendants over their inheritance, which accentuated these regional divides (the civil war among Attila's sons and cousins), and new foreign invasions from the east in the form of the Magyars and Vikings (Oghur invasions into Hunnic territory in the 460s).[141] The gradual diminution of royal power was then followed by the fall of the dynasty itself after the ephemeral reunion of the Frankish realm for the last time under Charles the Fat in AD 884 (reunion then dissolution under Dengizich and Ernak).[142]

Thus in effect the arrival of the Huns marked the beginning of intense political changes across the whole breadth of the European landmass, culminating in the establishment of state-level entities in all of central, eastern and northern Europe, where before their arrival there had been no tradition of political unity and state organization.[143] The political culture of early medieval Europe was in essence a Hunnic-derived version of the common Central Eurasian political *koine* fused together with the residues of Roman political institutions.[144]

The impact of the Huns and other Inner Asians who came with them on early medieval 'Europe' was, then, quite extraordinary. Every major Germanic state entity took its form only after coming into close contact with the Huns and other Inner Asians. The great Ibn Khaldun in his remarkable *Muqaddimah* once remarked 'The Vanquished always want to imitate the victor in his distinctive characteristic, his dress, his occupation, and all his other conditions and customs.'[145] The Germanic tribes of the

The birth of a new Europe 149

West definitely displayed the truth of this observation. We have already discussed the Franks above and also the case of the Alamanni/Suebi in an earlier chapter. The first Germanic political entity to emerge within Roman territory, that of the Visigoths,[146] was also the direct, political consequence of the Hunnic invasion of Moesia in AD 395 which provided the momentum for Visigothic 'ethnogenesis' (or rather military centralization) under Alaric, who took advantage of the large-scale Gothic movement into the southern Balkans (to escape the Hunnic invasion) to elevate himself into a leadership role and subsequently kingship.[147]

However, the Visigoths, although they fled from Hunnic political domination, imitated Hunnic–Alanic practices wholesale. A drastic shift away from infantry-based warfare to mounted warfare of the steppe type occurred[148] and a Hunnic–Sarmatian element in the Visigothic military hierarchy soon emerged in the person of Athaulf, brother-in-law of Alaric, who was intimately connected with the Huns in some way and managed to persuade a contingent of Huns to fight with him for Alaric.[149] Athaulf would succeed Alaric as king of the Visigoths and put to death a Goth/Sarmatian named Sarus[150] who had earlier massacred the Hunnic bodyguards of Stilicho.[151] Later he was himself murdered by the supporters of Sarus among the Visigoths.[152]

We have already noted above that Frankish political institutions in Gaul were probably influenced by Hunnic political culture. It is to be wondered whether the very similarly organized Visigothic realm with its notion of the sacrosanctity of the monarch (i.e. divine charisma of the ruler),[153] relatively small bureaucracy and limited taxation,[154] and a dominant, highly militarized nobility ruling the conquered masses in a quasi-feudal structure[155] that is dependent on land ownership[156] and more rigid social stratification,[157] like the Merovingian kingdom (though obviously much less so than the Franks) was imitating the Central Asian political culture of the Huns.[158] Like the Franks, the Visigoths in the early decades of their existence as a political entity had a system of appointing vice-kings in the Hunnic manner.[159] The new feudal Europe of these Germanic kings was characterized like the steppe world by the dominance of the military nobility.[160] All previously secular/civilian, Roman, aristocratic hierarchies became progressively military[161] under the new regimes in ways reminiscent of the Xiongnu and other steppe militarized societies.[162] Thus in Merovingian Gaul during the successive partitions of territory among royal heirs, Theudebert I in 533 would need the support of his *leudes*,[163] or military retainers (sworn followers), to counter the ambitions of his uncles and cousins. Gundovald in AD 585 was eliminated when he lost support and was abandoned by his military retinue.

The Lombards were also dominated by a military nobility. After the deaths of Alboin and Cleph the nobles do not elect a king for ten years until military necessity forces them to elect Authari in 584.[164] Gradually these military nobles throughout Germanic Europe developed into the more familiar medieval feudal lords with vested interests in lands granted to them by the king.[165]

The earlier Ostrogothic king Theodoric had maintained better control by ensuring that his military subordinates attended court regularly to receive the king's gifts, following thereby the practices of his Hunnic forebears and a tradition that goes back as far as the Achaemenid Persian monarchs.[166] The Ostrogoths under Theodoric would also practise a type of feudalism by appointing semi-independent lords who held sway over frontier provinces in Italy.[167] An intermediate level of leaders existed between the king and his people as in steppe confederacies. As among the Franks, Visigoths and other Germanic peoples possibly influenced by the Huns, the Ostrogoths ran a parallel military administration of Gothic counts beside local Roman administrators,[168] which in turn resembles the Xiongnu and Kushan practice, mentioned earlier in the book, of running a parallel military administration (whose members had overall authority both military and civil[169]) beside a civil administration run by bureaucrats recruited from among the sedentary, conquered population (who ran the mundane, day-to-day administration).[170] The mobility of the Ostrogothic kings, their itinerant kingship,[171] also mimics the behaviour of steppe and Iranian kings mentioned earlier.

By way of another example the Lombards, who would later become rulers of most of Italy following the collapse of the Ostrogoths, were also first organized into a viable tribal confederation with their own king (i.e. politically organized) only upon their encounter with the Bulgars (i.e. Huns).[172] The first Lombard king Agelmund was supposedly killed by the Bulgars (Huns) and the new king Lamissio then supposedly took revenge and defeated the Bulgars.[173] The episode in Paul the Deacon shows evidence of common memory of Hunnic conquest, the identification of Huns with the contemporary Bulgars among the Lombards, and a break of sorts with the Hunnic Empire presumably after Nedao. However, the story of Lombard victory and independence at a very early stage from Hunnic influence is probably a distortion of actual reality. This is borne out by the fact that the Hunnic/Alanic practice[174] of artificial, decorative, cranial deformation was practised among the Germanic elite in Bohemia (home of the Lombards) even after the Battle of Nedao in AD 454,[175] an indication perhaps that at least among the elite Hunnic influence or even physical presence was not a passing phenomenon.[176]

In fact the Lombards even after Nedao may have been influenced by the Hunnic-controlled Rugians, whose lands they later occupied after the destruction of the Rugian kingdom by Odoacer. In the *Life of Saint Severinus* (1.9.31) the Rugians are shown to have exercised considerable power in Noricum and also in surrounding areas, taxing Roman cities in Noricum and offering protection from the Heruli, Alamanni, Thuringians and other bandit tribes.[177] Even after their movement into Rugiland the Lombards were for a long time militarily inferior even to the Heruli.[178] The far more formidable Rugii could therefore have exerted some control over the neighbouring Lombards until their downfall at the hands of Odoacer. The Thuringians, the immediate northern neighbours of the Lombards, like the Goths and the Gepids practised Hunnic cranial deformation much more intensively it seems than the Lombards[179] and this may be indicative of a strong Hunnic element in their ruling upper stratum.[180] Cranial deformation is even found among the Burgundians still further west, also in all likelihood due to the impact of Hunnic domination of the Burgundians in the fifth century.[181]

The later Lombards would actually have a strong Bulgar Hunnic element and these formed a part of Alboin's army that marched into Italy.[182] Imitation of actual Hunnic political practices might be discernible in the Lombard practice of acknowledging six pre-eminent dukes among their thirty-six nobles. This may well be an imitation of the Xiongnu–Hun–Bulgar institution of the six corners mentioned earlier.[183] Quite revealingly Alboin, the Lombard king, when he defeats his rival the king of the Gepids makes a goblet out of his vanquished enemy's head.[184] This is a steppe custom that was first practised among the Inner Asian Scythians[185] and Xiongnu (Huns).[186] The skill with which Odoacer and Theodoric, the predecessors of the later Lombard kings, managed Italy and exploited existing Roman administration and bureaucracy was also likely due to the Scirian and Ostrogothic experience of Hunnic imperial rule.[187] The tribute collection system that was employed by the Ostrogoths, Franks and to a lesser extent the Lombards also resembles the tribute collection that was practised in the Hunnic Empire and conforms to the general Inner Asian model of tributary empires[188] (for instance the Sassanid Empire of Iran and the Xiongnu Empire of Turkestan, both of which were built on tribute collection from vassal states and peoples).[189]

The Huns and Alans also profoundly influenced both Germanic and Roman military organization. We see in the Vandal kingdom and also among the Ostrogoths the presence of chiliarchs (*millenarii*), reflecting the radical re-organization of armies on the basis of the already familiar steppe decimal system. Such re-organization along steppe lines also had a profound political and social effect on the two above-mentioned peoples. Instead of the old clan-based, undisciplined mob fighting in units of different sizes, which usually defined a Germanic army, we find a more tightly organized military force which in turn allowed for a greater degree of political control by the king over his subjects.[190] This social and military revolution facilitated political evolution and state formation which had until the arrival of the Huns eluded the Germanic peoples.

The success and superiority of steppe cavalry was noted early by the Romans in the context of their collisions with the Parthians. However, it was only after the military successes of the Huns and Alans that imitation of their tactics and practices became pervasive in the Roman army.[191] Vegetius would even complain about the decline in the quality of the Roman infantry due to excessive focus on the improvement of the cavalry wing of the army.[192] Heavy and light cavalry and more importantly mounted archers were introduced into the Roman military system to allow the army to implement necessary tactical changes to meet the new threat from the steppe. The Hunnic arrival also meant the excessive concentration of military resources in the east along the Danube and the Euphrates fronts, to counter the double menace of the Sassanids and the European Huns. This led to the weakening of the Empire's western borders in the fourth century and this altered strategic situation contributed to the fall of the Western Empire.[193]

The important role of the Alans, the first western steppe people to be conquered by the Huns, in the dissemination of Central Asian Hunno-Iranian culture in western Europe must also be further emphasized.[194] As mercenaries in the service of the Roman Empire the contribution of the Alans to the maintenance of imperial rule was by no mean negligible. Despite the anti-Alan bias of Jordanes mentioned earlier, the Alans appear to have been among the federated troops at least the most loyal upholders of Roman authority. Alaric was defeated repeatedly by the Alan cavalry under their general Saul who died in the service of Stilicho in the defence of Italy from the Goths.[195] Alan military prowess would later translate into actual political power in the Eastern Empire. Aspar, the son of the Alan general Ardaburius (who had distinguished himself by defeating the Persians in Arzanene in AD 421 and then again later at Nisibis[196]), would turn himself into the effective kingmaker in the East and exercise immense power. Even the great Marcian and his successor Leo were the hand-picked choices of the Alan generalissimo.[197]

It is noteworthy that the western Germans such as the Visigoths were from the very beginning of their sojourn in the Roman Empire in intimate contact with the Alans. As mentioned in earlier chapters, many Gothic leaders have

The birth of a new Europe

Alanic names.[198] Alaric's successor Athaulf would be betrayed by his Alan allies during the siege of Vasatae in AD 414, when the Alans switched sides and joined the Romans.[199] The Alan kings Respendial and later Addax were also the lords of the tribal confederation of the Alans, Vandals and Suebi.[200] It is due to Alan influence that the Vandals subsequently adopted mounted warfare in preference to their traditional focus on infantry.[201] The Alans who remained in Gaul became an important part of the landholding warrior elite of medieval Gaul and Italy.[202] In Gaul they became part of the Armoricans and allied themselves with Aegidius against the Visigoths and also Childeric whom they repulsed from the Orléanais (AD 466).[203] Childeric's son Clovis (502–3) would also be defeated by the Armoricans under Alan leadership,[204] but later with the approval of the Eastern Roman emperor Anastasius, to whom the Alans remained loyal, he managed to gain the allegiance of thousands of Alan horsemen who made up a key element of his army and played a decisive role in finally vanquishing the Visigoths.[205]

The impact of the Huns and Alans[206] on medieval European culture can be seen in various ways. One of the most visible traces of their influence can be found in the aristocratic equestrian tradition of mounted knights in medieval Europe. Heavily armed cavalry was first created among the Romans to counter the tactical problems posed by Central Asian cavalry.[207] The medieval mounted knight, synonymous with the class of nobility,[208] is thus most likely the descendant, if not direct then at the very least collateral, of the heavy armoured cataphract cavalry that originated in the Eurasian steppe.[209] Tactics such as the feigned retreat employed by William the Conqueror at Hastings and other mounted troops in western France are clearly imitations of Hunnic and Alanic steppe tactics.[210] The favourite sport of the medieval elite, hunting on horseback,[211] is also an imitation of Iranian and nomadic steppe customs.[212] In fact one of the most renowned hunting dogs of medieval Europe was called Alanus and the canine breed actually derived from the Caucasus where the Alans had their abode before their intrusion into Gaul.[213] The markers of medieval aristocratic behaviour outlined by Odo of Cluny in the case of Gerard of Aurillac were hunting, archery and falconry,[214] the typical sports of steppe nobility.[215] It has even been suggested that the medieval aristocratic Germanic practice of meat-eating (practised heavily among the Franks among others), which differed markedly from traditional Roman upper-class meals,[216] was also influenced by steppe dietary practices that focused almost exclusively on meat-eating.[217]

The Eurasian steppe had long been a culturally interconnected area. In the Sarmatian period and also the Gotho-Alanic interlude before the onset of the Huns, most noticeably in the third century AD, eastern motifs and art styles start to have a profound impact on western Eurasian steppe art. Thus the diadem of gold with decoration in pearls, garnets and amethysts, so typical of later early medieval art,[218] first makes its appearance during this period in the west. On the upper rim of this diadem are '*cervidae* and trees showing the taste and manner of all the ornaments which are characteristic of the art of the steppe'[219] further to the east. Thus the thighs of the animals depicted are hollowed into pear-shaped sockets for precious stones in a style that appears also in the silver belts and other objects worked in precious metal from Siberia and especially from the region of Lake Baikal north of Mongolia, the old eastern territory of the Huns/Xiongnu.[220] Other Sarmatian objects from the same century, such as scabbard-ornaments in the form of sledges or ringed sword-pommels, are also based on Eastern steppe prototypes.[221]

This gradual influx of artistic influences from the Eastern steppe by the fourth century AD yielded a degree of artistic homogeneity perhaps unseen before across the whole of the steppe region from Ordos and Mongolia in the east to the Gothic areas in the west[222] and it is remarkable that this homogeneity coincided with the gradual Hunnic expansion west. The eastern influences that had their beginnings before the Hunnic invasions in the fourth century AD, in the following fifth century in Europe became a flood.[223] The fifth century saw a universal art style develop in the Danubian region which mingled Hunnic, Alanic, Germanic and Roman forms and motifs.[224]

This was in essence the art of the Hunnic Empire and regardless of ethnic differentiation[225] this art was shared in common by all previous inhabitants of Attila's empire: Goths, Lombards, Thuringians, Gepids,[226] Franks,[227] Alamanni etc.,[228] an indication of the impact of Hunnic imperial rule in the west[229] which managed to impose a degree of uniformity in physical culture within its territory.[230] The art form that we call Gothic[231]/Germanic, early medieval or Danubian was in fact a later manifestation of the same art form that had been in existence in the Eurasian steppe centuries earlier among the Sarmatians[232] and the Huns (Xiongnu).[233] Thus knives, cauldrons, jewels in glassware, fibulae, clasps, perforated baldric-plates, pins with animal heads, all items that are characteristic of the art of early medieval Europe, are 'nothing if not the ancient art of the steppes' that had 'overflowed over Europe'.[234]

We discover later for instance that Aquitainian style of ornamentation found in some 134 artefacts across the whole of France (particularly in the Orléanais, Armorica and southern Gaul) mostly on belt buckles from the sixth and seventh centuries AD, depicts Central Asian motifs of Hunno-

The birth of a new Europe

Alan provenance.[235] The Hunno-Alanic (i.e. steppe, Central Asian) sword cult that symbolized political control and military prowess in a religious context also, according to one critic, could have influenced later Western traditions such as the famous story of King Arthur's magic sword Excalibur.[236] The practice of decorating jewellery and weapons with precious stones to create a polychrome (cloisonné) style,[237] so characteristic of Gothic and later Germanic art, also originates in the steppe.[238] The finest objects of this style of steppe-influenced art, not surprisingly, date to the fifth century and were produced in the lower Danubian region, the core territory of the Huns.[239] The most distinctive of the stones used in this new type of jewellery was the garnet, some of which may have originated from India via again Central Asian and Iranian (Sassanian) intermediaries.[240] The Huns and their Alan subjects/rivals thus brought with them to Western Europe not only a new political tradition, but also new imageries, values and cultural styles that made the Middle Ages distinct from the Classical civilization that had preceded it.[241]

Conclusion

The fall of the Western Roman state has captured the attention of historians and the general public for centuries. Lost in all that flurry of scholarly and media frenzy over the fall of Rome and interest in the new Germanic Europe that emerged afterwards, was the not so insignificant role of the Huns in bringing about this cataclysmic transformation. The Huns were sidelined largely due to mistaken preconceptions that defined the Eurasian steppe as a political and cultural backwater. It is hoped that through the evidence presented in this book, those misconceptions among many Classicists and Ancient Historians can finally be dispelled.

The Eurasian steppe was home to a sophisticated political culture that time and again produced great empires. It was from this complex political and cultural milieu that the Huns emerged as they expanded their empire into Europe. It has been demonstrated that the Huns while they were still in Central Asia were constantly surrounded by and eventually conquered peoples with complex political structures. The comparative analysis of Hunnic practices in Europe and other contemporary Inner Asian political systems has also yielded the conclusion that the Huns were not an exception to the political complexity of Inner Asian polities. They were absolutely not the primitive mob that they have been thought to be. Their empire was a politically advanced military state that united the disparate tribes and ethnic groups of eastern and central Europe into a complex state-level entity.

The impact of this Inner Asian empire in Europe on the Roman state has also been reassessed and it has been argued that the Huns played a far more significant role in the dissolution of the Western Roman state than has been thought possible by many scholars until recently. Critics have often pointed out that the Roman Empire neither declined nor fell.[1] This is largely true. The empire of the Romans, both its western half and eastern half, was definitely not a moribund, decadent state, ripe for destruction. The empire also did not 'fall' entirely, since its eastern half survived for another thousand years! However, it is equally impossible to deny that the western half of this mighty empire suddenly failed and completely disintegrated in the fifth century AD. It has been demonstrated that this failure of the imperial government to effectively handle the 'barbarian' problem (in vivid constrast to its successful handling of a similar crisis in the third century AD) was due largely to the military losses inflicted on the empire by the Huns. The Huns time and again prevented the empire from taking effective military measures against the barbarians by sapping the military resources of both halves of the empire, precisely at a time when they were needed most to rid North Africa of the Vandals, and by ending all vestiges of Roman military supremacy in Gaul through the destruction of the army of Aetius, the 'last Roman'.

It has also been argued that many of the leaders of post-Roman Europe were either Hunnic or mixed Hunnic in origin. The Huns certainly did not just disappear into oblivion. They left visible political and cultural traces that facilitated the transformation of Roman Europe into early medieval Europe. The eastern half of their state survived the civil wars following the death of Attila and would transform itself into various successor states in the Ukraine and the Balkans.

In fact to the eyes of Eurasian nomads such as the Huns there never was such a thing as a European continent. Europe as we know it is merely a long peninsula that stretches out of the Eurasian mainland.[2] Indeed in the fifth century AD and arguably for a long time before the great invasions of the Huns there was no Europe and no Asia for the ancient residents of the 'European' landmass, but rather a culturally distinct Mediterranean world of the Roman Empire to the south and the culturally less alien Eurasian world to the north stretching from the Rhine to Mongolia. Arguably even this distinction was a rapidly diminishing one. In any case this, rather than the abstract and unrealistic geographical distinction of Europe and Asia, was the more visible and pertinently real divide. The western fringes of this Eurasia were forcibly incorporated into the Mediterranean world by the Romans in the first centuries BC and AD. However, this artificial union was cut short by the Eurasian Huns, who by ending the Western Roman *Imperium* severed the tenuous political links between the Mediterranean world and the region that would later constitute Western Europe. By dividing the western fringe of Eurasia (the area that later became the Frankish Empire[3]) from the Mediterranean and then collapsing (i.e. failing to fill the power vacuum) the Huns essentially both allowed and forced the western rim to develop a separate identity, an artificial, 'European' one.

What indeed was this 'European' identity? The early medieval culture that ultimately gave rise to modern European nation states was brought about by a fusion of Hunno-Danubian (i.e. eastern Eurasian culture of the steppe brought to the west by the Hunnic Empire and the Alans) aristocratic culture and the surviving residues of Roman civilization in western Eurasia. The elite of the Frankish, Burgundian, Ostrogothic, Lombard and other states in the West patronized this hybrid culture that later became the dominating ethos of medieval 'Europe'. The Hunnic Empire was thus essential in the creation of this separate Europe and, ironically, by infusing the West with Eastern cultural styles and practices, allowed Europe to develop its own distinct cultural characteristics that distinguished it from its prior Roman precedents.

Where indeed does Europe end? In Austria? At the Caucasus and the Urals? In Turkey? All these boundaries are politically sensitive in the Europe of today. How far is the East and how close is the West? This research suggests that history does not validate many of these boundaries. To divide Europe and Asia is, both geographically and historically, a pointless exercise in tortuous, ideological illusions.[4] The sooner it is recognized that there is a Eurasian history and not a separate Asian and European history, the better it will be for both the study of history and the political realities of today. The cosmopolitan nature of the Hunnic and the Roman Empires, the worlds in which ethnicity or race was not a barrier to inclusion or active participation in the running of the state,[5] surprisingly provide a model that is more compatible with our modern vision of a multicultural world and pluralistic state order, a model that the modern world, including 'Europe', might perhaps benefit from imitating.

Notes

CHAPTER I: INTRODUCTION

1. Cited in Allsen (2001a), 83 ff.
2. See Findley (2005), 91. See also Adshead (1993), 76.
3. See Rossabi (2007).
4. For the difficulties involved in writing world history see Hodgson (1993), 247–66. See also Manning (2003), 313–23.
5. See also Beckwith (2009), 93.
6. See Sinor (1990a), 1–18.
7. For the history of the Toba Xianbei conquest of Northern China see Holmgren (1982).
8. Hodgson (1993), 12–28. Liu (2010), 62, argues that cultural exchange and trade across the whole of Eurasia reached maturity only after the conquest of all sedentary empires by the Huns and Xianbei in the 5th century AD.
9. Chase-Dunn and T. Hall (1997), 149.
10. See Rossabi (1989), 81 ff., for a nuanced discussion on the Central Asian caravan trade and what he sees as the less than decisive impact the discovery of new trade routes between Europe and East Asia in the fifteenth century had on this trade. He rightly emphasizes that the impact of political disruptions and religious and social changes in Eurasia itself must not be overlooked as one of the root causes for the demise of the so-called Silk Road. See also Beckwith (2009), 216 ff. Whatever the circumstances, after the sixteenth century this trade route, which had been the primary instrument of cultural dissemination and exchange in Eurasia, gradually ceased to function in its former capacity. With its demise the role of steppe empires in world history also gradually faded. Extended discussion of the Silk Road, fascinating as it is, is beyond the scope of this book.
11. Chase-Dunn and Hall (1997), 149. See also Christian (1998), 426.
12. Allsen (2001a), 14 and (2009), 135–54. See also Beckwith (2009), 183–203, and Di Cosmo, Frank and Golden (2009), 3, for assessments of the *Pax Mongolica*. For the effect that this *Pax* had on trade and exchange see Martinez (2009), 100–8. See Bentley (1993), 27, for the role of Turco-Mongols and their vast trans-regional empires that sponsored regular and systematic interactions between peoples of different cultural traditions. See also Abu-Lughod (1989), 170, and Seaman (1991), 1–16.

13. For a rare attempt at a revisionist stance see Weatherford (2004), xxiii–xxiv.
14. Ever since the days of the great Central Asian scholar Chokan Valikhanov in the nineteenth century when Eurocentrism was in full swing, the history of the steppe has received relatively scant attention from mainstream Western historians. Many of these, until the beginning of the twentieth century (!), displayed a condescending attitude towards evidence derived from writings of Eastern authors. Even today when studying events such as the invasion of the Huns from Central Asia, historians of Classical Antiquity and Medieval Europe rarely, if ever, consult in depth Central Asian sources, relying instead on highly limited and scanty Greek sources. See Sulejmenov (1989), 30.
15. An admirable starting point is Amitai-Preiss and Morgan (2000), *The Mongol Empire and its Legacy*, and the recent *Cambridge History of Inner Asia: The Chinggisid Era* (2009) by Di Cosmo, Frank and Golden. See also the assessment of Hall (1991), 34–5, of the importance of Eurasian nomads in the restructuring of the old Eurasian world order, which in turn acted as a catalyst for the emergence of what we now call the modern world. See also Christian (1998), 9.
16. See Sinor (1990b), 290.
17. The Southern Xiongnu who initiated the rule of the 'barbarians' in Northern China were part of the Chinese political landscape by this stage and resembled the federated barbarians of the contemporary Roman Empire to the west. However, their conquest of the Jin dynasty was the catalyst for all subsequent incursions into China by other related steppe peoples from beyond China's political sphere of influence.
18. See Hookham (1962), for the most detailed biography of Timur and also Manz (1999). The Manchu Empire of the seventeenth century and the formidable Ottoman Turks, the Empire of Nader Shah the Afsharid, the Turkmen Qajar state of Iran which survived into the twentieth century, were all created by Inner Asian peoples. However, by this stage Inner Asia was no longer the only dominant force in global politics, as in the centuries of Turco-Mongol hegemony under Chinggis Khan and Timur.
19. Johanson (2006), 1–14 and Golden (2006b), 21–6. Turkic, Iranian and Mongolic are all primarily references to language families, not racial categories. In other words they refer to groups (sometimes with a pronounced ethnic identity) that spoke certain languages that belong to a certain language family (Turkic, Mongolic etc.).
20. Darwin (2007), 5–6.
21. The era of Tang expansionism was actually even shorter, though the dynasty would linger on until AD 907. From its very beginnings the ruling Li clan of the Tang Empire was related by marriage to the Turks and used Turkish cavalry to unify China after the collapse of the previous, short-lived Sui Dynasty. See Lattimore (1979), 485, and Pulleyblank (2000b), 82–3. Many of the powerful border magnates along the Great Wall could speak Turkish or were Turks commanding Turkish troops in imperial service. The most famous among them An Lushan, a Turkish general in Tang service, would destroy the stability of the empire through his massively destructive rebellion in AD 755, an event which made the later Tang emperors dependent on Uighur Turkish support

for their very survival. See Mackerras (1990), 317–18. For the impact of Turk political organization on the Tang Empire see Beckwith (2009), 138. In fact the northern Zhou, which provided the foundations on which the Yang family of the Sui and the Li clan of the Tang (both imperial houses had a strong admixture of nomadic, non-Chinese blood) unified China, was itself a Xianbei (Mongolic) dynasty ruled by the Yuwen clan, who also provided the Sui dynasty with most of its top-ranking generals. The Yang clan of the Sui dynasty came to power by virtue of being related by marriage to the Yuwen emperors. Chinese power then barely lasted a century, if it was ever really Chinese. The Arabs would hold onto power for roughly 200 years before being overwhelmed by the Buyids and the Samanids (Iranians) who were themselves extinguished by the Turks (Seljuks, Karakhanids and the Ghaznavids) in the tenth and eleventh centuries AD. See Golden (1990a), 359–65.

22. Beckwith (2009), 75 ff., argues that this situation had existed even earlier during the period of Proto-Indo-European conquests in the Bronze Age and calls the Hunnic conquests and Germanic migrations the 're-central Eurasianization of Europe', pp. 109 ff. The Bronze Age is, however, well beyond the scope of this book and we cannot realistically overlook the 'Roman and Han Chinese interlude' in between the Proto-Indo-Europeans and the Huns. Nonetheless, it does provide an interesting precedent for later Central Asian dominance of much of Eurasia and given the astonishing similarities between Scytho-Sarmatians and Xiongnu-Huns, it is an area that deserves to be researched in much greater detail. See also Frank (1992), 1–52, and Hodgson (1993), 26–8.
23. A representation that has to some extent been corrected in recent scholarship on the Mongols in particular. See Allsen (2009), 141–8.
24. The destruction and butchery caused by the nomads are arguably grossly exaggerated in most of our hostile sedentary sources. See Khazanov (2001), 6. Most famously the decline of agriculture in Khwarezm in Uzbekistan and in Iraq was attributed to the destruction of irrigation networks by the Mongols, but there is ample evidence that in Khwarezm this was actually due to the salinization of the soil and in Iraq irrigation systems had been in decline since the tenth century AD, long before the Mongol invasion.
25. See Bosworth (1988) for an in-depth discussion on the destruction caused by the Macedonian conquest.
26. There is controversy over whether the Macedonians were Greek or a Balkan ethnic group. See Hammond and Griffith (1979), vol. II, 39–54.
27. See Dani and Bernard (1994), 67–72.
28. See Beckwith (2009), 202–3, 229–31; Soucek (2000), 132–8; Adshead (1993), 135–49, for the Mongol Il-Khanid and Timurid Renaissance (consult also Findley (2005), 102–3; Manz (2009), 194–6; and Dale (2009), 207–17, for the artistic and cultural brilliance of the Timurid era, especially under Husayn Bayqara and Babur). See also Allsen (2009), 148 for the centrality of the Mongols in the selection and transmission of transcontinental cultural traffic in the thirteenth and fourteenth centuries, especially, but not exclusively, in the domains of military technology (perhaps most famously gunpowder (pp. 150–1),

used by Mongol armies in western campaigns as early as the 1220s) and administrative methods.
29. Martynov (1990), 187–91.
30. Bell-Fialkoff (2000), 1. Beckwith (2009), 320 ff., in a reaction against the excessive demonization of steppe polities in 'sedentary' literature, even asserts that Central Asia is the home of modern civilization (p. 319) and downplays the brutality of central Eurasian conquests of their periphery. Although he is right to criticize the excessive exaggeration of some of our sources, it does not lead us anywhere to inaccurately minimize the power and belligerence of steppe peoples. For instance, attributing the Hunnic conquest of the Goths to Gothic aggression (p. 331) hardly makes sense and is not supported by any serious interpretation or reading of our sources. His emphasis on the weaknesses of steppe polities, which is designed to minimize their aggressive potential vis-à-vis sedentary states and thus refute some of the negative press that attributes unrelenting belligerence to the steppe, has some validity when applied to the later and more recent history of the steppe in the seventeenth to nineteenth centuries AD when Central Asia was conquered and divided by the Manchus and the Russians (p. 339). However, the impressions derived from Central Asia in decline can hardly be applied to the millennium of Central Asian dominance that came before it. Attila, Chinggis Khan and Timur fighting to avenge grievances inflicted on their people by sedentary populations? That is surely going too far and though the motive is understandable, as our analysis of the Hunnic Empire will subsequently show, the notion of relative weakness of steppe empires vis-à-vis sedentary states is pure fiction in these earlier centuries. They were the elite military powers of the day and did not shy from using their potential in the most brutal fashion conceivable, just as the Romans, Greeks and the Persians did before them.
31. There has been an extensive and ongoing debate on the controversial issue of the ethnic provenance of the Huns and their links to the Xiongnu. The Xiongnu connection will be discussed later. However, it is necessary to note here that the Huns were from very early on in their history a highly heterogeneous people (probably with a heavy mixture of Tokharians and Scytho-Sarmatians (linguistically belonging to the Iranian language family) whom they conquered before their entry into Europe). There are, however, good reasons for regarding at least their ruling, dominant tribes as one of the very first Turkic (linguistic category) groups to enter Europe. The region from which the Huns derived, the Altai region, and southern Siberia, by the late first and early second centuries AD (when the region was overrun by refugees from the Northern Xiongnu confederation fleeing Xianbei pressure) was predominantly occupied by Turkic nomads. Oghuric Turkic groups, the so-called Ding-ling (see Pulleyblank 1983, 455–6), elements of which later became the Tiele Turkic confederation that dominated much of Kazakhstan after the end of Hunnic rule over large parts of Europe in the fifth century AD, were already in close proximity to this region as early as the second century BC when they were conquered by the Xiongnu (Golden 1992, 61, 78–9), the most probable

progenitors of the Huns. The original Xiongnu in Mongolia, however, according to Pulleyblank, may have spoken a Palaeo-Siberian language, Kettic to be precise (Pulleyblank 1962, 242–3). But it is highly unlikely that the Huns spoke Kettic by the time they entered Europe. Maenchen-Helfen (1973), 23, 402–3, 438–9, 453–4, identifies reasonable Turkic etymologies in the names of tribes ruled by the Huns, in particular the Alpidzuri and Tuncarsi, and also in personal names of Hunnic rulers. More on this later.
32. As Beckwith (2009), 325, 341–2 accurately points out, the so-called 'nomadic' empires of Central Asia, including that of the Huns, had their own urban and agricultural resources and were definitely not the quintessentially parasitical predators they are often viewed as. The population of these states consisted of not only pastoralists, but urbanites and sedentary farmers. They were therefore largely self-sufficient and could produce their own metalware, clothes, food and weapons. For a good list of export items from Central Asia during the Middle Ages see p. 327. More discussion on the limited nature of nomadism in steppe empires will follow later.
33. See also Di Cosmo, Frank and Golden (2009), 4. Bentley (1993), 27 and 163, attributes the cause of the decline of Eurasian empires, their economy, agricultural and industrial production, trade and communications, to the disruptions caused by the bubonic plague. See also Christian (1998), 426–7. For a view with greater stress on economic factors see Adshead (1993), 178–9, 194–201.
34. See Fletcher (1979–80), 236–51.
35. See also Findley (2005), 86–7, for the remarkable stimulus provided by steppe empires for trans-Eurasian exchanges in trade, material goods and, most importantly, ideas. This all eventually led to the formation of a 'unified conceptualization of the world' (p. 89). For a discussion on the integration of information brought about by the Mongolian unification of Eurasia see Adshead (1993), 53, 70–7.
36. Chen (1966), 252.
37. Beckwith (2009), 111.
38. For an extensive discussion of Iranian languages see Sims-Williams (1998), 125–53, particularly p. 4, and Haig (2008), 4–5. For Germanic Languages see König and van der Auwera (1994). For Turkic Languages see Johanson and Csató (1998).
39. See Smith (1986), who argues that ethnicity is a historical phenomenon that is not exclusively confined to the Modern era.
40. Kim (2009), 7–10.
41. Barth (1969).
42. Smith (1986), 12.
43. See Jones (1997), 65, for a good discussion of the two approaches to ethnicity.

CHAPTER 2: ROME'S INNER ASIAN ENEMIES BEFORE THE HUNS

1. As a territorial concept, not ethno-linguistic.
2. Strabo (11.9.2, 515C; 6.4.2, 288C) and Justin (41.1.1) compare Parthia to Rome in military power. See also Ehrhardt (1998), 295–307.

3. Kuhrt (1998), 532. Though strongly vouched for by Olbrycht (1998), 11–43, esp. 31 ff. For the steppe culture of the early Parthians and their steppe 'Scythian' pointed hats, see Curtis (2007), 8. See also Lerner (1999), 16–18.
4. Dandamayev (1994), 35; Cook (1983), 4.
5. For the presence of a strong nomadic, pastoral element among the Persians see Hdt. 1.125; Cook (1983), 58.
6. Vogelsang (1992), 174–7, 305. See also Lubotsky (2002), 189–202, for direct Scythian influence on Old Persian via their intrusions into the Middle East. The Achaemenids themselves later exerted a strong cultural influence on Inner Asia. This can be seen in the famous Pazyryk carpet in far away western Siberia which was decorated with Achaemenid motifs. See Frye (1996), 91; Rudenko (1970), 295–304; Gryaznov (1969), 158–9. For superb photos of these carpets see Gryaznov (1969), 117–35.
7. Vogelsang (1992), 241–4, 303. The Inner Asian influence on Achaemenid military practices in particular seems to have been long-term and consistent. See Harmatta (1994a), 486. The seasonal migrations of the Achaemenid kings also appear distinctly Inner Asian and point to their nomadic, steppe origins. See Tuplin (1998), 63–114.
8. See Cook (1983), 62, 64, 260.
9. Cook (1983), 76, 152.
10. Vogelsang (1992), 244, 311–14, hence the title King of Kings borne by the Achaemenid kings. In Old Persian inscriptions we frequently encounter the term *abara* to denote the act of bearing tribute (*baji*) to the Great King (*DPe* 9–13, *DNa* 19–20, *DSe* 18), Balcer (1979), 10, and Herrenschmidt (1989), 107. In Persian-controlled Babylonia in the western half of the empire, the Persian loanword *baru* was also used to denote taxes due from bow lands (*bit qasti*), fields or gardens held in what amounted to a quasi-feudal tenure, whose owner(s) (usually soldiers (*qasti* is a reference to archers)) were responsible for the annual delivery of certain amounts of staples produced in their holdings. See Oppenheim (1985), 573–4, and Stolper (1989).
11. For a good definition of feudalism see Reynolds (1994), 2–3
12. For a discussion on feudalism as an economic system and its evolution from antiquity to the late medieval period the rather outdated work of Anderson (1974) is still sometimes useful. For a good summary of the political system of feudal vassalage and investiture of fiefs in medieval Europe see Bloch (1961), 163–73.
13. Wallace-Hadrill (1962), 7.
14. Wickham (2009), 522–3, 126–8. See also Anderson (1974), 148, and Wiet, Elisseeff, Wolff and Naudou (1975), 197–8, for descriptions of later decentralized feudalism.
15. Cribb (1991), 42.
16. See Reynolds (1994), 12, 48–74. I will for the sake of convenience use the term 'fief' as a synonym for appanage and grants of large territories by the king to his close vassals.
17. Cook (1983), 248, 254, 256, 257–8; Briant (1984), 75–6.

18. Hdt. 7.61; Cook (1983), 168. They would also possess six pre-eminent noble families, allegedly descending from the six conspirators (seven including Darius who was enthroned as King) who deposed Smerdis, Hdt. 3. 84, Dandamayev (1989), 104–5. Interestingly most, if not all, of these six nobles were representatives of the old Persian tribal nobility, i.e. their dominance of power in the Persian system had long-established precedents, probably originating from the time when the Persian tribal confederacy was still part of the political *koine* of Inner Asian steppe cultures.
19. Widengren (1956), 158.
20. Cook (1983), 213.
21. Xenophon, *Cyropaedia* 1.5.5, Widengren (1956), 165.
22. Dandamayev (1994), 41. See also Olbrycht (1998), 19. For the later political sophistication of Chorasmia in the early centuries AD before the great Hunnic invasions and the heavy Sassanian Persian cultural influence on Chorasmia and beyond, see Zeimal (1983), 257–8. For the impact of Achaemenid and Chorasmian cultures on the Massagetae and the Sarmatians see Sulimirsky (1970), 58–61. For the role of Scythian/Sacan nomads of the Aral sea region in the formation of Chorasmian civilization of Central Asia in the seventh and sixth centuries BC see Tolstov (1961), 51–2.
23. For the cultural links and similarities between the Parthians and other Central Asian nations, which were frequently controlled by steppe empires such as the Kangju and the Huns, see Wang (2007), 95. For the existence of political organization and advanced social hierarchy in the Eurasian steppe and southern Siberia (especially the Altai region and eastern Kazakhstan from which later the Huns would begin their trek west) long before the latter half of the first millennium BC, see Gryaznov (1969), 93–4, 136.
24. For the origins of Arsaces see Curtis (2007), 7. All subsequent Parthian rulers took the throne name Arsaces, p. 8. See also Drijvers (1998), 285, and Wolski (1993), 52–7.
25. Colledge (1967), 24–5. For more information on the Inner Asian origins of the Parthians see Bader, Gaibov and Koshelenko (1998), 24, and also Sarianidi (1998), 22–3.
26. Strabo (11.7.1, 508C; 11.82, 511C). Pourshariati (2008), 19. See also Blois and Vogelsang (1991), 158–62, Alonso-Núñez (1988–9), 133–4, and Wolski (1993), 37–51. For the theory that the Parthian royal house was in some way linked to the Alans or the Yuezhi who founded the Kushan Empire, see Lozinsky (1984), 127–8. This is a possibility, but the state of the current evidence leaves the theory in the realm of conjecture.
27. Colledge (1967), 28 ff., and Wolski (1993), 79 ff.
28. See Curtis (2007), 11. The Tochari were in all probability the Yuezhi or included the Yuezhi mentioned in our Chinese sources, Beckwith (2009), 380–3. A more in-depth discussion of the Yuezhi and Saka invasions and their political institutions will be postponed until the next chapter.
29. The later weakness of the Parthians in the second century AD, the century that saw the apogee of Kushan power, may well be the consequence of Kushan

pressure in the East coupled with the devastating invasions of the Inner Asian Alans from 72 AD (when the Parthians were even forced to ask Rome for aid) to the last recorded invasion during the reign of Vologases III in *c.* 135–6 AD. See Litvinsky, Shah, and Samghabadi (1994), 473, 475, Colledge (1967), 52, 166–7, and also Curtis (2007), 13.
30. For the military reforms under Mithradates II (123–88 BC) and the abandonment of Seleucid, Mediterranean type armaments in favour of Inner Asian, steppe military institutions, see Colledge (1967), 65.
31. See Olbrycht (1998), 32, and Colledge (1967), 35, for the involvement of the Sacaraucae and other Saka in the enthronement of Sinatruces and also their meddling in Parthian affairs during the reigns of Phraates IV, Artabanus II and Gotarzes II. See also Bivar (2007), 29, and van Wickevoort Crommelin (1998), 271. For the impact of Scythian or rather Saka steppe concepts and culture on the Parthians see Invernizzi (2007), 168–70.
32. See Colledge (1967), 37–43.
33. See Koshelenko and Pilipko (1994), 145.
34. Tacitus, *Ann.* 6.42.4. See Ehrhardt (1998), 299, and Bivar (2007), 27. Pourshariati (2008), 29, cites Simocatta, who lists seven nobles, not six, but this is probably an archaizing anachronism, since Simocatta is obviously thinking of the seven conspirators who helped Darius gain the throne in the Achaemenid era. See Hdt. Book 3.76. Moses Khorenatsi in his *History of the Armenians* 2.28, asserts that the Suren and Karen families in particular were related by blood to the Arsacid royal house and had the right to produce a king should the royal line become extinct. See Thomson (1978), 166.
35. Bivar (2007), 28. See also Wolski (1993), 89, and Koshelenko and Pilipko (1994), 133.
36. The origins of heavily armoured cavalry (the mounted knights of medieval legends) are probably to be found in the Central Asian steppe among possibly the Sarmatians. See Tacitus' description of cataphract Sarmatian aristocracy, *Hist.* 1.79.1–4.
37. See Wolski (1993), 103. Slaves according to Plutarch and Justin, but actually indicative of dependent population or peasants who are subject to great landowners or quasi-feudal lords, i.e. closer to medieval serfs than to the Classical model of slaves.
38. Bivar (2007), 28.
39. Plutarch, *Crassus* 24. 1. Bivar (2007), 29, Wolski (1993), 90, and Colledge (1967), 62. For the later involvement of the Suren family in Parthian politics and also in India, e.g. the career of Abdagases, see Bivar (2007), 32–4.
40. Bader *et al.* (1998), 24–5, 28–9. For a detailed treatment of the image of kingship, royal ceremonials and the ideological foundations of kingship in the Iranian world, especially under the Sassanians who succeeded the Arsacids, see Abka'i-Khavari (2000).
41. *Nat. Hist.* 6.29. Colledge (1967), 57; Lukonin (1983), 700–1, 728. See also Wolski (1993), 111, and Koshelenko and Pilipko (1994), 146.

Notes to pages 13–14

42. The Karens were allocated 'fiefs' at Nihavand in Media, the Gew family in Hyrcania, the great Mihrans on Rhagae. They were all hereditary quasi-feudal lords, different from the Achaemenid satraps who were not, at least initially, hereditary rulers. See Pourshariati (2008), 25, Lukonin (1983), 729–30, and also Colledge (1967), 61.
43. Colledge (1967), 60–1. See also Koshelenko and Pilipko (1994), 145. The election of the king by an elite council consisting of royal kinsmen and high-ranking nobles/priests among the Parthians (another feature which we find repeatedly in steppe empires, e.g. the Mongol Kuriltai), is noted by both Justin (42.4.1; 42.5.4; 42.5.6), who refers to a *Senatus Parthicus*, and Strabo 11.9.3, *synedrion*. See Lukonin (1983), 690, 707–8. Brother-to-brother succession was also possible. See Wolski (1993), 110–12, and Drijvers (1998), 287–8. See also Widengren (1976), 239, on Parthian sacred kingship.
44. Though by no means was the Parthian Empire as chaotic as late medieval Europe. The Parthian brand of quasi-feudalism, like that of other Inner Asian polities was 'centralized feudalism' of the early medieval sort. See Neusner (1963), 43, and Pourshariati (2008), 25. For the significance of 'serfdom' in Parthia see Colledge (1967), 86. For the Parthian control of vassal princedoms and kingdoms see Wiesehöfer (2007), 47.
45. See Litvinsky *et al.* (1994), 475.
46. Colledge (1967), 59.
47. Lozinski (1984), 128–9, argues that this only reflects the situation in the western half of the Parthian Empire and that there were two further divisions in the east forming a total of four (two in the east, two in the west, again we will see a mirror image of this system among the Xiongnu in the next chapter; the Xiongnu Empire also had four divisions within their two principal wings (east and west, each with a subdivision)). The geography of Moses Khorenatsi records that Sassanian Persia was divided into four parts, see Marquart (1901), 161.
48. More on this shortly.
49. For a brief analysis of references to Parthians in Armenian sources see Kettenhofen (1998), 325–53.
50. Hunting and horse-riding were such an integral part of Parthian identity that king Vonones who had been educated in Rome was dethroned for lacking interest in these steppe-derived pursuits of the Parthian nobility. See Colledge (1967), 94. Feasting, polo and epic composition among bards were the other leisure activities of this Inner Asian elite, all reminiscent no doubt of the pursuits of medieval European feudal lords. In the Sassanian period the hunt also mirrored warfare and was the symbol of battle readiness of the warriors. See Allsen (2006), 37–41, 125, 211, and Daryaee (2009), 51.
51. Strikingly enough the Xiongnu in the east would, like the Parthians, also have their own four great nobles (kings) who each held authority over one fourth of the empire, see de Crespigny (1984), 176. The Sassanian Empire seems to have had a similar system of dividing the state into four large military and administrative districts, governed by the so-called rulers of the sides (north, south, east and west), see Lukonin (1983), 731–2. However, the practice of dividing the

state into four divisions is first attested rather late in the Sassanian Empire during the reign of Khusrow I. See Pourshariati (2008), 95.
52. Colledge (1967), 64.
53. Rubin (2000), 638.
54. Moses Khorenatsi 2.71, tells us that the Suren family were jealous of the Arsacids and willingly collaborated with the Sassanids, Thomson (1978), 218.
55. Pourshariati (2008), 37. See also McDonough (2011), 298–9.
56. Pourshariati (2008), 3.
57. McDonough (2011), 295–6. The now outdated works of Toumanoff (1963), 39, Altheim and Stiehl (1954), 131–74, and Widengren (1956), 79–81, 89–95, 114, are still sometimes useful for insights on vassalage, 'fief' allocation, heredity, investiture and homage in Sassanian Iran. Iranian vassal–lord relations involved a contract and oath of loyalty from the vassal to his lord. This contract could be made redundant by the rebellion of the vassals which would justify confiscation of 'fiefs' that had been distributed.
58. Rubin (2000), 653.
59. Pourshariati (2008), 63.
60. Pourshariati (2008), 8.
61. Daryaee (2009), 46.
62. Rubin (2000), 653, usually senior members of the royal dynasty.
63. Rubin (2000), 653.
64. McDonough (2011), 300.
65. Daryaee (2009), 10.
66. Daryaee (2009), 53.
67. Abka'i-Khavari (2000), 39, 81–2. Similar entertainment was to be found even earlier at the court of the Achaemenids, Cook (1983), 210.
68. See Altheim (1959), vol. IV, 65–6. Burns (1984), 51, suggests that the Huns were influenced by Sassanid ceremonial practices which contributed to the formation of Hunnic concepts of monarchy and symbols of power that were then transmitted to the Germanic, Gothic successors of the Huns, who in turn mingled these ideas with Roman practices. Altheim (1948), 21–2, argues that descriptions of Hunnic buildings in Priscus and later archaeological remains of Bulgar palaces show evidence of Parthian and Sassanian influence. This is debatable. However, the cultural impact of the Iranian world on the Huns and other Oghuric Turks before they entered Europe seems to have been not insubstantial. See Altheim (1959), vol. I, 7. Many Huns and later Hunnic Bulgars would also bear Iranian names. For instance the name of the founder of Danubian Bulgaria was Asparouk, which is old Iranian in origin (Altheim (1959), vol. I, 10).
69. Allsen (2006), 37–41, 125, 211. See also Tafazzoli and Khromov (1996), 82, and Abka'i-Khavari (2000), 82–90.
70. The linguistic category of peoples and polities that use Iranian languages.
71. For the possible Yuezhi influence on the Huns see Wendelken (2000), 192. For trade routes and commerce that may have facilitated the spread of ideas and especially material culture from Persia to the Inner Asian heartland of the Huns

(i.e. Sogdian merchants and the Silk Routes) see Litvinsky *et al.* (1994), 484. For detailed information on Sogdian merchants see La Vaissière (2002). See also Olbrycht (1998), 29, for the intensive use of the northern trade route from Turfan, via Dayuan (Ferghana), to Kangju and Yancai (Alans), which became particularly active after the first century BC. There was also a southern route that went from Yarkand via Bactria to Parthia. For the intensity of Kushan–Sassanian cultural and political interactions, especially during the Kushano-Sassanian phase (following the conquest of the Kushans by the Sassanians) in the third and early fourth centuries AD, see Tanabe (1998), 93–100. For direct Sassanian contacts with the Huns before the Hunnic invasion of Europe see Bivar (1998), 103–8.

72. The region of northeastern Kazakhstan from which the Huns originated was exposed to Persian influence as early as Achaemenid times as the discoveries of Achaemenid inspired motifs on carpets in the magnificent burial remains of Pazyryk in Eastern Kazakhstan and the Altai region show. See Rudenko (1970), 295–304. See also Rubinson (1992), 69–71, who highlights early contacts between this region and China. The region was by no means a cultural backwater. See also Aalto (1971) and von Gabain (1979), 86, for discussion on the Iranian influence on the early Turkic speaking peoples in Central Asia. Brown (1971), 160–1, accurately highlights the role of Central Asia in disseminating Iranian culture to areas further east. In fact, as Brown points out, Persia was above all a 'Central Asian power'. See Rice (1965a), 107–14, 121, for Sassanian and Parthian artistic influence on Central Asia, particularly Sogdia and Chorasmia, regions conquered by the Huns before their expansion into Europe.

73. Altheim (1959), vol. IV, 52–3, suggests that the Hunnic taxation system in Europe may have been influenced by Partho-Sassanian precedents.

74. Curta (2006), 78–9. For similarities between this grave complex and contemporary elite Avar burials in Hungary see Smilenko (1965).

75. As noted in the introduction 'Germanic' denotes mainly the linguistic category of Germanic speaking peoples.

76. Brown (1971), 20.

CHAPTER 3: THE HUNS IN CENTRAL ASIA

1. Heather (1995a) of course argues that the 'Hunnic revolution' was the indirect strategic cause for the fall of the West, but even he attributes only a subsidiary role to the Huns in the process and views Hunnic expansion solely from the perspective of the Goths and other Germanic tribes. In the minds of most scholars the Huns were in no way part of the process of the transformation of the Western world, simply the annoying nuisance that set the process in motion from a distance. I will argue henceforth that the Hunnic revolution featured not the Germans as the main actors, but the Huns themselves.

2. Ammianus Marcellinus 31.2.3; 31.2.9. Not surprisingly all archaeological discoveries from Hunnic tombs have yielded arrowheads made of iron, not bone.

See Maenchen-Helfen (1973), 13; Matthews (1989), 338. The use of bone-tipped arrows occasionally as cheap substitutes for iron-tipped arrows is certainly not out of the question. However, Ammianus exaggerates their usage to create the overall impression of primitive barbarism. Although it is not explicitly stated, Ammianus deliberately creates the false impression that the Huns lack basic metal tools due to their 'technological backwardness'. In fact earlier Roman writers compliment the excellent quality of the arms produced by Central Asian 'nomads'. Quintus Curtius Rufus (4.9.3) makes reference to coats of mail (of course made of iron) and Arrian (3.13.4) was impressed by Central Asian cataphract horsemen carefully covered with coats of mail and armed with various iron weaponry.

3. Ammianus Marcellinus 31.2.7. The translation is from the Loeb Classical Library edition by J. C. Rolfe.
4. Thompson (1948), 41–3. The Massagetae who inhabited the Kazakh steppe and the Sarmatians (among whom the Alans are often included) who inhabited the Pontic steppe before the Huns, used metal armour including coats of iron mail and helmets. In fact iron goods were common throughout the entire steppe region by the fourth century BC, Christian (1998), 146, 188. To envisage the Huns even getting out of Central Asia without advanced iron weapons is absurd.
5. Maenchen-Helfen (1973), 6–20. See also Alemany (2000), 32–8, Kürsat-Ahlers (1994), 42, and Kelly (2009), 22, 26.
6. Kradin (2002).
7. Kradin (2002), 368–88. See also his 2011 article, in particular p. 82, where he reiterates his stated position and calls the Xiongnu a centralized imperial confederation, a stateless empire. See also p. 94. A much looser definition of the state provided by Krader (1978), 93–108, who argues convincingly that all steppe empires were state-level polities, is more sensible. However, in order to avoid any confusion or accusations of inaccurate generalization, I will adhere to Kradin's definition.
8. Di Cosmo (2011), 44–5.
9. Kradin (2011), 94–5, number of functionaries were limited he argues.
10. For discussion on what constitutes an 'early state' see Claessen and Skalnik (1978b), 22–3, and also Scheidel (2011), 114. The majority of Xiongnu experts – Pritsak (1954c), Dorzhsüren (1961), Taskin (1973), Davydova (1975), Khazanov (1984), Sükhbaatar (1980), Kürsat-Ahlers (1994), Kychanov (1997), Di Cosmo (2002, 2011) – are in agreement that a form of early statehood for the Xiongnu polity is beyond any doubt.
11. Di Cosmo (2011), 44–5. On this Kradin is also in agreement (2011).
12. Kradin (2011), 80, defines the Hunnic Empire in Europe as a quasi-imperial nomadic statehood formation that was smaller than an empire. It will be argued later that the Hunnic state was not a quasi-imperial entity, but a full-fledged empire.
13. Kelly (2009), 28 and 47, recognizes the possibility that the Huns may have been better organized and economically more advanced than Ammianus suggests,

but he does not go far enough in his analysis of Central Asian history and thus characterizes the Huns as a highly mobile, loose (i.e. politically primitive) confederation of clans. He characterizes even the later Hunnic Empire under Attila as a 'protection racket on a grand scale' and sees an administrative void in the Hunnic realm.
14. For an in-depth discussion on the name and location of the various Scythian peoples (Saka) in both Europe and Asia see Szemerényi (1980), 4–46.
15. Hartog (1988), 202.
16. Hartog (1988), 19.
17. A Sogdian source, which we will discuss in detail shortly, from the fourth century AD suggests that the Xiongnu (modern Chinese reading of the glyphs representing their name, which in its EMC reading was in all probability the same as the name Hun, see note below) were actually called Huns. Their connection with the European Huns has always been a highly contentious issue, but there are compelling reasons for assuming that this identification is accurate. See first Torday (1997), 172.
18. Golden (2009b), 83.
19. See Melyukova (1990), 101–2, and Torday (1997), 88. See also Golden (1982), 50 ff., for a later example of state formation, social hierarchy and administration of the Turkish Khaganate.
20. The empire in that year was divided by civil war into two warring factions, the Northern Xiongnu and the Southern Xiongnu.
21. Barfield (1981), 59. As Tapper (1991), 525, in his analysis of nomads in Safavid and Qajar Iran points out, nomadism by no means implies lack of fixed boundaries or less organizational capacity. If anything the existence of well-defined territories and regular movements under an authoritative leader was essential for the survival of the nomadic tribal community in a very fragile ecological environment. For an in-depth study of the agro-pastoral conditions under which historical steppe polities emerged, the capacity of these states to control large territories, and the importance and durability of the political tradition that was initiated by the Xiongnu, see Honeychurch and Amartuvshin (2006a), 255–78, in particular p. 262.
22. De Crespigny (1984), 178; Pritsak (1954a), 239.
23. The supreme ruler and the equivalent of the Turco-Mongol Khagan. For discussion see Kürsat-Ahlers (1994), 268–70.
24. Watson (1961), vol. II, 163–4.
25. Pulleyblank (2000a), 64, also the origin of the Turkic title Tarkhan and the Mongol Daruga.
26. The designation 'horns' or 'angles' appears only later in the *Hou Hanshu* (covering the history of the later Han dynasty (AD 25–220)) and not the *Shiji* passage quoted above. The designation and possibly also the six further titles called the six horns (angles) that do not appear in the *Shiji*, but, according to Mori, were only gradually created after 97 BC (the date of the completion of the *Xiongnu liezhuan* in the *Shiji*), may only have been firmly established in the Xiongnu political system by the time of the Southern Xiongnu. See Mori (1973),

22–3. However, Mori's view, as he himself points out (p. 34), has not been proven beyond doubt and has been criticized. Mori acknowledges G. Uchida's valid critique of his views and concedes that there are grounds for uncertainty since the slight differences in the titles given in the *Hou Hanshu* and the earlier *Shiji* and *Hanshu* could simply be an indication that the Han Chinese of the Hou Han period observed Xiongnu government practices more correctly than their predecessors in the earlier Qian Han period. Thus the possible differences in titles may or may not be indicative of reforms in the governmental organization of the Xiongnu over time. See also Kradin (2011), 89.

27. Christian (1998), 194.
28. De Crespigny (1984), 176–7. The concept of four pre-eminent sub-kings is also found among the later Volga Bulgars (Hunnic descendents in Europe), Pritsak (1954b), 379, and also among the Gokturks who succeed the Huns and Rouran as masters of the steppe, Pritsak (1954c), 186.
29. See note 26 above. See also Kradin (2011), 92.
30. *Hou Hanshu* 79. 2944. According to Mori (1973), 30–1, the office was later passed from the hands of the Chanyu's family to those of the Huyan clan who were related to the Chanyu through marriage.
31. de Crespigny (1984), 177. The hierarchy and political ranks of aristocratic and royal clans, as mentioned above, may have changed somewhat among the Southern Xiongnu whose political organization after the Xiongnu civil war that split the empire in two informed much of the details we find in the *Hou Hanshu*. In other words there may have been regional developments or changes over time that altered the political fabric of Southern Xiongnu society and made it slightly different from the former Xiongnu political system. However, it is clear that even these later developments, if they were of any significance, derived from the political traditions of the original Xiongnu Empire, see Brosseder and Miller (2011a), 20.
32. Pritsak's (1954c) extended discussion on the twenty-four lords is criticized quite mercilessly by Daffinà (1982), and should be read with caution. See also Kürsat-Ahlers (1994), 276.
33. See Ishjamts (1994), 158, and Kollautz and Miyakawa (1970), 44, though it is also clear that some former rulers of conquered peoples were allowed to remain kings/chiefs as well under appropriate Xiongnu overlordship and over-kings. For the government of the more distant Western regions the Xiongnu created the office of the 'Commandant in charge of Slaves' (Yü 1990, 127), which under the aegis of the Xiongnu Ri-zhu king had the power to tax states such as Karashar and Kalmagan and to conscript corvée labour (pp. 127–8). Also certain Chinese defectors were appointed kings, e.g. Wei Lu as king of the Ding Ling and Lu Wan of the Donghu. However, the upper echelons of power and positions of political, administrative and military importance close to the Shanyu and key strategic areas, were almost exclusively reserved for members of the imperial clan and a few select Xiongnu aristocratic families. See also Golden (2009b), 110. For the later Mongol system of provincial administration and state organization in Central Asia, which closely resembles the Xiongnu model, see Biran (2009), 61.

34. Ishjamts (1994), 158. Kradin (2011), 93, argues that originally there was a tripartite administrative system within the Xiongnu Empire that gradually by the time of the civil war that split the Xiongnu into two rival groups had evolved into a dual system.
35. Barfield (1981), 48–9.
36. See Markley (forthcoming), 22, for a discussion on Xiongnu quasi-'feudalism'. See also Kollautz and Miyakawa (1970), 44. For the notion of the tribe functioning as a territorial unit in its allocated place within the confederacy of a steppe empire see Cribb (1991), 54–5.
37. Barfield (1981), 49. For archaeological evidence of a highly sophisticated social hierarchy among the Xiongnu see Honeychurch and Amartuvshin (2006a), 264–5. Kürsat-Ahlers (1994), 289–90, argues for a Xiongnu bureaucracy in the form of a military organization.
38. Christian (1998), 194.
39. See Pulleyblank (2000a), 53, for the possible Scythian impact on early Xiongnu culture.
40. Khazanov (1984), 178. The Xiongnu would develop three aristocratic clans linked via family/marriage ties to the Shanyu: the Huyan, Lan and Xubu (the imperial clan was the Xulianti/Luanti clan which descended from the early Shanyus Touman and Modun, Kollautz and Miyakawa (1970), 44), which formed the ruling, upper stratum of Xiongnu society. See also Pulleyblank (2000a), 68. These ruling clans, along with the royal family, led separate subdivisions of nomads. See also Kürsat-Ahlers (1996), 138, and Golden (1992), 64–6, for discussion on the nature of the Xiongnu state.
41. Ivantchik (1999a), 145.
42. Ivantchik (1999a), 145–7.
43. Ivantchik (1999a), 160.
44. See Ivantchik (1999a), 164–5 where he gives a detailed account of the legend of the three sons of Zoroaster. The eldest son became the priest, the second the farmer and the third the warrior. This corresponds perfectly with the etymologies suggested for the names of the three sons of Targitaus, as in Indo-Iranian cosmology the sky (soleil) is identified with the warrior caste (Colaxais, the youngest), the earth (montagne) with the priestly caste (Lipoxais, the eldest), and the underworld (l'eau) with the productors/farmers (Arpoxais, the second son), p. 158. See also Corcella (1993), 232; Abetekov and Yusupov (1994), 28.
45. Khazanov (1978), 425–40; Kürsat-Ahlers (1996), 139.
46. Bichler (2000), 97. For an in-depth analysis of the capacity of steppe pastoralists to rapidly mobilize and organize complex military and political structures that can influence vast territories see Christian (1998), 85–9.
47. Hartog (1988), 200. For the depiction of royal power in Scythian art see Bader, Gaibov and Koshelenko (1998), 25.
48. Yü (1990), 123.
49. Yü (1990), 124.
50. See Harmatta (1970), 14.

51. Bichler (2000), 90. See Abetekov and Yusupov (1994), 25–6 for the analysis of archaeological evidence which supports the existence of an aristocratic elite and political hierarchy among the Scythians. See also Kürsat-Ahlers (1994), 179–93, 198–227.
52. Christian (1998), 129–31.
53. There is some evidence of Persian influence in the Saka steppe of Central Asia. Persian goods do appear occasionally in areas such as Eastern Kazakhstan in the Altai region. See Christian (1998), 167.
54. The putative Chinese influence on the Xiongnu is contested by Di Cosmo (2011), 47–8, who regards resemblances and similarities in administrative and cultural practices to be largely the result of a shared set of associations that may go back to a more ancient cultural stratum.
55. Kollautz and Miyakawa (1970), 45. For Xiongnu elite governance and feudalism see McGovern (1939), 118; Yü (1990), 135–6.
56. For details see Pritsak (1954b), 377–9; (1955b), 256–9. Amazingly this north–south orientation is also evident in the placement of human remains in a Hunnic grave discovered in the Crimean steppe, see de Vingo (2000), 156.
57. Pulleyblank (2000a), 70. This will also be of significance for the Huns in Europe as we shall see later in the book.
58. See Melyukova (1990), 110–17, for a short discussion on the Sarmatians. For a more detailed treatment see Batty (2007), 225–36.
59. Wendelken (2000), 202. See also Batty (2007), 368–72.
60. Though in their heyday Strabo would report that king Spadinus of the Aorsi could field an army of 200,000 men (Strabo 11.5.8). An exaggeration no doubt.
61. *Geography* 7.3.17. See also Ptolemy 5.9.16.
62. Harmatta (1970), 12, 14–15. We will see a mirror image of this later in the Hunnic Empire where the core of the empire is also surrounded by a protective ring of vassal tribes.
63. Lucian, *Toxaris* 51; Moses Khorenatsi, *History of the Armenians* 2.50, 58; see Thomson (1978), 191. See also Alemany (2000), 287–9.
64. P'austos Buzand, *History of the Armenians* 3. 6–7.
65. Yatsenko (2003), 93.
66. Tacitus *Ann.* 12.17–18.
67. Yatsenko (2003), 93. For further references to Alan rulers and the special status of queens in Alan society see Dio Chrysostom, *Or.* 36.3.5; Polyaenus, *Strat.* 8.56.
68. Yatsenko (2003), 94.
69. Ptolemy 3.15.3, see Alemany (2000), 8.
70. Scheidel (2009), 18.
71. Maenchen-Helfen (1944–5); (1961); (1973), 367, and Sinor (1997), 5.
72. See Henning (1948), 601–45. Altheim (1959), 37, argues that the Huns were a branch of the Xianbei and that the Chinese references to them as Xiongnu in the fourth century AD are anachronistic. This is highly unlikely.
73. Sinor (1990c), 179.
74. Maenchen-Helfen (1973), 441.

75. Bailey (1954), 12–21.
76. La Vaissière (2005), 7.
77. La Vaissière (2005), 8.
78. La Vaissière (2005), 9.
79. La Vaissière (2005), 11–15.
80. Pulleyblank (2000a), 60–1, agrees on the basis of phonetic evidence that there is no alternative but to accept that the European Huns had the same name as the Xiongnu. So does de Crespigny (1984), 174. See also Wright (1997) and Hill (2009), 73–4, for further information on phonetic and other evidence in favour of Xiongnu–Hun identification.
81. Hambis (1958), 262; Maenchen-Helfen (1973), 330–1; La Vaissière (2005), 17; Bona (1991), 140; Érdy (1995), 5–94. See Czeglédy (1983), 91, for a more sceptical approach.
82. La Vaissière (2005), 17.
83. See La Vaissière (2007), 129. For evidence of the existence of the same cult also among the White Huns in Central Asia, which could be another indicator of the common origins of the European and Central Asian Huns, see the same reference.
84. Extremely difficult to reject in fact given the abundant archaeological evidence which clearly suggests cultural and religious continuities between the Xiongnu and the Huns, see Érdy (1995), 7.
85. Their expansion seems to have been as follows: (1) Altai region to northeastern Kazakhstan and Southern Siberia (a very gradual absorption of Oghuric Turkic speaking Dingling/Oghurs and perhaps Ugrian speakers) by the late third century AD; (2) conquest of the Kangju and Wusun in Uzbekistan and the Ili Basin respectively, by the mid fourth century AD; (3) conquest of the Alans (Volga Region and the Kuban Steppe) and Bactria (from the Sassanian Kushanshahs), 460–70s AD. The Oghurs left behind in western Kazakhstan after the Hunnic departure into Europe seem to have become the Saraghurs, Urogs (a Byzantine scribal error for Ugor/Ogur/Uigur says Hamilton (1962), 34) and Onoghurs (Priscus fr. 40) who would later cause trouble for the Huns in the 460s. The original Hunnic territory stretching from the Altai region to southwestern Siberia seems to have been occupied by the mid fifth century AD at the latest by the Sabirs who were perhaps under pressure from the Rouran further to the east. This forced the remaining Huns (the Weak Huns: Chuban Huns) in the area to relocate to the Ili basin (former Wusun lands) and physically separated the European Huns from the Asian Huns. Then a further incursion by the Avars in the mid fifth century AD triggered the flight of the Sabirs and the various Oghurs into Europe.
86. Defeated Xiongnu groups migrated west into Dzungaria and Kazakhstan in successive waves from the first century AD onwards following the collapse of Xiongnu power in Mongolia. The first such migration actually took place even earlier in the first century BC. *Han-shu pu-chu* B, 1a, 10–2a, 1, records that supporters of a pretender to the Xiongnu throne fled in 57–6 BC to the northwest to an area northeast of Kangju, see Daffinà (1982), 32 (see also

Czeglédy (1983), 55–6; Golden (2009a), 83, for further discussion on early Xiongnu movements into Kazakhstan and Dzungaria in the late first century BC). The Wusun (in the Zhetysu region) were also subjected to repeated Xiongnu attacks during this early migration. In AD 91 the Shanyu of the Northern Xiongnu fled to the Ili valley and the Altai region where later the Huns and also the so-called Weak Huns (Yueban/Chuban) would originate. See Yü (1990), 147. See also Golden (1992), 62–3, and Hambis (1958), 251.

87. Pulleyblank (1962); (2000a), 62–5; Vovin (2000). This is questioned by Benjamin (2007), 49, who sees the Xiongnu as either Proto-Turks or Proto-Mongols, who spoke a language related to the clearly Turkic Dingling further west.

88. This Yeniseian element seems to have retained a dominant role in the Southern Xiongnu, who were geographically closer to the heartland of the Chinese Empire in Shaanxi (Northern China), right into the fourth century AD. That is if Vovin's (2000), 92, identification of the language of the Southern Xiongnu (in particular the Jie tribe which constituted one of the core tribes of the confederation), preserved in the form of a Xiongnu poem found in the *Jin Shu* (95.2486), with Yeniseian, is correct. However, although the Jie tribe is certainly part of the Xiongnu nation that invaded the Chinese Empire, it is unclear whether they were part of the original Xiongnu governing elite. So whether their language reflects the old Xiongnu language of the elite is uncertain. A different argument is provided by Pritsak (1976b), 480–2, that the name of the tribe *Jie* itself is Hunno-Bulgar in origin, not Yeniseian. I tend to agree with Pulleyblank and Vovin to the extent that the original Xiongnu ruling elite do not seem to have spoken either an Iranian or a Turkic language, but it is equally uncertain whether they spoke a Yeniseian language and there is no firm consensus on the matter. The tribe's name, Jie, also suggests that it originated in the area around the city of Tashkent in the far west of the Xiongnu empire (Pritsak (1976b), 479).

89. Proper names and etymologies are, however, often inaccurate guides to the genetic affiliation of a people or a historical personality. If they were, anyone bearing a Hebrew name in Western Europe would become Jewish, thereby vastly inflating the number of Jews in the world, or the Hungarians with a national name deriving from the Turkic Onoghurs (see Szádeczky-Kardoss (1990), 224) would become Turks, not Magyars.

90. For the presence of the Turkic Dingling within the Northern Xiongnu federation in the West see Yü (1990), 148, Golden (2009a), 87, and Duan (1988), 111–13. For the possibility that the Hu-chieh, west of the Wusun in central Kazakhstan, conquered by Modun in the second century BC, were from the reconstruction of Early Middle Chinese pronunciation and transliteration Oghur/Oghuz (i.e. Turks), see Torday (1997), 220–1.

91. According to the *Weilue* = *Sanguozhi* 30.863–4, some Turkic tribes (Dingling) were definitely present in the Kazakh steppe, north of the Kangju and west of the Wusun by the third century AD. See also Golden (2006–7), 27; (2009a), 87. For their presence among the Southern Xiongnu see Pulleyblank (1990a), 21. The Dingling from the fourth century onwards would be known as the Gaoche

(highcarts)/Chile or Tiele (see Czeglédy (1983), 62–4, and Duan (1988), 16–18, 197), enemies of the nascent Rouran Empire in Mongolia. Their political disunity would make them vulnerable to first Xiongnu/Hun and then Rouran conquest. See Pulleyblank (1990b), 22–5. Their foundation legend, as it is preserved in the *Wei Shu* 103.2307, or the myth regarding their elite, tells of a union between the daughter of the Xiongnu/Hun Shanyu and a wolf that produced the Gaoche, indicative of the conquest or influence that the Huns had over the Dingling in previous centuries. See de Groot (1910), 266, and Sinor (1990b), 295. The *Wei Shu* also tells us that the Xiongnu spoke the same language as the Gaoche/Dingling (Turkish), which is problematic since the original Xiongnu probably spoke Kettic. It may well be a reference to the complete Turkification of contemporary Xiongnu/Huns, e.g. the Yueban Xiongnu (*Wei Shu* 102.2268) who by the fifth century, when information later noted down in the *Wei Shu* was being gathered, had the same customs and language as the Gaoche. By the fifth century the Gaoche too would centralize their political system to produce a supreme ruler who bore the title *ulug bägräg* (Great Lord/Prince), see Pulleyblank (1990a), 25.
92. Golden (2006b), 31.
93. Érdy (1995), 53.
94. Hambis (1958), 258; Brosseder and Miller (2011a), 30; Di Cosmo (2011), 40–2.
95. See Brosseder and Miller (2011a), 26–7, 30–1, and de Crespigny (1984), 174.
96. See also Christian (1998), 227. He suggests not only ethnic, but strong cultural influences from China, Iran and Central Asia on the Huns while they were still in Kazakhstan.
97. Heather (2006), 330. Maenchen-Helfen (1973), 386–9, also thinks that these names are the Germanic or Germanicized names of Turkic Huns. However, there is no consensus on the matter among scholars. Golden (1992), 90, citing Pritsak (1956), 404–19, argues that the name Attila derives from the Turkic word for the river Volga which was Atil (referred to as Attilan in Menander Protector fr. 10.4, Blockley (1985), 124). Shippey (1982), 66–7, has also argued that the assertion that the name Attila is Gothic is a product of nineteenth-century Germanic romantic, philological revisionism.
98. Bona (1991), 35, argues that the name Bleda is Turkic, Bildä/Blidä meaning 'wise ruler', and bears only superficial resemblance to the Gothic Blaedila. The name of Attila is also likely to be a title deriving from the Turkic name for the river Volga (Atil), meaning literally 'great river' (Pritsak (1956), 415), implying 'universal, oceanic ruler' (p. 419). See also Alemany (2000), 183.
99. Maenchen-Helfen (1973), 389.
100. For an in-depth discussion of the Hunnic rather than Germanic origin of this name in particular see Schramm (1960), 139–40.
101. The last two names are likely to be titles of offices held by these two men, not real names. For all these etymologies see Bona (1991), 33.
102. Maenchen-Helfen (1973), 392–415. See also Bona (1991), 33–5; Pritsak (1956), 414; La Vaissière (2007), 129. Most known Hunnic tribal names are also Turkic, Maenchen-Helfen (1973), 427–41, e.g. Ultincur, Akatir etc. The *-cur*

suffix in many of these names is a well-known Turkic title and as Beckwith (1987), 209, points out the To-lu or Tardus tribes (Hunnic in origin) of the western Turkish On Oq were each headed by a Cur (noble). Zieme (2006), 115, adds the fact that the title 'cur' belongs to a pre-Turkic Tocharian stratum of the Turkic language, again highlighting the heterogeneity of Central Asian peoples and even languages. See also Aalto (1971), 35.
103. See also Sinor (1990c), 202.
104. For Oghuric Turkic see Czeglédy (1983), 113, and Golden (2006/7), 28.
105. More on this later.
106. For the frequent bilingualism among steppe peoples see Golden (2006–7), 19, and Moravcsik and Jenkins (1967), 172.
107. Priscus, fr. 13.3, Blockley, (1983), 289. Iranian, though not mentioned by Priscus, was also certainly spoken in the empire, and was possibly as influential as Hunnic or Gothic, especially in the east. The name of the Hunnic leader who in 465/6 raided Dacia Ripensis and Mediterranea, Hormidas, is Iranian, Maenchen-Helfen (1973), 390.
108. Zeimal (1996), 132.
109. See Pritsak (1976c), 22, for the polyglot, multilingual nature of all nomadic empires. See also Hdt. 4.24, where Herodotus discusses the use of seven different languages and a corresponding number of interpreters in Scythia for mutual comprehension among the various ethnic groups.
110. Markley (forthcoming), 16.
111. There were tribes within the Xiongnu federation even in the Far East that possessed Caucasian facial features, e.g. the Jie soldiers in the Southern Xiongnu confederation who had high noses and full beards. See Maenchen-Helfen (1973), 372, n. 94.
112. Kürsat-Ahlers (1994), 305. For a brief summary of the history of the Xianbei state and its absorption of nearly 100,000 Xiongnu families see Ishjamts (1994), 155–6. The name Xianbei in its EMC form Sirbi/Serbi is also probably connected with the name Sabir (Pritsak 1976a, 22, 28–9) which we shall see later.
113. Biswas (1973), 9; Golden (1992), 63.
114. Czeglédy (1983), 64–5.
115. The Yueban or Chuban Huns would conclude a military alliance with the northern Wei (AD 448) against the Rouran, indicating that they were in the mid fifth century still a military force to be reckoned with in western Turkestan. See Hambis (1977), 17–18, and Czeglédy (1983), 65. The *Wei Shu* 102.2268, indicates that the forebears of the Yueban were a horde of the northern Shanyu of the Xiongnu. When the northern Xiongnu were defeated by the Han imperial armies they fled westward, but the weak elements among them were left in the area north of Qiuci. Afterwards this weak group of Xiongnu is said to have moved further and subjected the land of the Wusun to form the state of Yueban. The stronger group were the Huns who erupted into Central Asia and Europe. See Yu (2004), 240, 286–7. Yu argues that the Yueban moved into Europe sometime after AD 448, under pressure from the Rouran (287). This, however,

does not seem likely since the Yueban Huns were separated from Europe by the dominion of the Sabirs.
116. See de Crespigny (1984), 329–37, for the career of Tian Shi-huai.
117. Pulleyblank (2000a), 59–60; Holmgren (1982), 7–9. However, dynasties with Xiongnu origins would still rule in the Tarim basin. The famous Chü-ch'ü dynasty of Kocho would survive until their destruction at the hands of the Rouran in AD 460. See Sinor (1990b), 294.
118. For possible Kushan expansion into the Tarim basin during the second century AD and heavy cultural influence on the area as a whole see Hitch (1988), 190–1.
119. For an overview of the Yuezhi conquest of Daxia (Bactria) see Yu (2004), 12–14.
120. Enoki, Koshelenko and Haidary (1994), 172, argue that Yuezhi in EMC should be read *zguja* i.e. Scythians. However, in private correspondences with the author, Professor Sam Lieu pointed out that this reading, though on the surface highly attractive, is unlikely. I agree with his opinion.
121. *Shiji* 123.3162, tells us that the Xiongnu Shanyu had the skull of the defeated Yuezhi king turned into a drinking cup; Benjamin (2007), 72–3; Narain (1990), 155; Hill (2009), 312–18.
122. See Liu (2001), 261–92.
123. For discussion on this identification see Benjamin (2007), 97–100, and Hill (2009), 537. For a good discussion on the Saka in Eastern Turkestan see Debaine-Francfort (1990), 81–95.
124. *Han Shu* 61 4B. Pulleyblank (1970), 158–60, thinks that these descriptions of Yuezhi collisions with the Sai and also the Wusun are 'arbitrary embellishments'. However, this is probably excessive, given the fact that the Saka invasions are also corroborated by our Greek sources. See also Rapin (2007), 50–1.
125. Strabo 11.8.4.
126. Benjamin (2007), 181–4.
127. *Han Shu* 61 5A.
128. Bivar (1983a), 192, identifies the Yuezhi of the Chinese sources with the Tochari of our Greek sources. This seems to be confirmed by the fact that Pompeius Trogus *Prologue* 41 talks about the conquest of Bactria and Sogdia (i.e. the region conquered by the Yuezhi in our Chinese sources) by the Asiani with whom the Tochari are closely associated. See however Benjamin (2007), 185–7, for an alternative reading of Trogus and the argument that the Asiani were none other than the Wusun who raided Bactria (*Han Shu* 61 5A) and should not be identified with the Tochari (Yuezhi), who came later.
129. Pompeius Trogus *Prologue* 42 states 'Reges Tocharorum Asiani'.
130. The Scythians who killed Phraates were likely to have been the Saka who had overrun Bactria. Those that killed Artabanus were possibly the Yuezhi or included the Yuezhi. See Czeglédy (1983), 28, and Van Wickevoort Crommelin (1998), 270.
131. For the later collisions between the Parthians and the 'Scythians', see Strabo (11.9.2). See also Enoki *et al.* (1994), 181–2.

180	*Notes to pages 32–3*

132. Hill (2009), 29. See also Frye (1996), 134.
133. For the Turkic appropriation of Iranian and Tocharian titles see Golden (2006b), 21. Iranian, Sogdian and Tocharian titles such as *Sad* (Middle Iranian/Sogdian/Saka for 'prince'), *Beg* (Iranian and Sogdian for 'Lord'), *Isbara* (Sanskrit and Tocharian for 'prince' or 'lord') were used by the Gokturks who also employed a large number of Sogdians in their imperial bureaucracy (p. 19). In fact the multicultural nature of all steppe empires allowed such heterogeneity to flourish. Of the fifty or so names of Turkish rulers in Chinese sources only a few have genuinely Turkic names. See Sinor (1990b), 290, and Beckwith (2009), 411. The Huns also undoubtedly included a strong Iranian element, given the appearance of Iranian names and cultural practices in their ruling elite, as we shall see later.
134. Pulleyblank (1995), 425; (1966), 28; Hill (2009), 587–90; Benjamin (1998), 37–8.
135. On the five *yabgus* see Grenet (2006).
136. Bivar (1983a), 192–3, argues that the Kushans were none other than the Asiani mentioned earlier who became kings of the Tochari.
137. See Grenet (2006), 339–40, Puri (1994a), 248–9, and Hill (2009), 29, 329–32.
138. See Narain (1990), 165, and Pugachenkova, Dar, Sharma, Joyenda, and Siddiqi (1994), 372. See also Wink (2001), 221, and Cribb (2007), 366, who notes the link between imperial Kushan coinage and nomad/Inner Asian identity.
139. Christian (1998), 211.
140. Yu (2004), 165–6.
141. See Sims-Williams (2008), 56–7.
142. Hill (2009), 31.
143. Puri (1994a), 263. See also Tapper (1991), 507, for an excellent discussion on the proclivity of tribal groups in Iran in later contexts to develop into powerful militaristic confederacies and restructure themselves into a community with what he calls a 'feudalistic' class structure. Conditions in the steppe were obviously more conducive to the formation of military leagues and confederacies that gave rise time and again to steppe empires. The Kushan case is however, closer to the later Iranian models of state formation in that, like the later Afshars, Zands and Qajars, there is a dominant steppe/pastoral aristocracy (military tribal confederation) that imposes a form of centralized quasi-feudal order upon the conquered sedentary population. See also Frye (1996), 141–4.
144. A very similar system of government is also found among the contemporary Sakas (also from Inner Asia) and the Pahlavas (Indo-Parthians) in India. Among the Saka rulers of Mathura in western India a senior king was assisted in his duties by a junior king in a highly developed system of joint rule and this is made manifest in the concept of *dvairajya* (double kingship) among them. The Saka and Parthian rulers of India also inherited the system of governing major districts through satraps from the Achaemenids, the *ksatrapas* (satraps) and *mahaksatrapas*. See Puri (1994b), 199–200.
145. Narain (1990), 167.
146. Czeglédy (1983), 91; Sinor (1990c), 202–3; Kollautz and Miyakawa (1970), 210–12; Narain (1990), 172–3.

Notes to page 33

147. For information on Kushan expanstion into the Tarim Basin in the second century AD see Hitch (1988) and Bivar (1983a), 208–9.
148. See Litvinsky *et al.* (1994), 479–80. See also Hill (2009), xxi, and Bivar (1983a), 203, 209.
149. Narain (1990), 169.
150. For the debate see Hill (2009), 311–12. See also Benjamin (1998), 33, Wood (2002), 64, and Abdullaev (2007), 75, who identifies the Asiani as the rulers of the Tochari mentioned in Justin's *Prologue* to Pompeius Trogus and then links them to the Kushans.
151. Pritsak (1976c), 6.
152. Pulleyblank (1995), 425, argues for a different location for Dayuan, but most scholars now accept the identification of Ferghana with Dayuan, see Benjamin (2007), 137.
153. The Kangju also later controlled much of Sogdia, Benjamin (2007), 137; Hill (2009), 373. See also Daffinà (1982), 323–4, for a discussion on the location of the Kangju.
154. Czeglédy (1983), 32. Trogus (*Prol.* 41, 7). See also Alemany (2000), 17. Hill (2009), 149, 152, suggests the possibility of linking the Asi with the Wusun, due to phonetic similarity in their names. The identification is also made by Tolstov (1961), 83. Sims-Williams (2002a), 240, argues that the Kushans were the royal family of the Asi.
155. Yu (2004), 1–6, and Czeglédy (1983), 46; the Kangju would also intermittently control areas north of the Oxus, Yu (2004), 6.
156. Hill (2009), 173.
157. See Hill (2009), 33, 175, 381. Alemany (2000), 400–2, is more cautious about the identification. The fact that the Kangju subdued or merged with the Alans seems, however, to be substantiated by the Old Turkic runic inscriptions of Kül Tigin (AD 732), where we find the name Kängäräs (Kängär (Kangju) + As (Alans)), Pritsak (1976c), 7–8.
158. Pulleyblank (1995), 427; Czeglédy (1983), 50; Zadneprovskiy (1994), 463, 466–7; Alemany (2000), 398; Kyzlasov (1996), 316. Professor La Vaissière in private correspondence with the author confirmed that it is entirely plausible that the Kangju exercised a degree of control over the Alans. To what extent is not entirely clear. On the possibility of Kangju domination over neighbouring Khwarezm he also expressed a carefully guarded affirmative opinion. However, he also pointed out that there is as yet insufficient evidence to prove any Kangju domination over Khwarezm.
159. Benjamin (2007), 155–6; Hill (2009), 182.
160. Grenet, Podushkin and Sims-Williams (2007), 1026; Benjamin (2007), 150–1; Hill (2009), 175; Hulsewé and Loewe (1979), 130–1; Daffinà (1982), 324.
161. Rapin (2007), 53, calls the Kangju a broadly 'nomad' empire with a system of fortified cities and capitals.
162. Czeglédy (1983), 52; Sims-Williams (2002a), 240. Rapin (2007), 59–62, argues for the deep Central Asian origins of the Alans and notes that Chinese mirrors were used by the Alans. He also identifies the Asi and Asiani as Alans who

formed a part of the Kangju Empire or a subdivision of it in southwestern Kazakhstan. See also Grenet and La Vassière (2005), 79–81. If Bivar's (1983a), 192–3, identification of the Asiani/Asi with the Kushans is also correct then we have the same or a related ruling clan or tribe ruling the Kushan Empire, Kangju Empire and the Alans. See also Vernadsky (1951), 345.

163. Hill (2009), 173; Hulsewé and Loewe (1979), 47.
164. Signs of Kangju–Xiongnu contacts can be seen in the discovery of a Xiongnu (Hunnic) style silver belt plaque at Kultobe in Kazakhstan, a site identified as belonging to the Kangju. See Grenet *et al.* (2007), 1019.
165. For a discussion on the location of the Wusun see Daffinà (1982), 326. For a general introduction on the Wusun see Yu (2004), 25–32. See also Gardiner-Garden (1986).
166. *Han Shu* 96B 1B; Benjamin (2007), 115. As a consequence part of the population ruled by the Wusun kings were Yuezhi (p. 120).
167. For the often strained relationship between the Xiongnu Huns and the Wusun, originally vassals of the Xiongnu, see Benjamin (2007), 114–19.
168. This type of pastoral economy and social stratification has been termed correctly by Cribb (1991), 42, as pastoral 'feudalism', where a small, powerful elite own vast numbers of animals that they farm out to 'tenant' households. Somewhat reminiscent of the structure of medieval European feudal society.
169. There also seems to have been at various stages a dual kingship of the Greater Kunmo and Lesser Kunmo, a typical feature of Inner Asian kingship. See Yu (2004), 40–1, 47–8, and Giele (2011), 60.
170. Zadneprovskiy (1994), 460. See also Yu (2004), 33.
171. Zadneprovskiy (1994), 461. The presence of the Yueban/Chuban kingdom which is without a doubt Xiongnu in origin in eastern Kazakhstan in the fifth century is further proof that the Huns were indeed Xiongnu in origin. See also Kyzlasov (1996), 320, and McGovern (1939), 364–5. See Sinor (1990b), 294, for further information on the Chuban alliance with the Toba Wei against the Rouran between AD 444 and 450.
172. *c.* AD 350 suggests Czeglédy (1983), 62. Around AD 300 at the hands of the Kidarite Huns suggests Zeimal (1996), 120. Grenet *et al.* (2007), 1030, suggest that the fragmentation of the Kangju state may have begun as early as the late second or early third century AD.
173. More on this shortly.
174. Zadneprovskiy (1994), 463, 470. The Kangju were at various times vassals of the Yuezhi to the south and the Xiongnu to the east. See Zeimal (1983), 243, and Hill (2009), 177.
175. Czeglédy (1983), 99.
176. Grenet *et al.* (2007), 1030.
177. Érdy (1995), 22.
178. Golzio (1984), 22–3.
179. See Holmgren (1982), 65–9.
180. More on this later.

181. Pulleyblank (1983), 453, has argued that in EMC Hua was pronounced *Var* and he further suggests that these Var are identical with the Wuhuan, a branch of the Donghu confederation (including also the Xianbei (*Serbi* or *Sirvi* in EMC) conquered by the Xiongnu. Wuhuan in EMC, he suggests, was *Agwan*, which due to the absence of the sound *r* in EMC was the contemporary rendering of Agwar or Avar. See also Czeglédy (1983), 95. However Professor La Vaissière in private correspondence with the author has suggested an alternative reading which would make Hua EMC for Ghor, a region of Afghanistan inhabited by the Hephtalites, rather than Var. As of today there is no consensus on the transliteration of Hua in EMC.
182. See Sinor (1990b), 298.
183. See La Vaissière (2007), 125. Sinor (1990b), 298, argues that the Hephtalites were the ruling dynasty of the Hua. The Hua were originally under Rouran overlordship, but later seem to have broken free from Rouran control according to the *Liangshu* cited above.
184. See Theophylact Simocatta, *Historiae* 7.7–8, ed. C. de Boor, 256.23–262.17, full text and translation in German in Haussig (1953), 281–90. Theophylact identifies the two leading tribes of the Oghurs (either the Hephtalite-controlled Turkic tribes in Kazakhstan or members of the Tiele (Chile) tribal confederacy in the same region) as Var and Khunni (i.e. Huns, see Haussig (1953), 347).
185. Czeglédy (1983), 34–5. The Rouran, probably in origin the Wuhuan (Avars?) from further east in Inner Mongolia, were found in the vicinity of Dunhuang, in close proximity to Turpan when they began their extraordinary rise under Shelun Khagan in the late fourth century, Christian (1998), 237. There is yet no evidence whatsoever that the Rouran expanded further west before Shelun's rise in the late fourth century AD, i.e. they appear too late on the scene to have been responsible for putting pressure on the Huns in the mid fourth century AD. The Hua or the Hephtalites, as noted above, became their vassals presumably some time in the late fourth century AD, but the Hua-Hephtalites are taken by La Vaissière (2007), 121, to be Oghuric Turkic Huns who were part of the Hunnic migration wave, not the Avars or Vars. The first Avar movement into what is now modern Kazakhstan (the original territory of the European Huns in the fourth century AD) should perhaps be dated to the time of the Toba Wei alliance with the Chuban Huns in the fifth century, which will be discussed further shortly.
186. Schlütz and Lehmkuhl (2007), 114.
187. Érdy (1995), 45. The presence of a group identified as Khunnoi by Ptolemy (3.5.10) already in the second century AD in the vicinity of the Sarmatian Bastarnae and Roxolani (situated in the Nogai steppe), also suggests strongly that the Hunnic expansion west commenced much earlier than their famous fourth-century eruption into the Pontic steppe recorded by Ammianus. The absorption of the Dingling or Oghuric Turkic tribes in Kazakhstan is likely to have been a long drawn-out process.
188. See La Vaissière (2007), 121. See also p. 124 for the text and translation of the crucial passages in the *Tongdian*, 5259, which provide the definite date for the

southward migration of the Huns from the Altai. The passages are based on the much earlier *Wei Shu*.
189. Could just be a reference to western Huns, see Kononov (1977), 62, 75, for the old Turkic runic term *kidirti* meaning west.
190. Whether the Kidarite dynasty was originally Hunnic or Iranian is disputed. Tremblay (2001), 188, thinks that they and the later Hephtalites, who overthrew them, are Iranians. Grenet (2002), 203–24, thinks likewise. However, it does seem more likely that they were part of the initial Hunnic wave into eastern Iran who became Iranian in culture after their conquest and claimed to be the heirs to the Kushan legacy (see Zeimal (1996), 120, 127, Frye (1996), 175, and La Vaissière (2007), 123). Priscus, fr. 33 and fr. 41, Blockley (1983), 336, 346, and 348, calls them Huns and mentions the Kidarite king Khunkas. Tremblay notes that the etymology for this name has to be *X(y)on-qan*, i.e. Hun Khan (Khan of the Huns), (2001), 188; Grenet (2002), 209. See also Biswas (1973), 15, Bivar (1983a), 212, and Frye (1975b), 38, who agree that they are Huns, though Frye is of the opinion that the Hephtalites had a powerful Iranian element in their ruling elite, which is likely to be true. Altheim (1959), 32–3, suggests probably correctly that the name Kidarite is an old Turkish designation for west (i.e. the western wing of the Hunnic polity, thus meaning exactly the same thing as White Huns (white being the colour designation for west in the steppe)). The Kidarites were pushed out of Sogdia in the fifth century and then destroyed in the Gandhara region by the Hephtalites towards the end of the fifth century, sometime between AD 477 (the date of their last embassy to the Toba Wei) and AD 520 (when Gandhara is definitely under Hephtalite control according to a Chinese pilgrim). See Enoki (1959), 27.
191. Bivar (1983a), 212. An Armenian source, P'austos Buzand, tells us that the Hon (Huns) under the Kidarite dynasty conquered the region before AD 367. See also Czeglédy (1983), 71, 84.
192. *Wei Shu* 102.2270. See Pritsak (1954a), 239. See also Érdy (1995), 21, for archaeological evidence (Hunnic–Xiongnu type cauldron found near the Amu Darya valley in the Khiva area and two Hunnic funerary cauldrons made of clay in the delta of the Syr Darya) that points to the Xiongnu identity of the White Huns. Related artefacts have also been found in the areas controlled by the European Huns which all point to the same conclusion that both the European and Central Asian Huns were Xiongnu in origin.
193. Czeglédy (1983), 73–4.
194. See Bivar (1983a), 211, and also Pritsak (1954a), 243.
195. After AD 437 at the earliest suggests Sinor (1990b), 299.
196. Chinese rendition of their name in the *Liangzhigongtu*. The *Liangshu* 54 calls them Yandaiyilituo/Hephtalite.
197. The Hunnic origin or self-identification of the Hephtalite dynasty is reflected in the form OIONO or HIONO, which appears in their coinage. See Golden (1992), 81. The *Liangshu* as noted above calls them or their country Hua (Var or Ghor). The most reliable analysis of the Hephtalite dynasty and its origins is that of La Vaissière (2007), 119–124. La Vaissière refutes much of the

erroneous views on the Hephtalites held by Enoki (1959); (1963), 12–32. See also Kollautz and Miyakawa (1970), 95. The Iranian origin of the Hephtalites vouched for by many scholars (most prominently Enoki), has now been largely discredited due to the discovery that the so-called Hephtalite language with Iranian affinities, used to justify the Iranian theory, was not introduced by the Hephtalites themselves, but was the indigenous language of the region conquered by the Hephtalites. See Sims-Williams (2002a), 234.

198. The Hephtalites are one of the two peoples sometimes identified with the Eurasian Avars (Vars) mentioned in our Byzantine sources. Theophylact 7.7 (Whitby and Whitby 1986, 189) would name the Var (Avars?) and Huns as Lords of the Oghurs. If the Hua-Hephtalites were Var (uncertain), this could possibly be a reference to the Hephtalite/Var conquest of the Oghurs (meaning 'tribes' in Oghuric Turkic) in what is now Kazakhstan, who had earlier been dominated by the Huns, hence the reference to the overlordship of the Vars and Huns over the Oghurs. Menander Protector refers to the Varkunites (Var-Huns, Menander fr. 19.1, Blockley (1985), 174), as does Pseudo-Moses of Chorene who calls them *Walxon* (again Var and Hun), Szádeczky-Kardoss (1990), 207. See also Czeglédy (1983), 92 ff. The Rouran Khaganate, however, which we will meet shortly, could also have been the Vars/Avars mentioned by our Byzantine sources. See Golden (2000), 284. In any case the Vars and the Huns seem to have been closely related, if not ethnically then at least culturally. We can note for instance the fact that one of the last Khagans of the Rouran, Anagui (AD 520–52) had the same name as a sixth-century Utigur Hun prince who lived around the same time, Anagaios (Menander Protector fr. 43, Alemany (2000), 187), Kollautz and Miyakawa (1970), 57.

199. Enoki (1959), 24, probably correctly connects them to the Hun-na-sha (king of the Huns) state/dynasty, who, according to Chinese sources, controlled Sogdia in the late fourth and early fifth centuries AD. See also Frye (1975b), 38 and Bivar (1983a), 211 on the Chionites.

200. Bivar (1983a), 211; Czeglédy (1983), 79.

201. Tremblay (2001), 188, thinks that the name is Iranian. It is also similar to the name of the later Bulgar Khan Krum. Haussig (2000), 273.

202. Ammianus Marcellinus 16.9.3–4; 19.1.7.

203. Altheim (1959), vol. 4, 28.

204. For details see Altheim (1959), vol. 2, 258–9.

205. Procopius 1. 4.35. See also Kollautz and Miyakawa (1970), 102.

206. The change from the Kidarites to the Hephtalites was a political upheaval among the White Hunnic migrants already in western Central Asia, not another invasion wave arriving from Inner Asia, see La Vaissière (2007), 123–4.

207. Kidarite expansion south into Gandhara and India occurred probably prior to AD 410, Zeimal (1996), 122. By the middle of the fifth century they were invading the territories of the Indian Gupta Empire and despite the triumphant rhetoric of victory found in Gupta records, the Kidarite Huns wrested control of the Punjab away from the Guptas (p. 124). Similar empty rhetoric

of non-existent victories will also be encountered later on in the Romans' records of their interactions with the European Huns.
208. Kollautz and Miyakawa (1970), 102, and Christian (1998), 220.
209. Bivar (1983a), 214; Litvinsky (1996b), 139–40.
210. Procopius 1.3.1–22; 1.4.1–14. See also Frye (1984), 148, and Rubin (2000), 642. Agathias 4.27.3–4, Frendo (1975), 130, provides much the same information and emphasizes that the Hephtalites are a Hunnic people.
211. Frye (1984), 149.
212. Procopius 1.6.10; Theophanes, AM 5968, Mango and Scott (1997), 189–91.
213. Procopius 1.7.1–3.
214. See La Vaissière (2007), 125, and also discussion on the extent of the Hephtalite state in Biswas (1973), 25.
215. Kollautz and Miyakawa (1970), 98. See also Miller (1959), 11–12.
216. Litvinsky (1996b), 142; Chakrabarti, K. (1996), 188; Wiet *et al.* (1975), 35–6.
217. Marquart (1901); Biswas (1973), 26; Pulleyblank (2000b), 93.
218. See Czeglédy (1983), 77. Considered dubious by some.
219. Procopius 1.3.2–7.
220. Procopius 1.3.4. There is endless, fruitless debate on whether the Hephtalites were mainly Turco-Mongol (Mongoloid) or Iranian (Caucasoid) in ethnic composition. Marquart (1901) and Grousset (1939) think they were Mongols. McGovern (1939) and La Vaissière (2007) argue for the Turks, which is likely to be correct, and Enoki (1959) for an Iranian origin. Humbach (1966–7), 30 and (1969), 33–52, esp. 34–6, argues that they were a combination of Alans and Huns. See Alemany (2000), 345–6 for further details. Alemany himself is cautious. As mentioned earlier they claimed to be Huns themselves. The confusion results largely from the multiple and conflicting origin theories provided by our Chinese sources (*Wei Shu* 102.2278–9, for instance, suggests both an Iranian origin via the Yuezhi and a Turkish alternative via Gaoche). Even if we were to just dismiss the reference to the Yuezhi as an anachronism, the confusion in the Chinese sources is in all likelihood actually indicative of the real ethnic heterogeneity of the Hephtalite state and even its elite. All the steppe empires of Eurasia were in fact made up of numerous ethnic groups. It is likely that the Hephtalite Empire included all three linguistic groups with perhaps a Turkic military elite. Hephtalite personal names, however, as Tremblay (2001) argues, for the most part seem to be Iranian, indicating a high degree of cultural and probably ethnic fusion. The same heterogeneity is of course a characteristic feature of the Xiongnu and also our European Huns.
221. Pulleyblank (1983), 452–3, also speculates that the Var (Hua) tribes, which along with the Huns may have constituted the ruling core of the Hephtalite state (Golden (1992), 80; Czeglédy (1983) 117–20), were connected to the Wuhuan confederacy of Inner Mongolia. For similarities in headdress and hairstyles between the Wuhuan and the Hephtalites, see Pulleyblank (2000b), 92. If his observations and transliterations are true this would make the Hephtalites at least in part Mongol speakers. Bivar (1983a), 213, on the other hand argues for an aristocracy that spoke Turkish, pointing out that the last

Hephtalite ruler to be recorded in history, a certain Nezak who ruled in the region of Badghis (northeast of Herat), bore the Turkic title of Tarkhan, Bivar (1983a), 215 (but Tarkhan was originally a Xiongnu (possibly non-Turkic) title, Golden (2006–7), 30; Grenet (2002), 214). The fact that the Hephtalites referred to themselves as Huns argues against an Iranian, sedentary origin in Badakhstan. However, the Iranization of the Hephtalites and the presence of an Iranian element in their confederacy from very early on are certainly possible. See also Bona (1991), 30, who argues that most European Huns were actually Caucasoid and that less than 20–25 per cent were Mongoloid.

222. Pulleyblank (2000b), 92. See Theophanes 446.21, Moravcsik (1958), vol. II, 158–9. Dani, Litvinsky, and Zamir Safi (1996), 169, identify the Hara (Kara) Huns with the red Huns (Kermichiones). Golden (1992), 81, and Sinor (1990b), 300–1, also agree that the designation white and black are common to nomadic confederations. It is, as mentioned above, indicative of the territorial divisions of the steppe polity and has nothing to do with skin complexion. Procopius was relying on hearsay like most Classical authors and his information on the Hephtalites 'expresses an antiquarian, somewhat Herodotean spirit' that is not always reliable, Matthews (1989), 62.

223. Pritsak (1954b), 382; (1955b), 259.

224. Olympiodorus fr. 19 (80, 173). See also Moravcsik (1958), vol. 2, 341.

225. See Holmgren (1982), 14–18, for a good, critical discussion on the *Wei Shu*.

226. The *Wei Shu* 103.2290, tells us that towards the beginning of the fifth century to the northwest of the Rouran there were in the vicinity of the Altai the remaining descendents of the Xiongnu. In 102.2278–9, as mentioned above, it gives details about the Yeda (i.e. Hephtalites, who are described as being either of the race of the Yuezhi or a branch of the Gaoche (Dingling Turks)) migration from the Altai mountains to the southwest into Central Asia. The Hephtalites became the ruling dynasty of the White Huns.

227. Hunnic archaeological remains have been found in this region from the first century AD onwards. See Pritsak (1954a), 243. Pritsak also argues that the core territory of these western Xiongnu/Huns before their great push further west into Iran and Europe in the fourth century was the Talas river and the area around the Issyk-kul. He also argues that a Hunnic Kurgan dating to the first or second century AD was discovered in the Volga region, seemingly confirming the presence of some Huns this far west already in the second century AD. More on this question in Chapter 4. Whether or not the Huns had really advanced this far west in the second century AD is still uncertain, but the Hunnic domination of the Zhetysu region (the territory usually assigned to the Wusun) before the fourth century vouched for by Pritsak needs some further consideration. The *Weilue* (*Sanguozhi* 30.863–4) seems to allocate this region in the third century AD to the Wusun, and the area to the west of this area and north of the Kangju to the Dingling. The Wusun and the Kangju are said to have neither expanded nor shrunk since Han times. Daffinà (1982), 327, notes that according to the *Wei Shu* 102, 9b, 5–6 = *Bei Shi* 97, 14b, 7–8, the remnants of the Wusun were forced to relocate to the Pamirs by AD 437/8. See also

Zadneprovskiy (1994), 461. By then the Zhetysu region was firmly in the hands of the Weak Huns (Yueban/Chuban). This would seem to suggest that the Huns only managed to conquer the Wusun and also the Kangju some time in the mid fourth century shortly before their expansion into Alan and Kushan/Sassanian territories to the west and south. Earlier Hunnic presence in neighbouring Dzungaria and continued presence in the region is confirmed by the discovery of a Hunnic cauldron (dated to the second century AD) in that area, see Érdy (1995), 45–6. The bulk of the Hunnic nation however seems to have been situated in the Altai region and certain elements also in areas further west corresponding to modern northern/northeastern Kazakhstan, Irtysh and Middle Ob region in the third century AD, Érdy (1995), 45, so bordering the Alans and Kangju to the west and southwest and the Wusun to the south.

228. La Vaissière (2005), 21.
229. For discussion see Hirth (1901), 91 (now certainly outdated); Shiratori (1923), 100–1; Enoki (1955), 43–62; Wright (1997), 96; Pulleyblank (2000b), 93.
230. See Pulleyblank (2000b), 91–2; Maenchen-Helfen (1944–5), 225–31; Miller (1959), 12.
231. Pulleyblank (2000b), 93–4.
232. Pulleyblank (2000b), 94. Pseudo-Styliten also identifies the European Huns as the same people as the western Huns who invaded Persia (Hephtalites), which suggests at the very least a close affinity between the two groups and most likely the common origins of both from the former Hunnic empire in Central Asia, Altheim (1959), 39.
233. Kollautz and Miyakawa (1970), 98.
234. Frye (1996), 176, and Grenet (2002), 210.
235. Czeglédy (1983), 78.
236. Grenet (2002), 212. The title *tegin* is likely to be Mongolic (i.e. Wuhuan/Xianbei) in origin, which would make perfect sense if we considered the Var element in the Hephtalite ruling elite to be Wuhuan. See Sims-Williams (2002a), 234, his discussion on Pulleyblank's early observations.
237. Dani *et al.* (1996), 172–3; Chakrabarti (1996), 189. Possible Kushan (also Inner Asian in origin) precedents for this quasi-feudal structure that the Huns probably built on cannot be denied (p. 194).
238. See Kyzlasov (1996), 321, for the career of this remarkable figure.
239. Duan (1988), 118–20, the Xiongnu survived in Mongolia as the Bayeqi until the early fifth century when they were fully incorporated into the Rouran Khaganate. See also Kyzlasov (1996), 322.
240. Golden (1992), 77. See also Pulleyblank (2000b), 84.
241. Pulleyblank (2000b), 79–82.
242. McGovern (1939), 407; Enoki (1959), 1; Biswas (1973), 34; Golden (1992), 79–80.
243. Kradin (2005), 154. This dualism would surface again and again in states ruled by steppe peoples. For the political division and organization of the Gokturk Khaganate into eastern and western halves in the sixth century and its maintenance until the eighth century, after the collapse of the Rouran in

the sixth, see Golden (1992), 127 ff., and Sinor (1990b), 304–5. The Turkish empires of the Karakhanids of Central Asia in the ninth to twelfth centuries (Golden (1992), 125, and Soucek (2000), 84) and the contemporaneous Seljuk Sultanate in the Middle East before its sedentarization under Malik Shah, would also practise dualism and clan rule (Golden 1992, 219), as would the Pecheneg tribes of the western steppe in the ninth to twelfth centuries AD in the same region inhabited previously by the Huns (p. 266). The Pechenegs, according to Constantine Porphyrogenitus, consisted of eight tribes/*themata* (provinces), four tribes situated on each side of the Dnieper river. Three of the eight tribes called the Kangar (Chabouxingyla, Iabdiertim and Kouartzitzour) ranked higher than the rest and the Iabdiertim reigned supreme. The eight tribes were in turn subdivided into forty districts. Each tribe would be associated with a colour (usually that of a horse) and their rulers would bear different titles indicating rank. Much the same as the Huns and the Turks before them (p. 266). See also Curta (2006), 182–3.
244. Kradin (2005), 155.
245. Exactly the same structure is found also in the Gokturk Khaganate that replaced the Rouran Khaganate in the mid sixth century AD and also among the later Khazars who controlled southern Russia and the Ukraine from the seventh to the tenth centuries AD as successors of the Western Turks, see Findley (2005), 43, 50. The Rouran and Gokturks also taxed tributary sedentary populations and the same system is also found among the western Huns.
246. See the anecdotes concerning Modun's punishment of the slightest infringements among his followers in *Shiji* 110.2888.
247. See Kradin (2005), 162, and also Kollautz and Miyakawa (1970), 63 and 89.
248. Kollautz and Miyakawa (1970), 89. Imperial governors in the succeeding Gokturk Ashina dynasty that replaced the Rouran also consisted entirely of members of the ruling dynasty. These governors were allocated 'fiefs' in the familiar appanage system which we find in the preceding Xiongnu and Rouran Empires. See Findley (2005), 44–5
249. Kradin (2005), 162.
250. A similar system of succession is also noted among the later Turkic Pechenegs in the Pontic steppe. According to Constantine Porphyrogenitus, the Pecheneg kings had no right to determine the succession which usually resulted in collateral succession within the same royal clan. No one, however, could succeed to the throne from outside the royal family. See Khazanov (1984), 179, and Golden (1992), 11. The Mongol Kuriltai (a diet of royals, nobles and worthies) would later in the thirteenth century elect a new Khan in a similar way to the Pechenegs, but with greater authority being given to the reigning Khagan depending on his prestige in a manner identical to earlier Rouran practice. For the Mongol law of succession see Bacon (1958), 56–7.
251. The Gokturks who replaced the Rouran as masters of their former empire would also adopt exactly the same policy towards their subjects and appointed members of the ruling Ashina clan as rulers or governors of important tribes, e.g. the Basmils. See Golden (1992), 142–3, 146, and Tekin (1968), Bilga Kagan

Inscription, p. 275 for Basmils and p. 278 for governors. See also Kürsat-Ahlers (1994), 352–3, who notes that the Turks imposed Ashina (royal clan) members as rulers on Karluks, Basmils, On Ok, Khazars and the Pechenegs (in their case a son-in-law, reminiscent of Aradaric, related by marriage to Attila, and vassal king of the Gepids in the Hunnic Empire, as we shall see later). The Gokturk Empire which stretched from the Black Sea to the borders of Korea, possibly at one point even as far as the Pacific, created a Pax Turcica that allowed for the free trade of goods between East and West, a forerunner to the grander empire of the Mongols in the thirteenth century. The Uighurs who supplanted the Gokturks also imposed governors on conquered tribes, the Basmils and Qarluks, Golden (2006–7), 33.

252. Kradin (2003), 80, points out correctly that the political structure of the nomadic steppe empire and the militarization of the entire population, which was its distinctive feature, could frequently lead to insurrection and desertion among disaffected tribes who enjoyed a degree of internal autonomy under the hegemony of the ruling tribe. Proximity to an agrarian, sedentary civilization which could finance such revolts or desertions and accommodate runaway fugitives from the steppe empire could exacerbate tensions within it. In the earlier Xiongnu Empire there were also cases of desertions of tribes who fled west to escape Xiongnu rule, e.g. the Yuezhi who fled into Bactria (*Han Shu* 96A: 14b–15a) and the Wusun into Kazakhstan (*Shiji* 123:9a–10a). Political dissidents also fled to Han China like the Hun-yeh king who defected with his entire tribe in 121 BC (*Shiji* 123: 9b–10a). See Barfield (1981), 49–50. It is also in such a context that we should interpret the saga of Radagaisus and also probably the Alans of AD 405–6 who departed the Danubian plains for Roman territory, away from Hunnic domination.

253. Kwanten (1979), 19–20.

254. The overriding importance of military success among steppe nomads as the instrument of legitimization is clearly brought to light in the steppe notion of charisma deriving from heavenly ordained good fortune – Iranian *farnah* and Turkic *kut*. See Frye (1989), 135–40, and Khazanov (2003), 43, for more details. This notion of charisma (i.e. the right to rule) deriving from good fortune (military success) was intimately linked to the ideology of divine kingship and the theory of the mandate of heaven. Ruling clans like the Xiongnu ruling house, the Turkic Ashina clan and the Mongol Chinggisids (Di Cosmo, Frank and Golden (2009), 1) all claimed the divine mandate to rule the earth bestowed by heaven on their chosen clan. The Ashina clan would even claim divine origin (see Golden 1982, 37–76, for an excellent discussion on imperial ideology among pre-Mongol steppe peoples) and a similar claim to a heavenly mandate can even be seen in the much earlier case of the Scythian royal horde which in its foundation legend claimed for its ancestor the heavenly gift of burning gold objects that fell from the sky, which he alone could access due to divine favour (Hdt. 4.5). Attila would of course also lay claims to divine favour by the discovery of the sword of Mars (God of war), Jordanes, *Getica* 35.183.

255. His name, as mentioned earlier, is the same as that of the sixth-century near contemporary Utigur Hunnic king Anagai in the Pontic steppe, Menander Protector, fr. 19.1, Blockley (1985), 172.
256. More on the origins of Onegesius and Orestes later.
257. Kradin (2005), 163.
258. For the importance of the wolf in early southern Siberian art, especially Altaian art and iconography in the first and second centuries AD (the region from which the Huns would later begin their long trek west), see Rice (1965a), 37–8.
259. Golden (2001a), 39.
260. More on this in the next chapter.
261. Di Cosmo (1994), 1092–1126; Markley (forthcoming), 15; Beckwith (2009), 341–2; Soucek (2000), 43; Christian (1998), 91, 128. See also Czeglédy (1983), 119, for the co-existence of urbanized and nomadic Hephtalites.
262. The strict dichotomy of nomads and sedentary peoples leads to all kinds of misunderstandings and confusions. The divide is not as clear-cut as is often believed. For a good definition of nomadic pastoralism see Cribb (1991), 15–20. Cribb also provides good examples of later Turkic and Kurdish tribal confederacies that possessed both nomadic and sedentary elements integrated into a single entity (26–7). See also Batty (2007), 31, and Gorbunova (1992), 33.
263. Archibald (2002), 56 ff. and Sulimirsky (1985), 152, 182–3.
264. Rolle (1989), 117, and Christian (1998), 140.
265. See also Minyaev (1996), 81.
266. Rolle (1989), 119.
267. Rolle (1989), 119, and Tsetskhladze (2007), 48. The Apasiakoi Saka of the Syr Darya delta, closer to the original home of the European Huns, were also sedentarizing pastoralists who engaged in agriculture and may even have built large towns and fortified settlements. The Saka may also have been instrumental in introducing urban culture to the Tarim basin futher east in the first millennium BC. See Christian (1998), 132 and 139. See also Abetekov and Yusupov (1994), 30, for evidence of ceramic production in the steppe region.
268. In fact as Golden (2009a), 91, points out pastoral nomadism itself probably 'evolved in agricultural communities in which animal husbandry became the dominant economic activity'.
269. See Lubo-Lesnichenko (1989), 47, and also Minyaev (2001), 3, who provide a description of the Ivolga complex near Ulan Ude which shows signs of agriculture and fortifications. See also Ishjamts (1994), 156–8, Honeychurch and Amartuvshin (2006a), 266–7, Brosseder and Miller (2011b), 27, and Batsaikhan (2011), 122–3.
270. For this symbiosis between farmers and pastoralists see Tapper (1991), 528.
271. See Dandamaev (1994), 41 and Diakonoff (1985), 129–31.
272. Mukhamedjanov (1994), 270. For urban development under the Kushans see Litvinsky (1994), 299 ff.
273. For the astonishing sophistication of the sedentary, Khwarezmian civilization with which the Huns were geographically adjacent before their irruption into Europe see Helms (1998), 77–96. See also Rapoport (1996), 161–185.

274. See Negmatov (1994), 444–451. See also Abdullaev (2007), 83–6, for evidence on 'nomad' city sites in Central Asia such as Kala-i Zakhoki Maron in the neighbourhood of Karshi in Uzbekistan, an area later absorbed by the Huns.
275. For the increasing importance of the sedentary element in the Kangju state see Grenet *et al.* (2007), 1027. See also Zadneprovskiy (1994), 464.
276. Zadneprovskiy (1994), 460.
277. For the surprising 'immobility' of many steppe pastoralists and so-called 'nomads' and their presence in a fixed locality over long, extended periods of time, a phenomenon which for centuries coincided with massive migrations across the Eurasian steppe, see Frachetti (2008), 8.
278. For the difficulty involved in defining what is urban, sedentary and what is pastoral, nomad in Central Asia, given the frequent existence of pastoral activity in the same area with agriculture and farming, e.g. in the Chaganian region, see Stride (2007), 115.
279. Fine (1983), 44–5.
280. Curta (2006), 65. John of Ephesus, *Ecclesiastical History* 5.32.256.
281. Kashgari would write his famous work in Arabic for the benefit of his Arab audience in Baghdad. The *Diwan* is dedicated to the Abbasid Caliph al-Muqtadi (AD 1075–94) whose reign coincided with the Seljuk (Oghuz) Turkish takeover of Iraq and Iran from the Shiite Persian Buwayid dynasty. The Arabs were eager to learn about their new masters and Kashgari obliged their curiosity. See Dankoff (1972), 23.
282. Dankoff (1972), 30–1.

CHAPTER 4: THE HUNS IN EUROPE

1. For more information on the political structure of steppe nomadic states, especially how its military character defined the norms of civil administration as well as military organization, see Vasjutin (2003), 53–8. Khazanov (2003), 43, provides an excellent overview of the political culture of steppe imperial states, which remained remarkably similar and uniform despite the passage of time and the transfer of power to different ethnic and linguistic milieux, from the time of the Scythians and the Xiongnu to the rise of the Mongols in the thirteenth century AD. See also Fletcher (1986), 16–32, and Allsen (1996), 116. Virtually all these empires possessed pretty much the same political system. A ruling clan with semi-divine status distributed among themselves and lesser nobles a plethora of imperial, noble and administrative titles. They shared a similar system of imperial symbolism that included colours, banners, rank traditions, practices associated with crowning, dressing, belting, special investiture ceremonies, sacred territories and cult centres. All shared the notion of collective or joint sovereignty. The state belonged not to the individual ruler, but to all members of the ruling clan. There was the typical overlapping of administrative systems with the military organization (tripartite or bipartite), which divided the imperial polity into left and right wings, corresponding to the principle military–political divisions of the empire. A decimal system of population control and

mobilization and a patrimonial mode of government that implied redistribution of various kinds of wealth and goods among vassals, followers and even commoners were quintessential features of the nomadic political entity.
2. For the steppe origins of the Toba Xianbei state of Northern Wei see chapter 1 of the *Wei Shu* in Holmgren (1982). See also Kwanten (1979), 15–16.
3. Wiet *et al.* (1975), 33, provide an excellent map of the great invasions from the steppe during the fourth and fifth centuries AD.
4. As Khazanov (2003), 43, rightly points out, 'such was the state of affairs in the Eurasian steppes for approximately two and a half thousand years'.
5. Bona (1991), 41. See also Haussig (2000), 257, who points out that Ammianus' description of the bone arrowheads of the Huns derives from first-century AD Greco-Roman ethnography on the tribes of the North-East. His attribution of raw flesh-eating to the Huns has its origins in ethnographic speculation that goes back as far as Herodotus in the fifth century BC who attributes this behaviour to his *eschatoi andrōn* and more closely to Ptolemy in his description of the Amadokoi. It is true that some steppe tribes are known to have occasionally used bone arrowheads, since metal was a precious commodity (see Yagodin (2007), 63). However, this certainly does not corroborate Ammianus' picture of a primitive society. See also Kelly (2008), 36, 85–6, on the unreliability of Ammianus' description of foreigners, which for the most part is not based on autopsy.
6. Heather (2009), 211.
7. Heather (2009), 215–16. Halsall (2007), 171–2, the other most recent critic to comment on the issue also believes in Ammianus' ethnic stereotypes. Even Kelly (2009), 17, whose work is an excellent introduction to the history of the Huns, begins his treatment of the Huns with the chapter heading 'a backward steppe', hardly an accurate description.
8. Heather (2006), 62, 98; Halsall (2007), 144–7.
9. Heather (2006), 248, 280.
10. Bona (1991), 29, is exceptional in that he envisages a Hunnic Empire that was well organized from the very moment of Hunnic entry into Europe. He points out that archaeology shows a Central Asian political power with a Persian–Sassanian style splendour and etiquette, with no doubt, I would argue, a highly developed imperial structure and military order. Unfortunately Bona does not elaborate on this excellent observation.
11. Maenchen-Helfen (1973), 62, though he acknowledges that the Huns were well organized, argues that even Attila did not rule all of the Huns. More on this later.
12. There is a school of thought represented by Barfield (1989), 9, who argues that steppe empires came into existence as a counterweight devised by nomads to resist and also efficiently exploit via military aggression the material wealth of unified sedentary empires, e.g. the case of the Xiongnu Empire and Han China, the objective being not outright conquest of a sedentary state, but securing a constant flow of tribute from it. Barfield's excessive focus on the role of sedentary states and the dependence of steppe empires on them is rightly criticized by Di

Cosmo (2002), 170, and Beckwith (2009), 329–30. The so-called nomadic empires, as pointed out earlier, were by no means entirely nomadic, but always possessed a sedentary element. Barfield's model of Han–Xiongnu relations, however, can be useful in interpreting the policies of the Huns vis-à-vis the Roman Empire and Hunnic military campaigns into Roman territory, which were, at least initially, mainly aimed at bringing about economically advantageous treaties for the Huns and not territorial gains. This may reflect the old Xiongnu policy of deliberate aggression from a distance to extract maximum concessions from Han China and their reluctance to annex any Chinese territory as this would upset the current balance of power which helped stabilize the Xiongnu economy (Barfield 1981, 54–5). The same policy can also be seen in the White Hun dealings with Sassanian Persia. The White Huns repeatedly defeat the Persians and even kill and dethrone Persian kings, but refrain from annexing Persia and instead subject it to regular payments of tribute. In other words, it was not a case of Attila being unable to conquer the Romans. He had sound economic reasons for keeping the Roman state alive.

13. Heather (2006), 343–4. This part of his argumentation is especially perplexing, given the fact that in his more recent (2009) publication Heather accepts the fact that the Avars, who replaced the Huns in the western steppe in the mid sixth century AD, allowed for the Slavicization of the Balkans by destroying East Roman military supremacy in the region, p. 608. If so, why wouldn't the Huns, who were as powerful as the Avars and possessed a very similar political and military culture in the preceding fifth century, have been any less effective against Western Roman armies?
14. Halsall (2007), 19, 74, 78–9, 162, 188, 214.
15. Other aspects of Goffart's ideas are however criticized by Halsall (2007), 18.
16. Goffart (1980), 230. For the settlement of barbarian troops in Roman territory see Matthews (1989), 316.
17. Halsall (2007), 283.
18. Heather (2006), 156–7.
19. It is certainly true that the tactical superiority and excellence of steppe horse archers were widely recognized in antiquity. Procopius certainly thinks very highly of them and identifies these archers (Hunnic mercenaries and troops modelled on them) as the backbone of Eastern Roman military strength, 1.1.8–17, 5.27.27–9. The Goths, Procopius notes, were defeated because their horsemen were not mounted archers and were thus inferior to the Romans and their Hunnic allies, despite their numerical superiority.
20. Priscus fr. 1, Blockley (1983), 224; Jordanes, *Getica* 24.126; Procopius 8.5.4, 7–12. Alpizuri, Alcilzuri etc. See Maenchen-Helfen (1973), 427–41, for a comprehensive list of Turkic tribes ruled by the Huns.
21. Heather (2006), 450–1.
22. Heather (2006), 63–4, argues for a minimum of an increase by a third of Roman military manpower in the late third to mid fourth century, from 300,000 to anywhere between 400,000 to 600,000 men. Not quite accurate argues Goldsworthy (2009), 289. However, there seems to be no doubt that at the

very least the army had not significantly shrunk in size. See also Wickham (2009), 9.
23. Halsall (2007), 74–7. This bureaucracy and administrative shakeup, which meant more taxes, has sometimes been regarded as the root of internal decay, population decline and military collapse by many historians. However, as Heather (2006) himself shows, the population of the empire was actually increasing in the fourth century and the rural economy was flourishing at the same time, hardly the image of a state in decline, p. 118–19.
24. Matthews (1989), 253.
25. Kelly (2004), 1, 7, 192–3.
26. Williams (1985), 15–23.
27. The increase in size of the Roman army and the re-organization of the Roman army in the late third century is regarded by Brown (1971), 25, as 'one of the finest achievements of Roman statecraft'.
28. Campbell (1999), 234.
29. A marked improvement from the days of the early empire when commanders of regiments and generals of armies had been for the most part civilians holding temporary commissions and were in reality amateurs who rarely had enough military experience, see Jones (1964), vol. II, 1037.
30. Williams (1985), 97. A minimum of fourteen new legions were raised by Diocletian in addition to the restoration of pre-existing legions to something approaching their former numbers and strength.
31. Lactantius, *De Mortibus Persecutorum* 7.5. John Lydus, *De Mensibus* 1.27, gives a total of 389,704 men in the army under Diocletian and 45,562 in the navy. Agathias, *The Histories*. 13.7–8, gives probably the exaggerated number of 645,000. See also Whitby (2000b), 292, for estimates of the size of the army. See also Boak (1955), 87–9, for a rough estimate of 400,000 men in total throughout the whole empire. Halsall (2007), 144–5, also agrees.
32. Lenski (2002), 372. Ferrill (1986), 22, claims that at the beginning of the fifth century the Western Roman army still numbered perhaps more than 200,000 men. Perhaps significantly fewer troops were in reality of any practical use to the West Romans, as Boak (1955), 100, rightly points out (though his picture of critical manpower shortages in the Western Roman Empire only seems plausible for the fifth century and not the previous fourth.). By and large the decline in population in the Roman Empire, perhaps a realistic scenario at least in the Western half (maybe in some ways exacerbated by over-taxation by the imperial government to support the army needed to counter the pressures from the barbarians, which in turn drove some peasants into poverty), was still in most areas not catastrophic, see Jones (1964), vol. II, 1040–5. In any case the Western Roman army at least in the late fourth century AD, especially the army in Gaul, was in good condition to repel the barbarians, see Elton (1992), 168. Roman military power both in the Eastern Empire and the Western Empire was by no means in irreversible decline in the late fourth century or even in the early fifth century AD. See also Demougeot (1979), 180–2, and Jones (1964), vol. II, 682–6.

33. Jones (1964), vol. II, 1037.
34. Boak (1955), 92; Williams (1985), 213; Cameron (1993), 51; Whitby (2007a), 520; Halsall (2007), 108–9.
35. Jones (1964), vol. II, 1038; Stickler (2007), 499. For the distinction between regular troops and federates see Liebeschuetz (1990), 32–4. For a detailed study of Germanic troops in Roman service in the fourth century AD see Waas (1965). See also Cameron (2012), 52–7, for information on barbarians in the late Roman army.
36. See Geary (1988), 22.
37. For more information on barbarians in the Roman army see Christie (2011), 56–64.
38. Cameron (1993), 84, 94, 99, 103.
39. Heather (2006), 97–8. Heather considers Germanic socio-economic advancement to have intensified in the fourth century and that a more entrenched and stratified military elite had developed which allowed the Germanic peoples to finally become a mortal threat to Rome, if only given a unity of purpose among the disparate tribal confederacies. This unity of purpose, he argues, was forced on them by the arrival of the Huns. In his estimation the Huns therefore were an indirect catalyst for the downfall of Rome by virtue of having awakened the Germans' latent potential for conquest (p. 450–1). The same opinion is held by Bell-Fialkoff (2000), 120, who argues for the formation of more specialized and long-lasting war-bands/confederacies among the Germans in the fourth century. The presence of a well-established and perhaps powerful elite among the Germanic tribes in the fourth century is certainly plausible, see Hedeager (1992), 251–2. However, how different these elites were from previous elites of the third century AD or even the first century AD described by Tacitus, *Germania* 7, 11, 13–14, who were representatives of kin-based groupings and leaders of autonomous war-bands with limited authority over their followers (these elites are identifiable from their often impressive burial remains, see Pearson (1989), 203–20), is all too unclear. The Germanic elite, including the chiefs/kings, ruled by persuasion rather than by command due to their limited power and could only keep together a large retinue in times of war. Rank within the military retinue of the chief was determined by military valour, says Tacitus. See Hachmann (1971), 84, for archaeological evidence of hierarchical, social differentiation among the Germanic tribes in the 1st century AD. See also Leube (1978), 514. Even if the fourth-century Germanic, aristocratic elite had evolved to a point where they possessed greater authority over their followers, except among the most eastern Gothic tribes who were under heavy steppe influence, the growth in power of this elite does not seem to have translated into greater political unity and better military organization than in earlier centuries, as we shall see shortly. If the Germanic tribal confederacies had become somewhat stronger, so too had the Roman army in the fourth century.
40. Goffart (2006), 31, and Heather (2006), 62. See also Dignas and Winter (2007), 70 ff. Goffart also rightly stresses the power of the Parthians, somewhat neglected by Heather. The impact of the Sassanians, though surely significant,

was not as radical as Heather would suggest. See Tacitus' narrative of the wars over Armenia in the earlier centuries of Roman imperial rule, *Ann.* 6.34–5, and also consider Roman reactions to the defeats of Crassus and Antony at the hands of the Parthians. These provide us with a more realistic, contemporary Roman assessment of Parthian strength somewhat downplayed in recent scholarship (see also Wolski 1993, 122–75), though it is true that a brief period of heightened Persian militancy under Sassanian leadership after a century of lethargy under the late Parthians gave Rome a scare.

41. For a good summary of the third-century crisis from a military perspective see Luttwak (1976), 146–54.
42. The more classical views of Jones (1964), vol. II, 1067–8, that 'internal weaknesses cannot have been a major factor' in the collapse of the West and that external pressures were of critical importance, is surprisingly closer to the mark than more recent analyses of the 'Decline', 'Transformation' or 'Fall' of the Western Empire. So is the observation that the internal weaknesses stressed by many critics were common to both halves of the empire. See Jones (1964), vol. II, 1027. Nor was the collapse of the Western Roman Empire an unmitigated disaster for civilization, as it is often presented to be. As Brown (1971), 19, points out 'it left the cultural power-house of Late Antiquity – the eastern Mediterranean and the Near East – unscathed'. Our views of Late Antiquity in general are clouded by an over-fixation with the political and cultural changes that occurred in the underdeveloped and generally poorer western periphery of the Roman world, the region that later became Western Europe.
43. Cameron (1993), 44–5, 51–2.
44. Williams (1985), 211.
45. See Demandt (1984), 44–492, for an exhaustive summary of all the various causal factors advocated since Late Antiquity. Ward-Perkins (2005), 44, sees Roman internal civil wars and usurpations as key causes that brought about the success of the Germanic invasions. Social unrest such as the rebellion of the Bagaudae too could have been a factor. The confusion of course made things easier for the invaders and reveals perhaps, as he argues, lack of leadership from some of the late emperors. However, our sources actually show that in the person of Aetius effective leadership was available to deal with the onslaught, provided the Romans had been left alone to deal with the Germanic problem, i.e. if there had been no Hunnic wars. Arguably far greater confusion characterized Roman politics in the third century, yet as mentioned above the empire managed to survive the torrent of barbarian incursions in that century, which suggests that incompetence or instability cannot be the main reasons behind the collapse of imperial power in the Western Empire in the fourth and fifth centuries AD. See Jones (1964), vol. II, 1032–3, who as usual provides a more accurate assessment than more recent critics.
46. Jones (1964), vol. II, 1066–7, suggests that the problem may have been more acute in the West than in the East, but also wisely voices caution with regard to this hypothesis. See also Collins (1999), 98, who rejects the possibility of determining with any certainty whether or not the great landed aristocracy of

the West were in any way more powerful than that those in the East. Brown (1971), 43, suggests more confidently that they were.
47. Cameron (1993), 55, 84, 89. A more radically Marxist and clearly outdated analysis that attributes the fall of the Empire to the over-exploitation of the peasantry by the 'idle mouths' (= aristocratic elite) can be found in Ste. Croix (1981), 502–3. See also Geary (1988), 28–38, for discussion on the rise of the regional aristocracy in the Western Empire that at times encouraged separatist tendencies. For a more positive, though by no means flattering evaluation of the role of the late Roman provincial elite, see Brown (1971), 36–7, 120–1, 126. According to Brown (pp. 40–1), it was in fact the influence of the much-maligned landowners and tax-collectors that brought about the Romanization of the western provinces, the transition from Celtic languages to 'Romance' languages and the increasing sense of 'Roman' identity among the peasantry. Overall the Roman Empire in the fourth century was a much wider franchise than before which embraced a greater portion of the residents of the empire who now considered themselves to be *Romanus*. Brown (p. 119) suggests, however, that the western senatorial elite and the Catholic church simply dissociated themselves from the fate of the Roman army in the fifth century and that that was the cause of the failure of imperial government. This is, however, an analysis based on actions taken by the elite after the disintegration of the Roman army, which forced the provincial elite to come to an accommodation with the new barbarian rulers. The senatorial elite of Gaul and Italy, though fractious, selfish and often incompetent were, as Brown himself points out, exceedingly patriotic in their own way and idealized Rome to an inordinate degree (pp. 120–1). They were certainly not glad to see the barbarians roaming about in Roman territory, suffered real losses in wealth and land due to the incursions (p. 126) and would have all too eagerly destoyed the barbarians if they could have done so. Yet the inability of the Roman military establishment to effectively keep these barbarians in check forced this class for the sake of self-preservation to reluctantly seek accommodation within a new political order set up by the barbarians. The defection of the aristocracy and the church, therefore, was the result of the failure of imperial government, not the cause of its failure.
48. Cameron (1993), 104–27; (2012), 104–27.
49. For instance the punitive expedition in the aid of the Western Empire against the Vandals in 441 AD, foiled by Hunnic intervention; Eastern Roman aid given to Aetius during the Hunnic invasion of Italy in 452 AD; another punitive campaign against the Vandals to aid the Western Empire in 468 AD (the disastrous Basiliscus expedition, allegedly sabotaged by the Alan general Aspar); Justinian's successful re-conquests.
50. Heather (2006), 86 ff.
51. Todd (1992), 30–1.
52. Heather (2006), 96, himself acknowledges this. Wenskus (1977), 496, argues that there are differences between the tribal leaders described by Tacitus and the later Germanic petty kings, those of the Alamanni for instance. This is

likely to be true and there was obviously an improvement in the organizational ability of some Germanic tribal groups after the early second century AD. However, there is nothing that would indicate that the systems of control exercised within the tribal confederacies underwent radical changes between the third and fourth centuries AD.
53. Todd (1992), 194, the lack of strong kingship among the Franks in the early fifth century AD.
54. Todd (1992), 207, loose and haphazard political organization without centralized authority among the Alamanni. For the general history of the Alamanni from the fourth to the early sixth century see Schmidt (1983a), 336–42.
55. Tacitus in his *Germania* 44, tells us that already in the first and second centuries AD the eastern Germans such as the Goths and the Rugii were under tighter control than the other Germans, but not inconsistently with freedom: *Gothones regnantur, paulo iam adductius quam ceterae Germanorum gentes, nondum tamen supra libertatem*.
56. See Longden (1954), 227–36.
57. Heather (2006), 86–98.
58. According to Capitolinus, *Vita Antonini Pii* 22.1–2 (ed. Hohl *BT* 1, 66–7; Chastagnol, 148), Alemany (2000), 18, the Marcommani colluded with the Alans and other Sarmatian tribes of the East to resist the Romans. See also Heather (2009), 96–107, and Schutz (2000), 10.
59. Twenty-five emperors were set up by the armies in forty-seven years! See Brown (1971), 24.
60. Alföldi (1965), 141–50; Demougeot (1979), 463–4; Bell-Fialkoff (2000), 126; Todd (1992), 150–2; Schutz (2000), 14–17; Kazanski (1991), 32–3; Kulikowski (2007), 18–20.
61. Brown (1971), 22. See also Potter (2004), 246.
62. The victory at Adrianople was in reality largely due to new military tactics introduced by the Alans and the Greutungs from the steppe. Luck also played a part in the encounter. Later collisions between the Romans and the Germanic barbarians actually show that the Roman army was far from inferior to the Germanic armies it faced in the fourth and fifth centuries. Stilicho's repeated victories over Alaric's Visigoths are telling.
63. Wenskus (1977), 318, points out correctly that more often than not Germanic kings before the fourth and in some instances, as among the Heruli, even after the fourth century AD were often merely *primi inter pares* rather than sovereign rulers.
64. Hummer (1998a). 9.
65. Ammianus Marcellinus 16.12.23–6. See Wickham (2009), 45, and Hummer (1998a), 8. See also Matthews (1989), 314–15 and Heather (2001), 42.
66. Ammianus Marcellinus 16.12.34. Wolfram (1997b), 67–8.
67. Ammianus Marcellinus 16.12.17. Hummer (1998a), 9. See also Drinkwater (1997), 1–16.
68. Hummer (1998a), 10; Leube (1978), 514. A similar situation seems to have existed among the slightly more centralized Tervingi Goths in Romania.

Among them there were also numerous *reiks* who ruled more or less independently over limited territory with associated peoples called *kuni*, see Lenski (2002), 120. In times of war they would united under the leadership of a *iudex* (judge).
69. Hummer (1998a), 22–6; Castritius (1990), 80. Heather (2009), 61, argues for a more sophisticated administrative capacity among fourth-century Germanic tribes, including the ability among the Alamanni and the Goths to levy perhaps taxation of sorts. However, it would be surprising if previous tribal confederations in the second and third centuries AD, whether they were Germanic, Sarmatic or Getic, lacked comparable capacities. If the Alamanni and the Goths did indeed possess such administrative capacity and had progressed further in the direction of statehood, it becomes even more apparent that the Huns must have possessed at the least comparable or superior levels of administrative capability in order to rule the fourth-century east Goths who were politically the most sophisticated among the Germanic peoples.
70. See James (1988), 52–4.
71. Geary (1999), 110.
72. Pohl (1997a), 39.
73. Christian (1998), 225; Matthews (1989), 325; Burns (1980), 37, 47, 49. Burns, however, argues for a gradual evolution of Gothic society into larger organizations based on ranking and sub-unit structures (p. 40). His theory is based on Ammianus' description of the Quadi (17.12.21), where a *subregulus* and *optimates et iudices* are mentioned. However, it is unclear as to whether this constitutes a clear ranking system or is just a reference to various tribal leaders commanding groups of warriors of different sizes, hence the designation *subregulus* (sub-petty king) to describe Agilmundus, a leader with a smaller retinue than the *regalis* Vitrodorus. Presumably the *optimates* and *iudices* are leaders with even smaller retinues. A development towards a more unified and hierarchical political structure among the east Germans in the mid fourth century AD is clearly a possibility and the Quadi, given their close proximity and mingling with Sarmatian tribes such as the Iazyges, according to Vernadsky (1951), 350, could have been imitating steppe Sarmatian practices and military arts. However, their organization was clearly not cohesive enough to withstand the Hunnic invasions. Whether the situation among the Quadi was a permanent state of affairs is doubtful and it may merely be a reflection of a temporary union such as that found among the Alamanni and Franks to the west in times of crisis or war. It will henceforth be argued that the Huns introduced a new, more cohesive political organization which accelerated this eastern Germanic, and later also western Germanic, trend towards larger social groupings and organization. It is highly doubtful whether centralized kingship over large confederations was becoming a more permanent institution among the Germans before the Hunnic arrival. Arguably it was the shock of defeat at the hands of the Huns and the following imitation among the Goths of Hunnic practices that triggered the 'unification' of the west Goths into a more cohesive confederation. The contribution of the Inner Asian Alans to the

political transformation of both the Visigothic and Vandal tribal groups into viable confederations must also not be underestimated and this will be discussed later in Chapter 6.
74. *Hist. eccl.* 4.33.
75. Geary (1999), 119.
76. Burns (1980), 47. This can be clearly seen in the election of Videricus, a grandson of Ermanaric, as king despite him being a minor, Ammianus Marcellinus 31.3.3.
77. Altheim (1959), 321; Vernadsky (1951), 361; Harmatta (1970), 49. The name *Greuntungi* according to Burns (1980), 34, means 'rulers of the steppe'. He is taking a bit of artistic licence in his etymological speculation. The less dramatic Vernadsky (1951), 353, and Pritsak (1968), 161, point out that it means literally 'sand people', i.e. presumably 'dwellers of the steppe', not rulers of the steppe. The name *Tervingi* means 'forest-people'. These very names suggest that rather than designating a coherent and organized political entity these appellations are blanket terms designating types of Goths living in Romania and the Ukraine, casting some doubt on the notion of greater political unity among Goths than among other Germanic peoples before the arrival of the Huns.
78. See Vernadsky (1951), 356. Intermarriages, especially among the elite, were widespread and intense acculturation took place between the Goths and Alans/Sarmatians. Prominent Gothic and Alanic figures in the fourth and fifth centuries AD were most often of mixed Alan–Goth heritage. For instance Maximinus had an Alan mother and a Gothic father, Aspar a Gothic mother and an Alan father, and Geiseric the Vandal king also might have had an Alan mother (p. 358). The east Gothic cavalry commanders who engineer the Visigothic triumph at Adrianople over the Romans, Alatheus and Saphrax (see Burns 1984, 41–1) both appear to possess Alanic names, as do the two Gothic kings Odotheus (386 AD) and Radagaisus (405–6 AD; the name Radagaisus is similar to the Sarmatian name Rathagosos, mentioned in an inscription at Olbia) who later try to break out of Hunnic domination with a group of Goths into Roman territory, Vernadsky (1951), 369, 373. See also Burns (1984), 38, who agrees that Alatheus and Saphrax were Sarmatian/Alan in origin.
79. Lozinski (1984), 127, raises the interesting hypothesis that the Massagetae mentioned first in Herodotus in the fifth century BC were none other than the Da Yuezhi mentioned in Chinese sources. Yuezhi, he argues, is an inaccurate transcription of the EMC reading which gives *Gweti, Gwoti, Goti* (Pulleyblank (2000b), 89, reads it as *Ywati* in order to make it approximate *Iatioi*, a variant he argues of *Asioi*, this seems rather forced). Add the Chinese *Da* (great) and we get 'Great Goti' which curiously enough is nearly identical with the name Massagetae (Great Getae). This is also the view of Tolstov (1961), 50, and Sulimirsky (1970), 81–2. The Yuezhi (Tocharians) as mentioned in Chapter 3 moved into western Central Asia under pressure from the Huns in the second century BC and one of their clans, the Kushans, ruled until the third century AD over most of Central Asia, Afghanistan and northwestern India. The Kushans had close ties with the rulers of the Kangju (the name of the region around Tashkent or Samarkand, later turned into an ethnonym,

e.g. Kangar, Kangly, see Tolstov (1961), 92), the Asi or Asiani, who for a while also controlled or were associated with the Alans further west. This leaves us with an interesting possibility. Were these Goti (Yuezhi), if the above reading of the Chinese characters is correct, involved in the ethnogenesis of the Goths in eastern Europe with the same name c. the first century AD or earlier? This would help explain the comment in Tacitus' *Germania* 44, where he says that the Goths were under tighter control than other Germans. The better organization that we consistently find among the Goths also in the third and fourth centuries AD may in some way be attributable to the possible Inner Asian origins of their ruling elite and provide the reason why the Sarmatians (superior in organization to the Germanic tribes in general) were defeated by the Goths, which could hardly make sense if the Goths were just haphazardly organized Germanic tribes migrating south from the Baltic region. Being an extreme minority, the core Inner Asian Goths would then have rapidly merged with the Sarmato-Germanic population of the region they conquered and in time adopted the language of the majority of their new subjects (east Germanic). Beckwith (2009), 380–3, suggests that the character *Yue* in Yuezhi in its EMC pronunciation can be read as *tokwar/togwar* (i.e. 'Tocharian'), but this is difficult to accept. Sam Lieu, an equally superb linguist, in private correspondences with the author has confirmed that the character *Da* (great) needs to be taken as a phonetic element in an ethnonym rather than as a simple magnifier for Da Yuezhi to read *togwar*. However, the reference in our Chinese sources to the *Xiao* (small) Yuezhi makes the reading of *Da* as part of an ethnonym unlikely.

80. Procopius 3.2.2–3; 3.3.1; 5.1.3. The extraordinary level of Inner Asian influence on so-called Gothic art and culture in the third and fourth centuries AD, which we will discuss in greater detail in Chapter 6, possibly bears witness to the Inner Asian origins (as discussed above) of the Gothic elite, as do the probable Alanic/Iranian names of the royal family Amal and other high-ranking Goths.
81. Vernadsky (1951), 359.
82. *Getica* 13.78, 14.79.
83. *Getica* 50.266. Jordanes' own father has the name Alanoviiamuth.
84. Vernadsky (1951), 359.
85. Christian (1998), 226.
86. Matthews (1989), 325–6.
87. Matthews (1989), 294; Todd (1992), 42.
88. Kelly (2009), 96.
89. Todd (1992), 45. Even then the Goths and Vandals failed to master the art of mounted archery, which left their cavalry at a constant disadvantage when facing Central Asian horsemen, p. 46.
90. Williams (1985), 212.
91. Priscus, fr. 11.2, Blockley (1983), 279. Earlier in the fourth century Aurelius Victor (*Epit*. 47, 3 (ed. Pichlmayr *BT*, p. 173)), Alemany (2000), 42, calls the Huns and the Alans the worst of all evils and *extremum periculum* to the name of Rome. See Sinor (1970), 100, 103–4, for the military superiority of steppe

empires and the observation that when united a nomadic empire of the steppe was virtually invincible due to the superior military skills (horsemanship and archery) of its soldiers and superior battle tactics employed by its generals.
92. Maenchen-Helfen, Heather, Sinor, etc., as mentioned earlier.
93. Priscus, fr. 11.2, Blockley (1983), 279. The discovery of Hunnic cauldrons along the Kama river and Attila's gift of furs to visiting ambassadors, according to Christian (1998), 229, suggest that the Hunnic tributary system reached deep into even the forest region of western Russia beyond the Pontic steppe. The presence of Hunnic princely graves, all identifiable by distinctive Hunnic artefacts such as the golden bow (an insignia of rank among the Huns), dating to the early fifth century AD, across a vast area stretching from the Rhine to areas east of the Dnieper provides archaeological evidence for Hunnic imperial rule over most of central and eastern Europe, see Sulimirsky (1970), 191–3.
94. Gordon (1960), 202; Blockley (1983), 386.
95. Priscus, fr. 11.2, Blockley (1983), 277.
96. Priscus, fr. 11.2, Blockley (1983), 277.
97. Priscus, fr. 11.2, Blockley (1983), 279.
98. Priscus, fr. 11.2, Blockley (1983), 279. Another contemporary source, the anonymous Gallic chronicler of 452, was also equally conscious of the magnitude of the danger to the empire posed by the Huns. See Muhlberger (1990), 183. This account of Attila's ambitions makes a mockery of suggestions that all he wanted was to take the place of Aetius as a Roman subject or secure for himself a similar position as the Roman general-in-chief, the opinion of Sinor (1993), 12. Stickler (2007), 502–3, accurately points out that the Huns posed a mortal threat to the Roman Empire precisely because they rejected any prospect of integration into the military or civil structure of the Roman Empire and offered the barbarian tribes beyond Rome's borders an alternative to Roman hegemony. In other words they enforced a separation between the Germanic tribes and the Romans and denied the Western Romans in particular their key areas of mercenary recruitment. This served to undermine the military power of the West in times of crisis.
99. Priscus, fr. 11.1, Blockley (1983), 245.
100. Similar arrangements are also found among the later Mongols who set up the institution of imperial bodyguards, the *keshig* formed out of *nökürs* (companions in arms or comitatus), an entire army that watched over the person of the Khagan, an elaborated version no doubt of earlier steppe institutions. See Golden (2009b), 113. Chinggis Khan adopted the policy of also stripping the tribes he conquered of their traditional leadership and replacing them with his vassals or family members. A less drastic, but very similar practice has already been noted in Chapter 3 among the Rouran and we will encounter the same practice among the Huns. We have also noted the fact that in the Rouran and Gokturk Empires that dominated the steppes in the fifth and sixth centuries AD these imperial bodyguards/retinue were known as *böri* (wolves) and identified with the spirit of the mythical wolf ancestor of the ruling Ashina clan (see Findley 2005, 38). We do not have firm evidence that

the imperial guard among the Huns were called wolves, but the proliferation of Germanic names with the element 'wolf' (-*ulf* suffix in Gothic names) in the fifth century is extremely suggestive and may indicate that the practice of adding this suffix to personal names was popularized by the Hunnic practice of calling their finest warriors wolves. The word *böri* used to refer to the ruler's retinue is not Turkic, but Iranian in origin (Findley 2005, 39), and this suggests the likelihood that the Huns, like the Rouran and Ashina Gokturks, may have taken over this usage from their Iranian subjects and then passed it on to the Goths.

101. See Thompson (1996), 179–200, for an extended discussion.
102. The Seljuk Sultan Malik-Shah would suffer a serious revolt of the Chigils and Karluks for failing to give the traditional customary feasts to these tribesmen. See Bosworth (1968), 92. The participation in these feasts was an important exercise in determining one's social status and honour before the ruler.
103. Altheim (1959), vol. IV, 284, argues that Onegesius is a Hellenized Hunnic name, Old Turkish *on-iyiz*. Onegesius was, he argues, more likely to have been a Hun, not a Roman defector. The name of Onegesius' brother Skottas, who if Onegesius is a Hun should likewise be a Hun, is presumed to be Gothic in origin, which tells us that ethnicity and names do not often go hand in hand. What is even more interesting is the suggestion (Altheim and Stiehl 1954, 259) that this name means 'der zehn zur Gefolgschaft hat', i.e. it is a reference to his position as a commander in the army organized in the typical steppe decimal system.
104. Somewhat like the all-powerful Persian *vizier* (bureaucrat) of the Seljuk Turkish Sultan Malik-Shah, Nizam al-Mulk. See Bosworth (1968), 66–86. Nizam al-Mulk, despite being a bureaucrat, also commanded armies for the Sultan (Bosworth 1968, 69). We see the same phenomenon with Onegesius who was employed in the punitive expedition against the Akatziri.
105. Priscus, fr. 13.1, fr. 11.2, Blockley (1983), 285, 259, 265–7, 241–3. See also Whitby (2000c), 705, for information.
106. Whitby (2000c), 711.
107. Altheim (1948), 21–2. Priscus fr. 11.2, Blockley (1983), 257, reports that Hunnic secretaries read out names of fugitives from a written list. Altheim argues that the writing that was read was definitely neither Greek nor Latin. He suggests that the Oghuric Turkic runic writing system of the later Hunnic Bulgars, which we know from inscriptions in Bulgaria, was brought into Europe from Central Asia by the Huns. The Bulgar script is most likely an adapted version of the old Sogdian alphabet to the Hunnic/Oghric Turkic language. Such a borrowing could only have happened while the Huns were still in Kazakhstan and in close proximity to the Iranian world, i.e before the late fourth century AD (see also Vasilyev 1992, 124). Further possible evidence for Hunnic writing can be found in the Syriac chronicle of Zacharias of Mitylene who writes that in 507 or 508 AD bishop Qardust of Arran went to the land of the Caucasian Huns where he remained for seven years. He returned bringing with him books in the Hunnic language (Altheim 1948, 30). See also Ishjamts (1994), 166–7, for information on the existence of a still

unproven early Xiongnu (Hun)–Xianbei runic writing which may have existed around the same time as the Sogdian script and been a part of the wider Eurasian runic script that later may have given rise to the Gokturk written script in the eighth century. See Vasilyev (1992), 119–22, for a good summary of the debate on the origin of Turkish runes.
108. Eunapius, Book 9. 60 (John of Antioch fr. 187 = *Exc. de Ins.* 79), Blockley (1983), 89.
109. For a good discussion on the career and work of Olympiodorus see Matthews (1970), 79–97.
110. Sinor (1990c), 186, denies that Donatus is a Hun and speculates that he is a member of the Donatist heresy who found refuge among the Huns. This is highly unlikely.
111. Olympiodorus fr. 19 (*Bibl. Cod.* 80.173), Blockley (1983), 182.
112. Marcellinus Comes 444–5.1, Croke (1995), 18, 87. More on this later.
113. Kouridachus later in his flattery to Attila compares the Hunnic king to the Sun god. As Vaday (2000), 218, points out, the cult of the Sun was fundamental to Alan religion. A reminder of the intensity of the integration and acculturation that had occurred between the Huns and Alans by this stage.
114. Priscus, fr. 11.2, Blockley (1983), 258.
115. Priscus, fr. 11.2, Blockley (1983), 258.
116. Burns (1984), 46–7, 189, comments correctly that the Huns built up a governmental apparatus that unlike the earlier Germanic confederacies in the West and even the Greutung confederacy of the Goths, resulted in a tighter political command structure, precise ranks among government officials and allocation of clearly defined roles to conquered peoples.
117. See also Pritsak (1954a), 240. This Hunnic system of 'fief' allocation, the gradation of rank among nobles and territorial/tribal lords and the allocation of office based on these ranks, is very similar to the system found later among the Merovingian and Carolingian Franks, who also divided their kingdom into counties and territorial principalities that were distributed as fiefs to royal family members and a class of ranked military nobles. See Bloch (1961), 394–5. More on this in Chapter 6.
118. Priscus fr. 25 (Jordanes, *Getica* 50.259–63), Blockley (1983), 319–21.
119. Probably a title and not a personal name. A Germanicized Hunnic name says Bona (1991), 63.
120. Burgess (2001b), 97; Maenchen-Helfen (1973), 388.
121. Bona (1991), 63.
122. Findley (2005), 33.
123. Karaton's name is also likely to be a title rather than a personal name. His name means possibly 'black people' (*qara tun*), i.e. according to the colour designation of steppe political organization, ruler of the northern people, see Altheim (1959), vol. 1, 27. The European Huns were in all likelihood the Black Huns, i.e. the northern wing of the Hunnic state in Central Asia.
124. *Getica* 35.180, *germani Octar et Roas, qui ante Attilam regnum tenuisse narrantur.* See Croke (1977), 353, and Bona (1991), 50.

125. Sinor (1990c), 188. The rise to power of the sons of Mundzuk, the brother of Rua and Oktar, who may have died early, was obviously not without problems. Bleda and then Attila would continue to demand the return of royal fugitives in their dealings with the Romans before and after Bleda's murder. See Croke (1981), 160, 164.
126. Priscus, fr. 21.1(*Chron. Pasch.* 587 f.), Blockley (1983), 308. See also Malalas 19, 5–12, Lakatos, *Quellenbuch* 55, Pohl (1980), 247. An indication perhaps that he had ruled mainly the western Germanic tribes centred on a Gepid core before he usurped the role of supreme king of the Hunnic state from Bleda. This would explain the prominence of Ardaric and his Gepids during his reign and also in the succession crisis after his death. Even after overthrowing Hunnic hegemony the Gepids retained the system of dual kingship. We will discuss this matter further in the next chapter, but it is likely that one of the two kings of the Gepids was a figurehead set up by Ardaric from among the members of the Hunnic royal house in order to give his regime a stamp of legitimacy. The widespread diffusion and lasting continuation of eastern, steppe customs among the Gepids, for instance Hunno-Alanic cranial deformation and the use of Hunnic ritual metal mirrors, point to a powerful Hunnic element among the Gepids, see Pohl (1980), 248.
127. The old Empire of Xiongnu was very much characterized by federalism and collective rule among members of the royal clan (see Barfield 1981, 47, 51), though it did have a supreme ruler who was an autocrat in theory. Tyranny or monopolization of power by an over-zealous Shanyu could and did at times lead to deadly rebellions and overthrow of the ruling monarch, e.g. the overthrow of Wu-yen-chü-t'i who tried to centralize all political power in violation of the traditional rights of the Xiongnu nobility (*Han Shu* 94A: 35b–38b). Attila's overthrow of Bleda and his autocracy, like that of Wu-yen-chü-t'i who was also a usurper, are likely to have been the root cause of the disorder that followed his death. Opposition to his authoritarianism was already manifest during his reign, as shown by the desertion of royal princes of the blood such as Mama and Atakam to the Romans. These were later handed over to Attila by the defeated emperor in Constantinople or killed by the Romans when they refused to be handed over to Attila, Priscus fr. 2; 9.3, Blockely (1983), 227, 238. See Whitby (2000c), 705; Thompson (1996), 85; Lindner (1982), 705.
128. Altheim (1948), 28, sees the title *praecipuus rex* as a translation of an Oghuric Turkic title for emperor *aniliki* (equivalent of the Rouran/Avar Khagan) found in the Schumen inscription of the Danubian Bulgars.
129. Priscus fr. 24, Blockley (1983), 318.
130. Altheim (1948), 27–8, argues that Priscus' words summarizing Attila's career at his death that Attila had ruled both Scythia and Germania and terrorized both Roman Empires, reflect the Hunnic/steppe ideology of the emperor/Khagan by heavenly mandate ruling over the four quarters of the world. Certainly this type of ideology appears in the later Turkic Orkhon inscriptions and there is no reason why it could not have existed among the Huns. However, the

division between Scythia and Germania is a Roman geographical concept, not a Hunnic one. Thus the likelihood of these words reflecting any Hunnic steppe ideology is rather low. Though there is the possibility that Priscus is Romanizing a Hunnic chant for their dead ruler and has interpreted for his Roman readers Hunnic geographical concepts in a Roman way. Altheim also suggests other similarities between words and concepts in Priscus' funerary chant of the Huns and those in the Turkic Orkhon inscriptions. For instance Attila is praised for his good fortune in Priscus fr. 24 by the mourning Huns. The Turkic Khagan in the Orkhon inscriptions holds the title *iduq qut*, literally 'holy luck/fortune'. The counting of regnal years among the later Hunnic Bulgars also seems to mimic East Asian practices found in China, which could be the result of the residual memory of borrowings from earlier Hunnic/Xiongnu interactions with the Chinese.

131. See Golden (1992), 103, for a discussion on the Bulgar prince list that has Attila and Ernak as the founding ancestors. More on this later. For the possibility of double kingship (dualism between the Khagan and Iugurrus) among the Inner Asian Avars who succeeded the Huns in Hungary see Pohl (1988), 293–300.

132. Priscus, fr. 13, Blockley (1983), 284. Again indicative of the Hunnic practice of distributing 'fiefs' to royal family members and top-ranking nobles. This whole political structure is, as Altheim (1959), vol. IV, 286, notes, quasi-feudal and a forerunner of later medieval European feudal polities. More discussion on this in Chapter 6.

133. Thompson (1996), 181. See also Demougeot (1979), 533, 541–2.

134. For information on similar functions (diplomatic missions and military assignments) performed by Xiongnu governors/sub-kings dispatched by the central government see Pritsak (1954c), 194.

135. Priscus fr. 11, Blockley (1983), 258. See Altheim (1959), vol. IV, 25, for the astute observation that these *logades* function in ways reminiscent of the later *missi regii* of the Carolingian Franks. See also Grierson (1965), 291, and Ganshof (1971), 56–8, 126–35, 166–7, 173, for more information on the *missi*. The political impact of the Hunnic Empire on later European medieval polities such as the Frankish kingdom will be discussed in greater detail in Chapter 6.

136. Priscus fr. 11, Blockley (1983), 244. Thompson (1996), 183. Revealingly the name of one of Ernak's kinsmen Emmedzur is, according to Altheim (1959), vol. I, 27, a Latinized corruption of a formal Hunnic title *ämäcur* which means 'horse lord'. This almost exactly matches the title given to the governors of the Xiongnu Empire, 'ten thousand horsemen'.

137. Thompson (1996), 182. See also Altheim (1959), vol. IV, 281–3.

138. The Muslim geographer Ibn Fadlan (AD 922) tells us that the Khazars and the Volga Bulgars (descendents of the Huns) also held the right (east) as the place of honour. Thus the most important princes of the realm were seated to the right of the ruler/Khagan. See Velidî Togan (1939), 43, 212. See also Pritsak (1954b), 379.

139. Priscus fr. 13; 14, Blockley (1983), 284, 290. That these *logades* were not a random selection of men but are identical with the ranked officials of a

traditional steppe empire such as the Xiongnu and the Rouran is confirmed by the later Byzantine use of the same term to describe graded officials within the Avar Empire that succeeded the Huns, see Pohl (1988), 186.
140. Thompson (1996), 182.
141. Chelchal the Hun later during Dengizich's invasion of the Roman Empire in the late 460s describes these Hunnic collections of taxes (tribute) from the Goths which caused discontent among the Goths in the Hunnic army, Priscus fr. 49, Blockley (1983), 356.
142. Thompson (1996), 197.
143. See Ishjamts (1994), 158, for a description of the six horns nobles. See also de Crespigny (1984), 177.
144. De Crespigny (1984), 177.
145. In Chuvash, the only living descendent of the Oghuric language of the Huns, *alti* ('six' in common Turkic) is rendered *ultta*, hence *ulticur* instead of *alticur*. This reconstruction is considered to be anachronistic by Doerfer (1973), 20, who on the basis of a Volga Bulgarian inscription from the thirteenth/fourteenth century where six is rendered as *alti*, not *ultta*, argues that the 'u' is a later development in Chuvash that does not reflect the form of six in Oghuric Turkic. However, his argument is based on weak premises, assuming that Volga Bulgarian of the thirteenth/fourteenth century is purely Oghuric Turkic. He fails to take into consideration the fact that the inscription dates from a time when Volga Bulgarian was undergoing a transformation into Kipchaq Turkic. The only language that probably reflects the language of the Hunnic-Bulgars is Chuvash.
146. Referred to as tribe in Agathias 5.11.2, Frendo (1975), 146. It is probably a reference not to a specific tribe, but to tribes led by the six lords. See Altheim (1959), vol. 1, 27.
147. Constantine Porphyrogenitus, *De Cerimoniis Aulae Byzantinae*, 2.47. See also Haussig (2000), 277.
148. Pritsak (1954b), 379.
149. Altheim (1959), vol. 1, 25–6, is of the opinion that Dulo is a reference to the origins of the Hunnic-Bulgars in Central Asia. Another tribal designation mentioned in the Bulgar prince list, Ermi, also refers to a location in Central Asia, the region of the Ermichions, which according to Theophanes 239.20, lies within the territory of the Avars (at this stage the region of western Turkestan).
150. Pritsak (1954a), 241, 245.
151. Pritsak (1952b), 55, and Pritsak (1955a), 64. Benjamin (2007), 120, agrees that there is probably a dynastic link between the old Xiongnu and the European Huns, but see also Altheim (1959), vol. 1, 20–6, who is sceptical about the dynastic links between the Bulgar Dulo clan and the old Xiongnu Empire. He argues that the Onogurs and Onoq are one and the same and that the Bulgar kings traced their origins to this Western Turkish tribal confederation in modern day Kazakhstan. He also argues (p. 27) that the Huns were a branch of the Xianbei (the other great steppe people who defeated the Xiongnu in Mongolia), not the Xiongnu. This seems highly unlikely.

152. Pritsak (1954a), 245.
153. On the possible Hunnic origin of Valamer, the founder of the Ostrogothic confederation, see the next chapter.
154. Wolfram (1988), 75.
155. It can be no accident that the sixth-century Utigur Hunnic prince bears the same name as the last Khagan of the Rouran *A-na-kuei* (Chinese transliteration), which in its original pronunciation corresponds exactly to *Anagai-os* (Greek transliteration). See Pulleyblank (2000b), 85. See also the comments of Kyzlasov (1996), 317, that the western Huns had a clear-cut military and administrative system like the Xiongnu with hereditary rulers, and Werner (1956), 2, who points out that the Hunnic state system and structure was not dissimilar to later steppe empires.
156. Altheim (1948), 24. More discussion on this in Chapter 6.
157. Thompson (1996), 54; Bell-Fialkoff (2000), 226; Sinor (1990c), 181; Geary (2002), 94–9; Heather (2009), 216–20.
158. Altheim (1959), vol. 1, 363, suggests likewise.
159. See Allsen (1996), 116–35, for a detailed analysis of ideology in the formation of political structures in the steppe.
160. Ammianus Marcellinus 31.3.3.
161. Maenchen-Helfen (1973), 23, 444–55. See also Altheim (1959), vol. 1, 8. These people continued to resist Hunnic domination even after retreating to the Danube well after AD 376. See Golden (2000), 282. Altheim (1959), vol. 1, 3–6, 12–13, Vernadsky (1951), 347, and Haussig (2000), 256, all agree that already in the second century AD a group of Huns or early Turkic speakers had entered Europe. They identify the Khunnoi in Ptolemy 3.5.10, who are seen in the company of the Sarmatian Bastarnae and Roxolani in the Nogai steppe, as early Turkic Huns. See also Batty (2007), 360, who also accepts this consensus. Haussig assumes that the Iazyges (probably Sarmatians) who later appear in Hungary along with the Bastarnae and the Roxolani are Turkish Huns and that this set a precedent for later Hunnic movements into this region, *Iazy* in old Turkish supposedly meaning 'plain/ plateau'. This is, however, highly speculative. The flight of parts of the northern Xiongnu in the second century AD to Kazakhstan also may corroborate the presence of some Huns in the west who could be the Khunnoi mentioned by Ptolemy. See also Sinor (1990c), 178, Thompson (1996), 25, and Christian (1998), 203.
162. Wolfram (1997b), 80–2. The existence and nature of this confederation, however, is highly disputed. The Huns (both the Huns invading from Central Asia and those with a similar name (Khunnoi) already residing in the Pontic steppe since the second century AD (who were probably by this stage completely sarmatianized)) as Maenchen-Helfen (1973), 29, points out, certainly do not appear to have participated in the battle of Adrianople. They may though have been induced by bribes to raid Roman territory further north along the Danube (p. 28). Randers-Pehrson (1983), 49, suggests the possibility that the name Saphrax is Hunnic. This is also suggested by Burns (1984), 38, but it is more likely that he was Alan.

163. Liebeschuetz (1990), 61; Demougeot (1979), 390.
164. Biswas (1973), 15.
165. The Roman Empire of the East that had survived the Hunnic conquest of its Western twin, would face a similar invasion of Turkic Seljuks in the eleventh century. The Seljuk Empire was a vast entity stretching from Central Asia to the Mediterranean and no one has ever suggested that this Empire of Inner Asian invaders from exactly the same area as the Huns was without a state structure or political organization. Yet when the Seljuks first invade the Eastern Roman Empire, small groups of Turkmen acting semi-independently of the Seljuk sultan sometimes enter Roman service, just like the 'other' Huns who fight independently of the main Huns in Europe. Later on in order to repel the Norman invasion of Greece the emperor Alexius I hires whole regiments of Turkish cavalry from the Seljuk sultan of Rum just as Theodosius, Stilicho and Aetius had hired Hunnic troops from the Hunnic kings in Europe six centuries earlier. See Norwich (1991), vol. III, 7, 21, 50. None of this suggests that the Seljuks were without political institutions or that they were primitively organized.
166. The later Pechenegs who occupied the same territory as the Huns and whose elite may have used the same Oghuric Turkic language as the Huns (Pritsak 1976c, 23) in the Ukraine between the ninth and eleventh centuries AD are also accused of being 'stateless' and poorly organized due to the mercenary activity of some of their constituent tribes, but facts speak for themselves. As Pritsak (1976c), 12–16, notes, the Pecheneg state was intricately organized with a complex system of precedence and ranks. Constantine Porphyrogenitus mentions that there was a dual Khaganate in the typical steppe manner ruled by the Thonuzoba charismatic clan, four provinces (*thema*, the word used to designate Byzantine provinces) in each wing with each province further divided into five districts (*meros*), for a total of eight provinces (of which three, being inhabited by the ruling Cangars, had precedence over the rest) and forty districts. It would be very difficult to argue that what we have here does not constitute a 'state', even if a rudimentary one. The myth of bad organization among nomads consistently leads historians to ignore the obvious inadequacy of their assessment of the political organization of steppe state entities.
167. Xu (2005), 7, 87.
168. *Wei Shu* 100. 2223; *Bei Shi* 94.3128.
169. *Sui Shu* 84.1881–2; *Xin Tangshu* 219.6168.
170. *Zizhi Tongjian* 185.5792.
171. *Zizhi Tongjian* 246.7967. For an excellent summary of Khitan relations with the Turks (Gokturks and Uyghurs) see Xu (2005), 188–205.
172. See Xu (2005), 83–102.
173. See Kwanten (1979), 76–7 for a good summary of Abaoji's career.
174. Xu (2005), 4.
175. Xu (2005), 260–1.
176. *Zizhi Tongjian* 266.8678–9.
177. Xu (2005), 257.

Notes to pages 63–7

178. Pritsak (1968), 162–3.
179. Standen (2005), 139–46.
180. Xu (2005), 141, 148–51.
181. Standen (2005), 131, 159.
182. Standen (2005), 146.
183. Standen (2005), 155–6. See also Standen (2009), 87–103, for a detailed history of the Khitan intervention in China and the seizure of the sixteen prefectures.
184. We will discuss all of the above in detail shortly.
185. Standen (2005), 135. For a very similar phenomenon among the Turkmen frontier guards of the Seljuk Sultanate of Rum in Anatolia see Köprülü (1992), 77–80.
186. See Kwanten (1979), 119–22.
187. For details see Kwanten (1979), 59–62.
188. Bosworth (1968), 16.
189. Christian (1998), 354–5. For an in-depth analysis of the early history of the Karakhanids see Pritsak (1951).
190. Pritsak (1953–4), 23; Christian (1998), 371; Kwanten (1979), 60.
191. Bosworth (1968), 11.
192. The Seljuks originally started off as allies/vassals of first the Oghuz Yabghu and then the Karakhanids, Pritsak (1952a), 288–9.
193. Bosworth (1968), 49; Findley (2005), 70.
194. Lambton (1968), 218–19.
195. Bosworth (1968), 50–1.
196. Bosworth (1968), 49.
197. Bosworth (1968), 61.
198. Pritsak (1951), 273, 285; Christian (1998), 371; Findley (2005), 75.
199. Pritsak (1952a), 281, 284–5, 287; Christian (1998), 355. See also Findley (2005), 68, and Kwanten (1979), 62.
200. Bosworth (1968), 17–19.
201. Bosworth (1968), 18.
202. Pritsak (1968), 163; (1952a), 290–1; Bosworth (1968), 66.
203. Lambton (1968), 217.
204. Bosworth (1968), 41.
205. Christian (1998), 375.
206. Bosworth (1968), 63.
207. Rice (1961), 51; Bosworth (1968), 43.
208. Bosworth (1968), 67; Kwanten (1979), 65.
209. Lambton (1968), 219.
210. Rice (1961), 43–50; Bosworth (1968), 67.
211. The Karakhanids were a fractious dynasty just like other Turco-Mongol dynasties in history, always prone to civil war due to disputes over fief allocations, and this limited their potential for extensive conquests. However, their internal organization was so sound that their dynasty would rule in Central Asia for nearly 400 year from the mid ninth century to AD 1212. See Pritsak (1953–4), 37–57.
212. Heather (2006), 202.

213. Maenchen-Helfen (1973), 31.
214. Zosimus 4.34.6.
215. Ambrose *Ep.* 24.8 (ed. PL 16, c. 1038). Alemany (2000), 31. Thompson (1996), 30, suggests that the Huns may also have conquered eastern Pannonia during this time from the Romans.
216. Maenchen-Helfen (1973), 46.
217. Orosius *Hist.* 7.38.3; 7.40.3. (ed. Arnaud-Lindet *CUF* 3, pp. 112, 118), Alemany (2000), 62–3.
218. Zosimus 5.26.4 (ed. Paschoud *CUF* 3, p. 39), Alemany (2000), 109–10.
219. More on this in the next chapter. Vandalarius (conqueror of the Vandals) and Hunimund (according to Jordanes, victorious over the Suebi), who I will argue were likely to have been Huns, appear on the scene around this time.
220. Uldin is called a *regulus* (a sub-king or petty king), which indicates that he was a minor Hunnic king rather than the principal king, see Schramm (1969), 143. That honour belonged to a monarch further east in line with the usual Inner Asian practice of privileging the east over the west.
221. See Burns (1984), 46. The imposition of Hunimund as king of the Goths and Suebi was probably the cause of the secession. More on this in the next chapter.
222. Sozomon, *Ecclesiastical History* 9.5. See Thompson (1996), 33–4, for more details, both regarding Uldin's campaign and the extraordinary countermeasures taken by the Romans after the invasion to prevent future invasions. Fortifications and the Roman fleet along the Danube were especially strengthened, demonstrating that the Huns had given the East Romans a scare despite the setback suffered by Uldin.
223. Heather (1996), 117.
224. Findley (2005), 81–3, the ability to mobilize manpower and tax conquered populations are key indicators of administrative efficiency. The Huns like the later Mongols possessed both capacities.
225. Tapper (1991), 508–9.
226. Tapper (1991), 514–15.
227. See Frye (1984), 142.
228. Maenchen-Helfen (1973), 52 ff.
229. Jerome, *Commentary on Ezekiel* 38.2, ed. J.-P. Migne, *Patrologia Latina* 25. 356A; *Epistolae* 77.8, records how the east trembled at the sight of their swift horses. Ephraim the Syrian is more dramatic and in a violent diatribe claims that the Huns ate children, drank the blood of women and were the reincarnation of the devil, Gog and Magog, Sinor (1993), 4.
230. For example there were defectors such as those mentioned by Priscus, and royal family members who were unwilling to take orders from Attila, fr. 9.3. See Bona (1991), 61. For the tradition of 'blood tanistry' among the Turco-Mongols of Inner Asia to determine the royal succession see Fletcher (1978).
231. Goldsworthy (2009), 417.
232. Thompson (1996), 237, and more recently Kelly (2009), 51, in a less polemical fashion, have categorized the Hunnic state as a parasitic entity that contributed

233. Hunnic mercenary service in the Roman payroll would occur as early as the beginning of the fifth century AD when Honorius employed an army of 10,000 Huns to attack Alaric, Thompson (1996), 54. Aetius in AD 425 employed an army of 60,000 (!) Huns to support the usurper John against the forces of Theodosius II, see Sinor (1990c), 187. The Huns would also participate in the destruction of the Burgundians in support of Aetius in 437 (Prosper, *Epitoma Chronicon* 1322, ed. Mommsen *MGH AA* 9, p. 475; *Chronica Gallica* of 452, 118, ed. Mommsen, p. 660) and again under Aetius defeat the Visigoths in AD 438, Collins (2000), 113. A small contingent of this western expedition would also aid Litorius against the Visigoths in 436 with success, relieving Narbonne. A later foray against the Visigoths in 439, however, failed leading to the death of Litorius who, according to Salvian, put his trust in the Huns, while the Goths put theirs in God! See also Schutz (2000), 58, and Collins (1999), 82–4. Huns were also employed in the capture of Tibatto, the leader of the Bagaudae in AD 437, Thompson (1996), 77–8.
234. On the Bacaudae see Drinkwater (1992), 208–17.
235. Jones (1964), vol. I, 189, Elton (1992), 170, Halsall (2007), 244, and Kelly (2009), 85.
236. Jones (1964), vol. I, 193.
237. Croke (1981), 167.
238. Priscus fr. 9.1, Blockley (1983), 235.
239. Maenchen-Helfen (1973), 110; Wickham (2009), 81.
240. Marcellinus Comes, Croke (1995), 19. As Whitby (2007b), 137–8, points out the Hunnic invasions of the 440s were a more serious crisis for the empire than the Gothic invasions of the 370s.
241. See Poulter (2007c), 39; (2007b), 71.
242. For an accurate assessment of the Persian threat to Rome in the fifth century, which was quite negligible due to pressures the Persian were under in the east of their empire, see Jones (1964), vol. II, 1030–1.
243. See Croke (1981), 161. This battle as well as the negotiations conducted by Anatolius after it (described in Priscus fr. 9.3, Blockley (1983), 236–40), dated by Thompson (1996), 93, to AD 442 cannot have taken place in that year, but must be dated to AD 447 as Maenchen-Helfen (1973), 114–18, explains. This also has important ramifications for assessing the nature of the East Roman contribution to the war effort of AD 452 against Attila, as we shall see later.
244. Theophanes, *Chron.* AM 5942.
245. Burgess (2001a), 80; Muhlberger (1990), 174. One hundred cities says Callinicus, *De Vita S. Hypatii*, 139.21 ff., see Croke (1995), 88. See also Kelly (2009), 104.
246. Theophanes, *Chron.* AM 5942. Theophanes confusingly jumbles the events of between AD 441 and 447 and places the death of Bleda (*c.* AD 444–5 at the earliest, see Croke (1995), 87) and various events belonging to two separate wars in a single account. See Maenchen-Helfen (1973), 113. The Huns and

later the Avars were the only two barbarian peoples to master siege warfare which made them all the more dangerous to Roman defences in the Balkans and elsewhere. See Whitby (2000b), 310–11. Most cities in the Balkans had survived the previous incursions of the Goths (in the late fourth and early fifth centuries AD), who were not skilled besiegers, but the impact of the Huns on the empire was serious, precisely because of their ability to capture fortified Roman positions as well as destroy Roman field armies, Whitby (2000c), 708–9.

247. Thompson (1996), 102; Heather (2007), 178.
248. Muhlberger (1990), 174.
249. See Lee (2000), 41–2, and Whitby (2000c), 709.
250. Marcellinus Comes 447.2, Croke (1995), 19; Thompson (1948), 94.
251. Priscus, fr. 9.3 (*Exc. de Leg. Gent.* 3), Blockley (1983), 236–40.
252. Thompson (1996), 172–3; Wolfram (1997b), 104. In the Western Empire the situation was much more serious and with a comparatively small income of some 40,000 pounds of gold the government in AD 450 on the eve of the Great Hunnic Invasion would have been forced to spend a staggering 60 percent of its annual tax revenue just to maintain an army of 30,000 men, Wolfram (1997b), 104.
253. For a counter-argument see Lee (2000), 41, 45.
254. Wickham (2009), 33.
255. Cameron (1993), 97.
256. Croke (1981), 163.
257. No less than four embassies were sent by Attila to Constantinople after AD 447, Croke (1981), 165.
258. Priscus fr. 9, Blockley (1983), 237. See also Croke (1983b), 297–308, for a discussion on this fragment.
259. Cameron (1993), 112.
260. Holmes and Evans (2006), 36.
261. Bury (1923), vol. 1, 293–4, obviously from a different perspective from the one adopted in this book, argues that the course of history would not have been altered if Attila had won the battle. It will henceforth be demonstrated that actually the Huns were probably victorious and that indeed the course of history was not altered, but that the new history of Europe was slightly different from the one that has been imagined by generations of historians.
262. Thierry (1856), 178. Murdoch (2006), 54, still argues that the victory 'saved European culture' and was 'a defining moment in Europe's history'.
263. The neglect of the Roman contribution to the battle is largely due to the battle narrative provided by Jordanes who in a speech that he attributes to Attila (clearly Jordanes' own) casts disparaging remarks on the effectiveness of Roman troops (*Getica* 39. 204–5). This has led Ferrill (1986), 152–3, to build an entire thesis about the supposed degeneration of Roman troops by the mid fifth century AD. This is however based on highly dubious assertions made by Jordanes and it is likely that the main enemy faced by the Huns in the great battle was the Western Romans, not the Visigoths.

264. Similar ideas were already being floated during the sixteenth century in Germany and France. See Kelley (1993), 164. For discussion on British 'Germanic' nationalism which triggered this type of racial stereotyping see Weinbrot (1997), 177.
265. Creasy (1943), 145. For the contribution of German nineteenth-century philology to racism and racial theories against the Huns in England and Germany as part of the nineteenth-century century reinvention of antiquity see Shippey (1982), 68. Quite amusingly William Morris, in the late nineteenth century, would consider the Goths to be very much the same as the English in status and turn the Huns into his Dusky men, the invading horde (Shippey (1982, 56). This later influenced Tolkien when writing his famous novels.
266. Fuller (1954), 286. This somewhat baffling hostility towards the Huns is matched by the equally baffling desire even in post-1940s scholarship to excuse the comparable brutality of the Goths and other Germanic invading tribes. Thus Alföldi (1965), in a publication as reputable as the *Cambridge Ancient History*, speaks in glowing terms of the might of the Goths who plundered the Mediterranean provinces of the empire in the third century AD. 'The Goths were men of a mighty stamp; their warriors were giants indeed – the attacking Germans were few in number and only able to gain the upper hand through the effeminate cowardice of the garrisons of Asia Minor or of the civil population', he says (p. 159). After indulging in both the inordinate exaltation of the Goths and unabashed orientalism towards the 'asiatics', he then goes out of his way to excuse the cruelty of the invading Goths. His analysis is so superbly rhetorical that it deserves a full quotation: 'Even in modern times war lets loose the basest passions. What wonder, then those children of nature revelled in sheer destruction? If they deliberately burn cities after sacking them, or murder such prisoners as are sick and decrepit? It would not be wholly just to charge them with the moral guilt of all this. The tragedy was not brought about by any ethical inferiority of the German race, but by the clash of two worlds at different levels of culture. As long as the Germans remained in their primitive environment, it was natural that they earn their daily bread, not in the sweat of the brow, but in blood: "volenti non fit iniuria." But when they turned the law of violence against the world-State, which was adapted for peace and had based its whole mighty organisation on a humane mode of life, their primitive morality proved disastrous to the higher morality of the Empire, little as they can be blamed for it. It is an observed fact that, the greater the friction, the greater the assimilation to one another of two surfaces in contact; and so even these destructive wars produced a pronounced assimilation of the opposing parties, which, for the Germans, acquired a decisive historical importance' (p. 161). But then surely one could say exactly the same things about Hunnic massacres.
267. Fuller (1954), 299.
268. Fuller (1954), 301.
269. Holmes and Evans (2006), 36–7.
270. Parker (1995), 64. See also Thompson (1996), 154–6.

271. Thompson (1996), 237. Kelly (2009), 51, unfortunately, despite his other great insights, repeats this line of thought and labels the Hunnic Empire a parasitic state.
272. *Getica* 35.182.
273. See Lindner (1982), 703, who rightly points out that it is pointless to talk about a Hunnic race or ethnic group given the varied origins of the people who made up the Hunnic people.
274. Ferrill (1986), 150, as late as 1986 would argue that the battle was significant as a conflict between Christians and heathens that saved Christian Europe. Surely this is preposterous.
275. Some Huns may have started converting to Christianity even before the reign of Attila. See Jerome (AD 403), *Ep.* 107.2 and Orosius (AD 417), 7.41.8, who mention Hunnic converts to Christianity.
276. More on this shortly in the following chapters.
277. Merrills and Miles (2010), 115, point out that the invasion of 451 led directly to the collapse of Aetius' power and ultimately to that of Valentinian III. Elton (1992), 171–2, argues quite erroneously that the military situation in Gaul did not change after the Hunnic invasion. He is thus left with the dilemma of explaining why the previously formidable Roman military establishment almost entirely loses control of Gaul within a decade of the invasion and relies completely on military support from the Visigoths, Burgundians and Franks to even maintain a semblance of authority.
278. For instance we know from another fragment of Priscus 21.1 (*Chron. Pasch.* 587 ff.), Blockley (1983), 308, that Theodorid, according to the original Priscan account, was killed by an arrow, not from a fall from his horse as Jordanes would have it. Jordanes' narrative is full of such embellishments and alterations of Priscus' original narrative. Therefore the account in the *Getica* is not at all reliable.
279. Jordanes, as Barnish (1992), 41, accurately observes, carried out 'a major pro-Gothic reshaping' of the original account of the invasion written by Priscus. Barnish also convincingly suggests that the narrative of the battle found in the *Getica* has been coloured by Cassiodorus. More on this later. Merrills and Miles (2010), 5, note correctly that Jordanes typically uses enemies of the Goths such as the Vandals as a literary device for highlighting the valour and greatness of his Goths. The reliability of his narrative is therefore highly questionable whenever battles involving Goths are discussed. Especially so since there is an instance where Jordanes even goes as far as to invent a phantom Vandal kingdom north of the Danube in the early fourth century AD in order to attribute a great victory over the Vandals to an equally fictitious ancient Gothic king called Geberich, *Getica* 22.113–5 (Merrills and Miles (2010), 28). Jordanes in *Getica* 31.161; *Romana* 322, even invents the bizarre scenario of the Alans and Vandals fleeing Pannonia and invading Gaul (AD 406) because they feared that the Visigoths might return, see Goffart (1988), 64. Vernadsky (1951), 378, suggests that the battle of Chalons was militarily indecisive.

Notes to pages 75–7

280. *Getica* 40.209.
281. In fact as Elton (1992), 173–4, points out, the Visigoths were militarily speaking markedly unsuccessful in Gaul in the fifth century. They rarely won battles and were defeated in most of the major field battles they fought against the Romans, Huns and the Franks. Their bad luck would continue even during the reign of Euric after they gained control of most of southern Gaul and after Roman power in Gaul as a whole had almost completely vanished.
282. *Getica* 41.216. Thompson (1996), 155–6; Kelly (2009), 197–8.
283. For the Visigothic expansion under Euric after the deaths of both Attila and Aetius see Giese (2004), 51–3.
284. The similarity of this ploy with the unending deceptions, underhandedness and intrigues of Themistocles in the Herodotean narrative of the Greek defeat of the Persians has been noted by Wallace-Hadrill (1962), 60–3. The Herodotean allusions throughout the battle narrative will be discussed below, all of which suggests that the information provided by Jordanes regarding the behaviour of the key figures in the battle is in many cases an artificial, literary construct, not factual at all.
285. The Visigoths of course eventually benefited from the defeat of the Romans and then the subsequent demise of Hunnic authority in the region after AD 453. Both empires (Roman and Hunnic) had vacated the scene and Gaul was ripe for the taking by either the Goths or the Franks who had suffered comparatively little from the Hunnic invasion.
286. Kelly (2009), 198, correctly observes that after the first day of the battle the Romans and the Goths could not be confident of victory the next day.
287. *Getica* 40.211.
288. *Getica* 40.212.
289. The sceptical Altheim (1959), vol. IV, 324–9, even goes as far as to argue that Jordanes' description of the battle is in fact modelled on Herodotus' description of the battle of Salamis. The behaviour of the main characters in the battle and the various stages of the battle are therefore, according to him, largely artificial constructs, literary fiction.
290. *Getica* 40.213.
291. *Getica* 40.212.
292. *Getica* 40.212, *sic bellicosissimus rex victores suos turbabat inclusus*.
293. Gregory of Tours 2.7; *Chronica Minora* I, p. 302. Thompson (1996), 156.
294. What is curious is that the *Gallic Chronicle of 452*, which should be the more reliable source of events in the fifth century given the fact that it is contemporary, talks about the *gravi clade inflicta* and nothing else. It attributes victory to the Romans. The later *Chronicle of 511* however, which without a doubt used the earlier chronicle as a source (Burgess 2001b, 86), does not mention a Roman victory or a Hunnic defeat and writes that the Patrician Aetius and Theodoric, King of the Goths, fought against Attila, King of the Huns, at Mauriacus where Theodoric and Laudaricus, a blood relative of Attila, were killed. It adds that there were innumerable corpses. The great deal of additional and accurate details that this latter chronicle provides, indicate

that it is based on a more reliable source/sources than the terse details provided in the *Chronicle of 452*, and reflects the actual situation. The fact that Attila chose to return with the bulk of his army to Hungary after the battle probably led chroniclers like the Gallic chronicler of 452 and Hydatius to attribute a pyrrhic victory to the Romans. More on this shortly.

295. *Gallic Chronicle of 511*, Burgess (2001b), 97; Bona (2002), 57; Marin (1990), 45; Érdy (1995), 17–18.
296. *Getica* 40.210.
297. Bachrach (1973), 66.
298. Bachrach (1973), 64–5.
299. The importance of which is rightly stressed by Bury (1923), vol. 1, 293–4, who argued that this was the decisive encounter, not the later battle of Chalons itself. I would argue that the siege was decisive in that it delayed the Hunnic advance into Gaul and compelled the Huns even after their costly victory at Chalons to withdraw to Hungary due to the close of the campaigning season that year, thereby allowing Roman historians to attribute a pyrrhic victory to the Romans of Aetius.
300. We can see a clear example of this in Jordanes' text itself. In *Getica* 43.227, Jordanes talks about another battle between the Huns and Thorismud's Visigoths after Chalons. Jordanes with his usual hyperbole says that Attila was dealt another humiliating defeat at the hands of the Visigoths. But then just after this in 228 he says: *Thorismud vero repulsis ab Alanis Hunnorum catervis sine aliqua suorum lesione* 'Now after the bands of the Huns had been repulsed by the Alani, without any hurt to his own men, Thorismud' departed for Tolosa, i.e the battle was fought by the Alans not the Visigoths and indeed the Huns were, as Jordanes himself acknowledges, attacking not the Visigoths but the Alans settled near the Loire river (226).
301. Bachrach (1973), 66–7.
302. *Getica* 41.214.
303. Hdt. 6.111–21.
304. *Getica* 36.184. Bona (2002), 67, rightly dismisses this as highly unlikely.
305. In fact Jordanes himself makes this bribery on the part of Geiseric superfluous by mentioning that Attila had already thought long about such a campaign, *Getica* 36.185. Merrills and Miles (2010), 115, regard this reference to Geiseric's involvement as an invention of a later historian. For further discussion on this episode see Clover (1967), 113–17, 127–8, and Berndt (2007), 136–7.
306. Priscus, fr. 20, 1 (*Exc. de. Leg. Gent.* 7), Blockely (1983), 304–6. The Priscan origin of this fragment is doubted by Christensen (2002), 340, on the grounds that its focus on Geiseric, thus Goths and Honoria, smacks of Cassiodorus/Jordanes, not Priscus.
307. Priscus, fr. 20, 3 (*Exc. de. Leg. Gent.* 7), Blockley (1983), 306.
308. The importance of the Franks in this whole invasion saga which is stressed by Priscus is almost erased from memory by Cassiodorus–Jordanes. See Barnish (1992), 41. Barnish also suggests that the narrative of the battle found in the *Getica* has been coloured by Cassiodorus' literary objective which was to

present his patron Theodoric the Great as a greater Aetius–Theodorid and Clovis, Theodoric's northern rival, as a lesser Attila (pp. 41–2).
309. This includes Thompson (1996), 144, who sees Toulouse as the original target, along with perhaps the aim of replacing Aetius as *magister militum* of the Western Roman Empire! As if the king of most of Europe who boasted that the Roman emperor was not even equal to his own generals would have considered this a desirable prospect.
310. Whitby (2000a), 482.
311. See Rogers (1996), 3–26.
312. Hardly a neutral observer, Sidonius in his panegyric attributes the 'victory' over the Huns not to Aetius but to Avitus (!), whom he was trying to flatter (*Carm.* 7.315–66), declaring that it was due to his diplomacy that the Goths were induced to come to the aid of Aetius and rescue his handful of auxiliaries from the Huns. The Roman army indeed was reduced to a handful of auxiliaries after the battle and the army that remained virtually intact and still potent after the battle was that of the Visigoths. The reason for this, however, and the Visigothic dominance in Gaul after the battle was, as discussed above, due to the fact that the Romans and Alans under Aetius bore the brunt of the battle and the casualties, while the Goths after the death of their king retired to safety, hence suffering minimal losses. Sidonius' panegyric that magnifies the role of the Goths to glorify Avitus, whom the Visigoths later raised to the position of emperor, would contribute to creating the false impression that the Goths were mainly responsible for the 'defeat' of the Huns. This impression would be amplified by Cassiodorus, Jordanes and Isidore of Seville, all of whom had a vested interest in stressing the role of the Goths.
313. Prosper a. 451, Murray (2000), 73.
314. See note 312.
315. Lebecq (2006), 329–30, argues that Adovacrius (Gregory of Tours, *Decem libri historiarum* 2.18) the ruler of the Saxon 'pirates' is different from Odovacrius (2.19), whom he sees as Odoacer, the ruler of Italy. However, the context of the passage seems to confirm that they are one and the same.
316. For information on the exaggeration of Aegidius' and Syagrius' authority in Gaul see Collins (2000), 118, James (1988), 70–1, and Bachrach (1972), 3. The realm of Soissons probably consisted of little more than Soissons and surrounding areas. See Demougeot (1979), 686. They certainly did not control North-western Gaul which was under Armorican-Alan rule. See also Wood (2000), 507. Chaos reigned north of the Loire before Frankish unification, Wood (2000), 509, because Roman imperial authority north of the Loire had all but vanished after the Hunnic invasion.
317. AD 469 says Geary (1988), 80.
318. The Franks north of the Loire, as Demougeot (1979), 674–5, points out, were not exactly the federates of the empire that some historians are inclined to assume. Allies indeed some of them were at different points with Aegidius and Paul against the Visigoths, but the Franks were by no means the dependants of Aegidius. The Frankish invasion (Sidonius *Carm.* 7.360–75) and takeover of

Roman territory in the mid 450s (perhaps tellingly, right after the end of the initial phase of the Hunnic civil war in the east, probably as a mop-up of conquests already effected by the Huns earlier in the decade in Germania I and Belgica Secunda) is highly informative and reveals the true nature of the Frankish dealings with the Romans (Demougeot 1979, 676–8). Aegidius was in fact in all probability dependent on Frankish military support rather than the other way around, as the battle against the Visigoths in AD 463 clearly shows. He is named as the victor by Hydatius and Priscus, but the *Gallic Chronicle* tells us that it was the Franks who did the fighting. See James (1988), 64. As James accurately puts it, the Kingdom of Syagrius is 'a figment of the modern historical imagination' (p. 72). Most of northern Gaul, after Attila's invasion and the exit of Odoacer to Italy, was in the hands of the Britons– Alans in Armorica, the Rhineland Franks in the east and the rest of the Franks under Childeric in the centre (the most powerful it seems of the three given the geographical scope of Childeric's campaigns from Angers in the west to Alaman territory in the east (p. 75)). The *Epistulae Austrasiacae*, 2, also tells us that Childeric ruled Belgica Secunda and that Clovis had inherited his position from his father, Wood (1994), 40–1. Now Belgica Secunda includes Soissons, which means that Syagrius was probably a minor ruler under the overlordship of the Franks of Childeric, or as Wood (1985), 262, suggests, he may have started establishing himself in a position of power after the enthronement of Clovis as the new king of the Franks, taking advantage of Clovis' youth and inexperience (Clovis was only 15 when he became king, says Gregory of Tours 2.43). A temporary weakening of the Frankish position in northern Gaul during the early years of Clovis' rule is highly likely.

319. Gregory of Tours, *Hist. Franc.*, *MGH, SS. Rer. Merov.*, 1.83.18 and 19.
320. So does Wood (2000), 510, Collins (1999), 103, and James (1988), 69–70. Reynolds and Lopez (1946), 47, think the Saxons that Adovacrius leads here are an error and should in fact be the Sciri, who are the people usually under Odoacer's leadership in our sources. However, this need not be the case. The continental Saxons had been conquered by the Huns like all other Germanic groups outside the Roman empire. The Hunnic onslaught was what probably triggered the Saxon exodus to Britain. However, many more remained in Germany under Hunnic domination and may have been given to the Hunnic noble Odoacer as his fief.
321. Bona (1991), 127.
322. Priscus fr. 20.3, Blockley (1983), 306.
323. The disputed Frankish succession is unlikely to have been a struggle among the Ripuarian Franks along the Rhine. The Franks under consideration are most likely to have been the Salian Franks, since all tribes east of the Rhine were already under Hunnic rule by this stage in the 450s. We cannot know for certain which group of Franks Priscus was referring to, but for what it is worth Jordanes in his list of tribes that supported Aetius in 451 distinguishes the Riparii (i.e. the Ripuarians) from the Franci by which he means the Salians (*Getica* 36.191).

324. Fredegar's *Chronicle* 3.11. See Murray (2000), 612; Bona (2002), 68; Demougeot (1979), 682.
325. Halsall (2001), 123, 125, argues that the Thoringi mentioned in Gregory of Tours (2.12) is a mistake for *Tungri*, the inhabitants of the area around Tongres in northern Gaul. He notes that Gregory elsewhere (*Hist.* 2.9) refers to this northern Gallic region as Thoringia and that he has made up the story of Childeric's flight to trans-Rhine Thuringia on the basis of the similarity between the name of his wife Basina and the Thuringian king Basinus/Bisinus (a name borne by a Thuringian king east of the Rhine, a common dynastic name among the Thuringians suggests Demougeot (1979), 750). Vanderspoel (2009), 427–9, argues along the same lines and postulates the year AD 456 as the date for Childeric's exile to the Thuringi and that this was triggered by foreknowledge among Salian Franks of the Ripuarian Frankish invasion of AD 457 that led to the capture of Cologne and Trier. He argues that Childeric started off as the vassal of the Roman general Aegidius and was under Roman protection. However, as mentioned earlier, the power of Aegidius was nowhere near as formidable as Halsall and Vanderspoel regard it to have been. Also evidence from Childeric's tomb filled with items strongly indicative of eastern, Danubian Hunnic influence (James (1988), 62; Périn and Feffer (1987), vol. 1, 114–34) suggests the likelihood that the Thuringia to which Childeric fled was indeed the Thuringia beyond the Rhine. See also Richter (1994), 20. We will later discuss in greater detail the intensity of Hunnic influence on the Thuringians in the fifth century. Halsall and Vanderspoel, on the basis of the report in Gregory of Tours that Aegidius ruled instead of Childeric over the Franks for eight years as king during Childeric's exile in Thuringia, date Childeric's exile to 456 and his return to 463, when he allies with the Romans against the Visigoths. However, this is in all likelihood an error. The dates simply do not make sense in the light of what we know about Aegidius' activities in Gaul and the 24-year reign attributed to Childeric (Demougeot 1979, 682). Gregory attributes a 30-year reign to him, James (1988), 79. Since Childeric was dead by AD 481, this would mean his reign or independence from whatever authority (Hunnic or Roman) began in AD 451 (if he reigned for 30 years) or AD 457 (if 24 years). Neither allows sufficient time for an 8-year Roman interregnum under Aegidius, since Aegidius became prominent as a general under Majorian in Gaul only *c.* AD 457, Périn and Feffer (1987), vol. 1, 106. Even if his prominence began under the earlier Avitus in AD 455, this still does not provide enough time. As Demougeot (1979), 683, points out, Childeric's exile is likely to have commenced earlier in AD 451 or perhaps I would argue even earlier than 451, i.e. around the time when Attila got involved in the succession dispute among the Franks. Demougeot, assuming that the Salian Franks under Childeric fought for the Romans at Chalons, attributes his exile to Frankish discontent over losses suffered at Chalons, but the fact that Childeric flees east to Hunnic territory suggests a different scenario. He was probably expelled by the Salian Franks sometime shortly after the defeat and death of King Chlogio/Chlodio at the hands of Aetius *c.* AD 449/450 (James

(1988), 57–8; AD 448 says Wood (1994), 37). Most Salians, except those that followed Childeric to Hunnic territory, would then have fought for the Romans as auxiliaries and possibly stayed in Roman service after Chalons under Avitus then possibly Aegidius until they invited Childeric back to rule them in AD 457. This would validate both the later tradition of him and his mother being 'abducted' by the Huns and that of him being in exile for eight years until his enthronement in AD 457. The 30-year reign may be referring to the commencement of his rule over a portion of eastern Franks who submitted to Attila in AD 451 well before he added the majority of the Salians to his rule. The attribution of kingship to Aegidius is possibly either a confusion of Aetius' domination of the Franks after his defeat of the Salian Frankish king Chlodio *c.* AD 448 (see Demougeot 1979, 489–90, for information on Chlodio) with the later alliance between the Franks of Childeric and Aegidius or, according to Demougeot (p. 683), the result of a temporary Roman military success involving maybe Aegidius under Avitus against the Salians during the war of 455–6, which led to their temporary submission to the Romans before the Salians recalled Childeric. Fredegar (*Chronicle* 3.11) claims that the Franks (Salians) revolted from Aegidius because he, having been tricked by Wiomad, tried to impose taxes on them, James (1988), 68. James for his part suggests that the memory of Franks having at one stage served under Roman leadership might have led Gregory to erroneously attribute kingship to Aegidius (p. 68). Wood (1994), 37–8, suggests that Childeric and his family actually originated in Thuringia, east of the Rhine. Hummer (1998b), 13, goes further and suggests a strong eastern, Danubian influence and perhaps even Pannonian origins of certain elements within the Frankish elite, perhaps even Childeric himself.

326. Bona (2002), 69.
327. Fredegar, *Chronicle* 3.11.
328. Bachrach (1972), 4; Wallace-Hadrill (1958), 541.
329. See note 325.
330. Fredegar, *Chronicle* 3.11. Wood (1994), 39–40; Wallace-Hadrill (1962), 85, 161. Obviously the emperor Maurice is chronologically impossible, but the presence of large quantities of Byzantine coins in Childeric's grave suggests that the record of him getting a vast treasure from some eastern source is accurate. Who else could have possessed a hoard of East Roman coins east of the Rhine other than Attila himself who collected an annual tribute from the East Romans and distributed the gold as reward to his vassals?
331. Fredegar, *Chronicle* 3.2.
332. Hummer (1998b), 14.
333. The Burgundians had been almost annihilated by the Huns earlier in the century in AD 436. See Schutz (2000), 53–9. The Franks also were mauled by the invading Alans in AD 405 and then by Aetius and the Huns. Jordanes lists the Franks and the Burgundians on the side of Aetius in the battle of Chalons, but Sidonius Apollinaris, *Panegyrics* 7.320–6, a contemporary, lists the Burgundians and Franks on the Hunnic side. Some Franks (most of the Salians, perhaps also some of the Rhineland Franks (see James 1988, 58)),

obviously those who opposed the elevation of the Hun-backed candidate to the kingship, would have fought with Aetius. Many like the Bructeri sided with Attila (for information on Hunnic-type princely graves found in the Rhineland and Alsace regions dating to the mid fifth century AD in Rhineland Frankish and Alamannic territory see Sulimirsky (1970), 191, who views them as burials of Hunnic governors, since they contain the Hunnic golden bow, an insignia of rank among the Huns). A small contingent of the Burgundians may also have fought for Aetius given the settlement of some of them in eastern Gaul (Sapaudia) as federates (after their massacre by the Huns) in AD 443 (see Schutz (2000), 59; James (1988), 55), but a substantial portion of them seem to have been under Hunnic rule at the time of the great battle. These eastern (Hunnic controlled) Burgundians would later cross the Rhine again and link up with the Burgundians in Sapaudia forming the second Burgundian kingdom. See Périn, and Feffer (1987), vol. 1, 97, 102–4, for discussion and also Hunno-Alanic cranial deformation among the Burgundians west of the Rhine.

334. So significant was the Hunnic invasion of Gaul for the Burgundians that it gave them a time limit on their lawsuits (*Lex Burgundionum* 17.1), Barnish (1992), 38.
335. Schutz (2000), 60, dismisses as Byzantine court gossip the perfectly logical proposition that the Franks and Bacaudae had requested Attila's intervention in Gaul.
336. This seems to have been standard practice among the Huns to settle their subjects in buffer zones between themselves and foreign powers as the settlement of troops under Ultzindur and Emnetzur, kinsmen of Attila and his son Ernak in Roman Dacia south of the Danube shows, Jordanes, *Getica* 50.266. Jordanes says that these generals took possession (*potiti sunt*) of the land (by force implied) while many other Huns swarming about everywhere betook themselves into Romania: *multique hunnorum passim proruentes tunc se in Romania dediderunt* (ed. Mommsen *MGH* (1961), 127).
337. Bachrach (1973), 68, suggests that Hunnic bands that remained in Gaul after the battle launched this attack on the Visigoths. See also Sinor (1990c), 196–7. Alemany (2000), 135, is more sceptical.
338. Bachrach (1973), 67, argues correctly that it was again the Alans who were the main combatants in this encounter with the Huns.
339. As Bachrach (1973), 68, notes the Visigoths did fight a big battle in 452, but not against the Huns. They attacked the Alans in northern Aquitaine, who had been seriously weakened by their two previous encounters with the Huns, and drove them north of the Loire.
340. More on this in the next chapter.
341. Apparently Childeric, after the breakup of the Hunnic Empire, embraced the Roman 'cause', at least superficially (hence his co-operation with Aegidius and later Paul), thereby receiving Roman official recognition of his occupation of former Roman lands west of the Rhine. The famous letter of Bishop Remigus of Rheims to Clovis tells us that Clovis' parents, i.e. Childeric, probably had

official Roman recognition for their administration of Belgica Secunda. See James (1988), 65, 67.

342. Quite fittingly perhaps the tomb of Childeric at Tournai was bedecked with artwork and goods made in the Danubian style of the Hunnic Empire, see Bona (2002), 69, Werner (1956), 32, James (1988), 62, and also Halsall (2001), 128. The practice of leaving behind vassals to mop up can also be seen in the aftermath of the Hunnic war against the Eastern Empire. The Hun lords Emnetzur and Ultzindur, already mentioned above, are said to have seized land in Dacia south of the Danube without Roman authorization. Exactly when this happened is unclear and Jordanes (*Getica* 50.266) makes it appear as if it occurred after the battle of Nedao in AD 454. However, the barbarian settlements mentioned by Jordanes, even the ones supposedly sanctioned by the Roman state such as those of the Ostrogoths in Pannonia and the Sarmatians in Illyricum, are likely to have happened under Attila's direction much earlier. The Romans after the breakup of the Hunnic Empire merely formalized a fait accompli. Revealingly one of the tribes mentioned in the so-called post-Nedao settlement, the Sadagarii, were actually already situated along the lower Danube (presumably in Little Scythia where Jordanes later places them) during the time of Julian and probably much earlier during the reign of Constantine, see Harmatta (1970), 57.

343. Muhlberger (1990), 122, 189. See also Collins (1999), 86.

344. Hydatius also calls the battle of Chalons a defeat for Attila. However, his attribution of victories to the Romans in both instances can hardly be called impartial or even factually accurate. See Burgess (1993), 83, 102. Hohlfelder (1984), 61, on the basis of this information provided by Hydatius of Lemica, *Chronicle* 154, which asserts that the Huns were defeated by the army of Marcian and plagues from heaven: *missi per Marcianum principem Aetio duce caeduntur auxiliis pariterque in sedibus suis et caelestibus plagis et per Marciani subiuguntur exercitum*, contemplates an invasion of Hunnic territory north of the Danube by Marcian's East Roman army and also a separate auxiliary force under an Eastern general called confusingly Aetius defeating the Huns in Italy. Obviously this is an over-extrapolation from the original Latin: *sedibus suis* does not mean 'north of the Danube'. Roman territory south of the Danube was still beyond Eastern Roman government control years later in the mid 450s; more on this later. It was under the control of the Huns and their subjects who moved into the area after or before the abrogation of the treaty agreed to between Attila and Anatolius and Nomus by Marcian in AD 450. Hydatius is probably indulging in wishful thinking in his account since there is no record elsewhere of any Roman resistance in Italy led by either the eastern or western Aetius. Furthermore, as we have seen above the great East Roman defeats at the hands of the Huns took place in AD 447, not 442. This simply does not leave enough time for the Eastern Empire to effectively marshal enough resources to take on the Huns in AD 452. Whatever the Eastern input to the defence of Italy was, it is likely to have been very insignificant. Prosper, for all the accusations thrown at him for his supposedly

anti-Aetius sentiments, is probably correct in saying that the emperor, senate and people of Rome could think of no other way out of the danger except submission and the payment of tribute to the Huns, a. 452, Murray (2000), 73–4. The *Gallic Chronicles* of 452 and 511 also have nothing to say about the efforts of Aetius and Marcian to defend Italy, which were undoubtedly negligible.

345. Howarth (1994), 135.
346. Thompson (1996), 160–1; Humphries (2000), 527. See Prosper a. 452, Murray (2000), 74.
347. All Western emperors after the Hunnic invasion are entirely dependent on independent, barbarian armies or the Eastern Empire. Avitus is enthroned by a Visigothic army, Majorian by the barbarian general Ricimer (part Suebi and part Visigoth) who has the support of the Burgundians, Severus by Ricimer, Anthemius by the Eastern Empire, Olybrius by Ricimer, Glycerius by the Burgundians under Gundobad, Nepos by the Eastern Empire, and finally Romulus by the ex-Hunnic army under Odoacer, see Collins (1999), 91–4, for a good summary of events. There is no longer a 'Roman' army to speak of in the West after AD 452.
348. Whitby (2000b), 298. But still led by Hunnic princes such as Odoacer.
349. Lee (2000), 43, or rather a joint candidate of Aspar and Zeno.
350. Priscus fr. 24.1, Blockley (1983), 317.
351. In fact the later Roman emperors had a habit of portraying military defeats as victories. Thus in AD 422 Theodosius, after suffering reverses against both the Huns under Rua and the Sassanids, negotiated peace by promising the annual payment of 350 pounds of gold to the Huns. After this had occurred the emperor put up an inscription (the Hebdomon inscription) claiming that he was victorious everywhere. See Croke (1977), 365–6. A military defeat was thus portrayed as a Roman triumph. Later in AD 434 a major Hunnic invasion under Rua devastated Thrace and threatened Constantinople. A major military disaster and a protracted siege of the Eastern Roman capital were only averted by the sudden, unexpected death of the Hunnic king. Theodosius again took credit for a 'military triumph'. We are of course reminded of the sudden death of Attila two decades later that saved the Roman Empire once again and allowed the Romans to boast of having 'defeated' the Huns. As with the so-called victory of Marcian in Italy over Attila, this earlier Roman 'triumph' over Rua was also attributed to a divine intervention via a plague that decimated the Hunnic army. See Kelly (2009), 65–8.
352. Maenchen-Helfen (1973), 161–2. See also Liebeschuetz (2007), 105, for the slow reconstruction of Roman fortifications in the Lower Danubian region which began only in the late 450s AD.
353. Thompson (1996), 170. Jordanes, *Getica* 50.264–6, provides a list of barbarian tribes from the Hunnic Empire who were settled south of the Danube within previously Roman territory. Jordanes says that the Romans gave these lands to these groups, presumably he means after Nedao, but as the conditions of the peace treaty after the war of AD 447 (Priscus fr. 11.1, Blockley 1983, 242) show,

the Romans had to accept the Hunnic occupation of a wide belt of territory south of the Danube stretching from Singidunum on the frontier of Pannonia to Novae, some 300 miles distance and five days' journey in depth, i.e. 100–120 miles. All of Dacia Ripensis and parts of three other Balkan provinces were thus in Hunnic hands (Thompson (1996), 108; Poulter (2007a), 71) and some of these groups mentioned by Jordanes were probably already settled in these areas by the Huns before Nedao as part of the regular process of relocating conquered tribes around the Hunnic core lands in Hungary. Croke (1981), 170, argues that the annexed territory south of the Danube was given back to the Romans by Attila after the embassy of Anatolius and Nomus in AD 449. Attila indeed did agree to withdraw from Roman territory. However, agreement and real action are two different things. Just as the Romans reneged on their agreement to hand over all Hunnic fugitives, subsequent events seem to show that Attila did not in fact abandon the Roman territory that he had occupied. Especially since Theodosius, with whom he had negotiated, died the following year and was succeeded by Marcian who immediately abrogated the terms of the treaty agreed between Attila and Theodosius. The influx of barbarian tribes into this area south of the Danube would have accelerated after Nedao and the Romans, clearly in no position to control this influx in any meaningful way, must have simply recognized a fait accompli.

354. Jordanes tells us that the Huns under Emnetzur and Ultzindur, kinsmen of Hernak, i.e. Hunnic minor princes, unlike the other barbarians who 'received' their land, i.e. gained recognition from the Romans, 'seized' Oescus, Utus and Almus in Dacia and the Huns poured into Romania (modern Bulgaria) south of the Danube without any authorization or consent from the Romans (*Getica* 50.266). Exactly when is uncertain, but this process, as discussed above, could have been initiated as early as AD 447 when Attila conquered the area. The Romans would in fact talk regularly about giving away land which they no longer controlled. For instance in the *De administrando* chapter 30, Constantine Porphyrogenitus claims that the emperor Heraclius gave land in the western Balkans, which was not under East Roman rule in the seventh century AD at all, but under Avar rule, to the Croats and Serbs. See Jenkins (1962), 114–15, Curta (2006), 137–8. Later we will also examine a similar instance of 'land-giving' recorded in Procopius about Justinian giving away land, again in the Balkan area that the empire no longer controls, to barbarians. Jordanes' own family (his grandfather Paria) were originally vassals of an Alanic king called Candac who held sway over a part of Moesia under Attila or after Nedao (*Getica* 50.266). See also Croke (1987), 118–19 and Demougeot (1979), 768–9. Altheim (1959), vol. v, 27, argues that the name Candac is etymologically linked to the Oghuric-Turkic name Candik, a name that is attested among the later Avars, and that it is Hunnic, not Alanic. This is difficult to confirm or reject. Candac was mostly likely a Hunno-Alanic leader of a group of Alans in Moesia, which concurs with the known Hunnic practice of distributing fiefs to Hunnic royals and nobles.

355. The argument that the two halves of the Roman Empire were in fact two separate states and therefore had no obligation whatsoever to support each other has been raised by some. However, the frequent involvement of Eastern military units in wars and succession struggles in the West seems to slightly qualify this belief in two separate states. In the reign of Theodosius II Eastern forces were dispatched on four occasions to the west. In AD 410, 4,000 troops were sent to Honorius to help in the defence of Italy against Alaric. In 424 Ardabur and his son Aspar intervened with Eastern forces to defeat the usurper John, the third time in a generation the Eastern army overthrew a Western usurper, Whitby (2000b), 296. In 431 again Eastern troops under Aspar were dispatched to halt the Vandal invasion of Africa. Finally in 441 a massive invasion force was sent west by the emperor to drive the Vandals out of Africa. See Lee (2000), 39. As Lee (2000), 39–40, notes, a mixture of dynastic solidarity among the descendants of Theodosius the Great and self-interest often allowed the two halves of the empire to co-operate in mutual defensive measures against the barbarians and internal rebels (solidarity would even be shown after the end of Theodosian rule in the East under Marcian, Lee (2000), 43). If it had not been for the Hunnic incursions that dictated Eastern foreign policy initiatives in the 440s, the Romans would undoubtedly have destroyed the Vandals and restored the integrity of the Western Empire.

356. Stickler (2007), 504, points out correctly that the Hunnic invasions made the organic development of the political and military relations between the Romans and the mass-migrating Germanic tribes impossible. Rome was repeatedly forced to react swiftly to mass intrusions that often overstressed the capabilities of its military structures on the border as well as its hinterlands. Faced with sudden and massive military threats, the age-old defensive system of the empire that had worked well in the past failed completely, not because of any inherent weaknesses in the Roman army of the fourth and fifth centuries AD, but because the enemy (the Hunnic Empire) was so much stronger than enemies Rome had faced before.

357. If money given as tribute or contributions by the Romans is an indicator at this stage of the comparative power of barbarian nations, then the Gepids who were by far the most powerful of the western barbarians at this juncture must be regarded as among the weakest because they were paid a paltry sum of only 100 pounds of gold per year, Bona (1976), 16. Clearly the amount of gold given to Theodoric Strabo is related to his distance from the imperial capital, not his actual military potential.

358. Heather (1991), 256. As noted above, Moesia Superior, Dacia Ripensis and Praevalitana were only reincorporated into the empire after AD 458, indicating the military impotence of Constantinople immediately after the Hunnic Wars of the 440s. Hunnic groups such as the one under Tuldila, who were persuaded in AD 457 to join the Roman army under Majorian, then marching into Italy, were still active in this area south of the Danube. See Thompson (1996), 174; Maenchen-Helfen (1973), 405. Even after this, Roman restoration in Dacia (western Bulgaria and northern Serbia) would prove to be ephemeral

and shaky at best. The region around Sirmium, south of the Danube, would fall under the rule of the Gepids after the flight of the Ostrogoths in the 470s (the Ostrogoths would regain this region under Theodoric, but the region was retaken by the Gepids during Justinian's re-conquest of Italy; Procopius, 7.33.7–8). Former Roman territory west of the Danube (modern Croatia and western Hungary), lands formerly held by Thiudimer's Ostrogoths until AD 470, would fall eventually into the hands of Odoacer, the Suebi and the Heruls. The Emperor Anastasius would later recognize the Herul control over the areas they controlled in Dacia around Singidunum (Belgrade) as a 'gift' to them; Procopius, 7.33.13.

359. See Wickham (2009), 78.
360. According to Krautschick (1986), Basiliscus himself might have been intimately linked to the family of Edeco the Hun. His nephew was none other than Armatus, *magister militum per Thracias*, who may have been the brother of Hunoulphus and Odoacer (for scepticism on the linking of Basiliscus with Odoacer see MacGeorge (2002), 284–5). Hunoulphus would join his brother in East Roman service after AD 469, Amory (1997), 282–3. Ironically, or perhaps in collusion, the uncle Basiliscus and the nephew Odoacer would seize the throne in both the Western and Eastern Empires in the same year! Basiliscus of course was the brother of Empress Verina, the wife of Emperor Leo, whose daughter Ariadne was the wife of the emperors Zeno and Anastasius. Basiliscus was thus likely to have been someone who originated in Attila's empire who after the Hunnic civil war in AD 454 took up service in the Eastern Roman army. He may even have been a Hun or a Scirian, depending on which side of Odoacer's family he was related to.
361. Procopius, 3.6.1–2, provides these absurd figures, but he is here relying on hearsay (*phasi*) originating from earlier sources and he displays his inaccurate knowledge of fifth-century events by placing Aetius' death before that of Attila, 3.24–35. See also Merills and Miles (2010), 122.
362. The size of the Eastern Roman army facing the most dangerous enemy of all, the Sassanian Persians, was usually 20,000 strong in the sixth century AD. See Whitby (2000b), 293, and Elton (2007), 536.
363. Whitby (2007a), 517, points out that the mobile Roman army of Late Antiquity numbered 20,000–30,000 men at the most. Interestingly John the Lydian, *De Magistratibus* 3.43, suggests that the invasion involved 10,000 ships. Now of course this is nonsense, but if we replace the ships with men it becomes far more intelligible.
364. It also put a severe strain on the state of the Eastern Empire's finances, see Jones (1964), vol. I, 224.
365. Hdt. 6.95.
366. Hdt. 7.89. They also echo the number of ships, 1,100, supposedly gathered to launch a campaign against the same Vandals in AD 441. See Thompson (1996), 87, and Merrills and Miles (2010), 112.
367. For the alleged expenditures on the campaign see Cameron (1993), 28, and also Mango and Scott (1997), 181.

368. Lee (2000), 47.
369. Priscus fr. 46 (*Exc. de Leg. Gent.* 18), Blockley (1983), 352. Indeed in fr. 47 we see the Saragurs, the main enemy of the Huns after Attila's death, who had defeated the Akatziri earlier in AD 463, invading Persia to the south, possibly due to resistance encountered in the west from the Huns under Ernak, which halted their expansion in that direction.
370. More on this in the next chapter.
371. Priscus fr. 49 (*Exc. de Leg. Gent.* 21), Blockley (1983), 356–8. Thompson (1996), 173, suggests that this engagement involving Chelchal was with a group of Goths and Huns separate from those with Dengizich. This does not seem likely.
372. He was possibly a nephew of Aspar's wife (Theophanes, *Chron.* AM 5964; 5970 (ed. C. de Boor, Leipzig, 1883, reprint, Stuttgart, 1972, 117 and 126)). See also Heather (1991), 255–6. ed. C. de Boor (Leipzig, 1883, reprint, Stuttgart, 1972)
373. Heather (1991), 261.
374. Demougeot (1979), 789.
375. Jones (1964), vol. I, 223.
376. *Getica* 54.277.
377. *Getica* 56.286–7. Thiudimer would die *c.* AD 474 leaving his son Theodoric to pick up where he left off, see Giese (2004), 67.
378. Heather (2007), 181.
379. Whitby (2000b), 300.
380. For information on the Isaurians see Elton (2000), 293–307.
381. See Wickham (2009), 96.
382. Jones (1964), vol. I, 226; Burns (1980), 68.
383. Heather (1991), 282–3.
384. Heather (2007), 183.
385. Heather (2009), 246.
386. Burns (1980), 69–71.
387. Demougeot (1979), 788.
388. Marcellinus Comes, Croke (1995), 28.
389. Heather (2009), 249–50.
390. Heather (2009), 250; Giese (2004), 69.
391. John of Antioch fr. 214.7; Zacharias of Mytilene, *Historia Ecclesiastica* 6.6; Wolfram (1988), 277; Heather (1991), 304; Demougeot (1979), 792–3.
392. John of Antioch fr. 214.8–9; Marcellinus Comes s.a. 487 (CM 2.93); Malalas, Bonn 383; Theophanes *Chron.* AM 5977 (131 de Boor); Michael the Syrian 9.6; Heather (1991), 305 ff.; Burns (1980), 76–7.
393. Jones (1964), vol. II, 1030.
394. Malalas, xiv, p. 358; *Chron. Pasch.* i, p. 587. See also Priscus, fr. 21, Blockley (1983), 309 and Jeffreys, Jeffreys and Scott (trans.) (1986), 195.

CHAPTER 5: THE END OF THE HUNNIC EMPIRE IN THE WEST

1. Heather (2009), 237, 254, 264.
2. Kelly (2009), 47.

3. Heather (2009), 359. A similar view of steppe polities and the belief that political power of the steppe ruler is dependent almost entirely on personal charisma, success in warfare and the distribution of booty (i.e. in this case 'subsidies'/tribute from a sedentary state, Rome) were held by the renowned Inner Asian historian Fletcher (1979–80), 236–51. However, Fletcher's political model for the Turco-Mongols derives from an over-simplification of steppe political history which fails to take into full consideration the symbiosis of nomadic and agricultural populations within most steppe empires, especially in the earlier political entities such as the Xiongnu, Royal Scythia, Kushans etc., as we have demonstrated earlier. The long political tradition of steppe empires and the sedentary elements within them provided steppe political entities with a stability that often, though not always, limited the usual 'tanistry' involved in imperial successions. It also made them by and large self-sufficient. The centrifugal tendencies of the nomadic element was thus kept in check and the ideology of the sacred and collective rights of the royal clan to rule, i.e. a legitimacy principle, kept the state intact in spite of the frequent distribution of fiefs. Fletcher himself was perceptive enough to acknowledge that the combination of the two elements could in fact provide remarkable stability, but he restricts this phenomenon to later steppe empires only (p. 237).
4. Golden (1992), 110.
5. The phenomenon, noted as early as the nineteenth century by Valikhanov (see Sulejmenov 1989, 31–2), of steppe imperial states and peoples not disappearing, as western historians have erroneously assumed, but merely undergoing a transformation as the dominant tribal group is overthrown by either an external intruder usurping leadership or more frequently a rebel tribe within the empire, can be observed throughout steppe history, e.g. the Turks overthrowing the Rouran and the Uighurs the Turks. Both these incidents were internal revolts that marked the reallocation of power within the same state, not the end of the previous existing political entity. See Sinor (1990b), 285–316. The steppe empire founded by the Rouran persisted under different leadership from the late fourth to the ninth century AD. Some five hundred years! In the Avar state, after the military defeat at the hands of the Byzantines in AD 626, the Bulgars demand that the Khaganate (office of emperor) should henceforth pass to their tribe and not the Avars, demonstrating the nature of the so-called end or creation of new states in the steppe. This led to a civil war and the eastern half of the Avar realm as a consequence seceded to form Great Bulgaria under Kubrat, who claimed descent from Irnik, the son of Attila. More on this later.
6. Kradin (2003), 85.
7. Heather (2006), 355–6.
8. See Bona (1976), 28 ff., for the archaeology and geography of Gepidia. Bona (p. 38) also notes that some Mongoloid features are found among the Gepids in the fifth and sixth centuries AD, no doubt the result of inter-mixing with the Huns. The Gepids of all the Germanic peoples other than the Goths were the most heavily influenced by the Huns. What does this tell us about the nature of their revolt? Even physically they were most similar to the original Huns from

Notes to pages 92–4

Asia. Hunnic cranial deformation is also extremely common among the Gepids (p. 38).
9. Todd (1992), 236.
10. Wolfram (1988), 258–9.
11. *Getica* 50.259.
12. John Malalas 14.10, Jeffreys *et al.* (1986), 195, where Attila is said to be of the race of the Gepids. Malalas then makes the puerile error of locating the battle of Chalons on the Danube.
13. Burgess (2001b), 97.
14. Maenchen-Helfen (1973), 388; Sinor (1946–7), 29; Schönfeld (1911), 277.
15. On the Gothic practice of adopting Hunnic names see Jordanes, *Getica* 9.58. Thompson (1996), 278–9, voices healthy scepticism about the claims that Huns possessed Gothic names. Rather it is more likely that Hunnic names were Germanicized by the Germanic subjects of the Huns.
16. For discussion see Schramm (1969), 148.
17. Maenchen-Helfen (1973), 389.
18. *Getica* 50.266.
19. Rorlich (1991), 278.
20. Golden (1992), 233.
21. Maenchen-Helfen (1973), 407; Pritsak (1953–4), 19; Moravcsik (1958), 136–7.
22. Maenchen-Helfen (1973), 415.
23. Maenchen-Helfen (1973), 407.
24. *Getica* 23.120; Bona (2002), 27.
25. *Chron. Pasch.*; Maenchen-Helfen (1973), 407.
26. *Getica* 9.58.
27. *Getica* 4.25.
28. Bona (2002), 27.
29. Though Maenchen-Helfen (1973), 406, tries to link this name to later Germanic names such as Beremod. I would argue that these are Gothic names deriving from an original Hunnic name.
30. The Huns had extensive contacts with Iranian populations even before their entry into Europe where they conquered yet another Iranian nation, the Alans. Consequently via a long process of intermarriages and acculturation many Huns and Alans turned Huns came to possess Iranian names. See Maenchen-Helfen (1973), 390–2. As mentioned earlier, among the eastern cousins of the European Huns, the Hephtalites, kings also often bore Iranian names.
31. For an in-depth discussion on the Sarmatian language see Harmatta (1970), 58–97.
32. Vernadsky (1951), 376.
33. *Getica* 38.199, 200. The element *ard* also had connotations of the divine in the Alan language, as in Ardabourios, Alemany (2000), 112, i.e. was associated with the sacred.
34. Bona (1976), 73. See Zieme (2006), 114–27, for the Central Asian use of hybrid names that combined elements from different languages as a means of political and social expediency. This is clearly what is happening in the Hunnic Empire and among the Germanic subjects of the Huns.

232   *Notes to pages 94–6*

35. Maenchen-Helfen (1973), 154, discusses this in some detail though he is strongly against the identification of Heithrek with Ardaric and considers the war between the Goths and Huns in the saga to be a memory of the post-Nedao conflict between Valamer's Ostrogoths and the remnants of the Huns.
36. Wolfram (1997b), 144. Mundo would have an eventful career first as an ally of the Ostrogothic king Theodoric (Haase 1991, 87) then later as commander of the Roman army in the Balkans as *magister militum per Illyricum*. He would achieve a tremendous military success by repulsing the Bulgar invasion of AD 530 and even capturing one of the kings of the Bulgars, who in the previous year had defeated and captured the Caucasian Hunnic king Askoum then commanding the Roman army (John Malalas 18. 21, Jeffreys *et al.* (1986), 254). See also Croke (1982a), 132. Croke (p. 130) attempts to force a translation of the words *de Attilani* (Jordanes' reference to the origins of Mundo in *Getica* 58.301) as designating not the family of Attila, but the whole tribal confederation of Attila including the Gepids, i.e. anyone from the former empire of Attila. This is highly implausible and Croke himself acknowledges the possibility that Mundo was somehow related to Attila by descent. His preoccupation with proving that Mundo was either a Gepid or a Hun is rather puzzling, since many barbarian leaders of the migration period possessed hybrid identities and blood lineages. For instance, as mentioned earlier, Attila was referred to as a Gepid Hun.
37. Pohl (1980), 290.
38. Maenchen-Helfen (1973), 152–3.
39. Pohl (1980), 261. Giesmos was a king in his own right in the Gepid kingdom and evidence from skeletal remains confirms the presence of a strong upper-class Hunnic element within the Gepid aristocracy even after Nedao (p. 295).
40. Interestingly the Suebi who were geographically close to the Gepids and were active in the post-Nedao competition for land in the Danubian region also had two kings Hunimund and Alaric, *Getica* 54.277.
41. Bona (1976), 70.
42. Bona (1976), 70. See also Curta (2006), 54.
43. Priscus fr. 11.2, Blockley (1983), 248.
44. Heather (1996), 152.
45. Reynolds and Lopez (1946), 36–54.
46. Anonymus Valesianus 10.45 (ed. Mommsen, *MGH*: AA 9:314), see also König (1997), 72.
47. John of Antioch fr. 209 (*FHG* 4:617).
48. Anonymus Valesianus 8.37 (*MGH*: AA 9:308); John of Antioch fr. 209.1 (*FHG* 4:617).
49. Jordanes *Romana* 344 (*MGH*: AA 1:44); *Getica* 46.242, 57.291.
50. *Auctarium Prosperi Hauniensis*, s.a. 476 (*MGH*: AA 9:308).
51. Marcellinus Comes, s.a. 476 (*MGH*: AA 9:91); Theophanes, *Chron.* AM 5965 (1:119 De Boor), clearly just guesswork on the part of Marcellinus and not to be taken seriously. See König (1997), 27, 112, for a complete list of sources on Odoacer's origins.

52. Anonymus Valesianus 8.38 (*MGH*: AA 9:310). However, the Anonymus does mention that Odoacer is the son of Edico/Edeco. He was obviously expecting this name to ring a bell amongst his readers.
53. K 693 (ed. Adler, 3:53).
54. Malchus, fr. 13, McBain (1983), 326.
55. Malchus, fr. 13, McBain (1983), 326.
56. Anonymus Valesianus 10.46.
57. Theophanes, *Chron.* AM 6020, Mango and Scott (1997), 267; Malalas 18.14, Jeffreys *et al.* (1986), 250. Czeglédy (1971), 148 sees him as being the ruler of the Akatziri situated north of East Roman possessions in the Crimea.
58. For Gordas or Grod, whose excessive missionary zeal among the Huns would backfire, see Golden (1992), 106. On the north Caucasian Huns who converted to Christianity, see Golden (1992), 107.
59. Bona (1991), 30.
60. On the origin of the Sciri see Reynolds and Lopez (1946), 40 ff. Vernadsky (1951), 350, in contrast views them as a Germanic people that lived under Sarmatian hegemony. See also Harmatta (1970), 11.
61. MacGeorge (2002), 284–6, the latest critic to comment on the issue, simply repeats McBain's argument about the Thuringians without a further thought.
62. Norwich (1991), vol. ii, 250; Bullough (1965a), 323–4. In fact we have examples of even earlier imperial marriages with Germanic princely houses: Bertha, the daughter of Hugh of Arles, king of Italy (died AD 948), was married to Romanus II, and Anna the half sister of the previous emperor Constantine Porphyrogenitus had married Lewis III of Provence, Norwich (1991), vol. ii, 187. All this no doubt led to a resurgence of Byzantine interest in the West.
63. *Historia Langobardorum* 1.1.
64. We will discuss the Hunnic ancestry of Theodoric and the Amals in the next chapter.
65. Priscus fr. 11, Blockley (1983), 249. Thompson (1948), 11; McBain (1983), 325.
66. The Sciri are noted here by Jordanes as having chosen to situate themselves closest to Ernak's Huns in Scythia Minor and Lower Moesia even after the defeat of the Attilids at the battle of Nedao in AD 454. If Edica their chieftain had no links to the Huns, why would the Sciri behave in this manner?
67. This variation of his name is given by Anonymus Valesianus 10.45.
68. Altheim (1948), 24.
69. Edgü-Timur is the name of a general who served Ogotai Khan in Iran in 1239. Spuler (1939), 39, 383. Reynolds and Lopez (1946), 48.
70. Royal graves attributed to the Scirian ruling family found at Bákod-puszta show strong signs of Hunnic influence, again possibly reinforcing the Hunnic origins of the Scirian royal family and Edeco himself, see Pohl (1980), 273–4.
71. See Reynolds and Lopez (1946), 48; Heather (2009), 228; Goffart (2006), 205; Thompson (1996), 171.
72. For further discusssion on the possible Hunnic/Turkic origins of the Torcilingi see below. The Heruli, another people closely associated with Odoacer, are also noted for their cranial deformation (Hunno-Alanic custom) and the presence

of partially Mongoloid peoples and eastern ritual mirrors among them, all indicative of a strong link with the Huns, see Pohl (1980), 277.
73. Anonymus Valesianus 8.37.
74. A similar confusion over the exact ethnic provenance of individuals originating from Attila's court or those descended from them can be found in the case of Mundo, the grandson of Attila, who is called a Gepid by Greek sources, but is called a Hun by the Goths, see Pohl (1980), 290.
75. *Getica* 46.242.
76. *Romana* 344.
77. Cahen (1973), 24–7.
78. *Getica* 46.242; *Getica* 57.291; *Romana* 344.
79. Most notably by Maenchen-Helfen (1973).
80. Reynolds and Lopez (1946), 39.
81. Pomponius Mela 1.116.
82. Pliny the Elder, *Natural History* 6.19.
83. Fredegar, *Chronicle* 3.2, Murray (2000), 593.
84. Wagner (1984), 407–10.
85. Ewig (1997), 824–5, 845–7.
86. Meserve (2008), 50.
87. Sinor (1990b), 309.
88. Cahen (1973), 24–7.
89. Pritsak (1968), 163.
90. Golden (1996a), 97–107; Pritsak (1976c), 27.
91. See Nicolle (2001), 21. Peoples bearing names astonishingly similar to the Torks/Turks are, as we have seen above, attested as early as the first century AD in Pomponius Mela and Pliny the Elder, which suggests that there is a high probability that a people with the ethnonym Tork or Turk existed in the Pontic steppe region well before the arrival of the Huns and that this group or some other easterly Turkic tribe that had accompanied the Huns in their migration west may have constituted the fief allocated to Odoacer. The name Tork/Turk was clearly much more widespread and in use much earlier than the famous rise of the great Gokturks in the mid sixth century AD. See Sinor (1990b), 286–7.
92. See also Vernadsky (1951), 360.
93. Tacitus, *Germania* 43.1.
94. Paul the Deacon, *Historia Langobardorum*, 1.19, identifies these Rugians with the Rugians also under Odoacer, which is rather baffling given Odoacer's history of conflict with the Rugians. Paul believes that Odoacer ruled a segment of the Rugians and fought other Rugians who opposed him in Noricum.
95. Reynolds and Lopez (1946), 43–4 .Both Jordanes and also Procopius spell their name with an 'o', not 'u': Procopius, 7.2.1–4.
96. *Romana*, 344.
97. *Getica* 57.291.
98. The Baltic Rugians are sometimes identified with the island of Rügen in the Baltic Sea.
99. Strabo, *Geographika* 7.1.3; Wolfram (1988), 38, n. 32. Tacitus, *Germania*, 44.1.

100. Wolfram (1988), 40. The Vandals are associated with the early Goths (Gotones) in Pliny the Elder, *Historia Naturalis*, 4.99.
101. Procopius, 6.14.10, says the Heruli were once lords of the Lombards, which indicates that before then they must have served the Rugii who were vastly superior to the Heruli before their defeat at the hands of Odoacer. Wickham (2009), 45, thinks that the Rugii of Noricum and also the Suebi in Pannonia in the fifth century AD are the descendants of the Quadi who had earlier been absorbed into the Hunnic Empire. This is plausible and is also compatible with the idea of a Hunnic elite being imposed on the conquered tribe now renamed Rogii/ Rugii after the conquering king, Ruga.
102. See Rives (1999), 311, for discussion.
103. Ptolemy, *Geographika* 2.11.12, mentions Rougion near the Baltic coast west of the Vistula and also a tribe called the Routikleioi in the same area.
104. Demougeot (1979), 251–2, speculates that they may have moved southwards down the Oder into Moravia during the fourth century, but this is a reconstruction based on the assumption that the Rugii of Noricum are the Rugii of the Baltic region.
105. Associated with the Gothic word *Hulmarugeis*, meaning 'island Rugii', Rives (1999), 311.
106. Wolfram (1988), 41.
107. *Getica* 3.24. See also Todd (1992), 226; Merrills (2005), 128–9.
108. Christensen (2002), 189, notes this geographical distinction and then interprets this to mean that Jordanes' account as a whole is unreliable.
109. As Geary (2002), 118–19, points out the Germanic peoples who emerge after the fourth- and fifth-century dislocations and conquests were new peoples with old names, fundamentally different in many cases from previous tribal confederations that bore the same names before the Hunnic invasions.
110. *Getica* 53.272, 50.266. Thompson (1996), 202.
111. Todd (1992), 177, Rugian prominence in Lower Austria and Noricum.
112. Eugippius, *Vita S. Severini* 44. See Alföldi (1974), 224.
113. *Vita S. Severini* 42, speaks of King Feva of the Rugii giving Favianis, one of the few towns which remained on the bank of the Danube, to his brother Ferderuchus as fief.
114. *Vita S. Severini* 31 records that the Rugii collected taxes from the Noricans and were powerful enough to protect them from the Heruls, Thuringians, Alamanni, bandits and others. See Wood (2000), 515, and Demougeot (1979), 736–41, for further details. See also Christie (1995), 20, and Burns (1980, 63.
115. Anonymus Valesianus 10.48.
116. Reynolds and Lopez (1946), 44–5.
117. Maenchen-Helfen (1973), 400.
118. Reynolds and Lopez (1946), 50.
119. Heather (1996), 115, that is unless Vinitharius, whom Valamer overthrew and whose grand-daughter he married, was in some way connected to Ermanaric. There is an odd medieval legend that makes a figure named Ermanaric the

uncle of Dietrich von Bern (Theodoric the Great, Valamir's nephew), who has usurped the throne from his nephew.
120. Heather (1991), 19, argues that Jordanes' genealogy of the Amals derives from Cassiodorus. This is disputed by Merrills (2005), 103–4, who argues, probably correctly, that Jordanes' Amal genealogy is only partially dependent on Cassiodorus and contains later additions.
121. Merrills (2005), 102–3.
122. Merrills (2005), 109. See also Golden (2009a), 74–5, 105.
123. Merrills (2005), 109.
124. Heather (1991), 21.
125. Schönfeld (1911), 142; Wolfram (1988), 31, 37.
126. Strikingly enough his name echoes the meaning of well-known Turco-Mongol names such as Temujin (Genghis Khan) and Timur (Tamerlane), man of iron.
127. Wolfram (1988), 31.
128. Heather (1991), 26; Goffart (2002), 33–4, 46–7; Gillett (2002), 87.
129. Heather (1991), 9, 18.
130. *Getica* 38.199. See Wolfram (1988), 142, and Heather (1991), 241, for discussion.
131. An excellent and by far the best analysis of both Jordanes and his principal source Cassiodorus is found in Christensen (2002), though the writer, somewhat justifiably, is extremely sceptical about the historical validity of Jordanes' Amal genealogy. He regards it as utterly unreliable, which is true if we understand the Amal kings to have been Goths from the beginning. However, as we shall demonstrate, if taken as a Hunnic dynasty, the later sections of the genealogy do fit in with known historical events and circumstances.
132. Mommsen, ed., *MGH*, 121–2.
133. All translations of the *Getica* are from Mierow (1915).
134. Schönfeld (1911), 250, Heather (1996), 114–15, (2003), 90, and Christensen (2002), 146, 154. See also Doerfer (1973), 34. The possibility is also raised by Wolfram (1988), 254, though he is more hesitant than the others. Heather (1995b), 148, asserts that the identification is correct, but that the attribution of Hunnic ethnicity to Balamber is probably a mistake. The etymology of the name is uncertain but it does seem to have an eastern origin. There was a Kidarite Hunnic city in fifth-century Central Asia called Βαλαάμ, see Moravcsik (1958), vol. II, 85, though connections with the name Balamer are hard to establish.
135. Heather (1988), 126.
136. Fine (1983), 25–6. The name Antes appears in Pliny the Elder's *Natural History* 6.35, and designates a people living between the Azov Sea and the Caspian, i.e. a Sarmatian group far to the east. See Dolukhanov (1996), 137. They seem to have migrated west sometime between the first and fifth century AD into what is now the northern Ukraine and merged with the Slavs in that area.
137. See Fine (1983), 25, Browning (1975), 32, and Curta (2006), 56–61. See also Heather (2009), 607. There are interesting references to the Limigantes, former slaves of the free Sarmatians during the time of Constantine and Constantius in Ammianus Marcellinus 17.13; 19.11; *Excerpta Valesiana* (in

Ammianus) 6.32. Vernadsky (1951), 345, claims that the name conceals a hidden form 'limig-antes'. However, even if the Limigantes were a type of Antes that existed in the fourth century further west than other Antes, they are situated not in the Ukraine or eastern Romania where the Amals could have engaged them but in the Tisza river region in Hungary further to the west. The bulk of the Antes are located in the northern parts of the Ukraine, northwest of the Kutrigur and Utigur Huns, by Procopius, 8.4.9, even in the mid sixth century AD.

138. Christensen (2002), 146, Vinitharius is a Latin or Latinized title, not a Gothic one, which raises the question, was he a real historical figure and if he was, was he a Goth or a Hun? Of course the Iranian Antes before they merged with the Slavs had been in the Pontic steppe region since the first century AD (Sulimirsky 1970, 155). However, the name Vinitharius (Wend-fighter) gives the game away. The Antes that are mentioned by Jordanes are Slavic Antes, not the earlier Iranian Antes mentioned by Pliny.

139. Mommsen, ed., *MGH*, 122–3.
140. More on this later.
141. More on this shortly.
142. Heather (1991), 25.
143. Eckhardt (1955), 43–4. Eckhardt also tries to link Vinitharius' campaigns against the Antes with the supposed conquests of Ermanaric, but as Christensen (2002) notes, Ermanaric's conquests listed in the *Getica* are largely fictitious (p. 196), the list of peoples he supposedly conquered is hardly an accurate reflection of peoples who actually lived in Scythia in the fourth century. The Aesti (or rather Hesti in Cassiodorus, equated with Aesti in Tacitus, *Germania* 45.4–9) who are mentioned among the conquered tribes actually sent an embassy to Ravenna during the lifetime of Cassiodorus, *Variae* 5.2, hence Jordanes' awareness of them and their inclusion in the inventive list of tribes subdued by Ermanaric (p. 191). The dimensions of this 'Gothic' empire are in fact a reflection of the later empire of Attila in Europe (p. 160).
144. Christensen (2002), 149.
145. Pritsak (1956), 404–19 argues convincingly that the name Attila is a Turkic name that combines two elements *as* ('great/big' in Chuvash, the only living descendant of the Hunno-Bulgarian language of the Huns) + *til* + *a* (river/sea + magnifier), meaning 'universal (ruler)'. This was Germanized into Attila. The fact that Priscus' interpreter was a Goth called Bigila explains why his name is rendered in its Gothic form in Priscus. Maenchen-Helfen's rejection of this etymology (1973), 386–7, is groundless. He suggests Gothic/Gepidic *Atta* (father) + diminutive suffix *-ila*.
146. The original form is given in Jordanes, *Getica* 35.180, *Mundzuco*.
147. Schramm (1969), 140. The Gothic form is provided by Priscus as Μουνδίουχος. This was simplified even further into Μούνδιος, a form found in Theophanes 102.15, Moravcsik (1958), vol. II, 194.
148. Pritsak (1956), 404–19.
149. Schönfeld (1911), 206.

150. Schönfeld (1911), 272.
151. Schönfeld (1911), 108, 245.
152. Maenchen-Helfen (1973), 404.
153. Maenchen-Helfen (1973), 422. Haussig (2000), 277, suggests that *Oult* or *Oulti* is a Greek rendering of the Oghuric Turkic word for the number six. What is interesting is the fact that in names such as Oultizouroi and Ultzincur above we have clearly two elements *Oulti* (six) + the Turkic title *Cur* (noble), meaning 'the six lords'. We have already observed how the Xiongnu possessed a political body called the six horns, an institution which is also found as the highest advisory council in the Later Hunnic Empire of the Bulgars. It is to be wondered whether Uldin was one of these six great nobles of the Hunnic Empire.
154. Schramm (1969), 146–55.
155. Christensen (2002), 139 ff.
156. Heather (1991), 26.
157. Wolfram (1988), 170, who takes Jordanes' account to be accurate, despite its absurd chronological distortions, assumes that the Huns restored the old ruling house of the east Goths, presented by Jordanes as the Amals, to their former position of authority among the Goths under Hunnic rule in order to prevent separatist movements such as the revolt of Radagaisus in AD 405. However, it is highly doubtful that the so-called Amals who appear in the mid fifth century as rulers of the Goths had any connections at all to Ermanaric.
158. *Getica* 48. 252–3.
159. Wolfram (1988), 251; 483. Division of the Goths between Valamer and his brothers, while recognizing the supremacy of Valamer as supreme king, is likely to be an imitation of the Hunnic, Inner Asian practice of 'fief' distribution among members of the royal family. See Prosper, *Epitoma Chronicon* a. 455, 1353, p. 480; Jordanes, *Getica* 35.180 ff. See also Thompson (1948), 81 ff.
160. Burns (1984), 53.
161. *Getica* 52.268–9.
162. Wolfram (1988), 261.
163. Theodoric celebrated the thirtieth year of his reign in AD 500, Wolfram (1988), 493, which must mean that he was elevated to kingship in AD 470/1. This coincides with his seizure of Singidunum and defeat of the Sarmatians. If Theodoric was born in AD 455/6 he would have been just fifteen when he led this campaign. This would then conflict with Jordanes' own assertion that Theodoric was already eighteen before he launched the attack on the Sarmatians, *Getica* 55.282.
164. *Getica* 52.271; Ennodius, *Panegyricus Dictus Clementissimo Regi Theoderico ab Ennodio Dei Famulo*, iii, ed., Vogel, *MGH*: AA, 7 (Berlin, 1885, reprint 1961), 204, Wolfram (1988), 262. Jordanes, *Getica* 55.282, tells us that Theodoric was eighteen when he returned to his father from Constantinople, so presumably c. AD 469, Wolfram (1997b), 196. This would mean he was twenty years old when he captured Singidunum at the head of his army in AD 471, Wolfram (1988), 262. Far more reasonable than as a fifteen-year-old boy. Even if

Theodoric was dispatched to Constantinople in AD 461, not AD 459 (the more likely date), this would mean he was born c. AD 453/4, again too early for Jordanes' distorted chronology.

165. Heather (2009), 223, taking Jordanes at his word, thinks Theodoric was born in the mid 450s. However, Wolfram's analysis which puts his birth at AD 451 is the correct one. Anonymus Valesianus 9.42 and 12.58, makes Theodoric the son of Valamer, not Thiudimer. The same information is also given by Malchus fr. 11, 14, Damascius, *Epitome Photiana* 46 = Photius, *Bibl.* 242, John of Antioch fr. 211, 4 = c. 95 (Boor), and Theophanes, *Chron.* AM 5977. All of which is an error, says König (1997), 30–1, who thinks that this was either because Theodoric, unlike Thiudimer who was a lesser king under Valamer, became the over-king of the Ostrogoths in succession to Valamer in Italy where he was proclaimed king or because Valamer when he sent Theodoric to Constantinople presented him to the East Romans as his son. This is quite intriguing and it seems that when Theodoric returned from Constantinople he took command of a separate force of Goths, some 6,000 says Jordanes (*Getica* 55.282), with which he attacked the Sarmatian king Babai and captured Singidunum, without the knowledge of his father, Thiudimer. Could it be that these 6,000 men were the former troops of Valamer that Theodoric, now that he had returned, inherited?

166. Interestingly Priscus, who usually uses the term Scythian to refer to Huns rather than Goths, calls Balamer (Valamer) a Scythian, fr. 37, Blockley (1983), 340.

167. Pohl (1980), 256; Wolfram (1988) 488; Thompson (1996), 168. In fact Theophanes, *Chron.* AM 5977, tells us that the sons of Attila were the rulers of the Ostrogoths before Valamer. As Pohl suggests, Ellac was actually the candidate backed by the Goths as successor to Attila's throne.

168. Maenchen-Helfen (1973), 164. The weakness of Eastern Roman power in the Balkans even at this stage is confirmed by the fact that rather than taking punitive measures against Valamer's Goths for their invasion of their territory the Eastern Romans chose to buy him off with a thinly veiled tribute of 300 pounds of gold per year, see Priscus fr. 37, Blockley (1983), 340.

169. Jordanes is extremely anxious throughout his account to explain away the long subjection of the Goths to the Huns, which he obviously found embarrassing. He thus argues that Valamer and his brothers, though more noble than the Hunnic king they served due to their glorious Amal lineage (*Getica* 53.199), did not break free from the Huns only because of the great power of Attila during whose lifetime no tribe in Scythia could defy the Huns (*Getica* 48.253). Having explained away the 'disgrace' of Valamer's subservience to the Huns with the once in a century phenomenon called Attila, Jordanes must have felt the pressing need to extricate his Amals from Hunnic control right after Attila's death.

170. *Getica* 50.266.
171. *Getica* 50.264.
172. Priscus fr. 37, Blockley (1983), 340. In other words, it was similar to the agreement made between the Huns and the Romans during the reign of Attila, but of course on a much smaller scale.

173. Demougeot (1979), 777.
174. Wolfram (1988), 259.
175. Mommsen, ed., *MGH*, 128–30.
176. Demougeot (1979), 770, argues that the Sadages were a Hunnic people situated north of the Sava river, placed there probably by Attila himself, and direct eastern neighbours of the Ostrogoths in Pannonia.
177. Priscus, fr. 45, Blockley (1983), 352.
178. Eckhardt (1955), 150.
179. Wolfram (1988), 259. Jordanes, *Getica*, 265. Pohl (1980), 261, argues that only a part of the Sciri sided with the Huns and most of them under Edeco sided with the Gepids. However, this is difficult to substantiate. The short-lived Scirian kingdom situated in the plain of the Tisza was only set up shortly before or after the defeat of Valamer's Goths by the Huns and the Sciri *c.* AD 465. The initial reverse at Nedao forced the Attilid Huns to retreat east into Lesser Scythia seized by Hernac. Oescus, Utus and Almus in Dacia were taken by his kinsmen Emnetzur and Ultzindur. The other pro-Attilid subjects established themselves to the west of Hernac and south of the Gepids. The Sciri, Sadagarii and some of the Alans were settled near Hernac in Scythia Minor and Lower Moesia (i.e. Bulgaria), the Ostrogoths in Pannonia around Sirmium (modern northern Serbia and Slovenia (Wolfram 1988, 260)) and the Sarmatians, Cemandri and 'some Huns' in Illyricum at Castra Martis. These were not, as has been assumed, Roman controlled regions at this stage. As noted earlier, Roman recovery of areas south of the Danube after AD 453 was slow and never really completed. As late as the mid 460s a small, independent Hunnic group in the Balkans under the rule of a minor princeling called Hormidac would capture Sardica (Sofia) well south of the Danube and could not be entirely vanquished by the imperial army under Anthemius, the future Western Roman emperor, and had to be brought to terms, Sidonius, *Carm.* 2.240 ff., Thompson (1996), 170.
180. Demougeot (1979), 770.
181. It is highly likely that after the death of Hunimund the Great, his fief that he had received from the Hunnic supreme king (Suebi and most of the Goths) was divided between his heirs, Suebi going to Hunimund the younger and the Goths going to Thorismud.
182. *Getica* 48.250. Jordanes again as usual says the Goths won the battle and defeated the Gepids. He, however, interestingly uses the same *topos* that he employs in his account of Theodorid's death at Chalons. Again the victorious king is killed in battle due to a nasty fall from his horse. The same thing also supposedly happened to the 'victorious' Valamer who was killed when he fell from his horse, *Getica* 53.276. Needless to say, this is all nonsense. The death of the king clearly means defeat in battle.
183. For other examples of Jordanes' pro-Amal or rather pro-Gothic bias see Heather (1991), 52. For the historical value of his *Getica* see pp. 34 ff.
184. Note that in Jordanes' account of both the war against the Huns and the Sciri (*Getica* 52.268; 54.278), on both occasions Valamer is taken by surprise and

fights the Huns and Sciri alone in the absence of his brothers. Clearly both accounts are duplicated references to one and the same event. That the Goths were the losers, not victors in this battle is made clear by Jordanes himself. After the usual nonsense about how the Goths even after the death of their king defeated their enemies, he says in 54.278, that after Valamer was dead the Goths 'fled' to his brother Thiudimer who then summoned Vidimer, the third brother, to help him.

185. Fr. 45 (*Exc. de Leg. Gent.* 17), Blockley (1983), 352.
186. Some may argue that the Goths mentioned in this fragment of Priscus (fr. 49, Blockley (1983), 356–8) are not the Amals or are some other Goths (Heather 2007, 174), but it is impossible to find evidence of the existence at this stage of any other substantial group of Goths in the Danubian region outside Roman control and near the Huns of Dengizich (in modern-day Romania) other than the Amal Goths. A group of Goths under a certain Bigelis (Jordanes, *Romana* 336) is said to have unsuccessfully invaded the Eastern Empire some time *c.* AD 466 (Heather 2006, 368) but they were defeated by the Romans and could not have been the Goths with Dengizich. They were possibly a breakaway group of Goths from the Ostrogoths under Valamer, who escaped Hunnic domination after the defeat of Valamer. The Crimean Goths indeed existed further away in the Ukraine, but this region was either independent of the Huns at this stage (due to the invasion of the Oghurs) or under the control of Ernak who opposed Dengizich's expedition against Constantinople, so they cannot be the Goths in question either.
187. *Getica* 48.251. Jordanes through his chronological distortion places this departure of Beremud in the early fifth century and attributes Valamer's accession to the throne of the Goths to his absence from the scene in Gaul. This is obviously absurd. Both Thorismud his father and Valamer his cousin were vassals of the Huns until at least AD 454. His father had died fighting for Ellac. So why would he have suddenly come to hate the rule of the Huns? The Hunnic rule that Beremud despised was obviously not the loose hegemony that the sons of Attila exercised before AD 461. It was the conquest of the Ostrogoths *c.* AD 465 that led to the death of Valamer.
188. Wolfram (1988), 256.
189. Maenchen-Helfen (1973), 165.
190. Priscus fr. 46 (*Exc. de Leg. Gent.* 18), Blockley (1983), 352.
191. Croke (1995), 98, argues that this occurred in AD 468 and that negotiations between Dengizich and the Romans broke down in 466/7. Pohl (1980), 265, places the event in AD 469, Marcellinus Comes a. 469; *Chronica Minora* 2, 90.
192. Signs of such revolt are already apparent in AD 467 among some of the Goths fighting under the Huns. Chelchal, the Hunnic officer in Roman service, incites a portion of Dengizich's troops, mainly Goths trapped by the Roman army, against the Huns leading them. The Goths take up arms against their masters and cause complete disorder which is then exploited by the Romans under Aspar, Anagast, Basiliscus and Ostrys, Priscus fr. 49, Blockley (1983), 356–8.

193. Schutz (2000), 72. It may also explain why there is an army of 6,000 Goths who obey Theodoric personally and not his father Thiudimer when Theodoric returns to his father. These 6,000 Goths were probably the leftovers from Valamer's former followers who had submitted to Dengizich and then rebelled in AD 467–8. That they recognize Theodoric as king before the death of Thiudimer (AD 473) in AD 471 is also intriguing. Only Jordanes among fifth- and sixth-century sources claim that Thiudimer is Theodoric's father. All the rest call Valamer his father. Could it be that Jordanes is wrong again as he usually is and that these troops obeyed Theodoric because he was the son of their previous lord Valamer? It could be that Jordanes has simply identified Thiudimer as Theodoric's father because Thiudimer was king after Valamer's death and following the logic of father to son succession, instead of uncle to nephew, he has made Thiudimer Theodoric's father.
194. Agathias, *The Histories* 2.13.3, Frendo (1975), 45–6, gives information about the elevation of Ragnaris the Hunnic Bittugur to kingship among the Ostrogoths in their final struggle against Narses.
195. *Getica* 55.280–1. Thiudimer's Gothic expansion in the direction of Noricum in AD 468 is reported by Sidonius, *Carm.* 2, 377. See also Alföldi (1974), 220. For a debate on the exact location of this Suebi–Alamanni confederacy see Hummer (1998b), 25. We also hear of the Goths in Lower Pannonia (i.e. those of Thiudimer) being hostile to the Rugii of king Flaccitheus in Noricum and plotting to kill the Rugian king in an ambush (*Vita S. Severini* 5).
196. The Gepids, formally the arch-enemy of the eastern Huns from this time onwards, consistently remain as allies of the Bulgar Huns and are seen fighting with the Bulgars against the Ostrogoths and the Eastern Empire, see Gyuzelev (1979), 13–14.
197. *Getica* 54.277–9, 55.282.
198. More on this shortly.
199. A further squabble among the remaining tribes along the Danube, unfortunately unrecorded, after AD 470 seems to have triggered the Torcilingian, some Rugian, Scirian and Herulian migration to Italy under Odoacer in AD 471/2, and the migration of a portion of the Suebi under Hunimund into the territory of the Alamans. *Vita S. Severini* 22, relates how a certain Hunimund, presumably the same Hunimund who fought against Thiudimer, attacked the city of Batavis (Passau) in Noricum some time after Vidimer's Goths had passed through Noricum *c.* AD 472.
200. Cassiodorus, *Variae* 9.25.4, pp. 291 ff., and 11.1.19, pp. 329ff. Wolfram (1988), 31, Christensen (2002), 75. Quite strikingly Jordanes only mentions Hunimund's fictitious links to Ermanaric in the context of succession to the Gothic throne, i.e. after the slaying of Vinitharius by Valamer and Gesimund (*Getica* 48.250). There is no mention of his links to Ermanaric in the passage directly before (*Getica* 48.248, the account of the defeat of Vinitharius), where he is called simply Hunimund the Great, father of Gesimund.
201. *Getica* 48.248.

202. This will probably be disputed by Heather who accepts the Gesimund/Gensemund identification, but thinks that Gensemund's adoption by the Amals signifies that he wasn't an Amal himself (1991, 26). Indeed Gensemund wasn't an Amal, but neither was Valamer originally. The legitimacy of both their claims to the Hunno-Gothic throne actually derived from their relationship to the previous king Hunimund, whose son/descendant and grandnephew, or more likely nephew, they respectively were.
203. *Getica* 24.121–2.
204. Wolfram (1988), 257; Merrills (2005), 164.
205. Reynolds and Lopez (1946), 49; Altheim (1959), 351.
206. The prestige of the Huns was such that even the Vandal king Gaiseric named his son Huneric, 'Hun-king'. It is quite obvious though that this did not imply that he was an ethnic Hun.
207. *Getica* 14.79.
208. As in *Türkmen ili* (the Turkmen people) and *Özbek ili* (Uzbek people). Such a term would not make sense as a personal name, but as we can see in the cases of Ostrogotha and Amal, these names are not personal names but eponymous attributions based on names of peoples and clans. See Tekin (1968), 334. Wolfram (1988) provides a rather forced Germanic etymology and interprets the name Hunuil as 'he who is immune to magic'. However, all Germanic names with the element Hun are compound names e.g. Hunulf, Huneric, Hunimund, and these names with the element Hun only occur after the Hunnic conquest and never before it. Thus the name Hunuil must be a post-Hunnic creation, not a pre-Hunnic Germanic name of the ancestor of the Amals.
209. The wide diffusion of names ending in *-ulf* after Hunuil may also be significant. The wolf, as mentioned earlier, is of course the Turco-Mongol totem and mythical ancestor. It was also the name given to imperial bodyguards in the Rouran and Gokturk Khaganates. For the importance of the wolf totem in early southern Siberian art, especially Altaian art and iconography in the first and second centuries AD (the same region from which the Huns would later begin their long trek west), see Rice (1965a), 37–8. See Pritsak (1953–4), 23, and Kollautz and Miyakawa (1970), 85. See also de Groot (1910), 266, for the origin myth of the Tiele (Gaoche) tribes in the old territory of the Huns: the union of a daughter of a Xiongnu shanyu and a wolf. Haussig (2000), 277, also points out that the wolf was the totemic ancestor of the Onoghurs who were intimately associated with the Attilid Bulgars. The Bulgar prince list calls the founding hero of Great Bulgaria (Kubrat) Kurt, meaning 'wolf' in Turkish (*qurt*), Altheim (1959), 227. In the Kül Tigin inscription (early eighth century) the Turks are repeatedly likened to wolves and their enemies to sheep, Tekin (1968), 265. The ancestress of the Ashina Gokturks is said to have been a she-wolf, Golden (2009a), 95–6; Sinor (1982), 223–31. In contrast there is simply no precedent for the wolf being recognized as an ancestor or holy animal among the Germanic peoples, though names with the element *ulf* do seem to predate the arrival of the

Huns. The popularization of names ending with -*ulf*, however, seems to begin during the Hunnic period. Hunuil's son is called Athal(a), (the form Athala is found in Cassiodorus 330.19, see Schönfeld (1911), 33), which Schönfeld links with the Germanic/Gothic word for nobility *Adel*, but there is also an Old Turkic etymology: *Adal* meaning 'take a name', commonly given to sons before they attain a name for themselves through a great deed (for this practice see Findley (2005), 45). As Bona (1976), 73, points out, Ostrogothic kings (who I argue here were Hunnic in origin) were similarly not given names in infancy. They earned their appellation (e.g. Theodoric/ 'king of the people', Thrasaric/'king of the warriors' etc.) in a manner that is strikingly similar to Turkic practices, and given the preponderance of actual titles in Hunnic names, it is likely that this was also true among the Huns. The name with the -*a* ending, Athala, also has an uncanny resemblance to Attila, says Golden in private email correspondence with the author. The similarity between the two names may have invited conflation when the Hunnic name was Germanicized.

210. *Getica* 4.25. Maenchen-Helfen (1973), 406. See also Merrills(2005), 118–19 for further discussion on Berig.
211. Christensen (2002), 302–17.
212. Isidore, *Historia Gothorum* (*Form. Prolix.*) 66. Not even the non-extant work of Ablabius, a Visigothic writer in the late fifth and early sixth century AD, seems to have contained any genuine Gothic traditions with regard to their early history, i.e. origins, Christensen (2002), 310, 345. It must also be noted that very frequently even up to the twelfth century AD when Saxo Grammaticus set about his work, in literary circles, both Greco-Roman and early Medieval, the Baltic Sea coast was often used interchangeably with or confused with the Scythian, i.e. Black Sea coastal region, due to geographical imprecision over the sea to the north which usually meant the Black Sea, but could also refer to the Baltic Sea. Thus Dacians/Dacia would even be identified with Danes/Denmark, Vernadsky (1951), 348.
213. Cassius Dio, *Historia Romana* 60.19.1. Christensen (2002), 303. See also Altheim (1959), 226.
214. Christensen (2002), 306, 346. See also Merrills (2005), 121, and Gillett (2009), 407, who argues that the Scandinavian origins of the Goths derive from the classicizing milieu of Constantinople, not Gothic traditions. Kulikowski (2007), 49–52, provides a detailed analysis of the problem of accepting Jordanes as a 'reliable' source for Gothic prehistory and supposed origins in Scandinavia. He argues that archaeological evidence is inconclusive and cannot prove that the Goths came from Scandinavia. He notes correctly that without preconceptions deriving from Jordanes, the so-called archaeological connections of the Goths to Scandinavia are far from self-evident (pp. 60–8).
215. Geary (1999), 108, notes how the legendary origins of the royal clan became often the legendary origin of the people and he lists the Goths, Salian Franks and Longobards as examples.

216. In fact in Jordanes there is an alternative Gothic leader who leads the Gothic migration south from the Baltic region where they are first sighted by Tacitus, Filimer (*Getica* 4.26–8), 'about the sixth since Berig', says Jordanes. This figure coupled with a fairly detailed itinerary of the Goths from the Baltic region to Oium is most probably the founding king of the original Gothic oral traditions and Ablabius cited by Jordanes. In contrast the reference to Berig is extremely brief and most likely a reference to the Hunnic royal ancestor of the Amals. As Merrills (2005), 124–5, correctly notes, the tradition of Ablabius and other sources cited by Jordanes associated the Goths with Scythia, some even with Britain, but the identification with Scandinavia is Jordanes' (possibly Cassiodorus') own addition. Thus the association of Berig the founding king with Scandinavia is also fiction. The name of this figure clearly points to the Hunnic origins of the Amals.
217. *Getica* 53.272.
218. This is rendered even more likely by the fact that whenever subsequently the Gepids find themselves threatened they are assisted by the Hunnic Bulgars ruled by eastern Attilids, e.g. the aid given by the Bulgars against Theodoric's invasion of Sirmium in 504–5, Collins (2000), 127, and then again by 12,000 Kotrigur Bulgars in AD 551 against the Lombards and the Romans, Whitby (2000c), 712, which probably suggests that the Gepids were vassals or allies of the Hunnic Bulgars.
219. Though he does not seem to have contributed much in terms of troops to Dengizich's invasion given the location of his fief in Croatia, far removed from the scene of the action (Bulgaria). The remnants of Valamer's army seem to have made up the mutinous Ostrogoths in Dengizich's army.
220. *Getica* 56.283–4.
221. That the Rugians were in conflict with the Goths while they were still in Pannonia is confirmed by *Vita S. Severini* 5, that mentions King Flaccitheus of the Rugii's fear of the hostility of the Goths towards him. This probably induced him to join the anti-Gothic alliance.
222. *Vita S. Severini* 17,4; Alföldi (1974), 220. Wolfram (1988), 263, places this siege around AD 468 when Thiudimer raided Noricum. However, Alföldi's date is more correct.
223. Wolfram (1988), 268; Demougeot (1979), 599, places his death at AD 472, which is probably an error. Unless the Vidimer who entered Italy was Vidimer the son, not the father.
224. *Getica* 48.251.
225. Sidonius Apollinaris, *Epistulae* 8.9.5 vv. 36–8.
226. Some of the Visigoths were in Italy with Avitus in AD 455–6 and one might argue that this reference to Ostrogothic victories against the Huns with Visigothic aid may be a reference to Valamer's clash with the sons of Attila *c.* AD 455–6 (which I have argued did not occur until the mid 460s). However, Avitus who employed the Visigoths was by no means on good terms with Valamer's Ostrogoths. In AD 455 the Ostrogoths actually inflicted a defeat on the Western Romans (i.e. the Visigoths who were fighting for him and other

Germanic mercenaries) under Avitus who tried to make a comeback into Pannonia, see Kazanski (1991), 105.
227. Sidonius, *Epistulae* 8.9.5 vv. 39–42, talks about how *c.* AD 476 the 'Roman' sought salvation from Euric against the hordes of the Scythian clime. This must be a reference to Odoacer's 'Scythians' who around then took over Italy from the last Western Roman emperor Romulus Augustulus.
228. Demougeot (1979), 598, John of Antioch, fr. 209, 1. John refers to the 'Scythians' of Odoacer. This could either be a generic reference to people from Scythia or a reference to actual Huns since Roman writers frequently referred to the Huns of the fifth century as Scythians (Demougeot 1979, 599).
229. *Getica* 54.277. Until this time and very likely until the 480s Odoacer and Feletheus-Feva of the Rugians, who were, as shown in the previous section, probably related Hunnic princes, were allies. Wolfram (1988), 266–7.
230. Refer back to section on Odoacer.
231. Alföldi (1974), 224.
232. Wood (2000), 515.
233. Wolfram (1988), 278; Haase (1991), 57.
234. The remaining Rugii under Fredericus joined Theodoric in his assault against Odoacer, but managed to remain distinct from the Ostrogoths as late as AD 541, Heather (1995b), 155. The remarkably stable transition from empire to kingdom under Odoacer and Theodoric was no mean achievement, when compared with the social dislocation that accompanied the barbarian takeover of Gaul, Spain and Britain, Humphries (2000), 532. Was this exceptionally smooth transition due to Odoacer's prior experience of Hunnic imperial administration?
235. See Maenchen-Helfen (1973), 416, for discussion on the origin of the name.
236. Heather (1996), 114–15, does not suggest this, but agrees that Balamber is Valamer.
237. It seems that all Gothic nobility were linked to this ancient king by Roman historians because of the fact that he is the only eastern Gothic king of any significance known from the fourth century. Jordanes also conflates him with Attila and makes him into a world conqueror of all barbaricum like Attila.
238. Heather (1996), 115; (1991), 58.
239. The Germanification of royal names during the time of Valamer, whose own name is probably the Iranian Balimber (see Wolfram 1988, 254), not at all surprising given the long association of the Huns with Iranians in Central Asia and also the Alans, but whose brothers and cousins all have Germanic sounding names, was probably part of this process of assimilation of Hunnic princes in the west. We have already encountered an example of this before in Laudaricus, the relative of Attila with a clearly Germanic name.
240. Croke (1983a), 85. Anonymus Valesianus 8.38.
241. Altheim (1948), 23. See also Murdoch (2006), 47.
242. For a good summary of Gundobad's career see Wood (2003), 252–4.
243. As Jones (1964), vol. 1, 244, points out, by this stage the Roman army in the West had 'dwindled to nothing'.

244. For a good summary of the careers of Orestes and his son Romulus Augustulus see Demougeot (1979), 605–8.
245. The latter account is favoured by Murdoch (2006), 77, and most other commentators.
246. *Getica* 46.242; *Romana* 344.
247. *History of the Wars*, 5.1.6.
248. Goffart (1988), 355.
249. König (1997), 27.
250. More on this below.
251. Wood (1994), 15; Périn and Feffer (1987), vol. I, 155.
252. Collins (1999), 94.
253. See Demougeot (1979), 602–3.
254. Murdoch (2006), 69.
255. Procopius, 5.1.4. For discussion on the nature of this land dispute and a critique of Procopius' claims see Goffart (1980), 58–76.
256. Demougeot (1979), 607. As Geary (1988), 13, points out, the office of emperor in the West had by this stage lost its meaning since almost all power and influence was in the hands of barbarian kings and the troops that they governed whose de facto positions were at times suitably enhanced by Roman titles granted to them by the Eastern emperors.
257. Marcellinus Comes, Croke (1995), 26–7, declares that the Roman Empire in the West perished with the deposition of Romulus by Odoacer.
258. See also the assessment of Vernadsky (1951), 380.
259. Croke (1983a), 86, 115. Silber (1971), 23, 33, also argues along the same lines. This is due to the attitudes of Roman sources that regarded or wanted to regard Odoacer and Theodoric as Roman *magistri militum*, no different from previous barbarian strongmen such as Ricimer and Gundobad, see Amory (1997), 197.
260. Cassiodorus in the *Variae* uses imperial vocabulary to refer to the Ostrogothic kingdom, calling it an *imperium* of Theodoric (1.42) and repeatedly uses the phrase *imperium italiae* (1.18.2, 12.22.5; Fanning (1992), 295). Clearly this reflects at least in part the understanding of Theodoric who considered his realm an *imperium* separate from the Roman Empire of the East and different from the Western Roman Empire that had preceded it. Both Theodoric and Odoacer, though at times adopting a subservient pose to deflect Eastern Roman intervention in Western affairs (e.g. when Anastasius tried to intervene in Western affairs *c.* AD 510 and offer diplomatic support to the Franks against the Visigoths while at the same time putting military pressure on Theodoric himself, see Heather (2009), 359–60), thus saw themselves as rulers of independent kingdoms. This is confirmed by the fact that Odoacer later on in his reign appointed his son Thela as Caesar without any authorization from Constantinople, Murdoch (2006), 106, 113–14. Clovis the Frank who was geographically more distant from Constantinople and as a consequence had little to fear from the East Romans was more brazen in his imperial pretensions, allowing his followers to hail him as Augustus in AD 507

and minting coins with his own name and image in the place of the emperor, see Dixon (1976), 77. For all the rhetoric of respecting the Roman emperor and Roman imperial traditions, the two Italian kings like Clovis in Gaul behaved independently in practice, but at the same time also harboured aspirations for recognition by the native Romans as legitimate rulers (due to the ever-present fear of eventual re-conquest by the Eastern Empire which caused both the kings great anxiety), hence their willingness to abide by, at least outwardly, established Roman precedents. See also Haase (1991), 55.

261. Malchus, fr. 10, actually tells us that the idea of invading Italy was first raised not by Zeno, but by Theodoric who in AD 479 proposed to Zeno that he would restore the deposed Nepos to Rome. Zeno showed no interest in the proposal then, but when Strabo died and the power of Theodoric Amal increased to such an extent that he was a real danger to Constantinople itself, then finally Zeno did 'commission' Theodoric to attack Odoacer, see König (1997), 120.

262. Croke (1983a), 115. See also Anonymus Valesianus 11.49. The fact that the Goths did not wait for any authorization from Constantinople before declaring Theodoric King of Italy (12.57, though he chose to call himself *Gothorum Romanorumque rex*, rather than *rex Italiae*, Haase (1991), 16) is proof that whatever links the Romans may have conjured up between the Eastern emperor and Theodoric, to the Goths themselves this was a mere formality that could either easily be ignored or utilized to their advantage depending on the context. See Wolfram (1988), 284, for discussion.

263. Malchus, frag. 20 (*FHG* 4:132). Zeno in this period did not even have the military capacity to destroy the minor Gothic warlord Theodoric Strabo in Thrace and of course Theodoric Amal who were rampaging all over the Balkans often within sight of Constantinople while the almost non-existent imperial forces lay impotent.

264. This is clearly reflected in the panegyric literature from the time of Theodoric. Ennodius for instance even regards or pretends to regard the Ostrogothic regime in Italy as the legitimate restoration of the Western Roman Empire and creates an image of Theodoric as the restorer of Roman power, see Amory (1997), 113; Haase (1991), 13.

265. Croke (1983a), 115. See also Demougeot (1979), 609–14.

266. Jones (1964), vol. 1, 253–4; Amory (1997), 8.

267. Burns (1980), 113. See also Collins (1999), 109–10.

268. Odoacer would send the imperial regalia from Italy to Zeno in Constantinople, Amory (1997), 313; Murdoch (2006), 5. For the ambiguity of Theodoric's relationship with the Eastern emperor see Bullough (1965b), 168. See also Demougeot (1979), 805–12, 820–2, and König (1997), 38.

269. Murdoch (2006), 100–1.

270. See Dandamaev (1989), 331.

271. See Briant (2002), 817–72, 875–6, on Alexander's takeover of Persia and the lasting continuation of Persian practices within the new Macedonian Empire. Nonetheless, the change of rulers cannot be said to have been insignificant or insubstantial.

272. The argument that Odoacer's army was a 'Roman' army and therefore his overthrow of the last Western emperor was no more than a military coup within the Roman system is also clearly invalid. For starters his army was no more 'Roman' than the army of the British East India Company was Mughal. Both were nominally subject to the emperors in Ravenna and Delhi, but in reality the foreign masters of both emperors. Furthermore, no barbarian military chief in Italy had ever declared himself king of Italy and governed without a resident puppet emperor in Ravenna (Ricimer had arguably set a precedent for this by governing alone for eighteen months (AD 465–7) between the reigns of Severus and Anthemius, but he soon reverted back to acknowledging an emperor resident in Italy). The notion that the powerless Nepos in Split, physically in exile, outside Italy and in no way affecting events in Italy even indirectly, was after AD 476 somehow still reigning emperor was of course pure fiction. To argue that the deposition of Romulus was not a turning point or that the later establishment of the Ostrogothic kingdom in Italy was just a continuation of Roman rule would be equivalent to saying that there was no significance to the overthrow of the last Mughal emperor of India, Bahadur Shah II, and that the British Raj was merely an Indian continuation of the Mughals. To be sure in some ways it was presented as such, Queen Victoria assuming the position of empress of India in the place of the deposed Bahadur Shah, and Zeno, comfortably far away, becoming the sole emperor of the 'united' Roman Empire. However, just as the British Raj was clearly a different political entity from the Mughal Empire, so was the 'barbarian' kingdom of Italy of Odoacer and Theodoric from the Western Roman Empire. It is certainly valid to speak of the transformation of Roman society, since social and economic changes in Italy, and other parts of the former Western Empire, were much more gradual than political upheavals under the two kings. Yet the transformation was neither deliberate nor natural for the former residents of the Roman Empire in the West. It was forced upon them by foreign conquerors who brought with them a new political system that radically altered 'European' history.
273. Kollautz and Miyakawa (1970), 113; Golden (1992), 78; Christian (1998), 237.
274. Haussig (2000), 275, however, is of the opinion that the Oghurs were actually Huns.
275. Pritsak (1976a), 28–9, argued that the Sabirs were a westerly tribe of the powerful Xianbei. The Xianbei were active as far west as the territory of the Central Asian Huns (before the Hunnic advance into Europe in the fourth century) and given the Wuhuan identification of the Var (Avars), whose original homeland was in Inner Mongolia, directly south of the Xianbei with whom they had a common Donghu (Mongolian) origin, the westerly drift of some of the Xianbei in the same direction as the Huns and the Avars is not at all unlikely. Pulleyblank (2000b), 71, reconstructs the name Xianbei in Early Middle Chinese as Särbi or Särvi. See also Golden (1990b), 235.
276. Priscus, fr. 30. See also Kollautz and Miyakawa (1970), 138–9.
277. Kollautz and Miyakawa (1970), 141, identify the *Sar-* prefix as etymologically linked to *sary* = 'white' (Turkish). See also Golden (2006–7), 37; Sinor (1946–7), 5.

250   *Notes to page 132*

278. See also Golden (1992), 88 and 92. The years leading up to AD 463 also saw the eruption of the Kidarite Huns of Central Asia into Sassanian Persia, doubtlessly also due to the pressures exerted by the Rouran (Avars). The Persians would request financial/military aid from the Romans in order to cope with the Kidarite threat, Priscus, fr. 41, Blockley (1983), 346. See Demougeot (1979), 772.
279. See also Czeglédy (1983), 98. See also Golden (2009a), 86, who dates the expansion of the Avars which triggered these migrations to *c.* AD 450.
280. AD 465–6 according to Maenchen-Helfen (1973), 165, and AD 468–9 according to Thompson (1996), 172–3.
281. Ernak seems to have had a measure of success in this regard by AD 466. Priscus, fr. 47, Blockley (1983), 352–4, records that in that year the Saragurs who had earlier attacked the Akatziri and other peoples to the west turned south into Persian-controlled Iberia and Armenia, leading to the dispatch of an embassy from Peroz, the Persian king (already seriously stretched due to his wars with the Central Asian Huns), to request Roman aid. The drive of the Saragurs, who after this disappear completely from the records, to the south is in all probability indicative of Ernak's military success against them in the mid 460s.
282. Priscus fr. 13.3, Blockley (1983), 288.
283. See Golden (1990c), 257; Kollautz and Miyakawa (1970), 157; Sinor (1990c), 199; Altheim (1948), 15, 21; Gyuzelev (1979), 11.
284. Bell-Fialkoff (2000), 229; Golden (1990c), 257. Clauson (1962), 39, suggests the possibility that certain Oghuric tribes may have already formed a part of the Hunnic nation before these later arrivals.
285. Both are identified as Bulgars by Halasi-Kun (1943), 80. See also Golden (1992), 99. For a different etymology for the name Kutrigur see Altheim (1959), 16. See also Clauson (1962), 38.
286. Golden (1992), 99.
287. Procopius, 8.5.21–2. Both these tribes were also later identified as Bulgars. See Fine (1983), 43. Menander Protector in his record of Justinian's diplomatic efforts to trigger a civil war between the Kutrigurs and Utigurs reports that Sandilkh the king of the Utigurs replied to Justinian that it would be unholy and altogether improper to destroy one's own fellow tribesmen. Sandilkh also calls the Kutrigurs his kin, again confirming the common origins of the two groups, Blockley (1985), 42–4.
288. Pritsak (1954a), 244. Justinian's letter to the Utigur Hunnic king Sandilch shows that he expected the eastern Hunnic king to have the ability to restrain the western king Zabergan of the Kutrigurs, hence gifts to the Huns were sent only to the Utigurs (Agathias 5.12.6–7, Frendo (1975), 147), which ended up offending the Kutrigurs. Justinian incites the Utigurs to punish the Kutrigurs by suggesting that the Kutrigurs had attacked the Roman Empire to demonstrate that they were superior to the Utigurs (i.e. were challenging the supremacy and overlordship of the eastern wing (Utigurs), traditionally the superior wing of a steppe confederacy/state). This angers Sandilch, who

Notes to pages 132–7

having learned of the Kutrigur expedition against the Romans wished, according to Agathias, to punish the Kutrigurs for their insolence (5.24–5, Frendo (1975), 160–2). All this suggest that the Utigurs and Kutrigurs were the constituent members of the same Hunnic confederation in the Pontic steppe, with the Utigurs as superior overlords. This is confirmed by the information that before this there had not been any open dissension between the two wings and war among the Kutrigur and Utigur Huns started from this time onwards.

289. Golden (1992), 233.
290. Christian (1998), 287.
291. Thompson (1996), 196.
292. Kwanten (1979), 174, 251; Adshead (1993), 86, 104.
293. Roemer (1986b), 43. For the later history of the Chaghatai Khanate, see *Tarikh-i-Rashidi* of Mirza Muhammad Haidar Dughlat.
294. See Petrushevsky(1968), 483–537.
295. Roemer (1986a), 2–3.
296. Roemer (1986a), 11–16.
297. See also Boyle (1968b), 413–17. For a good summary of the history of the disintegration of the Ilkhanate see Kwanten (1979), 244–9.
298. Heather (2009), 223 argues that after the death of Dengizich the Huns ceased to exist as an independent force in the Trans-Danubian world. This is simply incorrect.

CHAPTER 6: THE LATER HUNS AND THE BIRTH OF EUROPE

1. Czeglédy (1983), 103.
2. Golden (1992), 104.
3. Golden (1992), 103; Pritsak (1954a), 244.
4. Golden (2000), 288. See also Croke (1980), 188.
5. Marcellinus Comes, Croke (1995), 32–3. Runciman (1930), 5; Golden (2000), 288; Browning (1975), 29. The Bulgar raid in AD 499 ended in a particularly embarrassing defeat for the Romans who lost more than 4,000 men and four military counts (Croke (1980), 189; Browning (1975), 29). At times the Bulgars were employed as mercenaries in the empire's service against other enemies such as the Ostrogoths and their ally Mundo (the Gepid grandson of Attila the Hun) in AD 505, Croke (1980), 190 and Collins (2000), 127.
6. Marcellinus Comes, Croke (1995), 37–8, the Caucasian Huns also raided Armenia, Cappadocia and Lycaonia the year after in AD 515. The Huns had certainly not disappeared as a people after Nedao.
7. Malalas 16.16, Jeffreys *et al.* (1986), 226, Vitalian here is supported by an army of Huns and Bulgars, again showing the intimate links between the two names. See also Runciman (1930), 6, and Golden (1990c), 258.
8. Procopius, 7.14.1–2. The Antes and the Sclaveni according to Procopius have no single ruler, but live under a 'democracy' (7.14. 22) and seem to be largely autonomous. Some of them in modern-day southern Romania agree to fight the

Huns on behalf of the Empire north of the Danube (7.14.33). Demougeot (1979), 759, suggests that they were vassalized by the Bulgars, which is probably correct.
9. Curta (2006), 53–4; Browning (1975), 34.
10. Procopius, 2. 4.4–11. Kollautz and Miyakawa (1970), 157.
11. Theophanes tells us that the Kutrigurs (Kotragoi) and Bulgars are of the same stock. See Mango and Scott (trans.) (1997), 498.
12. Croke (1982b), 63.
13. Golden (1992), 100. In the western Balkans the Bulgars would penetrate as far south as the Isthmus of Corinth. See Whitby (2000c), 715.
14. Liebeschuetz (2007), 112.
15. Croke (1980), 192. See also Malalas 18.21, Jeffreys *et al.* (1986), 254, where Malalas uses the term general and king interchangeably to describe the two commanders of the the Bulgar Hunnic raids into the Roman Empire. These are in all likelihood references to sub-kings in the Hunnic feudal hierarchy.
16. Original Oghuric Turkic name may actually have been Kurt, according to the Bulgarian Prince List, suggests Fine (1983), 48.
17. Another Byzantine chronicler Nicephorus (35.1) identifies the Ounnogoundours with the Huns and Bulgars (Mango and Scott 1997, 500), suggesting close affinity between Huns, Bulgars and Onogurs, which were all probably names of the same tribal confederacy, either at different sub-tribal or supra-tribal levels and time periods. Agathias calls them Onogurs Huns (3.5.6, Frendo (1975), 72).
18. The name Ounnogoundour (Onogur) Bulgars clearly shows that the Onogurs were a subdivision within the wider Bulgar confederation. See Moravscik (1958), vol. II, 219, who calls the name Onogur a '*Beiname der Bulgaren*'. It also explains why in certain lists of peoples in the Pontic steppe the Bulgars are mentioned and the Utigurs/Kutrigurs are omitted and in others the latter are mentioned while the Bulgars are omitted. They were one and the same. Theophanes 357.8–10, Moravcsik (1958), vol. II, 98, locates the *urheimat* of the Bulgars (Great Bulgaria) in the area around lake Maeotis and the Kuban steppe, exactly the area where Procopius places the Utigurs and Kutrigurs.
19. Theophanes, *Chron.*, 1, 357, de Boor; AM 6171, Mango and Scott (1997), 497. See Golden (1992), 244–5 and Kollautz and Miyakawa (1970), 159. See also Czeglédy (1983), 112.
20. Agathias, *Agathiae Myrinaei historiarum libri quinque*, ed. Keydall (1967), 177; Golden (1992), 98.
21. See Browning (1975), 47, 123, where he comments that the Bulgars inherited from their nomadic past a complex and stable social and military hierarchy, a strong political organization, a developed system of officers of state and a tradition of government. The aristocratic council of the six great boyars/nobles would feature prominently in the political landscape of the Bulgar state as it did in the Xiongnu and Hunnic Empires that preceded it (p. 125).
22. Moravcsik (1958), vol. II, 107.
23. Gyuzelev (1979), 17, argues quite plausibly that Jordanes clearly views the Utigurs and Kutrigurs as simply Bulgars and hence does not mention them

in his list of nations in the Pontic steppe. They clearly represent branches of the same political entity. The name Bulgar, as well as the more political name Hun, was a blanket term for all tribes living under Attilid domination.

24. Procopius, Agathias and Menander all call the Utigurs and Kutrigurs Huns. Menander, as Blockley (1985), 9, points out, does not use the name Hun in a generic sense, but to designate a distinct grouping of tribes. The Emperor Justin when replying to the Avar ambassador Targites is also reported to have declared that he would not pay to the Avars the tribute Justinian had earlier paid to the Huns. He then mentions the Kutrigurs and Utigurs by name (fr. 12.6, Blockley (1985), 138–40). This indicates that both the Avars and the Romans regarded the contemporary Kutrigurs and Utigurs to be Huns, not in an anachronistic sense, but in reality and that these later sixth-century groups and the earlier fifth-century Huns were regarded as being one and the same by sixth-century Byzantines. The use of the name Hun in a truly generic sense for northern pontic nomads only begins with Theophylact Simocatta in the seventh century who calls both the Avars and the Turks Huns, see Whitby and Whitby (1986), 23.
25. Procopius 8.3.5. These Huns were separated from the rest of the Huns due to the establishment of the Sabir realm in the Volga region. See Czeglédy (1983), 98. The Sabirs, who according to Malalas (ed. Dindorf, 430–1) were a powerful confederacy that could field an army of 100,000 horsemen (an exaggeration no doubt, but indicative of their importance in Byzantine estimations), would co-exist with the Greater Hunnic state to the west in the Kuban steppe and southern Ukraine and the mini-state of the Caucasian Huns to the south in Dagestan.
26. The Sabirs entered Europe *c.* AD 506. See Czeglédy (1983), 103.
27. Procopius, 1.8.19.
28. Procopius, 1.12.1–9. Here an East Roman ambassador, Probus, is sent to the Huns who occupy all the territory between Cherson and the Bosphorus (probably the Utigur wing of the Bulgar Huns), to win over with money a Hunnic army to aid Constantinople's Iberian allies. The Utigurs, however, refuse to accept the proposal and instead a general by the name of Peter is sent to Lazica by the emperor with some Huns (presumably mercenaries recruited among certain elements of the Caucasian Huns more sympathetic to the Romans) to aid the Iberian king Gourgenes.
29. Malalas 18.13, Jeffreys *et al.* (1986), 249–50; Theophanes AM 6020, Mango and Scott (1997), 266–7.
30. Golden (1992), 106.
31. Also regarded as Sabirs rather than Huns by Czeglédy (1971), 147.
32. Croke (1980), 191.
33. See Golden (1992), 107, for a comprehensive analysis of the Armenian and Byzantine sources on these Huns. See also Kollautz and Miyakawa (1970), 153, and Sinor (1990c), 200–1.
34. Arguably until much later than the sixth century, since in the Khazar Empire (seventh–eleventh centuries AD) which dominated the Pontic steppe after the

Huns and Avars there were seven hereditary kingdoms, one of which was called Hun, a kingdom located in the basin of the Sulak river to the north of Derbent. Its capital was Varač'an (in Armenian sources) and Balangar in Islamic. See Pritsak (1978), 263. The realm of the Hunnic tribe Akatziri also seems to have persisted into Khazar times, since it is listed as a kingdom under direct Khazar control (Khotzir-Akatzir, Pritsak 1978), 263), as did those of the Volga Bulgars and Onogurs. The *Sui Shu* (covering the history of China from AD 581–617), 84, 8, also tells us that in the Tiele (Chili) tribal confederacy (descended, according to the same text, from the Xiongnu, though the accuracy of this observation is debatable, the territory of the confederation spanned a vast area, stretching from the Baikal region in the east to the Black Sea in the west) there was a tribe called Xun (Hun), Hamilton (1962), 54.

35. That the Utigurs and Kutrigurs formed the two main wings of the same steppe confederacy is proved by the foundation legend told by Procopius regarding the ethnogenesis of the two tribal groupings. He states that before the formation of both entities power in the steppe was concentrated in the hands of a single ruler (presumably he is referring here to Ernak, son of Attila), who then divided the power/empire between his two sons called Utigur and Kutrigur. The peoples allocated to the two sons were then called Utigurs and Kutrigurs, with the Utigurs clearly possessing precedence in the typical Inner Asian manner, being mentioned first and occupying the senior position to the east of the confederacy/ state, 8.5.1–4. This passage is clearly an allusion to real historical processes which took place in the late fifth century AD when Ernak united the steppe and then in the usual Inner Asian manner divided his realm into two wings. Procopius, again the most reliable source on these matters and who encountered real Huns during his military career under Belisarius, locates the Utigurs in the Kuban steppe and the Kutrigurs in 'the greater part of the plains' west of the Sea of Azov, i.e. southern Ukraine, 8.5.22–3. Menander 2.24–32, also notes that the Utigurs hesitated about fighting the Kutrigurs because they were 'our kin', Whitby (2007b), 153.

36. That the various Oghur tribes of the Pontic steppe were ruled by the Attilids is confirmed by the record left by Theophylact Simocatta (ed. de Boor, 256.23–262.17) who tells us that the Oghurs had two leading clans the Vars (later fifth- and sixth-century intruders into regions formally ruled by the Huns) and the Huns (Χουννὶ), and that their domination was not a recent development but long-established, παλαίτατοι ἔξαρχοι.

37. For discussion on these Hunnic names see Alemany (2000), 206–7.

38. Procopius, 1.14.39–50. Allied Hunnic mounted archers under the overall command of Aigan (by birth a Hun) and led by Sinnion and Balas, 600 in all, despite their small numbers would play a decisive role in the Eastern Roman re-conquest of North Africa as well and become the terror of the Vandals, 3.11.11–12; 18.12–19. Their reluctance to adhere to Roman military discipline, however, due to their status as allies, not subjects, would cause Belisarius problems throughout the campaign, 3.12.8–10, 4.1.5–11, 4.3.7–16. The Vandals under Gelimer in the latter passages try to win over disaffected Huns within Belisarius' army and Belisarius

in response has to win them back to his side with gifts, banquets and 'every other manner of flattering attention every day' in order to bring the campaign to a successful conclusion. The Hunnic cavalry is of such importance to the Roman army that victory or defeat hangs on their loyalty to the Roman cause. Althias would later defeat the army of Iaudas, king of the Moors, with a force of just seventy Huns, 4.13.1–17, again demonstrating the effectiveness of Hunnic troops. See Elton (2007), 537 and Greatrex (2000), 268, who argues that Althias was in all probability a Hun himself. As Whitby (2000b), 310, notes, the Hunnic cavalrymen were the best individual soldiers in the Roman army and the Roman cavalry itself was modelled on fifth-century Hunnic mobile armies. Two hundred Hunnic allies would again participate in Belisarius' conquest of Italy and in the process earn a formidable reputation, 5.5.4, 6.1.1–10, 7.30.6. By some historical irony the grandson of Attila, Mundo, in Roman service would command the other wing of the Roman advance against the Ostrogoths into Dalmatia 5.5.11 ff., 5.7.1–8. Huns would later form an important part of the great army with which Narses finished off Totila, 8.26.
39. Procopius, 1.15.1. See also 2.29.15.
40. Agathias 5.11.2, Frendo (1975), 146, where Agathias records that all the barbarian peoples east of Lake Maeotis were referred to by the general name of Scythians or Huns, whereas individual tribes had their own particular names. Of the two general designations, Scythian is clearly the anachronistic name used by Romans alone, whereas the name Hun was probably still very much in usage among the steppe tribes as either a tribal name in the case of the Caucasian Huns and the Hephtalites or as a blanket reference to the political overlordship of the Attilids.
41. Procopius, 1.21.11–16, 27–8.
42. See Greatrex (2000), 269–74, for the complexity of the designation Roman in Late Antiquity and also its broad political overtones and applications that transcended ethnic boundaries. In short, anyone who was politically loyal to the Roman state and the emperor was considered a Roman. The same applied to the designation Hun.
43. See Sulejmenov (1989), 29–30, for the views of the Shaybanid prince scholar Valikhanov and his theory of same tribes with different names succeeding one another in the Pontic steppe.
44. In any case these new arrivals were closely related to the Dingling (later Tiele and Oghurs) whose tribes already formed a part of the original Hunnic invasion wave in the fourth century AD. The situation we find among the fifth- and sixth-century Huns is very similar to the situation we find later among the Kipchaq Turks and the Pechenegs who settled the same area (Pontic steppe) as the Huns from the ninth to the thirteenth centuries AD. The Kipchaqs (Turkic, 'people of the sand-steppe, desert') were also known by an alternative name Cumans/Kun, the name of their ruling tribe (Pritsak 1968, 161), and the Pechenegs (meaning 'brother-in-law', indicative of their status as the confederation ruled by the brother-in-law of the Turkish Ashina Khagan/emperor, Pritsak (1976c), 6–7) by the name Kangar, again that of the ruling tribe. The alternative names have

sometimes confused historians without thorough grounding in Inner Asian history into thinking that there were multiple, different tribes in the steppe when in fact the appellations referred to a single tribal confederation. Thus in our sources the names Kutrigur, Bulgar and Hun are used interchangeably and refer in all probability not to separate groups but one group. Kutrigur, Utigur, Onogur, and possibly also Akatziri, are designations given to the four main divisions of the steppe confederation (Utigurs and Kutrigurs forming the main two wings and the Akatziri and Onogurs functioning as subsidiary hordes to the two main divisions, a fact seemingly confirmed by the information in Jordanes, *Getica* 5.37, that the Hunuguri (Onogurs) were inferior to their more powerful neighbours) all ruled by branches of the same ruling dynasty (Attilid), Bulgar (mixed ones, like the name Kipchaq (sand-people) and Pecheneg (brothers-in-law)) being the name of the confederation as a whole, often used interchangeably with the name Hun designating the imperial status of this confederation and the origins of its ruling elite.

45. That the name Hun and later also that of Avar denoted imperial status and greatness among the steppe peoples is revealed by the account in Theophylact 7.8.259, where the Ogurs (i.e. Turkic-speaking tribes) are said to have named their ruling clans after their oldest (i.e. the most important) rulers Hun and Var. See also Pohl (1988), 221–2.

46. In a similar way again the various tribes of the western steppe would later claim to be Turks because of the prestige of the name Turk which referred back to the great Gokturk Empire of the sixth to eighth centuries AD.

47. Two possible etymologies have been suggested for this tribe, either Aq-Qazir ('white Khazars', i.e, the western Khazars), see Hamilton (1962), 33 or Ayač-eri (forest-dwellers), Haussig (1953), 360, which seems more reasonable since the location of the Akatziri seems to be to the northwest of the Bulgars (beyond the pontic steppes occupied by the Altziagiri, Kutrigurs and Utigurs and in the forest zone of northern Ukraine).

48. Christian (1998), 277; Pohl (1988), 25. The two tribal groups are described in Menander as kinfolk who speak the same language, Menander, Blockley (1985), 43. It is significant that Jordanes mentions the Bulgars and then does not bother to mention the Kutrigurs and Utigurs. To him they were clearly one and the same.

49. Moravcsik (1958), vol. II, 230, mentions that some scholars have suggested the possibility that these Altziagiri are none other than the Ultzinzurs mentioned above, the tribes led by the six lords.

50. Christian (1998), 278.

51. Possibly related in some way with the Eastern Xianbei, Christian (1998), 279.

52. Pohl (1988), 25, thinks the identification is contentious. Hamilton (1962), 39, argues that the Onogurs were the western elements of the Onuygurs further to the east in Mongolia (the Selenga region), who are mentioned in the eighth-century inscription of Šine-usu. The Onuygur tribal confederation gave birth to the Great Uygur Khaganate which replaced the Gokturk Khaganate in the mid eighth century AD. It seems to represent roughly the same tribal union or is

a later development of an earlier tribal confederacy which also contained the Uyghurs, the Toquz-Oghuz, which led the Tiele Turkic tribes of the area between Lake Baikal and eastern Kazakhstan in the resistance against Gokturk domination, see Hamilton (1962), 29. What is interesting is the fact that Uyghur tribal names resemble closely the names of Oghuric Turkic tribes that appear in the western Pontic steppe in the fifth and sixth centuries AD, e.g. Sarig Uygur (Saragurs), Onuygur (Onogur), Uturqar (Utigur), Orqundur (Ogundur), Qasar (Akatziri), Abar (Avar), Bular (Bulgar), Hamilton (1962), 49. The similarities between these names may in some cases be suggestive of real links, in others they are clearly pure coincidences. Yet what is more relevant for our purposes is the observation (also mentioned by Pohl (1988), 25–6) that like the various tribes listed as forming the greater Uyghur Khaganate or the earlier western Turkish Khaganate (On Oq, meaning 'ten tribes'), the tribes of the western steppe listed separately and giving the false impression of anarchy and total independence may in fact be constituent tribes or tribal divisions of a larger confederacy, Onogur says Hamilton (1962), 48. It seems more likely that the general name for the greater political entity was Bulgar rather than Onogur, as the name Great Bulgaria (Theophanes AM 6171, 357.8–14; Nikephoros 33, 14–20, see Pohl (1988), 270) given to the state founded by the Bulgar Hunnic king Kubrat, which was formed under the leadership of the Onogurs (with the support of the Kutrigurs), shows. Pohl (1988), 26 is absolutely correct to observe that the various names with the element Oghur with a colour (as in Saragur 'yellow Oghur') or numerical prefix (On-oghur '10 Oghurs', Utur-gur '30 Oghurs', Kutur-gur/Toquz-Oguz '9 Oghurs/Oguz'), do not necessarily denote ethnic groups, but originate from the organizational structure of steppe empires.

53. *Getica*, 5.36–7. Christian (1998), 278. Kwanten (1979), 26, thinks that the Onogurs merged with the Bulgar Huns in the Pontic steppe. This is highly plausible.
54. Pohl (1988), 25.
55. See Alemany (2000), 393. For a detailed discussion on Book 12.7 of Pseudo-Zacharias Rhetor, see Czeglédy (1971).
56. Marquart (1903), 365, n. 1. See also Alemany (2000), 394; Czeglédy (1971), 137.
57. Czeglédy (1971), 143.
58. Presumably a new Turkic-speaking tribe entering the region with or independently of the Avars, see Alemany (2000), 393. Dani, Litvinsky and Zamir Safi (1996), 181, see them as a branch of the Hephtalite Huns residing in Central Asia.
59. Czeglédy (1971), 142.
60. Czeglédy (1971), 142, argues that the name was borrowed from Eustathius who compiled a chronicle of events up to AD 502.
61. As demonstrated earlier the Utigurs and Kutrigurs were definitely part of the same confederacy and, as Procopius' observation makes clear, they were the most powerful tribes in the Pontic steppe.
62. Also mentioned in Theophylact 7.9, Whitby and Whitby (1986), 190, as among the three easternmost peoples of the Pontic steppe. They were situated in close proximity to the Sabirs and the Onogurs.

63. The Onogurs are also known to have possessed an urban settlement called Bakath that was destroyed by an earthquake, Theophylact 7.8, Whitby (1986), 191. Czeglédy (1971), 147, sees them as being connected with the Bulgars and place both of them in the Kuban steppe, i.e. where the Utigurs were located. He further speculates that they were under Sabir domination at this stage, which is somewhat unlikely.
64. The astonishing sophistication of the Proto-Bulgar political system with its feudal political structure, bureaucracy and a native writing system (see Altheim and Stiehl 1954, 269–72), argues against a slide among the Hunno-Bulgars into uncontrolled anarchy after the defeat at Nedao suggested by many critics.
65. Pohl (1988), 21: (1997b), 93.
66. On the language of the Avars see Harmatta and Yilmaz (1988), 17–19 and 45. The Avars seem to have spoken an eastern Turkic language that was related, but slightly different from the Oghuric Turkic spoken by the Bulgar Huns. They were also highly heterogeneous.
67. Golden (1992), 100. The Avars who entered Europe numbered merely 20,000 men. Kollautz and Miyakawa (1970), 144.
68. The Avars had a powerful Hunnic element, as their ethnonym Var-Hun shows. See Czeglédy (1983), 107 ff. Many of the peoples who formed a part of their imperial confederation could also speak Hunnic (Oghuric Turkic). When the East Romans with Theognis negotiate with the Avar Khagan Bayan interpreters are said to have translated Greek into Hunnic to Bayan (Menander fr. 27.2, Blockley (1985), 239).
69. See Bona (1976), 100–2, for an assessment of the armaments, composition and military power of the Avar armies. Heavy cavalry armed with Central Asian (Persian says Bona) cataphract armour, 'East Asian' single-edged cavalry swords and most significantly of all iron stirrups (the first introduction of this innovation in Europe) which allowed the armoured knight to add extra force to his lance thrusts and also freely use his composite bow, formed the core of this army. No contemporary western army, even that of the East Romans could beat this formidable force on the open plains. The Avar army of mounted warriors numbered just 20,000 men (Curta 2006, 62), but were supplemented by subject peoples such as the Bulgars who provided the bulk of the light cavalry (also mounted archers) and the various Slavs who made up the infantry (Bona 1976, 101). See also Szádeczky-Kardoss (1990), 211, for the Byzantine description of Avar military tactics and equipment in the *Strategicon*.
70. Golden (1992), 109.
71. Golden (1992), 111, and Szádeczky-Kardoss (1990), 207.
72. Christie (1995), 58 ff.
73. Whitby (2000c), 721; Liebeschuetz (2007), 114–20; Pohl (1988), 58–89. The Avar conquest stretched as far south as Athens, Corinth and the Peloponnese. See also Szádeczky-Kardoss (1990), 208–9 and Curta (2006), 69 and 109. In AD 584 the East Romans were forced to pay a tribute of 80,000 *solidi*, Theophylact 1.6.6. An Avar ruling elite would linger on in areas such as Greece until AD 805–6, Szádeczky-Kardoss (1990), 215.

74. Szádeczky-Kardoss (1990), 212, 457. The heterogeneous nature of the Avar Khaganate and even the Avar ethnos (if it existed as a distinct entity) is borne out by grave finds in Pannonia which show various ethnic types dressing and fighting in Avar style, but also with Germanic cultural traits, Christie (1995), 65–6.
75. Pohl (2003), 574.
76. Szádeczky-Kardoss (1990), 213, Pohl (1988), 248–55, and Fine (1983), 42–3. For more information on Avar invasions of the Eastern Roman Empire see Whitby (2000c), 720–1. The Avar Empire like the Hunnic Empire before it possessed the same combination of nomadic and sedentary population base, Curta (2006), 65 and Whitby (2000c), 720.
77. For the civil war between the Avars and Bulgars over who would succeed to the office of Khagan see the *Chronicle* of Fredegar, Book 4.72, Wallace-Hadrill (1960), 60–1.
78. For the fascinating possibility of links between the historical Kubrat and his five sons and the Croatian foundation legend of Chrobatos and his five brothers, see Grégoire (1944–5), 88–118. See also Pohl (1988), 265.
79. Possibly derived from the five Tu-lu tribes that formed the eastern wing of the western Turk Kaghanate, see Sinor (1990b), 309.
80. Curta (2006), 76–9. For a detailed history of the Ogurs, Onogurs and the Bulgars see Golden (2000), 286–9.
81. Szádeczky-Kardoss (1990), 217–20. See also Curta (2006), 94, and Ganshof (1971), 20–1.
82. Fine (1983), 78. See also Kristó (2000), 370–2.
83. See Pritsak (1976a), 21.
84. Pohl (1997d), 69.
85. Curta (2006), 243–7.
86. Heather (2009), 385.
87. Beckwith (2009), 111.
88. Strzygowski (1923).
89. Heather (2009), 365.
90. Heather (2009), 383–4 and 618.
91. See Urbańczyk (2005), 143–5, and Heather (2009), 401. The Slavs of central and southeastern Europe experienced a long period of Avar domination and the first independent kingdom among them, according to the *Chronicle* of Fredegar Book 4.48, Wallace-Hadrill (1960), 39–40, was brought about by the rebellion of the sons of the Huns born from the wives and daughters of the Slavs: *Filii Chunorum quos in uxores Winodorum et filias generaverant tandem non subferentes maliciam ferre et oppressionem, Chunorum dominationem negantes – ceperunt revellare.* See also Pohl (1988), 257. This suggests that the Avars had a significant impact on early Slavic political organization and state foundation, Urbańczyk (1997b), 42. See also Brachmann (1997), 27–8, who notes a significant Turkic-speaking (i.e. Avar) element in the establishment of political structures and dynasties in the western Slavic world. The wendish 'dukedoms' that the Franks encounter in central Europe were no doubt either set up by the

Avars or like the so-called Blatnica-Mikulčice group dominated by elites who clearly had inherited Avar political practices, Urbańczyk (2005), 145.
92. The political culture of the east Slavs was also so heavily influenced by steppe polities that the earliest rulers of the Rus Khaganate, which preceded the Kievan Rus state of the Rurikids, called their ruler Khagan (a title first introduced into Europe by the Avars) in the Avar/Khazar manner. See Golden (2001c), 29–32, on the blood ties between the Rus Khagans and the Khazar Khagans. See also Noonan (2001), 87, who notes that even a late tenth-century ruler like Vladimir was referred to by Rus sources as 'our Khagan'. The Rus princes aspired to be recognized as the legitimate successors of the imperial tradition of the steppe empire of the Khazars and Bulgars (p. 89). Indeed Rus dualism may be an imitation of Khazar dualism (p. 92). Wickham (2009), 485–7, too argues that the Rus princes borrowed the techniques of rule over their territory from contemporary Turkic hegemonies: the Volga Bulgars and the Khazars. The title of Khagan, the system of tribute collection, the construction of an extensive network of long-distance defensive ramparts in the Kievan region (in imitation of Bulgar models), and the *druzhina* or military entourage of the princes, may all be imitations of Bulgar–Khazar practices. Kiev, the capital of Rus, is also likely to have been originally a Khazar garrison town and its Rus rulers like their steppe predecessors regarded the state as a family inheritance, not that of a particular individual. The collegial, familial nature of Rus political life necessitated family/aristocratic conferences that closely resemble the Mongol Kuriltai, Christian (1998), 290, 366–7.
93. Sulimirsky (1985), 152.
94. Sulimirsky (1985), 186. See also Bashilov and Yablonsky (2000), 10.
95. Sulimirsky (1985), 161.
96. Melyukova (1990), 106; Sulimirsky (1985), 154.
97. Sulimirsky (1985), 167.
98. Hdt. 4.25, 49, 78, 100.
99. Sulimirsky (1985), 183–4; Genito (1992), 61. See also Metzner-Nebelsick (2000), 160–73, who argues for a gradual assimilation of eastern (Thraco-Cimmerian) ideas and cultural practices rather than massive immigration of easterners into central Europe. She is probably correct in pointing out that there was no major change in population during the period under consideration in central Europe, but the radical transformation of local cultures in the Hungarian plains cannot be explained purely in terms of cultural exchange and networks. The intrusion of an eastern element, however small, into central Europe that Sulimirsky and other scholars advocate, is surely correct.
100. Sulimirsky (1985), 173, 192–3.
101. Genito (1992), 62–3.
102. See Findley (2005), 32.
103. Khazanov (2001), 4–5.
104. Though disputed, some historians argue that Denmark by the ninth century at least was ruled under a system of dual kingship, see Garipzanov (2008), 113–14, for the debate. Can it be a mere coincidence that the Danes possessed a

political system that resembles the steppe institution of dual kingship? Given the great distance in time between the Hunnic domination of Scandinavia (fifth century) and the first attestation of this political order in Denmark (ninth century), no firm conclusions can be made. However, it is worth further consideration and research. Interestingly among the Danes, as among steppe peoples, any male member of the ruling house was considered eligible for kingship and his power was dependent on both his claims to a certain sacred charisma and the support of his military retinue, 'home-receivers'/ *hempægar* (comitatus), see Roesdahl (1982), 25. Apparently there were two royal lineages in early Denmark and there were at times multiple kings (brothers) who ruled as a collective, Randsborg (1980), 13, 16.

105. We find this principle of collective rule among members of the royal clan as far north as northeastern Germany among the Polabian Slavs such as the Weletians who in the eighth and ninth centuries AD had a supreme prince Dragowit (*rex*) who had authority over other *reguli* in the tribal confederacy/ kingdom, and later supreme prince Liub (*totius regni summa*) who shared his authority with his brothers, each of whom controlled a *regio* (a federation of clans headed by a prince). Interestingly there were four *regiones* /subdivisions among the Weletians as among earlier and contemporary steppe confederations. As in a steppe empire, in this Slavic political entity a single dynasty had exclusive rights to the princely throne, see Lübke (1997), 120–1. See also Gringmuth-Dallmer (2000), 65. For the inference that many of these northwestern Slavs, the Sorbs and the Abodrites, were heavily influenced by former dissidents of the Avar Empire who moved to this region see Pohl (1988), 119.

106. Constantine Porphyrogenitus, *De Adminstrando Imperio* 41, Moravcsik and Jenkins (1967), 181. See also Bowlus (1994), 161. For a detailed study of Slavic Moravia that succeeded the Avar Khaganate see Boba (1971). See also Třeštík (2000a), 193, for the Moravian adoption of the Avar title of Zhupan and the Avar influence on Moravia. See Wolfram (1997a), 56, for Avar/Inner Asian influence on other Slavonic political entities in the area dominated later by the Moravians.

107. For the tradition of collective rule by members of the royal family in Poland see Shepard (2005), 256–7. See also Manteuffel (1982), 56, 118. For the Avar impact on early Polish political organization see Urbańczyk (1997b), 42.

108. The description of the system in early Bohemia is rather murkier than those for the neighbouring and more famous Greater Moravia, but we do hear of Bohemian dukes ruling collectively. We also learn that two of the princes (Spytihnev and Vitislav) by the late ninth century at least were pre-eminent, which reminds us of Inner Asian/Hunnic dual kingship. Given the paucity of details available it is impossible to ascertain whether or how these early princes were related and whether the pre-eminence of two princes was temporary or a long-established tradition. Later still in AD 936 before Premyslid unification we also hear of a certain *vicinus subregulus* (neighbouring sub-king) and of the largely autonomous Slavnikid ducal family who were in some way related to the Premyslids (maybe a collateral branch of the Premyslids, see Sláma

(2000), 282), but were removed from power by the Premyslids. See Žemlička (2000a), 235; (2000b), 274–6; Urbańczyk (2005), 146; Třeštík (2000b), 228. Early Bohemia was also under significant Avar cultural and social influence, Třeštík (2000b), 228.
109. Steinhübel (2000), 200.
110. Golden (2001), 39–40. Urbańczyk (2005), 145–6, and Heather (2009), 532–3 and 544, note correctly that political structures that allowed for the emergence of complex state entities in Slavic Europe following the collapse of the Avar Khaganate in the 790s AD, are likely to have been generated under Avar influence. The various dukedoms that immediately become visible in Bohemia and Moravia when the Franks enter the region are most likely entities that arose within the context of Avar imperial rule.
111. Sims-Williams (2002a), 234, the title was used in the White Hun Empire to refer to a minor official. See also Curta (2006), 164; Pohl (1988), 266, 305; Altheim and Stiehl (1954), 272. The south Slavic title *ban* may also derive from the Avar name Bayan. See Róna-Tas (1999), 115; Jenkins (1962), 121.
112. Anderson (1974), 231.
113. Fine (1983), 51–2. The possible Sarmatian (Iranian) origins of the early Croatian and Serbian governing elite has also been postulated, which could explain the great impact of steppe political systems on the early Serbo-Croatians (pp. 56–8). See also Jenkins (1962), 115 and 118, for the White Croats.
114. See Khazanov (2001), 4–5; Krader (1958), 79. See also Stepanov (2001), 17, for the Bulgar stress on the divine origins of their ruling dynasty. See Chen (2002), 293–6, for evidence of the pervasiveness of the concept of sacral kingship among the Kushans, the Turkic tribes of the fifth century AD and also among the Rouran (*Wei Shu* 103.2294 = *Bei Shi* 98.3255). Oosten (1996), 226–9, calls this Indo-European ideological tradition, but it is more accurate to call it Inner Asian.
115. Schutz (2000), 153, 163. We also see the same phenomenon among the Hunno-Gothic confederation of the Ostrogoths among whom the royal house of the Amals are given semi-divine status (*Getica* 13.78). See Heather (1995b), 166–7. Becher (2011), 184, sees the foundation of Merovingian dynastic power as being intrinsically rooted in Roman and Christian traditions. This is true to a certain extent, but is only part of the picture that is incomplete without the Hunnic influence pointed out here.
116. Wickham (2009), 113; Kaiser (1993), 83–5. For a more detailed account see Wallace-Hadrill (1962), 158–248. Curiously enough the sixth-century eastern neighbours of the Franks, the Hunno-Avars who ruled in central and eastern Europe, were noted by the East Romans for their long 'snaky' hair. Corippus in his *Laudem Justini Augusti Minoris*, line 262, talks about how the Avars 'filled the spacious halls with their long hair'. Agathias in his *Histories* 1.3.4 actually compares the long hair of the Avars with that of the Franks, though unfavourably, and says that whereas the long hair of the Franks is washed and clean, that of the Avars is dirty and unkempt. Still the similarity in customs is

quite remarkable. See Pallas-Brown (2000), 315–16, and Demougeot (1979), 775.
117. Ganshof (1971), 87.
118. Richter (1994), 13. See Geary (1988), 55–6, 61–2, for discussion on early Germanic kingship.
119. Oosten (1996), 222–3. Hummer (1998b), 12, perceptively points out that strong kingship among the Franks was triggered by influences from the Eurasian steppes. No doubt Roman political and administrative precedents (Wallace-Hadrill 1962, 1) helped secure and stabilize Frankish kingship once it was established, but they were not the main catalysts for its conception. It is noteworthy that in the divisions of territory among Frankish kings and sub-kings large former-Roman administrative centres were often turned into centres of royal power, Geary (2002), 136. Yet Roman provincial boundaries (i.e. larger administrative divisions) played no role whatsoever in the whole process, see Kaiser (1993), 28. This implies that while the Frankish kings adopted certain facets of Roman administration when it suited them, their non-Roman political tradition (the Inner Asian political practice of distributing appanages) took precedence over any former Roman administrative norms.
120. Ganshof (1971), 88–9; Kaiser (1993), 68–71.
121. Bachrach (1972), 18; Kaiser (1993), 28; Wood (1994), 50. Clovis himself was also not the only king of the Franks. There were three other kings (a total of four again): Sigibert (King of the Ripurian Franks to the east), Chararic and Ragnachar (a cousin of Clovis who ruled at Cambrai), whom he gradually, like Attila before him, eliminated, James (1988), 88–91; Périn and Feffer (1987), vol. 1, 159–60. Strangely enough the division of the realm into four parts, an Inner Asian political practice (recall the four main divisions of the Xiongnu Empire with sub-divisions in each half of the dual system and also the same division among the later Pechenegs mentioned earlier), is repeated again and again in Frankish history. The Franks also like steppe polities have two main divisions (Salian and Ripurian, later Neustria and Austrasia). Later on the Franks would add Burgundy to their realm and from then onwards we have three *regna*. However, besides Neustria, Austrasia and Burgundy we sometimes find Aquitaine being governed separately as a fourth kingdom (Geary (1988), 157; Goetz (2003), 326). Maybe this is merely a coincidence, but more research might yield some surprising revelations. For an argument that the division of the realm into four parts reflects Roman imperial tradition see Geary (1988), 95. This is highly unlikely given the fact that the tetrarchy of the late third and early fourth centuries AD was a one-off experiment that failed and was never repeated. It is also to be wondered how the Franks could even have known about this after 200 years. There is also the interesting phenomenon of the Alan-dominated tribal confederacy in Spain which also had four territorial divisions: the dominant Alans with the greatest share, nearly half of Spain (Lusitania and Carthaginensis), Suebi (half of Gallaecia), Siling Vandals (Baetica) and Hasding Vandals (the other half of Gallaecia), see Arce (2003), 138–40.
122. James (1988), 171.

123. Wood (1994), 56.
124. Wickham (2009), 113–14.
125. Geary (1988), 117.
126. See Widdowson (2009), 3, Schutz (2000), 183–4, and Lasko (1965), 213.
127. As explained earlier in the book 'feudalism' in the political sense of a formal division of state power between the king and his subordinate great vassals (sub-kings and great nobles) within the upper aristocratic elite (see Krader 1958, 77), and not the political-economic system which we identify with later medieval Europe, the *seigneurie* or manorialism.
128. Wallace-Hadrill (1962), 7, calls early Frankish 'feudalism', 'incipient feudalism' that allowed the king to increase his power by distributing land to his followers, thereby gaining their loyalty, but bestowing on the ruler the right to take the lands back. See Wickham (2009), 522–3, for this transition from Frankish centralized 'feudal' rule to 'seigneurial-type' power structures in the tenth century, the so-called 'feudal revolution'. Interestingly the earlier Frankish nobility in much the same way as their later Mongol peers to the Chingizid dynasty were overwhelmingly committed to the Merovingian political system and the dynasty of Clovis. This was because power in Francia as in the Mongol and Hunnic Empires was not local, but seen as royal. It came from holding office or being near to the king. This held the kingdom together, in spite of the centrifugal tendencies arising from the appointment of sub-kings and partitions among royal heirs. See Wickham (2009), 126–8. See also Anderson (1974), 148, and Wiet *et al.* (1975), 197–8, for descriptions of later decentralized feudalism.
129. The word *fief* has different connotations for different historians. See Reynolds (1994), 12, 48–74. I have for the sake of convenience used the term as a synonym for appanage and grants of large territories by the king to his close vassals.
130. Wickham (2009), 116–19.
131. Grierson (1965), 290; Ganshof (1971), 278; McKitterick (1983), 53.
132. Geary (1988), 118–19; James (1988), 105–6; Wood (1994), 159–64; McKitterick (1983), 17–18, 23.
133. It is therefore insufficient to categorize Merovingian Gaul as just sub-Roman, a poor imitation of Roman political and administrative precedents, lacking in any originality or imagination, as Wallace-Hadrill (1962), 9, and Hollister (1966), 188–9, do.
134. See Jordanes *Getica* 48.248, where Gesimund and the Goths with him support the Hunnic king Balamber because Gesimund was mindful of his oath of fidelity to the Hunnic king.
135. Wickham (2009), 122–3.
136. For information on Xiongnu–Hun assemblies see Batsaikhan (2011), 127. Naturally the great impact of existing Roman administrative structures must also be taken into account in the overall assessment of the Frankish political order. A certain degree of hybridity that mingled Roman institutions with new steppe-derived political practices and hierarchy best describes the Frankish political system. For the impact of Roman administrative precedents on the Merovingians see Lewis (2000), 73–4, and Wood (1996), 361–2.

137. Geary (1988), 100.
138. Ganshof (1971), 96; Reuter (1985), 75–6.
139. For a detailed history see Calmette (1978), 62–204.
140. Wickham (2009), 402.
141. Ganshof (1971), 290–1; McKitterick (1983), 172–9; Dixon (1976), 106–9.
142. Wickham (2009), 401–2.
143. Heather (2009), 610, attributes most of this to the Avars.
144. The impact of pre-existing Roman institutions on the Franks and other Germanic peoples must again not be underestimated, e.g. the Frankish use of the watered-down version of the Roman taxation system in Gaul (Ganshof 1971, 99). However, such Roman practices/institutions that had survived the conquest were almost always fused together or forced to co-exist with new practices introduced from outside the Roman Empire (which I would argue were of Inner Asian, steppe origin) such as the tributary system. One cannot therefore understand the nature of Germanic Europe of the early Middle Ages without examining the impact of steppe political institutions and practices.
145. Ibn Khaldun, *Muqaddimah*, Rosenthal (1967), 116.
146. A highly heterogeneous entity from the very beginning, see Collins (2004), 22.
147. See Schutz (2000), 34, and Kelly (2009), 40.
148. Geary (1999), 119. This shift had occurred earlier among the eastern Goths due to their proximity to the Sarmatians in the Pontic steppe. See Demougeot (1979), 354, for Sarmatization of the Goths. Gothic culture in the east was also under heavy steppe influence from the third century AD onwards. The presence of a relatively stable dynasty/dynasties of kings among the east Goths is probably a reflection of Gothic imitation of Sarmatian/Alan political practices. The names of prominent east Goths such as Alatheus, who acts as guardian for the young king Videric, and also Saphrax are Alan (p. 355), suggesting a strong Sarmatian, steppe element in the Gothic hierarchy.
149. Zosimus 5.37.1; Schutz (2000), 60; Thompson (1996), 38. Demougeot (1979), 453, suggests that Athaulf was Gotho-Sarmatian in origin. His ability to recruit some Huns for Alaric is striking, especially when we consider the fact that Uldin, the western Hunnic king of this time, was favourably disposed towards Alaric's enemy Stilicho and aided him to destroy the Goths of Radagaisus and also restrain Alaric (p. 423). Stilicho of course had a bodyguard of Huns. It is uncertain when Athaulf managed to get his contingent of Huns to support Alaric. Presumably this was after Stilicho's assassination and the murder of his Hunnic bodyguards in AD 408 (p. 454). The presence of an Alanic and also Hunnic element in the Visigothic polity is also acknowledged by Heather (2008), 27.
150. Perhaps he was like Athaulf of mixed Gothic–Sarmatian origin. See Demougeot (1979), 45, n. 12, where he cites Philost., 12.4.1 (*Griech. Christl. Schrift.* 21, J. Bidez, ed., Berlin, 1913), who calls him a Sarmatian in origin.
151. Halsall (2007), 213. For the feud between Sarus and Athaulf see Liebeschuetz (1990), 38–9.
152. Olympiodorus fr. 26, Blockley (1983), 188. See Todd (1992), 161–2, for the career of Athaulf.

153. Culican (1965), 193.
154. Wickham (2009), 103, and Heather (2000), 444–5. For a similar deficiency in the size of the administrative personnel needed to govern the kingdom among the Franks see Ganshof (1971), 90–1.
155. Heather (2000), 441, 443. See also Wickham (2009), 79, 105, and Geary (2002), 130–1. A similar system can also be found in Ostrogothic Italy. Regional military commands distributed among Ostrogothic nobles were a key factor in the Gothic governance of Italy, see Burns (1980), 113–14, 117–18.
156. Liebeschuetz (2000), 235. Kings were often obliged to reward services with land (Heather 2000, 444–5), which gradually diminished their ability to pay for a professional army and maintain a large bureaucracy. Compare this to the Sassanian model where reward for military service was also land grants, Rubin (2000), 654. However, the king's power lay more in his status as the primary distributor of patronage. The king's gifts such as garnet-encrusted cloisonné jewellery (Heather 2000, 446) carried prestige value and strengthened the support of the nobility. Furthermore, until the time of the Carolingian Empire land grants among the Franks, especially large territorial commands such as counties, marches and duchies were mostly non-hereditary grants and not even necessarily lifelong allocations. They could be revoked at any time and these measures checked any centrifugal tendencies in the Frankish state. Only later when central control broke down entirely did temporary grants of large territories become permanent and hereditary. See Bloch (1961), 192, and Reynolds (1994), 111–14. Yet, such liberal distribution of gifts, monetary rewards and grants of land or peoples was expected of a 'barbarian' king and has clear Hunnic, steppe parallels and is also a defining feature of earlier Persian–Parthian–Sassanian 'feudalism' discussed at the beginning of the book.
157. Heather (2000), 461–2. See also Weber (1983), 668–70. One could also argue that the social stratification already in existence in the Roman world at the time of the barbarian invasions made it much easier for the barbarians to fit in by simply replacing or absorbing the existing social elite into their own ranks and imposing a new feudal order on the conquered Roman population who were already used to the rule of powerful landowning magnates.
158. The Visigoths were, among the Germanic tribes, the most Romanized and their kings thus tried to rule in imitation of Roman imperial precedents. Thus it seems reasonable to conjecture that their kingdom, especially after its entrenchment in Spain, was of all the Germanic kingdoms, minus that of the Vandals, even further removed from continental Europe, the least affected by Central Asian, Hunnic/Alanic influence. See Wickham (2009), 148. However, the military aristocracy of the Visigothic kingdom was very similar to those of the Franks and Lombards. The burial practices of the Visigoths mentioned in *Getica* 30.158, further reflect borrowings from steppe cultures. See Altheim (1948), 25.
159. Wolfram (1997b), 151. For instance Frideric shared the kingship with Theodoric the Visigothic king of Toulouse.
160. Bloch (1961), 289–90. This warrior nobility was also distinguished from lower social classes by being mounted on horseback during battles.

161. Wickham (2009), 106. Vasjutin (2003), 53 points out that the political system of steppe nomads was created by their military organization. In steppe empires the bureaucracy functioned essentially as part of the military and in the judicial sphere. This is strikingly similar to the type of system we find in early medieval, Germanic Europe.
162. Strikingly enough in Xianbei-controlled northern China (Toba Wei, AD 386–534) the Inner Asian conquerors of the Chinese dominated their subjects via a 'feudal' administration run by a 'barbarian' military aristocracy assisted by native bureaucrats in ways remarkably similar to what we find among the western successor states of the Roman and Hunnic Empires. Virtually every former civilian institution in northern China was militarized by the Toba Xianbei. Over 150 years the northern Wei emperors distributed nearly 850 appanages to reward their military aristocracy and royal princes. Over three quarters of these 'fiefs' were granted to ethnically Toba nobles. See Kwanten (1979), 16. This gives us some idea of how fiefs in the Hunnic Empire would have been distributed.
163. For a short description of these military retainers (comitatus) of the Merovingian princes see Bloch (1961), 150, and Wood (1994), 64. See also Bachrach (1972), 72, 77, 90. 124. For similar military retinues closely linked to or at the very least clearly reminiscent of the Inner Asian, steppe tradition of comitatus (military retinue) in Kievan Rus, Piast Poland and Premyslid Bohemia see Font (2005), 285.
164. Wood (1994), 56–60; Wickham (1981), 30–2. Whitby (2000a), 471–2.
165. Oosten (1996), 224.
166. Whitby (2000a), 472; Heather (1995b), 145–73.
167. Heather (1995b), 154.
168. Heather (1995b), 160
169. Burns (1984), 174, points out that the Gothic *comites* were also the supreme government officials whenever present and had precedence over any civil officials.
170. See Yü (1990), 127–8, for the Xiongnu practice of appointing an overall governor titled 'Commandant in Charge of Slaves' with the power, if necessary, to directly tax and conscript corvée labour from the sedentary population of the Tarim basin. This was an official with overall military and civil authority. However, day-to-day administration of the region, as in Ostrogothic Italy, was left in the hands of vassal kings (in Italy, the Roman senatorial elite) and local administrators. For the Kushan Lords who also had overall authority (military and civil) over India in the Inner Asian Kushan Empire see Puri (1994a), 263.
171. Heather (1995b), 163.
172. Christie (1995), 14.
173. Paul the Deacon, *Historia Langobardorum* 1.16–17. See also Jarnut (2003), 414.
174. Cranial deformation may have initially been an East Iranian/Tocharian custom that the Huns adopted while they were still in Central Asia. As mentioned earlier, it was practised by the Kushans and later the Hephtalite

Huns in Central Asia. See Vernadsky (1951), 366–7, Altheim and Haussig (1958), 38, and Werner (1956), 11. See also Randers-Pehrson (1983), 42–3.
175. Christie (1995), 17.
176. Schutz (2000), 341, argues that the Lombards were heavily influenced by eastern nomads and that this is discernible in their personal ornaments: ear-hangings, mirrors and weapons, as well as Hunnic cranial deformation that was designed to create a clear physical distinction between the Lombard nobility and the general populace. Christie (1995), 21, identifies Hunnic traits in the fifth century among the Rugians, who may have initially included the Longobards, and also along much of the middle Danubian region mixed with the largely Germanic and Roman native culture. Spectacular warrior graves dating from the period of Attila's rule have been found in what later became Rugian territory.
177. See also Haberl and Hawkes (1973), 97–156; Menghin (1985), 23–9. For general information on the Danubian region as a whole and also archaeological evidence see Menghin, Springer and Wamers (1987).
178. Paul the Deacon, *Historia Langobardorum* 1.20.
179. Werner (1956), 15; Schmidt (1983b), 541–2. Christie (1995), 17, 42, is contradictory and acknowledges cranial deformation in Bohemia (the original Lombard homeland), but denies that it was practised among the Lombards themselves. There is no doubt that the Thuringians who would continue to rule an extensive kingdom to the north of Lombards until the 520s practised Hunnic cranial deformation like the Ostrogoths (Vernadsky (1951), 366–7; Schutz (2000), 290–1) and the Gepids (Buchet 1988, 61).
180. Schutz (2000), 411, notes the pervasive influence of the Huns among the Thuringians, which was far from a brief passing phenomenon. The military armaments and equestrian culture of the Thuringians were clearly adaptations of eastern steppe models.
181. Heather in Thompson (1996), 259. Buchet (1988), 58–64, argues that the Burgundians could have taken over the practice of artificial cranial deformation from other peoples like the Goths and Alans and not necessarily the Huns, since their submission to the Huns was relatively short and the Burgundians were fighting against the Huns at the battle of Chalons. However, as indicated earlier, many Burgundians, especially those to the east of the Rhine, were on the Hunnic side during this battle. They certainly had plenty of time and the incentive to be both receptive to and influenced by the Huns.
182. Christie (1995), 64, 98–100; Collins (1999), 203; Jarnut (1990), 100. Paul the Deacon mentions a group of Bulgars under their Duke Alzec who joined the Lombards during the time of king Grimoald and were given land in Benevento. These Bulgars would continue to speak their own Hunnic tongue in preference to Latin well into the eighth century (5.29). See also Todd (1992), 245. A Hunnic lineage also may have existed within the Lombardic royal family via the marriage of Audoin the father of Alboin to the granddaughter of Amalafrida, the sister of Theodoric, the Hunno-Gothic king of Italy. See Wolfram (1997b), 106.

183. Paul the Deacon, *Historia Langobardorum*, 2.31–2; Cleph, originally a Duke under Alboin who later became king (followed by his son Authari after a ten-year interregnum), Zaban of Ticinum (Pavia), Wallari of Bergamus (Bergamo), Alichis of Brexia (Brescia), Euin of Tridentum (Trent), Gisulf of Forum Julii (Cividale). After Cleph's death for ten years these dukes presided over thirty other dukes and ruled the Lombards until the election of Authari as king. See also Hodgkin (1895, reprint 2002), 106.
184. Bullough (1965b), 172.
185. Hdt. 4.65.
186. *Shiji* 110, tells of how the Xiongnu Shanyu made a drinking cup out of the skull of the defeated king of the Yuezhi. A similar fate befell the head of the defeated Eastern Roman emperor Nicephorus I in the early ninth century AD at the hands of the Bulgar Khan Krum, Attila's heir in the Balkans. Such was the 'popularity' of this custom that it is last recorded in the sixteenth century when the Turkic king of Persia Shah Ismail turned the head of the Uzbek Shaybani Khan into a goblet to celebrate his victory.
187. Impressively smooth transition from empire to kingdom, Humphries (2000), 532. For Ostrogothic rule of Italy under Theodoric and exploitation of its sophisticated civilian infrastructure see Christie (1995), 109.
188. Findley (2005), 35; Di Cosmo (1999c), 29–30.
189. Pohl (1997b), 118–20, for discussion on the tribute in early medieval Germanic Europe. The Franks in ways reminiscent of Inner Asian steppe empires would collect yearly tribute from vassal kingdoms and tribes such as the Saxons, Sicily, the Burgundians and the Lombards. In Ostrogothic Italy tribute, as in the Xiongnu, Sassanid and Hunnic Empires, referred to the taxes owed by the regions and cities to the central government.
190. Vernadsky (1951), 369–70, 375.
191. Maurice, *Strategikon* 1.2, 2.1, tells us that this respect for steppe warfare and tactics reached a fever pitch in the late sixth century AD when the Romans imitated everything in the arsenal of their Hunno-Avar opponents from tents and flexible battle array to bows and armour. See Whitby (2000b), 310; Dennis (1984), 12–13. Agathias 1.22.1, also describes how Narses used the Hunnic tactic of the feigned retreat to defeat the Franks, Frendo (1975), 30. See Curta (2006), 66–7, for information on the Byzantine/East Roman imitation of Avar stirrups in the *Strategikon*. See also Campbell (1999), 230. For the impact of Central Asian stirrups on later medieval feudal armies in western Europe see Bloch (1961), 153. Some residents of Constantinople in the sixth century went so far as imitating Hunnic dress as a mark of fashion. See Greatrex (2000), 276.
192. Vegetius, *De rei militari*, 1.20, 3.26. See also Halsall (2007), 105.
193. Campbell (1999), 232; Vernadsky (1951), 386. 389.
194. For the Inner Asian origins of Alan culture and its close affinity with the culture of the Huns see Sulimirsky (1970), 116–17, 144–7. The Alans before the Hunnic conquest had already adopted elements of Hunnic weaponry and other eastern cultural traits making them difficult to distinguish from the Huns, at least culturally.

195. Bachrach (1973), 34–5.
196. Bachrach (1973), 42. Priscus fr. 20; Evagrius, 2.1; and Socrates, 7.18.
197. Whitby (2000b), 308, and Bachrach (1973), 45.
198. Alemany (2000), 42.
199. Paulinus of Pella, *Eucharisticos* 377–85 (ed. Moussy SC 209, p. 84; Brandes CSEL XVI.1, 305–6), Alemany (2000), 67.
200. Hydatius, *Cont.* 68 (ed. Mommsen MGH AA XI, p. 19; Tranoy SC 218, p. 122), Alemany (2000), 54. See also Merrills and Miles (2010), 44, and Vernadsky (1951), 374.
201. Bachrach (1973), 58.
202. Bachrach (1973), 73.
203. Gregory, *Hist.*, 2.19, where he confuses Alamans with Alans. Bachrach (1973), 77.
204. Bachrach (1973), 85, notes that Armorican cavalry developed out of Alan horsemen.
205. Bachrach (1973), 78.
206. The close geographical proximity of the two groups and mutual cultural influence on each other even before the great Hunnic expansion west (see Altheim 1959, 9) justify regarding the Alans and Huns as forming a single closely linked Central Asian cultural unit, though they were at times politically and ethnically distinct. As Rudenko (1970), 88, points out, in terms of dress and apparel there was little to distinguish between a Sarmatian (Alan) and a Hun.
207. Vernadsky (1951), 367–8; Bachrach (1999), 293; Sulimirsky (1970), 31–2.
208. Bloch (1961), 291.
209. Khazanov (2001), 2; Christian (1998), 147; Gills and Thompson (2006), 2.
210. Bachrach (1973), 91. Quite fittingly the person who executed the manoeuvre at Hastings was Count Alanus of the Bretons serving under William. See Sinor (1995), 5.
211. The royal hunt of highly militarized kings and aristocrats dressed in Hunnic/Danubian style (with abundant gold ornaments and Central Asian belts) was a regular occurrence among the Franks. Wickham (2009), 189.
212. See Allsen (2006), 16, 40, 189, 266, 269.
213. Bachrach (1973), 118.
214. Bloch (1961), 303–4; Wickham (2009), 524. See also Allsen (2006), 59. Quite strikingly these are also the activities that preoccupied the Achaemenid Persian nobility of Inner Asian origin more than a thousand years earlier. The Persian nobility was expected to be proficient in riding, archery, hunting and tracking on horseback. See Cook (1983), 197.
215. Findley (2005), 31.
216. Wickham (2009), 100.
217. Recall Attila eating just meat and nothing else during Hunnic banquets. For information on nomad diet based almost exclusively on meat see Frenkel (2005), 212–13, and Christian (1998), 142. For more discussion on Hunnic etiquette and court ceremonials that closely echo later medieval court practices and also the uncanny resemblance between Hunnic and Sassanian court

ceremonials see Bona (1991), 78. For the interesting suggestion that the word 'beer' has a Hunnic origin, see Altheim (1959), vol. IV, 60.
218. Bona (1991), 150. See also Bona (2002), 29, 96–9, for samples of early Saka-Hunnic diadems in the same style discovered in Kanattas near Lake Balkash in eastern Kazakhstan, close to the homeland of the European Huns, and comparable samples found in the Ukraine and Hungary that reflect the Hunnic migration west. See also Boardman (2007), 14–24, for an extended discussion on the Kargaly diadem discovered in east Kazakhstan, the homeland of the Wusun and the Huns.
219. Halphen (1965), 100. See also Werner (1956), 66–8.
220. Halphen (1965), 100–1.
221. Halphen (1965), 101. For other eastern 'influences' or presence in a Sarmatian context possibly via migration waves from the east see Brosseder (2011), 412.
222. Halphen (1965), 102.
223. Bona (1991), 136–7; Werner (1956), 90.
224. See Christie (1995), 45, and also Bona (1976), 54–5, for the impact of oriental motifs introduced by the Huns that allowed this art to emerge as an independent style during the Hunnic Empire. See also Kazanski (1993), 213.
225. Kazanski (1993), 213. See also Bona (1976), 59 ff., for discussion on Germanic animal art style in the Danubian region. See also Heather (2009), 253–4.
226. For the use of Hunnic bronze mirrors among the Gepids see Demougeot (1979), 531.
227. The Franks and the Burgundian military aristocracy of the west imitated the mode of dress, art and customs of the royal Hunnic court on the Danube. See Marin (1990), 51–3. Marin notes that the great prestige of the Hunnic court on the Danube allowed for the vast diffusion of the Danubian style in western as well as eastern Europe (p. 49). See also Lasko (1965), 211–12, for the critical influence of eastern, Inner Asian art on Frankish and early medieval 'western, Germanic' art.
228. Werner (1956), 32.
229. Musset (1975), 200–1, discusses how the Hunnic/Germanic invasions coincided with the triumph of a new set of aesthetics in western European applied arts, the inspiration for which came from the steppe. He calls this a 'revolution in taste', a shift away from Greco-Roman norms to oriental influences of a Persian sort via the steppe. See also Altheim (1959), vol. I, 198, who emphasizes the Persian (or rather east Iranian) influence on Hunnic art. The new art spread out from southern Russia to the west via the Huns, Alans and Goths. See also Altheim (1959), vol. I, 200–2, for the influence of Hunnic weapons technology on the Franks and Alamanni.
230. Heather in Thompson (1996), 260. See also Marin (1990), 62, for the diffusion of Hunnic saddles across a vast area between the Volga and areas west of the Rhine, indicative also of the wide distribution of Hunnic influence.
231. East 'Gothic' art of the Ukraine was actually the successor of the earlier Sarmato-Bosporan art that derived from the steppe and had absorbed elements of Greco-Roman art, see Sulimirksy (1970), 203.

232. See Vernadsky (1951), 362–4, for a good summary of what he calls the Sarmatian roots of early Gothic art. See also Heather and Matthews (1991), 94–5. To talk about Gothic art without mentioning the overwhelming influence of Sarmatian and other steppe art would be the equivalent of discussing Roman art without mentioning its debts to Greek art. Also noteworthy is the fusion of Sarmatian and Hunnic culture (in the late centuries of the first millennium BC and early centuries of the first millennium AD) in the Altai region, Khudyakov (1997), 342. The Altai had originally been part of the cultural sphere of the Saka before the Huns moved into the area, see Davis-Kimball (2000), 89, 93. The fusion of Hunnic and Iranian (Saka-Sarmatian) culture of the steppe thus began almost five centuries before the eruption of the Huns into Europe. See also Minyaev (2000), 295. The Huns and other Oghuric Turkic peoples had already mixed with the Iranian population in Kazakhstan long before their entry into Europe to such an extent that the Huns began practising the Eastern Alanic–Central Asian Kushan custom of cranial deformation (it is rather unclear which people first started the custom, but by the early centuries AD it was widespread among the Huns and Alans in Kazakhstan, see Sulimirsky (1970), 36–8) and Hunnic remains become increasingly difficult to distinguish from those of the Sarmato-Alans. Only a few artefacts such as the bronze Hunnic cauldron stand out as being different and this has led some scholars to identify only the remains with which these cauldrons and some typically 'Hunnic' military equipment are found to be genuinely Hunnic, but obviously this is an error. The name Hun referred to a ruling dynasty (of eastern steppe origin) and the state that they governed. Yet within this state from very early on the vast majority of the population consisted of Oghuric Turks, Iranians and possibly some Ugrians from southern Siberia, i.e. the culture and art of the Huns even before they entered Europe was already hybrid and had a strong Iranian (Sarmato-Alan) flavour.

233. Halphen (1965), 108. See also Häusler (1983), 651–2, who calls the influence of Hunno-Sarmatian art vaguely 'Scythian' and 'oriental', and attributes the later Danubian style of art to Germanic craftsmen working under the direction of the Huns. Germanic craftsmen were no doubt involved in the production of these art works, but the heterogeneous nature of the Hunnic state on the Danube means that the art is equally heterogeneous and as much Hunnic and Alanic as Germanic. The Danubian art form is a later manifestation of the Sarmato-Hunnic, steppe art shared in common by residents of the western steppe stretching from modern-day Kazakhstan to the Ukraine (of course with regional variations and specificity and with some Germanic and even Roman input) where Huns, Alans, Sarmatians and Goths intermingled. Hence the difficulty in determining precisely the differences between Hunnic and Sarmatian remains and art in Central Asia and later Germanic and Hunno-Alanic art works and graves in Hungary.

234. Häusler (1983), 651–2. See also Werner (1956), 4, and Wiet *et al.* (1975), 82. Kelly (2009), 48–51, with no justification whatsoever, argues that there was little steppe influence on Gothic culture and art and that Gothic culture

remained largely unchanged during Hunnic rule because the Huns adopted Gothic culture and customs. He even argues that the Huns became an imperial power because they abandoned their own customs (nomadism) and took up Gothic customs, more precisely put, through the exploitation (the Hun Empire being a 'parasitic state') of existing Gothic society. This argument is baffling given the fact that experts of Central Asian art provide compelling evidence that the art of Germanic Europe was indeed heavily influenced by steppe art. True it is difficult to distinguish what is Hunnic/Alanic (steppe) and what is Gothic in the archaeological remains of the Danubian region (see Cribb 1991, 65, for the difficulties involved in archaeologically identifying a steppe nomadic/pastoral culture, especially when adjacent 'sedentary' populations possess very similar material culture), but that is not because the Huns became Goths, but rather due to the practice among historians of Roman history of classifying most artefacts in the Danubian region and further west as Gothic/Germanic without giving due regard to the heterogeneous nature of the art that we find in these areas. (For much more reasonable assessments see Bona (2002), 114–15, Harhoiu (1980), 106–7, Genito (1992), 64, Sulimirsky (1970), 163–4, and Kazanski (1993), 212–13. See also Érdy (1995), 13, who highlights one such erroneous observation regarding Hunnic diadems and cauldrons found in the west. The elaborate handle designs on Hunnic cauldrons and mushroom shaped decorative elements which resemble parts of fibulae were wrongly attributed by earlier archaeologists to Germanic influence on the Huns. More evidence from the east found in the Baikal, Altai and Ural regions have proven that this was a style of art developed much earlier further to the east.) For instance the 'Gothic' plate brooches found in France, Spain and Central Europe, which are always without any hesitation identified as Gothic, are often not Gothic at all but Alan in provenance, see Sulimirsky (1970), 185–6. The brooches were probably originally a Gothic form of art, but were adopted by the Alans as well before the great Hunnic invasions. In the Danubian region in particular what we have is an amalgam of artistic styles (most of which were already under the influence of steppe art: Hunnic, Sarmatian, Alan, Gothic) that occurred under Hunnic patronage. Is this art then Gothic? But did the Goths even exist as a people during this time? The so-called 'Ostrogothic art' which is attributed to the Goths in Hungary dates to the first half of the fifth century AD (i.e. when the Goths were under Hunnic domination) and only reached full maturation by the time of Theodoric the Great in the second half of the fifth century, Burns (1980), 55. The Ostrogoths were the creation of the Hunnic prince Valamer after the demise of the Hunnic Empire in the west. At this earlier stage what we have is a Hunnic nation on the Danube that was multiethnic and the art of the Danubian region was thus not Gothic, but Imperial Hunnic.

235. Aberg (1947), 40–69. Parallel animal ornamentation is also found in Hungary and the Ukraine, the traditional territory of the Huns. See Bachrach (1973), 99–100. Interestingly in the seventh and eighth centuries AD similar Turkic

decorated belts also spread over a vast area stretching from Iraq to China. In China, especially under the partly Turkic dynasty of the Tang (Lewis 2009, 149), even Chinese dress styles were altered due to heavy steppe influence. See Khazanov (2001), 2. Steppe arms, ornaments, and modes of fashion were being imitated by a broad sway of sedentary cultures across the whole of Eurasia during the early medieval period.
236. Bachrach (1973), 109–12. For the survival of the memory of Hunnic rule in later Germanic traditions and literature see Wirth (1999), 145–50.
237. See Bullough (1965b), 167, 171, for the polychrome-style art developed in the Danube/Black Sea region in the late fourth century AD which later became the inspiration for Gothic and Lombard art. See also Seyer (1983), 180–1, for discussion. The cloisonné technique itself was first developed by the Sumerians and the Egyptians, see Arrhenius (1985), 79.
238. See Werner (1956), 91, Kazanski (1991), 72, 76, and Arrhenius (1985), 44. See Gryaznov (1969), 166–70, for samples of cloisonné-style artefacts from as early as the late first millennium BC found in the Altai region, the urheimat of the Huns. See also Bader and Usupov (1995), 30, in the same volume Invernizzi (1995), plate VIII, for earrings (third century AD) decorated with pearls and semi-precious stones using the cloisonné technique from the Uzboy Region in Turkmenistan, and Vernadsky (1951), 362, for discussion on Sarmatian polychrome-style art. See also Sulimirsky (1970), 156, for the first-century AD Sarmatian gold diadem in the polychrome style from the Khokhlach–Novocherkassk barrow grave. All of these pre-date the first samples of Gothic polychrome-style art in the fourth century AD. The metal mirrors that were adopted by the Gepids and Lombards who were under intense Hunnic influence in the Danubian basin are also likewise steppe, Hunnic in origin, Werner (1956), 24. The impact of the very distinctive polychrome cloisonné style of Central Asian art was also noted in the artefacts found in the tomb of Childeric the Merovingian king and contemporary Alamannic, Gepid and Thuringian artefacts. They exhibit unmistakable signs of Hunnic/steppe influence, see Bona (2002), 69–70.
239. Todd (1992), 129, 139. Though steppe influence that led to the evolution of Germanic art may already have commenced due to the impact of the Sarmatians as early as the third century AD, the Hunnic arrival greatly accelerated this process and through their conquests and influence Danubian art spread far afield as far north as Scandinavia and as far west as Gaul. The role of the Huns in also bringing about a fusion of various Germanic styles of art and elements of material culture into a common Danubian style is also noted by Heather (2009), 229.
240. Arrhenius (1985), 34, 37, 46, 54–5, 64; Todd (1992), 139. Domed garnets and heart-shaped garnets, according to Arrhenius (1985), 46–8, were first produced by Hellenistic craftsmen and then spread east into Iran and India due to Hellenistic contacts with the east. The practice of using the garnet for ornamentation was soon also taken up by the Sarmatians in the western steppe and then passed on to the Goths and other Germanic peoples further to the west.

Notes to pages 155–8

For garnets in Frankish aristocratic and royal (Childeric) tombs see Todd (1992), 197–9. See also Bona (1991), 128–32, Périn and Kazanski (1996), 173, and Heather (2009), 307, 322 and 328, for discussions on the adoption of Hunnic–Danubian burial practices among the Franks, as evidenced in the tomb of Childeric, presumably to signal the grandeur of Childeric's rule by associating him with Hunnic imperial precedents. Similarly grandiose burials for leaders following the Hunnic model would become widespread in Western Europe in the sixth century.
241. Wickham (2009), 96.

CONCLUSION

1. Cameron (2012), 57, 211.
2. Fernández-Armesto (1995), 135.
3. See Staab (1996), 10, 21–2, who calls the Franks the '*Wegbereiter Europas*', the pioneers of Europe, which they indeed were. The impact of the Huns and other eastern Eurasians on the foundation and political organization of the Frankish kingdoms and therefore on later 'Europe', however, has not received the attention that it deserves.
4. Hodgson (1993), 39.
5. Robertson and Inglis (2006), 40–4.

Bibliography

Aalto, P. (1971) 'Iranian Contacts of the Turks in Pre-Islamic Times', in L. Ligeti, ed., *Studia Turcica* (Bibliotheca Orientalis Hungarica 17). Budapest, 29–37.
Aalto, P. and Pekkanen, T. (1975, 1980) *Latin Sources on North-Eastern Eurasia* (Asiatischer Forschungen 44, 57). Wiesbaden.
Abdullaev, K. (1995) 'Nomadism in Central Asia: The Archaeological Evidence (2nd–1st centuries B.C.)', in A. Invernizzi, ed., *In the Land of the Gryphons: Papers on Central Asian Archaeology in Antiquity*. Firenze, 151–61.
  (2007) 'Nomad Migration in Central Asia', in J. Cribb and G. Herrmann, eds., *After Alexander: Central Asia before Islam*. Oxford, 73–98.
Aberg, N. (1947) *The Occident and the Orient in the Art of the Seventh Century*, part 3. Stockholm.
Abetekov, A. and Yusupov, H. (1994) 'Ancient Iranian Nomads in Western Central Asia', in J. Harmatta, ed., *History of Civilizations of Central Asia*, vol. II: *The Development of Sedentary and Nomadic Civilizations*. Paris, 23–33.
Abka'i-Khavari, M. (2000) *Das Bild des Königs in der Sasanidenzeit: schriftliche Überlieferungen im Vergleich mit Antiquaria*. Hildesheim, Zürich and New York.
Abu-Lughod, J. (1989) *Before European Hegemony: The World System* A.D. 1250–1350. Oxford.
Adas, M. (2001) *Agricultural and Pastoral Societies in Ancient and Classical History*. Philadelphia.
Adshead, S. A. M. (1988) *China in World History*. New York.
  (1993) *Central Asia in World History*. Basingstoke.
Agarwal, A. (1986) 'A Cultural Study of the Western Kshatrapa Inscriptions', *Journal of Indian History* 64, parts 1–3, 53–67.
Ahmad, M. A. (1949) *Political History and Institutions of the Earliest Turkish Empire of Delhi, 1206–1290* A.D. Lahore.
Alemany, A. (2000) *Sources on the Alans: A Critical Compilation*. Leiden, Boston and Köln.
Alföldi, A. (1965) 'The Invasions of Peoples from the Rhine to the Black Sea', in *The Cambridge Ancient History*, vol. XII. Cambridge, 138–64.
Alföldi, G. (1974) *Noricum*. London and Boston.

Allsen, T. T. (1996) 'Spiritual Geography and Political Legitimacy in the Eastern Steppe', in H. J. M. Claessen and J. C. Oosten, eds., *Ideology and the Formation of Early States*. Leiden, 116–35.
  (2001a) *Culture and Conquest in Mongol Eurasia*. Cambridge.
  (2001b) 'Sharing out the Empire: Apportioned Lands under the Mongols', in A. M. Khazanov and A. Wink, eds., *Nomads in the Sedentary World*. Padstow, Cornwall, 172–90.
  (2006) *The Royal Hunt in Eurasian History*. Philadelphia.
  (2009) 'Mongols as Vectors for Cultural Transmission', in N. Di Cosmo, A. J. Frank and P. B. Golden, eds., *The Cambridge History of Inner Asia: The Chinggisid Age*. Cambridge, 135–54.
Alonso, C. R. (ed. and trans.) (1975) *Las historias de los godos, vándalos y suevos de Isidoro de Sevilla*. Leon.
Alonso-Núñez, J. M. (1988–9) 'The Roman Universal Historian Pompeius Trogus on India, Parthia, Bactria and Armenia', *Persica* 13, 125–45.
Altheim, F. (1948) *Hunnische Runen*. Saale.
  (1959) *Geschichte der Hunnen*. Berlin.
Altheim, F. and Haussig, W. (1958) *Die Hunnen in Osteuropa*. Tübingen.
Altheim, F. and Stiehl, R. (1954) *Ein asiatischer Staat: Feudalismus unter den Sasaniden und ihren Nachbarn*. Wiesbaden, 131–74.
Amitai, R. (2001) 'Turko-Mongolian Nomads and the Iqta System in the Islamic Middle East (ca. 1000–1400 A.D.)', in A. M. Khazanov and A. Wink, eds., *Nomads in the Sedentary World*. Padstow, Cornwall, 152–71.
Amitai, R. and Biran, M. (eds.) (2005) *Mongols, Turks, and Others: Eurasian Nomads and the Sedentary World*. Leiden.
Amitai-Preiss, R. and Morgan, D. O. (2000) *The Mongol Empire and its Legacy*. Leiden.
Amory, P. (1997) *People and Identity in Ostrogothic Italy, 489–554*. Cambridge.
Anderson, P. (1974) *Passages from Antiquity to Feudalism*. London.
Anderson, T. (1995) 'Roman Military Colonies in Gaul, Salian Ethnogenesis and the Forgotten Meaning of *Pactus Legis Salicae* 59.5', *Early Medieval Europe* 4, 129–44.
Anderson, W. B. (ed. and trans.) (1968) *Sidonius, Carmina, Epistulae* (Loeb Classical Library), 2 vols. Cambridge, MA.
Arapov, D. Y. (2003) 'The Chinggisids and their Status in Central Asia and East Europe', in N. N. Kradin, D. Bondarenko and T. Barfield, eds., *Nomadic Pathways in Social Evolution*. Moscow, 158–64.
Arce, J. (2003) 'The Enigmatic Fifth Century in Hispania: Some Historical Problems', in H. Goetz, J. Jarnut and W. Pohl, eds., *Regna and Gentes: The Relationship between Late Antique and Early Medieval Peoples and Kingdoms in the Transformation of the Roman World*. Leiden, 135–59.
Archibald, Z. H. (2002) 'The Shape of the New Commonwealth: Aspects of the Pontic and Eastern Mediterranean Regions in the Hellenistic Age', in G. Tsetskhladze, ed., *Greek Settlements in the Eastern Mediterranean and the Black Sea*. Oxford, 49–72.

Arnason, J. P. and Raaflaub, K. A. (eds.) (2011) *The Roman Empire in Context: Historical and Comparative Perspectives*. Oxford.
Arnaud-Lindet, M. (ed. and tr.) (1990) *Orosius, Historiarum Adversus Paganos Libri Septem*. Paris.
Arrhenius B. (1985) *Merovingian Garnet Jewellery: Emergence and Social Implications*. Stockholm.
Aruz, J. (ed.) (2000) *The Golden Deer of Eurasia: Scythian and Sarmatian Treasures from the Russian Steppes*. New York.
Aruz, J., Farkas, A., and Valtz Fino, E. (eds.) (2006) *The Golden Deer of Eurasia: Perspectives on the Steppe Nomads of the Ancient World*. New York.
Ascherson, N. (1995) *Black Sea*. London.
Asimov, M. S. *et al.* (eds.) (1981) *Ethnic Problems of the History of Central Asia in the Early Period*. Moscow.
Aubin, J. (1976) 'Le khanat de Čaġatai et le Khorasan (1334–1380)', *Turcica* 8, 16–60.
Azarpay, G. (1981) *Sogdian Painting*. Berkeley.
Bachrach, B. S. (1969) 'The Origin of Armorican Chivalry', *Technology and Culture* 10 (2), 166–71.
  (1972) *Merovingian Military Organization 481–751*. Minneapolis.
  (1973) *A History of the Alans in the West*. Minneapolis.
  (1999) 'Early Medieval Europe', in K. Raaflaub and N. Rosenstein, eds., *War and Society in the Ancient and Medieval Worlds*. Cambridge, MA, 271–307.
Bacon, E. (1958) *Obok: A Study of Social Structure of Eurasia* (Viking Fund Publications in Anthropology 25). New York.
Bader, A. N., Gaibov, V. and Koshelenko, G. (1998) 'Monarchic Ideas in Parthian Margiana as Shown on Seals', in V. S. Curtis, R. Hillenbrand and J. M. Rogers, eds., *The Art and Archaeology of Ancient Persia: New Light on the Parthian and Sasanian Empires*. London and New York, 24–37.
Bader, A. N. and Usupov, K. (1995) 'Gold Earrings from North-West Turkmenistan', in A. Invernizzi, ed., *In the Land of the Gryphons: Papers on Central Asian Archaeology in Antiquity*. Firenze, 23–38.
Bagge, S. (2008) 'Division and Unity in Medieval Norway', in I. H. Garipzanov, P. J. Geary and P. Urbańczyk, eds., *Franks. Northmen, and Slavs: Identities and State Formation in Early Medieval Europe*. Turnhout, 145–66.
Bailey, H. W. (1954) 'Harahuna', in *Asiatica: Festschrift Friedrich Weller*. Leipzig, 12–21.
  (1979) *Dictionary of Khotan Saka*. Cambridge.
  (1981) 'Iranian in Xiongnu', in *Monumentum Georg Morgenstierne*, vol. *1* (Acta Iranica 21, 2e série: Hommages et opera minora 7), 22–6.
  (1982) *The Culture of the Sakas in Ancient Iranian Khotan*. Delmar, NY.
  (1985) *Indo-Scythian Studies* (Khotaneses Texts 7). Cambridge.
Balcer, J. M. (1985) 'Fifth Century B.C. Ionia: A Frontier redefined', *Revue des études anciennes* 87, 31–42.
  (1989) 'Ionia and Sparda under the Achaemenid Empire: The Sixth and Fifth Centuries B.C. Tribute, Taxation and Assessment', in P. Briant and C. Herrenschmidt, eds., *Le Tribut dans L'Empire Perse*. Paris, 1–27.

Baldwin, B. (1980) 'Priscus of Panium', *Byzantion* 50, 18–61.
Balsdon, J. P. V. D. (1979) *Romans and Aliens*. Liverpool.
Balzer, M. M. (1990) *Shamanism: Soviet Studies of Traditional Religion in Siberia and Central Asia*. New York.
Banchich, T. and Lane, E. (trans.) (2009) *The History of Zonaras: From Alexander Severus to the Death of Theodosius the Great*. London.
Bandy, A. C. (ed. and trans.) (1982) *Ioannes Lydus On Powers*. Philadelphia.
Bang, P. F. and Bayly, C. A. (eds.) (2011) *Tributary Empires in Global History* (Cambridge Imperial and Post-Colonial Studies). Basingstoke and New York.
Barber, N. (1973) *The Lords of the Golden Horn: From Suleiman the Magnificent to Kamal Ataturk*. London.
Barclay, D. E. (1994) 'Medievalism and Nationalism in Nineteenth-Century Germany', in L. J. Workman, ed., *Studies in Medievalism*. Cambridge, 5–22.
Barfield, T. (1981) 'The Hsiung-nu Imperial Confederacy: Organization and Foreign Policy', *Journal of Asian Studies* 41 (1), 45–61.
  (1989) *The Perilous Frontier: Nomadic Empires and China*. Oxford.
  (1993) *The Nomadic Alternative*. Englewood Cliffs, NJ.
  (2001) 'Steppe Empires, China, and the Silk Route: Nomads as a Force in International Trade and Politics', in A. M. Khazanov and A. Wink, eds., *Nomads in the Sedentary World*. Padstow, Cornwall, 234–49.
Barlow, J. (1995) 'Kinship, Identity and Fourth-century Franks', *Historia* 45, 223–39.
Barnes, T. D. (1982) *The New Empire of Diocletian and Constantine*. Cambridge, MA.
  (1993) 'Ammianus Marcellinus and his world', *Classical Philology* 88, 55–70.
Barnish, S. (1992) 'Old Kaspars: Attila's Invasion of Gaul in the Literary Sources', in J. Drinkwater and H. Elton, eds., *Fifth-century Gaul: A Crisis of Identity?* Cambridge, 38–52.
Barrett, J. C., Fitzpatrick, A. P., and Maccines, L. (eds.) (1989) *Barbarians and Romans in North-West Europe from the Later Republic to Late Antiquity*. Oxford.
Barth, F. (ed.) (1969) *Ethnic Groups and Boundaries: The Social Organization of Cultural Difference*. Oslo.
Barthold V. V. (1956–62) *Four Studies on the History of Central Asia*, 3 vols. Leiden.
Barthold, W. (1977) *Turkestan Down to the Mongol Invasion*, 4th edn., trans. T. Minorsky. London.
Bartlett, R. (1993) *The Making of Europe: Conquest, Colonization, and Cultural Change 950–1350*. Princeton.
Bashilov, V. A. and Yablonsky, L. T. (2000) 'Some Current Problems Concerning the History of Early Iron Age Eurasian Steppe Nomadic Societies', in J. Davis-Kimball, E. M. Murphy, L. Koryakova and L. T. Yablonsky, eds., *Kurgans, Ritual Sites, and Settlements: Eurasian Bronze and Iron Age*. Oxford, 9–12.
Basilov, V. N. (ed.) (1989) *Nomads of Eurasia*, trans. M. F. Zirin. Seattle and London.
Basilov, V. N. and Zhukovskaya, N. L. (1989) 'Religious Beliefs', in V. N. Basilov, ed., *Nomads of Eurasia*. Seattle and London, 161–81.
Batsaikhan, Z. (2011) 'The Xiongnu: Progenitors of the Classical Nomad Civilization', in U. Brosseder and B. K. Miller, eds., *Xiongnu Archaeology:*

Multidisciplinary Perspectives of the First Steppe Empire in Inner Asia (Bonn Contributions to Asian Archaeology 5). Bonn, 121–8.

Batty, R. (2007) *Rome and the Nomads: The Pontic-Danubian Realm in Antiquity*. Oxford.

Bäuml, F. M. (1993) 'Attila in Medieval German Literature', in F. M. Bäuml and M. D. Birnbaum, eds., *Attila the Man and the Image*. Budapest, 57–64.

Bäuml, F. M. and Birnbaum, M. D. (1993) *Attila the Man and the Image*. Budapest.

Bazin, L. (1948) 'Un texte proto-turc du 4e siècle', *Oriens* 1, 208–19.

  (1975) 'Turcs et Sogdiens: les enseignements de l'inscription du Bugut (Mongolie)', in *Mélanges linguistiques offerts à E. Benveniste*. Paris, 37–46.

  (1983) 'Reflections sur le problème turco-mongol', *Turcica* 15, 31–58.

Beasley, W. G. and Pulleyblank, E. G. (eds.) (1961) *Historians of China and Japan*. Oxford.

Becher, M. (2011) 'The Franks: Rome's heirs in the West', in J. P. Arnason and K. A. Raaflaub, eds., *The Roman Empire in Context: Historical and Comparative Perspectives*. Oxford, 179–98.

Beck, L. (1986) *The Qashqa'i of Iran*. New Haven.

Beckwith, C. I. (1987) *The Tibetan Empire in Central Asia*. Princeton.

  (2009) *Empires of the Silk Road: A History of Central Eurasia from the Bronze Age to the Present*. Princeton.

Belenitsky, A. (1968) *Central Asia*. Geneva.

Bell-Fialkoff, A. (2000) *The Role of Migration in the History of the Eurasian Steppe: Sedentary Civilizations vs. "Barbarian" Nomad*. New York.

Benario, H. W. (1975) *An Introduction to Tacitus*. Athens, GA.

  (1990) 'Tacitus' Germania and Modern Germany', *Illinois Classical Studies* 15, 163–75.

Benjamin, C. (1998) 'Introduction to Kushan Research', in D. Christian and C. Benjamin, eds., *Worlds of the Silk Roads: Ancient and Modern* (Silk Road Studies 2). Turnhout, 31–49.

  (2007) *The Yuezhi: Origin, Migration and the Conquest of Northern Bactria* (Silk Road Studies 15). Turnhout.

Benson, L. and Svanberg, I. (1998) *China's Last Nomads: The History and Culture of China's Kazaks*. Armonk, NY and London.

Bentley, J. H. (1993) *Old World Encounters: Cross-Cultural Contacts and Exchanges in Pre-Modern Times*. Oxford.

  (1998) 'Hemispheric Integration, 500–1500 C.E.', *Journal of World History* 9 (2), 237–54.

Berndt, G. M. (2007) *Konflikt und Anpassung: Studien zu Migration und Ethnogenese der Vandalen* (Historische Studien 489). Husum.

Berthemann, L. and Waitz, G. (eds.) (1878) *Pauli Historia Langobardorum* (Monumenta Germaniae Historica, Scriptores Rerum Langobardicarum et Italicarum saec. VI–IX). Hannover.

Betts, A. V. G. (2007) 'The Aralo-Caspian Region', in V. N. Yagodin, A. V. G. Betts and S. Blau, eds., *Ancient Nomads of the Aral-Caspian Region: The Duana Archaeological Complex*. Leuven, 1–10.

Beveridge, A. (ed. and trans.) (1921) *Babur-nama*. London.
Bichler, R. (2000) *Herodots Welt*. Berlin.
Bidez, J., Festugière, A., and Sabbah, G. (eds. and trans.) (1983) *Sozomène: Histoire ecclésiastique*. Paris.
Bielenstein, H. (1980) *The Bureaucracy of Han Times*. Cambridge.
Biran, M. (2009) 'The Ögödeid and Chaghadeid realms', in N. Di Cosmo, A. J. Frank and P. B. Golden, eds., *The Cambridge History of Inner Asia: The Chinggisid Age*. Cambridge, 46–66.
Birnbaum, M. D. (1993) 'Attila's Renaissance in the Fifteenth and Sixteenth Centuries', in F. M. Bäuml and M. D. Birnbaum, eds., *Attila the Man and the Image*. Budapest, 82–96.
Biswas, A. (1973) *The Political History of the Hunas in India*. New Delhi.
Bivar, A. D. H. (1981) 'Gondophares and the Shahnama', *Iranica Antiqua* 16, 141–51.
  (1983a) 'The History of Eastern Iran', in E. Yarshater, ed., *The Cambridge History of Iran*, vol. III, part 1: *The Seleucid, Parthian and Sasanian Periods*. Cambridge, 181–231.
  (1983b) 'The Political History of Iran under the Arsacids', in E. Yarshater, ed., *The Cambridge History of Iran*, vol. III, part 1: *The Seleucid, Parthian and Sasanian Periods*. Cambridge, 21–99.
  (1998) 'The Sasanian Princes at Bamiyan', in V. S. Curtis, R. Hillenbrand and J. M. Rogers, *The Art and Archaeology of Ancient Persia: New Light on the Parthian and Sasanian Empires*. London and New York, 103–10.
  (2007) 'Gondophares and the Indo-Parthians', in V. S. Curtis and S. Stewart, eds., *The Age of the Parthians*. London and New York, 26–36.
Bloch, M. (1961) *Feudal Society*. London.
Blockley, R. C. (1983) *The Fragmentary Classicising Historians of the Later Roman Empire: Eunapius, Olympiodorus, Priscus and Malchus*. Liverpool.
  (1985) *The History of Menander the Guardsman*. Liverpool.
  (1988) 'Ammianus Marcellinus on the Persian Invasion of A.D. 359', *Phoenix* 42, 244–60.
  (2003) 'The Development of Greek Historiography: Priscus, Malchus, Candidus', in G. Marasco, ed., *Greek and Roman Historiography in Late Antiquity: Fourth to Sixth Century A.D.* Leiden, 289–315.
Blois, F. and Vogelsang, W. (1991) 'Dahae', in E. Yarshater, ed., *Encyclopaedia Iranica*. New York, 158–2.
Boak, A. E. R. (1955) *Manpower Shortage and the Fall of the Roman Empire in the West*. Ann Arbor.
Boardman, J. (2007) 'Central Asia: West and East', in J. Cribb and G. Herrmann, eds., *After Alexander: Central Asia before Islam*. Oxford, 9–25.
Boba, I. (ed.) (1967) *Nomads, Northmen and Slavs*. Paris and The Hague.
  (1971) *Moravia's History Reconsidered*. The Hague.
Bokovenko, N. A. (1997) 'Asian influence on European Scythia', *Ancient Civilizations from Scythia to Siberia* 3, 97–122.
Bona, I. (1976) *The Dawn of the Dark Ages: The Gepids and Lombards in the Carpathian Basin*. Budapest.

(1991) *Das Hunnenreich*. Stuttgart.
  (2002) *Les Huns: le grand empire barbare d'Europe* (IVe–Ve siècles), trans. K. Escher. Paris.
Bonamente, G. (2003) 'Minor Latin Historians of the Fourth Century A.D.', in G. Marasco, ed., *Greek and Roman Historiography in Late Antiquity: Fourth to Sixth Century A.D.* Leiden, 85–125.
Boor, C. de (ed.) (1887, reprint 1972) *Theophylact Simocatta, Historiae*. Stuttgart.
Bopearachchi, O. and Boussac, M. F. (2005) *Afghanistan: ancien carrefour entre l'est et l'ouest*. Turnhout.
Bosworth, A. B. (1988) *Conquest and Empire: The Reign of Alexander the Great*. Cambridge.
Bosworth, C. E. (1963) *The Ghaznavids: Their Empire in Afghanistan and Eastern Iran 994–1040*. Edinburgh.
  (1968) 'The Political and Dynastic History of the Iranian World (A.D. 1000–1217)', in *The Cambridge History of Iran*, vol. V: *The Saljuk and Mongol Periods*. Cambridge, 1–202.
Bowles, G. T. (1977) *Peoples of Asia*. New York.
Bowlus, C. R. (1994) *Franks, Moravians and Magyars: The Struggle for the Middle Danube, 788–907*. Philadelphia.
Boyle, J. A. (1958) *The History of the World-Conqueror*. Cambridge, MA.
  (ed.) (1968a). *The Cambridge History of Iran*, vol. V: *The Saljuk and Mongol Periods*. Cambridge.
  (1968b) 'Dynastic and Political History of the Il-Khans', in *The Cambridge History of Iran*, vol. V: *The Saljuk and Mongol Periods*. Cambridge, 303–421.
  (trans.) (1971) *The Successors of Genghis Khan, Translated from the Persian of Rashid Al-Din*. New York; London.
  (1977) *The Mongol World Empire, 1206–1370*. London.
Brachmann. H. (1997) 'Tribal Organizations in Central Europe in the 6th–10th centuries A.D.: Reflections on the ethnic and political development in the second half of the first millennium', in P. Urbańczyk, ed., *Origins of Central Europe*. Warsaw, 23–37.
Bradley, M. (2010) *Classics and Imperialism in the British Empire: Classical Presences*. Oxford and New York.
Brakke, D., Deliyannis, D., and Watts, E. (eds.) (2012) *Shifting Cultural Frontiers in Late Antiquity*. Farnham and Burlington, VT.
Brauer, R. W. (1995) *Boundaries and Frontiers in Medieval Muslim Geography* (Transactions of the American Philosophical Society 85/6). Philadelphia.
Braund, D. (1984) *Rome and the Friendly King: The Character of the Client Kingship*. London, Canberra and New York.
Bregel, Y. (1982) 'Tribal Tradition and Dynastic History', *Asian and African Studies* 16, 357–98.
  (1995) *Bibliography of Islamic Central Asia*, 3 vols. Bloomington.
  (1996) *Notes on the Study of Central Asia* (Papers on Inner Asia 28). Bloomington.
Briant, P. (1984) *L'Asie centrale et les royaumes proche-orientaux du premier millénaire*. Paris.

(1999) 'The Achaemenid Empire', in K. Raaflaub and N. Rosenstein, eds., *War and Society in the Ancient and Medieval Worlds*. Cambridge, MA, 105–28.
  (2002) *From Cyrus to Alexander: A History of the Persian Empire*. Winona Lake, IN.
Brodka, D. (2008) 'Attila, Tyche und die Schlacht auf den Katalaunischen Feldern: eine Untersuchung zum Geschichtsdenken des Priskos von Panion', *Hermes* 136, 2, 227–245.
Brooks, E. W. (ed.) (1924) *Historia Ecclesiastica Zachariae Rhetori vulgo adscripta*. Louvain.
Brosseder, U. (2011) 'Belt Plaques as an Indicator of East–West Relations in the Eurasian Steppe at the Turn of the Millennia', in U. Brosseder and B. K. Miller, eds., *Xiongnu Archaeology: Multidisciplinary Perspectives of the First Steppe Empire in Inner Asia* (Bonn Contributions to Asian Archaeology 5). Bonn, 349–424.
Brosseder, U. and Miller, B. K. (2011a) 'State of Research and Future Directions of Xiongnu Studies' in U. Brosseder and B. K. Miller, eds., *Xiongnu Archaeology: Multidisciplinary Perspectives of the First Steppe Empire in Inner Asia* (Bonn Contributions to to Asian Archaeology 5). Bonn, 19–33.
  (eds.) (2011b) *Xiongnu Archaeology: Multidisciplinary Perspectives of the First Steppe Empire in Inner Asia* (Bonn Contributions to to Asian Archaeology 5). Bonn.
Brown, P. (1971) *The World of Late Antiquity from Marcus Aurelius to Muhammad*. London.
  (1978) *The Making of Late Antiquity*. Cambridge, MA and London.
  (1998) *Late Antiquity*. Cambridge, MA.
  (2012) *Through the Eye of a Needle: Wealth, the Fall of Rome, and the Making of Christianity in the West, 350–550 AD*. Princeton.
Browning, R. (1975) *Byzantium and Bulgaria: A Comparative Study across the Early Medieval Frontier*. Berkeley, Los Angeles and London.
Brzezinski, Z. (2004) *The Choice: Global Domination or Global Leadership*. New York.
Buchet, L. (1988) 'La déformation crânienne en Gaule et dans les régions limitrophes pendant le haut Moyen Age: son origine – sa valeur historique', *Archéologie médiévale* 18, 55–71.
Bullough, D. (1965a) 'The Empire under the Ottonians', in D. T. Rice, ed., *The Dark Ages*. London, 299–326.
  (1965b) 'The Ostrogothic and Lombard Kingdoms', in D. T. Rice, ed., *The Dark Ages*. London, 157–74.
Burgess, R. (ed. and trans.) (1993) *The Chronicle of Hydatius and the Consularia Constantinopolitana: Two Contemporary Accounts of the Final Years of the Roman Empire*. Oxford.
  (ed.) (2001a) 'The Gallic Chronicle of 452: A New Critical Edition with a Brief Introduction,' in R. W. Mathisen and D. Shanzer, eds., *Society and Culture in Late Antique Gaul: Revisiting the Sources*. Aldershot, 52–84.
  (ed.) (2001b) 'The Gallic Chronicle of 511: A New Critical Edition with a Brief Introduction', in R. W. Mathisen and D. Shanzer, eds., *Society and Culture in Late Antique Gaul: Revisiting the Sources*. Aldershot, 85–100.

Burn, A. R. (1984) *Persia and the Greeks: The Defence of the West, c. 546–478 B.C.*, 2nd. edn. London.
Burnham, P. (1979) 'Spatial Mobility and Political Centralization in Pastoral Societies', in Équipe écologie et anthropologie des sociétés pastorals (ed.), *Pastoral Production and Society/ Production pastorale et société: Proceedings of the International Meeting on Nomadic Pastoralism, Paris 1–3 Dec. 1976*. Cambridge, 349–60.
Burns, T. S. (1980) *The Ostrogoths: Kingship and Society* (Historia Einzelschriften 36). Wiesbaden.
  (1984) *A History of the Ostrogoths*. Bloomington.
  (1994) *Barbarians within the Gates of Rome: A study of Roman Military Policy and the Barbarians, ca. 375–425 A.D.* Bloomington and Indianapolis.
Burstein, S. M. (2010) 'New Light on the Fate of Greek in Ancient Central and South Asia', *Ancient West and East* 9, 181–92.
Bury, J. B. (1923) *History of the Later Roman Empire*. London.
Cahen. C. (1973) 'Frédegaire et les Turcs', in *Économies et sociétés au Moyen Âge: mélanges offerts à Édouard Perroy*. Paris, 24–7.
Calmette, J. (1978) *L'Effondrement d'un empire et la naissance d'une Europe ixe–xe siecles*. Geneva.
Cameron, Alan (1970) *Claudian: Poetry and Propaganda at the Court of Honorius*. Oxford.
Cameron, Alan and Long, J. (1993) *Barbarians and Politics at the Court of Arcadius*. Berkeley, Los Angeles and Oxford.
Cameron, Averil (1993) *The Mediterranean World in Late Antiquity, AD 395–600*. London.
  (2012) *The Mediterranean World in Late Antiquity, AD 395–700*. London.
Cameron, G. C. (1948) *Persepolis Treasury Tablets*. Chicago.
Campbell, B. (1999) 'The Roman Empire', in K. Raaflaub and N. Rosenstein, eds., *War and Society in the Ancient and Medieval Worlds*. Cambridge, MA, 217–40.
Campbell, G. L. (2006) *Strange Creatures: Anthropology in Antiquity*. London.
Canduci, A. (2010) *Triumph and Tragedy: The Rise and Fall of Rome's Immortal Emperors*. Millers Point.
Canepa, M. P. (ed.) (2010a) *Theorizing Cross-Cultural Interactions among the Ancient and Early Medieval Mediterranean, Near East and Asia* (Ars Orientalis 38). Washington, DC.
  (2010b) 'Distant Displays of Power: Understanding Cross-cultural Interactions among the Elites of Rome, Sasanian Iran, and Sui-Tang China', in M. P. Canepa, ed., *Theorizing Cross-Cultural Interactions among the Ancient and Early Medieval Mediterranean, Near East and Asia* (Ars Orientalis 38). Washington, DC, 121–54.
Canfield. R. L. (1991) *Turko-Persia in Historical Perspective*. Cambridge.
Cary, E. (ed. and trans.) (1914–27) *Cassius Dio: Roman History* (Loeb Classical Library, 9 vols.). Cambridge, MA.

Castritius, H. (1990) 'Von politischer Vielfalt zur Einheit: zu den Ethnogenesen der Alemannen', in H. Wolfram and W. Pohl, eds., *Typen der Ethnogenese unter besonderer Berücksichtigung der Bayern*, vol. 1. Wien, 71–84.

Cataudella, M. R. (2003) 'Historiography in the East', in G. Marasco, ed., *Greek and Roman Historiography in Late Antiquity: Fourth to Sixth Century* A.D. Leiden, 391–447.

Chakrabarti, K. (1996) 'The Gupta Kingdom', in B. A. Litvinsky, ed., *History of Civilizations of Central Asia*, vol. III, *The Crossroads of Civilizations:* A.D. *250–750*. Paris, 185–206.

Chaliand, G. (2004) *Nomadic Empires: From Mongolia to the Danube*, trans. A. M. Berrett. New Brunswick, NJ and London.

Chang, C. S. (1966) 'Military Aspects of Han Wu-ti's Northern and Northwestern Campaigns', *Harvard Journal of Asiatic Studies* 26, 148–73.

Chang, K. C. (1986) *The Archaeology of Ancient China*, 4th edn. New Haven, CT.

Chapman, J. and Dolukhanov, P., eds. (1993) *Cultural Transformations and Interactions in Eastern Europe*. Aldershot.

Chard, C. S. (1974) *Northeast Asia in Prehistory*. Madison, WI.

Charles, R. H. (trans.) (1916) *The Chronicle of John, Bishop of Nikiu*. Oxford.

Chase-Dunn, C. and Hall, T. (1997) *Rise and Demise: Comparing World-Systems*. Boulder, CO.

Chavannes, E. (1895) *Les mémoires historiques de Se-ma-Tsien*. Paris.

Chen, S. (2002) 'Son of Heaven and Son of God: Interactions among Ancient Asiatic Cultures Regarding Sacral Kingship and Theophoric Names', *Journal of the Royal Asiatic Society*, Series 3, 12 (3), 289–325.

Chen, Y. (1966) *Western and Central Asians in China under the Mongols: Their Transformation into Chinese*, trans. H. Ch'ien and L. Carrington Goodrich. Los Angeles.

Chernenko, E. V. (1994) 'Investigations of the Scythian Tumuli in the Northern Pontic Steppe', *Ancient Civilizations from Scythia to Siberia* 1, 45–53.

Christ, K. (1965) 'Germanendarstellung und Zeitverständnis bei Tacitus', *Historia* 14, 62–73.

Christensen, A. S. (2002) *Cassiodorus, Jordanes and the History of the Goths: Studies in a Migration Myth*. Copenhagen.

Christian, D. (1994) '"Inner Asia" as a unit of World History', *Journal of World History* 5 (2), 173–211.

(1996) 'State Formation in the Steppes', in J. Perkins and J. Tampke, eds., *Europe: Prospects and Retrospects*. Sydney, 243–58.

(1998) *A History of Russia, Central Asia and Mongolia*, vol 1: *Inner Eurasia from Prehistory to the Mongol Empire* (The Blackwell History of the World). Oxford.

(2000) 'Silk Roads or Steppe Routes? The Silk Roads in World History', *Journal of World History* 11 (1), 1–26.

Christian, D. and Benjamin, C. (2000) *Realms of the Silk Roads: Ancient and Modern* (Proceedings from the third Conference of the Australasian Society

for Inner Asian Studies, ASIAS, Macquarie University, 18–20 September 1998). Sydney.
Christie, N. (1995) *The Lombards: The Ancient Longobards*. Oxford and Cambridge, MA.
  (2007) 'From the Danube to the Po: The Defence of Pannonia and Italy in the Fourth and Fifth Centuries AD', in A. G. Poulter, ed., *The Transition to Late Antiquity on the Danube and Beyond*. Oxford, 547–78.
  (2011) *The Fall of the Western Roman Empire: An Archaeological and Historical Perspective*. London and New York.
Chrysos, E. (1997) 'The Empire in East and West', in L. Webster and M. Brown, eds., *The Transformation of the Roman World AD 400–900*. London, 9–18.
Chrysos, E. and Schwarcz, A. (1989) *Das Reich und die Barbaren*. Vienna and Cologne.
Chun, A. J. (1990) 'Conception of Kinship and Kingship in Classical Chou China', *T'oung Pao* 76, 16–48.
Claessen, H. J. M. and J. G. Oosten (eds.) (1996) *Ideology and Formation of Early States*. Leiden.
Claessen, H. J. M. and Skalnik, P. (eds.) (1978a) *The Early State* (New Babylon: Studies in the Social Sciences 32). The Hague.
  (eds.) (1978b) 'The Early State: Theories and Hypotheses', in H. J. M. Claessen and P. Skalnik, eds., *The Early State* (New Babylon: Studies in the Social Sciences 32). The Hague, 3–30.
Clarke, K. (2008) 'Text and Image: Mapping the Roman World', in F. Mutschler and A. Mittag, eds., *Conceiving the Empire: China and Rome Compared*. Oxford, 195–214.
Clauson, G. (1962) *Turkish and Mongolian Studies*. London.
  (1964) 'Turks and Wolves', *Studia Orientalia* 28 (2), 3–22.
  (1970) 'The Origins of the Turkish Runic Alphabet', *Acta Orientalia* (Copenhagen) 32, 51–76.
  (1972) *An Etymological Dictionary of Pre-Thirteenth-Century Turkish*. Oxford.
Cleaves, F. W. (1982) *The Secret History of the Mongols*. Cambridge MA and London.
Clifford, A. (2012) *Imperial Rome AD 193 to 284: The Critical Century*. Edinburgh.
Clover, F. M. (1967) 'Geiseric and Statesman: A Study of Vandal Foreign Policy', PhD thesis, University of Chicago.
  (ed. and trans.) (1971) *Flavius Merobaudes: A Translation and Historical Commentary* (Transactions of the American Philosophical Society, n.s. 61). Philadelphia.
  (1972) 'Geiseric and Attila', *Historia* 22, 104–17.
Cohen, R. and Service, E. R. (eds.) (1978) *The Origin of the State: The Anthropology of Political Evolution*. Philadelphia.
Colledge, M. A. R. (1967) *The Parthians*. London.
Collins, R. (1999) *Early Medieval Europe 300–1000*. Basingstoke and London.

(2000) 'The western Kingdoms', in A. Cameron, B. Ward-Perkins and M. Whitby, eds., *The Cambridge Ancient History*, vol. XIV: *Late Antiquity: Empire and Successors, A.D. 425–600*. Cambridge, 112–34.
(2004) *Visigothic Spain 409–711*. Malden, MA and Oxford.
Cook, J. M. (1983) *The Persian Empire*. New York.
Cook, S. A., Adcock, F. E., Charlesworth, M. P., and Baynes, N. H. (eds.) (1965) *The Cambridge Ancient History*, vol. XII: *The Imperial Crisis and Recovery A.D. 193–324*. Cambridge.
Corcella, A. (1993) *Erodoto, Le Storie. Libro IV: La Scizia e la Libia*. Milan.
Cowley, A. (1923) *Aramaic Papyri of the Fifth Century B.C.* Oxford.
Creasy, E. S. (1943) *Fifteen Decisive Battles of the World*. Harrisburg.
Creel, H. G. (1970) *The Invention of Statecraft in China*. Chicago and London.
Cribb, J. (1997) 'Shiva images on Kushan and Kushano-Sassanian coins', in K. Tanabe, J. Cribb and H. Wang, eds., *Studies in Silk Road Coins and Culture: Papers in Honour of Professor Ikuo Hirayama on his 65th birthday*. Kamakura, 11–66.
(2007) 'Money as a Marker of Cultural Continuity and Change in Central Asia', in J. Cribb and G. Herrmann, eds., *After Alexander: Central Asia before Islam*. Oxford, 333–75.
Cribb, J. and Herrmann, G. (eds.) (2007) *After Alexander: Central Asia before Islam*. Oxford.
Cribb, R. (1991) *Nomads in Archaeology*. Cambridge.
Croke, B. (1977) 'Evidence for the Hun Invasion of Thrace in A.D. 422', *Greek, Roman and Byzantine Studies* 18, 347–367.
(1980) 'Justinian's Bulgar Victory Celebration', *Byzantinoslavica* 41, 188–95.
(1981) 'Anatolius and Nomus: Envoys to Attila', *Byzantinoslavica* 42, 159–79.
(1982a) 'Mundo the Gepid: From Freebooter to Roman General', *Chiron* 12, 125–35.
(1982b) 'The Date of the 'Anastasian Long Wall' in Thrace', *Greek, Roman and Byzantine Studies* 20, 59–78.
(1983a) 'A.D. 476: The Manufacturing of a Turning Point', *Chiron* 13, 81–119.
(1983b) 'The Context and Date of Priscus Fragment 6', *Classical Philology* 78, 297–308.
(1992) *Christian Chronicles and Byzantine History, 5th–6th Centuries*. Aldershot.
(trans.) (1995) *The Chronicle of of Marcellinus: A Translation and Commentary*. Sydney.
(1987) 'Cassiodorus and the *Getica* of Jordanes', *Classical Philology* 82, 117–34.
(2003) 'Latin Historiography and the Barbarian Kingdoms', in G. Marasco, ed., *Greek and Roman historiography in Late Antiquity Fourth to Sixth Century A.D.* Leiden, 349–89.
Croke, B. and Emmett, A. M. (eds.) (1983) *History and the Historians in Late Antiquity*. Sydney.
Csikszentmihalyi, M. (2003) 'Constructing lineages and inventing traditions through exemplary figures in early China', *T'oung Pao* 89 (1–3), 59–99.

Csorba, M. (1996) 'The Chinese Northern Frontier: Reassessment of the Bronze Age Burials from Baitu', *Antiquity* 70, 564–87.
Cuisenier. J. (1976) 'Kinship and Social Organisation in the Turko-Mongolian Cultural Area', in R. Forster and O. Ranum, eds., *Family and Society: Selections from the Annales*. Baltimore.
Culican, W. (1965) 'Spain under the Visigoths and Moors', in D. T. Rice, ed., *The Dark Ages*. London, 175–96.
Curta, F. (2001) *The Making of the Slavs: History and Archaeology of the Lower Danube Region c. 500–700*. Cambridge.
  (ed.) (2005) *East Central and Eastern Europe in the Early Middles Ages*. Ann Arbor.
  (ed.) (2006) *Southeastern Europe in the Middle Ages 500–1250*. Cambridge.
Curtin, P. D. (1985) *Cross-Cultural Trade in World History*. Cambridge.
Curtis, J. E. and Tallis, N. (2005) *Forgotten Empire: The World of Ancient Persia*. Berkeley.
Curtis, V. S. (2007) 'The Iranian Revival in the Parthian Period', in V. S. Curtis and S. Stewart, eds., *The Age of the Parthians*. London, 7–25.
Curtis, V. S., Hillenbrand, R., and Rogers, J. M. (eds.) (1998) *The Art and Archaeology of Ancient Persia: New Light on the Parthian and Sasanian Empires*. London and New York.
Curtis, V. S. and Stewart, S. (eds.) (2007) *The Age of the Parthians*. London.
Czeglédy K. (1971) 'Pseudo-Zacharias Rhetor on the Nomads', in L. Ligeti, ed., *Studia Turcica*. Budapest, 133–48.
  (1983) 'From East to West: The Age of Nomadic Migrations in Eurasia', trans. P. Golden, *Archivum Eurasiae Medii Aevi* 3, 25–156.
Daffinà, P. (1982) 'The Han Shu Hsi Yü Chuan Re-translated: A Review Article', *T'oung Pao* 68 (4/5), 309–39.
Dahmus, J. (1983) *Seven Decisive Battles of the Middle Ages*. Chicago.
Daim, F. (2003) 'Avars and Avar Archaeology: An Introduction', in H. Goetz, J. Jarnut and W. Pohl, eds., *Regna and Gentes: The Relationship between Late Antique and Early Medieval Peoples and Kingdoms in the Transformation of the Roman World*. Leiden, 463–570.
Dale, S. (2009) 'The later Timurids c.1450–1526', in N. Di Cosmo, A. J. Frank and P. B. Golden, eds., *The Cambridge History of Inner Asia: The Chinggisid Age*. Cambridge, 199–217.
Dandamaev, M. A. (1989) *A Political History of the Achaemenid Empire*. Leiden.
  (1994) 'Media and Achaemenid Iran', in J. Harmatta, ed., *History of Civilizations of Central Asia*, vol. II: *The Development of Sedentary and Nomadic Civilizations*. Paris, 35–65.
Dandamaev, M. A. and Lukonin, V. G. (1989) *The Culture and Social Institutions of Ancient Iran*. Cambridge.
Dani, A. H. and Masson, V. M. (1992) *History of Civilizations of Central Asia* vol. I: *The Dawn of Civilization*, Paris.
Dani, A. H. and Litvinsky, B. A. (1994) 'The Kushano-Sassanian kingdom', in B. A. Litvinsky, ed., *History of Civilizations of Central Asia*, vol. III: *The Crossroads of Civilizations, A.D. 250 to 750*. 103–18.

Dani, A. H., Litvinsky B. A., and Zamir Safi, M. H. (1996) 'Eastern Kushans: Kidarites in Gandhara and Kashmir, and Later Hephthalites', in B. A. Litvinsky, ed., *History of Civilizations Central Asia*, vol. III: *The Crossroads of Civilizations: A.D. 250 to 750*. Paris, 163–183.
Daniel, G. (1965) *The Medes and the Persians*. London.
Dankoff, R. (1972) 'Kasgari on the Tribal and Kinship Organization of the Turks', *Archivum Ottomanicum* 4, 27–49.
Dankoff, R. and Kelly, J. (trans.) (1982–5) *Compendium of the Turkic Dialects (Dîwân Luġat al-Turk)*. Cambridge, MA.
Darwin, J. (2007) *After Tamerlane: The Global History of Empire since 1405*. London.
Daryaee, T. (2009) *Sasanian Persia: The Rise and Fall of an Empire*. London; New York.
Davis-Kimball, J. (2000) 'The Beiram Mound: A Nomadic Cultic Site in the Altai Mountains (Western Mongolia)', in J. Davis-Kimball, E. M. Murphy, L. Koryakova, and L. T. Yablonsky, eds., *Kurgans, Ritual Sites, and Settlements: Eurasian Bronze and Iron Age*. Oxford, 89–105.
Davis-Kimball, J., Bashilov, V., and Yablonsky, L. (eds.) (1995) *Nomads of the Eurasian Steppes in the Early Iron Age*. Berkeley, CA.
Davis-Kimball, J., Murphy, E. M., Koryakova, L., and Yablonsky, L. T. (eds.) (2000) *Kurgans, Ritual Sites, and Settlements: Eurasian Bronze and Iron Age*. Oxford.
Debaine-Francfort, C. (1990) 'Les Saka du Xinjiang avant les Han (206 av.-220 ap. J.-C): Critères d'identification', in Francfort, H. P., ed., *Nomades et Sédentaires en Asie Centrale: apports de l'archéologie et de l'ethnologie* (Actes du colloque franco-soviétique Alma Ata (Kazakhstan) 17–26 Octobre 1987). Paris, 81–95.
de Crespigny, R. (1984) *Northern Frontier. The Policies and Strategies of the Later Han Empire*, Canberra.
Defarri, R. J. (1964) *Orosius: Seven Books of History Against the Pagans*. Washington.
Deguignes, J. (1756–1824) *Histoire générale des Huns, des Turcs, des Mogols et des autres Tartares occidentaux ... avant et depuis Jésus-Christ jusqu'à présent*, 5 vols. Paris.
Demandt, A. (1984). *Der Fall Roms*. Munich.
Demougeot, E. (1979) *La formation de L'Europe et les invasions barbares*. Paris.
Dennis, G. T. (1984) *Maurice's Strategikon: Handbook of Byzantine Military Strategy*. Philadelphia.
Dewing, H. B. (ed. and trans.) (1914a) *Procopius, De Aedificiis* (Loeb Classical Library). Cambridge, MA.
  (ed. and trans.) (1914b) *Procopius, Anecdota* (Loeb Classical Library). Cambridge, MA.
  (ed. and trans.) (1914c) *Procopius, De Bello Gothico* (Loeb Classical Library). Cambridge, MA.
Diakonoff, I. M. (1985) 'Media', in I. Gershevitch, ed., *The Cambridge History of Iran*, vol. II: *The Median and Achaemenian Periods*. Cambridge, 36–148.
Di Cosmo, N. (1994) 'Ancient Inner Asian Nomads: The Economic Basis and its Significance in Chinese History', *The Journal of Asian Studies* 53 (4), 1092–1126.

(1999a) 'The Northern Frontier in Pre-Imperial China', in M. Loewe and E. L. Shaughnessy, eds., *The Cambridge History of Ancient China*, vol. 1: *From the Origins of Civilization to 221 BC*. Cambridge, 885–966.
(1999b) 'Review of J. Janhunen, *Manchuria: An Ethnic History* (1996)'. *Bulletin of the School of Oriental Studies, University of London* 62 (1), 180–2.
(1999c) 'State Formation and Periodization in Inner Asian History', *Journal of World History* 10 (1), 1–40.
(2002) *Ancient China and its Enemies: The Rise of Nomadic Power in East Asian History*. Cambridge.
(2011) 'Ethnogenesis, Coevolution and Political Morphology of the Earliest Steppe Empire: The Xiongnu Question Revisited', in U. Brosseder and B. K. Miller, eds., *Xiongnu Archaeology: Multidisciplinary Perspectives of the First Steppe Empire in Inner Asia* (Bonn Contributions to Asian Archaeology 5). Bonn, 35–48.
Di Cosmo, N., Frank, A. G., and Golden, P. B. (eds.) (2009) *The Cambridge History of Inner Asia: The Chinggisid Era*. Cambridge.
Di Cosmo, N. and Wyatt, D. J. (eds.) (2003) *Political Frontiers, Ethnic Boundaries and Human Geographies in Chinese History*. London.
Dignas, B. and Winter, E, (2007) *Rome and Persia in Late Antiquity: Neighbours and Rivals*. Cambridge.
Dindorf, L. (ed.) (1831) *Ioannis Malalae Chronographia* (Corpus Scriptorum Historiae Byzantinae). Bonn.
Dittrich, U. (1984) *Die Beziehungen Roms zu den Sarmaten und Quaden im vierten Jahrhundert n. Chr.(nach der Darstellung des Ammianus Marcellinus)*. Bonn.
Dixon, P. (1976) *Barbarian Europe*. Oxford.
Dmitriev, S. V. (2003) 'Political Culture of the Turkic-Mongolian Nomads in Historical and Ethnological Perspective', in N. N. Kradin, D. Bondarenko and T. Barfield, eds., *Nomadic Pathways in Social Evolution*. Moscow, 148–57.
Dodgeon, M. H. and Lieu, N. C. (1991) *The Roman Eastern Frontier and the Persian Wars* AD *226–363: A Documentary History*. London and New York.
Doerfer, G. (1973) 'Zur Sprache der Hunnen', *Central Asiatic Journal* 17 (1), 1–51.
Dolukhanov, P. M. (1996) *The Early Slavs: Eastern Europe from the Initial Settlement to Kievan Rus*. London.
Dorey, T. A. (1969) '"Agricola" and "Germania"', in T. A. Dorey, ed., *Tacitus*. London, 1–18.
Dorzhsüren, T. (1961) *Umard Khünnü* (Ertnii sudlalyn shinzhilgee) (Studia Archeologica Tomus I, Fasciculus 5). Ulaanbaatar.
Dowsett, C. J. E. (1961) *The History of the Caucasian Albanians by Movsês Dasxuranci*. Oxford.
Drews, R. (2004) *Early Riders: The Beginning of Mounted Warfare in Asia and Europe*. New York and London.
Drijvers, J. W. (1998) 'Strabo on Parthia and the Parthians', in J. Wiesehöfer, ed., *Das Partherreich und seine Zeugnisse*. Stuttgart, 279–93.

(1999) 'Ammianus Marcellinus' Image of Arsaces and Early Parthian History', in J. W. Drijvers and D. Hunt, eds., *The Late Roman World and its Historian: Interpreting Ammianus Marcellinus*. London and New York, 193–206.
Drijvers, J. W. and Hunt, D. (eds.) (1999) *The Late Roman World and its Historian: Interpreting Ammianus Marcellinus*. London and New York.
Drinkwater, J. F. (1992) 'The Bacaudae of Fifth-century Gaul', in J. Drinkwater and H. Elton, eds., *Fifth-century Gaul: A Crisis of Identity?* Cambridge, 208–217.
(1997) 'Julian and the Franks and Valentinian I and the Alamanni: Ammianus on Romano-German relations', *Francia* 24 (1), 1–16.
(1999) 'Ammianus, Valentinian and the Rhine Germans', in J. W. Drijvers and D. Hunt, eds., *The Late Roman World and its historian: interpreting Ammianus Marcellinus*. London and New York, 127–37.
Drinkwater, J. F. and Elton, H. (ed.) (1992) *Fifth-century Gaul: A Crisis of Identity?* Cambridge.
Duan, L. (1988) *Dingling, Gaoju Yu Tiele*. Shanghai.
Dunlop, D. M. (1954) *The History of the Jewish Khazars*. New York.
Eberhard, W. (1942) *Lokalkulturen im alten China*. Leiden.
(1949) *Das Toba-Reich Nord Chinas*. Leiden.
(1950) *A History of China from the Earliest Times to the Present Day*. London.
(1970) *Conquerors and Rulers: Social Forces in Medieval China*. Leiden.
(1982) *China's Minorities: Yesterday and Today*. Belmont, CA.
Eckhardt. K. (1955), 'Die Nachbenennung in der Königshäusern der Goten', *Sudöst-Forschungen* 14, 34–55.
(1975) *Bibliotheca Rerum Historicarum, Studia*, vol. II: *Merovingica*. Aalen.
Efimov, V. G., Pauls, E. D., and Podolsky, M. L. (1996) 'Ancient Knights of the Minusine Steppes on Engraved Plaques from Vault Burials', *Ancient Civilizations from Scythia to Siberia* 2 (2), 238–50.
Ehrhardt, N. (1998) 'Parther und parthische Geschichte bei Tacitus', in J. Wiesehöfer, ed., *Das Partherreich und seine Zeugnisse*. Stuttgart, 295–307.
Elias, N. and Ross, E. D. (eds. and trans.) (1895) *The Tarikh-i-Rashidi of Mirza Muhammad Haidar, Dughlat: A History of the Moghuls of Central Asia. An English Version. (Originally composed in Persian in 1541–2). Edited, with Commentary, Notes, and Map*. London.
Elisseeff, V. (1998) 'Approaches Old and New to the Silk Roads', in V. Elisseeff, ed., *The Silk Roads: Highways of Culture and Commerce*. Paris, 1–2.
Elton, H. (1992) 'Defence in fifth-century Gaul', in J. Drinkwater and H. Elton, eds., *Fifth-century Gaul: A Crisis of Identity?* Cambridge, 167–83.
(1996) *Frontiers of the Roman Empire*. Bloomington and Indianapolis.
(2000) 'The Nature of the Sixth-Century Isaurians', in S. Mitchell and G. Greatrex, eds., *Ethnicity and Culture in Late Antiquity*. London, 293–307.
(2007) 'Army and Battle in the Age of Justinian (527–65)', in P. Erdkamp, ed., *A Companion to the Roman Army*. Malden, MA, 532–50.
Enoki, K. (1951) 'Efutaru minzoku no kigen' [The Origins of the Hephtalites], in *Wada hakase kanreki kinen Toyoshi ronso*. Tokyo.

(1952) 'Efutaru minzoku ni okeru iranteki yosu' [Iranian elements in the Hephtalite People], *Shigaku zasshi* 61, 1–26.
(1955) 'Sogdiana and Hioung-nous', *Central Asiatic Journal* 1, 43–62.
(1959) 'On the Nationality of the Ephthalites', *Memoirs of the Research Department of the Toyo Bunko* 18, 1–58.
(1963) '*Ryo shokko zu ni tsuite*' [A Study of the *Chih-kung-t'u* of Liang], Tohogaku 26, 31–46.
(1970) 'The Liang shih-kung-t'u on the Origin and Migration of the Hua or Ephthalites', *Journal of the Oriental Society of Australia* 7, 1–2, 37–45.
Enoki, K., Koshelenko, G. A., and Haidary, Z. (1994) 'The Yüeh-chih and their Migrations', in J. Harmatta, ed., *History of Civilizations of Central Asia*, vol. II. Paris, 171–89.
Erdkamp, P. (ed.) (2007) *A Companion to the Roman Army*. Malden, MA.
Érdy, M. (1995) 'Hun and Xiong-nu Type Cauldron Finds throughout Eurasia', *Eurasian Studies Yearbook* 67, 5–94.
Ertürk, K. A. (ed.) (1999) *Rethinking Central Asia*. Reading.
Esin, E. (1980) *A History of Pre-Islamic and Early-Islamic Turkish Culture*. Istanbul.
Ewig, E. (1997) 'Le mythe troyen et l'histoire de France', in M. Rouche, ed., *Clovis, histoire et mémoire: Baptême de Clovis, l'événement*. Paris, 817–47.
Fairbank, J. K. (1968) *The Chinese World Order*. Cambridge MA.
Faizrakhmanov, G. (2000) *Ancient Turks in Sibiria and Central Asia*. Kazan.
Fanning, S. (1992) 'Emperors and Empires in Fifth-century Gaul', in J. Drinkwater and H. Elton, eds., *Fifth-century Gaul: A Crisis of Identity?* Cambridge, 288–97.
Federov, M. (2004) 'On the Origin of the Kushans with Reference to Numismatic and Anthropological Data', *Oriental Numismatic Society Newsletter* 181, 30–2.
Fehling, D. (1989) *Herodotus and his 'Sources': Citation, Invention, and Narrative Art*, trans. J. G. Howie. Leeds.
Fernández-Armesto, F. (1995) *Millennium*. London.
Ferrill, A. (1986) *The Fall of the Roman Empire: The Military Explanation*. London.
Findley, C. V. (2005) *The Turks in World History*. Oxford.
Fine, J. V. A., Jr. (1983) *The Early Medieval Balkans: A Critical Survey from the Sixth to the Late Twelfth Century*. Ann Arbor.
Finlay, V. (2006) *Buried Treasure: Travels through the Jewel Box*. London.
Fischer, K. (1968) 'Zum Einfluss zentralasiatischer Nomaden und halbnomaden auf den Verlauf der indischen Feudalperiode', in *Das Verhältnis von Bodenbauren und Viehzüchtern in historischer Sicht*. Berlin, 53–60.
Fletcher, J. F. (1978) 'Blood Tanistry: Authority and Succession in the Ottoman, Indian Muslim and Later Chinese Empires', *The Conference for the Theory of Democracy and Popular Participation*, Bellagio.
(1979–80) 'Turco-Mongolian monarchic tradition in the Ottoman Empire', in I. Sevcenko and F. E. Sysyn, eds., *Eucharisterion: Essays Presented to Omeljan Pritsak* (Harvard Ukranian Studies 3–4). Cambridge MA, 236–51.
(1986) 'The Mongols: Ecological and Social Perspectives', *Harvard Journal of Asiatic Studies* 46, 11–50.
(1995) *Studies on Chinese and Islamic Inner Asia*. Aldershot.

Flower. M. (2006) 'Herodotus and Persia', in C. Dewald and J. Marincola, eds., *The Cambridge Companion to Herodotus*. Cambridge, 274–89.
Fodor, I. (1982a) *In Search of a New Homeland: The Prehistory of the Hungarian People and the Conquest*, trans. H. Tarnoy. Budapest.
 (1982b) 'On Magyar–Bulgar–Turkish Contacts', in A. Rona-Tas, ed., *Chuvash Studies*. Budapest, 45–81.
Font, M. (2005) 'Missions, Conversions, and Power Legitimization in East Central Europe at the Turn of the First Millennium', in F. Curta, ed., *East Central and Eastern Europe in the Early Middle Ages*. Ann Arbor, 283–96.
Foulke, W. D. (trans.) (1907) *Paul the Deacon: History of the Lombards*. Philadelphia.
Frachetti, M. D. (2008) *Pastoralist Landscapes and Social Interaction in Bronze Age Eurasia*. Berkeley, Los Angeles and London.
Frank, A. G. (1992) *The Centrality of Central Asia* (Comparative Asian Studies 8). Amsterdam.
Frendo, J. D. (1975) *Agathias: The Histories*. Berlin and New York.
Frenkel, Y. (2005) 'The Turks of the Eurasian Steppes in Medieval Arabic Writing', in R. Amitai and M. Biran, eds., *Mongols, Turks and Others: Eurasian Nomads and the Sedentary World*. Leiden, 201–41.
Fried, M. (1975) *The Notion of Tribe*. Menlo Park, CA.
Frye, R. N. (1962) 'Some Early Iranian Titles', *Oriens* 15, 352–9.
 (1973) *The Heritage of Persia*. Cleveland and New York.
 (ed.) (1975a) *The Cambridge History of Iran*, vol. IV: *From the Arab Invasion to the Saljuks*. Cambridge.
 (1975b) *The Golden Age of Persia: The Arabs in the East*. London.
 (1984) *The History of Ancient Iran*. Munich.
 (1989) 'Central Asian Concepts of Rule on the Steppe and Sown', in G. Seaman, ed., *Ecology and Empire: Nomads in the Cultural Evolution of the Old World*. Los Angeles, 135–40.
 (1996) *The Heritage of Central Asia: From Antiquity to the Turkish Expansion*. Princeton.
Fudjita, T. (1968) *On the Name of the Rouran State and Titles of Khaganes* (Toe gakuhao 13). Kyoto.
Fukuyama, F. (1992) *The End of History and the Last Man*. London.
Fuller, J. F. C. (1954) *Decisive Battles of the Western World*. London.
Fussman, G. (1998) 'L'inscription de Rabatak et l'origine de l'ère saka', *Journal asiatique* 286, 571–651.
Gabain, A. von (1949a) 'Steppe und Staat im Leben der ältesten Türken', *Der Islam* 29 (1), 30–62.
 (1949b) Review of L. Bazin, 'Un texte proto-turc du 4e siecle', *Der Islam* 29, 244–6.
 (1979) *Einführung in die Zentralasienkunde*. Darmstadt.
Gafurov, B., Asimov, M. *et al.* (eds.) (1970) *Kushan Studies in the USSR*. Calcutta.
Galloway, P. (2006) *Practicing Ethnohistory*. Lincoln, NE.
Ganshof, F. L. (1971) *The Carolingians and the Frankish Monarchy: Studies in Carolingian History*, trans. J. Sondheimer. Ithaca, NY.

Gardiner, K. H. J. (1973) 'Standard Histories, Han to Sui', in D. Leslie, C. Mackerras and G. Wang, eds., *Essays on Sources for Chinese History*. Canberra, 42–52.

Gardiner-Garden, J. R. (1986) 'Chang-Ch'ien and Central Asian Ethnography', *Papers of Far Eastern History* (Australian National University Institute of Advanced Studies Department of Far Eastern History) 33, 23–79.

(1987a) *Greek Conceptions of Inner Asian Geography and Ethnography from Ephorus to Eratosthenes* (Papers on Inner Asia 9). Bloomington.

(1987b) *Herodotus' Contemporaries on Scythian Geography and Ethnography* (Papers on Inner Asia 10). Bloomington.

(1987c) *Ktesias on Early Central Asian History and Ethnography* (Papers on Inner Asia 6). Bloomington.

Garipzanov, I. H. (2008) 'Frontier Identities: Carolingian Frontier and the Gens Danorum', in I. H. Garipzanov, P. J. Geary and P. Urbańczyk, eds., *Franks. Northmen, and Slavs: Identities and State Formation in Early Medieval Europe*. Turnhout, 113–43.

Garipzanov, I. H., Geary, P. J., and Urbańczyk, P. (eds.) (2008). *Franks. Northmen, and Slavs: Identities and State Formation in Early Medieval Europe*. Turnhout.

(2008) 'Introduction: Gentes, Gentile Identity, and State Formation in Early Medieval Europe', in I. H. Garipzanov, P. J. Geary, and P. Urbańczyk, eds., *Franks. Northmen, and Slavs: Identities and State Formation in Early Medieval Europe*. Turnhout, 1–14.

Gärtner, H. A. and Ye, M. (2008) 'The Impact of the Empire's Crisis on Historiography and Historical Thinking in Late Antiquity', in F. Mutschler and A. Mittag, eds., *Conceiving the Empire: China and Rome Compared*. Oxford, 323–45.

Gassowski, J. (1997) 'Cult and Authority in Central Europe', in P. Urbańczyk, ed., *Origins of Central Europe*. Warsaw, 59–64.

Geary, P. J. (1988). *Before France and Germany: The Creation and Transformation of the Merovingian World*. New York and Oxford.

(1999) 'Barbarians and Ethnicity', in G. W. Bowersock, P. Brown and O. Grabar, eds., *Late Antiquity: A Guide to the Postclassical World*. Cambridge, MA and London, 107–29.

(2002) *The Myth of Nations: The Medieval Origins of Europe*. Princeton and Oxford.

Genito, B. (1992) 'Asiatic Steppe Nomad Peoples in the Carpathian Basin: A Western Backwater of the Eurasian Nomadic Movement', in G. Seaman, ed., *Foundations of Empire: Archaeology and Art of the Eurasian Steppes*. Los Angeles, 59–67.

Ghirshman, R. (1979) 'La Formation quadripartite des Tribus perses', in J. Harmatta, ed., *Prolegomena to the Sources on the History of Pre-Islamic Central Asia*. Budapest, 73–83.

Gibbon, E. (1776–89) *The History of the Decline and Fall of the Roman Empire*. London.

Giele, E. (2011) 'Evidence for the Xiongnu in Chinese Wooden Documents from the Han Period', in U. Brosseder and B. K. Miller, eds., *Xiongnu Archaeology: Multidisciplinary Perspectives of the First Steppe Empire in Inner Asia* (Bonn Contributions to to Asian Archaeology 5). Bonn, 49–75.

Giese, W. (2004) *Die Goten*. Stuttgart.
Gillett, A. (2002) 'Was Ethnicity Politicized in the Earliest Medieval Kingdoms?', in A. Gillett, ed., *On Barbarian Identity: Critical Approaches to Ethnicity in the Early Middle Ages*. Turnhout, 85–121.
  (2009) 'The Mirror of Jordanes: Concepts of the Barbarian, Then and Now', in P. Rousseau, ed., *A Companion to Late Antiquity*. Malden, MA, 392–408.
Gills, B. K. and Thompson, W. R. (2006) 'Globalizations, Global Histories and Historical Globalities', in B. K. Gills and W. R. Thompson, eds., *Globalization and Global History*. London and New York, 1–17.
Goetz, H. (2003) '*Gens*, King and Kingdoms: The Franks', in H. Goetz, J. Jarnut and W. Pohl, eds., *Regna and Gentes: The Relationship between Late Antique and Early Medieval Peoples and Kingdoms in the Transformation of the Roman World*. Leiden, 307–44.
Goetz, H., Jarnut, J., and Pohl, W. (eds.) (2003). *Regna and Gentes: The Relationship between Late Antique and Early Medieval Peoples and Kingdoms in the Transformation of the Roman World*. Leiden.
Goetz, H., Patzold, S., and Welwei, K. (eds.) (2006) *Die Germanen in der Völkerwanderung: Auszüge aus den antiken Quellen über die Germanen von Mitte des 3. Jahrhunderts bis zum Jahre 453 n. Chr.*, 2 vols. Darmstadt.
Goffart, W. (1980) *Barbarians and Romans, A.D. 418–584: The Techniques of Accommodation*. Princeton.
  (1988) *The Narrators of Barbarian History (A.D. 550–800): Jordanes, Gregory of Tours, Bede, and Paul the Deacon*. Princeton.
  (2002) 'Does the Distant Past Impinge on the Invasion Age Germans?', in A. Gillett, ed., *On Barbarian Identity: Critical Approaches to Ethnicity in the Early Middle Ages*. Turnhout, 21–37.
  (2006) *Barbarian Tides: The Migration Age and the Later Roman Empire*. Philadelphia.
Golden, P. B. (1982) 'Imperial Ideology and the Sources of Political Unity amongst the Pre-Činggisid Nomads of Western Eurasia', *Archivum Eurasiae Medii Aevi* 2, 37–76.
  (1990a) 'The Karakhanids and Early Islam', in D. Sinor, ed., *The Cambridge History of Early Inner Asia*. Cambridge, 343–70.
  (1990b) 'The Peoples of the Russian Forest belt', in D. Sinor, ed., *The Cambridge History of Early Inner Asia*. Cambridge, 229–55.
  (1990c) 'The Peoples of the South Russian Steppes', in D. Sinor, ed., *The Cambridge History of Early Inner Asia*. Cambridge, 256–84.
  (1991) 'Nomads and their Sedentary Neighbors in Pre-Činggisid Eurasia', *Archivum Eurasiae Medii Aevi* 7, 41–81.
  (1992) *An Introduction to the History of the Turkic Peoples: Ethnogenesis and State Formation in Medieval and Early Modern Eurasia and the Middle East*. Wiesbaden.
  (2000) 'Nomads of the Western Steppes: Oγurs, Onoγurs and Khazars', in H. R. Roemer, ed., *History of the Turkic Peoples in the Pre-Islamic Period* (Philologiae et Historiae Turcicae Fundamenta 1). Berlin, 282–302.

(2001a) *Ethnicity and State Formation in Pre-Činggisid Turkic Eurasia*. Bloomington.
(2001b) 'Nomads and Sedentary Societies in Medieval Eurasia', in M. Adas, ed., *Agricultural and Pastoral Societies in Ancient and Classical History*. Philadelphia, 71–115.
(2001c) 'Nomads in the Sedentary World: The Case of Pre-Činggisid Rus and Georgia', in A. M. Khazanov and A. Wink, eds., *Nomads in the Sedentary World*. Padstow, Cornwall, 24–75.
(2006a) 'The Černii Klobouci', in Á. Berta, B. Brendemoen and S. Schönig, eds., *Symbolae Turcologicae: Studies in Honour of Lars Johanson on his Sixtieth Birthday* (Swedish Research Institute in Istanbul, Transactions 16). Stockholm, 97–107.
(2006b) 'Turks and Iranians: An Historical Sketch', in L. Johanson and C. Bulut, eds., *Turkic–Iranian Contact areas: Historical and Linguistic Aspects*. Wiesbaden, 17–38.
(2006–7) 'Cumanica V: The Basmils and Qipčaqs', *Archivum Eurasiae Medii Aevi* 15, 13–42.
(2009a) 'Ethnogenesis in the Tribal Zone: The Shaping of the Türks', *Archivum Eurasiae Medii Aevi* 16, 73–112.
(2009b) 'Migration, Ethnogenesis', in N. Di Cosmo, A. J. Frank and P. B. Golden, eds., *The Cambridge History of Inner Asia: The Chinggisid Age*. Cambridge, 109–19.
(2011) *Central Asia in World History*. Oxford.
Goldsworthy, A. (2009) *The Fall of the West: The Slow Death of the Roman Superpower*. London.
Golzio, K. (1984) *Kings, Khans and Other Rulers of Early Central Asia*. Cologne.
Goody, J. (1996) *The East in the West*. Cambridge.
Gorbunova, N. G. (1992) 'Early Nomadic Pastoral Tribes in Soviet Central Asia During the First Half of the First Millennium A.D.', in G. Seaman, ed., *Foundations of Empire: Archaeology and Art of the Eurasian Steppes*. Los Angeles, 31–48.
Gordon, C. D. (1960) *The Age of Attila*. Ann Arbor.
Grant, J. (1999) 'Rethinking the Ottoman "Decline": Military Technology Diffusion in the Ottoman Empire, Fifteenth to Eighteenth Centuries', *Journal of World History* 10 (1), 179–201.
Grant, M. (1998) *From Rome to Byzantium: The Fifth Century AD*. London.
Greatrex, G. (2000) 'Roman Identity in the Sixth Century', in S. Mitchell and G. Greatrex, eds., *Ethnicity and Culture in Late Antiquity*. London, 267–92.
Greatrex, G., Phenix, R. R., and Horn, C. B. (2010) *The Chronicle of Pseudo-Zachariah Rhetor: Church and War in Late Antiquity* (Translated Texts for Historians 55). Liverpool.
Grégoire, H. (1944–5) 'L'origine et le nom des Croates et des Serbes', *Byzantion* 17, 88–118.
Grenet, F. (2002) 'Regional Interaction in Central Asia and Northwest India in the Kidarite and Hephtalite Periods', in N. Sims-Williams, ed., *Indo-Iranian Languages and Peoples*. Oxford, 203–24.

(2006 [2007]) 'Nouvelles données sur la localisation des cinq yabghus des Yuezhi: l'arrière plan politique de l'itinéraire des marchands de Maès Titianos', *Journal Asiatique* 294 (2), 325–41.
Grenet, F. and La Vassière, E. de (2005) 'L'empire kouchan: histoire, civilization, religion', *Livret-Annuaire* 19, 2003–2004 (Paris, École Pratique des Hautes Études, section des sciences historiques et philologiques), 79–81.
Grenet, F., Podushkin, A., and Sims-Williams, N. (2007) 'Les plus anciens monuments de la langue sogdienne: les inscriptions de Kultobe au Kazakhstan', *Comptes rendus de l'Academie des Inscriptions et Belles-Lettres* 151, 1005–33.
Grierson, P. (1965) 'Charlemagne and the Carolingian Achievement', in D. T. Rice, ed., *The Dark Ages*. London, 269–98.
Gringmuth-Dallmer, E. (2000) 'Settlement Territories, Settlement and Economy among the Western Slavs between the Elbe and Oder', in A. Wieczorek and H. Hinz, eds., *Europe's Centre around AD 1000*. Stuttgart, 65–8.
Grønbech, K. (1958) 'The Steppe in World History', *Acta Orientalia* 23, 53–5.
Groot, J. J. M. de (1910) *The Religious Systems of China*. Leiden.
 (1921) *Die Hunnen der vorchristlichen Zeit,* vol. 1 of *Chinesische Urkunden zur Geschichte Asiens*. Berlin and Leipzig.
Grousset, R. (1939) *L'Empire des Steppes*. Paris.
Gryaznov, M. P. (1969) *The Ancient Civilization of Southern Siberia*, trans. J. Hogarth. Geneva.
Gumilev, L. N. (1960) *Chunnu*. Moscow.
Gumilev, L. N. (1967) *Drevnie Tyurki* [Ancient Turks]. Moscow.
 (1987) *Searches for an Imaginary Kingdom*, trans. R. E. F. Smith. Cambridge.
Gupta, P. L. and Kulashreshtha, S. (1994) *Kusana Coins and History*. New Delhi.
Gyuzelev, V. (1979) *The Proto-Bulgarians*. Sofia.
Haarder, A. (1982) *The Medieval Legacy: A Symposium*. Odense.
Haase, B. S. (1991) *Ennodius' Panegyric to Theodoric the Great: A Translation and Commentary*. Ottawa.
Haberl, J. and Hawkes, C. (1973) 'The Last of Roman Noricum: St. Severin on the Danube', in C. Hawkes and S. Hawkes, eds., *Greeks, Celts, Romans*. London, 97–156.
Hachmann, R. (1971) *The Germanic Peoples*. London.
Haig, G. I. J. (2008) *Alignment Change in Iranian Languages: A Construction Grammar Approach*. Berlin and New York.
Halasi-Kun (1943), 'A magyarság kaukázusi története'[The History of the Hungarians in the Caucasus] in L. Ligeti (ed.), *A magyarság östörténete* [Hungarian Prehistory]. Budapest, 71–99.
Haldon, J. (1999) 'The Byzantine World', in K. Raaflaub and N. Rosenstein, eds., *War and Society in the Ancient and Medieval Worlds*. Cambridge, MA, 241–70.
Hall, T. D. (1991) 'Civilizational Change and Role of Nomads', *Comparative Civilizations Review* 24, 34–57.
Hallock, R. T. (1969) *Persepolis Fortification Tablets*. Chicago.
Halm, C. (ed.) (1877) *Salvian, De gubernatione Dei* (Monumenta Germaniae Historica, Auctores Antiquissimi 1). Berlin.

Halphen, L. (1965) 'The Barbarian Background', in S. A. Cook, F. E. Adcock, M. P. Charlesworth and N. H. Baynes, eds., *The Cambridge Ancient History*, vol. XII: *The Imperial Crisis and Recovery* A.D. *193–324*. Cambridge, 96–108.

Halsall, G. (2001) 'Childeric's Grave, Clovis' Succession, and the Origins of the Merovingian Kingdom', in R. W. Mathisen and D. Shanzer, eds., *Society and Culture in Late Roman Gaul*. Aldershot, 116–33.

(2007) *Barbarian Migrations and the Roman West, 376–568*. Cambridge.

Hambis, L. (1958) 'Le Problème des Huns', *Recherches historiques* 220, 249–70.

(1977) *L'Asie Centrale: Histoire et Civilisation*. Paris.

Hamilton, F. J. and Brooks, E. W. (trans.) (1899) *The Syriac Chronicle: Known as that of Zachariah of Mitylene*. London.

Hamilton, J. (1962) 'Toquz-oγuz et On-uyγur', *Journal Asiatique* 250, 23–63.

Hammond, N. G. L. and Griffith, G. T. (1979) *A History of Macedonia 550–336 B.C.*, vol. II. Oxford.

Harhoiu, R. (1980) 'Das Norddonauländische Gebiet im 5. Jahrhundert und seine Beziehungen zum spätrömischen Kaiserreich', in H. Wolfram and F. Daim, eds., *Die Völker an der mittleren und unteren Donau im fünften und sechsten Jahrhundert*. Vienna, 101–15.

Harmatta, J. (1970) *Studies in the History and Language of the Sarmatians*. Szeged.

(1979) *Prolegomena to the Sources on the History of Pre-Islamic Central Asia*. Budapest.

(1994a) 'Conclusion', in J. Harmatta, ed., *History of Civilizations of Central Asia*, vol. II: *The Development of Sedentary and Nomadic Civilizations*. Paris, 485–92.

(1994b) *History of Civilizations of Central Asia*, vol. II: *The Development of Sedentary and Nomadic Civilizations*. Paris.

Harmatta, J. and Yilmaz, G. (1988) *De la question concernant la langue des Avars: inscriptions runiques Turques en Europe orientale*. Ankara.

Harries, J. (2000) 'Legal Culture and Identity in the Fifth-century West', in S. Mitchell and G. Greatrex, eds., *Ethnicity and Culture in Late Antiquity*. London, 45–57.

Harris, W. V. (2005) *Rethinking the Mediterranean*. Oxford.

Harrison, T. (2000) *The Emptiness of Asia*. London.

Hartog, F. (1988) *The Mirror of Herodotus: The Representation of the Other in the Writing of History*, , trans. J. Lloyd. Berkeley and London.

Hauptmann, L. (1935) 'Kroaten, Goten und Sarmaten', *Germanoslavica* 3, 95–127, 315–53.

Häusler, A. (1983) 'Die Zeit der Völkerwanderung und ihre Bedeutung für die Geschichte Europas', in B. Krüger, ed., *Die Germanen: Geschichte und Kultur der germanischen Stämme in Mitteleuropa*, vol. II. Berlin, 647–59.

Haussig, H. W. (1953) 'Theophylakt's Exkurs über die skythischen Völker', *Byzantion* 23, 275–462.

(1956) 'Die Quellen über die zentralasiatische Herkunft der europäischen Awaren', *Central Asiatic Journal* 2, 21–43.

(1983) *Die Geschichte Zentralasiens und der Seidenstrasse in vorislamischer Zeit*. Darmstadt.

(2000) 'Herkunft, Wesen und Schicksal der Hunnen', in H. R. Roemer, ed., *History of the Turkic Peoples in the Pre-Islamic Period* (Philologiae et Historiae Turcicae Fundamenta 1). Berlin, 256–81.
Hayashi T. (1990) 'The Development of a Nomadic Empire: The Case of the Ancient Türks (Tujue)', *Bulletin of the Ancient Orient Museum* 11, 164–84.
Heather, P. (1988) 'Cassiodorus and the Rise of the Amals: Genealogy and the Goths under Hun Domination', *Journal of Roman Studies* 78, 103–28.
(1991) *Goths and Romans 332–489*. Oxford.
(1995a) 'The Huns and the End of the Roman Empire in Western Europe', *English Historical Review* 110, 4–41.
(1995b) 'Theodoric, King of the Goths', *Early Medieval Europe* 4 (2), 145–73.
(1996) *The Goths*. Oxford.
(2000) 'State, Lordship and Community in the West (c. A.D. 400–600)', in A. Cameron, B. Ward-Perkins and M. Whitby, eds., *The Cambridge Ancient History*, vol. XIV: *Late Antiquity: Empire and Successors, A.D. 425–600*. Cambridge, 437–68.
(2001) 'The Late Roman Art of Client Management: Imperial Defence in the Fourth Century West', in W. Pohl, I. Wood and H. Reimitz, eds., *The Transformation of Frontiers: From Late Antiquity to the Carolingians*. Leiden, 15–68.
(2003) '*Gens* and *Regnum* among the Ostrogoths', in H. Goetz, J. Jarnut and W. Pohl, eds., *Regna and Gentes: The Relationship between Late Antique and Early Medieval Peoples and Kingdoms in the Transformation of the Roman World*. Leiden, 85–133.
(2006) *The Fall of the Roman Empire: A New History of Rome and the Barbarians*. Oxford and New York.
(2007) 'Goths in the Roman Balkans c. 350–500', in A. G. Poulter, ed., *The Transition to Late Antiquity on the Danube and Beyond*. Oxford, 163–90.
(2008) 'Ethnicity, Group Identity, and Social Status in the Migration Period', in I. H. Garipzanov, P. J. Geary and P. Urbańczyk, eds., *Franks. Northmen, and Slavs: Identities and State Formation in Early Medieval Europe*. Turnhout, 17–49.
(2009) *Empire and Barbarians: The Fall of Rome and the Birth of Europe*. Oxford.
Heather, P. and Matthews, J. (1991) *The Goths in the Fourth Century*. Liverpool.
Hedeager, L. (1987) 'Empire, Frontier and the Barbarian Hinterland: Rome and Northern Europe from AD 1–400', in M. Rowlands, M. Larsen and K. Kristiansen, eds., *Centre and Periphery in the Ancient World*. Cambridge, 125–40.
(1992) *Iron-Age Societies: From Tribe to State in Northern Europe, 500 BC to AD 700*, trans. J. Hines. Oxford and Cambridge, MA.
Heinzelmann, M. (1996) 'Gregor von Tours: die ideologische Grundlegung fränkischer Königsherrschaft', in Reiss-Museum Mannheim, *Die Franken Wegbereiter Europas Vor 1500 Jahren: König Chlodwig und seine Erben*, vol. 1. Mainz, 381–88.
Helms, S. (1998) 'Ancient Chorasmia: The Northern Edge of Central Asia from the 6th Century B.C. to the mid-4th Century A.D.', in D. Christian and

C. Benjamin, eds., *Worlds of the Silk Roads: Ancient and Modern* (Silk Road Studies 2), 77–96.
Hen, Y. (2007) *Roman Barbarians: The Royal Court and Culture in the Early Medieval West*. Basingbroke.
Henkelman, W. and Kuhrt, A. (eds.) (2003) *A Persian Perspective: Essays in Memory of Heleen Sancisi-Weerdenburg* (Achaemenid History 13). Leiden.
Henning, W. B. (1948) 'The Date of the Sogdian Letters', *Bulletin of the School of Oriental and African Studies* 12, 601–45.
Herrenschmidt, C. (1989), 'Le tribut dans les inscriptions en vieux-Perse et dans les Tablettes Élamites', in P. Briant and C. Herrenschmidt, eds., *Le Tribut dans L'Empire Perse*. Paris, 107–20.
Hildinger, E. (1997) *Warriors of the Steppe: A Military History of Central Asia 500 B.C. to 1700 A.D.* Cambridge, MA.
Hill, J. E, (2004) *The Peoples of the West from the Weilüe by Yu Huan: A Third Century Chinese Account Composed between 239–265 CE, quoted in zhuan 30 of the Sanguozhi. Published in 429 CE*. Draft English translation: http://depts.washington.edu/silkroad/texts/weilue/weilue.html.
  (2009) *Through the Jade Gate to Rome: A Study of the Silk Routes during the Later Han Dynasty 1st to 2nd Centuries CE, An Annotated translation of the Chronicle on the 'Western Regions' from the Hou Hanshu*. Lexington, KY.
Hinge, G. (2003) 'Scythian and Spartan Analogies in Herodotus' representation: Rites of Initiation and Kinship Groups', in P. G. Bilde, J. M Højte and V. F. Stolba, eds., *The Cauldron of Ariantas: Studies Presented to A. N. Sceglov on the Occasion of his 70th birthday*. Aarhus, 62–8.
Hinsch, B. (2004) 'Myth and the Construction of Foreign Ethnic Identity in Early and Medieval China (Xiongnu, Xianbei and Koreans in China)', *Asian Ethnicity* 5 (1), 81–103.
Hirth, F. (1901) 'Hunnenforschungen' *Keleti Szemle* 2, 81–91.
  (1909) 'Mr. Kingsmill and the Hsiung-nu', *The Journal of the American Oriental Society* 30, 32–45.
Hitch, D. A. (1988) 'Kushan Tarim Domination', *Central Asiatic Journal* 32 (3–4), 170–93.
Hodgkin, T. (1895, reprint 2002) *The Barbarian Invasions of the Roman Empire:* vol. v.: *The Lombard Invasion 553–600*. London.
Hodgson, M. G. S. (1993) *Rethinking World History: Essays on Europe, Islam, and World History*. Cambridge.
Hohlfelder, R. L. (1984) 'Marcian's Gamble: A Reassessment of Eastern Imperial Policy towards Attila AD 450–3, *American Journal of Ancient History* 9, 54–69.
Hollister, C. W. (1966) 'Twilight in the West', in L. White, ed., *The Transformation of the Roman World*. Berkeley and Los Angeles, 179–205.
Holmes, R. and Evans, M. (2006) *Battlefield: Decisive Conflicts in History*. Oxford.
Holmgren, J. (1982) *Annals of Tai: Early T'o-pa History According to the First Chapter of the Wei-shu*. Canberrra.
  (1986) 'Yeh-lü, Yao-Lien and Ta-ho: Views of the Hereditary Prerogative in Early Khitan Leadership', *Papers on Far Eastern History* 34, 37–81.

Holotová-Szinek, J. (2005) 'Les Relations entre l'empire des Han et les Xiongnu: vestiges archéologiques et textes historiques', *Etudes Chinoises* 24, 221–31.
  (2011) 'Preliminary Research on the Spatial Organization of the Xiongnu Territories in Mongolia', in U. Brosseder and B. K. Miller, eds., *Xiongnu Archaeology: Multidisciplinary Perspectives of the First Steppe Empire in Inner Asia* (Bonn Contributions to to Asian Archaeology 5). Bonn, 425–40.
Honey, D. B. (1990) *The Rise of the Medieval Hsiung-nu: The Biography of Liu-Yüan* (Papers on Inner Asia 15). Bloomington.
  (1999) 'The *Han-shu*, Manuscript Evidence and the Textual Criticism of the *Shih-chi*: The Case of the "Hsiung-nu *lieh-chuan*"', *Chinese Literature: Esssays, Articles, Reviews* 21, 67–97.
Honeychurch, W. and Amartuvshin, C. (2006a) 'States on Horseback: The Rise of Inner Asian Confederations and Empires', in M. T. Stark, ed., *Archaeology of Asia*. Malden MA and Oxford, 255–78.
  (2006b) 'Survey and Settlement in Northern Mongolia: The Structures of Intraregional Nomadic Organisation', in D. L. Peterson, L. M. Popova and A. T. Smith, eds., *Beyond the Steppe and the Sown*. Leiden, 183–201.
Hookham, H. (1962) *Tamburlaine the Conqueror*. London.
Hoops, J. (1968) *Reallexikon der germanischen Altertumskunde*. Berlin.
Hopwood, K. (1999) 'Ammianus Marcellinus on Isauria', in J. W. Drijvers and D. Hunt, eds., *The Late Roman World and its Historian: Interpreting Ammianus Marcellinus*. London and New York, 224–35.
Howarth, P. (1994) *Attila, King of the Huns: The Man and the Myth*. London.
Howorth, H. H. (1876–1927) *History of the Mongols from the 9th to the 19th century*, 4 vols. London.
Hsu, C. Y. and Linduff, K. M. (1988) *Western Chou Civilization*. New Haven and London.
Hulsewé, A. F. P. and Loewe, M. A. N. (1979) *China in Central Asia: The Early Stage 125 BC–AD 23: An Annotated Translation of Chapters 61 and 96 of the History of the Former Han Dynasty*. Leiden.
Humbach, H. (1966–7) *Baktrische Sprachdenkmäler* 1. Wiesbaden.
  (1969) 'Die historische Bedeutsamkeit der alanischen Namen', *Studia Classica et Orientalia Antonino Pagliaro Oblata* 3, 33–52.
Hummer, H. J. (1998a) 'The Fluidity of Barbarian Identity: The Ethnogenesis of Alemanni and Suebi, A.D. 200–500', *Early Medieval Europe* 7, 1–27.
  (1998b) 'Franks and Alamanni: A discontinuous Ethnogenesis', in I. Wood, ed., *Franks and Alamanni in the Merovingian Period: An Ethnographic Perspective*. Woodbridge, 9–32.
Humphrey, C. (1979) 'The Uses of Genealogy: A Historical Study of the Nomadic and Sedentarized Buryat', in Équipe écologie et anthropologie des sociétés pastorals (ed.), *Pastoral Production and Society/Production pastorale et société: Proceedings of the International Meeting on Nomadic Pastoralism, Paris 1–3 Dec. 1976*. Cambridge, 235–60.

(1994) 'Shamanic Practices and the States in Northern Asia: Views from the Center and Periphery', in N. Thomas and C. Humphrey, *Shamanism, History and the State*. Ann Arbor, 191–228.
Humphries, M. (2000) 'Italy, A.D. 425–605', in A. Cameron, B. Ward-Perkins and M. Whitby, eds., *The Cambridge Ancient History*, vol. XIV: *Late Antiquity: Empire and Successors, A.D. 425–600*. Cambridge, 525–51.
Hung, C. (1981) 'China and the Nomads: Misconceptions in Western Historiography on Inner Asia', *Harvard Journal of Asiatic Studies* 41, 597–628.
Hutton, M. and Warmington, E. H. (eds. and trans.) (1970) *Tacitus, Germania* (Loeb Classical Library). Cambridge, MA.
Invernizzi, A. (ed.) (1995) *In the Land of the Gryphons: Papers on Central Asian Archaeology in Antiquity*. Florence.
  (2007) 'The Culture of Parthian Nisa between Steppe and Empire', in J. Cribb and G. Herrmann, eds., *After Alexander: Central Asia before Islam*. Oxford, 163–77.
Irons, W. (1979) 'Political Stratification among Pastoral Nomads' in Équipe écologie et anthropologie des sociétés pastorals (ed.), *Pastoral Production and Society/Production pastorale et société: Proceedings of the International Meeting on Nomadic Pastoralism, Paris 1–3 Dec. 1976*. Cambridge, 361–74.
  (2003) 'Cultural Capital, Livestock Raiding, and the Military Advantage of Traditional Pastoralists', in N. N. Kradin, D. Bondarenko and T. Barfield, eds., *Nomadic Pathways in Social Evolution*. Moscow, 63–72.
Isaac, B. (1990) *The Limits of Empire: The Roman Army in the East*. Oxford.
Ishjamts, N. (1994) 'Nomads in Eastern Central Asia, in J. Harmatta, ed., *History of Civilizations of Central Asia*, vol. II. Paris, 151–69.
Ivantchik, A. I. (1999a) 'Une légende sur l'origine des Scythes (Hdt. IV, 5–7) et le problème des sources du «scythicos logos» d'Hérodote', *Revue des études grecques* 112 (1), 141–92.
  (1999b) 'The Scythian 'Rule over Asia': The Classical Tradition and Historical Reality', in G. Tsetskhladze, ed., *Ancient Greeks West and East*. Leiden, 497–520.
  (2001) *Kimmerier und Skythen: kulturhistorische und chronologische Probleme der Archäologie der osteuropäischen Steppen und Kaukasiens in vor- und frühskythischer Zeit* (Steppenvölker Eurasiens 2). Moscow.
Iwamura, S. (1962) 'Nomads and Farmers in Central Asia', *Acta Asiatica* 3, 44–56.
Jackson, P. and Lockhart, L. (eds.) (1986) *The Cambridge History of Iran*, vol. VI: *The Timurid and Safavid Periods*. Cambridge.
Jacobson, E. (1987) *Burial Ritual, Gender and Status in South Siberia in the Late Bronze–Early Iron Age* (Papers on Inner Asia 7). Bloomington.
Jagchid, S. (1977) 'Patterns of Trade and Conflict between China and the Nomadic Peoples of Mongolia', *Zentralasiatische Studien* 11, 177–204.
Jagchid, S. and Symons, V. J. (1989) *Peace, War and Trade along the Great Wall: Nomadic–Chinese Interaction through Two Millennia*. Bloomington and Indianapolis.
Jairazbhoy, R. A. (1963) *Foreign Influence on Ancient India*. Bombay.

James, E. (1980) *Visigothic Spain*. Oxford.
  (1988) *The Franks*. Oxford.
Janhunen, J. (1996) *Manchuria: An Ethnic History*. Helsinki.
Jarnut, J. (1990) 'Die langobardische Ethnogenese', in H. Wolfram and W. Pohl, eds., *Typen der Ethnogenese unter besonderer Berücksichtigung der Bayern*, vol. I. Vienna, 97–102.
  (2003) '*Gens, Rex* and *Regnum* of the Lombards', in H. Goetz, J. Jarnut and W. Pohl, eds., *Regna and Gentes: The Relationship between Late Antique and Early Medieval Peoples and Kingdoms in the Transformation of the Roman World*. Leiden, 409–27.
Jeffreys, E., Jeffreys, M., and Scott, R. (trans.) (1986) *The Chronicle of John Malalas* (Australian Association for Byzantine Studies, Byzantina Australiensia). Melbourne.
Jenkins, R. J. H. (ed.) (1962) *Constantine Porphyrogenitus, De Administrando Imperio*, vol. II: *Commentary*. London.
Jettmar. K. (1951) 'The Altai before the Turks', *Museum of Far Eastern Antiquities, Stockholm, Bulletin* 23, 135–223.
  (1966) 'Mittelasien und Sibirien in vortükischer Zeit', in B. Spuler, ed., *Handbuch der Orientalistik*, part I, vol. V: *Geschichte Mittelasiens*. Leiden, 1–105.
Johanson, L. (2006) 'Historical, Cultural and Linguistic aspects of Turkic–Iranian Contiguity', in L. Johanson, and C. Bulut, eds., *Turkic–Iranian Contact Areas: Historical and Linguistic Aspects*. Wiesbaden, 1–14.
Johanson, L. and Bulut, C. (2006) *Turkic–Iranian Contact Areas: Historical and Linguistic Aspects*. Wiesbaden.
Johanson, L. and Csató, E. A. (1998) *The Turkic Languages*. London.
Jones, A. H. M. (1964) *The Later Roman Empire 284–602*, vols., I, II and III. Oxford.
Jones, S. (1997) *The Archaeology of Ethnicity*. London and New York.
Jung, B. J. (trans.) (1994) *Sima Qian: Shiji with Commentaries*, 7 vols. Seoul.
Jung, S. I. (2001a) *Silkroadhak* [Study of the Silk Road]. Seoul.
  (2001b) *Godeh Munmyung Gyoryusa* [The History of Cultural Exchange in the Ancient World]. Seoul.
Kagan, D. (ed.) (1978) *The End of the Roman Empire: Decline or Transformation*, 2nd edn. Lexington, MA.
Kaiser, R. (1993) *Das römische Erbe und das Merowingerreich*. Munich.
Kappeler, A. (1976) 'L'ethnogénèse de peoples de la Moyenne-Volga (Tatars, Tchouvaches, Mordves, Maris, Oudmourtes) dans les recherches soviètiques', *Cahiers du Monde Russe et Soviètique* 17, 311–34.
Kaufman, S. J., Little, R., and Wohlforth, W. C. (2007) *The Balance of Power in World History*. Basingstoke and New York.
Kazanski, M. (1991) *Les Goths (Ier–VIIe siècles ap. J.-C.)*. Paris.
  (1993) 'The Sedentary Elite in the "Empire" of the Huns and its Impact on Material Civilization in Southern Russia during the Early Middle Ages (5th–7th Centuries AD)', in J. Chapman and P. Dolukhanov, eds., *Cultural Transformations and Interactions in Eastern Europe*. Aldershot, 211–35.

Kazanski, M. and Legoux, R. (1988) 'Contribution a l'étude des témoignages archéologiques des Goths en Europe Orientale à l'époque des Grandes Migrations: la chronologie de la Culture Černjahov récente', *Archéologie Médiévale* 18, 55–71.

Kelley, D. R. (1993) '*Tacitus Noster*: The *Germania* in the Renaissance and Reformation', in T. J. Luce and A. J. Woodman, eds., *Tacitus and the Tacitean Tradition*. Princeton, 152–67.

Kelly, C. (2004) *Ruling the Later Roman Empire*. Cambridge MA and London.

(2009) *Attila the Hun: Barbarian Terror and the Fall of the Roman Empire*. London.

Kelly, G. (2008) *Ammianus Marcellinus, the Allusive Historian*. Cambridge.

Kent, R. G. (1950) *Old Persian: Grammar, Texts, Lexicon*. New Haven.

Kessler, A. T. (1994) *Empires byond the Great Wall: The Heritage of Genghis Khan*. Los Angeles.

Kettenhofen, E. (1998) 'Die Arsakiden in den armenischen Quellen', in J. Wiesehöfer, ed., *Das Partherreich und seine Zeugnisse*. Stuttgart, 325–53.

Keydall, R. (ed.) (1967) *Agathiae Myrinaei historiarum libri quinque*. Berlin.

Khazanov, A. M. (1978) 'The Early State among the Scythians', in H. J. M. Claessen and P. Skalnik, eds., *The Early State*. The Hague, 425–40.

(1981) 'The Early State among the Eurasian Nomads', in H. J. M. Claessen and P. Skalnik, eds., *The Study of the State*. The Hague, 155–76.

(1982) 'The Dawn of Scythian History', *Iranica Antiqua* 17, 49–63.

(1984) *Nomads and the Outside World*. Cambridge.

(2001) 'Nomads in the History of the Sedentary World', in A. M. Khazanov and A. Wink, eds., *Nomads in the Sedentary World*. Padstow, Cornwall, 1–23.

(2003) 'Nomads of the Eurasian Steppes in Historical Perspective', in N. N. Kradin, D. Bondarenko and T. Barfield, eds., *Nomadic Pathways in Social Evolution*. Moscow, 25–49.

Khazanov, A. M. and Wink, A. (eds.) (2001) *Nomads in the Sedentary World*. Padstow, Cornwall.

Khudyakov, Y. S. (1997) 'Problems of the Genesis of Culture of the Hunnic Period in the Altai Mountains', *Ancient Civilizations from Scythia to Siberia* 3 (2–3), 329–46.

Kim, H. J. (2009) *Ethnicity and Foreigners in Ancient Greece and China*. London.

(2010) 'Herodotus' Scythians Viewed from a Central Asian Perspective: Its Historicity and Significance', *Ancient West and East* 9, 115–34.

King, C. (1987) 'The veracity of Ammianus Marcellinus' description of the Huns', *American Journal of Ancient History* 12, 1, 77–95.

Klausner, C. L. (1973) *The Seljuk Vizierate: A Study of Civil Administration*. Cambridge, MA.

Koga, N. (1990) 'A Brief History of Ch'in and Han Studies in Japan', *Acta Asiatica* 58, 90–119.

Kohl, P. L. (1981) *The Bronze Age Civilization of Central Asia: Recent Soviet Discoveries*. Armonk, NY.

Kollautz, A. and Miyakawa, H. (1970) *Geschichte und Kultur eines völkerwanderungszeitlichen Nomadenvolks: die Rouran der Mongolei und die Awaren in Mitteleuropa*, 2 vols. Klagenfurt.

König, E. and van der Auwera, J. (1994) *The Germanic Languages*. London.
König, I. (1997) *Aus der Zeit Theoderichs des Grossen: Einleitung, Text, Übersetzung und Kommentar einer anonymen Quelle*. Darmstadt.
Kononov, A. N. (1977) 'Terminology of the Definition of Cardinal Points at the Turkic Peoples', *Acta Orientalia Academiae Scientiarum Hung* 31 (1), 61–76.
Konov, S. (1912) 'Goths in Ancient India', *The Journal of the Royal Asiatic Society of Great Britain and Ireland* 44 (new series), 379–85.
Köprülü, M. F. (1992) *The Origins of the Ottoman Empire*, trans. G. Leiser. Albany, NY.
Koshelenko, G. A. and Pilipko, V. N. (1994) 'Parthia', in J. Harmatta, ed., *History of Civilizations of Central Asia, vol.* II. Paris, 131–50.
Krader, L. (1958) 'Feudalism and the Tatar Polity of the Middle Ages', *Comparative Studies in Society and History* 1, 76–99.
  (1963) *Social Organization of the Mongol-Turkic Pastoral Nomads*. The Hague.
  (1968) *Formation of the State*. Englewood Cliffs, N.J.
  (1978) 'The Origin of the State among the Nomads of Asia' in J. M. Claessen and P. Skalnik, eds., *The Early State*. The Hague, 93–108.
  (1979) 'The Origin of the State among the Nomads of Asia', in Équipe écologie et anthropologie des sociétés pastorals (ed.), *Pastoral Production and Society/ Production pastorale et société: Proceedings of the International Meeting on Nomadic Pastoralism, Paris 1–3 Dec. 1976*. Cambridge, 221–34.
Kradin, N. N. (1992) *Kochevye obshchestva*. Vladivostok.
  (1995) 'The Origins of the State among the Pastoral Nomads', in D. Schorkowitz, ed., *Ethnologische Wege und Lehrjahre eines Philosophen: Festschrift für Lawrence Krader zum 75. Geburstag*. Frankfurt am Main, 163–77.
  (2000) 'Nomadic Empires in Evolutionary Perspective', in N. N. Kradin, A. V. Korotayev, et al., eds., *Alternatives of Social Evolution*. Vladivostok, 274–88.
  (2002) 'Nomadism, Evolution, and World-Systems: Pastoral Societies in Theories of Historical Development', *Journal of World-System Research* 8, 368–88.
  (2003) 'Nomadic Empires: Origins, Rise, Decline', in N. N. Kradin, D. Bondarenko and T. Barfield, eds., *Nomadic Pathways in Social Evolution*. Moscow, 73–87.
  (2005) 'From Tribal Confederation to Empire: The Evolution of the Rouran Society', *Acta Orientalia Academiae Scientiarum Hungaricae* 58 (2), 149–69.
  (2011) 'Stateless Empire: The Structure of the Xiongnu Nomadic Super-Complex Chiefdom', in U. Brosseder and B. K. Miller, eds., *Xiongnu Archaeology: Multidisciplinary Perspectives of the First Steppe Empire in Inner Asia* (Bonn Contributions to to Asian Archaeology 5). Bonn, 77–96.
Kradin, N. N., Bondarenko, D. and Barfield, T. (2003) *Nomadic Pathways in Social Evolution*. Moscow.
Krautschick, S. (1986) 'Zwei Aspekte des Jahres 476', *Historia* 35, 344–71.
Kristó, G. (2000) 'The Arpads and the Hungarians', in A. Wieczorek and H. Hinz, eds., *Europe's Centre around AD 1000*. Stuttgart, 370–2.
Krüger, B. (ed) (1978, 1983) *Die Germanen: Geschichte und Kultur der germanischen Stämme in Mitteleuropa*, 2 vols. Berlin.

Krusch, B. (ed.) (1888) *Fredegarii et aliorum chronica: vitae sanctorum* (Monumenta Germaniae Historica, Scriptores Rerum Merovingicarum 2). Berlin.

Krusch, B. and Levison, W. (eds.) (1951) *Gregory of Tours, Historiae* (Monumenta Germaniae Historica, Scriptores Rerum Merovingicarum 1.1). Berlin.

  (eds.) (1885) *Gregory of Tours, Decem Libri Historiarum* (Monumenta Germaniae Historica, Scriptores Rerum Merovingicarum 1.2). Berlin.

Kuhrt, A. (1998) 'Concluding Remarks', in J. Wiesehöfer, ed., *Das Partherreich und seine Zeugnisse: The Arsacid Empire: Sources and Documentation* (Historia Einzelschriften 122). Stuttgart, 529–34.

Kulikowski, M. (2007) *Rome's Gothic Wars: From the Third Century to Alaric*. Cambridge.

Kürsat-Ahlers, E. (1994) *Zur frühen Staatenbildung von Steppenvölkern*. Berlin.

  (1996) 'The Role and Contents of Ideology in the early Nomadic Empires', in H. J. M. Claessen and J. C. Oosten, eds., *Ideology and the Formation of Early States*. Leiden, 136–52.

Kwanten, L. (1979) *Imperial Nomads: A History of Central Asia 500–1500*. Philadelphia.

Kychanov, E. I. (1997) *Kochevye gosudarstva ot gunnov do man' chzhurov* [Nomadic State from Hun to Manchu]. Moscow.

  (2001) 'Nomads in the Tangut State of His-Hsia (982–1227 AD)', in A. M. Khazanov and A. Wink, eds., *Nomads in the Sedentary World*. Padstow, Cornwall, 191–210.

Kyzlasov, L. R. (1996) 'Northern Nomads' in B. A. Litvinsky, ed., *History of Civilizations of Central Asia*, vol. III. Paris, 315–25.

Lamberg-Karlovsky, C. C. (1994) 'The Oxus Civilization: The Bronze Age of Central Asia' *Antiquity* 68, 353–4.

  (1994) 'The Bronze Age *Khanates* of Central Asia', *Antiquity* 68, 398–405.

Lambert, D. (2000) 'The Barbarians in Salvian's *De Gubernatione Dei*', in S. Mitchell and G. Greatrex, eds., *Ethnicity and Culture in Late Antiquity*. London, 103–15.

Lambton, A. K. S. (1986) 'Mongol Fiscal Administration in Persia', *Studia Islamica* 64, 79–99.

  (1968) 'The Internal Structure of the Saljuq Empire', in *The Cambridge History of Iran*, vol. v: *The Saljuk and Mongol Periods*, Cambridge 203–82.

Lanfranchi, G. B., Roaf, M., and Rollinger, R. (2003) *Continuity of Empire (?): Assyria, Media, Persia*. Padova.

Lasko, P. (1965) 'The Frankish kingdom from the Merovingians to Pepin', in D. T. Rice, ed., *The Dark Ages*. London, 197–218.

Lattimore, O. (1940) *Inner Asian Frontiers of China*. New York and London.

  (1962) *Inner Asian Frontiers of China*. Boston.

  (1979) 'Herdsmen, Farmers, Urban Culture', in Équipe écologie et anthropologie des sociétés pastorals (ed.), *Pastoral Production and Society/Production pastorale et société: Proceedings of the International Meeting on Nomadic Pastoralism, Paris 1–3 Dec. 1976*. Cambridge, 479–90.

La Vaissière, E. de (2002) *Histoire des marchands sogdiens*. Paris.

(2005) 'Huns et Xiongnu', *Central Asiatic Journal* 49, 3–26.
La Vaissière, E. de (2007) 'Is There a "Nationality" of the Hephtalites?', in M. Ghose, É. de la Vaissière, *Hephtalites, Bulletin of the Asia institute* 17, 119–32.
Lebecq, S. (2006) 'The Two Faces of King Childeric: History, Archaeology, Historiography', in T. F. X. Noble, ed., *From Roman Provinces to Medieval Kingdoms*. New York and Abingdon, 327–44.
Lee, A. D. (2000) 'The Eastern Empire: Theodosius to Anastasius', in A. Cameron, B. Ward-Perkins and M. Whitby, eds., *The Cambridge Ancient History*, vol. XIV: *Late Antiquity: Empire and Successors, A.D. 425–600*. Cambridge, 33–62.
Lee, C. and Zhang, L. (2011) 'Xiongnu Population History in Relation to China, Manchuria, and the Western Regions', in U. Brosseder and B. K. Miller, eds., *Xiongnu Archaeology: Multidisciplinary Perspectives of the First Steppe Empire in Inner Asia* (Bonn Contributions to to Asian Archaeology 5). Bonn, 193–200.
Legrand, J. (1979) 'Conceptions de l'espace, division territoriale et divisions politiques chez les Mongols de l'époque post-impériale (xiv–xvii siecles)', in Équipe écologie et anthropologie des sociétés pastorals (ed.), *Pastoral Production and Society/Production pastorale et société: Proceedings of the International Meeting on Nomadic Pastoralism, Paris 1–3 Dec. 1976*. Cambridge, 155–170.
Lehmann, W. P. (1986) *A Gothic Etymological Dictionary*. Leiden.
Lendon, J. E. (2005) *Soldiers and Ghosts: A History of Battle in Classical Antiquity*. New Haven.
Lenski, N. (2002) *Failure of Empire: Valens and the Roman State in the Fourth Century A.D.* Berkeley, Los Angeles and London.
Leppin, H. (2003) 'The Church Historians (I): Socrates, Sozomenus and Theodoretus, in G. Marasco, ed., *Greek and Roman Historiography in Late Antiquity: Fourth to Sixth Century A.D.* Leiden, 219–54.
Lerner, J. D. (1999) 'The Impact of Seleucid Decline on the Eastern Iranian Plateau: The Foundations of Arsacid Parthia and Graeco-Bactria', *Historia Einzelschriften* 123, 1–139.
Lerouge, C. (2007) *L'image des Parthes dans le monde gréco-romain: du début du 1er siècle av. J.-C. jusqu'à la fin du Haut-Empire romain* (Oriens et Occidens 17). Stuttgart.
Leslie, D. D., Mackerras, C., and Wang, G. (eds.) (1973) *Essays on the Sources for Chinese History*. Canberra.
Leube, A. (1978) 'Die Gesellschaft, Entwicklung und Strukturen', in B. Krüger, ed., *Die Germanen: Geschichte und Kultur der germanischen Stämme in Mitteleuropa*, vol. I. Berlin, 508–28.
Lewis, C. M. (2000) 'Gallic Identity and the Gallic Civitas from Caesar to Gregory of Tours', in S. Mitchell and G. Greatrex, eds., *Ethnicity and Culture in Late Antiquity*. London, 69–81.
Lewis, G. (1982) *The Book of Dede Korkut*. Singapore.
Lewis. M. (2009) *China between Empires: The Northern and Southern Dynasties*. Cambridge.

Li, Jihe (2003) 'A Research on Migration of Northwestern Minorities Between Pre-Qin to Sui and Tang'. Beijing.
Li, Rongxi (1996) *The Great Tang Dynasty Record of the Western Regions*. Berkeley.
Li, X. (1985) *Eastern Zhou and Qin civilizations*, trans. K. C. Chang. New Haven and London.
Li, Yanshou (1958) *Pei Shi*. Beijing.
Liebeschuetz, J. H. W. G. (1990) *Barbarians and Bishops: Army, Church, and State in the Age of Arcadius and Chrysostom*. Oxford.
  (2000) 'Administration and Politics in the Cities of the Fifth to the Mid-Seventh Century: 425–640', in A. Cameron, B. Ward-Perkins and M. Whitby, eds., *The Cambridge Ancient History*, vol. XIV: *Late Antiquity: Empire and Successors, A.D. 425–600*, 207–37.
  (2007) 'The Lower Danube Region under Pressure: from Valens to Heraclius', in A. G. Poulter, ed., *The Transition to Late Antiquity on the Danube and Beyond*. Oxford, 101–34.
Lindner, R. (1981) 'Nomadism, Horses and Huns', *Past and Present* 92, 3–19.
  (1982) 'What was a Nomadic Tribe', *Comparative Studies in Society and History* 24 (4), 689–711.
  (1983) *Nomads and Ottomans in Medieval Anatolia*. Bloomington.
Lindsay, W. M. (ed.) (1911) *Isidore, Etymologiarum Sive Originum Libri* XX (Oxford Classical Texts). Oxford.
Linduff, K. (1995) 'Zhukaigou, Steppe Culture and the Rise of Chinese Civilization', *Antiquity* 69, 133–45.
  (2006) 'Why have Siberian Artefacts Been Excavated within Ancient Chinese Dynastic Borders?', in D. L. Peterson, L. M. Popova and A. T. Smith, eds., *Beyond the Steppe and the Sown*. Leiden, 358–70.
Lipták, P. (1983) *Avars and Ancient Hungarians*. Budapest.
Lister, R. P. (1969) *The Secret History of Genghis Khan*. London.
Litvinsky, B. A. (1989) 'The Ecology of the Ancient Nomads of Soviet Central Asia and Kazakhstan', in G. Seaman, ed., *Ecology and Empire: Nomads in the Cultural Evolution of the Old World*. Los Angeles, 61–72.
  (1994) 'Cities and Urban Life in the Kushan Kingdom', in J. Harmatta, ed., *History of Civilizations of Central Asia*, vol. II. Paris, 291–312
  (ed.) (1996a) *History of Civilizations of Central Asia*, vol. III: *The Crossroads of Civilizations: A.D. 250–750*. Paris.
  (1996b) 'The Hephtalite Empire', in B. A. Litvinsky, ed., *History of Civilizations of Central Asia*, vol. III. Paris, 135–62.
  (2002) 'Copper Cauldrons from Gilgit and Central Asia: More about Saka and Dards and Related Problems', *East and West* 52, 127–49.
Litvinsky, B. A. and Bromberg, C. A. (eds.) (1996) *Archaeology and Art of Central Asia* (Studies from the Former Soviet Union, New Series 8). Bloomfield Hills, MI.
Litvinsky, B. A., Shah, M. H., and Samghabadi, R. S. (1994) 'The Rise of Sasanian Iran', in J. Harmatta, ed., *History of Civilizations of Central Asia*, vol. II. Paris, 473–84.

Liu, X. (2001) 'Migration and Settlement of the Yuezhi-Kushan: Interaction and Interdependence of Nomadic and Sedentary Societies', *Journal of World History* 12 (2), 261–92.
  (2010) *The Silk Road in World History*. Oxford.
Liu, X. and Shaffer, L. N. (2007) *Connections Across Eurasia: Transportation, Communication, and Cultural Exchange on the Silk Roads*. New York.
Loewe, M. (1993) *Early Chinese Texts: A Bibliographical Guide*. Berkeley.
  (2006) *The Government of Qin and Han Empires: 221 BCE–220 CE*. Indianapolis and Cambridge.
Loewe, M. and Shaughnessy, E. (ed.) (1999) *The Cambridge History of Ancient China: From the Origins of Civilization to 221 B.C.* Cambridge.
Löfstedt, L. (1993) 'Attila, the Saintmaker in Medieval French Vernacular', in F. M. Bäuml and M. D. Birnbaum, eds., *Attila the Man and the Image*. Budapest, 65–74.
Longden, R. P. (1954) 'The Wars of Trajan', in J. Bagnell Bury, S. A. Cook, and F. E. Adcock, eds., *The Cambridge Ancient History*, vol. XI: *The Imperial Peace, A.D. 70–192*. Cambridge, 223–52.
Lozinski, B. P. (1984) 'The Parthian Dynasty', *Iranica Antiqua* 19, 119–39.
Lübke, C. (1997) 'Forms of Political Organisation of the Polabian Slavs (until the 10th Century A.D.' in P. Urbańczyk, ed., *Origins of Central Europe*. Warsaw, 115–24.
Lubo-Lesnichenko, E. I. (1989) 'The Huns, Third Century B.C. to Sixth Century A.D.', in V. N. Basilov, ed., *Nomads of Eurasia*. Seattle and London, 41–54.
Lubotsky, A. (2002) 'Scythian Elements in Old Iranian', in N. Sims-Williams, ed., *Indo-Iranian Languages and Peoples*. Oxford, 189–202.
Luce, T. J. and Woodman, A. J. (1993) *Tacitus and the Tacitean Tradition*. Princeton.
Lukonin, V. G. (1983) 'Political, Social and Administrative Institutions, Taxes and Trade', in *The Cambridge History of Iran*, vol. III, part 2: *The Seleucid, Parthian and Sasanian Periods*. Cambridge, 681–746.
Lund, A. A. (1990) *Zum Germanenbild der Römer: eine Einführung in die antike Ethnographie*. Heidelburg.
Luttwak, E. N. (1976) *The Grand Strategy of the Roman Empire from the First Century A.D. to the Third*. Baltimore and London.
Ma, Y. (1989) *China's Minority Nationalities*. Beijing.
MacDowall, D. W. (1977) 'The Context of Rajuvula the Satrap', *Acta Antiqua Academiae Scientiarum Hungaricae* 25, 187–195.
MacGeorge, P. (2002) *Late Roman Warlords*. Oxford.
Mackerras, C. (1972) *The Uighur Empire According to the Tang Dynastic Histories*. Canberra.
  (1990) 'The Uighurs', in D. Sinor, ed., *The Cambridge History of Early Inner Asia*. Cambridge, 317–42.
Maenchen-Helfen, J. O. (1939) 'The Ting-ling', *Harvard Journal of Asiatic Studies* 4, 77–86.
  (1944–5) 'Huns and Hsiung-Nu', *Byzantion* 17, 222–43.
  (1959) 'The Ethnic Name Hun', in S. Egerod and E. Glahn, eds., *Studia Serica Bernhard Karlgren Dedicata*. Copenhagen, 223–38.

(1961) 'Archaistic Names of the Hiung-nu', *Central Asiatic Journal* 6, 249–61.
(1973) *The World of the Huns*, Berkeley and London.
Mair, V. (ed.) (1998) *The Bronze Age and Early Iron Age Peoples of Eastern Central Asia*. Washington, DC.
(2007) 'Horse Sacrifices and Sacred Groves among the North(west)ern Peoples of East Asia', *Eurasian Studies* 6, 22–53.
Mallory, J. P. (1973) 'A Short Survey of the Indo-European Problem', *Journal of Indo-European Studies* 1, 21–65.
(1989) *In Search of the Indo-Europeans*. London.
(2002) 'Archaeological Models and Asian Indo-Europeans', in N. Sims-Williams, ed., *Indo-Iranian Languages and Peoples*. Oxford, 19–42.
Mallory, J. P. and Mair, V. H. (2000) *The Tarim Mummies: Ancient China and the Mystery of the Earliest Peoples from the West*. London.
Mallowan, M. (1985) 'Cyrus the Great (558–529 B.C.)', in *The Cambridge History of Iran*, vol. II: *The Median and Achaemenian Periods*. Cambridge, 392–419.
Man, J. (2005) *Attila: A Barbarian King and the Fall of Rome*. London.
Mango, C. and Scott, R. (trans.) (1997) *The Chronicle of Theophanes Confessor: Byzantine and Near Eastern History AD 284–813*. Oxford.
Manning, P. (2003) *Navigating World History: Historians Create a Global Past*. New York and Basingstoke.
Manteuffel, T. (1982) *The Formation of the Polish State: The Period of Ducal Rule 863–1194*, trans. A. Gorski. Detroit.
Manz, B. F. (1999) *The Rise and Rule of Tamerlane*. Cambridge.
(2009) 'Temür and the early Timurids to c. 1450', in N. Di Cosmo, A. J. Frank and P. B. Golden, eds., *The Cambridge History of Inner Asia: The Chinggisid Age*. Cambridge, 182–98.
Marasco, G. (2003) *Greek and Roman Historiography in Late Antiquity: Fourth to Sixth Century A.D.* Leiden.
Mariana, I. (1992) 'The Steppes of the Aral Sea in Pre- and Early Scythian Times', in G. Seaman, ed., *Foundations of Empire: Archaeology and Art of the Eurasian Steppes*. Los Angeles, 49–58.
Marin, J. (1990) *Attila, les influences danubiennes dans l'ouest de l'Europe au v e siècle*. Caen.
Markley, J. B. (forthcoming) *Peace and Peril: Sima Qian's Portrayal of Han-Xiongnu Relations*. Brepols.
Marquart, J. (1901) 'Eranšahr nach der Geographie des Ps. Moses Xorenac'i'. Berlin.
(1903) *Osteuropäische und ostasiatische Streifzüge: Ethnologische und historisch-topographische Studien zur Geschichte des 9. und 10. Jahrhunderts (ca. 840–940)*. Leipzig.
Marsadolov, L. (2000) 'The Cimmerian Traditions of the Gordion Tumuli (Phrygia) Found in the Altai Barrows (Bashadar, Pazyryk)', in J. Davis-Kimball, E. M. Murphy, L. Koryakova and L. T. Yablonsky, eds., *Kurgans, Ritual Sites, and Settlements: Eurasian Bronze and Iron Age*. Oxford, 247–58.
Marshak, B. I. and Negmatov, N. N. (1996) 'Sogdiana', in B. A. Litvinsky, ed., *History of Civilizations of Central Asia*, vol. III. Paris, 233–80.

Marshak, B. I. and Raspopova, V. I. (1990) 'Les nomads et la Sogdiane', in H. P. Francfort, ed., *Nomades et Sédentaires en Asie Centrale: Apports de l'archéologie et de l'ethnologie (Actes du colloque franco-soviétique Alma Ata (Kazakhstan) 17–26 Octobre 1987)*. Paris, 179–85.
Marshall, R. (1993) *Storm from the East*. Los Angeles.
Martinez, A. P. (2009) 'Institutional development, revenue and trade', in N. Di Cosmo, A. J. Frank, and P. B. Golden, eds., *The Cambridge History of Inner Asia: The Chinggisid Age*. Cambridge, 89–108.
Martynov, A. J. (1990) 'La civilization pastorale des steppes du 1er millénaire avant notre ère', in H. P. Francfort, ed., *Nomades et Sédentaires en Asie Centrale: Apports de l'archéologie et de l'ethnologie (Actes du colloque franco-soviétique Alma Ata (Kazakhstan) 17–26 Octobre 1987)*. Paris, 187–91.
Matthews, J. F. (1970) 'Olympiodorus of Thebes and the History of the West (A.D. 407–425)', *The Journal of Roman Studies* 60, 79–97.
  (1986) 'Ammianus and the Eastern Frontier: A Participant's View', in P. Freeman and D. Kennedy, eds., *The Defence of the Roman and Byzantine East: Proceedings of a Colloquium Held at the University of Sheffield in April 1986*. Oxford, 549–64.
  (1989) *The Roman Empire of Ammianus*. London.
  (2000) 'Roman Law and Barbarian Identity in the late Roman West', in S. Mitchell and G. Greatrex, eds., *Ethnicity and Culture in Late Antiquity*. London, 31–44.
Mattingly, D. J. (2011) *Imperialism, Power, and Identity: Experiencing the Roman Empire* (Miriam S. Balmuth Lectures in Ancient History and Archaeology). Princeton and Oxford.
Mazlish, B. and Buultjens, R. (1993) *Conceptualizing Global History*. Boulder, CO and Oxford.
McBain, B. (1983) 'Odovacer the Hun?', *Classical Philology* 78, 4, 323–7.
McDonough, S. (2011) 'The Legs of the Throne: Kings, Elites and Subjects in Sasanian Iran', in J. P. Arnason and K. A. Raaflaub, eds., *The Roman Empire in Context: Historical and Comparative Perspectives*. Oxford, 290–321.
McGovern, W. M. (1939) *The Early Empires of Central Asia: A Study of the Scythians and the Huns and the part they played in World History*. Chapel Hill, NC.
McKitterick, R. (1983) *The Frankish Kingdoms under the Carolingians, 751–987*. Harlow.
Meineke, A. (ed.) (1898–9) *Strabo, Geographica*. Leipzig.
Melyukova, A. I. (1990) 'The Scythians and Sarmatians', in D. Sinor, ed., *The Cambridge History of Early Inner Asia*. Cambridge, 97–117.
  (1995) 'Scythians of Southeastern Europe', in J. David-Kimball, V. Bashilov and L. Yablonsky, eds., *Nomads of the Eurasian Steppes in the Early Iron Age*. Berkeley, 28–61.
Menges, K. H. (1955) 'The South Siberian Turkic Languages I', *Central Asiatic Journal*, 107–36.
  (1956) 'The South Siberian Turkic Languages II', *Central Asiatic Journal*, 161–75.
  (1995) *The Turkic Languages and Peoples: An Introduction to Turkic Studies*. Wiesbaden.

Menghin, W. (1985) *Die Langobarden: Archäologie und Geshichte*. Stuttgart.
Menghin, W., Springer, T., and Wamers, E. (eds.) (1987) *Germanen, Hunnen und Awaren, Schätze der Völkerwanderungszeit: Die Archäologie des 5. und 6. Jahrhunderts an der mittleren Donau und der östlich-merowingische Reihengräberkreis*. Nürnberg.
Merrills, A. H. (2005) *History and Geography in Late Antiquity*. Cambridge.
Merrills, A. H. and Miles, R. (2010) *The Vandals*. Chichester.
Meserve, M. (2008) *Empires of Islam in Renaissance Historical Thought*. Cambridge MA.
Metzner-Nebelsick, C. (2000) 'Early Iron Age Pastoral Nomadism in the Great Hungrarian Plain-Migration or Assimilation? The Thraco-Cimmerian Problem Revisited', in J. Davis-Kimball, E. M. Murphy, L. Koryakova and L. T. Yablonsky, eds., *Kurgans, Ritual Sites, and Settlements: Eurasian Bronze and Iron Age*. Oxford, 160–84.
Meuli, K. (1962) 'Skythica', in W. Marg, ed., *Herodot: eine Auswahl aus der neueren Forschung*. Munich, 455–70.
Michels, C. (2008) *Kulturtransfer und monarchischer 'Philhellenismus': Bithynien, Pontos und Kappadokien in hellenistischer Zeit*, vol. IV of *Schriften zur politischen Kommunikation*. Göttingen.
Mielczarek, M. (1997) 'Remarks on the Numismatic Evidence for the Northern Silk Route: The Sarmatians and the Trade Route Linking the Northern Black Sea Area with Central Asia', in K. Tanabe, J. Cribb and H. Wang, eds., *Studies in Silk Road Coins and Cultures*. Kamakura, 131–48.
Mierow, C. C. (trans.) (1915) *The Gothic History of Jordanes*. Princeton.
  (trans.) (1963) *The Letters of Saint Jerome* (Ancient Christian Writers 33). Westminster, MD.
Millar, F. (1966) *The Roman Empire and its Neighbours*. London.
Miller, B. K. (2011) 'Permutation of Peripheries in the Xiongnu Empire', in U. Brosseder and B. K. Miller, eds., *Xiongnu Archaeology: Multidisciplinary Perspectives of the First Steppe Empire in Inner Asia* (Bonn Contributions to Asian Archaeology 5). Bonn, 559–78.
Miller, D. H. (1993) 'Ethnogenesis and Religious Revitalization beyond the Roman Frontier: The Case of Frankish Origins', *Journal of World History* 4 (2), 277–85.
Miller, K. (ed.) (1849) *Dexippus, Fragments* (Fragmenta Historicorum Graecorum 3). Paris.
Miller, R. A. (trans.) (1959). *Accounts of Western Nations in the History of the Northern Chou Dynasty*. Berkeley and Los Angeles.
Millward, J. A. (2007) *Eurasian Crossroads: A History of Xinjiang*. New York.
Minorsky, V. F. (1970) 'On the Ancient Turkish Title (šaδ)', in *Gururājamañjarikā: studi in onore di Giuseppe Tucci*. Napoli, 167–93.
Minyaev, S. (1985) 'The Origin of the Hsiung-nu', *International Association for the Study of the Cultures of Central Asia Information Bulletin* 9, 69–78.
  (1996) 'Les Xiongnu', *Dossiers d'Archeologie* 212, 73–83.

(2001) 'Art and Archaeology of the Xiongnu: New Discoveries in Russia', *Circle of Inner Asian Art* 14, 3–9.
(2000) 'The Origins of the "Geometric Style" in Hsiung nu Art', in J. Davis-Kimball, E. M. Murphy, L. Koryakova and L. T. Yablonsky, eds., *Kurgans, Ritual Sites, and Settlements: Eurasian Bronze and Iron Age*. Oxford, 293–303.
Mitchell, S. (2007) *A History of the Later Roman Empire AD 284–641: The Transformation of the Ancient World*. Malden and Oxford.
Mitchell, S. and Greatrex, G., (2000) *Ethnicity and Culture in Late Antiquity*. London.
Mittag, A. and Ye, M. (2008) 'Empire on the Brink: Chinese Historiography in the Post-Han Period', in F. Mutschler and A. Mittag, eds., *Conceiving the Empire: China and Rome Compared*. Oxford, 347–69.
Molè, G. (1970) *T'u-yü-hun from the Northern Wei to the Time of the Five Dynasties*. Rome.
Mommsen, T. (ed.) (1882, reprint 1961) *Iordanis Romana et Getica* (Monumenta Germaniae Historica, Auctores Antiquissimi 5, l.) Berlin.
(ed.) (1892) *Chronica Minora 1* (Monumenta Germaniae Historica, Auctores Antiquissimi 9). Berlin.
(ed.) (1894) *Chronica Minora 2* (Monumenta Germaniae Historica, Auctores Antiquissimi 11). Berlin.
Moorhead, J. (2001) *The Roman Empire Divided: The Post-Roman World, 400–700*. Harlow.
Moravcsik, G. (1930) 'Zur Geschichte der Onoguren', *Ungarische Jahrbücher* 10, 53–90.
(1958) *Byzantinoturcica*, 2 vols. Berlin.
(1967) *Studia Byzantina*. Amsterdam
Moravcsik, G. (ed.) and Jenkins, R. J. H. (trans.) (1967) *De Administrando Imperio* (Corpus Fontium Historiae Byzantinae 1). Washington, DC.
Morgan, D. (1986) *The Mongols*. Oxford.
Mori, M. (1973) 'Reconsideration of the Hsiung-nu State: A Response to Professor O. Pritsak's Criticism', *Acta Asiatica* 24, 20–34.
Muhlberger, S. (trans.) (1984) 'The Copenhagen Continuation of Prosper', *Florilegium* 6, 71–95.
(trans.) (1990) *The Fifth Century Chroniclers: Prosper, Hydatius, and the Gallic Chronicler of 452*. Leeds.
(trans.) (1992) 'Looking Back from Mid Century: The Gallic Chronicler of 452 and the Crisis of Honorius' Reign', in J. Drinkwater and H. Elton, eds., *Fifth-century Gaul: A Crisis of Identity?* Cambridge, 28–37.
Mukhamedjanov, A. R. (1994) 'Economy and Social System in Central Asia', in J. Harmatta, ed., *History of Civilizations of Central Asia*, vol. II. Paris, 265–90.
Müller, K. (ed.) (1851) *John of Antioch, Fragments* (Fragmenta Historicorum Graecorum 4). Paris.
Müller, K. E. (1972) *Geschichte der antiken Ethnographie und ethnologischen Theoriebildung*: vol. 1: *Von den Anfängen bis auf die byzantinischen Historiographen*. Wiesbaden.

Mullie, J. L. M. (1968) 'Les Chan-Joung ou Joung des montagnes', *Central Asiatic Journal* 12, 159–80.
  (1969) 'Les Sien-pi', *Central Asiatic Journal* 13, 24–51.
Murail, P., *et al.* (2000) 'The Man, the Woman and the Hyoid Bone: From Archaeology to the Burial Practices of the Xiongnu People', *Antiquity* 74 (285), 531–36.
Murdoch, A. (2006) *The Last Roman: Romulus Augustulus and the Decline of the West*. Stroud.
Murray, A. C. (ed. and trans.) (2000) *From Roman to Merovingian Gaul: A Reader*. Peterborough, Ontario.
Musset, L. (1975) *The Germanic Invasions: The Making of Europe AD 400–600*. London.
Mutschler, F. and Mittag, A. (eds.) (2008) *Conceiving the Empire: China and Rome Compared*. Oxford.
Narain, A. K. (1989) *On the "First Indo-Europeans": The Tokharian-Yuezhi and their Chinese Homeland* (Papers on Inner Asia 2). Bloomington.
  1990 'Indo-Europeans in Inner Asia', in D. Sinor, ed., *The Cambridge History of Early Inner Asia*. Cambridge, 151–76.
Neelis, J. (2007) 'Passages to India: Saka and Kushana Migrations in Historical Contexts', in D. M. Srinivasan, ed., *On the Cusp of an Era: Art in the Pre-Kusana World*. Leiden, 55–94.
Negmatov, N. N. (1994) 'States in North-western Central Asia', in J. Harmatta, ed., *History of Civilizations of Central Asia*, vol. II. Paris, 441–56.
Németh, G. (1940) *Attila és hunjai* [Attila and the Huns]. Budapest.
  (1966) 'The Runiform Inscription from Nagy Szent Miklós and the Runiform Scripts of Eastern Europe', *Acta Linguistica Academiae Scientiarum Hungaricae* 21, 1–51.
Neusner, J. (1963) 'Parthian Political Ideology', *Iranica Antiqua* 3, 40–59.
Nicolle, D. (2001) *Armies of Medieval Russia 750–1250*. Oxford.
Nienhauser, W. H. (ed.) (1994) *The Grand Scribe's Records*, vols. I and VII. Bloomington.
  (ed.) (2002). *The Grand Scribe's Records*, vol. II. Bloomington.
  (1995a) 'The Study of the Shih chi (*The Grand Scribe's Records*) in the People's Republic of China', in *Das Andere China*. Wiesbaden, 381–403.
  (1995b) 'Historians of China', *Chinese Literature: Essays, Articles, Reviews* 17, 207–16.
  (1996) 'A Century (1895–1995) of Shih chi Studies in the West', *Asian Culture Quarterly* 24 (1), 1–51.
Noonan, T. S. (1995–7) 'The Khazar Economy', *Archivum Eurasiae Medii Aevi* 9, 253–318.
  (2001) 'The Khazar Qaghanate and its Impact on the Early Rus State: The Translatio Imperii from Itil to Kiev', in A. M. Khazanov and A. Wink, eds., *Nomads in the Sedentary World*. Padstow, Cornwall, 76–102.
Norden, E. (1962) *Alt-Germanen: Völker-und Namengeschichtliche Untersuchungen*. Stuttgart.

Norwich, J. J. (1991) *Byzantium*, 3 vols. London.
Obolenski, D. (1971) *The Byzantine Commonwealth*. London.
Olbricht, P. (1954) 'Uchida's Prolegomena zu einer Geschichte der Jou-jan', *Ural-Altaiische Jahrbücher* 26, 90–100.
Olbrycht, M. (1998) 'Die Kultur der Steppengebiete und die Beziehungen zwischen Nomaden und der sesshaften Bevölkerung (der arsakidische Iran und die Nomadenvölker)', in J. Wiesehöfer, ed., *Das Partherreich und seine Zeugnisse: The Arsacid Empire: Sources and Documentation* (Historia Einzelschriften 122). Stuttgart, 11–43.
Olsen, J. S. (1998) *An Ethnohistorical Dictionary of China*. London.
Onon, U. (1997) *The History and the Life of Chinggis Khan*. Leiden.
Onyshkevych, L. (1999) 'Scythia and the Scythians', in E. D. Reeder, ed., *Scythian Gold*. New York, 23–36.
Oosten, J. (1996) 'Ideology and the Development of European Kingdoms', in H. J. M. Claessen and J. C. Oosten, eds., *Ideology and the Formation of Early States*. Leiden, 220–41.
Oppenheim, A. L. (1985) 'The Babylonian Evidence of Achaemenian Rule in Mesopotamia', in I. Gershevitch, ed., *The Cambridge History of Iran*, vol. II: *The Median and Achaemenian Periods*. Cambridge, 529–87.
Ostrowski, D. (1990) 'The Mongol Origins of Muscovite Political Institutions', *Slavic Review* 49 (4), 525–42.
 (1998) *Muscovy and the Mongols: Cross-cultural Influences on the Steppe Frontier, 1304–1589*. Cambridge.
Pallas-Brown, R. (2000) 'East Roman Perception of the Avars in the Mid- and Late Sixth Century', in S. Mitchell and G. Greatrex, eds., *Ethnicity and Culture in Late Antiquity*. London, 309–29.
Parker, E. H. (1895; reprint 1996) *A Thousand Years of the Tartars*. London and New York.
Parker, G. (1995) *The Cambridge Illustrated History of Warfare: The Triumph of the West*. Cambridge.
Paschoud, F. (ed. and trans.) (1971–89) *Zosimus, Historia Nova*. Paris.
Patkanoff, S. (1900) 'Über das Volk der Sabiren', *Keleti Szemle* I, 258–77.
Pearson, M. P. (1989) 'Beyond the Pale: Barbarian Social Dynamics in Western Europe', in J. C. Barrett, A. P. Fitzpatrick and L. Maccines, eds., *Barbarians and Romans in North-West Europe from the Later Republic to Late Antiquity*. Oxford, 198–226.
Périn, P. and Feffer, L. (1987). *Les Francs*, 2 vols. Paris.
Périn, P. and Kazanski, M. (1996) 'Vom Kleinkönigtum zum Grossreich: Das Grab Childerichs I', in Reiss-Museum Mannheim, *Die Franken Wegbereiter Europas Vor 1500 Jahren: König Chlodwig und seine Erben*, vol. 1. Mainz, 173–82.
Peters, E. (1989) *Europe and the Middle Ages*. Englewood Cliffs, NJ.
Petrushevsky, I. P. (1968) 'The Socio-Economic Condition of Iran under the Il-Khans', in *The Cambridge History of Iran*, vol. V: *The Saljuk and Mongol Periods*, Cambridge, 483–537.
Phillips, E. D. (1965) *The Royal Hordes: Nomad Peoples of the Steppe*. London.

P'iankov, I. V. (1996) 'The Ethnic History of the Sakas' in B. A. Litvinsky and C. A. Bromberg, eds., *Archaeology and Art of Central Asia*. (Studies from the Former Soviet Union, New Series 8). Bloomfield Hills, MI, 37–46.

Piggot, S. (1969) *Ancient Europe*. Chicago.

Pirazzoli-t'Serstevens, M. (2008) 'Imperial Aura and the Image of the Other in Han Art', in F. Mutschler and A. Mittag, eds., *Conceiving the Empire: China and Rome Compared*. Oxford, 299–317.

Pirenne, H. (1925) *Medieval Cities: The Origins and the Revival of Trade*. Princeton.

Planhol, Y. de (1979) 'Saturation et sécurité: sur l'organisation des societés de pasteurs nomades' in Équipe écologie et anthropologie des sociétés pastorals (ed.), *Pastoral Production and Society/Production pastorale et société: Proceedings of the International Meeting on Nomadic Pastoralism, Paris 1–3 Dec. 1976*. Cambridge, 29–42.

Platnauer, M. (ed. and trans.) (1922) *Claudian, Opera*, 2 vols. (Loeb Classical Library(. Cambridge, MA.

Pogrebova, M. N. and Raevskij, D. S. (1989) 'Concerning the "Breakaway" Scythian', *Vestnik drevnej istorii* 1,188, 40–65.

Pohl, W. (1980) 'Die Gepiden und die *Gentes* an der mittleren Donau nach dem Zerfall des Attilareiches', in H. Wolfram, H. and F. Daim, eds., *Die Völker an der mittleren und unteren Donau im fünften und sechsten Jahrhundert*. Wien, 239–305.

(1988) *Die Awaren: Ein Steppenvolk in Mitteleuropa 567–822 n. Chr.* Munich.

(1990) 'Verlaufsformen der Ethnogenese-Awaren und Bulgaren', in H. Wolfram and W. Pohl, eds., *Typen der Ethnogenese unter besonderer Berücksichtigung der Bayern*, vol. 1. Wien, 113–24.

(1997a) 'The Barbarian Successor States', in L. Webster and M. Brown, eds., *The Transformation of the Roman World 400–900*. London 33–47.

(1997b) 'The Empire and the Lombards' in *Kingdoms of the Empire: The Integration of Barbarians in Late Antiquity*. Leiden, 75–133.

(1997c) *Kingdoms of the Empire: The Integration of Barbarians in Late Antiquity*. Leiden.

(1997d) 'The Role of the Steppe Peoples in Eastern and Central Europe in the First Millennium A.D.', in P. Urbańczyk, ed., *Origins of Central Europe*. Warsaw, 65–78.

(2000) *Die Germanen*. Munich.

(2003) 'A Non-Roman Empire in Central Europe: The Avars', in H. Goetz, J. Jarnut and W. Pohl, eds., *Regna and Gentes: The Relationship between Late Antique and Early Medieval Peoples and Kingdoms in the Transformation of the Roman World*. Leiden, 571–95.

Pohl, W., Wood, I., and Reimitz, H. (eds.) (2001) *The Transformation of Frontiers: From Late Antiquity to the Carolingians*. Leiden.

Poly, J. (1993) 'La corde au cou: les Francs, La France, et la loi salique', in *Genèse de l'état moderne en Méditerranée: approches historiques et anthropologiques des pratiques et des représentations* (Collection de l'École française de Rome 168). Rome, 287–320.

Poppe, N. (1965) *Introduction to Altaic Linguistics*. Wiesbaden.
Potter, D. S. (2004) *The Roman Empire at Bay, AD 180–395*. London.
Potts, D. (2008) 'Puzur-Inšušinak and the Oxus Civilization (BMAC): Reflections on Šimaški and the Geo-political Landscape of Iran and Central Asia in the Ur III Period', *Zeitschrift für Assyriologie und Vorderasiatische Archäologie* 98, 165–94.
  (2011) 'Nomadismus in Iran von der Frühzeit bis in die Moderne: eine Untersuchung sowohl aus archäologischer als auch historischer Sicht', *Eurasia Antiqua* 16, 1–19.
Poulter, A. G. (ed.) (2007a) *The Transition to Late Antiquity on the Danube and Beyond*. Oxford.
  (2007b) 'The City, A Fort and the Countryside', in A. G. Poulter, ed., *The Transition to Late Antiquity on the Danube and Beyond*. Oxford, 51–97.
  (2007c) 'The Transition to Late Antiquity', in A. G. Poulter, ed., *The Transition to Late Antiquity on the Danube and Beyond*. Oxford, 1–50.
Pourshariati, P. (2008) *Decline and Fall of the Sasanian Empire: The Sasanian–Parthian Confederacy and the Arab Conquest of Iran*. London and New York.
Previté-Orton, C. W. (1933) *Outlines of Medieval History*. Cambridge.
Pritsak, O. (1951) 'Von den Karluk zu den Karachaniden', *Zeitschrift der Deutschen Morgenländischen Gesellschaft* 101, 270–300.
  (1952a) 'The Decline of the Empire of the Oghuz Yabghu', *The Annals of the Ukrainian Academy of Arts and Sciences in the U.S.* 2, 279–92.
  (1952b) 'Stammesnamen und Titulaturen der altaischen Völker', *Uralaltaische Jahrbücher* 24.
  (1953–4) 'Die Karachaniden', *Der Islam* 31, 17–68.
  (1954a) 'Orientierung und Farbsymbolik', *Saeculum* 5, 376–83.
  (1954b) 'Die 24 Ta-ch'en: Studie zur Geschichte des Verwaltungsaufbaus der Hsiung-nu Reiche', *Oriens Extremus* 1, 178–202.
  (1954c) 'Kultur und Sprache der Hunnen', in *Festschrift für Dmytro Cyzevs'kyj*. Berlin, 238–49.
  (1955a) *Die bulgarische Fürstenliste und die Sprache der Protobulgaren*. Wiesbaden.
  (1955b) 'Qara: Studie zut türkischen Rechtssymbolik', in *Zeki velidi Togan'a Armağan*, Istanbul, 239–63.
  (1956) 'Der Titel Attila', in *Festschrift für Max Vasmer*, Berlin, 404–19.
  (1959) 'Xun, der Volksname der Hsiung-nu', *Central Asiatic Journal* 5, 27–34.
  (1968) 'Two Migratory Movements in the Eurasian Steppe in the 9th–11th centuries', *Proceedings of the 26th International Congress of Orientalists, New Delhi 1964*, vol. II. New Delhi, 157–63.
  (1976a) 'The Hsiung-nu Word for 'Stone'', *Tractata Altaica: Denis Sinor ... dedicate*. Wiesbaden, 479–85.
  (1976b) 'From the Säbirs to the Hungarians', *Hungaro-Turcica: Studies in Honour of Julius Németh*. Budapest, 17–30.
  (1976c) 'The Pečenegs: A case of Social and Economic Transformation', (*Archivum Eurasiae Medii Aevi* I (1975), 211–35). Lisse, 4–29.

(1978) 'The Khazar Kingdom's Conversion to Judaism', *Harvard Ukrainian Studies* 2, 261–81.
(1981) *Studies in Medieval Eurasian History*. London.
(1982) 'The Hunnic Language of the Attila Clan', *Harvard Ukrainian Studies* 6, 428–76.
Průšek, J. (1971) *Chinese Statelets and the Northern Barbarians in the Period 1400–300 B.C.* Dordrecht, Holland.
Psarras, S. (1994) 'Exploring the North: Non-Chinese Cultures of the late Warring States and Han', *Monumenta Serica* 42, 1–125.
Pugachenkova, G. A., Dar, S. R., Sharma, R. C., Joyenda, M. A., and Siddiqi, H. (1994) 'Kushan Art', in J. Harmatta, ed., *History of Civilizations of Central Asia*, vol. II. Paris, 331–95.
Pulleyblank, E. G. (1962) 'The Consonantal System of Old Chinese', *Asia Major* 9, 58–144, 206–65.
(1966) 'Chinese and Indo-Europeans', *Journal of the Royal Asiatic Society of Great Britain and Ireland* 98, 9–39.
(1970) 'The Wu-sun and Sakas and the Yüeh-chich Migration', *Bulletin of the School of Oriental and African Studies, University of London* 33 (1), 154–60.
(1983) 'The Chinese and their Neighbours in Prehistoric and Early Historic Times', in D. N. Keightley, ed., *The Origins of Chinese Civilization*. Berkeley, 411–66.
(1990a) 'The Name of Kirgiz', *Central Asiatic Journal* 34 (1–2), 98–108.
(1990b) 'The High Carts': A Turkish speaking people before the Türks', *Asia Major*, 3rd Series, 3, 21–6.
(1991) *Lexicon of Reconstructed Pronunciation in Early Middle Chinese, Late Middle Chinese, and Early Mandarin*. Vancouver.
(1995) 'Why Tocharians?', *Journal of Indo-European Studies* 23 (3/4), 415–30.
(2000a) 'The Hsiung-nu', in H. R. Roemer, ed., *History of the Turkic Peoples in the Pre-Islamic Period* (Philologiae et Historiae Turcicae Fundamenta 1). Berlin, 52–75.
(2000b) 'The Nomads in China and Central Asia in the Post-Han Period', in H. R. Roemer, ed., *History of the Turkic Peoples in the Pre-Islamic Period* (Philologiae et Historiae Turcicae Fundamenta 1). Berlin, 76–94.
(2002) *Central Asia and Non-Chinese Peoples of Ancient China*. Aldershot.
Puri, B. N. (1994a) 'The Kushans', in J. Harmatta, ed., *History of Civilizations of Central Asia*, vol. II. Paris, 247–63.
(1994b) 'The Sakas and Indo-Parthians', in J. Harmatta, ed., *History of Civilizations of Central Asia*, vol. II. Paris, 191–207.
Raaflaub, K. and Rosenstein, N. (eds.) (1999) *War and Society in the Ancient and Medieval Worlds*. Cambridge, MA.
Rackham, H., Jones, W. H. S., and Eichholz, D. E. (ed. and trans.) (1947–52) *Pliny, Historia Naturalis* (Loeb Classical Library), 10 vols. Cambridge, MA.
Randers-Pehrson, J. D. (1983) *Barbarians and Romans: The Birth Struggle of Europe, A.D. 400–700*. Norman, OK.
Randsborg, K. (1980) *The Viking Age in Denmark: The Formation of a State*. London.

Ranov, V. A. and Gupta, S. P. (1979) *Archaeology of Soviet Central Asia, and the Indian Borderlands*. Delhi.

Rapin, C. (2007) 'Nomads and the Shaping of Central Asia: From the Early Iron Age to the Kushan Period' in J. Cribb and G. Herrmann, eds., *After Alexander: Central Asia before Islam*. Oxford, 29–72.

Rapoport, I. A. (1996) 'The Palaces of Topraq-Qal'a' in B. A. Litvinsky and C. A. Bromberg, eds., *Archaeology and Art of Central Asia* (Studies from the Former Soviet Union, New Series 8). Bloomfield Hills, MI, 161–85.

Ratchnevsky, P. (1991) *Genghis Khan: His Life and Legacy*, trans. T. N. Haining. Oxford.

Rawson, J. (1980) *Ancient China, Art and Archaeology*. London.
  (1989) 'Statesmen or Barbarians? The Western Zhou as Seen through their Bronzes', *Proceedings of the British Academy* 75, 71–95.

Reiss-Museum Mannheim (1996) *Die Franken Wegbereiter Europas Vor 1500 Jahren: König Chlodwig und seine Erben*, 2 vols. Mainz.

Reuter, T. (1985) 'Plunder and Tribute in the Carolingian Empire', *Transactions of the Royal Historical Society* 35, 75–94.

Reynolds, R. L. and Lopez, R. S. (1946) 'Odoacer: German or Hun?', *The American Historical Review* 52 (1), 36–53.

Reynolds, S. (1994) *Fiefs and Vassals: The Medieval Evidence Reinterpreted*. Oxford.

Rice, D. T. (1965) *The Dark Ages*. London.

Rice, T. T. (1957) *The Scythians*. London.
  (1961) *The Seljuks in Asia Minor*. London.
  (1965a) *Ancient Arts of Central Asia*. London.
  (1965b) 'Eastern Europe and the Rise of the Slavs', in D. T. Rice, ed., *The Dark Ages*. London, 139–56.

Richter, M. (1994) *The Formation of the Medieval West: Studies in the Oral Culture of the Barbarians*. Dublin.

Ridley, R. T. (1982) *Zosimus: New History*. Canberra.

Rives. J. B. (1999) *Tacitus, Germania*. Oxford.

Robertson, R. and Inglis, D. (2006) 'The Global Animus: In the Tracks of World Consciousness', in B. K. Gills and W. R. Thompson, eds., *Globalization and Global History*. London and New York, 33–47.

Robinson, C. F. (2003) *Islamic Historiography*. Cambridge.

Roemer, H. R. (1986a) 'The Jalayirids, Muzaffarids and Sarbadars' , in P. Jackson and L. Lockhart, eds., *The Cambridge History of Iran*, vol. VI: *The Timurid and Safavid Periods*. Cambridge, 1–41.
  (1986b) 'Timur in Iran', in *The Cambridge History of Iran,* vol. VI: *The Timurid and Safavid Periods*. Cambridge, 42–97.
  (ed.) (2000) *History of the Turkic Peoples in the Pre-Islamic Period/Histoire des peuples turcs a l'époque pré-islamique* (Philologiae et Historiae Turcicae Fundamenta 1). Berlin.

Roesdahl, E. (1982) *Viking Age Denmark*. London.

Rogers, G. (1996) 'An Examination of Historians' Explanations for the Mongol Withdrawal from East Central Europe', *East European Quarterly* 30 (1), 3–26.

Rolfe, J. C. (ed. and trans.) (1935–9) *Ammianus Marcellinus* (Loeb Classical Library). Cambridge, MA.
  (ed. and trans.) (1939) *Anonymous Valesianus, Pars Posterior, Ammianus Marcellinus*, vol. III (Loeb Classical Library). Cambridge, MA, 530–69.
Rolle, R. (1989) *The World of the Scythians*, trans. G. Walls. London.
Róna-Tas, A. (1970) 'Some Problems of Ancient Turkic', *Acta Orientalia* (Copenhagen) 32, 209–29.
  (1974) 'Tocharische Elemente in den altaischen Sprachen' in *Sprache, Geschichte und Kultur der Altaischen Völker* (Protokollband der 12. Tagung der Permanent International Altaistic Conference 1969). Berlin, 499–504.
  (1978) 'Julius Németh: Life and Work', *Acta Orientalia Academiae Scientiarum Hungaricae* 32 (3), 261–84.
  (1982) 'The Periodization and Sources of Chuvash Linguistic History', in A. Róna-Tas, ed., *Chuvash Studies*, 113–69.
  (1991) *An Introduction to Turkology*. Szeged.
  (1999) *Hungarians and Europe in the Early Middle Ages: An Introduction to Early Hungarian History*. Budapest.
Rorlich, A. (1991). 'The Volga Tatars: Modern Identities of the Golden Horde', in S. Seaman and D. Marks, eds., *Rulers from the Steppe: State Formation on the Eurasian Periphery*. Los Angeles, 274–290.
Rosenthal, F. (trans.) (1967) *Ibn Khaldun, The Muqaddimah: An Introduction to History*. London.
Rossabi, M. (1975) *China and Inner Asia from 1368 to the Present Day*. New York.
  (1983) *China Among Equals*. Berkeley.
  (1989) 'The "Decline" of the Central Asian Caravan Trade' in G. Seaman, ed., *Ecology and Empire: Nomads in the Cultural Evolution of the Old World*. Los Angeles, 81–102.
  (1998) 'The Ming and Inner Asia', in D. Twitchett and F. W. Mote, eds., *The Cambridge History of China*, vol. VIII: *The Ming Dynasty, 1398–1644*, part 2. Cambridge, 221–71.
  (2007) *The Mongols and Global History*. New York and London.
Rota, S. (ed. and trans.) (2002) *Magno Felice Ennodio, Panegirico del dementissimo re Teoderico*. Rome.
Rowlands, M., Larsen, M. and Kristiansen, K. (eds.) (1987) *Centre and Periphery in the Ancient World*. Cambridge.
Roy, D. T. and Tsien, T. S. (1978) *Ancient China: Studies in Early Civilization*. Hong Kong.
Rubin, Z. (2000) 'The Sassanid Monarchy', in A. Cameron, B. Ward-Perkins and M. Whitby, eds., *The Cambridge Ancient History*, vol. XIV: *Late Antiquity: Empire and Successors, A.D. 425–600*. Cambridge, 639–61.
Rubinson, K. (1975) 'Herodotus and the Scythians', *Expedition* 17, 16–20.
  (1992) 'A Reconsideration of Pazyryk', in G. Seaman, ed., *Foundations of Empire: Archaeology and Art of the Eurasian Steppes*. Los Angeles, 68–76.
Rudenko, S. I. (1969) *Die Kultur der Hsiung-nu und die Hügelgräber von Noin Ula*. Bonn.

Rudenko, S. I. (1970) *Frozen Tombs of Siberia: The Pazyryk Burials of Iron Age Horsemen*. London.
Rudgley, R. (2002) *Barbarians*. London and Oxford.
Runciman, S. (1930) *The History of the First Bulgarian Empire*. London.
Said, E. (1979) *Orientalism*. New York.
Sarianidi, V. (1998) 'Traces of Parthian Culture in the Cemetary of Tillya Tepe (Afghanistan)' in V. S. Curtis, R. Hillenbrand and J. M. Rogers, eds., *The Art and Archaeology of Ancient Persia: New Light on the Parthian and Sasanian Empires*. London and New York, 20–3.
Scheidel, W. (2009) *Rome and China*. Oxford.
  (2011) 'The Xiongnu and the Comparative Study of Empire', in U. Brosseder and B. K. Miller, eds., *Xiongnu Archaeology: Multidisciplinary Perspectives of the First Steppe Empire in Inner Asia* (Bonn Contributions to Asian Archaeology 5). Bonn, 111–20.
Schlütz, F. and Lehmkuhl, F. (2007) 'Climatic Change in the Russian Altai, Southern Siberia, Based on Palynological and Geomorphological Results, with Implications for Climatic Teleconnections and Human History Since the Middle Holocene', *Vegetation History and Archaeobotany* 16, 101–18.
Schmauder, M. (2003) 'The Relationship between Frankish *Gens* and *Regnum*: A Proposal Based on the Archaeological Evidence', in H. Goetz, J. Jarnut and W. Pohl, eds., *Regna and Gentes: The Relationship between Late Antique and Early Medieval Peoples and Kingdoms in the Transformation of the Roman World*. Leiden, 271–306.
  (2009) *Die Hunnen: Ein Reitervolk in Europa*. Darmstadt.
Schmidt, B. (1983a) 'Die Alamannen', in B. Krüger, ed., *Die Germanen: Geschichte und Kultur der germanischen Stämme in Mitteleuropa*, vol. II. Berlin, 336–60.
  (1983b) 'Die Thüringer', in B. Krüger, ed., *Die Germanen: Geschichte und Kultur der germanischen Stämme in Mitteleuropa*, vol. II. Berlin, 502–48.
Schmitt, R. (2000) *The Old Persian Inscriptions of Naqsh-i Rustam and Persepolis*. London.
Schneider, R. (1996) 'König und Herrschaft', in Reiss-Museum Mannheim, *Die Franken Wegbereiter Europas Vor 1500 Jahren: König Chlodwig und seine Erben*, vol. I. Mainz, 389–95.
Schneider, R. M. (2008) 'Image and Empire: The Shaping of Augustan Rome', in F. Mutschler and A. Mittag, eds., *Conceiving the Empire: China and Rome Compared*. Oxford, 269–98.
Schönfeld, M. (1911) *Wörterbuch der altgermanischen Personen- und Völkernamen*. Heidelburg.
Schramm, G. (1969) 'Eine hunnisch-germanische Namenbeziehung?' *Jahrbuch für fränkische Landesforschung* 20, 129–55.
Schutz, H. (2000) *The Germanic Realms in Pre-Carolingian Central Europe, 400–750*. New York.
Seaman, G. (1989) *Ecology and Empire: Nomads in the Cultural Evolution of the Old World*. Los Angeles.

Seaman, G. and Marks, D. (eds.) (1991) *Rulers from the Steppe: State Formation on the Eurasian Periphery*. Los Angeles.
  (1991) 'World Systems and State Formation on the Inner Eurasian Periphery', in G. Seaman and D. Marks, eds., *Rulers from the Steppe: State Formation on the Eurasian Periphery*. Los Angeles, 1–20.
  (ed.) (1992) *Foundations of Empire: Archaeology and Art of the Eurasian Steppes*. Los Angeles.
Seaman, G. and Marks, D. (eds.) (1991) *Rulers from the Steppe: State Formation on the Eurasian Periphery*. Los Angeles.
Seeck, O. (ed.) (1876) *Notitia dignitatum*. Paris.
Segal, D. (1993) 'Echoes of Attila in Twentieth Century Russia', in F. M. Bäuml and M. D. Birnbaum, eds., *Attila the Man and the Image*. Budapest, 106–16.
Sellwood, D. (1983) 'Minor States in Southern Iran', in E. Yarshater, ed., *The Cambridge History of Iran*, vol. III, part 1: *The Seleucid, Parthian and Sasanian Periods*. Cambridge, 299–321.
Semenov, V. and Chugunov, K. (1996) 'New Evidence of the Scythian-type Culture of Tuva', *Ancient Civilizations from Scythia to Siberia*, 2 (3), 311–34.
Seyer, R. (1983) 'Die Kunsthandwerkliche Produktion', in B. Krüger, ed., *Die Germanen: Geschichte und Kultur der germanischen Stämme in Mitteleuropa*, vol. II. Berlin, 173–204.
Shaw, B. D. (1982–3) '"Eaters of Flesh, Drinkers of Milk": The Ancient Mediterranean Ideology of the Pastoral Nomad', *Ancient Society*, 13–14.
  (2001) 'War And Violence', in G. W. Bowersock, P. Brown and O. Grabar, eds., *Interpreting Late Antiquity*. Cambridge MA and London, 130–69.
Shayegan, M. R. (2011) *Arsacids and Sasanians: Political Ideology in Post-Hellenistic and Late Antique Persia*. Cambridge.
Shen, Youliang (1998) *A Research on Northern Ethnic Groups and Regimes*. Beijing.
Shen, Yue (1958) *Song shu*. Beijing.
Shepard, J. (2005) 'Conversions and Regimes Compared: The Rus' and the Poles, ca. 1000', in F. Curta, ed., *East Central and Eastern Europe in the Early Middle Ages*. Ann Arbor, 254–82.
Shepherd, G. (1999) 'Fibulae and Funales: Intermarriage in the Western Greek colonies and the evidence from the cemeteries', in G. Tsetskhladze, ed., *Ancient Greeks West and East*. Leiden, 267–300.
Sherratt. A. (ed.) (1980) *Cambridge Encyclopedia of Archaeology*. Cambridge.
Shippey, T. A. (1982) 'Goths and Huns: The Rediscovery of the Northern Cultures in the Nineteenth Century', in A. Haarder et al., eds., *The Medieval Legacy: A Symposium*. Odense, 51–69.
Shiratori, K. (1923) 'Sur l'origine des Hiong-nou', *Journal Asiatique* 1, 71–81.
  (1930) 'On the Territory of the Hsiung-nu Prince Hsiu-t'u Wang and his Metal Statues for Heaven Worship', *Memoirs of the Research Department of the Toyo Bunko* 5, 1–78.
Silay, K. (1996) *An Anthology of Turkish Literature*. Bloomington.

Silber, M. (1971) *The Gallic Royalty of the Merovingians in its Relationship to the "Orbis Terrarum Romanus" during the 5th and the 6th Centuries* A.D. Bern and Frankfurt.
Simons, G. (1968) *Barbarian Europe*. New York.
Sims-Williams, N. (1998) 'The Iranian Languages', in A. Giacolone Ramat and P. Ramat, eds., *The Indo-European Languages*. London, 125–53.
　(2002a) 'Ancient Afghanistan and its Invaders: Linguistic Evidence from the Bactrian Documents and Inscriptions', in N. Sims-Williams, ed., *Indo-Iranian Languages and Peoples*. Oxford, 224–42.
　(ed.) (2002b) *Indo-Iranian Languages and Peoples*. Oxford.
　(2008) 'The Bactrian Inscription of Rabatak: A New Reading', *Bulletin of the Asia Institute* 18, 53–68.
Sinor, D. (1946–7) 'Autour d'une migration du peuples au Ve siècle, *Journal Asiatique*, Paris, 1–78.
　(1970) 'Central Eurasia', in D. Sinor, ed., *Orientalism and History*, 2nd edn. Bloomington, 93–119.
　(1972) 'Horse and Pasture in Inner Asian History', *Oriens Extremus* 19, 171–84.
　(1977) *Inner Asia and its Contacts with Medieval Europe*. London.
　(1982) 'The Legendary Origins of the Türks', in E. V. Zygas and P. Voorheis, eds., *Folklorica; Festschrift for Felix J. Oinas* (IUUA 141). Bloomington, 223–57.
　(1985) 'Some Components of the Civilization of the Türks', in G. Jarring and S. Rosén, eds., *Altaistic Studies* (25th Meeting of the Permanent International Altaistic Conference, June, 1982, Kungl. Vitterhets Historie och Antikvitets, Akademiens Konferenser, 12). Stockholm, 145–59.
　(1990a) *The Cambridge History of Early Inner Asia*. Cambridge.
　(1990b) 'The Establishment and Dissolution of the Türk Empire', in D. Sinor, ed., *The Cambridge History of Early Inner Asia*. Cambridge, 285–316.
　(1990c) 'The Hun Period', in D. Sinor, ed., *The Cambridge History of Early Inner Asia*. Cambridge, 177–205.
　(1990d) 'Introduction: the concept of Inner Asia, in D. Sinor, ed., *The Cambridge History of Early Inner Asia*. Cambridge, 1–18.
　(1993) 'The Historical Attila', in F. M. Bäuml and M. D. Birnbaum, eds., *Attila the Man and the Image*. Budapest, 3–15.
　(1995) 'Languages and Cultural Interchange along the Silk Roads', *Diogenes* 171, vol. 43/3, Oxford, 1–13.
　(1997) *Studies in Medieval Inner Asia*. Norfolk.
Skalmowski, W. and Van Tongerloo, A. (1984) *Middle Iranian Studies* (Orientalia Lovaniensia Analecta 16). Leuven.
Skrynnikova, T. D. (2003) 'Power among Mongol Nomads of Chinggis Khan's Epoch', in N. N. Kradin, D. Bondarenko and T. Barfield, eds., *Nomadic Pathways in Social Evolution*. Moscow, 135–47.
Sláma, J. (2000) 'Premyslids and Slavnikids', in A. Wieczorek and H. Hinz, eds., *Europe's Centre around AD 1000*. Stuttgart, 282–3.
Smagulov, E. A. (1997) 'Finds of Sasanian Gems in the Otrar Oasis', *Ancient Civilizations from Scythia to Siberia* 3 (2–3), 253–9.

Smilenko, A. T. (1965) *Glodos'ki skarbi* [The Hlodosy hoard]. Kiev.
Smirnow, A. P. (1979) *Die Skythen*. Dresden.
Smith, A. D. (1986) *The Ethnic Origin of Nations*. Oxford.
Smith, J. M. (1970) 'Mongol and Nomadic Taxation', *Harvard Journal of Asiatic Studies* 30, 46–85.
  (1975) 'Mongol Manpower and Persian Population', *Journal of the Economic and Social History of the Orient* 18, 271–99.
  (1978) 'Turanian Nomadism', *Iranian Studies* 11.
So, J. F. and Bunker, E. C. (1995) *Traders and Raiders on China's Northern Frontier*. Seattle and London.
Soucek, S. (2000) *A History of Inner Asia*. Cambridge.
Spuler, B. (1939) *Die Mongolen in Iran*. Leipzig.
Staab, F. (1996) 'Die Franken-Wegbereiter Europas', in Reiss-Museum Mannheim, *Die Franken Wegbereiter Europas Vor 1500 Jahren: König Chlodwig und seine Erben*, vol. 1. Mainz, 10–22.
Standen, N. (2005) 'What Nomads Want', in R. Amitai and M. Biran, eds., *Mongols, Turks and Others: Eurasian Nomads and the Sedentary World*. Leiden, 129–74.
  (2009) 'The Five Dynasties', in D. Twitchett and P. J. Smith, eds., *The Cambridge History of China*, vol. v. Cambridge, 38–132.
Ste. Croix, G. E. M. de (1981) *The Class Struggle in the Ancient Greek World from the Archaic Age to the Arab Conquests*. London.
Steensgaard, N. (1973) *The Asian Trade Revolution of the Seventeenth Century*. Chicago.
Stein, A. M. (1921) *Serindia: Detailed Report of Explorations in Central Asia and Westernmost China*, 5 vols. London and Oxford.
Steinhübel, J. (2000) 'The Nitran Principality in Great Moravia and Hungary', in A. Wieczorek and H. Hinz, eds., *Europe's Centre around AD 1000*. Stuttgart, 200–1.
Stepanov, T. (2001) 'The Bulgar Title ΚΑΝΑΣΥΒΙΓΙ: Reconstructing the Notion of Divine Kingship in Bulgaria, AD 822–836', *Early Medieval Europe* 10 (1), 1–19.
  (2005) 'Ruler and Political Ideology in *Pax Nomadica*: Early Medieval Bulgaria and the Uigur Qaganate', in F. Curta, ed., *East Central and Eastern Europe in the Early Middle Ages*. Ann Arbor, 152–61.
Stickler, T. (2007) 'The Foederati', in P. Erdkamp, ed., *A Companion to the Roman Army*. Malden, MA and Oxford, 495–514.
Stolper, M. W. (1989) 'On Interpreting Tributary Relationships in Achaemenid Babylonia', in P. Briant and C. Herrenschmidt, eds., *Le tribut dans l'empire perse*. Paris, 147–56.
Strayer, J. R. (1970) *On the Medieval Origins of the Modern State*. Princeton.
Stride, S. (2007) 'Regions and Territories in Southern Central Asia: What the Surkhan Darya Province tells us about Bactria', in J. Cribb and G. Herrmann, eds., *After Alexander: Central Asia before Islam*. Oxford, 99–117.
Strzygowski, J. (1923) *Origin of Christian Church Art*, trans. O. M. Dalton and H. J. Braunholtz. Oxford.

Sükhbaatar, G. (1980) *Mongolchuudyn ertnii övög Khünnü naryn azh akhui, niiigmiin baiguulal, soel, ugsaa garal*. Ulaanbaatar.
Sulejmenov, R. B. (1989) 'Chokan Valikhanov: Explorer of the Nineteenth Century Asian Nomadic Peoples', in G. Seaman, ed., *Ecology and Empire: Nomads in the Cultural Evolution of the Old World*. Los Angeles, 29–40.
Sulimirsky, T. (1970) *The Sarmatians*. Southampton.
  (1985) 'The Scyths', in I. Gershevitch, ed., *The Cambridge History of Iran*: vol. II, *The Median and Achaemenid Periods*. Cambridge, 149–99.
Swidler, N. (1972) 'The Development of the Kalat Khanate', in W. Irons and N. Dyson-Hudson, eds., *Perspectives on Nomadism*. Leiden, 115–21.
Syme, R. (1958) *Tacitus*, 2 vols. Oxford.
Szádeczky-Kardoss, S. (1990) 'The Avars', in D. Sinor, ed., *The Cambridge History of Early Inner Asia*. Cambridge, 206–55.
Szemerényi, O. (1980) *Four Old Iranian Ethnic Names: Scythian-Skudra-Sogdian-Saka*. Wien.
Tafazzoli, A. and Khromov, A. L. (1996) 'Sasanian Iran: Intellectual Life' in B. A. Litvinsky, ed., *History of Civilizations of Central Asia*, vol. III. Paris, 79–102.
Tanabe, K. (1997) 'The Kushano-Sasanian Kings Hidden in Roman and Chinese Literary Sources', in K. Tanabe, J. Cribb and H. Wang, eds., *Studies in Silk Road Coins and Culture: Papers in Honour of Professor Ikuo Hirayama on his 65th Birthday*. Kamakura, 75–88.
  (1998) 'A newly located Kushano-Sasanian Silver Plate: The Origin of the Royal Hunt on Horseback for Two Male Lions on "Sasanian" Silver Plates', in V. S. Curtis, R. Hillenbrand and J. M. Rogers, *The Art and Archaeology of Ancient Persia: New Light on the Parthian and Sasanian Empires*. London and New York, 93–102.
Tanabe, K., Cribb, J., and Wang, H. (eds.) (1997). *Studies in Silk Road Coins and Culture: Papers in Honour of Professor Ikuo Hirayama on his 65th Birthday*. Kamakura.
Tao, J. S. (1983) 'Barbarians or Northerners: Northern Sung Images of the Khitans', in M. Rossabi, ed., *China Among Equals*. Berkeley and Los Angeles, 66–86.
Tapper, R. L. (1979a) 'The Organisation of Nomadic Communities in Pastoral Societies of the Middle East', in Équipe écologie et anthropologie des sociétés pastorals (ed.), *Pastoral Production and Society/Production pastorale et société: Proceedings of the International Meeting on Nomadic Pastoralism, Paris 1–3 Dec. 1976*. Cambridge, 43–65.
  (1979b) 'Individuated Grazing Rights and Social Organisation among the Shahsevan Nomads of Azerbaijan', in Équipe écologie et anthropologie des sociétés pastorals (ed.), *Pastoral Production and Society/Production pastorale et société: Proceedings of the International Meeting on Nomadic Pastoralism, Paris 1–3 Dec. 1976*. Cambridge, 95–114.
  (1991) 'The Tribes in Eighteenth- and Nineteenth-century Iran', in P. Avery, G. Hambly and C. Melville, eds., *The Cambridge History of Iran*, vol. VII: *From Nadir Shah to the Islamic Republic*. Cambridge, 506–41.

Taskin, V. S. (1973) *Materialy po istorii siunnu* (po kitaiskim istochnikam) [Material about Xiongnu (Chinese Sources)], trans. with introduction and comments by V. S. Taskina, vol. II. Moscow.

Tavernier, J. (2007) *Iranica in the Achaemenid Period (ca. 550–330 B.C): Lexicon of Old Iranian Proper Names and Loanwords, Attested in Non-Iranian Texts*. Leuven, Paris and Dudley, MA.

Teitler, H. (1999) 'Visa vel Lecta? Ammianus on Persia and the Persians', in J. W. Drijvers and D. Hunt, eds., *The Late Roman World and its Historian: Interpreting Ammianus Marcellinus*. London and New York, 216–23.

Tekin, T. (1968) *A Grammar of Orkhon Turkic*. Bloomington.

Thierry, A. (1856) *Histoire d'Attila*, vol. I. Paris.

Thomas, N. and Humphrey, C. (1994) *Shamanism, History, and the State*. Ann Arbor.

Thompson, E. A. (1948) *A History of Attila and the Huns*. Oxford.

(1965) *The Early Germans*. Oxford.

(1982) *Romans and Barbarians: The Decline of the Western Empire*. Madison.

(1996) *The Huns*, revised and with an afterword by Peter Heather. Oxford.

Thompson, W. R. (1999) 'The Military Superiority Thesis and the Ascendancy of Western Eurasia in the World System', *Journal of World History* vol. 10 (1), 143–78.

Thomson, R. W. (trans.) (1978) *Moses Khorenats'i:, History of the Armenians*. Cambridge, MA and London.

Thorley, J. (1979) 'The Roman Empire and the Kushans', *Greece and Rome*, 2nd series, 26 (2), 181–90.

Thorpe, L. (1974) *Gregory of Tours: The History of the Franks*. London.

Todd, M. (1992) *The Early Germans*. Guildford.

Tolstov, S. P. (1961) 'Les Scythes de l'Aral et le Khorezm', *Iranica Antiqua* I, 42–92.

Torday, L. (1997) *Mounted Archers: The Beginnings of Central Asian History*. Edinburgh.

Toshio, H. (1990) 'The Development of a Nomadic Empire: The Case of the Ancient Türks (Tujue)', *Bulletin of the Ancient Orient Museum* 11, 164–84.

Toumanoff, C. (1963) *Studies in Christian Caucasian History*. Gerogetown.

Townsend, J. (1996) 'Chinese Nationalism', in J. Unger, ed., *Chinese Nationalism*. New York, 1–30.

Toynbee, A. (1958) *East to West: A Journey Round the World*. London.

(1961) *Between Oxus and Jumna*. London.

(1973) *Constantine Porphyrogenitus and his World*. London.

Traina, G. (2009) *428 AD: An Ordinary Year at the End of the Roman Empire*. Princeton.

Treadgold, W. (1988) *The Byzantine Revival 780–842*. Stanford.

Tremblay, X. (2001) *Pour une histoire de la Sérinde: le manichéisme parmi les peuples et religions d'Asie Centrale d'après les sources primaires*. Vienna.

(2005) Irano-Tocharica et Tocharo-Iranica', *Bulletin of the School of Oriental and African Studies* 68 (3), 421–49.

Třeštík, D. (2000a) 'The Creation of a Slavic Empire: The Great Moravian Example', in A. Wieczorek and H. Hinz, eds., *Europe's Centre around AD 1000*. Stuttgart, 193–5.
  (2000b) 'The Czechs', in A. Wieczorek and H. Hinz, eds., *Europe's Centre around AD 1000*. Stuttgart, 227–34.
Trever, C. (1932) *Excavations in Northern Mongolia (1924–1925)*. Leningrad.
Tryjarski, E. (1985) 'Alte and neue Probleme der runenartigen Inschriften Europas. Ein Versuch der Entzifferung der Texte aus Murfatlar und Pliska', in K. Röhrborn and W. Veenker, eds., *Runen, Tamgas und Graffiti aus Asiens und Osteuropa* (Veröffentlichungen der Societas Uralo-Altaica 19). Wiesbaden, 53–80.
Tsetskhladze, G. (2007) 'Pots and Pandemonium: The Earliest East Greek Pottery from the North Pontic Native Settlements', *Pontica* 40, 37–70.
Tuplin, C. (1996) *Achaemenid Studies*. Stuttgart.
  (1998) 'The Seasonal Migration of Achaemenid Kings: A Report on Old and New Evidence', in M. Brosius and A. Kuhrt, eds., *Studies in Persian History: Essays in Memory of David M. Lewis* (Achaemenid History 11). Leiden, 63–114.
Twitchett, D. and Fairbank, J. K. (gen. eds.) (1979–) *The Cambridge History of China*, vols. I–III and VI–XIII. Cambridge.
Tymowski, M. (1996) 'Oral Tradition, Dynastic Legend and Legitimation of Ducal Power in the Process of the Formation of the Polish State', in H. J. M. Claessen and J. C. Oosten, eds., *Ideology and the Formation of Early States*. Leiden, 242–55.
Uchida, G. (1957) 'Some Notes on the Jou-jan', in *Studia Altaica: Festschrift für Nikolaus Poppe*. Wiesbaden.
Unger, J. (1993) *Using the Past to serve the Present: Historiography and Politics in Contemporary China*. New York and London.
Urbańczyk, P. (ed.) (1997a) *Origins of Central Europe*. Warsaw.
  (1997b) 'Changes of Power Structure During the 1st Millennium A.D. in the Northern Part of Central Europe', in P. Urbańczyk, ed., *Origins of Central Europe*. Warsaw, 39–44.
  (2005) 'Early State Formation in East Central Europe', in F. Curta, ed., *East Central and Eastern Europe in the Early Middle Ages*. Ann Arbor, 139–51.
  (2008) 'Slavic and Christian Identities During the Transition to Polish Statehood', in I. H. Garipzanov, P. J. Geary and P. Urbańczyk, eds., *Franks, Northmen, and Slavs: Identities and State Formation in Early Medieval Europe*. Turnhout, 205–22.
Vaday, A. (2000) 'The World of Beliefs of the Sarmatians', *Specimina Nova Universitatis Quinqueecclesiensis* 16, 215–26.
Vanderspoel, J. (2009) 'From Empire to Kingdoms in the Late Antique West', in P. Rousseau, ed., *A Companion to Late Antiquity*. Malden, MA, 426–40.
Vasilyev, D. D. (1992) 'Turkic Runic Inscriptions on Monuments of South Siberia', in G. Seaman, ed., *Foundations of Empire: Archaeology and Art of the Eurasian Steppes*. Los Angeles, 117–26.

Vasjutin, S. A. (2003) 'Typology of Pre-States and Statehood Systems of Nomads', in N. N. Kradin, D. Bondarenko and T. Barfield, eds., *Nomadic Pathways in Social Evolution*. Moscow, 50–62.
Velidî Togan, A. Z. (1939) *Ibn Fadlans Reisebericht*. Leipzig.
Vernadsky, G. (1951) 'Der sarmatische Hintergrund der germanischen Völkerwanderung', *Saeculum* 2, 340–92.
  (1953) *The Mongols and Russia*. New Haven.
Vignet-Lunz, J. (1979) 'A propos des Bédouins: une réévaluation des rapports "nomades-sédentaires"', in Équipe écologie et anthropologie des sociétés pastorals (ed.), *Pastoral Production and Society/ Production pastorale et société: Proceedings of the International Meeting on Nomadic Pastoralism, Paris 1–3 Dec. 1976*. Cambridge, 467–78.
Vingo, P. de (2000) 'Historical and Archaeological Sources Relating to the Migration of Nomadic Peoples towards Central and Southern Europe during the Imperial Age (1st to 5th centuries AD)', in J. Davis-Kimball, E. M. Murphy, L. Koryakova and L. T. Yablonsky, eds., *Kurgans, Ritual Sites, and Settlements: Eurasian Bronze and Iron Age*. Oxford, 153–9.
Volkov, V. V. (1995) 'Early Nomads of Mongolia', in J. Davis-Kimball, V. Bashilov and L. Yablonsky, eds., *Nomads of the Eurasian Steppes in the Iron Age*. Berkeley, 319–33.
Vogel, F. (ed.) (1885) *Ennodius, Vita Epiphanius* (Monumenta Germaniae Historica, Auctores Antiquissimi 7). Berlin.
Vogelsang, W. J. (1985) 'Early Historical Arachosia in South-east Afghanistan; Meeting-place between East and West, *Iranica Antiqua* 20, 55–99.
  (1988) *Review of* La Bactriane sous les Kushans: problèmes de l'histoire et de culture [Kushanskaja Baktrija, problem istorii i kul'tury], trans. P. Bernard. Paris, *Persica* 13, 161–6.
  (1992) *The Rise and Organisation of the Achaemenid Empire: The Eastern Iranian Evidence*. Leiden.
Vos, M. F. (1963) *Scythian Archers in Archaic Attic Vase-Painting*. Groningen.
Vovin, A. (2000) 'Did the Xiongnu speak a Yeniseian Language?' *Central Asiatic Journal* 44 (1), 87–104.
Waas, M. (1965) *Germanen in römischen Dienst im 4. Jh n. Chr.* Bonn.
Wagner, M. (1984) 'Die Torci bei Fredegar', *Beiträge zur Namenforschung* 19, 402–10.
Wagner, N. (2008) 'Odovacar, die "T(h)orcilingi" und die "Thuringi"', *Beiträge zur Namenforschung* 43, 1, 13–20.
Waldron, A. N. (1983) 'The Problem of the Great Wall of China', *Harvard Journal of Asiatic Studies* 43, 643–63.
Wallace-Hadrill, J. M. (1958) *Fredegar and the History of France*. Manchester.
  (1960) *The Fourth Book of the Chronicle of Fredegar with its Continuations*. London.
  (1962) *The Long-Haired Kings*. London.
  (1967) *The Barbarian West 400–1000*, 3rd edn. London.
  (1975) *Early Medieval History*. Oxford.
Wang, H. (1982) 'Apa Qaghan, Founder of the Western Turkish Khanate, the Splitting up of the Turkish Khanate and the Formation of the Western Turkish Khanate', *Social Sciences in China* 2, 124–52.

Wang, T. (2007) 'Parthia in China: A Re-examination of the Historical Records', in V. S. Curtis, *The Age of the Parthians*. London, 87–104.
Ward, D. J. (1993) 'Attila, King of the Huns in Narrative Lore', in F. M. Bäuml and M. D. Birnbaum, eds., *Attila the Man and the Image*. Budapest, 38–44.
Ward-Perkins, B. (2005) *The Fall of Rome and the End of Civilization*. Oxford.
Watson, B. (1961) *Records of the Grand Historian of China (Shih chi)*, vol. II. New York.
Watson, W. (1971) *Cultural Frontiers in Ancient East Asia*. Edinburgh.
Weatherford, J. (2004) *Genghis Khan and the Making of the Modern World*. New York.
Weber, S. (1983) 'Die gesellschaftliche Entwicklung bei den germanischen Stämmen in der Endphase der Gentilordnung und am Überzeugung zum Feudalismus', in B. Krüger, ed., *Die Germanen: Geschichte und Kultur der germanischen Stämme in Mitteleuropa*, vol. II. Berlin, 660–82.
Webster, L. and Brown, M. (eds.) (1997) *The Transformation of the Roman World AD 400–900*. London.
Weinbrot, H. D. (1997) 'Politics, Taste, and National Identity: Some Uses of Tacitism in Eighteenth Century Britain', in T. J. Luce and A. J. Woodman, eds., *Tacitus and the Tacitean Tradition*. Princeton, 168–84.
Wells, P. S. (1999) *The Barbarian Speaks: How the Conquered Peoples Shaped Roman Europe*. Princeton.
Wendelken, R. W. (2000) 'Horses and Gold: The Scythians of the Eurasian Steppe, in A. Bell-Fialkoff, ed., *The Role of Migration in the History of the Eurasian Steppe: Sedentary Civilizations vs. "Barbarian" Nomad*. New York, 189–206.
Wenskus, R. (1977) *Stammesbildung und Verfassung: das Werden der frühmittelalterlichen gentes*. Cologne.
Werner, J. (1956) *Beiträge zur Archäologie des Attila-Reiches* (Bayerische Akademie der Wissenschaften 38 A). Munich.
West, S. (1988) 'The Scythian Ultimatum (Herodotus 4.131, 132)', *Journal of Hellenic Studies* 108, 207–11.
  (2004) 'Herodotus and Scythia', in V. Karageorghis and I. Taifacos, eds., *The World of Herodotus*. Nicosia, 73–89.
Whitby, M. (2000a) 'Armies and Society in the Later Roman World', in A. Cameron, B. Ward-Perkins, and M. Whitby, eds., *The Cambridge Ancient History*, vol. XIV: *Late Antiquity: Empire and Successors, A.D. 425–600*. Cambridge, 469–95.
  (2000b) 'The Army, c. 420–602', in A. Cameron, B. Ward-Perkins and M. Whitby, eds., *The Cambridge Ancient History*, vol. XIV: *Late Antiquity: Empire and Successors, A.D. 425–600*. Cambridge, 288–314.
  (2000c) 'The Balkans and Greece 420–602', in A. Cameron, B. Ward-Perkins, and M. Whitby, eds., *The Cambridge Ancient History*, vol. XIV: *Late Antiquity: Empire and Successors, A.D. 425–600*. Cambridge, 701–30.
  (ed.) (2000d) *The Ecclesiastical History of Evagrius Scholasticus*. Liverpool.
  (2007a) 'Army and Society in the Late Roman World: A Context for Decline?', in P. Erdkamp, ed., *A Companion to the Roman Army*. Malden, MA, 515–22.

(2007b) 'The Late Roman Army and the Defence of the Balkans', in A. G. Poulter, ed., *The Transition to Late Antiquity on the Danube and Beyond*. Oxford, 135–61.
Whitby, M. and Whitby, M. (trans.) (1986) *The History of Theophylact Simocatta*. Oxford.
White, L. (1966a) *Medieval Technology and Social Change*. Oxford.
  (ed.) (1966b) *The Transformation of the Roman World: Gibbon's Problem after Two Centuries*. Berkeley and Los Angeles.
Whitfield, S. (1999) *Life along the Silk Road*. Berkeley and Los Angeles.
Wickevoort Crommelin, B. van (1998) 'Die Parther und die parthische Geschichte bei Pompeius Trogus-Iustin', in J. Wiesehöfer, ed., *Das Partherreich und seine Zeugnisse*. Stuttgart, 259–77.
Wickham C. (1981) *Early Medieval Italy: Central Power and Local Society 400–1000*. London.
  (2009) *The Inheritance of Rome: A History of Europe from 400 to 1000*. New York.
Widdowson, M. (2009) 'Merovingian Partitions: A Genealogical Charter?', *Early Medieval Europe* 17, 1–22.
Widengren, G. (1956) 'Recherches sur le féodalisme iranien', *Orientalia Suecana* 5, 79–182.
  (1969) *Der Feudalismus im alten Iran*. Cologne and Opladen.
  (1976) 'Iran, der grosser Gegner Roms: Königsgewalt, Feudalismus, Militärwesen', *Aufstieg und Niedergang der romischen Welt* II (9.1), 219–306.
Wieczorek, A. and Hinz, H. (eds.) (2000) *Europe's Centre around AD 1000*. Stuttgart.
Wiedemann, T. E. J. (1986) 'Between Men and Beasts: Barbarians in Ammianus Marcellinus', in I. S. Moxon , J. D. Smart and A. J. Woodman, eds., *Past Perspectives: Studies in Greek and Roman historical Writing*. Cambridge, 189–201.
Wiesehöfer, J. (ed.) (1998) *Das Partherreich und seine Zeugnisse*. Stuttgart.
  (2007) 'Fars under Seleucid and Parthian rule', in V. S. Curtis and S. Stewart, eds., *The Age of the Parthians*. London, 37–49.
Wiet, G., Elisseeff, V., Wolff, P., and Naudou, J. (1975) *The Great Medieval Civilizations*, 3 vols. London.
Wilkinson, E. (1973) *The History of Imperial China: A Research Guide*. Cambridge, MA.
Williams, S. (1985) *Diocletian and the Roman Recovery*. London.
Wink, A. (2001). 'India and the Turco-Mongol Frontier', in A. M. Khazanov and A. Wink, eds., *Nomads in the Sedentary World*. Padstow, Cornwall, 211–33.
Wirth, G. (1999) *Attila: Das Hunnenreich und Europa*. Stuttgart.
Wolf, E. R. (1982) *Europe and the People without History*. Berkeley.
Wolfram, H. (1988) *History of the Goths*, trans. T. J. Dunlap. Berkeley.
  (1993) 'The Huns and the Germanic Peoples', in F. M. Bäuml and M. D. Birnbaum, eds., *Attila the Man and the Image*. Budapest, 16–25.
  (1997a) 'The Ethno-Political Entities in the Region of the Upper and Middle Danube in the 6th–9th Centuries A.D.', in P. Urbańczyk, ed., *Origins of Central Europe*. Warsaw, 45–57.

(1997b) *The Roman Empire and its Germanic Peoples*, trans. T. Dunlap. Berkeley.
Wolfram, H. and Daim, F. (eds.) (1980) *Die Völker an der mittleren und unteren Donau im fünften und sechsten Jahrhundert*. Wien.
Wolfram, H. and Pohl, W. (eds.) (1990) *Typen der Ethnogenese unter besonderer Berücksichtigung der Bayern*, vol. 1. Wien.
Wolski, J. (1993) *L'empire des Arsacides*. Leuven.
Wood, F. (2002) *The Silk Road*. London.
Wood, I. (1985) 'Gregory of Tours and Clovis', *Revue Belge de Philologie et d'histoire* 63, 249–72.
  (1990) 'Ethnicity and the Ethnogenesis of the Burgundians', in H. Wolfram and W. Pohl, eds., *Typen der Ethnogenese unter besonderer Berücksichtigung der Bayern*, vol. 1. Wien, 53–69.
  (1994) *The Merovingian Kingdoms 450–751*. London and New York.
  (1996) 'Die Franken und ihr Erbe-"Translatio Imperii"', in Reiss-Museum Mannheim, *Die Franken Wegbereiter Europas Vor 1500 Jahren: König Chlodwig und seine Erben*, vol. 1. Mainz, 358–64.
  (ed.) (1998) *Franks and Alamanni in the Merovingian Period: An Ethnographic Perspective*. Woodbridge.
  (2000) 'The North-Western Provinces', in A. Cameron, B. Ward-Perkins and M. Whitby, eds., *The Cambridge Ancient History*, vol. XIV: *Late Antiquity: Empire and Successors, A.D. 425–600*. Cambridge, 497–524.
  (2003) 'Gentes, Kings and Kingdoms – The Emergence of States: The Kingdom of the Gibichungs', in H. Goetz, J. Jarnut and W. Pohl, eds., *Regna and Gentes: The Relationship between Late Antique and Early Medieval Peoples and Kingdoms in the Transformation of the Roman World*. Leiden, 243–69.
Workman, L. J. (ed.) (1994) *Medievalism in Europe*. Cambridge.
Wriggins, S. H. (1996) *Xuanzang: A Buddhist Pilgrim on the Silk Road*. Boulder.
Wright, D. C. (1997) 'The Hsiung-nu-Hun Equation Revisited', *Eurasian Studies Yearbook* 69, 77–112.
Wright, J., Honeychurch, W., and Amartuvshin, C. (2009) 'The Xiongnu Settlements of Egiin Gol, Mongolia', *Antiquity* 83, 372–87.
Xu E. (2005) *Historical Development of the Pre-dynastic Khitan*. Helsinki.
Xu, P. F. (2001) 'The Archaeology of the Great Wall of Qin and Han', *The Journal of East Asian Archaeology* 3 (1–2), 259–81.
Xue, Zongzheng (1992) *A History of Turks*. Beijing.
Yablonsky, L. T. (2000) '"Scythian Triad" and "Scythian World"', in J. Davis-Kimball, E. M. Murphy, L. Koryakova and L. T. Yablonsky, eds., *Kurgans, Ritual Sites, and Settlements: Eurasian Bronze and Iron Age*. Oxford, 3–8.
Yagodin, V. N. (2007) 'The Duana Archaeological Complex', in V. N. Yagodin, A. V. G. Betts, and S. Blau, eds., *Ancient Nomads of the Aral-Caspian Region: The Duana Archaeological Complex*. Leuven, 11–78.
Yagodin, V. N., Betts, A. V. G., and Blau, S. (eds.) (2007) *Ancient Nomads of the Aral-Caspian Region: The Duana Archaeological Complex*. Leuven.
Yamada, N. (1985) 'The Original Turkish Homeland', *Journal of Turkish Studies* 9, 243–46.

Yao Silian (1958) *Liang shu*. Beijing.
Yatsenko, S. A. (2003) 'Peculiarities of Social Development of the Sarmato-Alans and their Image in the Evidence of Other Cultures', in N. N. Kradin, D. Bondarenko and T. Barfield, eds., *Nomadic Pathways in Social Evolution*. Moscow, 88–99.
Yi, G. R. (trans.) (1998) *Samguksagi* [The History of the Three Kingdoms]. Seoul.
Yu, T. (1998) 'A Study of Saka History', *Sino-Platonic Papers* 80.
  (2004) 'A History of the Relationships between the Western and Eastern Han, Wei, Jin, Northern and Southern Dynasties and the Western Regions', *Sino-Platonic Papers* 131.
Yü, Y. S. (1967) *Trade and Expansion in Han China: A Study in the Structure of Sino-Barbarian Economic Relations*. Berkeley.
  (1986) 'Han Foreign Relations', in *The Cambridge History of China*, vol. I. Cambridge, 377–462.
  (1990) 'The Hsiung-nu', in D. Sinor, ed., *The Cambridge History of Early Inner Asia*. Cambridge, 118–50.
  (2002) 'Nomads and Han China', in W. F. Kasinec and M. A. Polushin, eds., *Expanding Empires: Cultural Interaction and Exchanges in World Societies from Ancient to Early Modern Times*. Wilmington, 133–41.
Zadneprovskiy, Y. A. (1994) 'The Nomads of Northern Central Asia after the Invasion of Alexander', in J. Harmatta, ed., *History of Civilizations of Central Asia*, vol. II. Paris, 457–72.
Zecchini, G. (2003) 'Latin Historiography: Jerome, Orosius and the Western Chronicles', in G. Marasco, ed., *Greek and Roman Historiography in Late Antiquity Fourth to Sixth Century* A.D. Leiden, 317–45.
Zeimal, E. V. (1983) 'The Political History of Transoxiana', in E. Yarshater, ed., *The Cambridge History of Iran*, vol. III, part 1: *The Seleucid, Parthian and Sasanian Periods* Cambridge, 232–62.
  (1996) 'The Kidarite Kingdom in Central Asia' in B. A. Litvinsky, ed., *History of Civilizations of Central Asia*, vol. III. Paris, 119–33.
Žemlička, J. (2000a) 'Centres and Organisation of Rule', in A. Wieczorek and H. Hinz, eds., *Europe's Centre around* AD *1000*. Stuttgart, 235–38.
  (2000b) 'The Premyslids and Bohemia', in A. Wieczorek and H. Hinz, eds., *Europe's Centre around* AD *1000*. Stuttgart, 274–7.
Zieme, P. (2006) 'Hybrid Names as a Special Device of Central Asian Naming', in L. Johanson, and C. Bulut, eds., *Turkic–Iranian Contact Areas: Historical and Linguistic Aspects*. Wiesbaden, 114–27.
Zuev, Y. (1977). 'Political History of Huns, Usuns and Kangyui (Kangar)' in *History of Kazakh SSR.*, vol. I. Alma-Ata, 284–93.
  (2002) *Rannie Tyurki: Ocerki istorii i ideologii* [Early Türks: Essays on History and Ideology]. Almaty.

Index

Achaemenids, 10, 12, 164, 168, 180
Aegidius, 80, 82, 153, 219, 221, 223
Aetius, 56, 63, 73, 75–80, 82–3, 197–8, 203, 210, 213, 216–22, 224, 228
Afshars, 68, 180
Agathias, 138, 186, 195, 208, 242, 250, 252–3, 255, 262, 269
Agelmund, 150
Akatziri, 56–7, 107, 122, 132–3, 135, 140–2, 204, 229, 233, 250, 254, 256–7
Alamanni, 49–52, 81, 120, 136, 149, 151, 154, 198–200, 235, 242, 271
Alans, 19, 25–6, 31, 33, 38, 42, 45–6, 49, 51–4, 59–60, 62, 67, 70, 74–5, 77, 82–3, 132, 143, 145–6, 151–3, 158, 165–6, 169–70, 175, 181, 186, 188, 190, 199–202, 205, 216, 218–20, 222–3, 226, 231, 240, 246, 263, 268–73
Alaric, 117, 149, 152–3, 199, 213, 227, 232, 265
Alatheus, 60, 201, 265
Alboin, 150–1, 268–9
Alemany, A., 170, 174, 177, 181, 185–6, 199, 202, 212, 223, 231, 254, 257, 270
Allsen, T. T., 159, 161, 167–8, 192, 209, 270
Altaic, 29
Altheim, F., 55, 127, 168–9, 174, 184–5, 188, 201, 204–9, 217, 226, 233, 243–4, 246, 250, 258, 262, 266, 268, 270–1
Althias, 255
Altziagiri, 141, 256
Amal, 53, 86, 96, 105–6, 108, 110–12, 118, 120–3, 125, 202, 236, 239–41, 243, 248
Amida, 37
Ammianus, 17, 19, 45, 51, 54, 60, 106, 110, 169–70, 183, 185, 193, 199–201, 209, 236
Anagast, 85, 241
Anagui, 41, 185
Anastasius, 228
Anatolius and Nomus, 224, 226
Andac, 53
Anonymus Valesianus, 96, 99, 234

Antes, 108, 110, 137, 236–7, 251
Anthemius, 128–9, 225, 240, 249
Arbogast, 52
Ardabur, 227
Ardaric, 30, 92, 94–5, 104, 106, 113–14, 118, 127, 132, 135–6, 206, 232
Areobindus, 70–1
Ariantes, 24, 26
Armatus, 228
Arnegisclus, 71, 85
Arpads, 142
Arrian, 170
Arsaces, 12–13, 165
Ashina, 41, 64, 189–90, 203, 243, 255
Asi, 32–3, 181, 202
Aspar, 71, 84, 86–7, 119, 152, 198, 201, 225, 227, 229, 241
Asparouk, 168
Athalaric, 109, 119
Athanaric, 52
Athaulf, 149, 153, 265
Avars, 35–6, 42, 89, 93, 132–3, 136, 138, 141–2, 145–7, 175, 183, 185, 194, 207–8, 214, 226, 230, 249–50, 253–4, 257–60, 262, 265

Babai, 115, 117, 120, 239
Bacaudae *see* Bagaudae
Bachrach B. S., 77, 218–19, 222–3, 263, 267, 270, 273–4
Bactrian, 28, 30, 32
Bagaudae, 197, 213
Balamber *see* Valamer
Ban Chao, 32
Barfield, T., 171, 173, 190, 193, 206
Barnish, S., 216, 218, 223
Barselts, 141
Barth, F., 7, 163
Basich *see* Basik
Basik, 30, 54, 93
Basiliscus, 85, 87, 198, 228, 241

333

Index

Batty, R., 174, 191, 209
Beckwith C. I., 159, 161–3, 165, 178, 180, 191, 194, 202, 259
Bei Shi, 37, 187, 210, 262
Belisarius, 85, 137, 139–40, 254
Beremud, 109, 119, 124, 126, 241
Berig, 123
Berik, 57–8, 94
Bittugurs, 86, 120
Black Huns, 37, 205
Bleda, 30, 37, 39–40, 56–7, 67, 92, 95, 134, 177, 206, 213
Blockley, R. C., 177–8, 184–5, 191, 194, 202–8, 213–14, 216, 218, 220, 225, 229, 232–3, 239–41, 250, 253, 256, 258
Boareks, 139
Bona, I., 45, 56, 81, 175, 177, 187, 193, 205, 212, 218, 220–22, 224, 227, 230–3, 244, 258, 271, 273–5
Brown, P., 198
Bulgars, 59, 74, 87, 91, 101, 132, 137–8, 140–2, 144, 146, 150, 168, 172, 204, 206–8, 230, 232, 238, 242–3, 245, 250–2, 254, 256, 258–60, 268
Burgundians, 70, 82, 129, 136, 151, 213, 216, 222–3, 225, 268–9

Candac, 53, 226
Carolingians, 147–8
Cassiodorus, 75, 77, 98, 106, 110, 121, 123, 126, 216, 218–19, 236–7, 242, 244–5, 247
Chagatai, 29, 134
Charaton *see* Karaton
Charlemagne, 147–8
Chase-Dunn, C. and Hall, T., 3, 159
Chelchal, 86, 208, 229, 241
Childeric, 80–3, 135, 153, 220–4, 274–5
Chinggis Khan, 1, 3, 39, 61, 160, 162, 203
Chionites, 5, 36, 185
Chonodomarius, 51
Chorasmia, 12, 16, 165
Christensen, A. S., 110, 123, 218, 235–8, 242, 244
Clovis, 80, 83, 147, 153, 219–20, 223, 247, 263, 264
Constantine Porphyrogenitus, 146, 189, 208, 210, 226, 233, 261
Constantius, Hunnic official, 55, 236
Croke, B., 205–6, 213–14, 225–6, 229, 232, 241, 246–8, 251–3
Czeglédy, 36, 175–86, 188, 191, 233, 250–3, 257–8

Daffinà, 172, 175, 181–2, 187
Danubian style, 154, 272
Dayuan, 33, 169, 181
de Crespigny R., 167, 171–2, 175, 177, 179, 208
Deguignes, J., 26

Demougeot, E., 195, 199, 207, 210, 219, 221, 226, 229, 235, 240, 245–8, 250, 252, 263, 265, 271
Dengizich, 30, 85–6, 92–3, 111, 117–19, 123–6, 132–3, 135, 137, 148, 208, 229, 241–2, 245, 251
Di Cosmo, N., 20, 159–60, 163, 170, 174, 177, 190–1, 194
Dingling, 28, 33, 35, 175–6, 183, 187, 255
Diocletian, 47, 195
Donatus, 55–6, 205
Drijvers, J. W., 165, 167
Dulo, 59, 142, 208
Dzungaria, 39, 175, 188

Edeco, 41, 55–7, 72, 81, 87, 96–100, 104–5, 117–18, 122, 125, 127–9, 135, 228, 233, 240
Ellac, 30, 56–7, 91–6, 107, 113, 118, 122, 126, 132, 135, 239, 241
Emmedzur, 93, 207
Emnetzur *see* Emmedzur
Ennodius, 96, 98, 238, 248
Enoki, K., 179, 184–6, 188
epitēdeioi, 41
Érdy, M., 36, 175, 177, 182–4, 188, 218, 273
Ermanaric, 53, 105, 107, 110–12, 121, 126, 201, 235, 237–8, 242
Ernak, 57, 59, 86, 93, 111, 118, 124, 126, 132–3, 137–8, 142, 148, 207, 223, 229, 233, 241, 250, 254
Eskam, 30
Euric, 80, 124, 217, 246
Eutharic, 109, 119, 124

Ferghana, 33, 169, 181
feudalism, 7, 10–11, 39, 69, 143, 147, 150, 164, 167, 173–4, 182, 264, 266
Findley, C. V., 159, 161, 163, 189, 203, 205, 211–12, 244, 260, 269–70
Fletcher, J. F., 163, 192, 212, 230
Fredegar, 81–2, 100, 221–2, 234, 259
Fritigern, 52
Frye, R. N., 164, 180, 184–6, 188, 190, 212

Gallic Chronicle of 452, 71, 203
Gallic Chronicle of 511, 217
Geary, P. J., 196, 198, 200–1, 209, 219, 235, 244, 247, 263–6
Geiseric, 70, 78, 84, 201, 218
Gelonus, 41
Gepids, 53, 57, 68, 86, 92, 95, 104, 114, 118, 120, 124–5, 135, 142, 151, 154, 190, 206, 227–8, 230–2, 240, 242, 245, 268, 271, 274
Gesimund, 108–10, 121–2, 126, 242–3, 264
Giesmos, 94–5, 232
Glones, 139
Glycerius, 124–5, 129–30, 225

Goffart, W., 46, 128, 194, 196, 216, 233, 236, 247
Gokturks, 40–1, 66, 172, 180, 189, 204, 210, 243
Golden, P. B., 132, 146, 159–63, 171–3, 176–8, 180, 184–91, 203, 207, 209, 230–1, 233–4, 236, 243, 249–53, 258–60, 262
Golden Horde, 29, 91
Goldsworthy, A., 69, 194, 212
Great Bulgaria, 91, 101, 142, 230, 243, 252, 257
Greatrex, G., 255, 269
Gregory of Tours, 81, 217, 220–1
Grenet, F., 180–2, 184, 187–8, 192
Greuthung Goths, 53
Grumbates, 37
Gundobad, 82, 127, 129–30, 225, 246–7
Guptas, 5, 38, 185

Halphen, L., 271–2
Halsall, G., 46, 193–6, 213, 221, 224, 265, 269
Han Empire, 25, 32–3, 35, 187
Hanshu, 172
Hara Huna, 37–8
Harmatta, J., 164, 173–4, 201, 224, 231, 233, 258
Hartog, F., 24, 171, 173
Heather, P., 29, 45–8, 50, 67–8, 86–7, 89, 106, 108, 110, 126, 144, 169, 177, 193–6, 198–200, 203, 209, 211–12, 214, 227, 229–30, 232–3, 235–41, 243, 246–7, 251, 259, 262, 265–8, 271–2, 274–5
Henning, W. B., 27, 174
Hephtalites, 2, 33, 35–9, 45, 54, 131, 140–1, 183–8, 191, 231, 255
Hermanaric *see* Ermanaric
Herodotus, 2, 12, 21, 24, 41, 77, 85, 166, 178, 193, 201, 217
Heruls, 84, 96, 103, 124–5, 127, 228, 235
Hormidac, 84, 240
Hou Hanshu, 23, 171–2
Hua, 35–6, 183–6
Hummer, H. J., 82, 199–200, 222, 242, 263
Hunimund, 52, 108–9, 112, 116–18, 121–6, 135, 212, 232, 240, 242–3
Hunoulphus, 41, 87, 96, 98, 104, 124–5, 129, 228
Huyan, Lan, Xubu, 58
Hydatius, 80, 83–4, 218, 220, 224, 270

Iazyges, 25, 200, 209
Idanthyrsus, 24
Illus, 87
Iranian, 3, 7, 11–12, 16, 24, 27, 29, 31, 37, 41, 53, 59, 62, 66, 68–9, 94, 97, 105, 143, 145–8, 150, 152–3, 155, 160, 162–3, 166, 168–9, 173, 178, 180, 184–7, 190, 202, 204, 231, 237, 246, 262, 267, 271–2
Ishjamts, N. J., 172–3, 191, 204, 208

Ivantchik, A. I., 24, 173

Jerome, 68, 212, 216
Jin Empire, 35
John of Antioch, 99, 128–9, 205, 229, 232, 246
John Malalas, 88, 231–2
Jones, A. H. M., 49
Jordanes, 53, 74–9, 81, 86, 91–4, 98–100, 102–4, 106–14, 118–29, 138, 140–1, 190, 194, 202, 205, 212, 214, 216–20, 222–6, 231–42, 245–6, 252, 256, 264
Justin, 10, 32, 163, 166–7, 181, 253
Justinian, 49, 70, 72, 109, 137, 139, 142, 198, 226, 228, 250, 253

Kangju, 16, 31, 33–7, 42, 62, 66, 165, 169, 175–6, 181–2, 187, 192, 201
Kanishka, 32
Karakhanids, 64–6, 161, 189, 211
Karaton, 30, 38, 56, 205
Karen, 14, 166
Kazanski, M., 199, 246, 271, 273–5
Kelly, C., 47, 89, 170, 193, 195, 202, 212–13, 216–17, 225, 229, 265, 272
Kermichiones, 38, 187
Khazanov, A. M., 161, 170, 173, 189–90, 193, 260, 262, 270, 274
Khazars, 93, 101, 132–3, 189–90, 207, 256, 260
Khitans, 61–4
Kidarites, 37, 39, 61, 131, 184–5
Koguryo, 39, 61
Kollautz A. and Miyakawa, H., 172–4, 185–6, 188–9, 243, 249–50, 252, 258
Kouridachus, 56, 205
Kradin, N. N., 20, 39, 91, 170, 172–3, 188–91, 230
Kubad, 37
Kubrat, 16, 101, 138, 142, 230, 243, 257, 259
Kujula Kadphises, 32
Kuriltai, 148, 189
Kursich *see* Kursik
Kursik, 30, 54, 93
Kushans, 12, 16, 31–4, 37, 42, 169, 180–2, 191, 201, 230, 262, 267
Kushanshahs, 33, 175
Kutrigurs, 57, 137–8, 140–2, 250, 253–4, 256–7

La Vaissière, E. de, 27–8, 36, 169, 175, 177, 181, 183–6, 188
Lactantius, 47, 195
Laudaricus, 30, 56, 77, 92, 217, 246
Leo, Roman emperor, 83, 119, 138, 152, 228
Liangshu, 35, 183–4
Litvinsky, B. A., 166–7, 169, 181, 186–8, 191, 257
logades, 55, 57–8, 134, 207

Lombards, 98, 130, 142, 148, 150–1, 154, 235, 245, 266, 268–9, 274

Maechen-Helfen, J. O., 163
Mahmud al-Kashgari, 42
Majorian, 221, 225, 227
Malchus, 87, 97, 233, 239, 248
Marcellinus Comes, 71, 88, 205, 213–14, 229, 232, 241, 247, 251
Marcian, 83–4, 114, 152, 224–7
Marcomanni, 51
Massagetae, 139, 165, 170, 201
Matthews, J. F., 47, 170, 187, 194–5, 199–200, 202, 205, 272
McBain, B., 96–8, 233
Menander Protector, 177, 191, 250
Merovingian, 81, 146–7, 149, 205, 262, 264, 274
Merrills, A. H. and Miles, R., 216, 218, 228
Modun, 24, 40, 59, 173, 176, 189
Mongol Empire, Mongols, 1, 3, 93, 122, 135, 160
Moravcsik, G., 252
Moses of Chorene, 14, 185
Mundo, 94, 138, 232, 234, 251, 255
Mundzuk, 30, 93, 105, 111, 206

Nagai, 40
Nanaivandak, 27–8
Nedao, 91–2, 97, 99, 104, 113–14, 118, 126, 132, 138, 150–1, 224–6, 232–3, 240, 258
Nepos, 129–31, 225, 248–9

Odo of Cluny, 153
Odoacer, 74, 80–2, 87–8, 96–100, 102–5, 124–5, 127–30, 151, 220, 225, 228, 232–5, 242, 246–9
Odotheus, 67
Oebarsius, 30, 58
Oghuric Turks, 33–4, 168, 272
Oghurs, 120, 132–3, 137, 139, 175, 185, 241, 249, 254–5, 257
Oghuz, 64–6, 69, 101, 176, 192, 211, 257
Oktar, 30, 56, 206
Olbia, 26, 201
Olbrycht, M., 164–6, 169
Olybrius, 225
Olympiodorus, 38, 55, 187, 205, 265
Onegesius, 41, 55, 57–8, 134, 191, 204
Onoghurs, 141, 175–6, 243
Orestes, 41, 55, 57, 96, 127–30, 134, 247
Orosius, 212, 216
Ostrogoths, 49, 53, 59, 67, 86, 95, 104–5, 109, 112–14, 118–20, 122–6, 129–30, 132, 135, 137, 150–1, 224, 228, 232, 239–42, 245–6, 251, 255, 262, 268, 273
Oultizouroi, 58, 138, 238

Parthian Empire, 9, 16, 42, 167
Paul, Roman general, 80, 219, 223
Paul the Deacon, 98, 150, 234, 267–9
Pazyryk, 164, 169
Pechenegs, 141, 189–90, 210, 255, 263
Peroz, 37, 250
Plutarch, 13, 166
Pohl, W., 94, 113, 200, 206–8, 232–4, 239–41, 256–9, 261–2, 269
Pompeius Trogus, 179, 181
Priscus, 30, 54–5, 57, 71–2, 75, 78, 81, 84, 86, 94, 96–7, 99, 119, 122–3, 127, 132, 168, 175, 178, 184, 194, 202–8, 212–14, 216, 218, 220, 225, 229, 232–3, 237, 239–41, 249–50, 270
Pritsak, O., 38, 59, 170–2, 174, 176–8, 181, 184, 187, 201, 205, 207–11, 231, 234, 237, 243, 249–51, 254–5, 259
Procopius, 37–8, 53, 88, 128–9, 132, 137–40, 185–7, 194, 202, 226, 228, 234–5, 237, 247, 250–5, 257
Prosper, 80, 213, 219, 224–5, 238
Ptolemy, 26, 60, 103, 123, 174, 183, 193, 209, 235
Pulleyblank, E. G., 28–9, 32, 38, 160, 162, 171, 173–6, 179–81, 183, 186–8, 201, 209, 249

Quintus Curtius Rufus, 170

Radagaisus, 40, 67, 112, 190, 201, 238, 265
Rashid al-Din, 1–3
Reynolds, R. L. and Lopez, R. S., 96, 100, 102, 104–5, 220, 232–5, 243
Ricimer, 82, 128–9, 225, 247, 249
Romulus Augustulus, 41, 55, 127, 130, 246–7
Rouran, 3, 35, 39–41, 43, 45, 55–6, 59, 61, 64–6, 69, 107, 131, 172, 175, 177–9, 182–3, 185, 187–9, 203, 206, 208–9, 230, 243, 250, 262
Royal Scythians, 12, 19, 24, 50, 145
Rua see Ruga
Ruga, 29, 59, 67, 92, 102, 104–5, 111, 125, 235
Rugii, 84, 86, 96, 100–5, 117, 120, 124–5, 128, 151, 235, 242, 245

Sabirs, 132, 138–9, 141–2, 175, 179, 249, 253, 257
Saint Severinus, 97, 129, 151
Saka, 10–13, 25, 32, 41, 165–6, 171, 174, 179–80, 191, 271–2
Sandilch, 142, 250
Sangiban, 77
Saphrax, 60, 201, 209, 265
Sarmatians, 25, 27, 47, 51, 53, 92, 108, 117, 120, 124, 145, 154, 161–2, 165–6, 170, 174, 201–2, 209, 224, 233, 236, 238, 240, 265, 272, 274

Sarus, 149, 265
Sassanians, 9, 14–16, 36–8, 48, 54, 71, 139, 142, 166, 169, 196
Scandza, 103, 123
Sciri, 41, 56–7, 67–8, 81, 83–4, 86, 96–7, 100, 103–4, 107, 114, 116–18, 120, 122–5, 127–9, 135, 220, 233, 240
Scythians, 12, 21, 24–6, 32, 41, 52, 58, 72, 125, 145, 151, 174, 179, 192, 246, 255
Seljuks, 4, 65–6, 69, 103, 135, 161, 210–11
Shelun, 39–40, 183
Shiji, 22–3, 171, 179, 189–90, 269
Sidonius Apollinaris, 80, 124
Sima Qian, 2, 22
Simmas and Ascan, 139
Sims-Williams, 163, 180–2, 185, 188, 262
Sinor, D., 27, 159–60, 174, 177–80, 182–4, 187, 189, 202–3, 205–6, 209, 212–13, 223, 230–1, 234, 243, 249–50, 253, 259, 270
Sogdian, 27, 30, 38, 55, 169, 171, 180, 204
Strabo, 10, 25, 163, 165, 167, 174, 179, 234
Styrax, 139
Suebi, 49, 52, 67, 70, 86, 92, 112, 117–23, 125, 135, 149, 153, 212, 225, 228, 232, 235, 240, 242, 263
Sulimirsky, T., 165, 191, 260, 273
Sunicas and Aigan, 139
Suren, 13–14, 166, 168
Surena, 12–13
Syagrius, 80, 219–20

Tacitus, 26, 101–3, 105, 166, 174, 196–9, 202, 234, 237, 245
Tashkent, 31, 33–4, 36, 176, 201
Tervingi, 50–2, 199, 201
Theodoric Amal, 53, 74, 86–8, 96, 98, 100, 103–4, 106, 108–9, 113–14, 119–20, 123–6, 130–1, 150–1, 217, 219, 228–9, 232–3, 236, 238–9, 242, 244–9, 266, 268–9, 273
Theodoric Strabo, 85–7, 227, 248
Theodorid, 75–8, 216, 219
Theodosius the Great, 55, 227
Theophanes, 71, 138, 186–7, 208, 213, 229, 232–3, 237, 239, 252–3, 257
Thiudimer, 86, 112–13, 115–18, 120, 124, 129, 228–9, 239, 241–2, 245
Thompson, E. A., 19, 57–8, 71, 74, 99, 170, 204, 206–9, 212–14, 216–17, 219, 225, 227–9, 231, 233, 235, 238–40, 251, 265, 268, 270–1
Thorismud, 75–6, 78, 82, 218
  Ostrogothic king, 109–10, 112, 118
Thuringian, 96, 98, 221, 274
Tiele, 132, 162, 177, 183, 243, 254–5, 257
Timur, 3, 135–6, 160, 162, 233, 236
Toba Wei, 36, 182–4, 267

Tochari, 12, 32, 165, 179–81
Toghril Beg, 65
Tokharians, 162
Torcilingi, 96–103, 124–5, 127–8, 233
Tuldila, 114, 227

Uighurs, 1, 39–40, 61, 190, 230
Uldin, 40, 58, 67, 111–12, 121, 125, 212, 238, 265
Ultzindur, 93, 103, 223–4, 226, 240
Urbańczyk, P., 259, 261
Utigurs, 57, 137–8, 140–2, 250, 252–4, 256–8

Vadamerca, 98, 108
Valamer, 86, 96, 98–9, 105–14, 117–21, 123, 125–7, 129, 132, 135, 209, 235, 238–43, 245–6, 273
Valerian, 16
Valikhanov, 160, 230, 255
Vandalarius, 109–12, 121, 212
Vandals, 49–50, 52–3, 67, 70, 84–5, 102, 112, 198, 202, 212, 216, 227–8, 235, 254, 263, 266
Vernadsky, G., 94, 182, 200–2, 209, 216, 231, 233–4, 237, 244, 247, 268–70, 272, 274
Vetericus, obscure Goth in Gaul, 119
Videric, son of Beremud, 119
Vidimer, 113, 115, 117, 120, 124–6, 129–30, 241–2, 245
Vinitharius, 107–12, 118, 121, 235, 237, 242
Visigoths, 49, 53, 70, 73, 75, 77, 79–83, 107, 109, 123–4, 149–50, 152, 199, 213, 216–19, 221, 223, 245, 247, 266
Vitalian, 137, 251
Vithericus, 110
Vithimeris, 110
Vogelsang, W. J., 10, 164–5
Volga Bulgaria, 58
Vovin, A., 29, 176
Vultuulf, 107, 111–12, 121

Wallace-Hadrill, J. M., 164, 217, 222, 259, 262–4
Wei Shu, 31, 36, 38, 177–8, 184, 186–7, 193, 210, 262
Werner, J., 209, 224, 268, 271–2, 274
Whitby, 185, 195–6, 204, 206, 213–14, 219, 225, 227–9, 245, 252–5, 257–9, 267, 269–70
White Huns, 2, 36–9, 45, 61, 69, 71, 140, 175, 184, 187, 194
Wickham, C., 72, 164, 195, 199, 213–14, 228–9, 235, 260, 262, 264–7, 270, 275
Widengren, G., 165, 167–8
Wolfram, H., 59, 113, 119, 199, 209, 214, 229, 231–2, 234–6, 238–9, 241–3, 245–6, 248, 261, 266, 268
Wolski, J., 165–7, 197

Wusun, 31, 33–5, 42, 66, 175–6, 178–9, 181–2, 187, 190, 271
Wuxing, 25

Xianbei, 3, 28, 31, 35, 39, 43, 61–2, 66, 159, 161–2, 174, 178, 183, 188, 193, 205, 208, 249, 267
Xiongnu, 3, 5, 10, 12, 14, 16, 19–23, 24, 25–9, 31–6, 38–43, 55–9, 61–2, 64, 65, 69, 79, 91, 93, 107, 132, 140–1, 149–51, 154, 160–2, 167, 170–6, 178–9, 182–4, 186–90, 192–3, 205–9, 230, 238, 243, 252, 254, 263–4, 267, 269

yabgu, 32–3
Yancai, 33, 169

Yellow Turban revolt, 35
Yeniseian, 29, 93, 176
Yueban, 31, 34, 176–8, 182, 188
Yuezhi, 12, 16, 31–4, 42, 165, 168, 179, 182, 186–7, 190, 201, 269

Zabergan, 137, 250
Zeno, 85, 87–8, 130, 137, 225, 228, 248, 249
Zercon, 30
Zhi-paye-zhi, 40
Zhizhi, 33
Zhupan, 146, 261
Zizhi Tongjian, 210
Zosimus, 67, 212, 265

Lightning Source UK Ltd.
Milton Keynes UK
UKHW022047041021
391676UK00002B/196